The Inflation-Targeting Debate

National Bureau of Economic Research—
Studies in Business Cycles
Volume 32

The Inflation-Targeting Debate

Edited by **Ben S. Bernanke and Michael Woodford**

The University of Chicago Press

Chicago and London

The University of Chicago Press, Chicago 60637
The University of Chicago Press, Ltd., London
© 2005 by the National Bureau of Economic Research
All rights reserved. Published 2005
Paperback edition 2006
Printed in the United States of America
14 13 12 11 10 09 08 07 06   2 3 4 5
ISBN: 0-226-04471-8 (cloth)
ISBN-13: 978-0-226-04472-9 (paper)
ISBN-10: 0-226-04472-6 (paper)

Library of Congress Cataloging-in-Publication Data

The inflation targeting debate / edited by Ben S. Bernanke and
   Michael Woodford.
       p. cm. — (National Bureau of Economic Research studies in
   business cycles ; v. 32)
    "This volume grew out of a National Bureau of Economic Research
   conference on inflation targeting held in Bal Harbour, Florida, in
   January 2003."
    Includes bibliographical references and index.
    ISBN 0-226-04471-8 (cloth : alk paper)
    1. Inflation (Finance)—Congresses. 2. Monetary policy—
Congresses. I. Bernanke, Ben. II. Woodford, Michael, Professor.
III. National Bureau of Economic Research. IV. Studies in business
cycles ; v. 32.

HG229 .I45636 2004
332.4'1—dc22   2004055352

Relation of the Directors to the
Work and Publications of the
National Bureau of Economic Research

1. The object of the NBER is to ascertain and present to the economics profession, and to the public more generally, important economic facts and their interpretation in a scientific manner without policy recommendations. The Board of Directors is charged with the responsibility of ensuring that the work of the NBER is carried on in strict conformity with this object.

2. The President shall establish an internal review process to ensure that book manuscripts proposed for publication DO NOT contain policy recommendations. This shall apply both to the proceedings of conferences and to manuscripts by a single author or by one or more co-authors but shall not apply to authors of comments at NBER conferences who are not NBER affiliates.

3. No book manuscript reporting research shall be published by the NBER until the President has sent to each member of the Board a notice that a manuscript is recommended for publication and that in the President's opinion it is suitable for publication in accordance with the above principles of the NBER. Such notification will include a table of contents and an abstract or summary of the manuscript's content, a list of contributors if applicable, and a response form for use by Directors who desire a copy of the manuscript for review. Each manuscript shall contain a summary drawing attention to the nature and treatment of the problem studied and the main conclusions reached.

4. No volume shall be published until forty-five days have elapsed from the above notification of intention to publish it. During this period a copy shall be sent to any Director requesting it, and if any Director objects to publication on the grounds that the manuscript contains policy recommendations, the objection will be presented to the author(s) or editor(s). In case of dispute, all members of the Board shall be notified, and the President shall appoint an ad hoc committee of the Board to decide the matter; thirty days additional shall be granted for this purpose.

5. The President shall present annually to the Board a report describing the internal manuscript review process, any objections made by Directors before publication or by anyone after publication, any disputes about such matters, and how they were handled.

6. Publications of the NBER issued for informational purposes concerning the work of the Bureau, or issued to inform the public of the activities at the Bureau, including but not limited to the NBER Digest and Reporter, shall be consistent with the object stated in paragraph 1. They shall contain a specific disclaimer noting that they have not passed through the review procedures required in this resolution. The Executive Committee of the Board is charged with the review of all such publications from time to time.

7. NBER working papers and manuscripts distributed on the Bureau's web site are not deemed to be publications for the purpose of this resolution, but they shall be consistent with the object stated in paragraph 1. Working papers shall contain a specific disclaimer noting that they have not passed through the review procedures required in this resolution. The NBER's web site shall contain a similar disclaimer. The President shall establish an internal review process to ensure that the working papers and the web site do not contain policy recommendations, and shall report annually to the Board on this process and any concerns raised in connection with it.

8. Unless otherwise determined by the Board or exempted by the terms of paragraphs 6 and 7, a copy of this resolution shall be printed in each NBER publication as described in paragraph 2 above.

Contents

Acknowledgments   ix

Introduction   1
Ben S. Bernanke and Michael Woodford

1. **What Has Inflation Targeting Achieved?**   11
   Mervyn King

I. OPTIMAL TARGETS

2. **Implementing Optimal Policy through
   Inflation-Forecast Targeting**   19
   Lars E. O. Svensson and Michael Woodford
   Comment: Bennett T. McCallum
   Discussion Summary

3. **Optimal Inflation-Targeting Rules**   93
   Marc P. Giannoni and Michael Woodford
   Comment: Edward Nelson
   Discussion Summary

4. **Inflation Targeting, Price-Path Targeting,
   and Output Variability**   173
   Stephen G. Cecchetti and Junhan Kim
   Comment: N. Gregory Mankiw
   Discussion Summary

5. **Imperfect Knowledge, Inflation Expectations,
   and Monetary Policy**   201
   Athanasios Orphanides and John C. Williams
   Comment: George W. Evans
   Discussion Summary

II. CRITICAL PERSPECTIVES

6. **Does Inflation Targeting Matter?**   249
   Laurence Ball and Niamh Sheridan
   Comment: Mark Gertler
   Discussion Summary

7. **Limits to Inflation Targeting**   283
   Christopher A. Sims
   Comment: Stephanie Schmitt-Grohé
   Discussion Summary

8. **Inflation Targeting in the United States?**   311
   Marvin Goodfriend
   Comment: Donald L. Kohn
   Discussion Summary

III. INFLATION TARGETING FOR EMERGING MARKETS

9. **Inflation Targeting in Transition Economies:
   Experience and Prospects**   353
   Jiri Jonas and Frederic S. Mishkin
   Comment: Olivier Blanchard
   Discussion Summary

10. **Inflation Targeting and Sudden Stops**   423
    Ricardo J. Caballero and Arvind Krishnamurthy
    Comment: Ben S. Bernanke
    Discussion Summary

    Contributors   447
    Author Index   451
    Subject Index   455

Acknowledgments

This volume grew out of a National Bureau of Economic Research (NBER) conference on inflation targeting held in Bal Harbour, Florida, in January 2003. We are grateful to many people who made the conference and the resulting volume possible. In particular, we would like to thank Martin Feldstein and the NBER for support; the NBER's conference staff for excellent logistical arrangements for the conference; and Helena Fitz-Patrick for shepherding the volume through the publication process. We would also like to thank Thomas Laubach for preparation of the summaries of the discussions at the conference and all of the contributors to the volume for the work they have done to bring insights from current research to bear on a topic of current practical importance.

Introduction

Ben S. Bernanke and Michael Woodford

Since about 1990, a significant number of industrialized and middle-income countries have adopted inflation targeting as their framework for making monetary policy. As the name suggests, in an inflation-targeting regime the central bank is responsible for achieving a publicly announced objective for the inflation rate, typically at a medium-term horizon of one to three years. Under "flexible" inflation-targeting regimes, now the norm in practice, central banks are able to pursue other objectives as well, such as output stabilization, as long as the inflation objective is achieved in the long run. Inflation-targeting central banks have also typically placed a heavy emphasis on communication, transparency, and accountability; indeed, the announcement of the inflation target is itself motivated in large part as a means of clarifying the central bank's objectives and plans for the public.

Countries that have adopted inflation targeting have generally experienced good macroeconomic outcomes, including low inflation and stable economic growth; and, as already noted, this approach has diffused around the globe. However, despite more than a decade of experience, important questions about inflation targeting remain unanswered. Among these are the following:

1. To what extent does inflation targeting, as practiced, correspond to an optimal form of monetary policy? Or, to put the question another way, could the framework of inflation targeting be redesigned in ways that

Ben S. Bernanke is the Howard Harrison and Gabrielle Snyder Beck Professor of Economics and Public Affairs at Princeton University and a member of the Board of Governors of the Federal Reserve System. Michael Woodford is professor of economics at Columbia University and a research associate of the National Bureau of Economic Research.

would provide better results? For example, should inflation targeting be strictly forward looking—that is, should it be interpreted as inflation-*forecast* targeting—or should current and lagged values of inflation and other variables affect the policy setting? Should central banks attempt to target inflation or the price level? Is there any theoretical reason to expect the enhanced communication aspect of inflation targeting to improve policy outcomes?

2. To what extent are the improvements in performance observed in countries that have adopted inflation targeting the direct result of the change in policy regime, as opposed to other causes? For example, many countries that did not adopt inflation targeting, or adopted only parts of the approach, also experienced substantial improvements in macroeconomic performance in the 1990s. Would these countries have done better if they had adopted full-fledged inflation targeting? Would the inflation-targeting countries have done as well if they had not gone the inflation-targeting route? Are there certain preconditions for inflation targeting to be helpful? Are there institutional or economic circumstances under which adopting inflation targeting can be counterproductive?

3. The early adopters of inflation targeting, such as New Zealand, the United Kingdom, Canada, and Sweden, were for the most part industrialized countries. More recently, both middle-income developing countries and transition economies have begun to experiment with this approach. Are these countries "ready" for inflation targeting, or would they be better advised to adopt some other type of monetary regime? What special issues does inflation targeting raise for developing and transition economies?

To try to answer these and other questions about inflation targeting, the National Bureau of Economic Research convened a conference in Miami, Florida, in January 2003, attended by academics, central bankers, and other experts in monetary policy. The proceedings of this highly stimulating conference are contained in this volume. In the rest of this introduction we give a brief overview of the keynote address and the papers that were presented.

The volume begins with remarks delivered by Mervyn King, the incoming governor of the Bank of England and longtime member of the Bank's Monetary Policy Committee, to open the conference. King reflects on the experience with inflation targeting in the United Kingdom. Although he acknowledges that the adoption of an inflation-targeting framework may not have been essential to the great improvement in macroeconomic performance in the United Kingdom since 1992, King argues that this framework at least made making the right decisions easier. He reviews the implementation of inflation targeting at the Bank of England and discusses what he sees as the important advantages of the approach. These include both a substantial increase in the professionalism of decision making and increased political acceptance of the delegation of technical judgments about the month-to-month conduct of policy to the Bank. Finally, he argues that inflation targeting should be viewed as "a way of thinking about policy" rather than as "an automatic answer to all the difficult policy questions." This insight proves to be a recurrent theme of the papers in this volume.

The papers from the conference fall naturally into three groups. The first set of papers considers the optimal formulation of an inflation-targeting policy. Indeed, King argues in his opening remarks that inflation targeting should be conceived of as "a way of implementing the optimal policy reaction function." Taking this charge seriously, the first group of papers examines how an inflation-targeting policy might be implemented in order to approach this ideal.

Lars E. O. Svensson and Michael Woodford (chap. 2) present a theoretical case for the view that inflation-forecast targeting, if conducted in an ideal manner, is an optimal monetary policy. Their paper is concerned not so much with the way in which inflation and other variables should evolve under an optimal policy—although a position on that question is a necessary starting point for their analysis—but rather with the question of the *implementation* of optimal policy, by which they mean the design of a decision procedure for policy that can be expected to bring about the desired equilibrium. They argue that an inflation-forecast targeting procedure can be designed that not only is consistent with an optimal equilibrium but also represents a desirable approach to implementation. Under such a procedure, the central bank considers in each decision cycle how its instrument must be set in order for the central bank's current projections regarding the future evolution of inflation and other variables to satisfy a certain *target criterion,* which defines what it means for policy to be "on track."

The authors judge alternative approaches to implementation according to several criteria. These include the transparency of the connection between the public description of the policy rule and ultimate policy goals; the robustness of the policy rule to model perturbations; and the degree to which a given policy rule excludes the possibility of alternative, much less desirable equilibria that arise as a result of self-fulfilling expectations. They argue that forecast-targeting procedures are especially desirable approaches to the implementation of optimal policy on the first two grounds. Determinacy of equilibrium is less easily ensured under such procedures than under commitment to a backward-looking instrument rule in the spirit of the Taylor rule; however, Svensson and Woodford argue that it is possible to design a "hybrid" procedure—under which the central bank commits itself to respond in a backward-looking way to departures of the economy's actual evolution from the desired equilibrium but follows a forecast-targeting procedure otherwise—that retains the transparency and robustness of a targeting procedure while ensuring determinacy of equilibrium as well.

Svensson and Woodford compare alternative approaches to the implementation of optimal policy in the context of a relatively simple "New Keynesian" model of the monetary transmission mechanism. Marc P. Giannoni and Michael Woodford (chap. 3) complement their analysis by discussing the form of the optimal target criterion in a range of more complicated models that introduce features found in many estimated models of the monetary transmission mechanism with optimizing foundations. They consider the question of which variables should be taken into account (in addition to the inflation projection) in an optimal target criterion. They also show what determines the appropriate relative weights that should be placed on various variables, the relative weights that should be placed on projections for different future horizons, and the degree to which the optimal target criterion should be history dependent. The main point of their paper is to show how the nature of the optimal target criterion varies depending on one's beliefs about the correct structural model of the monetary transmission mechanism, and on the numerical values assigned to the parameters of one's model.

Giannoni and Woodford illustrate their approach by estimating a small quantitative model of the U.S. monetary transmission mechanism and computing an optimal targeting procedure for the estimated model. Like a number of other recent empirical models, their estimated model incorporates staggering of both wages and prices; indexation of both wages and prices to a lagged price index; predetermined wages, prices, and real private expenditure for one quarter following an unexpected change in monetary policy; and habit persistence. The optimal policy rule is found to correspond to a multistage inflation-forecast targeting procedure. Under the optimal procedure, the degree of projected future inflation that should be acceptable depends on the central bank's current projections for future real wages and real activity (relative to a time-varying natural rate of output) and also on past projections. The degree to which actual U.S. policy over the past two decades would have conformed to the optimal target criteria is considered, on the assumption that projections at each point in time would have corresponded to the forecasts implied by a small, unrestricted vector autoregression (VAR) model. Some systematic departures of actual policy from the optimal criteria are identified, but these seem to have been relatively modest over the period in question.

Steven G. Cecchetti and Junhan Kim (chap. 4) consider a particular issue in the design of an optimal targeting regime, namely, the degree to which overshoots of the long-run target inflation rate should be followed by intentional undershoots, in order to "undo" part or all of the undesired increase in prices. Under a simple (purely forward-looking) inflation target of the kind presumed in much theoretical discussion of inflation targeting, as well as typically used in practice, the central bank "lets bygones be bygones" by setting an inflation target that is independent of past successes or failures in hitting the target. Under a "price-path target," by contrast, the central bank would seek to keep the price level near some preannounced target path that rises deterministically at the long-run target inflation rate. The latter approach would require that excess inflation eventually be completely reversed, in order for the price level not to remain permanently away from the target path.

Cecchetti and Kim define a class of "hybrid" targeting rules that nests the extremes of pure inflation targeting and pure price-path targeting as polar cases. They assume that the central bank is assigned a quadratic loss function that it is expected to seek to minimize in a discretionary fashion. The loss function includes both an output-gap stabilization objective and a term proportional to squared deviations of the actual price level from a time-varying target, which is a weighted average of the previous actual price level and the previous target, increased by the long-run inflation target. Cecchetti and Kim consider which objective in this family would be best to assign to a central bank, from the point of view of minimizing a true social welfare function that penalizes both inflation and output-gap variability but assigns no intrinsic significance to the stationarity of the absolute price level. A stabilization objective other than pure inflation targeting may nonetheless be optimal because of the suboptimality of the discretionary equilibrium from the point of view of the loss function assigned to the central bank.

Cecchetti and Kim characterize the optimal hybrid central-bank objective as a function of model parameters and then estimate the relevant parameters for twenty-three countries. They conclude that a hybrid rule that is fairly close to price-path targeting would be optimal for most of the countries in their sample. As between the simple alternatives of pure inflation targeting and pure price-path targeting, they argue for the desirability of price-path targeting, not only because their estimated parameter values imply that it would be better for most countries but also because their numerical analysis indicates that price-path targeting is a more robust choice against variation in the values of the estimated parameters.

The papers just mentioned all consider the implications of alternative approaches to the conduct of monetary policy under the assumption of rational expectations on the part of the private sector. Athanasios Orphanides and John C. Williams (chap. 5) instead consider the important practical question of the extent to which performance under a given policy rule may deteriorate if people do not have rational expectations but must base their forecasts on extrapolation from the statistical patterns that they have already observed. They then ask how a concern for robustness against this kind of imperfect knowledge should modify the recommendations that are made for the conduct of monetary policy.

In the context of a simple model of the inflation-output trade-off, Orphanides and Williams find not only that the degree to which it is possible for the central bank to stabilize inflation and the output gap is reduced in the case of imperfect knowledge on the part of the private sector, but also that the same policies are no longer optimal. In particular, they find that the optimal policy (in the case of particular assumed relative weights on the two stabilization goals) allows less response of inflation to cost-push shocks than would be optimal in the case of rational expectations. When the private sector forms its inflation expectations by estimating a regression model of inflation dynamics using recently observed data, allowing inflation to rise temporarily in response to a cost-push shock runs the risk of being (incorrectly) interpreted by private agents as an indication of a higher long-run average rate of inflation. It is therefore necessary for the central bank to target inflation more tightly than would be optimal under rational expectations, in order to prevent the losses that would result from allowing inflation expectations to drift. A conclusion that can be drawn from this analysis is that "stricter" inflation targeting is more appropriate in the case of economies where central-bank credibility has not yet been established.

The results of Orphanides and Williams also shed light on the question of why a public inflation target is desirable, rather than simply letting the public infer the central bank's policy commitments from its observed behavior. Orphanides and Williams show that when private agents are assumed to know the long-run average inflation rate associated with central bank policy (i.e., the central bank's long-run inflation target), rather than having to estimate it—although they still must estimate the dynamics of transitory departures from this long-run target—a more favorable trade-off between inflation and output-gap variability becomes attainable. Hence announcement of an inflation target—if it can be made credible to the private sector that the announced target represents the central bank's true goal—can improve macroeconomic performance, by anchoring inflation expectations to a greater extent in the face of short-run fluctuations in inflation due to cost-push shocks. The model of Orphanides and Williams thus provides theoretical results regarding the benefits of an explicit inflation target that are consistent with the experience that Mervyn King emphasizes in his remarks about the United Kingdom.

The second group of papers offers critical evaluations of inflation targeting as a general approach, especially as it has been implemented in practice thus far. Laurence Ball and Niamh Sheridan (chap. 6) compare the macroeconomic performance of inflation-targeting and non-inflation-targeting countries. Specifically, they compare seven OECD countries that adopted inflation targeting in the early 1990s with thirteen that did not, with respect to the behavior of inflation, output, and interest rates. Many commentators have remarked upon the substantial, sustained reductions in both the average level and the volatility of inflation by the inflation-targeting countries during the 1990s, as well as the fact that this improvement was achieved without any evident increase in instability of the real economy, and proposed these achievements as testimony to the benefits of inflation targeting as a monetary policy strategy. Ball and Sheridan, however, find that macroeconomic performance improved along similar dimensions for both targeters and nontargeters over this period of time, leading them to suggest that some of the improvements in macroeconomic stability in the inflation-targeting countries may have been unrelated to the adoption of inflation targeting. In particular, once they control for initial macroeconomic conditions (such as higher inflation, on average, in the countries that adopted inflation targeting), they find little evidence of greater improvement due to the adoption of inflation targeting. To the extent that they find greater absolute improvements in performance in inflation-targeting countries, they ascribe the result to "mean reversion": that is, these countries typically had worse initial conditions and thus were likely to improve more than countries that were in better shape at the beginning of the sample, independent of choice of policy regime.

These results indicate that some caution in interpreting the experience with inflation targeting thus far is appropriate. The proper interpretation of the results of Ball and Sheridan will doubtless be the subject of considerable further debate. As Gertler notes in his comment, it is arguable that a number of the non-inflation-targeting countries also changed their monetary policies in substantial ways in the 1990s, in respects that may have involved important features of inflation targeting, even if these countries did not have official inflation targets. (As argued by Goodfriend in this volume, the United States has adopted a number of features of inflation targeting in recent years.) Disentangling the different aspects of a given country's monetary policy regime in a way that can clarify which elements are most important in achieving better performance will be an important topic for further study.

Christopher A. Sims (chap. 7) cautions against dangers that may result from prescribing inflation targeting as an approach to monetary policy without regard to a country's fiscal situation and to the degree of independence of the central bank. A monetary policy rule that incorporates a target for inflation, and that commits the central bank to vigorous reaction to departures from the target inflation rate (as under the Taylor rule), will not necessarily result in an equilibrium in which inflation remains near the target rate. Under certain assumptions about fiscal policy and about the connection between the respective balance sheets of the central bank and the government, such a monetary rule may fail to prevent the existence of other equilibria (such as self-fulfilling deflations) or may even require the equilibrium inflation rate to diverge from the target rate (in a hyperinflationary spiral).

Sims argues, as a result, that inflation targeting may be least useful in exactly those countries that have had the greatest difficulties controlling inflation in the past; it should therefore not be oversold as a general solution to the problem of chronic inflation. In drawing attention to the importance of a suitable institutional framework and fiscal position for the success of an inflation-targeting rule, the paper echoes an important theme of the work by Jonas and Mishkin (discussed below) as well. This need not mean that inflation targeting should remain a fashion suited only to countries with few serious problems of macroeconomic stability to begin with. But a complete theory will surely place inflation targeting within the context of a broader program of institutional and policy reform, and the proper target criterion for an inflation-targeting central bank is unlikely to be independent, in this more general theory, of the degree of success that can be anticipated in reforming other aspects of policy.

Marvin Goodfriend (chap. 8) considers the case for adoption of inflation targeting in the United States. He argues that in several important senses the Federal Reserve already practices "implicit inflation targeting." Under Chairman Greenspan, the Fed clearly assigns priority to maintaining a low and stable inflation rate; it has achieved considerable credibility in this regard, and as a result of this credibility the Fed has gained flexibility in stabilizing the real economy without losing control of inflation. Nonetheless, Goodfriend argues that it would be desirable for the Fed to make its commitment to maintaining a low inflation rate more explicit. This would help to ensure that the credibility achieved by the Fed under the leadership of Paul Volcker and Alan Greenspan can be maintained through changes of personnel and improve the democratic accountability of the Fed as well. Finally, Goodfriend considers practical aspects of the way in which inflation targeting could be adopted in the United States given the current legislative mandate of the Fed, and he also addresses practical objections to the adoption of inflation targeting—arguing, for example, that such a commitment would not prevent the Fed from pursuing an efficient countercyclical stabilization policy.

In his comment on Goodfriend's paper, Kohn presents a skeptical view of the need for inflation targeting in the United States at this time. While Kohn agrees that the Fed's accumulation of credibility for maintenance of low inflation has been a very positive development, he denies that current policy is properly characterized as implicit inflation targeting, and he argues that adoption of explicit inflation targeting would substantially restrict the flexibility that has been essential to the success of recent U.S. policy. In his view, the Fed's current approach has already achieved the main benefits of inflation targeting (such as successful anchoring of inflation expectations) without any need for the straitjacket of a formal inflation target, and it would be wise to continue an approach that has worked well thus far.

These contrasting briefs—each presented by one of the most articulate proponents of the position in question—bring into focus a number of central issues that must be addressed in evaluating the potential of inflation targeting. How important are explicit as opposed to implicit commitments on the part of a central bank? How important is flexibility, and can flexibility of the crucial sort be reconciled with the existence of an explicit target for policy, if the nature of the commitment to that target is properly defined? These are critical issues for further analysis, and further reflection upon the experiences of central bankers in the United States and elsewhere will surely play an important role in settling them.

The third and final group of papers concerns the special problems of monetary policy in emerging markets. Jiri Jonas and Frederic S. Mishkin (chap. 9) examine the experiences of three transition economies that have recently adopted inflation targets: the Czech Republic, Poland, and Hungary. Transition economies such as these have a number of unusual features that pose special problems for the conduct of inflation targeting. The economies are in the midst of radical restructuring. They are new democracies, and relations between the government and the central bank in particular are not yet clearly defined. Furthermore, they are about to join the European Union and are thus prospective future members of the European Monetary Union (EMU); the requirements for entry to EMU thus pose additional constraints on the conduct of monetary policy. While these special circumstances make inflation targeting more difficult in these countries, and the three countries have often missed their targets by large margins, Jonas and Mishkin find that the strategy has been relatively successful in bringing about disinflation, and they argue that other possible strategies for inflation control would also be at least as problematic under these circumstances. Hence they remain optimistic about the usefulness of inflation targeting as a strategy for transition economies.

Several lessons are proposed regarding the appropriate conduct of inflation targeting by transition economies. Jonas and Mishkin argue that it is more than usually important in these economies that the central bank avoid undershooting (as well as overshooting) its inflation target, in order not to endanger the fragile political support for the central bank. It is also especially important in these economies that the inflation target be defined as a medium-term objective, allowing room for substantial short-run departures from the medium-term target in response to unforeseen shocks, and that the central bank be able to communicate effectively with the public about the goals of inflation targeting, the limits of what it can achieve, and the reasons for the target misses that occur.

Ricardo J. Caballero and Arvind Krishnamurthy (chap. 10) are concerned with special problems resulting from the vulnerability of emerging-market economies to volatile international capital flows—specifically, to the occurrence of "sudden stops," in which foreign lenders are suddenly unwilling to lend to the country at any interest rate. They present a model of a small open economy in which a central bank that is unable to commit itself in advance will choose to use monetary policy to defend the value of its currency too aggressively when a sudden stop occurs. That is, after the fact, the central bank will exhibit "fear of floating." However, this policy is distinctly suboptimal relative to the best policy under commitment. The optimal state-contingent commitment from an ex ante point of view would instead provide the private sector with a greater incentive to accumulate foreign-currency assets (or reduce foreign-currency borrowing), by allowing foreign-currency assets to increase in value (in terms of the domestic currency) during the crisis.

Caballero and Krishnamurthy show that a central bank operating under discretion can be induced to behave in a more desirable way if it is assigned a state-contingent inflation target (rather than a constant target) or if the inflation target is defined in terms of a measure of inflation that assigns greater weight to the prices of nontraded goods. That is, an appropriate ex ante inflation target may help to ameliorate the effects of sudden stops and steer the economy and the central bank away from the inferior fear-of-floating equilibrium. The paper also contributes to theoretical discussion of the appropriate price index to target in the case of an open economy, an important issue in the theory of inflation targeting for advanced economies as well.

To conclude this introduction, we return to Mervyn King's point that inflation targeting should be viewed as "a way of thinking about policy" rather than "an automatic answer to all the difficult policy questions." Or, as Ben Bernanke and Frederic Mishkin put it in an early essay on the subject, inflation targeting is "a framework, not a rule." Inflation targeting offers a number of the basic elements of a successful monetary policy framework, including a clearly defined nominal anchor, a coherent approach to decision making, the flexibility to respond to unanticipated shocks, and a strategy for communicating with the public and financial markets. However, as in any other framework, making good policy requires sensitivity to the specific economic and institutional environment in which policymakers find themselves, as well as the technical capability to modify and adapt the framework as needed. We hope that the research contained in this volume will be useful to monetary policymakers and their staff in their efforts to achieve economic stability.

1

What Has Inflation Targeting Achieved?

Mervyn King

In the United Kingdom, in rather the same way as Marvin Goodfriend described the U.S. experience, we went through a postwar period of first stop/go and then three severe recessions. There was the "great inflation" in which inflation peaked at 27 percent in the mid-1970s—and averaged 13 percent a year right through the whole of that decade. It even averaged over 7 percent a year right through the 1980s under Mrs. Thatcher. Only since 1992 has inflation been consistently below 4 percent, and in fact it has averaged a fraction under 2.5 percent of our target for the past ten years, with growth averaging 2.5 percent a year and a little above the historical trend. Inflation has been low and stable. Unemployment came down from double-digit levels to 5 percent. And there have been forty-two consecutive quarters of positive economic growth, which I think is unprecedented, at least in our history.

But the question is, was inflation targeting necessary to that achievement? Whatever the answer to that question, I do think that inflation targeting made our job easier by reducing the cost of making the right decisions. Why is that? I think that monetary stability, or macroeconomic stability more generally, is a bit like healthy living: you need to find a sustainable way of doing it. There is no point alternating between a crash diet and bingeing. That is the boom/bust syndrome. The key is to find a way of setting policy that can be sustained. I think it is helpful to devise procedures, whether they be thought of as monetary policy rules or whether they are institutions that remove temptation, to help the weaker brethren explain themselves to others.

Mervyn King is governor of the Bank of England and is chairman of the Monetary Policy Committee.

Let me very briefly summarize what happens in the United Kingdom. We have a target for consumer price inflation, which is a measure of retail price inflation excluding the interest component on mortgages—the so-called RPIX inflation—and we are instructed to aim at 2.5 percent. And we are meant to aim for that at all times. It is a symmetric target; that is quite clear in the remit. That is relevant, I think, to the paper by Jonas and Mishkin (chap. 9, which I will discuss later), in which they see some problems in transition economies from the lack of symmetry.

Crucially, this target is set by the government. We do not set it ourselves at the Bank of England. It is given to us by government. The decisions on interest rates are then made by the Monetary Policy Committee, which meets once a month by statute on fixed dates, all announced well in advance. There are nine members of the committee, each with one vote. Dissenting votes are common. It is rare to have a unanimous vote from the committee.

We spend a long time on the forecast procedure using a range of models. Sometimes I think that we have more econometric models than one could possibly want. In the end, however, the judgment of the committee has to play a key role, and we can come back to that later. We publish our minutes thirteen days after the announcement of the decision. The minutes contain the voting pattern, and they contain a description of the arguments that were given during the discussion to justify views on particular parts of the analysis or indeed on the final judgment on interest rates. Once a quarter, we publish a formal forecast for inflation in our *Inflation Report.*

This systematic process should be contrasted with what went before in the United Kingdom. No notice of when policy decisions would be made was given. The financial markets had no notice of when interest rates would be decided, so it could be any day. That certainly kept them glued to the screens.

Of course, in this setting a serious economic discussion did not carry much weight. It was the ability to swing the argument on the basis of what happened at the time. And politics intruded a very great deal. So what has happened in Britain is that we switched, for better or worse—and I think it is clearly for the better—to a much more systematic professional procedure, which you have had in the Federal Open Markets Committee (FOMC) for a very long time. Now, I think this may well be part of the success of inflation targeting in other countries as well.

There are four key points I want to make. One is about constrained discretion and inflation expectations. A second is about inflation targeting and the committee process itself. A third is about transparency and accountability, and a fourth is one that Martin Feldstein has alluded to, which is that inflation targeting does not give all the answers. That is, there are many difficult aspects of the economic outlook that are all about serious economics and discussing what is likely to happen in the future, but that are made no easier by having an inflation-targeting framework than they would be by any other framework.

On the first point, constrained discretion and inflation expectations, any monetary policy can be thought of as a combination of an inflation target in the medium term and a response to shocks as they occur. In that sense, any coherent policy reaction found can be described as inflation targeting. I like to see inflation targeting as being about—to use Ben Bernanke and Frederic Mishkin's phrase—"constrained discretion." It sets up a process in which the Central Bank has to explain what it is doing. Now, this has two implications, I think. One is that it is easier, I believe, to influence inflation expectations. Certainly part of our success has been that we have brought inflation expectations down; whether you measure them by bond yields, index-linked versus conventional yields, or surveys, inflation expectations in Britain are now pretty well anchored on the 2.5 percent target. And that makes monetary policy easier by giving monetary policy a bit more time to respond. We are not worried that an inflationary shock is likely to lead immediately to an upward revision or downward revision of inflation expectations, feeding through very quickly as it might have done before into inflation expectations, wage bargaining, and then prices. This point is stressed in the paper by Orphanides and Williams (chap. 5), which we are going to discuss. It matters because if you let inflation expectations drift too far away from the target, you can end up in quite serious difficulty with a costly process to bring them back again.

Another aspect of our process is that it is one in which economists have some comparative advantage. This is unlike the old British amateur tradition, in which mystery and mystique were the essence of central banking. In the United Kingdom, this has been something of a sea-change. This may or may not be true elsewhere. In Britain, however, the central bank is now seen as an institution that is about making professional economic judgments in a way that it was not before, and I think that really matters.

I have always thought of inflation targeting as a way of implementing the optimal policy reaction function, setting the optimal policy by means of constrained discretion within the inflation-targeting framework. In chapter 2, Lars Svensson and Michael Woodford are going to explain why it is just a bit more complicated than I used to think. Nevertheless, I still think that the idea of a framework is to get as close as possible to what you, the theorist, think of as optimal monetary policy. This should be done in a way that forces the central bank to explain and, by accountability, helps to keep it on track and make the right decisions. That is the first point.

The second point is the committee process. This is a pure observation based on the U.K. experience. Even with nine professional economists, my belief is that in a committee without a clear objective there would be scope for people to set their own agenda. Members might try to argue that their view of the objective is the right one and other people's the wrong one. This could divert the committee from spending its time discussing the state of the economy and the technical judgments needed to hit a given target.

What is clearly true about our Monetary Policy Committee, and I do not think this was obvious ex ante, is that the entire discussion is focused on a technical economic judgment about what it is necessary to do to hit the inflation target. Now, you can talk about whether the target is desirable or not, but in terms of making sure that people around the table do what they are supposed to do, this is highly effective. Many committees I have sat on have had the property that people often try to gain leadership of the community by moving toward the center, forming a consensus in which they exercise some leadership. They are never judged on whether the outcome of the decision is good or bad; instead, they are judged according to whether they are strong committee people.

Individual accountability, allied to the fact that the target is given to us from outside, means that the nature of our discussions is absolutely, solidly focused on the state of the economy and what we need to do to interest rates to keep inflation on track to hit the target. We have a two-day meeting in which the first day is about the diagnosis of the economy, and the second day is the treatment, the level of interest rates. Those meetings are more successful than any other meetings I have been to at committees because there is a very clear objective.

The third point concerns transparency, accountability, and legitimacy. Our split between the government setting the target and the central bank making decisions is of course instrument independence, to use Stan Fischer's phrase. But we go out around the country and to Parliament to explain why our policy decisions will help to meet the target, and having a clear target gives us a natural focus. I would say that this delegation of decisions to the Monetary Policy Committee, which actually came in May 1997, has in fact proved very popular. This was not to be expected. Many people thought that no government would make the Bank independent because Parliament would complain that it had lost control. The press would complain that there was no democratic mandate and that people would feel that we were unaccountable.

That has turned out not to be the case. First of all, the business community likes to feel that there is a group of people who actually know what they are talking about setting monetary policy. In fact, it is the only thing we are supposed to be talking about. Second, we are accountable in well-defined ways, and I think that the pressure we have been put under to explain ourselves has actually benefited us.

One of the great benefits of having a committee is that people can see what the issues are, and even if members of the committee disagree and put different arguments, I think the great success of our system and that which has been a real lesson to us has been never to claim that the decision was obvious. Always point out that there were arguments on each occasion for and against the action that was taken, explain what the arguments were, and then everyone feels that at least the relevant arguments are being put on the table.

Finally, on the last point, inflation targeting, as I said, is a way of thinking about policy. It is not an automatic answer to all the difficult policy questions. I think the asset price question is probably the best example of that. We have faced major asset price movements, so it is not as if we have not actually been challenged in our framework so far. We have had a rise in the effective exchange rate index of more than 20 percent, both nominal and real, in the early part of the period, which has persisted almost until now. We had the sharp rise in stock prices and then a sharp fall in stock prices. More recently, we have had increases in house prices of between 25 and 30 percent.

I think the difficulty is to work out what these movements mean for the risks in the future. My feeling is that any policy decision has to take into account the entire distribution of future outcomes for inflation and output, and not just the expected values in some exact future period. In my speech in November 2003 at the London School of Economics, I talked about the fact that inflation targeting as a framework can, I think, provide a way to discuss this. Sharp asset price movements raise risks that mean there is a potential trade-off between the risk of a small shortfall of the inflation target now relative to a bigger risk of a large deviation of inflation from the target in the future. In the conventional discussion, there is a trade-off between the volatility of inflation and the volatility of output. Similarly, in choosing the horizon over which you bring inflation back to the target, there is a choice about whether to accept in the short run inflation a little short of the inflation target, but to do so knowingly, against the risks involved in a potentially large deviation of inflation from target further ahead at a longer horizon.

I think this is a tricky question to which there is no simple answer. It is not something that is peculiar to inflation targeting, and other frameworks have other methods of dealing with it. But I don't think it is inconsistent with inflation targeting, although it does merit some separate discussion.

We have spent a good deal of time and effort building a constituency for low inflation. This involves trying to build public support for low inflation, which I think is important because of the very interesting work done on Germany showing that the more distant were the hyperinflation episodes, the more the younger generations lacked commitment to low inflation. Thus, you cannot just rely on the memory of boom and bust in the past to keep people committed to low inflation. We need a positive program to persuade people, and having a clear inflation target has helped. Like the Federal Reserve, we have our competition for schools, and ours is called Target 2.5.

Martin Feldstein had six issues to discuss, whereas I have five questions that I would like to put. First, I would be interested to know whether people would agree that inflation targeting makes it easier for the weaker brethren—that is, most people in central banking—to do the right thing.

Second, why is it that countries that have adopted inflation targeting are generally very happy with it? Is it just that they have benefited from a very benign period, or have they found this a sustainable, healthy way of living?

Third, what is it that a central bank should be trying to communicate? Is it a policy reaction function, or is it something more complicated? Is it what central banks are learning about the economy, in addition to a policy reaction function? I often think that Alan Greenspan's speeches are almost a conversation with the public about the issues that arise when thinking about the economy. I think we have tried to do some of that, too.

Fourth, how serious are the problems posed by issues such as asset price inflation and about the horizon over which inflation should be brought back to target? Finally, how can we focus the attention of both decision makers and the public much more on the risks around the central projection than on just the central projection of a forecast for the expected value of our projection?

I

Optimal Targets

2

Implementing Optimal Policy through Inflation-Forecast Targeting

Lars E. O. Svensson and Michael Woodford

2.1 Introduction

In recent years, many central banks have adopted inflation-targeting frameworks for the conduct of monetary policy. These have proven in a number of countries to be effective means of first lowering inflation and then maintaining both low and stable inflation and inflation expectations, without negative consequences for the output gap. Thus, the new approach to monetary policy has been judged quite successful, as far as its consequences for the average level of inflation and the output gap are concerned.

It has been less clear how effective these procedures are as ways of bringing about desirable transitory fluctuations in inflation and output in response to exogenous shocks.[1] But this is also a relevant question in the choice of a framework for the conduct of monetary policy; moreover, the expectation that inflation-targeting procedures will perform well in this respect is often cited as one of their leading advantages over other approaches to the maintenance of low inflation and the achievement of cred-

Lars E. O. Svensson is a professor of economics at Princeton University and a research associate of the National Bureau of Economic Research. Michael Woodford is professor of economics at Columbia University and a research associate of the National Bureau of Economic Research.

We have benefited from discussions with and comments from Giovanni Favara, Mark Gertler, Peter Ireland, Henrik Jensen, Mervyn King, Kai Leitemo, Bennett McCallum, Glenn Rudebusch, John Taylor, and participants in the conference and in seminars at Bank of Canada, Georgetown University, NBER's Monetary Economics Program, New York University, Princeton University, Université de Montréal and NBER's preconference. We also thank Giovanni Favara for research assistance and Christina Lönnblad, Kathleen DeGennaro, and Kathleen Hurley for editorial and secretarial assistance. Remaining errors and expressed views are our own.

1. See, for instance, Svensson (1999b), especially footnote 43.

ibility. For example, King (1997a) argues the superiority of inflation targeting over commitment to a money-growth rule on the ground that, while either approach should equally serve to maintain low average inflation and low inflation expectations, inflation targeting *also* results in optimal short-run responses to shocks, while money-growth targeting does not. Here we consider how inflation targeting should be conducted in order to achieve this goal.

2.1.1   Disadvantages of Purely Forward-Looking Policy Making

In King's analysis, inflation targeting is associated with decision making under discretion. However, that discretion is constrained by a clear objective, involving inflation stabilization around the inflation target and output-gap stabilization around an output-gap target. In particular, the output-gap target is modified (relative to the output-gap target that would reflect true social preferences) to equal zero, so as to be consistent with the natural output level. This modification of the output-gap target suffices to eliminate the "average inflation bias" associated with discretionary policy making, and in the simple Barro-Gordon model that King assumes, this also suffices to make the outcome of discretionary optimization fully optimal—that is, consistent with the optimal equilibrium under commitment, including optimal responses to transitory shocks.

However, this result is quite special to the simple model that King uses. As a number of authors have pointed out, in the presence of forward-looking private-sector behavior (of the kind that naturally results from dynamic optimization by the private sector), discretionary optimization by a central bank generally results not only in average inflation bias, when the output-gap target is positive, but also in inefficient *responses to shocks* (what is sometimes called "stabilization bias"), regardless of whether the output-gap target is positive or not.[2]

The reason is simple. In general, forward-looking behavior implies that the bank's short-run trade-offs (between, say, its inflation stabilization and output-gap stabilization) following a shock can be improved if it can be arranged for private-sector *expectations* about future inflation and output to adjust in the right way in response to the shock. However, this can occur—when the private sector has rational expectations—only if subsequent central bank policy does in fact change as a result of the past shocks, in such a way as to bring about the alternative evolution that it was desired

---

2. Jonsson (1997) and Svensson (1997b) point out that stabilization bias and conditional inflation bias, as distinct from average inflation bias, arise in a Barro-Gordon model with output persistence—that is, with an endogenous state variable. Flodén (1996); Clarida, Galí, and Gertler (1999); and Woodford (1999b) show that stabilization bias arises with a Calvo-type forward-looking Phillips curve. The problem goes beyond a mere contemporaneous response to shocks of the wrong size. Instead, as stressed by Woodford (1999a,b), discretionary optimization also generally leads to a suboptimal degree of persistence of the effects of shocks as well—the problem of inadequate history dependence discussed below.

that people would expect. Under discretionary optimization, however, it will *not,* as the central bank will reoptimize afresh at the later date and care nothing about past conditions that no longer constrain what it is possible for it to achieve at that date. This problem can exist, and generally does, even when the output-gap target is consistent with steady inflation at the inflation target so that there is no *average* inflation bias.

As Woodford (1999a) stresses, the suboptimal responses to shocks characteristic of discretionary optimization also characterize *any* decision procedure for monetary policy that is purely forward looking. By a "purely forward-looking" procedure we mean one in which *only* factors that matter for the central bank's forecast of the future evolution of its target variables, conditional upon its current and future policy actions, play any role in its decisions. Any such procedure has the property that, *if* it determines a unique equilibrium, that equilibrium is one in which the evolution of the target variables depends only upon the factors just mentioned. In particular, the equilibrium paths of the target variables will be independent of past conditions that no longer matter for current equilibrium determination except insofar as the central bank may condition its policy upon them. But, as Woodford (1999b) emphasizes, in general forward-looking private-sector behavior implies that an optimal equilibrium will involve additional *history dependence.* This is because it is optimal for the path of the target variables to depend upon past conditions—even when these no longer constrain currently feasible outcomes—because of the effects of the prior *anticipation* of such dependence upon the path of the target variables at earlier dates.[3]

Purely forward-looking approaches to monetary policy are also more easily prone to another problem, which is *indeterminacy* of rational-expectations equilibrium. Most inflation-targeting central banks (as, indeed, most central banks nowadays) use a short-term nominal interest rate as the policy instrument or "operating target." But as Sargent and Wallace (1975) first stressed, interest rate rules may allow a large multiplicity of rational-expectations equilibrium paths for real and nominal variables, including equilibria in which fluctuations occur that are unrelated to any variation in economic "fundamentals." This indeterminacy is plainly undesirable—at least if alternative policy rules are available that are equally consistent with the best equilibrium but do not allow the bad ones—since some of the possible equilibria will be very bad, from the point of view of any objective that penalizes unnecessary variation in the target variables.[4]

---

3. The history dependence of equilibria resulting from optimal policy under commitment in the case of a forward-looking system has been observed since the early treatments by, for instance, Backus and Driffill (1986) and Currie and Levine (1993).

4. This criterion for choice among alternative monetary policy reaction functions is also stressed in Bernanke and Woodford (1997); Christiano and Gust (1999); Clarida, Galí, and Gertler (1998); Kerr and King (1996); Rotemberg and Woodford (1999); and Woodford (1999b, 2003, chap. 4).

In the case of many forward-looking models derived from private-sector optimization, as with the rational-expectations IS-LM model analyzed by Sargent and Wallace (1975), one can show that commitment to *any* reaction function that determines the path of the nominal interest rate purely as a function of exogenous factors (that is, without any feedback from endogenous variables such as the rate of inflation) implies indeterminacy of the equilibrium price level.[5] However, this does not mean that interest rate–setting procedures as such must lead to this outcome; as McCallum (1981) first noted, a sufficient degree of dependence (of the right sort) of the central bank's interest rate operating target upon endogenous variables can render equilibrium *determinate,* in the sense of there existing a unique nonexplosive solution to the equilibrium conditions. It is important, though, to choose an interest rate–setting procedure that involves sufficient dependence of this kind.

One example of the kind of dependence that suffices for determinacy in the simple forward-looking model used below is that assumed in the well-known reaction function proposed by Taylor (1993): making the nominal interest rate an increasing function of the observed inflation and output gap, with a positive coefficient on the output gap and a coefficient greater than 1 on inflation. This sort of reaction function has also been found to lead to a determinate equilibrium in a variety of other types of forward-looking models.[6]

The kind of dependence that is needed for determinacy may not be possible in the case of a purely forward-looking procedure of the kind often assumed in discussions of inflation-forecast targeting. To make this point in an especially sharp way, we here consider a simple forward-looking model in which no lagged endogenous variables matter for the determination of future inflation and output. In this case, a purely forward-looking monetary policy procedure—by which (in line with Woodford 2000 and Giannoni and Woodford 2002) we mean one under which the decision at each point in time depends only on the set of possible future paths for the economy, given its current condition—must make the central bank's instrument choice a function solely of information about the future evolution of the exogenous disturbances. Under the further assumptions that (a) all information about the exogenous disturbances that is available to the private sector is also directly observed by the central bank, and (b) the central bank must choose its current instrument setting before observing the private sector's current choices of endogenous variables and its current expectations, this means that the nominal interest rate will evolve solely as a function of exogenous state variables, independent of the paths of any of the

5. See Woodford (1999b) for a result of this kind in the context of a model closely related to that used here.
6. See Christiano and Gust (1999); Levin, Wieland, and Williams (1999); Rotemberg and Woodford (1999); and Woodford (1999b).

endogenous variables. But such a rule implies indeterminacy of the equilibrium paths of both inflation and output.[7]

Thus, we conclude once again that a decision procedure that can be relied upon to achieve the optimal equilibrium under commitment must be history dependent in a way that purely discretionary decision-making procedures are not, as well as insuring determinacy of the equilibrium. Our task in this paper is to consider to what extent various alternative forms of inflation targeting can avoid stabilization bias, incorporate history dependence of the proper sort, and result in determinacy of the equilibrium.

2.1.2 Monetary Policy Rules and Approaches to Policy Implementation

Since we will discuss the details of alternative decision frameworks for monetary policy, it is practical to have a consistent classification of such decision frameworks. In this paper, as in Svensson (1999b, 2003), a "monetary policy rule" is interpreted broadly as a "prescribed guide for monetary policy conduct." We give particular attention to a special type of policy rules, which we call "targeting rules." "Target variables" are endogenous variables that enter a loss function, a function that is increasing in the deviations of the target variables from prescribed "target levels." "Targeting" is minimizing such a loss function. "Forecast targeting" refers to using forecasts of the target variables effectively as intermediate target variables, as in King's (1994) early characterization of inflation targeting.

A "general targeting rule" is a high-level specification of a monetary policy rule that specifies the target variables, the target levels, and the loss function to be minimized. A complete description of such a procedure also requires specification of the exact procedure used to determine the actions that should minimize the loss function, such as the one that we propose in section 2.3 below.

A "specific targeting rule" is instead expressed directly as a condition for the target variables, a "target criterion." Under certain circumstances,

---

7. Studies such as Clarida, Galí, and Gertler (1998) and Woodford (2003, chap. 4), find that equilibrium may be determinate, in a forward-looking model closely related to our own, under commitment to a rule that makes the nominal interest rate a sufficiently sharply increasing function of current and/or expected *future* inflation and output gaps over some horizon. But their result is obtained by assuming that the desired relation between expected inflation and output and the nominal interest rate can be imposed as an equilibrium condition: the bank's ability to ensure that it necessarily holds in equilibrium is not questioned. Such a condition, however, is an *implicit instrument rule* and does not represent a fully operational specification of the monetary policy rule, as the central bank's instrument is expressed as a function of endogenous variables (conditional expectations of future inflation and output) that themselves depend upon current monetary policy. In practice, the bank would have to forecast the paths of the endogenous variables, given its contemplated action. If this forecast depends only on information about the exogenous disturbances and the bank's contemplated policy, then an operational version of the policy rule, an *explicit instrument rule,* in which the bank's decision procedure is completely specified as an algorithm, is equivalent to a rule that sets the nominal interest rate as a function of the exogenous disturbances, and leads to indeterminacy.

commitment to a general targeting rule may be equivalent to a particular specific targeting rule, which describes conditions that the forecast paths must satisfy in order to minimize a particular loss function. Nonetheless, it may be important to distinguish between the two ways of describing the policy commitment, on grounds either of differing efficiency as means of communicating with the public or of differing degrees of robustness to changes in the model of the economy used to implement them. Furthermore, a specific targeting rule need not be equivalent to any intuitive general targeting rule,[8] and indeed one of our primary reasons for our interest in such specifications here will be their greater flexibility, which makes it easier to introduce history dependence of the sort required to solve the problems introduced in the previous section.

Any policy rule implies a "reaction function," which specifies the central bank's instrument as a function of predetermined endogenous or exogenous variables observable to the central bank at the time that it sets the instrument. This "implied reaction function" should not, in general, be confused with the policy rule itself; for example, the implied reaction function associated with a given policy rule will generally change in the case of changes in the model of the economy used in implementing the rule. However, an "explicit instrument rule" is a low-level specification of the monetary policy rule, in the form of a prescribed reaction function. Proposals such as the policy rule advocated by Taylor (1993) are of this form.

We are interested in decision procedures for monetary policy that can achieve (or at least come close to) the optimal equilibrium under commitment. In fact, there is no single policy rule that is uniquely consistent with the optimal equilibrium. Many rules may be consistent with the same equilibrium, even though they are not equivalent insofar as they imply a commitment to different sorts of out-of-equilibrium behavior. Furthermore, even rules that specify the same actions in all circumstances, given a particular model of the economy, may deserve separate consideration because they would no longer be equivalent if the bank's model of the economy were to change.

We shall not here attempt to enumerate all of the possible types of policy rules that could achieve the optimal equilibrium. Instead, we shall seek approaches to this problem that preserve, to the greatest extent possible, the attractive features of inflation-forecast targeting, the procedure currently used (in one variant or another) by the most prominent inflation-targeting central banks.[9] For example, we shall prefer approaches in which the decision process has as transparent a connection as possible with the central bank's ultimate objectives. A procedure like inflation-forecast tar-

8. One can always find a trivial general targeting rule for any specific targeting rule by simply letting the loss function be the square of the specific targeting rule written as a target criterion equal to zero.

9. See, for instance, Svensson (1997a, 1999b, 2003) for discussion of procedures of this general type.

geting, in which the entire decision process is organized around the pursuit of an explicit objective defined in terms of the ultimate goal variables, has several advantages. Focus upon such an objective helps to ensure that policy is made in a coherent fashion; it facilitates communication with the public about the intended consequences of the bank's policy, even when the full details of the implementation of the policy may be too complex to describe; and it favors accountability by indicating the way in which the policy's success can appropriately be measured. We shall inquire as to the extent to which we can preserve this sort of transparency while introducing the sort of history dependence required for a determinate equilibrium with optimal responses to shocks.

Another criterion for a good policy rule is robustness of the rule specification to possible changes in the details of the bank's model of the economy. A full analysis of the question of robustness would necessarily be numerical, as in general one cannot expect *any* rule to be completely unaffected by possible model changes, and the question will be which kinds of rules are less affected. Nonetheless, we here consider robustness of a somewhat special kind, which is the possibility that a rule may continue to be optimal under some particular (restricted) class of perturbations of the model. On this ground, we shall consider a policy rule better if it continues to be optimal under a larger class of perturbations than is true for another rule.

This, too, is a desirable feature of inflation-forecast-targeting proposals. These tend to be high-level specifications of monetary policy, with the details of implementation depending upon the details of the particular model of the economy used by a particular central bank. In some cases, changes in the model require no change in the high-level description of optimal policy. For example, Svensson (1997a, 2003) shows how a targeting rule defined in terms of desired features of the forecast paths for inflation and the output gap may correspond to a first-order condition that characterizes the optimal equilibrium. An advantage of this way of describing the optimal equilibrium is that the form of the first-order condition is invariant under certain changes in the model, notably changes in the assumed character of (additive) stochastic disturbances. Here we shall give attention to policy specifications that share this property, although they involve history dependence sufficient to eliminate the problems just mentioned with purely forward-looking procedures.[10]

With these desiderata in mind, we explore the possibility of implementing the optimal equilibrium in each of three possible ways. Our highest-level policy specification is in terms of a general targeting rule, a loss function that the central bank is committed to seeking to minimize through a forecast-based dynamic optimization procedure. In the case of this way of specifying

---

10. In Svensson (1997a), problems of stabilization bias and lack of history dependence do not arise, owing to the absence of forward-looking elements in the simple model used to expound the idea.

policy, the history dependence necessary for optimality must be introduced through a modification of the central bank's loss function, which must be made history dependent in a way that the true (social) loss function is not.

Our second, intermediate-level policy specification is in terms of a specific targeting rule, specifying a criterion that the bank's forecast paths for its target variables must satisfy. This kind of rule specifies a relation involving one or more endogenous variables that cannot be directly observed at the time that policy is chosen and that instead must be forecasted. Furthermore, in the case of a forward-looking model, even forecasting endogenous variables a short time in the future will in general require solving for the model's equilibrium into the indefinite future; thus, a forecast of the entire future paths of the various variables is required. A decision procedure of this kind is therefore still organized around the construction of forecast paths conditional upon alternative policies, even if explicit optimization is not undertaken. In the case of such a targeting rule, the history dependence necessary for determinacy and optimality must be introduced through commitment to a rule that involves *lagged* endogenous variables as well as forecasts of their future values.

Finally, our lowest-level specification of policy is in terms of an explicit instrument rule, specifying the setting of the central bank's instrument as a function of variables that are exogenous or predetermined at the time. Implementation of this kind of policy rule is no longer dependent upon either a model of the economy or an explicit objective function. We find that such rules are less transparently related to the ultimate objectives of policy than in the other two cases, also when we consider the possibility of instrument rules that are relatively robust to changes in model specification, owing to their derivation from first-order conditions that characterize the optimal equilibrium. Such rules also differ from the other two cases in that they are purely backward looking; as a result, introduction of the dependence upon lagged endogenous variables required for determinacy and optimality is straightforward.

Our analysis leads us to more than one example of a policy rule that both renders equilibrium determinate and achieves the optimal equilibrium, if the central bank's commitment to it can be made credible to the private sector. These include history-dependent variants of inflation-forecast targeting. We thus conclude that the need for history dependence in policy, for the reasons just sketched, is consistent with a suitably designed forecast-targeting procedure.

The paper is organized as follows. In section 2.2, we introduce a simple forward-looking model that allows us to make the above remarks more concrete. We characterize the optimal equilibrium in such a model and show that it involves history dependence of a kind not consistent with purely discretionary decision making. We also show that the problem of indeterminacy of equilibrium arises in this model and needs to be considered in the specification of the different policy rules.

In sections 2.3, 2.4, and 2.5, we then take up the three successively lower-level specifications of policy described above. In each case, we consider ways in which the sort of history dependence in policy required for consistency with the optimal equilibrium can be introduced. We also treat the issue of determinacy of equilibrium for each of the policies analyzed. Finally, in section 2.6, we compare the advantages and disadvantages of the various proposals taken up in the previous sections. Here we also briefly discuss the transparency of the connection to policy goals and the robustness of our various policy specifications. We conclude that a variant of inflation-forecast targeting, modified to include a commitment by the central bank to respond to deviations of private-sector expectations from those it had forecasted, represents an especially attractive procedure from the point of view of these several criteria.

2.2   The Model

The model is a variant of a standard forward-looking model used, for example, in Clarida, Galí, and Gertler (1999) and Woodford (1999b, 2003). In the variant that we use here, inflation and output are both predetermined for one period, as in Bernanke and Woodford (1997), Rotemberg and Woodford (1997, 1999) and Svensson (2003), except for an unforecastable random error term that cannot be affected by monetary policy. Optimizing private-sector behavior is represented by two structural equations, an aggregate-supply equation (derived from a first-order condition for optimal price-setting by the representative supplier) and an "expectational IS curve" (derived from an Euler equation for the optimal timing of purchases).[11]

The forward-looking aggregate-supply (AS) equation takes the form

$$(1) \qquad \pi_{t+1} = \beta \pi_{t+2|t} + \kappa x_{t+1|t} + u_{t+1},$$

where π_{t+1} is inflation between periods t and $t + 1$ (also referred to as inflation in period $t + 1$), x_t is the output gap, indicating the percentage by which output exceeds potential, $0 < \beta < 1$ is a discount factor, κ is a positive coefficient, and u_{t+1} is an exogenous disturbance term, the value of which is realized only in period $t + 1$.[12] For any variable z and any horizon $\tau \geq 0$, we use the notation $z_{t+\tau|t} \equiv E_t z_{t+\tau}$ to denote private-sector expecta-

11. See Woodford (2003) for general discussion of the microeconomic foundations of the class of models to which ours belongs.

12. Here we assume, as in standard expositions of the Calvo pricing model, that prices remain fixed in monetary terms between the occasions on which they are reoptimized. It is worth noting, however, that if we were to assume a constant rate of increase in prices between the occasions on which prices are reoptimized, as in Yun (1996), the AS relation would take the same form, but with π_{t+1} interpreted as inflation in excess of that "normal" rate. Our conclusions below as to the character of optimal policy would also all have direct analogs in that case, allowing for the possibility of optimal targeting rules in which the inflation target could differ from zero.

tions regarding $z_{t+\tau}$ conditional on information available in period t; for example, $\pi_{t+2|t}$ denotes private-sector inflation expectations in period t of inflation between periods $t + 1$ and $t + 2$. This variant of the Calvo-Rotemberg AS relation differs from that used, for example, in Woodford (1999b) in that the conditional expectations of x_{t+1} and π_{t+2} are taken in period t rather than $t + 1$. This is because, except for the surprise component $u_{t+1} - u_{t+1|t}$, we assume that prices are determined one period in advance. As a result of this decision lag, the first-order condition for "voluntary" price changes is the same as in the simpler case but conditioned upon an earlier information set. This has the consequence that, as is often assumed, monetary policy changes will have no effect upon inflation within the period in which the change first becomes public. We assume that measured inflation differs from the average of "voluntary" price changes by an error term that need not be forecastable when the "voluntary" price changes are determined; this might be interpreted either as measurement error in the price index or as a time-varying markup of retail prices over the predetermined wholesale prices.[13] We allow for the existence of a "surprise" component of inflation in order to avoid the counterfactual implication that inflation is known with perfect certainty one period in advance.

Our specification also differs from the simplest one in that we allow for a forecastable "cost-push" shock $u_{t+1|t}$, which shifts the distance between "potential output" (with respect to which our "output gap" is defined) and the level of output that would be consistent with zero "voluntary" inflation. Thus, we assume that some exogenous shifts in the aggregate supply curve do not correspond to changes in the efficient level of output (an example would be exogenous variation in the markup over wholesale prices); these shifts are not considered to represent variation in "potential output" (so that the social loss function can still be expressed in terms of our output-gap variable), and thus they appear as a residual in equation (1). Allowance for such a shock creates a conflict between inflation stabilization and output-gap stabilization, so that optimal policy does not take the relatively trivial form of completely stabilizing the predictable components of both variables. A special case is when the cost-push disturbance is a first-order autoregression—or AR(1)—process,

$$(2) \qquad\qquad u_{t+1} = \rho u_t + \varepsilon_{t+1},$$

where $0 \le \rho < 1$ and ε_{t+1} is an exogenous independently and identically distributed (i.i.d.) shock.[14]

13. Which interpretation we take has no consequences for our analysis of optimal policy, since the surprise component of inflation makes in any event only an exogenous and constant contribution to the expected losses computed below.

14. Here we assume that the same shock ε_{t+1} represents both the surprise component of inflation in period $t + 1$ and the innovation in period $t + 1$ in the distortion $u_{t+1|t+1}$ that affects "voluntary" inflation in period $t + 2$. These could be the same process, if, for example, both

The forward-looking aggregate-demand (IS) equation takes the form

(3)
$$x_{t+1} = x_{t+2|t} - \sigma(i_{t+1|t} - \pi_{t+2|t} - r^n_{t+1}),$$

where i_t, the "instrument rate," is a short nominal interest rate and the central bank's instrument, σ, is a positive coefficient (the intertemporal elasticity of substitution), and r^n_{t+1} is an exogenous disturbance. Again, conditional expectations are taken one period earlier than in the standard Euler equation, because interest-sensitive private expenditure is assumed to be predetermined for one period. This "time to plan" (argued in Christiano and Vigfusson 1999 and Edge 2000 to be realistic at least in the case of investment spending) is included in order to obtain the implication that monetary policy changes have no effect upon output, either, during the period of the change. Again, we allow for a "surprise" component of output, which may be interpreted as exogenous variation in some other component of aggregate expenditure, such as government purchases, that are not predetermined.

The forecastable component of the disturbance process, $r^n_{t+1|t}$, represents exogenous variation in the Wicksellian "natural" (real) rate of interest, the real interest rate consistent with a zero output gap. This represents a composite of disturbances that affect the desired timing of expenditure and disturbances that affect potential output, since our IS equation is written in terms of the output gap rather than output.[15] As long as our stabilization objectives can be defined in terms of inflation and the output gap (rather than output directly), only the effect of such factors upon the natural rate of interest matters for our analysis. A special case is when the natural rate of interest is an AR(1) process,

(4)
$$r^n_{t+1} = \bar{r} + \omega(r^n_t - \bar{r}) + \eta_{t+1},$$

where $0 \le \omega < 1$, $\bar{r}$ is the average natural real rate, and η_{t+1} is an exogenous i.i.d. shock in period $t + 1$.[16]

The inclusion of the decision lags in our structural relations implies that inflation and the output gap fulfill

(5)
$$\pi_{t+1} = \pi_{t+1|t} + u_{t+1} - u_{t+1|t},$$

(6)
$$x_{t+1} = x_{t+1|t} + \sigma(r^n_{t+1} - r^n_{t+1|t}),$$

---

are due to exogenous variation in the retail markup. More generally, however, all that really matters for our subsequent analysis is that the forecastable component $u_{t+1|t}$ is assumed to be an AR(1) process. Allowing a "surprise inflation" term that is independent of this process makes no difference for our conclusions.

15. See Woodford (2003, chap. 4), for discussion of how various types of real disturbances affect this variable.

16. Once again, it does not necessarily make sense to equate the "surprise" component of the output gap with the innovation in the natural rate, but this notational economy does not affect any of our subsequent conclusions.

so that both inflation and the output gap are determined one period in advance, up to surprise terms that are completely exogenous. Thus, policy should be aimed solely at influencing the evolution of the *forecastable components* of inflation and the output gap, the private sector's inflation and output-gap "plans," $\pi_{t+1|t}$ and $x_{t+1|t}$. Thus, taking the expectation in period t of equations (1) and (3), we can interpret them as describing how private-sector *plans* in period t for inflation and the output gap in period $t + 1$, $\pi_{t+1|t}$ and $x_{t+1|t}$, are determined by *expectations* of (a) inflation and the output gap in period $t + 2$, $\pi_{t+2|t}$ and $x_{t+2|t}$, (b) the interest rate in period $t + 1$, $i_{t+1|t}$, and (c) the cost-push shock and natural interest rate in period $t + 1$, $u_{t+1|t}$ and $r^n_{t+1|t}$. This modification of the basic model thus emphasizes, in equation (3), that monetary policy affects the economy not through the value set for the current short interest rate but rather by the expectations created regarding *future* interest rates.[17] Actual inflation and the output gap in period $t + 1$ are then determined by equations (5) and (6).

It follows from this last observation that there is no reason for surprise variations in the short-term interest rate to ever be chosen by the central bank. Such surprises can have no advantages in terms of improved stabilization of inflation or output, and if there is even a tiny degree of preference for less interest rate variability (for reasons such as those discussed in Woodford 2003, chap. 6), it will therefore be optimal to make the interest rate perfectly forecastable one period in advance. We shall therefore restrict our attention to decision-making procedures under which the central bank's instrument is predetermined. One way to ensure this is for the central bank to make a decision in period t, denoted $i_{t+1,t}$, regarding the interest rate to be set in period $t + 1$; several of the policy frameworks considered below incorporate this feature. This illustrates the more general point that a desirable decision-making framework may require the bank to decide, during the period-t decision cycle, about matters in addition to the current setting of its instrument i_t.

We assume an intertemporal social loss function of the form

(7)
$$E \sum_{t=t_0}^{\infty} \beta^{t-t_0} L_t,$$

the expected value of the sum of discounted future period losses, starting in an arbitrary initial period t_0. (The question of the information with respect to which it is appropriate to condition in evaluating alternative policies is considered below.) The period losses are given by a period loss function of the form

(8)
$$L_t = \frac{1}{2}[\pi_t^2 + \lambda(x_t - x^*)^2],$$

---

17. This is also largely the case in the standard model, as is emphasized in Rotemberg and Woodford (1999) and Woodford (1999b), since expected future interest rates enter indirectly via the expectations of future inflation and output gaps that enter equations (1) and (3).

where λ is the nonnegative relative weight on output-gap stabilization and x^* is the socially optimal output gap (for simplicity's sake assumed to be constant), which is positive if potential output on average, due to some distortion, falls short of the socially optimal output level.[18] The discount factor β in equation (7) is assumed to be the same as the coefficient appearing in equation (1). Woodford (2003, chap. 6) shows that this form of loss function can be derived as a quadratic approximation to the (negative of) expected utility of the representative household in the same optimizing sticky-price model as is used to derive structural relations (1) and (3). And apart from this, it is a commonly assumed representation of the objectives of a central bank engaged in flexible inflation targeting (for instance, King 1997a and Svensson 1999b).

We assume that the private sector and the central bank have the same information. Specifically, we assume that both observe the current realization u_t in period t and have the same information in period t about the future evolution of the exogenous disturbances; thus, for example, the private sector's conditional expectation $u_{t+\tau|t}$, regarding any period $\tau > 0$, is assumed to also be the expectation regarding that exogenous variable conditional upon the central bank's information during its period-t decision cycle. We also assume that any random element in the central bank's period-t decisions is revealed to the private section in period t. The only asymmetry is that in our discussion of specific central bank decision procedures we assume that the central bank makes its period-t decisions (such as its commitment $i_{t+1,t}$) without being able to observe the values of period-t *forward-looking* variables, such as private-sector plans $\pi_{t+1|t}$ and $x_{t+1|t}$. This allows us to avoid the circularity of supposing that the central bank can directly respond in period t to forward-looking variables that themselves depend upon the central bank's period-t decisions. However, in a rational-expectations equilibrium, the period-t forward-looking variables will be functions of the current values of predetermined and exogenous variables (about which the bank and the private sector have the same information), and thus the bank has sufficient information to allow it to perfectly forecast the period-t variables that it does not directly observe. We also compute the equilibria associated with alternative central-bank decision procedures on the assumption that these procedures are perfectly understood by the private sector; this includes a correct understanding by the private sector of the central bank's model of the economy, insofar as this model is used in the bank's decisions. When the bank's model matters, we assume that it is the same as the true model of the economy (described by equations [1] and [3] and the stochastic processes governing the exogenous

---

18. Note that time variation in the optimal output gap has been allowed for by the inclusion of the "cost-push" disturbance term in equation (1). Following prior literature, we separately consider the consequences of a nonzero mean distortion and the consequences of random variation in the distortion.

disturbances, [2] and [4] in the special case), which is to say, the model with which private-sector expectations are assumed to be consistent.

The model assumed here, while familiar, has some features that are worthy of comment. Both the AS and IS equations incorporate important forward-looking elements. In particular, the trade-off that the central bank faces in period t between alternative values for the forecastable components of inflation and the output gap in period $t+1$ ($\pi_{t+1|t}$ and $x_{t+1|t}$, respectively) depends upon private-sector expectations regarding equilibrium in still later periods (due to the $\pi_{t+2|t}$ term in equation [1]) and hence upon expectations regarding future policy. This gives rise to a "conditional" or "stabilization bias" in the responses to shocks resulting from discretionary optimization, as we show explicitly below.

Indeed, our simple model is extremely forward-looking, in that the equations that determine $\pi_{t+\tau|t}$ and $x_{t+\tau|t}$ for all $\tau > 0$ involve no other variables, except period-t expectations regarding future central bank actions $i_{t+\tau|t}$. and regarding the evolution of the exogenous disturbances $u_{t+\tau|t}$, $r^n_{t+\tau|t}$. This means a purely forward-looking decision procedure for monetary policy—one that depends simply upon the central bank's forecasts in period t of the future evolution of its target variables—will result in period-t decisions that depend only upon period-t expectations regarding the evolution of the exogenous disturbances, and not upon any current or lagged *endogenous* variables at all.[19]

This feature of our model is undoubtedly highly special, but it allows us to contrast the history dependence that is required in order to implement optimal policy with the results of purely forward-looking procedures in an especially sharp way. In a more realistic model, many sorts of intrinsic dynamics would also probably be present, as a result of which lagged endogenous variables would matter for conditional forecasts of the future evolution of the target variables. But our general points about the generic inefficiency of purely forward-looking procedures would remain valid; the *quantitative* significance of the inefficiency in more complex, but more realistic, models remains a topic for future research.

2.2.1   Optimal Equilibrium Responses to Shocks

By an "equilibrium" of this model, we mean a triple of stochastic processes for inflation, the output gap, and the interest rate that satisfy equations (1) and (3). Note that our concept of equilibrium does not include any

---

19. An advantage of our allowance for one-period decision lags in both spending and pricing decisions is that feedback from even the current quarter's inflation rate and output gap, as in the rule proposed by Taylor (1993), is here clearly an example of dependence upon variables that are irrelevant under a purely forward-looking procedure. This allows us a sharp contrast between purely prospective procedures, such as those often recommended in the literature on inflation targeting, and purely backward-looking rules such as the Taylor rule. We believe that this feature of our model is quite realistic (assuming the "period" to be a typical length of time between central bank decision cycles) and thus worth the minor complication involved. In fact, inflation and output may be largely predetermined for significantly longer periods of time.

assumption that the central bank behaves optimally, as our task is in fact to investigate the equilibria associated with alternative candidate policy-making procedures on the part of the central bank.

We first consider the equilibrium from some period t_0 onward that is *optimal* in the sense of minimizing equation (7). In this calculation, the expectation is conditional upon the state of the world in period t_0, denoted E_{t_0}, when we imagine being able to choose among equilibria that remain possible from that period onward. Let us call this "t_0-optimality"; it corresponds to the type of optimal plan with which the literature on dynamic Ramsey taxation, for example, is typically concerned. (We shall subsequently also define optimality from a "timeless perspective" that we shall argue is more appropriate when choosing among policy rules.)

We begin by observing that, conditional upon information available one period in advance, the period-$t + 1$ loss function may be written

$$E_t L_{t+1} = \frac{1}{2} E_t[\pi_{t+1|t}^2 + \lambda(x_{t+1|t} - x^*)^2] + \frac{1}{2} E_t[(\pi_{t+1} - \pi_{t+1|t})^2$$

$$+ \lambda(x_{t+1} - x_{t+1|t})^2]$$

$$= \frac{1}{2} E_t[\pi_{t+1|t}^2 + \lambda(x_{t+1|t} - x^*)^2] + \frac{1}{2} E_t[(u_{t+1} - u_{t+1|t})^2$$

$$+ \lambda \sigma^2 (r_{t+1}^n - r_{t+1|t}^n)^2],$$

using equations (5) and (6). The second term on the right-hand side of the second line is independent of policy, as it depends only upon the exogenous disturbance processes. Thus (using also the fact that $E_{t_0} L_{t+1} = E_{t_0}[E_t L_{t+1}]$ for all $t \geq t_0$), we may replace each term of the form $E_{t_0} L_{t+1}$ in equation (7) by the conditional expectation of the first term on the right-hand side above, plus a positive constant. Since the initial term $E_{t_0} L_{t_0}$ is also independent of policy (given predetermined initial values for $\pi_{t_0|t_0-1}$ and $x_{t_0|t_0-1}$), our problem may equivalently be defined as that of choosing paths for the *forecastable components* of inflation and the output gap, the private-sector one-period-ahead plans for inflation and the output gap, $\{\pi_{t+1|t}\}_{t=t_0}^{\infty}$ and $\{x_{t+1|t}\}_{t=t_0}^{\infty}$, so as to minimize

$$E_{t_0} \sum_{t=t_0}^{\infty} \beta^{t+1-t_0} \frac{1}{2}[\pi_{t+1|t}^2 + \lambda(x_{t+1|t} - x^*)^2].$$

Note that once we have determined the optimal paths for the forecastable components, we shall have determined the optimal paths for inflation and the output gap as well, because of equations (5) and (6).

We thus need ask only what constraints the equilibrium relations (1) and (3) impose upon the possible paths of the forecastable components of these two variables. One such constraint is

(9) $\pi_{t+1|t} = \beta \pi_{t+2|t} + \kappa x_{t+1|t} + u_{t+1|t},$

obtained by taking the conditional expectation of equation (1) one period in advance. This is in fact the only constraint. For given any processes for the forecastable components satisfying equation (9), the inflation processes implied by equation (5) then necessarily satisfies equation (1); and given any processes for inflation and the output gap, one can solve equation (3) for a forecastable interest rate process $\{i_{t+1|t}\}_{t=t_0}^{\infty}$ that satisfies that condition as well.

Thus, we form the Lagrangian

$$(10) \quad \mathscr{L}_{t_0} \equiv E_{t_0} \sum_{t=t_0}^{\infty} \beta^{t+1-t_0}$$

$$\left\{ \tfrac{1}{2}[\pi_{t+1|t}^2 + \lambda(x_{t+1|t} - x^*)^2] + \Xi_{t+1}[\beta\pi_{t+2|t} + \kappa x_{t+1|t} + u_{t+1|t} - \pi_{t+1|t}] \right\},$$

where Ξ_{t+1} is the Lagrange multiplier associated with the constraint (9).[20] We note that Ξ_{t+1} depends on period-t information only. Differentiating with respect to $\pi_{t+1|t}$ and $x_{t+1|t}$ for any $t \geq t_0$ gives the first-order conditions

$$(11) \qquad\qquad \pi_{t+1|t} - \Xi_{t+1} + \Xi_t = 0,$$

$$(12) \qquad\qquad \lambda(x_{t+1|t} - x^*) + \kappa\Xi_{t+1} = 0,$$

for all $t \geq t_0$, with the initial condition

$$(13) \qquad\qquad \Xi_{t_0} = 0.$$

We eliminate Ξ_t from equations (11) and (12) and get the consolidated first-order condition

$$(14) \qquad\qquad \pi_{t+1|t} + \frac{\lambda}{\kappa}(x_{t+1|t} - x_{t|t-1}) = 0$$

for $t > t_0$ and

$$(15) \qquad\qquad \pi_{t+1|t} + \frac{\lambda}{\kappa}(x_{t+1|t} - x^*) = 0$$

for $t = t_0$.

In order to determine the stochastic processes for $\pi_{t+1|t}$ and $x_{t+1|t}$, we use equations (14) and (15) to eliminate $\pi_{t+1|t}$ and $\pi_{t+2|t}$ in equation (9). For $\lambda > 0$, this yields a second-order difference equation for $x_{t+1|t}$ for $t \geq t_0$,

$$(16) \qquad x_{t+2|t} - 2ax_{t+1|t} + \frac{1}{\beta}x_{t|t-1} = \frac{\kappa}{\beta\lambda}u_{t+1|t},$$

where

$$(17) \qquad\qquad 2a \equiv 1 + \frac{1}{\beta} + \frac{\kappa^2}{\beta\lambda}$$

and equations (13) and (15) give rise to an initial condition,

---

20. Relative to the formulation in Woodford (1999a), the Lagrange multiplier is defined with the opposite sign, so as to be interpreted as marginal losses rather than gains.

(18)
$$x_{t_0|t_0-1} \equiv x^*,$$

where we emphasize that the notation $x_{t_0|t_0-1}$ is here temporarily used only to introduce the initial condition (18) in equation (16), corresponding to the initial condition (13), rather than to denote the one-period-ahead output-gap plan in period $t_0 - 1$. The characteristic equation,

(19)
$$\mu^2 - 2a\mu + \frac{1}{\beta} = 0,$$

has two roots (eigenvalues of the dynamic system), $c \equiv a - \sqrt{a^2 - 1/\beta}$ and $1/(\beta c)$, such that $0 < c < 1 < 1/\beta < 1/(\beta c)$. Then, by standard methods, the solution can be written

(20)
$$x_{t+1|t} = -\frac{\kappa}{\lambda}c\sum_{j=0}^{\infty}(\beta c)^j u_{t+1+j|t} + cx_{t|t-1}$$

for $t \geq t_0$.

Under the assumption in equation (2), the term $\sum_{j=0}^{\infty}(\beta c)^j u_{t+1+j|t}$ is given by $\rho u_t/(1 - \beta\rho c)$, and equation (20) becomes

(21)
$$x_{t+1|t} = -\frac{\kappa}{\lambda}\frac{\rho c}{1 - \beta\rho c}u_t + cx_{t|t-1}$$

(22)
$$= -\frac{\kappa}{\lambda}\frac{\rho c}{1 - \beta\rho c}\sum_{j=0}^{t-t_0}c^j u_{t-j} + c^{t+1-t_0}x^*,$$

where the last step uses equation (18). Given this solution for $x_{t+1|t}$, we can then use equation (14) to find equilibrium values of $\pi_{t+1|t}$. We thus obtain

(23)
$$\pi_{t+1|t} = \frac{\rho c}{1 - \beta\rho c}u_t + \frac{\lambda}{\kappa}(1 - c)x_{t|t-1}$$

(24)
$$= \frac{\rho c}{1 - \beta\rho c}\left[u_t - (1 - c)\sum_{j=1}^{t-t_0}c^{j-1}u_{t-j}\right] + \frac{\lambda}{\kappa}(1 - c)c^{t-t_0}x^*,$$

again simplifying by assuming equation (2).

For $\lambda = 0$, we directly have the simple solution

$$x_{t+1|t} = -\frac{1}{\kappa}u_{t+1|t},$$

$$\pi_{t+1|t} = 0$$

to equations (14) and (15). Since $c \to 0$ when $\lambda \to 0$, this can be shown to be the limit of equations (21)–(24).

2.2.2 Optimality from a "Timeless Perspective"

This equilibrium, however, specifies inflation and output-gap processes that depend upon how long it has been since the period t_0 in which the "t_0-optimal" equilibrium was chosen. Obviously, exactly the same criterion would lead one to choose a *different* equilibrium in some later period, rather than the continuation of the equilibrium chosen as optimal in period t_0. This is just the familiar problem of time inconsistency of optimal plans in problems of this kind, first identified by Kydland and Prescott (1977). Formally, it results from the fact that initial condition (13) is specified for period t_0, although the solution generally involves $\Xi_t \neq 0$ in later periods.

What this means, intuitively, is that the proposed criterion for optimality allows one to select an equilibrium from period t_0 onward that exploits the fact that private-sector expectations in earlier periods are *already given* when the paths from t_0 onward are chosen. This allows one to choose a surprise inflation for "just this once" while committing never to do so again, as one would suffer all of the consequences of *anticipated* inflation if one chose an equilibrium in which inflation is planned for a period well after t_0. Of course, if one allows oneself to exploit preexisting expectations in this way, it would be equally appealing to allow "one last unexpected inflation" in some later period as well. This is the reason for the time inconsistency of optimal policy in this sense.

It therefore makes sense not to demand of a monetary policy rule that commitment to it from some date t_0 onward be expected to implement an equilibrium that is "t_0-optimal." Instead, we consider optimality from the "timeless perspective" recommended by Woodford (1999a) and Giannoni and Woodford (2002). A policy rule is optimal from a timeless perspective if (a) it has a time-invariant form and (b) commitment to the rule from any date t_0 onward determines an equilibrium that is optimal, subject to at most a finite number of constraints on the initial evolution of the endogenous variables. Regarding constrained optimality as sufficient weakens the sense in which the rule is required to be optimal, but there may be no time-invariant policy that would be optimal in an unconstrained sense (that is, that would be t_0-optimal). Furthermore, the fact that the economy's expected evolution under commitment to the rule is optimal subject *only* to a constraint on its short-run evolution (and not, for example, any constraint that requires long-run outcomes to resemble short-run outcomes) means that the constraints on short-run outcomes are ones that an optimizing central bank would wish to be subject to—and in particular, would wish for the private sector to expect it to be subject to—in the future. Acceptance of such a constraint thus means conformity to a rule of behavior to which it would have been optimal to commit oneself in the past. Acting in conformity with such a rule is a way of making it more credible that one will also act in conformity with it in the future, and the central bank has an interest in creating the latter expectation. Note that a policy rule that satisfies this criterion in period t_0 will also satisfy it if the matter is reconsidered in any later period; thus this approach to policy choice eliminates the problem of time-inconsistency.[21]

---

21. Of course, this property alone does not eliminate the incentive to deviate from such a policy commitment in order to reduce expected losses conditional upon the state of the world

The definition just given does not identify the constraints on the economy's short-run evolution that should be accepted, and so there need not be a unique state-contingent evolution from date t_0 onward that can qualify as optimal from a timeless perspective. Nonetheless, the constraints on the initial evolution of the economy are not arbitrary, for most constraints on short-run outcomes have the property that even if one is subject to them, it would be optimal to choose an equilibrium that does not satisfy them in the future. The requirement that the equilibrium chosen be implementable through commitment to a time-invariant policy imposes a strong self-consistency requirement on the choice of the initial constraints, although it does not uniquely determine them. In fact, in a linear-quadratic policy problem of the kind considered here (or in Giannoni and Woodford 2002), all policy rules that are optimal from a timeless perspective lead to the same long-run average values of endogenous variables such as output and inflation and to the same equilibrium responses to unexpected shocks that occur at date t_0 or later. The equilibria that are implemented by these rules differ only in a transitory, deterministic component of the equilibrium paths of variables like inflation and output.

In the example considered here, a rule that is optimal from a timeless perspective must bring about an equilibrium from date t_0 onward that minimizes equation (7), subject to the constraints that equations (1) and (3) hold for each $t \geq t_0$, and the additional constraint

(25)
$$\pi_{t_0+1|t_0} = \bar{\pi}_{t_0},$$

where the constraint value $\bar{\pi}_{t_0}$ is selected in a time-invariant way, as a function of the economy's state in period t_0 (after the realization of the exogenous disturbances, but before the determination of the endogenous variables). Furthermore, the rule for selecting $\bar{\pi}_{t_0}$ must be one that is satisfied by $\pi_{t+1|t}$ for all $t > t_0$ in the constrained optimal equilibrium from the standpoint of period t_0. Here we give two examples of rules for selecting the constraint on short-run outcomes that have the desired property; this will suffice both to show that it is possible to satisfy the self-consistency requirement and to illustrate the point that the constraint need not be uniquely defined.[22]

We first observe that if a t_0-optimal equilibrium has been chosen at a date t_0 that is now infinitely far in the past, equations (22) and (24) reduce to

---

at the time of the contemplated deviation. We do not here attempt to model the mechanism that makes it possible for a central bank to commit itself to a decision procedure other than unconstrained discretionary optimization. However, even granting the possibility of commitment, it remains more credible that an institution should feel bound by a past commitment when the logic of its own past analysis does not *itself* justify deviation at a later date.

22. Giannoni and Woodford (2002) provide a general approach to the choice of policy rules that are optimal from a timeless perspective, in the context of a broad class of linear-quadratic policy problems.

(26)
$$x_{t+1|t} = -\frac{\kappa}{\lambda}\frac{\rho c}{1 - \beta\rho c}\sum_{j=0}^{\infty} c^j u_{t-j}$$

and

(27)
$$\pi_{t+1|t} = -\frac{\rho c}{1 - \beta\rho c}\left[u_t - (1 - c)\sum_{j=1}^{\infty} c^{j-1}u_{t-j}\right].$$

This suggests one possible specification of a pair of constraints of the form of equation (25): one requires that $\pi_{t_0+1|t_0}$ satisfy equation (27) for $t = t_0$. In fact, one easily sees that the evolution of expected inflation and output from date t_0 onward that minimizes equation (7) subject to this constraint is just the one that satisfies equations (26) and (27) for all $t \geq t_0$.[23] Hence, this is an example of a self-consistent constraint on the economy's short-run evolution of the kind discussed above. A time-invariant policy rule that yields the evolution of equations (26) and (27) as a determinate equilibrium will therefore be optimal from a timeless perspective.

However, this is not the only state-contingent evolution from date t_0 onward that can be considered optimal from a timeless perspective. We may also select the constraints on short-run outcomes in a way that depends on the initial values of predetermined endogenous variables, rather than being a function solely of the history of exogenous disturbances as above. For example, suppose that in equation (25) we use the value

(28)
$$\overline{\pi}_{t_0} = \frac{\rho c}{1 - \beta\rho c}u_{t_0} + \frac{\lambda}{\kappa}(1 - c)x_{t_0|t_0-1},$$

where $x_{t_0|t_0-1}$ here denotes the actual output-gap plan in period $t_0 - 1$. (Our choice of this specification of the initial condition is motivated by the observation that $\pi_{t_0+1|t_0}$ would have to satisfy equation [23] in any τ-optimal equilibrium chosen at a date $\tau < t_0$.[24]) Under this specification, the equilibrium that minimizes equation (7) subject to constraint (25) is given by

(29)
$$x_{t+1|t} = -\frac{\kappa}{\lambda}\frac{\rho c}{1 - \beta\rho c}\sum_{j=0}^{t-t_0} c^j u_{t-j} + c^{t+1-t_0}x_{t_0|t_0-1}$$

(30)
$$\pi_{t+1|t} = \frac{\rho c}{1 - \beta\rho c}\left[u_t - (1 - c)\sum_{j=1}^{t-t_0} c^{j-1}u_{t-j}\right] + \frac{\lambda}{\kappa}(1 - c)c^{t-t_0}x_{t_0|t_0-1},$$

for all $t \geq t_0$.

The constraint (28) is observed to be self-consistent. The solutions (29) and (30) imply equations (21) and (23) for any $t \geq t_0$. Hence, we find once

---

23. The problem reduces to finding a solution to the system consisting of equations (1) and (3) together with equations (11) and (12), with the initial condition (25) replacing equation (13). Our method of derivation of equations (27) and (26) makes it obvious that they satisfy all of these equations.

24. A generalization of the approach used here is developed in Giannoni and Woodford (2002).

again that a time-invariant rule that yields the evolution of equations (29) and (30) as a determinate equilibrium is optimal from a timeless perspective.

For most values of the initial condition $x_{t_0 | t_0 - 1}$, these state-contingent paths for expected inflation and expected output in equations (29) and (30) will be different from those in equations (26) and (27)—except asymptotically, when they coincide as $c^{t+1-t_0} \to 0$. They similarly both differ from the t_0-optimal equilibrium, described by equations (22) and (24), except asymptotically. However, both examples of a timelessly optimal equilibrium agree with one another, and with the t_0-optimal equilibrium, in the linear terms involving the exogenous disturbances in periods $t \geq t_0$. These several alternative conceptions of the optimal state-contingent evolution from period t_0 onward differ only in certain deterministic components of the equilibrium levels of inflation and output, that in each case become negligible for t sufficiently greater than t_0.

The examples of timelessly optimal equilibria just discussed are only two of an infinite number of possibilities. More generally, we observe that the equilibrium resulting from adoption of a timelessly optimal policy rule must satisfy conditions (11) and (12) for all $t \geq t_0$, for *some* value of Ξ_{t_0}. However, the value of Ξ_{t_0} need not satisfy equation (13) in general. Instead, Ξ_{t_0} is selected as some function of the state of the world, denoted h_{t_0-1}, in the previous period. For future reference, we define the state of the world in period t as $h_t \equiv \{u_t, r_t^n, i_t, i_{t+1|t}, \pi_{t+1|t}, x_{t+1|t}; u_{t-1}, r_{t-1}^n, i_{t-1}, i_{t|t-1}, \pi_{t|t-1}, x_{t|t-1}; \ldots\}$.

Our characterization of optimal equilibrium already allows us to reach one important conclusion about optimal policy. This is that a *purely forward-looking* decision procedure cannot be used to implement an optimal equilibrium. In the current model, the equations that determine the expected future values of the goal variables, $\pi_{t+\tau|t}$ and $x_{t+\tau|t}$ for $\tau \geq 1$, for any given expected future path of the central bank's instrument, depend only upon expectations in period t of the future paths of the exogenous disturbances. Thus, if the central bank does not itself plan to condition its decisions in period t or later on information other than information about the exogenous disturbance processes, then its forecasts of the future evolution of the target variables will be independent of any other information (specifically, the value of any lagged endogenous variables). Under a purely forward-looking decision procedure, its decisions during the period-t decision cycle should similarly be independent of any such "irrelevant" information. Then, if a correct private-sector understanding of this policy rule results in a determinate rational-expectations equilibrium, the equilibrium will be one in which the evolution of the target variables is independent of "irrelevant" lagged endogenous variables.[25]

---

25. Even if equilibrium is indeterminate, if one expects that the equilibrium that should result in practice will be selected by a "minimum-state-variable" (MSV) criterion, like that sug-

But we have seen that an optimal equilibrium is necessarily *not* of this kind. In the case that equations (2) and (4) hold, all information about the future evolution of the disturbances is summarized by the current disturbances u_t and r_t^n. Thus, an equilibrium that could be implemented using a purely prospective decision procedure would have to make $\pi_{t+1|t}$ and $x_{t+1|t}$ functions of u_t and r_t^n. Our above solutions do not have this character; instead, $x_{t|t-1}$ and, therefore, the entire history $\{u_{t-j}\}_{j=1}^{\infty}$, back at least to period t_0, affect the optimal values of both variables. Thus, a decision procedure that can implement an optimal equilibrium must involve a degree of *history dependence* not allowed for in the types of purely prospective policy procedures often assumed in discussions of inflation targeting. Examples of suitable sources of history dependence are presented in sections 2.3 through 2.5.

2.2.3   Interest Rates in an Optimal Equilibrium

To each of the optimal paths for inflation and the output gap just characterized there corresponds an optimal path for the nominal interest rate. Taking the conditional expectation of equation (3) in period t and solving for $i_{t+1|t}$, we obtain

$$(31) \qquad i_{t+1|t} = r_{t+1|t}^n + \pi_{t+2|t} + \frac{1}{\sigma}(x_{t+2|t} - x_{t+1|t}).$$

Substitution of equation (14), which holds for all $t > t_0$ in a t_0-optimal equilibrium and in the equilibrium associated with any timelessly optimal policy rule, into equation (31) then yields

$$i_{t+1|t} = r_{t+1|t}^n + \frac{\lambda\sigma - \kappa}{\lambda\sigma}\pi_{t+2|t}$$

for all $t > t_0$. Finally, substitution of the equilibrium values of $\pi_{t+2|t}$ discussed above yields a stochastic process for the forecastable component of the interest rate.

For example, in the case of a timelessly optimal policy resulting in the equilibrium described by equations (26) and (27), the associated forecastable component of the interest rate is given by $i_{t+1|t} = i_{t+1}^*$, where

$$(32) \quad i_{t+1}^* \equiv \bar{r} + \omega(r_t^n - \bar{r}) + \frac{\lambda\sigma - \kappa}{\lambda\sigma}\frac{\rho c}{1 - \beta\rho c}\left[\rho u_t - (1 - c)\sum_{j=0}^{\infty}c^j u_{t-j}\right].$$

(Here we also assume equation [4], allowing us to replace $r_{t+1|t}^n$ with $\bar{r} + \omega[r_t^n - \bar{r}]$.) Note that the exogenous process $\{i_{t+1}^*\}_{t=t_0}^{\infty}$ also indicates how the expected interest rate must evolve, as a function of the history of exogenous

---

gested by McCallum (1999), then the equilibrium selected will not depend upon the "irrelevant" lagged endogenous variables, and the argument in the text goes through. If one admits that non-MSV equilibria may occur, then the equilibria that may occur will include a large number of equilibria other than the optimal one.

disturbances, in *any* optimal equilibrium that has been in existence for a long enough period of time.

Alternatively, in the case of a timelessly optimal policy resulting in the equilibrium described by equations (21) and (23), the expected interest rate is given by $i_{t+1|t} = \bar{\imath}_{t+1}$, where

$$(33) \quad \bar{\imath}_{t+1} \equiv \bar{r} + \omega(r_t^n - \bar{r}) + \frac{\lambda\sigma - \kappa}{\lambda\sigma} \frac{\rho c}{1 - \beta\rho c}(p + c - 1)u_t + fx_{t|t-1},$$

where

$$(34) \qquad\qquad f \equiv \frac{\lambda\sigma - \kappa}{\kappa\sigma}(1 - c)c.$$

Note that in equation (33) we have expressed the endogenous process $\bar{\imath}_{t+1}$ as a *time-invariant* function of the state of the world h_t, a representation that will be useful for our discussion below of associated reaction functions; a corresponding expression for $i_{t+1|t}$ as a function of h_{t_0-1} and the exogenous disturbances in periods t_0 through t can be obtained by substituting expression (29) for $x_{t|t-1}$ into equation (33). Once again, we observe that, if initial conditions h_{t_0-1} are consistent with the stationary optimal equilibrium presented in equations (26) and (27), processes (32) and (33) will coincide exactly at all times. (This can be seen by observing that if one instead uses equation [26] to substitute for $x_{t|t-1}$ in equation [33], one obtains equation [32].)

None of our optimality conditions place any restrictions upon the path of the *unforecastable* component of the interest rate, and indeed, from the point of view of the objective assumed above, its path is completely arbitrary, as it has no effect upon either spending or pricing decisions in this model. However, it is plausible to assume that one should prefer less variable interest rates, other things being equal.[26] It follows that it can never be desirable to have any unforecastable interest rate fluctuations; thus we stipulate that an optimal policy will imply that $i_{t+1} = i_{t+1|t}$ at all times. With this additional stipulation, we can now derive unique equilibrium interest rate processes associated with each of the possible optimal equilibria. These are given by the above equations, with i_{t+1} replacing $i_{t+1|t}$.

This result still only tells us how it is desirable for interest rates to evolve in equilibrium, as a function of the disturbances that hit the economy; it does not tell us what form of policy rule should be adopted by the central bank in order to bring about an equilibrium of the desired character. Simply committing to set interest rates as the specified function of the history of disturbances is not the only type of policy rule that would be con-

---

26. Woodford (2003, chap. 6) discusses reasons why one may even be willing to accept somewhat more variable inflation and output gaps for the sake of improved interest rate stabilization. Svensson (2003, section 5.6) expresses skepticism about those reasons. We abstract from such concerns here in order to simplify the algebra in our analysis.

sistent with an equilibrium of the desired kind, and in fact we shall argue that this would *not* be a desirable approach to the implementation of optimal policy—it would be inferior to other approaches, both on the ground of nonrobustness of the policy rule to changes in the model of the economy and on the ground that equilibrium will not be determinate under such a rule.

Still, this characterization of optimal equilibrium interest rate paths can help to identify possible forms of policy rules that will be consistent with one or another of the optimal equilibria just discussed. In particular, any given explicit decision procedure will imply a *reaction function*

$$(35) \qquad\qquad i_{t+1} = F(s_{t+1}, h_t)$$

indicating the way in which the central bank's instrument is set as a function of the information available to it in decision cycle $t + 1$, consisting of all exogenous disturbances, $s_{t+1} \equiv (u_{t+1}, r^n_{t+1})$, in period $t + 1$ and the state of the world, h_t, in period t.[27] Recall that we assume that all exogenous disturbances s_{t+1} realized in period $t + 1$ are already known to the central bank before its instrument setting for period $t + 1$ must be chosen, but that period-$t + 1$ endogenous variables, the inflation and output-gap plans $\pi_{t+1|t}$ and $x_{t+1|t}$, that generally depend upon the bank's action, cannot be directly responded to; instead, the bank can respond only to its *forecasts* of how these variables should evolve. However, all elements of h_t, including period-t endogenous variables, are assumed to be public information prior to the bank's period-$t + 1$ decision cycle; thus i_{t+1} may respond to them.

In this study we shall restrict our attention to decision procedures of two broad types, targeting rules and explicit instrument rules. Each of these classes implies a further restriction upon the possible form of the reaction function. In the case of a *targeting rule,* the setting of i_t chosen during the period-t decision cycle is not expected to affect the period-t target variables, π_t and x_t, since these are assumed to be predetermined; only the private sector's *forecast* of the setting during previous periods matters for the period-t target variables. Hence, the targeting procedure must instead be used to choose a *commitment* $i_{t+1,t}$ regarding the interest rate setting to be adopted in the following period; the interest rate itself is simply set in accordance with the commitment made during the previous decision cycle: $i_{t+1} = i_{t+1,t}$. It then follows that under any such rule the interest rate i_{t+1} will be a function of information available to the central bank during its period-t decision cycle. Under our information specification, this means a function

---

27. In general, the vector s_{t+1} includes all information as of period $t + 1$ about the paths of the exogenous disturbances in periods $t + \tau$ for $\tau \geq 1$. In the special case that both disturbances are Markovian, as assumed in equations (2) and (4), the vector s_{t+1} has only two elements, u_{t+1} and r^n_{t+1}.

of variables that are *predetermined* in period t, or *exogenous* variables realized in period t, so that the implied reaction function associated with such a policy must be of the more restricted form

(36) $$i_{t+1} = F(s_t, h_{t-1}).$$

Given that the reaction function must have the form of equation (36), we can *uniquely* identify the implied reaction function that must be implied by any targeting rule that is consistent with a particular equilibrium from the adoption date t_0 onward. To do this, we simply read off our solution, above, for i_{t+1} as a function of s_t and h_{t-1}. Thus, a targeting rule consistent with the equilibrium in equations (26) and (27) must yield the implied reaction function

(37) $$i_{t+1} = \bar{i}_{t+1}^{*},$$

where i_{t+1}^{*} is defined in equation (32), while a targeting rule consistent with the equilibrium in equations (21) and (23) must yield the implied reaction function

(38) $$i_{t+1} = \bar{i}_{t+1},$$

where $\bar{i}_{t+1}$ is defined in equation (33). Of course, these reaction functions do not yet uniquely identify the form of the policy rule; alternative high-level policy prescriptions might imply the same reaction function. We give examples below of targeting procedures that imply each of these reaction functions.

In the case of an *explicit instrument rule,* instead, the policy rule is just a commitment to set the instrument in accordance with a particular reaction function. One advantage of this way of specifying the policy rule is that the instrument setting in period $t + 1$ need no longer be a function solely of information available at the time of the period-t decision cycle; it can instead make use of information available only by the time of the period–$t + 1$ decision cycle. Because unforecastable interest rate movements are undesirable, an optimal instrument rule will nevertheless necessarily be of the restricted form

(39) $$i_{t+1} = F(h_t)$$

rather than of the form in equation (35). Yet there remains an advantage of family (39) over the even more restrictive family (36), which is that it allows i_{t+1} to respond to endogenous variables realized in period t—information that we assume is available to the private sector when making its period-t decisions, but *not* during the central bank's period-t decision cycle. This can be useful in that it allows the central bank to respond in period $t + 1$ to private-sector decisions in period t, $\pi_{t+1|t}$ and $x_{t+1|t}$, that are inconsistent with the equilibrium that it is trying to bring about (and thus inconsistent with its own forecasts of those variables during its period-t decision cycle). A commitment to such responses can be useful, as we show later, in excluding unwanted alternative rational-expectations equilibria.

In the case of the more flexible specification (39), we can no longer uniquely determine the reaction function from our above solution for the equilibrium interest rate process. Our discussion above allowed us to determine how i_{t+1} must depend upon s_t and h_{t-1} in the equilibrium that we wish to implement. However, many endogenous variables in h_{t-1} in the equilibrium that we wish to implement. However, many endogenous variables in h_t will also be functions of these variables, and (assuming that the variables co-move as in the desired equilibrium) the desired variation in interest rates can therefore be arranged by setting i_{t+1} as a function of these variables rather than by setting it as a direct function of the variables observed by the central bank by the time of its period-t decision cycle. There will thus generally be a large number of possible instrument rules consistent with a given equilibrium, even though there is a one-to-one correspondence between instrument rules and reaction functions.

2.2.4   The Problem of Indeterminacy

One aspect of the problem of implementing optimal policy is finding a decision procedure that is consistent with an optimal equilibrium, as characterized above. But even when we find a procedure that satisfies this criterion—say, a targeting rule that implies reaction function (37) or (38)—there remains the question whether the optimal equilibrium is the *only* equilibrium consistent with the specified policy rule. In addressing this question, it suffices to characterize a policy rule in terms of the reaction function that it implies.[28] Our question is then whether the system of equations consisting of equations (1), (3) and either (36) or (39) has a unique bounded (or nonexplosive) rational-expectations equilibrium.[29] In this

28. Note, however, that for some other questions—notably the analysis of robustness—the reaction function is *not* a sufficient description of a policy rule. It is for this reason that we are careful in this paper not to *identify* policy rules with their implied reaction functions.

29. We shall not demand the existence of a unique solution to our linear equation system, when even explosive solutions are counted. In general, in a forward-looking model, *no* policy rule will have that property. The apparent explosive solutions may not correspond to true rational-expectations equilibria. One reason is that the conditions for optimality in the private-sector decision problems underlying our structural equations (1) and (3) include transversality conditions as well as the first-order conditions to which our structural equations correspond. These additional requirements for optimality are necessarily satisfied by any bounded solution but may not be satisfied by an explosive solution. Furthermore, our structural equations are really only log-linear approximations to the true (nonlinear) equilibrium conditions; bounded solutions to the log-linearized equations approximate solutions to the exact conditions (in the case of small enough disturbances), but explosive solutions may not correspond to any additional solutions to the exact conditions. Finally, determinacy as defined here implies at least *local* uniqueness of the equilibrium that we consider, which may be considered a reason for greater confidence that the private sector should coordinate its expectations upon the equilibrium than in the case where a very large number of equilibria exist arbitrarily close to one another (the case of indeterminacy).

case, we shall say that equilibrium is *determinate,* and we shall assume that the coordination of private-sector expectations upon the determinate equilibrium is unproblematic.

One case in which this condition fails to be satisfied is when the reaction function makes the interest rate a function solely of *exogenous* state variables. In this case, equilibrium is *indeterminate,* for essentially the same reason as in the analysis of Sargent and Wallace (1975). When i_{t+1} is an exogenous process, the endogenous variables $\{\pi_{t+1|t}\}_{t=t_0}^{\infty}$ and $\{x_{t+1|t}\}_{t=t_0}^{\infty}$ are determined solely by a pair of difference equations obtained by taking the expectation of equations (1) and (3) conditional upon information in period t. This system can be written in vector form as

(40) $$\mathbf{z}_{t+1|t} = \mathbf{M}\mathbf{z}_t + \mathbf{N}\tilde{\mathbf{s}}_t$$

for $t \geq t_0$, where the column vectors $\mathbf{z}_t$ and $\tilde{\mathbf{s}}_t$ are defined as

(41) $$\mathbf{z}_t \equiv \begin{bmatrix} \pi_{t+1|t} \\ x_{t+1|t} \end{bmatrix}, \qquad \tilde{\mathbf{s}}_t \equiv \begin{bmatrix} u_{t+1|t} \\ r^n_{t+1|t} - \bar{r} \\ i_{t+1|t} - \bar{r} \end{bmatrix},$$

the matrix $\mathbf{M}$ is defined as

$$\mathbf{M} \equiv \begin{bmatrix} 1/\beta & -\kappa/\beta \\ -\sigma/\beta & 1 + \kappa\sigma/\beta \end{bmatrix},$$

and the matrix $\mathbf{N}$ has elements that do not matter for our argument.

Using standard methods, this system has a unique bounded solution for the process $\{\mathbf{z}_t\}_{t=t_0}^{\infty}$ if and only if both eigenvalues of the matrix $\mathbf{M}$ have modulus greater than 1 (in which case the solution would be obtained by "solving forward"). The characteristic equation of $\mathbf{M}$ is given by

(42) $$\mu^2 - \frac{1 + \beta + \kappa\sigma}{\beta}\mu + \frac{1}{\beta} = 0,$$

which is easily seen to have two real roots satisfying $0 < \mu_1 < 1 < 1/\beta < \mu_2$. Because $|\mu_1| < 1$, the condition for determinacy is not satisfied, and instead there is an infinite number of bounded solutions. Since each solution for the forecastable components can be used to construct an equilibrium process for inflation and the output gap using equations (5) and (6), we find that equilibrium is indeterminate.[30]

---

30. In particular, let e be the right eigenvector of M associated with eigenvalue μ_1, and let $\{\bar{z}_t\}_{t=t_0}^{\infty}$ be any bounded solution to equation (40). Then consider the alternative process defined by

$$z_t = \bar{z}_t + e\delta_t, \qquad \delta_t = \mu_1\delta_{t-1} + \xi_t,$$

where $\{\xi_t\}_{t=t_0}^{\infty}$ is *any* bounded random variable such that $\xi_{t+1|t} = 0$. Then the process $\{z_t\}_{t=t_0}^{\infty}$ constructed in this way is another bounded solution to equation (40). Note that this method works no matter what correlation ξ_t may have with innovations in "fundamental" distur-

This means that one cannot implement an optimal equilibrium simply by determining how interest rates should evolve in that equilibrium, as a function of the history of exogenous disturbances, and then committing to that functional relation as a rule for setting the interest rate. Such a policy rule would lead to indeterminacy. But there is a further immediate consequence as well: in this model, any purely forward-looking decision procedure implies a reaction function that results in indeterminacy of equilibrium if the central bank is committed to this procedure. For as argued above, any purely forward-looking procedure implies a reaction function that responds solely to information about the exogenous disturbance processes.

Thus, the desire to obtain a determinate equilibrium is another reason why a desirable policy rule must involve some degree of history dependence. In particular, we may now furthermore clarify that it must involve some degree of dependence upon lagged *endogenous* variables—whereas the mere criterion of consistency with an optimal equilibrium might be satisfied by a policy rule that involved dependence solely upon lagged exogenous disturbances (such as a commitment to equation [37] as an instrument rule).

As a simple example of how dependence upon lagged endogenous variables can bring about determinacy, we may consider a Taylor-type rule that prescribes that the interest rate be set each period at the value

$$(43) \qquad i_{t+1} = \bar{r} + g_\pi \pi_{t+1|t} + g_x x_{t+1|t},$$

for some coefficients $g_\pi, g_x \geq 0$.[31] Substituting this rule into equation (3) to eliminate the interest rate, we again obtain an equation system of the form of equation (40), with the vector z_t defined as in equation (41), but in this case the matrix $\mathbf{M}$ is given by

---

bances at date t and no matter how large the variability of ξ_t may be. Thus there is an infinite set of bounded equilibria; there is an infinite set of additional equilibria arbitrarily close to any given equilibrium; and these equilibria include ones in which the target variables fluctuate in response to completely nonfundamental sources of uncertainty ("sunspot equilibria"), as well as an infinite set of equilibria in which they respond solely to "fundamental" uncertainty but in differing ways. Furthermore, some of the equilibria involve arbitrarily large variability of both inflation and the output gap, and so arbitrarily large values for the expected loss function in equation (7). Thus, such a policy rule is quite unappealing, if one worries at all about the possibility of one of the less attractive equilibria being the one that results.

31. Note that if we assume that prices and output are both entirely predetermined, as in Rotemberg and Woodford (1997, 1999), this rule specifies the interest rate as a function of current inflation and output, as in Taylor's (1993) original formulation. In the case that these variables are not entirely predetermined, direct dependence upon current inflation and output would not be possible, as these are not yet observed during the bank's period-t decision cycle. We might allow dependence upon the bank's estimates of those variables, $\pi_{t+1|t}$ and $x_{t+1|t}$—which estimates will in fact always be perfectly accurate, because of equations (5) and (6)—but such a rule would be dominated by the one proposed in the text, because of the undesirability of unforecastable interest rate movements. It should be noted that the analysis of determinacy would proceed in exactly the same way for either version of the rule.

(44)
$$\mathbf{M} \equiv \begin{bmatrix} 1/\beta & -\kappa/\beta \\ -\sigma/\beta + \sigma g_\pi & 1 + \kappa\sigma/\beta + \sigma g_x \end{bmatrix}.$$

One then observes that both roots of the characteristic equation have modulus greater than 1, so that equilibrium is determinate, if and only if

(45)
$$g_\pi + \frac{1-\beta}{\kappa} g_x > 1.$$

Thus, a sufficiently strong response to fluctuations in *either* inflation or the output gap suffices for determinacy.[32]

Note that a reaction function of the form of equation (43) must be interpreted as an instrument rule rather than as an implied reaction function associated with a targeting rule, because it involves dependence on endogenous variables realized only in period t. The possibility of such dependence is an advantage of instrument rules, from the point of view of ensuring determinacy. Note that it is not equivalent for the central bank to commit to responding in this way to its own forecast of these variables during its period-t decision cycle, even though all period-t exogenous disturbances are assumed to be observed at that time. This is because a commitment to respond in period $t + 1$ to private-sector actions in period t that deviate from the equilibrium expected by the central bank may be useful in ensuring that equilibria *other* than that one are not equally consistent with private-sector optimization.

However, as we illustrate below, it is not necessary for determinacy that there be feedback from period-t endogenous variables in the setting of i_{t+1}; thus, reaction functions of the form of equation (36) may also imply a determinate equilibrium.[33] However, our Taylor-type example shows that in the case of an instrument rule, determinacy can be achieved even with a rule that involves no dependence of the instrument upon lagged variables more than one period in the past; in the case of a targeting rule, determinacy requires that the reaction function (and hence the central bank's targets themselves) depend on endogenous variables in period $t - 1$ or earlier. Thus, there is a sense in which the required degree of history dependence is even *greater* in the case of a targeting rule.

We turn now to an analysis of the consequences of particular decision procedures for monetary policy. We pay particular attention to forecast-

---

32. Note that the coefficients called for by Taylor (1993), namely $g_\pi = 1.5$ and $g_x = 0.5$, necessarily imply determinacy. More generally, such a rule results in determinacy if and only if it respects what Woodford (2003, chap. 2) calls the "Taylor principle": the requirement that a sustained increase in the rate of inflation must eventually result in an increase in the nominal interest rate of an even greater size. Since equation (1) implies that a unit permanent increase in inflation implies a permanent increase in the output gap of $(1 - \beta)/\kappa$ units, a rule of the form of equation (43) satisfies this principle if and only if equation (45) holds.

33. See the analysis in section 2.4 of determinacy in the case of a reaction function of the form of equation (38).

targeting rules, given the reasons for interest in this class of procedures noted in section 2.1.

2.3   Commitment to a Modified Loss Function

In this section, we discuss our highest-level policy specification, a general targeting rule, which is in terms of a loss function that the central bank is committed to seeking to minimize, through a forecast-based dynamic optimization procedure. We first specify how the central bank computes its forecasts and show the outcome for the optimal forecasts if the central bank uses the social loss function to evaluate these. We show that selecting the optimal forecasts under complete discretion results in a time-consistency problem. One way to restore time consistency is to apply dynamic programming and resort to forecasts consistent with the inefficient equilibrium resulting from discretionary optimization (as characterized, for example, using the method of Söderlind 1999). A more attractive way to restore time consistency is a general targeting rule in the form of a modified loss function, the minimization of which results in forecasts consistent with the optimal equilibrium. We then discuss issues connected with implementation of the optimal equilibrium under this approach.

2.3.1   Forecast Targeting

All of the procedures that we discuss in this section involve a particular approach to dynamic optimization that we call "forecast targeting." Under forecast targeting, the central bank first constructs conditional inflation, output-gap, and interest-rate forecasts corresponding to alternative feasible policies and then chooses the preferred scenario according to the specified loss function. (A similar procedure is used in the case of our discussion in the next section of specific targeting rules, except that the preferred scenario is chosen as the one that satisfies a specified target criterion.) Let $i^t \equiv \{i_{t+\tau,t}\}_{\tau=1}^{\infty}$ denote such an interest rate path considered in period t, where $i_{t+\tau,t}$ denotes the interest rate considered for period $t + \tau, \tau \geq 1$. Let $\pi^t \equiv \{\pi_{t+\tau,t}\}_{\tau=1}^{\infty}$ and $x^t \equiv \{x_{t+\tau,t}\}_{\tau=1}^{\infty}$ denote conditional (mean) inflation and output-gap forecasts (forecast paths) considered in period t. We use the notation $\pi_{t+\tau,t}$ and $x_{t+\tau,t}$ to distinguish the central bank's internal forecast in period t for period $t + \tau$ from private-sector inflation and output-gap expectations in period t for period $t + \tau, \pi_{t+\tau|t}$ and $x_{t+\tau|t}$.

The forecast paths in period t will be related according to the central bank's forecast model,

(46) $$\pi_{t+\tau,t} = \beta\pi_{t+\tau+1,t} + \kappa x_{t+\tau,t} + u_{t+\tau,t},$$

(47) $$x_{t+\tau,t} = x_{t+\tau+1,t} - \sigma(i_{t+\tau,t} - \pi_{t+\tau+1,t} - r^n_{t+\tau,t}),$$

for $\tau \geq 1$. Here $u^t \equiv \{u_{t+\tau,t}\}_{\tau=1}^{\infty}$ and $r^{nt} \equiv \{r^n_{t+\tau,t}\}_{\tau=1}^{\infty}$ denote the central bank's (mean) forecasts of the exogenous shocks to the AS equation and the natural interest rate, conditional on information available in period t (that is, $u_{t+\tau,t} \equiv E_t u_{t+\tau}$ and $r^n_{t+\tau,t} \equiv E_t r^n_{t+\tau}$ for $\tau \geq 1$). The paths satisfying these conditions are the ones over which the bank then optimizes.[34]

2.3.2 Discretionary Minimization of the Social Loss Function

Let us first examine the situation when the central bank uses the social loss function to evaluate alternative forecast paths and chooses as its preferred forecast the one that minimizes the corresponding expected loss. In this case, the central bank's period loss function over the conditional forecasts can be written

$$(48) \qquad L_{t+\tau,t} = \frac{1}{2}[\pi^2_{t+\tau,t} + \lambda(x_{t+\tau,t} - x^*)^2]$$

for $\tau \geq 1$, where in equilibrium $L_{t+\tau,t}$ will differ from $E_t L_{t+\tau}$ by a constant. Thus, in period t the central bank wishes to find the combination (i^t, π^t, x^t) of an interest rate path and conditional forecasts that fulfills (46) and (47) and minimizes

$$(49) \qquad L_t + \sum_{\tau=1}^{\infty} \beta^\tau L_{t+\tau,t},$$

where L_t, given by equation (8), is predetermined.

Note that once the central bank has determined its forecasts of the cost-push shock and the natural interest rate, u^t and r^{nt}, this is a deterministic optimization problem, in contrast to the stochastic optimization problem examined above in section 2.2.1. Furthermore, for any conditional forecasts π^t and x^t, the corresponding interest rate path i^t can be constructed from equation (47) by solving for $i_{t+\tau,t}$,

$$(50) \qquad i_{t+\tau,t} = r^n_{t+\tau,t} + \pi_{t+\tau+1,t} + \frac{1}{\sigma}(x_{t+\tau+1,t} - x_{t+\tau,t}).$$

Therefore, the central bank can solve the problem in two steps. First, it considers $x_{t+\tau,t}$ as a control variable and chooses it so that x^t and π^t fulfill equa-

---

34. Constructing conditional forecasts in a backward-looking model (that is, a model without forward-looking variables) is straightforward. Constructing such forecasts in a forward-looking model raises some specific difficulties, discussed in Svensson (1999b, appendix A). The conditional forecasts for an arbitrary interest rate path derived in the present paper and in Svensson assume that the interest rate paths are "credible"—that is, anticipated and allowed to influence the forward-looking variables. A different approach to constructing conditional inflation forecasts for arbitrary interest rate paths is used by Leeper and Zha (1999), who assume that these interest rate paths result from unanticipated deviations from a normal reaction function.

tion (46) and minimize equation (49). Second, it calculates the corresponding i^t according to equation (50).

The first step can be executed by formulating the Lagrangian

(51) $\mathcal{L}_t \equiv$

$$\sum_{\tau=1}^{\infty} \beta^{\tau} \left\{ \tfrac{1}{2} [\pi_{t+\tau,t}^2 + \lambda(x_{t+\tau,t} - x^*)^2] + \Xi_{t+\tau,t}[\beta\pi_{t+1+\tau,t} + \kappa x_{t+\tau,t} + u_{t+\tau,t} - \pi_{t+\tau,t}] \right\},$$

where $\Xi_{t+\tau,t}$ is the Lagrange multiplier for the constraint (46) for period $t +$
τ, considered in period t. Differentiating with respect to $\pi_{t+\tau,t}$ and $x_{t+\tau,t}$
gives the first-order conditions

(52) $$\pi_{t+\tau,t} - \Xi_{t+\tau,t} + \Xi_{t+\tau-1,t} = 0,$$

(53) $$\lambda(x_{t+\tau,t} - x^*) + \kappa\Xi_{t+\tau,t} = 0$$

for $\tau \geq 1$, together with the initial condition

(54) $$\Xi_{t,t} = 0.$$

Eliminating the Lagrange multipliers in equations (52) and (53) leads to
the consolidated first-order condition

(55) $$\pi_{t+\tau,t} + \frac{\lambda}{\kappa}(x_{t+\tau,t} - x_{t+\tau-1,t}) = 0$$

for $\tau \geq 2$ and

(56) $$\pi_{t+1,t} + \frac{\lambda}{\kappa}(x_{t+1,t} - x^*) = 0$$

for $\tau = 1$. Thus, finding the optimal forecasts reduces to the problem of
finding π^t and x^t that satisfy equations (46), (55), and (56).

As noted in Woodford (1999a), these first-order conditions define a decision procedure that will not be time consistent. This can be seen from the
fact that the first-order condition for $\tau = 1$, equation (56), is different from
that for $\tau \geq 2$, equation (55). This results because, in deciding on $\pi_{t+1,t}$, the
central bank takes the previous period's forecast $\pi_{t+1,t-1}$ as given and lets
$\pi_{t+1,t}$ deviate from it without assigning any specific cost to doing so. As a result, the forecasts in period t are not generally consistent with the forecasts
made in period $t - 1$, even if no new information is received in period t.

To see this, suppose that the forecasts π^{t-1} and x^{t-1} were constructed in period $t - 1$ so as to minimize the intertemporal loss function (49) with $t - 1$
substituted for t. The same procedure in period $t - 1$ as above then resulted
in the same first-order conditions (55) and (56), although with $t - 1$ substituted for t. Thus, in period $t - 1$, the first-order condition for $\tau = 2$ was

(57) $$\pi_{t+1,t-1} + \frac{\lambda}{\kappa}(x_{t+1,t-1} - x_{t,t-1}) = 0.$$

Without any new information in period t relative to period $t-1$, we should have $\pi_{t+1,t} = \pi_{t+1,t-1}$ and $x_{t+1,t} = x_{t+1,t-1}$ for intertemporal consistency. From equations (56) and (57) it is apparent that this will not be the case, unless by chance $x_{t,t-1} = x^*$.

This illustrates that the period-t forecasts for period–$t+1$ inflation under the above procedure will generally differ from the forecasts of period–$t+1$ inflation in period $t-1$. This also implies that when there is reoptimization in period $t+1$, with new optimal forecasts constructed then, the period–$t+1$ forecast of period–$t+2$ inflation, $\pi_{t+2,t+1}$, would normally differ from the period-t forecast. Thus, the above procedure will not result in time-consistent forecasts and will violate the intuitive condition stated in Svensson (1999a), according to which "if no new information has arrived, the forecasts and the interest rate path [should be] the same, and interest setting [should follow] the same interest rate path."

2.3.3 A Dynamic-Programming Procedure

One way to make the forecasts time consistent would be for the central bank to recognize in period t that the forecasts will be reoptimized in period $t+1$ and to incorporate this in its forecasts in period t. This would amount to application of the dynamic-programming approach assumed in standard expositions of the Markov equilibrium resulting from discretionary optimization in a model like ours (such as Söderlind 1999). Under this alternative approach, the first-order conditions (52) and (53) for the forecasts in period t will instead take the form

$$(58) \qquad \pi_{t+\tau,t} - \Xi_{t+\tau,t} = 0$$

and

$$(59) \qquad \lambda(x_{t+\tau,t} - x^*) + \kappa\Xi_{t+\tau,t} = 0,$$

or, equivalently,

$$(60) \qquad \pi_{t+\tau,t} + \frac{\lambda}{\kappa}(x_{t+\tau,t} - x^*) = 0,$$

for $\tau \geq 1$.

Using equation (60) in equation (46) and solving in the usual manner, we find in this case that the optimal forecast paths are given by

$$x_{t+\tau,t} = \frac{\lambda(1-\beta)}{\kappa^2 + \lambda(1-\beta)}x^* - \frac{\kappa}{\kappa^2 + \lambda(1-\beta\rho)}\rho^\tau u_t,$$

$$\pi_{t+\tau,t} = \frac{\lambda\kappa}{\kappa^2 + \lambda(1-\beta)}x^* + \frac{\lambda}{\kappa^2 + \lambda(1-\beta\rho)}\rho^\tau u_t.$$

One may verify that in this case the forecasts are now intertemporally consistent.

The corresponding instrument path i^t is then given by equation (50). It follows that in the period-t decision cycle the central bank will plan to set the interest rate in period $t + 1$ according to

$$(61) \quad i_{t+1} = i_{t+1,t} = \frac{\lambda\kappa}{\kappa^2 + \lambda(1 - \beta)} x^* + \bar{r} + \omega(r_t^n - \bar{r}) + \frac{\rho\lambda + (1 - \rho)\dfrac{\kappa}{\sigma}}{\kappa^2 + \lambda(1 - \beta\rho)} \rho u_t.$$

In at least one possible equilibrium associated with this procedure, private-sector plans agree with the forecasts, $\pi_{t+1|t} = \pi_{t+1,t}$ and $x_{t+1|t} = x_{t+1,t}$. In this equilibrium, the forecastable components of inflation and the output gap evolve according to

$$(62) \quad x_{t+1|t} = \frac{\lambda(1 - \beta)}{\kappa^2 + \lambda(1 - \beta)} x^* - \frac{\kappa}{\kappa^2 + \lambda(1 - \beta\rho)} \rho u_t,$$

$$(63) \quad \pi_{t+1|t} = \frac{\lambda\kappa}{\kappa^2 + \lambda(1 - \beta)} x^* + \frac{\lambda}{\kappa^2 + \lambda(1 - \beta\rho)} \rho u_t.$$

This equilibrium differs from the optimal equilibrium, described by equations (26) and (27), in several respects. First, as long as $x^* > 0$, there is an average inflation bias, since $E[\pi_{t+1}] > 0$. Second, the average output gap is positive, $E[x_t] > 0$.[35] Third, the equilibrium lacks history dependence, since $\pi_{t+1|t}$ and $x_{t+1|t}$ do not depend on the past output-gap plan $x_{t|t-1}$ or past disturbances u_{t-j}. Fourth, the coefficients on u_t are different, illustrating the "stabilization bias" discussed in Jonsson (1997); Svensson (1997b); Clarida, Galí, and Gertler (1999); and Woodford (1999b).

We shall not examine the actual implementation of such an equilibrium further. Let us just note that equation (61) implies that the interest rate will be a function of the exogenous disturbances. If the private sector perceives of this setup as just being characterized by the reaction function (61) and the model equations (1) and (3), then it follows from the argument of section 2.2.4 that equilibrium is indeterminate. Suppose instead that the private sector forms expectations in accordance with the belief that, in a discretion equilibrium, inflation and the output gap in period $t + 2$ should only depend on the exogenous disturbances. Then the private-sector expectations $\pi_{t+2|t}$ and $x_{t+2|t}$ in equations (1) and (3) are given exogenously, and private-sector expectations $i_{t+1|t}$ determine the plans $\pi_{t+1|t}$ and $x_{t+1|t}$ uniquely. Then the equilibrium is determinate, and the equilibrium described by equations (62) and (63) will result.

---

35. The aggregate-supply equation (1) has the property that the long-run Phillips curve is positively sloped, $E[\pi_t] = \kappa E[x_t]/(1 - \delta)$. This is because the assumption in the standard Calvo setup is that firms between optimizing price changes keep their nominal price fixed. If instead, as in Yun (1996), it is assumed that prices between optimizing price changes are indexed to the average inflation rate, the long-run Phillips curve is vertical. (Similarly, in the standard Rotemburg setup, it is assumed that any price change is costly, making the long-run Phillips curve positively sloped. If instead it is assumed that any price change different from the average inflation rate is costly, the long-run Phillips curve is vertical.)

2.3.4   Sequentially Constrained Optimization

We now show that a forecast-based optimization procedure can be rendered consistent with the optimal equilibrium, through a suitable modification of the way in which the central bank evaluates alternative forecast paths. As indicated in our discussion in section 2.2.1, a suitable procedure must incorporate history dependence of a kind that is lacking in the procedures discussed in the previous section. One way of introducing the sort of history dependence that is required is for the central bank to commit itself to internalize the cost of systematically departing from its own previous forecasts. As we have seen in the previous section, the existence of a motive for such deviations is the reason for the suboptimality of a procedure aimed at minimization of the social loss function.

In the case of a deterministic environment, it would be sufficient to add the condition

$$\pi_{t+1,t} = \pi_{t+1,t-1}$$

to the bank's decision problem in period t. However, this would be inefficient in the more realistic case where there is some new information each period, and hence good reason to let $\pi_{t+1,t}$ deviate from $\pi_{t+1,t-1}$, albeit in an unforecastable way. But we may instead imagine a procedure in which the central bank chooses the forecast path that is optimal subject to a constraint of the form

$$(64) \qquad \pi_{t+1,t} = \overline{\pi}_t(u_t),$$

where the value of $\overline{\pi}_t(u_t)$ for each possible realization of the disturbance u_t is chosen as part of the bank's period–$t - 1$ decision.

It is clear that a dynamic-programming approach of this kind can create the necessary history dependence, at least in principle. As discussed in section 2.2.2 above, a timelessly optimal equilibrium involves an expected evolution from any date t onward that is optimal subject to a constraint of the form of equation (25). Furthermore, as just discussed, the evaluation of expected losses in any possible equilibrium from date t onward requires only a computation of the associated forecast paths. Hence, the choice of $i_{t+1,t}$ that should be made at date t in order to implement the timelessly optimal equilibrium can be made solely on the basis of an evaluation of the alternative forecast paths that are consistent with the constraint (64), assuming that, in each possible state at date t, $\overline{\pi}(u_t)$ takes the same value as in equation (25).

In the case of both of the examples of timelessly optimal equilibria discussed in section 2.2.2, the required constraint is of the form

$$(65) \qquad \overline{\pi}_t(u_t) = \overline{\pi}_{t,t-1} + \frac{\rho c}{1 - \beta\rho c}(u_t - u_{t,t-1}),$$

where the intercept $\bar{\pi}_{t,t-1}$ depends only on the state of the economy in period $t - 1$.[36] Thus we may imagine that the central bank commits itself in period $t - 1$ to subject itself in the following decision cycle to a constraint of the form in equation (65), where the value of $\bar{\pi}_{t,t-1}$ is chosen in period $t - 1$. It is the choice of $\bar{\pi}_{t,t-1}$ on the basis of the economy's state in period $t - 1$ that creates the desired history dependence of subsequent policy.

Because it is only $\bar{\pi}_{t,t-1}$ that must be chosen as part of the bank's period-$t - 1$ decision cycle, the choice can be made purely on the basis of a selection among alternative possible forecast paths at that time. (Note that the intercept in equation [65] that is consistent with the timelessly optimal equilibrium is just the forecast value $\pi_{t+1,t-1}$ associated with the constrained-optimal forecast path selected by the central bank in its period–$t - 1$ decision cycle.) Furthermore, the bank's choice of the appropriate value for $\bar{\pi}_{t,t-1}$, like its choice of the appropriate value for $i_{t,t-1}$, follows from its desire to bring about the constrained optimal equilibrium from among those projected to be possible in its period–$t - 1$ desired cycle. If and only if the bank selects the value of $\bar{\pi}_{t,t-1}$ in this way will it expect its own constrained optimization procedure in the following decision cycle to lead it to choose to continue the forecast path selected as constrained-optimal in the current decision cycle.

We thus obtain a sequential forecast-based optimization procedure that is consistent with an equilibrium that is optimal from a timeless perspective. (Either of the two timelessly optimal equilibria discussed in section 2.2.2 can be shown to be consistent with a procedure of this form, as long as one starts with the appropriate constraint in the first period that the procedure is followed.) However, a possible disadvantage of the procedure, from the point of view of communication with the public, is that the determination of which among the feasible forecast paths at a given time are consistent with constraint (64) depends on an evaluation of the current disturbance u_t, and the extent to which this differs from what was previously expected. This means that the numerical value of this disturbance (that is not meaningful outside the context of the bank's structural model) must be discussed as part of the decision about which among the feasible forecast paths should be selected, and not only in the course of generating the set of feasible forecast paths. Furthermore, the procedure requires the bank to discuss its forecast for this variable, and not simply the forecast paths of the target variables (inflation and the output gap) about which the public cares.

36. Note that the coefficient on u_t is the same in both equations (27) and (30). This is not accidental; the coefficient must be the same in the case of any timelessly optimal equilibrium. For in any such equilibrium, the evolution of the economy from date t onward satisfies the system consisting of equations (1), (3), (11), and (12) for some initial condition Ξ_{t-1}; alternative equilibria differ only in the way that the initial condition is selected. But the initial condition cannot depend on the realized value of u_t, nor does the equilibrium response of inflation forecasts to unexpected variation in u_t depend on the value assigned to Ξ_{t-1}.

The need to explicitly discuss this variable and its consequences for constraint (64), if the public is to be able to verify that the central bank is indeed basing its deliberations upon its putative objective, may be considered a difficulty for practical implementation of the proposal.

2.3.5   Minimization of a Modified Loss Function: "Commitment to Continuity and Predictability"

A closely related approach, which nonetheless avoids the difficulty just mentioned, is to modify the loss function that the central bank uses to evaluate alternative forecast paths, rather than restricting attention to forecast paths that satisfy a constraint of the form of equation (64). It follows from familiar Kuhn-Tucker theory that the constrained optimum of the previous section can alternatively be characterized as the optimum of a loss function that includes an additional term corresponding to the constraint. This dual approach is of particular interest in the present case, because the Lagrange multiplier associated with constraint (64) is independent of the value of u_t.[37] This means that the central bank can choose the value of the Lagrange multiplier that will modify its period-t decision problem as part of its period-$t - 1$ decision cycle and again make this decision solely on the basis of a selection among feasible forecast paths at that time. In this case, however, there is no need in period t to adjust the value of the multiplier in response to any surprise that may have occurred in the realization of u_t.

Suppose that the central bank modifies the period loss function $L_{t+\tau,t}$ for $\tau = 1$ by adding the term $\Xi_{t,t-1}(\pi_{t+1,t} - \pi_{t+1,t-1})$, hence substituting

$$(66) \qquad \tilde{L}_{t+1,t} \equiv \frac{1}{2}[\pi_{t+1,t}^2 + \lambda(x_{t+1,t} - x^*)^2] + \Xi_{t,t-1}(\pi_{t+1,t} - \pi_{t+1,t-1})$$

for $L_{t+1,t}$, where $\Xi_{t,t-1}$ is the corresponding Lagrange multiplier from the decision in period $t - 1$.[38] Then the first-order conditions are equations (52) and (53) for $\tau \geq 1$, where the initial condition (54) for $\tau = 1$ is replaced by

$$(67) \qquad \Xi_{t,t} = \Xi_{t,t-1}.$$

Since $\Xi_{t,t-1}$ fulfills equation (53) for $\tau = 1$ and t replaced by $t - 1$,

$$(68) \qquad \Xi_{t,t-1} = -\frac{\lambda}{\kappa}(x_{t,t-1} - x^*),$$

the consolidated first-order condition (56) for $\tau = 1$ becomes

---

37. This follows from the fact that the constraint (64) corresponds to the self-consistent constraint (25) associated with a timelessly optimal equilibrium.

38. Adding a linear term to the loss function is similar to the linear inflation contracts discussed in Walsh (1995) and Persson and Tabellini (1993). Indeed, the term added in equation (66) corresponds to a state-contingent linear inflation contract, which, as discussed in Svensson (1997b), can remedy both stabilization bias and average-inflation bias.

(69)
$$\pi_{t+1,t} + \frac{\lambda}{\kappa}(x_{t+1,t} - x_{t,t-1}) = 0$$

instead of equation (56). That is, the consolidated first-order condition (55) holds for $\tau \geq 1$ and not just for $\tau \geq 2$, with the initial condition

(70)
$$x_{t,t} = x_{t,t-1}$$

for $\tau = 1$. Comparison of these first-order conditions with equations (11) and (12) indicates that the optimal forecasts π^t and x^t chosen in period t under this procedure correspond to the optimal equilibrium. Hence, choice of $i_{t+1,t}$ to be consistent with these optimal forecast paths will result in a commitment to an interest rate that is consistent with continuation of the stationary optimal equilibrium.

What is the economic interpretation of the multiplier $\Xi_{t,t-1}$? From the Lagrangian equation (51), we see that $\Xi_{t,t-1}$ is the marginal loss in period $t-1$ resulting from an increase in the inflation forecast $\pi_{t+1,t-1}$. Adding the term $\Xi_{t,t-1}(\pi_{t+1,t} - \pi_{t+1,t-1})$ to the period-t loss function means that the central bank internalizes this cost when making decisions in period t. This is perhaps a somewhat abstract consideration for the purposes of practical policy making, but it is very much in line with the continuity, predictability, and transparency emphasized in actual inflation targeting (see, for instance, King 1997b). Hence, we refer to this case as a "commitment to continuity and predictability."

An Explicit Decision Procedure

We turn now to an explicit, algorithmic description of the central bank's decision procedure under this proposal. At the beginning of the period-t decision cycle, we suppose that the central bank observes the current realizations of the exogenous disturbances, which it may use as an input for its decisions; in particular, it observes the values of the current conditional expectations u^t and r^{nt}. It also recalls its commitment $i_{t,t-1}$, chosen during the previous cycle, and the value assigned to $\Xi_{t,t-1}$.

The first step in the decision procedure is the computation, using the bank's forecasting model, of the set of possible conditional forecasts π^t and x^t that are consistent with the model, given the conditional expectations u^t and r^{nt}. In our example, these are the paths consistent with equation (46) for all $\tau \geq 1$. It then evaluates the modified loss function, obtained by substituting equation (66) into equation (49), for each possible joint forecast path. In this way, the optimal forecasts are determined as well as the new value of the Lagrange multiplier, $\Xi_{t+1,t}$.

In our example, these optimal forecasts are the ones that satisfy the consolidated first-order condition (55) for all $\tau \geq 1$, with the initial condition (70). Using condition (55) to eliminate $\pi_{t+\tau,t}$ in equation (46) for $\tau \geq 1$, we get the same second-order difference equation for $x_{t+\tau,t}$ as obtained above for $x_{t+1|t}$—namely, equation (16)—but with the initial condition (70) instead of condition (18). Thus, the characteristic equation again has the two eigenvalues c and $1/(\beta c)$, where $0 < c < 1$, and the solution can be written

$$(71) \qquad x_{t+\tau,t} = -\frac{\kappa}{\lambda} c \sum_{j=0}^{\infty} (\beta c)^j u_{t+\tau+j,t} + c x_{t+\tau-1,t}$$

for $\tau \geq 1$.

Since the forecasts $u_{t+\tau,t}$ are given by the true (exogenous) conditional expectations $u_{t+\tau|t}$, which are assumed to be known to the bank as an input to the process, the term $\sum_{j=0}^{\infty} (\beta c)^j u_{t+\tau+j,t}$ has a uniquely determined value. Under assumption (2), this value is simply $\rho^\tau/(1 - \beta\rho c)$ times the current disturbance u_t, and equation (71) becomes

$$(72) \qquad x_{t+\tau,t} = -\frac{\kappa}{\lambda} \frac{c\rho^\tau}{1 - \beta\rho c} u_t + c x_{t+\tau-1,t}$$

$$(73) \qquad \qquad = -\frac{\kappa}{\lambda} \frac{\rho c}{1 - \beta\rho c} \frac{c^\tau - \rho^\tau}{c - \rho} u_t + c^\tau x_{t,t-1}$$

for each $\tau \geq 1$. From equation (55) it then follows that the optimal forecast of inflation is given by

$$(74) \qquad \pi_{t+\tau,t} = \frac{\rho c \rho^\tau}{1 - \beta\rho c} u_t + \frac{\lambda}{\kappa}(1 - c)x_{t+\tau-1,t}$$

$$(75) \qquad \qquad = \frac{\rho c}{1 - \beta\rho c} \frac{(1 - \rho)\rho^{\tau-1} - (1 - c)c^{\tau-1}}{c - \rho} u_t + \frac{\lambda}{\kappa}(1 - c)c^{\tau-1}x_{t,t-1},$$

for each $\tau \geq 1$.

In a third step, the central bank calculates the corresponding forecast path for its instrument, i^t, according to equation (50). From equation (55), this must satisfy

$$(76) \qquad i_{t+\tau,t} = r^n_{t+\tau,t} + \frac{\lambda\sigma - \kappa}{\lambda\sigma} \pi_{t+\tau+1,t}$$

for $\tau \geq 1$. The forecast path for the natural rate of interest is given by the true conditional expectations (exogenous and known to the bank), while the forecast path for inflation is determined as above. In the case that the disturbance processes satisfy both equations (2) and (4), the interest-rate path is given by

$$(77) \qquad i_{t+\tau,t} = \bar{r} + \omega^\tau(r^n_t - r) + \frac{\lambda\sigma - \kappa}{\lambda\sigma} \frac{\rho c}{1 - \beta\rho c} \frac{(1 - \rho)\rho^\tau - (1 - c)c^\tau}{c - \rho} u_t$$
$$+ f c^{\tau-1}x_{t,t-1}$$

for each $\tau \geq 1$.

Finally, the central bank makes its decisions. Its action—the setting of its operating target i_t for the current period—is determined by the commitment made during the previous decision cycle: it simply sets $i_t = i_{t,t-1}$. Its non-trivial current decisions are the selection of a commitment $i_{t+1,t}$ for its action in the following period, and a value for the Lagrange multiplier $\Xi_{t+1,t}$ to be used in the following period's modified loss function. These values are both obtained as initial elements of the forecast paths just computed. Thus, in the case of AR(1) disturbances the decisions are

$$(78) \quad i_{t+1,t} = \bar{r} + \omega(r_t^n - \bar{r}) + \frac{\lambda\sigma - \kappa}{\lambda\sigma} \frac{\rho c}{1 - \beta\rho c}(c + \rho - 1)u_t + fx_{t,t-1}$$

$$\Xi_{t+1,t} = -\frac{\lambda}{\kappa}(x_{t+1,t} - x^*)$$

$$(79) \qquad = \frac{\lambda}{\kappa}x^* + \frac{\rho c}{1 - \beta\rho c}u_t - \frac{\lambda}{\kappa}cx_{t,t-1},$$

where we have used equations (53) and (73) for $\tau = 1$. These decisions are recorded for use as inputs in the following decision cycle. At the beginning of period $t + 1$, the new realizations of the exogenous disturbances are observed and the cycle is repeated.

Several comments about this modified forecast-targeting process are appropriate. One is that the forecast paths that are constructed in successive decision cycles are now *time consistent,* in the sense that the forecasts made in decision cycle t coincide with the forecast that the bank would make in period t of what it will forecast using this procedure during any later decision cycle. For example, the bank's forecast in period t of the forecast path for inflation π^{t+1} during the following decision cycle, denoted $[\pi_{t+\tau,t+1}]_{,t}$, should be

$$[\pi_{t+\tau,t+1}]_{,t} = \frac{\rho c}{1 - \beta\rho c} \frac{(1 - \rho)\rho^{\tau-2} - (1 - c)c^{\tau-2}}{c - \rho}u_{t+1,t}$$

$$+ \frac{\lambda}{\kappa}(1 - c)c^{\tau-2}x_{t+1,t}$$

$$(80) \qquad = \frac{\rho c}{1 - \beta\rho c} \frac{(1 - \rho)\rho^{\tau-2} - (1 - c)c^{\tau-2}}{c - \rho}\rho u_t$$

$$- (1 - c)c^{\tau-2}\left[\frac{\rho c}{1 - \beta\rho c}u_t + \frac{\lambda}{\kappa}cx_{t,t-1}\right]$$

$$(81) \qquad = \frac{\rho c}{1 - \beta\rho c} \frac{(1 - \rho)\rho^{\tau-1} - (1 - c)c^{\tau-1}}{c - \rho}u_t + \frac{\lambda}{\kappa}(1 - c)c^{\tau-1}x_{t,t-1},$$

for each $\tau \geq 2$. Here we have used equation (75) to substitute for $\pi_{t+\tau,t+1}$ in the first line and equation (73) to substitute for $x_{t+1,t}$ in the second. Note that the final line agrees exactly with equation (75), so that the forecasting procedure is consistent.

Furthermore, the bank's forecasts are also consistent with *at least one* possible equilibrium associated with this policy. The forecasts are, by construction, consistent with equations (46) and (47), which are conditions that the true conditional expectations must satisfy in a rational-expectations equilibrium. In fact, one can show that there exists an equilibrium, consistent with the bank's pattern of action under this procedure, in which the true conditional expectations coincide at all times with the bank's forecasts ($\pi_{t+\tau|t} = \pi_{t+\tau,t}$, and so on). Checking this amounts simply to verifying that the processes

$$\pi_{t+1} = \pi_{t+1,t} + u_{t+1} - u_{t+1|t},$$

$$x_{t+1} = x_{t+1,t} + \sigma(r^n_{t+1} - r^n_{t+1|t}),$$

$$i_{t+1} = i_{t+1,t}$$

satisfy equations (1) and (3), when the bank forecasts are constructed as described above.

The equilibrium with this property is also observed to be one that is optimal from the point of view of the timeless perspective defined in section 2.2.2. Specifically, if the policy regime begins in some period t_0, with the initial conditions Ξ_{t_0,t_0-1} and i_{t_0,t_0-1} consistent with the stationary optimal equilibrium, and is expected to continue forever, the equilibrium just described for periods $t \geq t_0$ corresponds to the continuation of the stationary optimal equilibrium. The hypothesized initial conditions are, by equations (53) and (26),

(82)
$$\Xi_{t_0,t_0-1} = -\frac{\lambda}{\kappa}(x_{t_0|t_0-1} - x^*)$$

(83)
$$= \frac{\lambda}{\kappa}x^* + \frac{\rho c}{1 - \beta \rho c}\sum_{j=0}^{\infty} c^j u_{t_0-j-1}$$

and $i_{t_0,t_0-1} = i^*$. Substitution of these initial conditions into the equations just derived is easily seen to result in exactly the stationary optimal equilibrium characterized in section 2.2.2. Furthermore, regardless of the initial conditions, the equilibrium involves the optimal responses to shocks that occur from period t_0 onward, as well as the optimal long-run average values for the endogenous variables.[39]

Note that this procedure need not require that the bank's decisions regarding $i_{t+1,t}$ and $\Xi_{t+1,t}$ be made public or that it announce any other aspects of the forecast paths that it constructs as part of the above decision

---

39. Note that modification of the loss function to include the additional term in equation (66), in line with the inflation contracts referred to in note 38, suffices to eliminate the average inflation bias resulting from discretionary minimization of the true social loss function, even when the central bank's loss function includes an output gap target $x^* > 0$. Thus there is no need to *also* modify the loss function in the way proposed by King (1997a), setting $x^* = 0$ even if that is not its true social value. It is thus an appealing feature of this approach that a single modification of the purely discretionary procedure cures *both* the problems of average inflation bias and stabilization bias.

procedure. It need simply set its instrument in the way that has been specified, and, if its decision procedure (or, rather, the consequences of the procedure) is correctly understood by the private sector, the optimal equilibrium becomes a rational-expectations equilibrium consistent with this policy. This is because under this procedure the central bank's forecasts (and actions) are a perfectly predictable function of the history of exogenous disturbances, which are already assumed to be observed by the private sector. Thus, revealing the forecasts, or the commitments chosen by the bank on the basis of them, reveals no additional information.[40]

Nonetheless, announcement of the bank's decisions regarding $i_{t+1,t}$ and $\Xi_{t+1,t}$ may be useful in practice. First of all, the bank's commitment to condition its future decisions upon these past findings may be more reliably fulfilled when the commitments have been made public. (Our analysis in the previous paragraph of the irrelevance of the information provided by the announcements treats the bank's commitment to the decision procedure as unproblematic.) Second, the ability of the private sector to accurately forecast future policy (upon which the above calculation of optimal policy relies) may be facilitated by such announcements of the bank's intentions with regard to future decision cycles. (Our analysis in the previous paragraph similarly takes the private sector's correct understanding of the bank's decision procedure as given.) Similar considerations apply with regard to publication of the bank's forecasts. The fact that past forecasts have been made public may strengthen the bank's commitment to minimizing the modified loss function rather than the true social loss function, for unconstrained discretionary optimization will result in outcomes that systematically disconfirm previous forecasts. And obviously publication of the bank's forecasts makes it easier for the private sector to coordinate its own forecasts with those of the bank and hence to act in the way assumed by the bank's analysis.[41]

The Implied Reaction Function and Determinacy

We turn now to the question of whether the optimal equilibrium just discussed is *necessarily* the one that results from a commitment to the above procedure. In order to analyze this question, it suffices to consider the implied reaction function of this policy rule—that is, the implied mapping from exogenous and predetermined variables (the information of the cen-

40. The bank's forecasts are predictable not simply given the relations between variables that should exist in equilibrium, but regardless of the equilibrium that happens to be realized, for the procedure described above takes as inputs *no* observations of external reality other than the evolution of the exogenous disturbances and involves no internal randomization either.

41. The central bank has no incentive to announce a different value for $\Xi_{t+1,t}$ in order to manipulate the outcome of subsequent decision cycles. Because doing so would affect private-sector expectations in period t of its future decisions, this would lead to a worse equilibrium from the point of view of period t.

tral bank at the beginning of each decision cycle) to the bank's setting of its instrument. In the example explicitly treated above, the reaction function of the policy rule is given by $i_{t+1} = i_{t+1,t}$, where $i_{t+1,t}$ is given by equations (78) and (79). Furthermore, by solving equation (73) for $\tau = 1$ backward, we get

$$x_{t,t-1} = -\frac{\kappa}{\lambda}\frac{\rho c}{1 - \beta\rho c}\sum_{j=0}^{\infty}c^j u_{t-j-1}.$$

Combining this with equation (78) makes it obvious that the implied reaction function is given by $i_{t+1} = i^*_{t+1}$, where i^*_{t+1} is defined above in equation (32). Thus, as discussed in section 2.2.4, this decision procedure results in indeterminacy.

Thus, while the optimal equilibrium is one possible equilibrium consistent with a commitment to this policy, it is only one of a very large set of possible equilibria, even if we restrict our attention to stationary equilibria. The others are *not* optimal, involving as they do suboptimal responses to disturbances (simply due to self-fulfilling expectations) or fluctuations in response to irrelevant "sunspot" variables, or both. Thus, the use of the modified loss function solves *one* of the problems associated with discretionary minimization of the true social loss function—the procedure is now consistent with the optimal equilibrium—but it does not eliminate the problem of indeterminacy of equilibrium.

Arguably, the likelihood of the economy's settling upon an inefficient equilibrium might be reduced by making public the complete forecast paths calculated by the central bank. In this case the coordination of private-sector expectations upon exactly those announced by the central bank might be a natural "focal point" for the coordination game faced by private-sector agents deciding which outcome to expect. Nonetheless, this would be only one among a very large set of other possible equilibria of that "game." An alternative policy rule that is equally consistent with the optimal equilibrium, and that makes it the *unique* (or at least the unique nonexplosive) equilibrium, is superior (in at least this respect) to a rule that can only make that equilibrium a "natural focal point" among a large set of possible equilibria.

2.3.6   A Hybrid Rule That Ensures Determinacy

Determinacy can, however, be ensured in a more reliable way—by committing the bank to a policy that, if correctly understood by the private sector, *excludes* other equilibria—if the pure targeting procedure described above is modified in a way that introduces some elements of commitment to an instrument rule.

Note that a targeting procedure, as defined above, makes the bank's actions dependent solely upon its own internal forecasts of what will happen as a result of alternative decisions on its part. Such a purely forecast-based procedure implies that the bank takes no note of whether realized inflation and output gaps deviate from its forecasts (in a systematic way) or, alternatively, of whether private-sector plans and expectations deviate from central-bank forecasts. But this is not necessarily reasonable behavior; indeed, actual inflation-targeting central banks do seem to monitor private-sector plans and expectations, as is apparent from their published inflation reports.

When private-sector plans and expectations and the realized equilibrium deviate systematically from the central bank's forecasts, one might well suppose that a forecast-targeting central bank should react to this, by letting its interest rate deviate from what it would otherwise have set. For example, a bank might commit itself not to set $i_{t+1} = i_{t+1,t}$ regardless of whether its forecasts turn out in the meantime to be confirmed, but instead to set the interest rate according to a rule of the form

$$(84) \qquad i_{t+1} = i_{t+1,t} + g_\pi(\pi_{t+1|t} - \pi_{t+1,t}) + g_x(x_{t+1|t} - x_{t+1,t}).$$

Here $i_{t+1,t}$ no longer represents a *commitment* made during the period-t decision cycle as to the value of i_{t+1} that will necessarily be set, but it is still the bank's *forecast* during that decision cycle as to the value that will be set, assuming that the economy continues to evolve in accordance with the bank's predictions.

Equation (84) no longer describes a pure targeting rule, in that the bank's instrument setting i_{t+1} no longer follows from a pure calculation of what the effects of one choice or another upon the target variables should be. Instead, it has an element of commitment to an instrument rule—an approach under which the central bank adjusts its instrument in a way that it has committed itself to in advance, not because it judges at the time that this action will have a desirable effect, but because it has judged at an earlier time that it would be desirable for the private sector to anticipate behavior of this kind. Nonetheless, this is not a pure instrument rule either (an approach considered further in section 2.5), as the rule for setting the interest rate involves a time-varying coefficient $i_{t+1,t}$, which is chosen by the central bank through a targeting procedure. It thus represents a sort of hybrid decision procedure.

The values of $i_{t+1,t}$, $\pi_{t+1,t}$, and $x_{t+1,t}$ in this equation are each chosen by the central bank during its period-t decision cycle. They are all determined through exactly the same forecasting exercise as has been described above. For in forming its forecasts, the bank *expects* its forecasts to be correct; thus, in computing what it expects the consequences of a given choice of $i_{t+1,t}$ to be, it still expects i_{t+1} to equal $i_{t+1,t}$ in equilibrium. Furthermore, this rule is consistent with continuation of the stationary optimal equilibrium, for the same reason that the specific targeting rule described above is; for in the case that equilibrium occurs (as forecast by the central bank), the actions prescribed by equation (84) are identical to those prescribed by the general targeting rule.

However, the two procedures do not prescribe identical behavior out of equilibrium, and they may differ as to the determinacy of equilibrium. When the central bank follows the explicit decision procedure outlined in the "Explicit Decision Procedure" section, which results in the implied reaction function $i_{t+1,t} = i^*_{t+1}$, equation (84) would correspond to

$$(85) \qquad i_{t+1} = i^*_{t+1} + g_\pi(\pi_{t+1|t} - \pi_{t+1,t}) + g_x(x_{t+1|t} - x_{t+1,t}).$$

This reaction function is such that the central bank first decides on the interest rate plan, $i^t = \{i_{t+\tau,t}\}^\infty_{\tau=1}$, consistent with achieving the optimal inflation and output-gap forecasts, $\pi^t = \{\pi_{t+\tau,t}\}^\infty_{\tau=1}$ and $x^t = \{x_{t+\tau,t}\}^\infty_{\tau=1}$, that minimize the intertemporal loss function modified according to equation (66), which results in $i_{t+1,t} = i^*_{t+1}$, as we have seen. If, after having announced this interest rate plan, it observes that private-sector plans for inflation and the output gap, $\pi_{t+1|t}$ and $x_{t+1|t}$, deviate from its forecasts, $\pi_{t+1,t}$ and $x_{t+1,t}$, it makes a further adjustment of the interest rate implemented in period $t + 1$ according to equation (85). (Note that this is still a reaction function of the form of equation (39), although it no longer satisfies the information restriction assumed in equation (36), as a pure targeting rule would.)

Let us now consider the determinacy of equilibrium under such a commitment. When equation (85) is combined with the expectation of equations (1) and (3), the dynamic system can again be written as in equation (40) with vector $\mathbf{z}_t$ defined as in equation (41), whereas the vector $\tilde{\mathbf{s}}_t$ of exogenous variables is now given by

$$\tilde{\mathbf{s}}_t \equiv \begin{bmatrix} u_{t+1|t} \\ r^n_{t+1|t} - \bar{r} \\ \pi_{t+1,t} \\ x_{t+1,t} \end{bmatrix},$$

where we exploit that the central bank forecasts $\pi_{t+1,t}$ and $x_{t+1,t}$ depend on the exogenous shocks only. The matrix $\mathbf{M}$ is given by equation (44). It follows that a sufficient condition for determinacy is that the coefficients g_π and g_x fulfill equation (45). Since the optimal equilibrium is one possible equilibrium, the unique equilibrium must be the optimal one.

In equilibrium, private-sector plans and central-bank forecasts will be equal, so the term in equation (84) that involves the coefficients g_π and g_x will always be zero. The commitment to deviate from i^*_{t+1} in proportion to any deviation of private-sector plans from central bank forecasts is an out-of-equilibrium commitment that will not be noted in the equilibrium. The direction of the deviation is intuitive; if private-sector plans for inflation and/or the output gap exceed the central-bank forecasts, the bank responds with tighter policy—a higher interest rate.

Thus, determinacy is possible in the case of a hybrid rule of this kind, regardless of the values of the model's structural parameters; one simply need to choose any values for g_π and g_x that fulfill equation (45)—for instance, Taylor's (1993) classic values 1.5 and .5, respectively. This illustrates the fact that a commitment to respond to variables that are predetermined, and hence irrevocable, by the time the bank responds to them may nonetheless be desirable.

2.4   Commitment to a Specific Targeting Rule

In this section, we introduce our second, intermediate-level policy specification. This is in terms of a specific targeting rule, specifying a criterion that the bank's forecast paths for its target variables must satisfy. This kind of rule specifies a relation involving one or more endogenous variables that cannot be directly observed at the time that policy is chosen and that instead must be forecasted. Furthermore, in the case of a forward-looking model, even forecasting endogenous variables a short time in the future will in general require solving for the model's equilibrium into the indefinite future; thus, a forecast of the entire future paths of the various variables is required. A decision procedure of this kind is therefore still organized around the construction of forecast paths conditional upon alternative policies, even if explicit optimization is not undertaken. In the case of such a targeting rule, the history dependence necessary for determinacy and optimality must be introduced through commitment to a rule that involves *lagged* endogenous variables as well as forecasts of their future values.

A natural candidate for such a specific targeting rule is the consolidated first-order condition (14) for all $t \geq t_0$. This condition is not only *consistent* with the optimality in a timeless perspective but also has the property that, if the central bank could arrange for equation (14) to hold for all $t \geq t_0$, this condition would determine a unique bounded solution for periods $t \geq t_0$ given by equations (29) and (30).

However, the central bank cannot directly ensure that such a relation between the paths of its target variables is satisfied. It can, however, adjust its policy so as to produce *forecast paths* that satisfy this condition. Thus, the targeting rule commits the bank to a policy under which its decisions in period t are chosen so that its forecasts satisfy the condition

$$(86) \qquad \left[\pi_{t+\tau \mid t+\tau-1} + \frac{\lambda}{\kappa}(x_{t+\tau \mid t+\tau-1} - x_{t+\tau \mid t+\tau-2}) \right]_{,t} = 0$$

for all $\tau \geq 1$. This is a targeting rule involving private-sector plans of one-period-ahead inflation and the output gap. Using the facts that, for $\tau \geq 1$, $[\pi_{t+\tau \mid t+\tau-1}]_t \equiv \pi_{t+\tau,t}$ and $[x_{t+\tau \mid t+\tau-1}]_t \equiv x_{t+\tau,t}$ (under the maintained assumption that the bank does not yet observe current private-sector plans or expectations at the time it makes its current forecast), whereas $[x_{t \mid t-1}]_t \equiv x_{t \mid t-1}$ (under the assumption that lagged private-sector plans and expectations are observable), this is equivalent to ensuring that the bank's period-t forecast paths satisfy the specific targeting rule

(87) $$\pi_{t+\tau,t} + \frac{\lambda}{\kappa}(x_{t+\tau,t} - x_{t+\tau,t} - x_{t+\tau-1,t}) = 0$$

for $\tau \geq 1$, with the convention that

(88) $$x_{t,t} \equiv x_{t|t-1}.$$

Thus, the condition depends upon actually observed past private-sector plans in period $t - 1$ for the output gap in period t, $x_{t|t-1}$. Note that this differs from the case of a commitment to a modified loss function in section 3.5; compare equation (70).[42]

In order to find the forecasts π^t and x^t that fulfill this specific targeting rule, the bank combines equations (87) and (88) with the aggregate-supply relation (46). Using equation (87) to eliminate $\pi_{t+\tau,t}$, it gets the same second-order difference equation for $x_{t+\tau,t}$ as obtained above in section 2.3.5, except that the initial condition is equation (88) rather than equation (70). This implies the same solutions, equations (73) and (75), except that they depend on the previous private-sector output-gap plan $x_{t|t-1}$ rather than the previous one-period-ahead central-bank output-gap forecast, $x_{t,t-1}$, that is,

(89) $$x_{t+\tau,t} = -\frac{\kappa}{\lambda}\frac{\rho c}{1 - \beta\rho c}\frac{c^\tau - \rho^\tau}{c - \rho}u_t + c^\tau x_{t|t-1},$$

(90) $$\pi_{t+\tau,t} = \frac{\rho c}{1 - \beta\rho c}\frac{(1 - \rho)\rho^{\tau-1} - (1 - c)c^{\tau-1}}{c - \rho}u_t + \frac{\lambda}{\kappa}(1 - c)c^{\tau-1}x_{t|t-1}.$$

Using this in equation (76) then results in the implied reaction function

(91) $$i_{t+1,t} = \bar{\imath}_{t+1},$$

where $\bar{\imath}_{t+1}$ is defined by equations (33) and (34). Thus, the implied reaction function differs from that in section 2.3.5, where it was given by $i_{t+1,t} = i^*_{t+1}$, where i^*_{t+1} is defined by equation (32).

2.4.1   Determinacy under the Specific Targeting Rule

We have already observed that the specific targeting rule in equation (87) and the implied reaction function in equation (91) are *consistent* with the equilibrium described by equations (30) and (29) and thus consistent with continuation of the stationary optimal equilibrium if one starts from initial conditions consistent with that equilibrium. However, it remains to be con-

---

42. Leitemo (1999) examines the consequences in a forward-looking model of another targeting rule, namely that a constant-interest-rate inflation forecast should equal the inflation target at a specified horizon.

sidered whether the proposed policy commitment *requires* this outcome, under the assumption that the private sector regards the commitment as fully credible.

When the reaction function defined by equations (33) and (38) is combined with the expectations of equations (1) and (3), the resulting dynamic system can be written as equation (40) but with the column vectors z_t and $\tilde{s}_t$ now defined as

$$(92) \qquad z_t \equiv \begin{bmatrix} \pi_{t+1|t} \\ x_{t+1|t} \\ x_{t|t-1} \end{bmatrix}, \qquad \tilde{s}_t \equiv \begin{bmatrix} u_{t+1|t} \\ r^n_{t+1|t} - \bar{r} \end{bmatrix},$$

and the matrix M given by

$$M \equiv \begin{bmatrix} 1/\beta & -\kappa/\beta & 0 \\ -\sigma/\beta & 1 + \kappa\sigma/\beta & \sigma f \\ 0 & 1 & 0 \end{bmatrix}.$$

The eigenvalues are given by the roots of the characteristic equation, which can be written

$$(93) \qquad \mu\left(\mu^2 - \frac{1 + \beta + \kappa\sigma}{\beta}\mu + \frac{1}{\beta}\right) - \sigma f\left(\mu - \frac{1}{\beta}\right) = 0.$$

For $f = 0$, we have the same roots μ_1 and μ_2 as in the case of an exogenous process for the interest rate (see section 2.2.4 above), and a third root $\mu_3 = 0$. Hence, by continuity, for small f we again have indeterminacy, since we don't have exactly two roots of modulus above unity. It can be shown that an interval of positive values of f gives determinacy. The necessary and sufficient conditions for determinacy of a dynamic system of this kind are derived in Woodford (2003, prop. C.2, appendix to chap. 4) and reproduced in the appendix. The interval of determinacy can be written

$$(94) \qquad \min(f_1, f_2) < f < \max(f_1, f_2),$$

where f_1 and f_2 are the values of f that correspond to equality in conditions (114) and (115), respectively. They are

$$(95) \qquad f_1 \equiv \frac{\kappa}{1 - \beta} \quad \text{and} \quad f_2 \equiv \frac{2}{\sigma} + \frac{\kappa}{1 + \beta}.$$

For the case $f_2 < f_1$, the corresponding eigenvalues fulfill $\mu_3 < -1 < 0 < \mu_1 < 1 < 1/\beta < \mu_2$.

Comparing equations (34), (94), and (95), it is clear that determinacy will at best result only in the case of certain (not obviously plausible) parameter values. Once again, a possible interpretation of this result is that it simply means that following the implied reaction function is not *by itself* sufficient for determinacy. The central bank may need to supply additional information to the private sector in order to facilitate the coordination of private-sector plans and expectations upon the optimal equilibrium. Thus, ensuring determinacy may provide an additional argument for *transparency* in central-bank decision making.

As discussed above in section 2.3, it may be useful for the central bank to announce all or part of its forecasts π^t, x^t, and i^t. If these announcements are credible, in the sense that private-sector plans and expectations agree with the announced forecasts or even expect that others will, the optimal equilibrium will result. Alternatively, the central bank may announce only the targeting rule (equation [86]) that it intends to follow. If this announcement is credible, in the sense that people expect the bank to succeed in bringing about the target condition or at least expect others to expect the condition to hold, the optimal equilibrium will again be the only outcome.

2.4.2   A Hybrid Rule Related to the Specific Targeting Rule

Determinacy can again also be ensured in a more reliable way, by a hybrid rule involving an intuitive out-of-equilibrium commitment. This can be done in a way directly related to the declared specific targeting rule of equation (87), so it is still very much in the spirit of a targeting rule.

Consider the special case of equation (84) in which $g_\pi = \kappa/\lambda g_x = g > 0$. Then the reaction function implied by the hybrid procedure (84) and the specific targeting rule takes the form

$$(96) \qquad i_{t+1} = \bar{i}_{t+1} + g\left[\pi_{t+1|t} + \frac{\lambda}{\kappa}(x_{t+1|t} - x_{t|t-1})\right],$$

where we have used the fact that central-bank forecasts satisfy equations (87) and (91) to obtain a reduced-form variant of equation (84). This reaction function is such that the central bank first decides on the interest rate consistent with achieving the specific targeting rule (87), corresponding to $i_{t+1,t} = \bar{i}_{t+1}$. If, after having announced this interest rate plan, it observes that private-sector plans for inflation and the output gap, $\pi_{t+1|t}$ and $x_{t+1|t}$, deviate from the targeting rule of equation (14), it makes a further adjustment of the interest rate implemented in period $t + 1$, in the proportion g of the deviation from equation (14). (Note that, again, this is still a reaction function of the form of equation [39], although it no longer satisfies the information restriction assumed in equation [36], as a pure targeting rule would.)

Let us now consider the determinacy of equilibrium under such a commitment. When equation (96) is combined with the expectation of equations (1) and (3), the dynamic system can again be written as in equation (40) with the definition of the vectors z_t and $\tilde{s}_t$ as in equation (92), but the matrix M is now given by

$$(97) \qquad M \equiv \begin{bmatrix} 1/\beta & -\kappa/\beta & 0 \\ -\sigma/\beta + \sigma g & 1 + \kappa\sigma/\beta + \lambda\sigma g/\kappa & \sigma f - \lambda\sigma g/\kappa \\ 0 & 1 & 0 \end{bmatrix}.$$

The corresponding characteristic equation can be written

(98) $\mu \left(\mu^2 - \dfrac{1 + \beta + \kappa\sigma}{\beta} \mu + \dfrac{1}{\beta} \right) - \sigma f \left(\mu - \dfrac{1}{\beta} \right)$

$$- \frac{\lambda\sigma}{\kappa} g \left(\mu^2 - 2a\mu + \frac{1}{\beta} \right) = 0,$$

where we have separated out the terms multiplied by g. We recognize that the quadratic equation in the parenthesis multiplied by g is the same as the characteristic equation (19) examined above, with roots c and $1/(\beta c)$ fulfilling $0 < c < 1 < 1/\beta < 1/(\beta c)$. Furthermore, the rest of the characteristic equation is the same as the characteristic equation (93) examined above. If f fulfills equation (94), we already have determinacy even if $g \equiv 0$. One can show that, regardless of whether f fulfills equation (94) or not, for any given value of f, there exists a value $\bar{g}(f)$ such that

(99) $g > \bar{g}(f)$

is sufficient for determinacy. The value of $\bar{g}(f)$ is given by

(100) $\bar{g}(f) \equiv \max\{g_1(f), g_2(f), \min[g_3(f), g_4(f)]\},$

where $g_1(f), g_2(f), g_3(f)$, and $g_4(f)$ are the lowest values such that condition (A3) holds for $g > g_1(f)$, condition (A4) for $g > g_2(f)$, condition (A5) for $g > g_3(f)$, and condition (A7) for $g > g_4(f)$, respectively. In some cases, the critical value is $g_1(f) \equiv 1 - (1 - \beta)f/\kappa$. Preliminary numerical analysis indicate that $\bar{g}(f)$ for most parameters need not be much different from 1 for determinacy.

Since the optimal equilibrium is one possible equilibrium, the unique equilibrium must be the optimal one. In equilibrium, equation (14) will be fulfilled. The commitment to deviate from $\bar{\imath}_{t+1}$ in proportion to any deviation from equation (14) is an out-of-equilibrium commitment that will not be noted in the equilibrium.

Thus, determinacy is possible in the case of a hybrid rule of this kind, regardless of the values of the model's structural parameters; if equation (94) is violated, one simply need to choose any value for g that fulfills equation (99). This illustrates, again, the fact that a commitment to respond to variables that are predetermined, and hence irrevocable, by the time that the bank responds to them may nonetheless be desirable. In section 2.5, we offer a more general discussion of what may be achieved through commitments of this kind.

2.4.3   A Commitment to an Equivalent Specific Price-Level Targeting Rule

As in Svensson (2003), the specific targeting rule in equation (87) can be expressed as an equivalent price-level targeting rule. Let p_t denote (the log of) the price level in period t (so $\pi_t \equiv p_t - p_{t-1}$). First, define a price-level target path in period t, $p^{*t} \equiv \{p^*_{t+\tau,t}\}_{\tau=0}^{\infty}$, according to

(101)
$$p^*_{t,t} \equiv p^*_{t,t-1} + p_t - p_{t|t-1},$$

(102)
$$p^*_{t+\tau,t} \equiv p^*_{t,t}.$$

This price-level target path is conditional on a given one-period-ahead price-level target in period $t - 1$, $p^*_{t,t-1}$, to be determined. The target is adjusted by the unanticipated shock to the price level in period t, $p_t - p_{t|t-1} = u_t - u_{t|t-1}$, so that some base drift is allowed to occur.

Second, consider the specific price-level targeting rule for period t,

(103)
$$p_{t+1|t} - p^*_{t+1,t} + \frac{\lambda}{\kappa}x_{t+1|t} = 0.$$

By first-differencing equation (103)—hence, assuming that it holds in period $t - 1$ and in all future periods—and using equations (101) and (102), we see that equation (103) implies the consolidated first-order condition (14). Third, if equation (103) holds for $p^*_{t,t-1}$ in period $t - 1$, this together with equations (101) and (102) implies

(104)
$$p^*_{t,t} = p_t + \frac{\lambda}{\kappa}x_{t|t-1}.$$

Thus, if the price-level-targeting rule (103) is initiated in a period t_0 and holds for all $t \geq t_0$, we can interpret equation (104) as determining the initial starting point $p^*_{t_0,t_0}$ as a function of the predetermined initial price level, p_{t_0}, and the previous one-period-ahead private-sector output-gap plan, $x_{t_0|t_0-1}$, after which the future price-level target paths are determined by equations (101) and (102).

Again, the central bank cannot directly insure that equation (103) is fulfilled, but it can produce forecast paths that fulfill the corresponding specific targeting rule for the price-level and output-gap forecast paths,

(105)
$$p_{t+\tau,t} - p^*_{t+\tau,t} + \frac{\lambda}{\kappa}x_{t+\tau,t} = 0$$

for $\tau \geq 1$. That is, the forecast of the price-level gap between the price level and the price-level target should be proportional to the negative of the output-gap forecast.

In order to find the optimal price-level and output-gap forecasts, $p^t = \{p_{t+\tau,t}\}_{\tau=1}^{\infty}$ and x^t, the central bank combines equation (105) with the aggregate-supply relation (46). This leads to the difference equation

$$\tilde{p}_{t+\tau+2,t} - 2a\tilde{p}_{t+\tau+1,t} + \frac{1}{\beta}\tilde{p}_{t+\tau,t} = -\frac{1}{\beta}u_{t+\tau+1,t}$$

for $\tau \geq 0$, where

$$\tilde{p}_{t+\tau,t} \equiv p_{t+\tau,t} - p^*_{t+\tau,t}$$

denotes the price-level gap forecast, the initial condition is

(106)
$$\tilde{p}_{t,t} = p_t - p^*_{t,t}$$
$$\equiv p_{t|t-1} - p^*_{t,t-1},$$

where we have used equation (101), and a is given by equation (17). Under the assumption of equation (2), the solution is

$$\tilde{p}_{t+\tau,t} = \frac{c\rho^\tau}{1 - \beta\rho c}u_t + c\tilde{p}_{t+\tau-1,t}$$

$$= \frac{\rho c}{1 - \beta\rho c}\frac{c^\tau - \rho^\tau}{c - \rho}u_t + c^\tau\tilde{p}_{t,t}$$

for $\tau \geq 1$. From equation (105), it then follows the output-gap forecast fulfills

$$x_{t+\tau,t} = -\frac{\kappa}{\lambda}\frac{c\rho^\tau}{1 - \beta\rho c}u_t - \frac{\kappa}{\lambda}c\tilde{p}_{t+\tau-1,t}$$

$$= -\frac{\kappa}{\lambda}\frac{\rho c}{1 - \beta\rho c}\frac{c^\tau - \rho^\tau}{c - \rho}u_t - \frac{\kappa}{\lambda}c^\tau\tilde{p}_{t,t}$$

and that the inflation forecast is given by

$$\pi_{t+\tau,t} = \frac{\rho c\rho^\tau}{1 - \beta\rho c}u_t - (1 - c)\tilde{p}_{t+\tau-1,t}$$

$$= \frac{\rho c}{1 - \beta\rho c}\frac{(1 - \rho)\rho^{\tau-1} - (1 - c)c^{\tau-1}}{c - \rho}u_t - (1 - c)c^{\tau-1}\tilde{p}_{t,t}.$$

Using this in equation (47) to find the optimal instrument rate decision in period t, $i_{t+1,t}$ gives

(107) $$i_{t+1,t} = \tilde{i}_{t+1} \equiv \bar{r} + \omega(r^n_t - \bar{r}) + \frac{\lambda\sigma - \kappa}{\lambda\sigma}\frac{\rho c}{1 - \beta\rho c}(c + \rho - 1)u_t + \tilde{f}\tilde{p}_{t,t},$$

where we have assumed equation (4) and where

(108) $$\tilde{f} \equiv -\frac{\kappa}{\lambda}f \equiv \frac{\kappa - \lambda\sigma}{\lambda\sigma}(1 - c)c.$$

Note that there is a relatively close relation between optimal inflation targeting under commitment and price-level targeting under discretion, previously discussed by Svensson (1999c); Clarida, Galí, and Gertler (1999); Svensson and Woodford (2003, section 5.2); Vestin (1999); and Smets (2000).

Note also that equations (106) and (107) imply that the instrument responds to the endogenous variable $p_{t|t-1}$ and exogenous shocks. This has implications for the determinacy of equilibrium. When the implied reaction function defined by equation (107) is combined with the expectations of equations (1) and (3), the resulting dynamic system can be written as equation (40) but with the column vectors z_t and $\tilde{s}_t$ now defined as

$$\mathbf{z}_t \equiv \begin{bmatrix} p_{t+1|t} \\ x_{t+1|t} \\ p_{t|t-1} \end{bmatrix}, \qquad \tilde{\mathbf{s}}_t \equiv \begin{bmatrix} u_{t+1|t} \\ r^n_{t+1|t} - \bar{r} \\ u_t - u_{t|t-1} \end{bmatrix}$$

and the matrix $\mathbf{M}$ given by

$$\mathbf{M} \equiv \begin{bmatrix} 1 + 1/\beta & -\kappa/\beta & -1/\beta \\ -\sigma/\beta & 1 + \kappa\sigma/\beta & \sigma\tilde{f} + \sigma/\beta \\ 1 & 0 & 0 \end{bmatrix}.$$

The eigenvalues are given by the roots of the characteristic equation, which can be written

$$(\mu - 1)\left(\mu^2 - \frac{1 + \beta + \kappa\sigma}{\beta} \mu + \frac{1}{\beta} \right) + \frac{\kappa\sigma}{\beta} \tilde{f} = 0.$$

For $\tilde{f} = 0$, we have the same roots $0 < \mu_1 < 1 < 1/\beta < \mu_2$ as in the case of an exogenous process for the interest rate (see section 2.2.4 above), and a third root $\mu_3 = 1$. One can show that a sufficient condition for determinacy is

(109) $$0 < \tilde{f} < \tilde{f}_2,$$

where

(110) $$\tilde{f}_2 \equiv 2 + \frac{4(1 + \beta)}{\kappa\sigma}.$$

(Conditions [A3] and [A5] imply $\tilde{f} > 0$ and $\tilde{f} < \tilde{f}_2$, respectively, and condition [A7] is always fulfilled.) Comparing equations (94), (95), and (108)–(110), we see that the determinacy conditions for the specific price-level targeting rule in equation (105) are different from those for the specific (inflation) targeting rule in equation (87). Once again, however, they need not be fulfilled for all reasonable parameter values.

A hybrid price-level targeting rule of the form

$$i_{t+1} = \bar{i}_{t+1} + g(p_{t+1|t} - p^*_{t+1,t} + \lambda x_{t+1|t})$$

can also be considered, with a corresponding condition on g for determinacy.

2.5 Commitment to an Explicit Instrument Rule

As a final possibility, we now consider monetary policy procedures that involve commitment to the achievement of a rule that links the bank's instrument to other variables that are all either exogenous or predetermined at the time that the instrument must be set. Such an explicit instrument rule represents a possible decision procedure that requires no explicit consideration of either forecasts or optimization problems for its implementation. A commitment of this highly specific kind would have the advantage of making private-sector forecasting of future policy, and monitoring of the degree to which the central bank fulfills its commitment, quite straightforward. It also makes it easy to incorporate into the policy rule the sort of history dependence that is necessary to achieve the optimal equilibrium, and the sort of dependence upon the realized paths of endogenous variables that is necessary in order for equilibrium to be determinate. A rule of this kind with appropriately chosen coefficients may result in a unique non-explosive rational-expectations equilibrium in which the responses to all shocks are optimal; indeed, in the absence of restrictions upon the central bank's information set, there will in general be a large multiplicity of instrument rules that are equally desirable in this regard.[43]

Here we are concerned in particular with whether there are explicit instrument rules that lead to a desirable equilibrium and that *also* have a relatively transparent relation to the central bank's objective. One respect in which this may be true is that the rule may make the instrument a function solely of the paths of target variables.[44] This is certainly the point of the well-known proposal of Taylor (1993), under which the instrument rate is made a simple function of current measures of inflation and the output gap. However, simply specifying that policy should respond to any and all deviations of target variables from their (constant) target levels does not necessarily make sense, given that in general complete stabilization of all target variables around the target values will not be feasible even in principle. A more sophisticated approach would instead respond to deviations from the particular pattern of fluctuations in the target variables that is optimal.

It is already clear that one type of explicit instrument rule that is definitely *not* desirable is a commitment to make the nominal interest rate the particular function i^*_{t+1} in equation (32) of the history of disturbances that is associated with the "timeless" optimal equilibrium. A policy rule of this kind makes the nominal interest rate evolve exogenously, with no feedback from the actual realizations of the endogenous variables; and as we have discussed above in section 2.2.4, any such rule results in indeterminacy. Indeed, commitment to this instrument rule would be equivalent to commitment to the modified dynamic-optimizing procedure described earlier, which as we saw leads to indeterminacy. In the case of a simple commitment to the implied reaction function (32), the absence of any possibility of

43. See Woodford (1999b) for further discussion of this point.
44. Of course, there is no general reason to expect that an optimal policy rule should involve responses only to information that is revealed by the history of the target variables, as is stressed in Svensson (1999b, 2003).

response to private-sector expectations, and of any opportunity for the central bank to persuade the private sector of its own forecasts, is all the clearer. Thus, the equilibrium paths of inflation and output will not be uniquely determined in this case. Rules in the spirit of the Taylor rule, which specify a response to fluctuations in endogenous variables, are clearly preferable from a determinacy point of view (although, if exactly of the form suggested by Taylor [1993], they would not be optimal for the economy considered here).

One way of characterizing undesirable fluctuations in the target variables that has the advantages of not requiring explicit reference to the particular exogenous shocks that have occurred and of being robust to alternative assumed shock processes, is to identify them with failures to satisfy the consolidated first-order condition (14), the specific targeting rule that characterizes the optimal equilibrium. A commitment to "make the condition hold" each period is not a possible explicit instrument rule; in the bank's period–$t + 1$ decision cycle, it is already a matter of fact whether condition (14) has held or not, whereas in its period-t decision cycle, the endogenous variables $\pi_{t+1|t}$ and $x_{t+1|t}$ are not yet observable (as they will depend upon the bank's period-t decision). Nonetheless, the central bank can commit itself to move its instrument *in response* to whether the first-order condition has been satisfied.

A simple example of such a rule would be

$$(111) \qquad i_{t+1} = \bar{r} + g\left[\pi_{t+1|t} + \frac{\lambda}{\kappa}(x_{t+1|t} - x_{t|t-1})\right],$$

where again $g > 0$ is a given response coefficient. Such a commitment is similar to a Taylor-type instrument rule, in which the bank responds to the change in the output gap rather than its current level, as in the characterizations of Fed policy during the Volcker period proposed by Judd and Rudebusch (1998) and Orphanides (1999). It is also necessary, of course, to respond to the forecastable components of inflation and the output gap rather than to the realized values of these variables in order for the instrument rule to be fully explicit.[45] Note that this rule is once again one that makes the central bank's action perfectly forecastable one period in advance ($i_{t+1} = i_{t+1|t}$), even though there is no advance announcement of the instrument setting (since the central bank does not yet observe $\pi_{t+1|t}$ and $x_{t+1|t}$ during its period-t decision cycle).

What kind of equilibrium would result from credible commitment to such a policy? Taking expectations of equations (1), (3), and (111) conditional upon public information in period t, and eliminating the variable

45. Taylor's formulation of his proposal is criticized by McCallum (1997) on exactly this point. Note that, if we were to assume that both inflation and output are completely predetermined, as in the analysis of Rotemberg and Woodford (1997, 1999), rule (111) can be expressed in terms of a direct response to the period–$t + 1$ inflation rate and output gap, like the policy rules analyzed in those papers.

$i_{t+1|t}$, one obtains a system of difference equations that can again be written in the form of equation (40), with the definition of the vectors z_t and $\tilde{s}_t$ as in equation (92) and with the matrix M is now given by

$$M \equiv \begin{bmatrix} 1/\beta & -\kappa/\beta & 0 \\ -\sigma/\beta + \sigma g & 1 + \kappa\sigma/\beta + \lambda\sigma g/\kappa & -\lambda\sigma g/\kappa \\ 0 & 1 & 0 \end{bmatrix}$$

(again, we do not need the details of the matrix N).

As usual, determinacy requires that M have exactly two eigenvalues with modulus greater than 1, corresponding to the two nonpredetermined elements of z_t. Whether this is true depends upon the size of the response coefficient g. The matrix M above is equal to that in equation (97) when $f = 0$. It follows that the characteristic equation is the same as equation (99) when $f = 0$. Thus, the condition for determinacy is $g > \bar{g}(0)$.

It follows that as long as $g > \bar{g}(0)$, there is a unique bounded solution for z_t, which depends solely upon the predetermined variable $x_{t|t-1}$ and expectations in period t regarding the future paths of the exogenous disturbances. In the case that both disturbances are AR(1) processes, equations (2) and (4), this solution is one in which both $\pi_{t+1|t}$ and $x_{t+1|t}$ are linear functions of $x_{t|t-1}$, u_t and r_t^n. The next question is the extent to which this equilibrium coincides with the optimal one. In fact, we know that it cannot coincide exactly with the optimal one (more precisely, even if we start from initial conditions consistent with the stationary optimal equilibrium, the equilibrium resulting from a commitment to equation [111] will not continue that optimal equilibrium). This is because we have already seen that the stationary optimal equilibrium requires that the term in brackets in equation (111) be zero at all times, while it also requires that $i_{t+1} = i^*_{t+1}$ at all times, a quantity that, by equation (32), is generally different from $\bar{r}$.

On the other hand, the determinate equilibrium associated with rule (111) may approximate an optimal equilibrium; in particular, one can show that as g is made sufficiently large, the approximation to the optimal equilibrium becomes arbitrarily close. (Specifically, one can show that in the limit as $g \rightarrow +\infty$, this equilibrium approaches the one described by equations [21] and [23] for each period, which is to say, the unique equilibrium in which condition [14] holds each period.) However, such a policy prescription is unappealing, because of the possibility that small amounts of noise in the bank's measurement of the forecastable components of the goal variables would lead in practice to highly volatile interest rates.[46]

46. Here we presume that the central bank's measurement error does not become apparent to the private sector, and so cannot affect private sector forecasts or behavior, until *after* the quantities in the square brackets in equation (111) have been determined. Note that the central bank's error need not become apparent to the private sector until the period–t + 1 interest rate is revealed, whereas the forecasts to which the central bank responds in setting i_{t+1} are all determined by the private sector in period t. For further discussion of the undesirability of this approach to stabilization, see Bernanke and Woodford (1997).

Alternatively, we can make the instrument rule in equation (111) consistent with the stationary optimal equilibrium by adding a time-varying intercept term,

$$(112) \qquad i_{t+1} = i_{t+1}^* + g\left[\pi_{t+1|t} + \frac{\lambda}{\kappa}(x_{t+1|t} - x_{t|t-1})\right].$$

This is now a rule that is consistent with the stationary optimal equilibrium, regardless of the value of g. Because the added term is an exogenous random process, the determinacy calculations remain the same as above, and we again find that for $g > \bar{g}(0)$, equilibrium is determinate. Since we already know that the optimal equilibrium is consistent with equation (112), it follows from determinacy that the unique bounded equilibrium is an optimal one.

As yet another alternative, we could modify equation (111) by adding an endogenous term that renders the rule consistent with the stationary optimal equilibrium, namely

$$(113) \qquad i_{t+1} = \bar{i}_{t+1} + g\left[\pi_{t+1|t} + \frac{\lambda}{\kappa}(x_{t+1|t} - x_{t|t-1})\right],$$

where once again $\bar{i}_{t+1}$ is defined by equation (33). This is identical to the reaction function (equation [96]) implied by the hybrid procedure considered above in section 2.4.2, although here we contemplate a direct commitment to bring about this reaction function as an explicit instrument rule. The determinacy analysis is the same as in the previous section. Thus, for $g > \bar{g}(f)$, equilibrium is determinate, and the unique bounded equilibrium is an optimal one.

These two examples illustrate the possibility of achieving the optimal equilibrium as a determinate outcome through commitment to an explicit instrument rule with bounded coefficients. They also illustrate an important general point. This is that the mere fact that the target variables are predetermined in the short run, and so not able to be affected by current central bank decisions, does *not* imply that the only effective procedure must be a forward-looking one, which aims to have a certain effect upon the future paths of the target variables. Instead, as long as the private sector is forward looking and the central bank's policy rule can be made credible, committing to respond in a purely backward-looking way to past deviations of the target variables from their desired path can be an effective way of reducing the size of those deviations in equilibrium. The anticipation that the central bank will later respond in this way is enough to achieve the desired effect, and indeed, in a model like that assumed here, it is only the private sector's expectations regarding future policy that can have any effect on the evolution of the target variables at all.

This seems an important principle to keep in mind in choosing a policy rule, especially insofar as the determinacy of equilibrium is a concern.

However, the explicit instrument rules proposed above remain unattractive on grounds of robustness. Note that a suitable specification of either the targeting rule in equation (86) or the hybrid rule in equation (96) depends only upon the slope coefficient κ of the aggregate supply relation, and not upon other coefficients of the bank's model of the economy or any details of the assumed specification of the exogenous shock processes. Instead, the term i_{t+1}^* in equation (112) depends also upon the slope coefficient σ of the model's IS relation and upon the parameters of the exogenous shock processes (for instance, in the AR[1] specification assumed in equation [32], upon the parameters ρ and ω). The same is true of the term $\bar{\imath}_{t+1}$ in equation (113). The presence of these terms also requires that one sacrifice one of the obvious advantages of simple instrument rules like the Taylor rule, which is ease of communication of the nature of the commitment to the general public. When the instrument rule involves reference to responses to exogenous disturbances (rather than simply to goal variables, which are better understood by the public and are publicly reported), there is no longer any particular advantage of this approach in terms of transparency.

The hybrid procedure defined by equation (96) is more attractive in both of these last regards, for that specification of the policy commitment depended only upon the specific value of κ, yet (in the case that the specific model assumed above is used) it implied an identical reaction function as the instrument rule in equation (113). It was also a specification that required no explicit reference to the exogenous disturbances. Such a hybrid approach thus combines several of the most attractive features of a specific targeting rule and of an explicit instrument rule.

2.6   Concluding Remarks

We now offer a few remarks on the degree to which the various decision procedures discussed above satisfy the desiderata for a desirable monetary policy rule mentioned in the introduction. Our first and most important criterion, of course, is consistency of the policy rule with the stationary optimal equilibrium characterized in section 2.2. As we have seen, the most naive approach to inflation-forecast targeting—a forecast-based discretionary optimizing procedure aimed at minimization of the true social loss function—fails to have this property. However, we have shown that there are many different ways in which one could introduce the sort of history dependence required for consistency with the optimal equilibrium. Possible methods include modification of the loss function that the forecast-based optimizing procedure seeks to minimize, commitment to a specific targeting rule such as equation (86), commitment to an instrument rule such as equation (112) or (113), or commitment to a hybrid procedure such as equation (84) or (96). Any of these approaches would be equally satisfactory from the point of view of consistency with the optimal equilibrium, assuming credibility of the bank's commitment to the rule in question.

Our second criterion was determinacy of equilibrium under the policy rule, so that one could count on the optimal equilibrium being the one that should result from a correct understanding of the central bank's commitment on the part of the private sector. This turned out to be a problem for the procedure discussed in section 2.3.5, directed toward the minimization of a modified loss function, the "commitment to continuity and predictability." In the case of our present model, such a procedure results in indeterminacy for all possible values of the model parameters. More generally, because such a procedure necessarily corresponds to an implied reaction function involving no dependence upon lagged endogenous variables except insofar as these are relevant to forecasts of the future evolution of the target variables, such rules are less likely to involve the dependence upon lagged endogenous variables that is necessary in order to exclude self-fulfilling expectations.

This problem may be mitigated by a sufficient degree of transparency of the bank's decision procedure, as this may facilitate the coordination of private-sector expectations upon the paths forecasted by the central bank. But this would still seem to be a weakness of our highest-level approach to the specification of a policy rule, relative to lower-level specifications that make the bank's decisions dependent upon lagged endogenous variables for reasons unrelated to their effect upon the bank's forecasts.

However, a way to achieve determinacy is to amend the general targeting procedure with a commitment to a particular instrument-rate response by the central bank, if the private-sector plans of inflation and the output gap deviate from the central bank's forecast. This is the hybrid rule discussed in section 2.3.6 and represented by equation (85). Since this is an out-of-equilibrium commitment, it will not have any observable consequences in equilibrium.

A specific targeting rule can introduce additional dependence upon lagged endogenous variables, through commitment to a target criterion that depends upon past as well as future paths of the target variables. However, in the case of the simple targeting rule in equation (86), indeterminacy is likely still to be a problem for reasonable parameter values. Achieving determinacy in this way may require an even greater degree of dependence of the target criterion upon the past history of the target variables. Again, one way to achieve determinacy is to amend the specific targeting rule with a commitment to a particular out-of-equilibrium instrument-rate response by the central bank, if the specific targeting rule is violated. A hybrid rule that serves this purpose has been discussed in section 2.4.2 and displayed in equation (96).

An alternative approach, which can easily result in a determinate equilibrium that is also optimal from our timeless perspective, is commitment to an explicit instrument rule that requires the central bank to respond to deviations of the target variables from a target criterion that it should satisfy in an optimal equilibrium. This is illustrated by the explicit instrument rules in equations (112) and (113), but the hybrid rule mentioned above works equally well in this regard.

However, it should be stressed that the magnitude of the determinacy problems above may be exaggerated by the extremely forward-looking character of the model assumed here, in which no lagged endogenous variables are relevant to the determination of current and future values of the target variables, except insofar as such dependence is introduced through the monetary policy rule. A consideration of the extent to which the decision procedures of the kind we have considered would still face indeterminacy problems in a more complex, and possibly more realistic, model with sources of intrinsic inertia in the endogenous variables remains a topic for further research.

There remain two further criteria for comparison of our candidate policies. As noted in the introduction, we prefer approaches to monetary policy in which the connection between the central bank's decision process and its ultimate objectives is as transparent as possible. From this point of view, our highest-level policy specifications, in terms of a procedure that aims to minimize a specified loss function, are most suitable. The most transparent procedure would be the naive approach of discretionary minimization of the social loss function, but this procedure, as we have seen, is inconsistent with an optimal equilibrium. Minimizing a modified loss function, the commitment to continuity and credibility discussed in section 2.3.5, is somewhat less transparent, although the idea of taking into account the shadow cost of the previous central-bank forecasts and private-sector expectations is arguably a direct consequence of the desire to minimize the social loss function, once the nature of the bank's optimization problem is properly understood. Such concerns are also arguably present already in the thinking and rhetoric of actual inflation-targeting central banks, given banks' emphasis on continuity and predictability (see, for instance, King 1997b). However, in a more complex model with a greater number of forward-looking variables, this approach would imply that the Lagrange multipliers of *all* of the (relevant) forward-looking variables would need to be recorded and taken into account in modifying the period loss function. This would make the approach far less transparent and perhaps less practical as well.

The specific targeting rule discussed in section 2.4 and described by equation (14), implying that the expected deviation between inflation and the inflation target should be proportional to the decrease in the predictable component of the output gap, is simple but somewhat less intuitive, and for that reason it is less transparently related to underlying policy goals.[47] The equivalent price-level targeting rule for the forward-looking model discussed in section 2.4.3 is arguably more intuitive, though. And in any event, because such a rule is still specified in terms of the desired behavior of the target variables, it scores better on this criterion than would instrument rules such as equations (112) and (113). The same is true of the hybrid variant of this procedure described by equation (96).

Because explicit instrument rules are formulated as rules of central-bank conduct that happen, generally for relatively indirect reasons, to have desirable consequences if anticipated by the private sector, rather than as descriptions of what the bank is trying to achieve, they rate lowest on the criterion of transparency. A rule such as equation (111), however, is more transparently related to the goals of policy than many other instrument rules would be, insofar as it prescribes response to failure of the target variables to satisfy a target criterion (indeed, the same criterion as is the basis for the specific targeting rule in equation [14]). However, as we have seen, equation (111) in its simplest form is not consistent with the optimal equilibrium. Modified instrument rules such as equations (112) and (113), which are consistent with optimality, involve fairly complex functions of lagged disturbances or endogenous variables that are clearly not related to the goals of policy in any transparent way.

Our final criterion is the robustness of the alternative monetary policy procedures to modifications of the assumed model of the economy. The general topic of robustness is beyond the scope of this study, but our results here do allow us to comment upon the sensitivity of the various specifications to changes in parameters while assuming the same basic model structure.

Clearly, the higher-order policy specifications are more robust to model perturbations. Our general approach in section 2.3.5 of modifying the loss function so as to make a discretionary optimizing procedure consistent with the optimal equilibrium is not dependent upon the details of the bank's model of the economy at all. Only the identification of the relevant forward-looking variables and their associated Lagrange multipliers is at all model dependent; nothing about the specification would need to be changed as a result of changes in model parameters that maintained the same basic form of equations (1) and (3) or changes in the assumed specification of the exogenous disturbance processes.

The specific targeting rule in equation (14) is less robust than this, but it still depends only upon the slope coefficient κ of the AS relation. The targeting rule is independent of the nature and number of the exogenous dis-

47. In at least some very simple models, a similar specific targeting rule derived from the first-order conditions that characterize the optimal equilibrium is more intuitive and, indeed, more similar to the sort of intuitive forecast-targeting rules followed by actual inflation-targeting central banks; see Svensson (1997a).

turbances in the AS equation. Moreover, as long as there is no weight on interest rate stabilization or smoothing in the loss function, the targeting rule is completely independent of both the form of the IS equation and the nature of its disturbances. Thus, the targeting rule arising in this model is quite robust to a number of model perturbations. This supports the conjecture arising in the backward-looking model of Svensson (1997a) that targeting rules are likely to be more robust than instrument rules.[48] The hybrid variant of this rule (equation [84]) is equally robust.

The instrument rules (112) and (113) are the least robust, since they depend on all of the parameters of the model and are not robust to any perturbations—except changes in the variances of the i.i.d. shocks, due to the certainty equivalence that holds in a linear model with a quadratic loss function.

Overall, we find that each of our general classes of policy specifications contains specifications that incorporate the kind of history dependence required for consistency with the optimal equilibrium. The lower-level specifications are most advantageous from the point of view of ensuring determinacy, whereas to the contrary, we find that the higher-level specifications are most advantageous from the standpoints of transparency and robustness. An intermediate-level policy specification, involving commitment to a specific targeting rule, may be the best overall compromise among these competing concerns. The hybrid procedure described in section 2.4.2 is perhaps the most attractive of the alternatives reviewed here, as it allows one to ensure determinacy regardless of the model parameters while at the same time being quite robust and retaining a more transparent relation to the goals of policy than is possible in the case of an explicit instrument rule.

References

Backus, David, and John Driffill. 1986. The consistency of optimal policy in stochastic rational expectations models. CEPR Discussion Paper no. 124. London: Centre for Economic Policy Research.
Bernanke, Ben, and Michael Woodford. 1997. Inflation forecasts and monetary policy. *Journal of Money, Credit, and Banking* 24:653–84.
Christiano, Lawrence J., and Christopher J. Gust. 1999. Taylor rules in a limited participation model. NBER Working Paper no. 7017. Cambridge, Mass.: National Bureau of Economic Research.
Christiano, Lawrence J., and Robert J. Vigfusson. 1999. Maximum likelihood in the

---

48. Svensson (2003) takes this argument further and shows that specific targeting rules are robust to the unavoidable use of judgment in practical monetary policy. Giannoni and Woodford (2002) show how robust targeting rules can be computed for a general class of linear-quadratic policy problems.

frequency domain: A time to build example. NBER Working Paper no. 7027. Cambridge, Mass.: National Bureau of Economic Research.

Clarida, Richard, Jordi Galí, and Mark Gertler. 1998. Monetary policy rules in practice: Some international evidence. *European Economic Review* 42:1033–67.

———. 1999. The science of monetary policy: A new Keynesian perspective. *Journal of Economic Literature* 37:1661–707.

Currie, David, and Paul Levine. 1993. *Rules, reputation and macroeconomic policy coordination.* Cambridge: Cambridge University Press.

Edge, Rochelle M. 2000. Time to build, time to plan, habit persistence, and the liquidity effect. International Finance Discussion Paper no. 2000-673. Washington, D.C.: Federal Reserve Board, July.

Flodén, Martin. 1996. The time inconsistency problem of monetary policy under alternative supply side modeling. Stockholm University, Institute for International Economic Studies. Working Paper. Available at [http://www.hhs.se/personal/floden/].

Giannoni, Marc. P., and Michael Woodford. 2002. Optimal interest-rate rules: I. general theory. NBER Working Paper no. 9419. Cambridge, Mass.: National Bureau of Economic Research, December.

Jonsson, Gunnar. 1997. Monetary politics and unemployment persistence. *Journal of Monetary Economics* 39:303–25.

Judd, John P., and Glenn D. Rudebusch. 1998. Taylor's rule and the Fed: 1970–1997. *Federal Reserve Bank of San Francisco Economic Review* 1998 (3): 3–16.

Kerr, William, and Robert J. King. 1996. Limits on interest rate rules in the IS model. *Federal Reserve Bank of Richmond Economic Quarterly* 1996 (Spring): 47–76.

King, Mervyn A. 1994. Monetary policy in the UK. *Fiscal Studies* 15 (3): 109–28.

———. 1997a. Changes in UK monetary policy: Rules and discretion in practice. *Journal of Monetary Economics* 39:81–97.

———. 1997b. The inflation target five years on. *Bank of England Quarterly Bulletin* 37 (4): 434–42.

Kydland, Finn E., and Edward C. Prescott. 1977. Rules rather than discretion: The inconsistency of optimal plans. *Journal of Political Economy* 85:473–91.

Leeper, Eric M., and Tao Zha. 1999. Identification and forecasting: Joint inputs to policy analysis. Indiana University, Department of Economics. Working Paper.

Leitemo, Kai. 1999. Targeting inflation by constant-interest-rate forecast. Working Paper. Oslo, Norway: Norges Bank.

Levin, Andrew, Volker Wieland, and John C. Williams. 1999. Robustness of simple monetary policy rules under model uncertainty. In *Monetary policy rules,* ed. John B. Taylor, 263–99. Chicago: University of Chicago Press.

McCallum, Bennett T. 1981. Price level determinacy with an interest rate policy rule and rational expectations. *Journal of Monetary Economics* 8:319–29.

———. 1997. Issues in the design of monetary policy rules. NBER Working Paper no. 6016. Cambridge, Mass.: National Bureau of Economic Research.

———. 1999. Role of the minimal state variable criterion. NBER Working Paper no. 7087. Cambridge, Mass.: National Bureau of Economic Research.

Orphanides, Athanasios. 1999. The quest for prosperity without inflation. Working Paper. Washington, D.C.: Federal Reserve Board.

Persson, Torsten, and Guido Tabellini. 1993. Designing institutions for monetary stability. *Carnegie-Rochester Conference Series on Public Policy* 39:53–84.

Rotemberg, Julio J., and Michael Woodford. 1997. An optimization-based econometric framework for the evaluation of monetary policy. In *NBER Macroeconomics Annual 1997,* ed. Ben S. Bernanke and Julio J. Rotemberg, 297–346.

———. 1999. Interest-rate rules in an estimated sticky-price model. In *Monetary policy rules,* ed. John B. Taylor, 57–119. Chicago: University of Chicago Press.

Rudebusch, Glenn D., and Lars E. O. Svensson. 1999. Policy rules for inflation targeting. In *Monetary policy rules,* ed. John B. Taylor, 203–46. Chicago: University of Chicago Press.

Sargent, Thomas J., and Neil Wallace. 1975. Rational expectations, the optimal monetary instrument, and the optimal money supply rule. *Journal of Political Economy* 83:241–54.

Smets, Frank. 2000. What horizon for price stability. ECB Working Paper no. 24. Frankfurt, Germany: European Central Bank.

Söderlind, Paul. 1999. Solution and estimation of RE macromodels with optimal policy. *European Economic Review* 43:813–23.

Svensson, Lars E. O. 1997a. Inflation forecast targeting: Implementing and monitoring inflation targets. *European Economic Review* 41:1111–46.

———. 1997b. Optimal inflation targets, "conservative" central banks, and linear inflation contracts. *American Economic Review* 87:98–114.

———. 1999a. How should monetary policy be conducted in an era of price stability? Paper presented at New Challenges for Monetary Policy: A Symposium Sponsored by the Federal Reserve Bank of Kansas City. 26–28 August, Jackson Hole, Wyoming.

———. 1999b. Inflation targeting as a monetary policy rule. *Journal of Monetary Economics* 43:607–54. Longer working paper version, including appendix, available at [http://www.princeton.edu/~svensson].

———. 1999c. Price-level targeting vs. inflation targeting: A free lunch? *Journal of Money, Credit, and Banking* 31:277–95.

———. 2003. What is wrong with Taylor rules? Using judgment in monetary policy through targeting rules. *Journal of Economic Literature* 41:426–77.

Svensson, Lars E. O., and Michael Woodford. 2003. Indicator variables for optimal policy. *Journal of Monetary Economics* 50:691–720.

Taylor, John B. 1993. Discretion versus policy rules in practice. *Carnegie-Rochester Conference Series on Public Policy* 39:195–214.

Vestin, David. 1999. Price-level targeting versus inflation targeting in a forward-looking model. Stockholm University, Institute for International Economic Studies. Working Paper.

Walsh, Carl. 1995. Optimal contracts for independent central bankers. *American Economic Review* 85:150–67.

Woodford, Michael. 1999b. Optimal monetary policy inertia. NBER Working Paper no. 7261. Cambridge, Mass.: National Bureau of Economic Research, July.

———. 1999a. Commentary: How should monetary policy be conducted in an era of price stability? Paper presented at New Challenges for Monetary Policy: A Symposium Sponsored by the Federal Reserve Bank of Kansas City. 26–28 August, Jackson Hole, Wyoming.

———. 2000. Pitfalls of forward-looking monetary policy. *American Economic Review Papers and Proceedings* 90:100–04.

———. 2003. *Interest and prices: Foundations of a theory of monetary policy.* Princeton, N.J.: Princeton University Press.

Yun, Tack. 1996. Nominal price rigidity, money supply endogeneity, and business cycles. *Journal of Monetary Economics* 37:345–70.

Appendix

The Necessary and Sufficient Conditions for Determinacy

Consider a system of difference equations of the form

$$\mathbf{z}_{t+1|t} = \mathbf{M}\mathbf{z}_t + \mathbf{N}\tilde{\mathbf{s}}_t,$$

where $\mathbf{z}_t$ denotes a vector of three endogenous variables, two of which are forward looking and one of which is predetermined, $\tilde{\mathbf{s}}_t$ denotes a vector of exogenous variables, and $\mathbf{M}$ and $\mathbf{N}$ are matrices of appropriate dimension. The solution to this system is *determinate* if and only if the matrix $\mathbf{M}$ has one eigenvalue with modulus less than 1 and two eigenvalues with modulus greater than 1.

The characteristic equation of the system will be cubic and can be written

$$\mu^3 + a_2\mu^2 + a_1\mu + a_0 = 0.$$

Woodford (2003, prop. C.2, appendix to chap. 4) shows that the solution to the system is determinate if and only if the coefficients of the characteristic equation fulfill *either* (case I)

(A1) $\qquad\qquad\qquad 1 + a_2 + a_1 + a_0 < 0$ and

(A2) $\qquad\qquad\qquad -1 + a_2 - a_1 + a_0 > 0;$

or (case II) and

(A3) $\qquad\qquad\qquad 1 + a_2 + a_1 + a_0 > 0,$

(A4) $\qquad\qquad\qquad -1 + a_2 - a_1 + a_0 < 0,$ and

(A5) $\qquad\qquad\qquad a_0^2 - a_0a_2 + a_1 - 1 > 0;$

or (case III) equations (A3) and (A4) hold, together with

(A6) $\qquad\qquad\qquad a_0^2 - a_0a_2 + a_1 - 1 < 0$ and

(A7) $\qquad\qquad\qquad |a_2| > 3.$

Comment   Bennett T. McCallum

I am grateful to the conference organizers for the opportunity of discussing the Svensson and Woodford paper, which is concerned with many impor-

Bennett T. McCallum is H. J. Heinz Professor of Economics at Carnegie Mellon University and a research associate of the National Bureau of Economic Research.

For helpful discussions, I am indebted to Marc Giannoni, Christian Jensen, Edward Nelson, and Alexander Wolman.

tant issues, some of which I have been interested in for a number of years. It is a long, rich, and highly sophisticated paper by two of the most prominent and accomplished of today's monetary economists, so my work on it has been a privilege as well as a pleasure.

There are several themes of the paper that I find very attractive, including its emphasis on history dependence via a form of "timeless" commitment by the central bank, the incorporation of various response lags, the recognition that actual central banks do not have complete information about current conditions, and some attention to the robustness of policy rules or procedures. Also, it almost goes without saying, the authors' use of a model based on optimizing behavior by the economy's individual agents seems highly desirable.[1]

Presumably, however, my main job is to spell out areas of reservation or possible disagreement, so most of the remainder of this discussion will be concerned with such items. There are three main topics, including (a) the precise concept of timeless-perspective optimality that is employed in the paper, (b) the claim of an alleged weakness of instrument rules, and (c) the way in which robustness is handled. I will discuss these in turn.

Timeless Perspective Optimality

The model that is used throughout the paper to illustrate its ideas can be written as

$$(1) \qquad \pi_t = \beta E_{t-1}\pi_{t+1} + \kappa E_{t-1}x_t + u_t$$

$$(2) \qquad x_t = E_{t-1}x_{t+1} - b(E_{t-1}i_t - E_{t-1}\pi_{t+1} - v_t),$$

where the symbols are as in Svensson and Woodford's chapter except that I use b in place of σ, v_t in place of r_t^n, and $E_t z_{t+j}$ instead of $z_{t+j|t}$ as the rational expectation of z_{t+j} based on information variables from period t and earlier. In the Svensson and Woodford (S&W) model, u_t and v_t are exogenous shock processes. For simplicity I will take them to be first-order autoregressive (AR[1]) processes with AR parameters ρ_u and ρ_v.

In this model, and presuming that the target value of π_t is zero, S&W consider a central bank loss function of the form

$$(3) \qquad E_0 \sum_{t=1}^{\infty} \beta^{t-1}L_t,$$

where the period loss function is

$$(4) \qquad L_t = 0.5[\pi_t^2 + \lambda(x_t - x^*)^2],$$

---

1. Initially I was also pleased by their adoption of a modified version of the Calvo price adjustment model, one that avoids the potential for a long-run inflation-output gap trade-off, but the final version of the paper does not utilize that modification.

with $\lambda \geq 0$ and x^* representing the "socially optimal output gap (for simplicity assumed constant)." In this mostly familiar setup, S&W find that the first-order optimality conditions are

(5)
$$E_{t-1}\pi_t + \frac{\lambda}{\kappa}(E_{t-1}x_t - E_{t-2}x_{t-1}) = 0$$

for all $t = 2, 3, \ldots$, with, however,

(6)
$$E_{t-1}\pi_t + \frac{\lambda}{\kappa}(E_{t-1}x_t - x^*) = 0$$

for $t = 1$. (The sum in equation [3] begins with $t = 1$, although the expectation operator is E_0, because central bank actions affect inflation and output only after a one-period-lag, by the assumed information and timing structure of the model.[2]) Conditions (5) and (6) are necessary for a full commitment optimum, but such a program would of course be dynamically inconsistent. That is, exactly the same procedure would, if applied anew at any later date, call for a different path rather than a continuation of the one chosen. Consequently, an equilibrium based on a full commitment policy is typically judged as implausible. The discretionary optimal condition, satisfaction of equation (6) for all $t = 1, 2, 3, \ldots$, is dynamically consistent but is unattractive because of several well-known inefficiencies that have been emphasized by Woodford (1999, 2003); Clarida, Galí, and Gertler (1999); McCallum and Nelson (2000); and several others.

Accordingly, S&W are led to consider policies that are optimal from what Woodford (1999) termed a "timeless perspective." Such policies do not eliminate the discrepancy between their paths and those that would be chosen in any later period by a fresh discretionary calculation, but they have the attractive property of *continuation:* if the same procedure were applied anew, it would call for no departure from the previously selected path.[3] One way in which a condition satisfying S&W's version of timeless-perspective (TP) optimality can be obtained is by applying equation (5) for all periods, $t = 1$ as well as $t = 2, 3, \ldots$. Clearly, if that choice had been made at some date t' in the very distant past, then policy behavior in the present would be almost the same as if the choice had been instead the fully optimal (from the perspective of t') plan of equations (5) and (6).

It is the case that there are various ways of behaving in the "first" or start-up period $t = 1$ of a TP policy plan.[4] This is emphasized by S&W. Their discussion of implementation focuses, nevertheless, on policies in which con-

---

2. This structure makes the analysis much more tedious, and more difficult to follow, than the more usual setup. But the authors have good reasons for their specification.

3. Assuming, that is, no change in the model or the objective function being utilized.

4. For example, instead of $E_0\pi_1 + (\lambda/\kappa)(E_0x_1 - E_{-1}x_0) = 0$, the start-up setting could be $E_0\pi_1 + (\lambda/\kappa)(E_0x_1 - E_{-2}x_{-1}) + E_{-1}\pi_{-1} = 0$, as if the start-up period had been with rule (5) one period in the past. See Dennis (2001) for more discussion.

dition (5) is applied in all periods $t = 1, 2, \ldots$. Conditional upon time-0 information, this scheme will not be fully optimal unless by chance $E_{-1}x_0 = x^*$, in which case equations (5) and (6) coincide. Since other rules could have been adopted instead, it is of interest to consider how well this particular TP rule performs on average, over all possible initial conditions. Accordingly, let us consider the criterion $E[E_0 \sum_{t=1}^{\infty} \beta^{t-1}L_t]$, the unconditional expectation of the conditional objective in equation (3). Interestingly, there is another "timeless" rule, not satisfying the S&W definition of TP, that performs better than equation (5) with respect to that criterion, namely,

$$(7) \qquad E_{t-1}\pi_t + \frac{\lambda}{\kappa}(E_{t-1}x_t - \beta E_{t-2}x_{t-1}) = 0.$$

This result is an extension of one, due to Jensen (2001), that has been exposited by Jensen and McCallum (2002).[5] Rule (7), applied in all periods $t = 1, 2, \ldots$, has the desirable properties of continuation and time invariance, and performs better than equation (5) on average, but does not meet the second half of the S&W definition of TP optimality.

It will be readily observed that $E[E_0 \sum_{t=1}^{\infty} \beta^{t-1}L_t] = E \sum_{t=1}^{\infty} \beta^{t-1}L_t$, so adoption of the former as a policy criterion is equivalent to optimization from an unconditional perspective. This makes it clear that rule (7) will also perform better on average than other TP rules. The problem with any TP rule is that it is based on a conditional perspective yet avoids full exploitation of the prevailing initial conditions, since such exploitation would eliminate the continuation property and seriously impair credibility. The unconditional perspective is, it might be recalled, the one taken in the past by monetarists and some other economists who stressed the desirability of "rules" over "discretion" in monetary policy. It is also the type of optimization utilized by Taylor (1979, 1988) and several other analysts, including Rotemberg and Woodford (1999).

Targeting Rules versus Instrument Rules

S&W devote the largest part of their paper to issues involving the implementation of policy procedures designed to yield TP optimality. In their section 2.3 there is an extensive discussion of procedures to be used with "general targeting rules," in Svensson's (2003) terminology, with detailed attention paid to indeterminacy issues. The analysis is much too complex to summarize here. One possible reservation is that schemes that require the central bank to optimize with respect to a "modified" loss function, which does not reflect its true objectives, are unattractive from a practical perspective. One reason is that they would seem to rank low in terms of

---

5. The result applies to the S&W model because of the equality stated in the next paragraph. A similar result has been obtained by Blake (2001), and some related analysis is provided by Dennis (2001).

transparency, especially when the modified loss function involves lagged values of Lagrange multipliers from an optimization calculation involving an unspecified model. The discussion in section 2.4, of specific targeting rules—that is, first-order optimality conditions for a particular model—is less lengthy but also too complex to be described here.

S&W's section 2.5 discussion of explicit *instrument rules* is, by comparison, rather brief and straightforward. It focuses critically on the idea, proposed by McCallum (1999, 1493) and utilized by McCallum and Nelson (2000), of using an instrument rule in a particular way to implement a specific targeting rule. The approach is to adopt a rule that has the central bank adjusting its interest rate instrument in response to departures of the relevant first-order optimality condition from being satisfied. The simplest example provided for the model equations (1) and (2) is the rule

$$(8) \qquad i_{t+1} = r + \mu_1 \left[E_t \pi_{t+1} + \frac{\lambda}{\kappa}(E_t x_{t+1} - E_{t-1} x_t) - 0 \right],$$

with $\mu_1 > 0$.[6] Of course, such a rule will not result in exact satisfaction of the first-order condition, but it will approximate the latter. Indeed, as S&W recognize, "one can show that as $[\mu_1]$ is made sufficiently large, the approximation to the optimal equilibrium becomes arbitrarily close," basically as Nelson and I have suggested. Nevertheless, S&W argue that such rules are "unappealing, because of the possibility that small amounts of noise in the bank's measurement of the forecastable components of the goal variables would lead in practice to highly volatile interest rates." This repeats, in milder language, the contention of Svensson (2003, 461) that it "is a dangerous and completely impractical idea [for] monetary policy to have reaction functions with very large response coefficients, since the slightest mistake in calculating the argument of the reaction function would have grave consequences and result in extreme instrument-rate volatility."

The intuitive basis for that suggestion is apparent, since μ_1 multiplies the policy error, but I wish to argue nevertheless that its implied message is basically incorrect.[7] The variability of the interest rate does tend to increase as μ_1 increases, but it approaches the level that prevails with the specific targeting rule itself—often remaining somewhat smaller for any finite μ_1. This conclusion assumes, of course, that the same amount of noise or error applies to the bank's forecast under both procedures, which is the only sensible way to make the comparison.[8]

---

6. I use μ_1 in place of S&W's symbol *g*. Also, I henceforth assume that $E\pi_t = 0$.

7. I include the qualifier "basically" because there is an alternative set of information assumptions that could justify the S&W claim; see note 11 below.

8. The comparison is between two methods of implementing the same first-order condition, presumably with the same instrument. Incidentally, Nelson and I actually do not argue for large values of coefficients such as μ_1; we merely state that they would permit targeting rules to be closely approximated.

To demonstrate this result, let us specify the instrument rule in the form used by McCallum and Nelson (2000), adjusted for the lagged-information restrictions of the S&W model. Thus, for the timeless perspective case we have

$$(9) \qquad i_{t+1} = r + E_t\pi_{t+1} + \mu_1\left[E_t\pi_{t+1} + \frac{\lambda}{\kappa}(E_t x_{t+1} - E_{t-1}x_t) + e_t\right],$$

where e_t is the central bank's error made in period t and pertaining to i_{t+1}. Initially let e_t be white noise; an AR specification will be considered below. The corresponding specific targeting rule is then

$$(10) \qquad E_t\pi_{t+1} + \frac{\lambda}{\kappa}(E_t x_{t+1} - E_{t-1}x_t) + e_t = 0.$$

For the numerical exercise to follow, assume that $\beta = 0.99$, $\kappa = 0.03$, and $b = 0.5$—all rather standard values in the literature (pertaining to a calibration for quarterly time periods). Also, let the policy parameter λ equal 0.1. For the shock processes, let the innovation standard deviations be $\sigma_{\varepsilon u}$ = 0.005, $\sigma_{\varepsilon v}$ = 0.02, and $\sigma_{\varepsilon e}$ = 0.02. Table 2C.1 reports values of the loss function, and the standard deviation of the interest rate i_t, each averaged over 400 simulations and each with a sample size (after discard of fifty-three start-up periods) of 200. The five different cases pertain to different assumptions about the autocorrelation parameters ρ_u, ρ_v, and ρ_e.

Table 2C.1   **Comparison of instrument and targeting rules with Model (1)(2)**

	Rule (9)				Rule (10)
	$\mu_1 = 0.5$	$\mu_1 = 1.0$	$\mu_1 = 5.0$	$\mu_1 = 50$	$\mu_1 = \infty$
$\rho_u = 0.0$ $\rho_v = 0.0$ $\rho_e = 0.0$	6.90 0.0029	7.96 0.0008	9.35 0.0010	9.80 0.0014	9.78 0.0015
$\rho_u = 0.8$ $\rho_v = 0.0$ $\rho_e = 0.0$	77.2 0.0179	65.2 0.0039	62.3 0.0043	62.2 0.0057	62.5 0.0059
$\rho_u = 0.9$ $\rho_v = 0.0$ $\rho_e = 0.0$	403 0.0381	303 0.0083	277 0.0095	274 0.0124	279 0.0129
$\rho_u = 0.9$ $\rho_v = 0.8$ $\rho_e = 0.0$	816 0.1189	448 0.0907	286 0.0600	285 0.0547	275 0.0539
$\rho_u = 0.9$ $\rho_v = 0.0$ $\rho_e = 0.8$	453 0.0437	352 0.0249	326 0.0242	327 0.0253	320 0.0251

Note: Entries are average loss times 10^3 and quarterly standard deviation of i_t. In all cases, $\sigma_{\varepsilon u}$ = 0.005, $\sigma_{\varepsilon v}$ = 0.02, $\sigma_{\varepsilon e}$ = 0.02, β = 0.99, κ = 0.03, b = 0.5, and λ = 0.1.

In the case in the first row there is no autocorrelation in any of the shocks, so the targeting rule is ineffective given the model's assumed structure and information lags.[9] In row 2, however, we assume that $\rho_u = 0.8$, so there is scope for monetary policy to reduce the variability of inflation or the output gap, so as to reduce the average loss. Thus as μ_1 increases, the average loss falls. With very small values of μ_1, increases in its value do not increase the variability of the interest rate instrument, but with moderate or high values the variance of i_t increases with μ_1, as suggested by S&W. But the variance magnitude evidently approaches the value that prevails with the targeting rule of equation (10) in effect, as stated above.[10]

In row 3 the value of ρ_u is increased to 0.9, which raises the loss and the variance of i_t, but again this variance approaches that of the targeting rule as μ_1 is increased. The same holds true in row 4, where the model is enriched by the addition of serial correlation to the IS shock v_t, with $\rho_v = 0.8$. Finally, in row 5 serial correlation is posited for the e_t policy-error process, in addition to the private behavioral shock u_t, with $\rho_e = 0.8$. Again, the variability of i_t approaches that of the targeting rule as $\mu_1 \to \infty$, rather than growing to excessive levels.

From these results, it should be apparent that the alleged weakness of an instrument rule, relative to a specific targeting rule, is nonexistent for the model at hand.[11] By embedding the desired first-order condition in a Taylor-style instrument rule, the performance of the specific targeting rule can be approximated as closely as is desired. It would appear that the same would hold true for other specific targeting rules in other models.

Robustness and Conclusion

S&W's expressed concern for robustness of policy rules, with respect to model specification, is laudable. I believe that their approach leaves much to be desired, however, since it is based entirely on optimal rule design for the particular model at hand.[12] I have expressed criticism of such an approach in the past (McCallum, 1999, 1490–92) and would prefer one whose strategy is to search for a rule that performs reasonably well in a variety of models. A sophisticated and up-to-date study in this spirit,

---

9. This is because $E_t x_{t+1}$ and $E_t \pi_{t+1}$ are the same for all values of μ_1.

10. The reported numbers are subject to some random "sampling" error, since they represent an average of simulation results. The magnitude of this randomness is acceptable for the purposes at hand.

11. In their note 46, S&W mention conditions under which their argument would be valid. Crucial is that the central bank's "error does not become apparent to the private sector . . . until *after* the [next period's] interest rate is revealed." This seems, however, to be inconsistent with their assumption that "any random element in the central bank's period-t decisions is revealed to the private sector in period t."

12. The optimality condition (5) is invariant to changes in the autocorrelation structure of u_t but is not invariant to the inclusion in equation (5) of a lagged inflation term, for example, or to other forms of price stickiness.

which utilizes formal optimization methods but emphasizes the need for competing "reference models," has recently been provided by Levin and Williams (2003).

In any event, the main robustness-related criticism of instrument rules expressed by S&W (section 2.5) is evidently inapplicable to the one considered above—that is, rule (9).[13] That rule also fares well in terms of determinacy, as is implied by S&W's results in section 2.5. Accordingly, an instrument rule of this type—which is simple and straightforward in conception—would seem to be a strong contender for policy use, under the entirely hypothetical assumption that a central bank is confident that some specific model (such as that in equations [1] and [2], although presumably more complex) actually provides a good description of the economy at hand.

References

Blake, Andrew. 2001. A timeless perspective on optimality in forward-looking rational expectations models. London: National Institute of Economic and Social Research. Working Paper.

Clarida, Richard, Jordi Galí, and Mark Gertler. 1999. The science of monetary policy: A new Keynesian perspective. *Journal of Economic Literature* 37:1661–707.

Dennis, Richard. 2001. Pre-commitment, the timeless perspective, and policymaking from behind a veil of uncertainty. Federal Reserve Bank of San Francisco. Working Paper.

Jensen, Christian. 2001. Optimal monetary policy in forward-looking models with rational expectations by policy design. Carnegie Mellon University, Graduate School of Industrial Administration. Working Paper.

Jensen, Christian, and Bennett T. McCallum. 2002. The non-optimality of proposed monetary policy rules under timeless-perspective commitment. *Economics Letters* 77:163–68.

Levin, Andrew, and John C. Williams. 2003. Robust monetary policy with competing reference models. *Journal of Monetary Economics* 50:945–75.

McCallum, Bennett T. 1999. Issues in the design of monetary policy rules. In *Handbook of macroeconomics*, ed. John B. Taylor and Michael Woodford, 1483–1530. Amsterdam: North Holland.

McCallum, Bennett T., and Edward Nelson. 2000. Timeless perspective vs. discretionary monetary policy in forward-looking models. NBER Working Paper no. 7915. Cambridge, Mass.: National Bureau of Economic Research.

Rotemberg, Julio J., and Michael Woodford. 1999. Interest rate rules in an estimated sticky price model. In *Monetary policy rules,* ed. John B. Taylor, 57–119. Chicago: University of Chicago Press.

Svensson, Lars E. O. 2003. What is wrong with Taylor rules? Using judgment in monetary policy through targeting rules. *Journal of Economic Literature* 41:426–77.

Taylor, John B. 1979. Estimation and control of a macroeconomic model with rational expectations. *Econometrica* 45:1377–85.

———. 1988. The treatment of expectations in large multicountry econometric models. In *Empirical macroeconomics for interdependent economies,* ed. R. C. Bry-

---

13. This rule would of course be specified with no error term, if that is possible.

ant, D. W. Henderson, G. Holtham, and S. A. Symansky, 161–79. Washington, D.C.: Brookings Institution.
Woodford, Michael. 1999. Commentary: How should monetary policy be conducted in an era of price stability? In *New challenges for monetary policy,* 277–316. Kansas City, Mo.: Federal Reserve Bank of Kansas City.
———. 2003. *Interest and prices.* Princeton, N.J.: Princeton University Press.

Discussion Summary

Frank Smets questioned whether the welfare losses incurred due to discretionary optimization of society's preferences, and hence the welfare gains from delegating a modified loss function to the central bank, were quantitatively important. If not, the trade-off between simplicity of the delegation scheme and efficiency might suggest delegation of society's preferences. He asked whether, in the Bank of England's experience, lack of history dependence by not taking into account its own past forecasts had been perceived as a problem.

George Evans pointed out that, while the paper paid a lot of attention to the problem of determinacy of a rational-expectations equilibrium under the various policy rules, it did not consider the issue of learnability by private agents. He emphasized that rules that lead to determinacy may not necessarily be learnable and that, in particular, the hybrid rules proposed in the paper might fall into this category.

Martin Uribe expressed concern that the analysis of determinacy of equilibrium in the paper was focused on determinacy within a small neighborhood around the steady state, leaving open the issue of global determinacy of the equilibrium.

Marvin Goodfriend argued that the framework considered in the paper might be more valuable for analyzing future monetary policy when central banks have acquired the degree of credibility assumed in the paper. Nevertheless, the central bank's ability to fine-tune inflation and inflation expectations assumed in the paper might be unrealistically high. He questioned whether identifying cost shocks with historical residuals from estimated Phillips curves may overstate their importance, as some of those residuals may not reflect cost shocks, but credibility problems.

Athanasios Orphanides argued that it was unrealistic to assume that agents know the true model of the economy, let alone the true parameter values. This raises the problem of how to generate the forecasts required by the modified objectives and specific targeting rules proposed in the paper.

Ben Bernanke asked whether the first-order condition in the specific targeting rule could be interpreted as a stipulation about the time horizon within which the central bank had to bring inflation back to its target following a shock.

Mervyn King responded that the Bank of England's Monetary Policy Committee (MPC) has not so far shown any inflation bias. A risk in his mind was that the U.K. inflation record since the adoption of an inflation target in 1992 has been too good to be easily sustainable, raising the question of how inflation expectations might react if a significantly larger shock to inflation occurred. He emphasized that uncertainty played a fundamental role in the MPC's presentations, both to parliamentary committees and to the public. For example, the Bank's inflation projections were presented by focusing on the distribution of outcomes instead of a point forecast. The MPC's use of econometric models in its deliberations was possibly risking spending too much time discussing the central tendency of the forecast and too little time on the risks around that central tendency.

In response to Bennett McCallum's comments, *Michael Woodford* elaborated on the optimality criterion applied in the paper. According to this criterion, an equilibrium is optimal if it is optimal among all rational-expectations equilibria satisfying a self-consistent constraint on the inflation rate in the period that the policy was adopted. By contrast, McCallum's suggested optimality criterion was restricting the optimization to a particular family of rules that include the lagged output gap, thus assuming the desirability of this form of history dependence instead of deriving it. He also argued that, in the presence of measurement error in the data, the extremely strong responses proposed in McCallum's instrument rule were dangerous, in contrast to the specific targeting rules proposed in the paper.

3

Optimal Inflation-Targeting Rules

Marc P. Giannoni and Michael Woodford

An increasingly popular approach to the conduct of monetary policy, since the early 1990s, has been inflation-forecast targeting. Under this general approach, a central bank is committed to adjust short-term nominal interest rates periodically so as to ensure that its projection for the economy's evolution satisfies an explicit target criterion—for example, in the case of the Bank of England, the requirement that the Retail Prices Index minus mortgage interest payments (RPIX) inflation rate be projected to equal 2.5 percent at a horizon two years in the future (Vickers 1998). Such a commitment can overcome the inflationary bias that is likely to follow from discretionary policy guided solely by a concern for social welfare, and can also help to stabilize medium-term inflation expectations around a level that reduces the output cost to the economy of maintaining low inflation.

Another benefit that is claimed for such an approach (e.g., King 1997; Bernanke et al. 1999)—and an important advantage, at least in principle, of inflation targeting over other policy rules, such as a *k*-percent rule for monetary growth, that should also achieve a low average rate of inflation— is the possibility of combining reasonable stability of the inflation rate (especially over the medium to long term) with optimal short-run responses to real disturbances of various sorts. Hence Svensson (1999) argues for the

Marc P. Giannoni is an assistant professor of finance and economics at Columbia Business School and a faculty research fellow of the National Bureau of Economic Research (NBER). Michael Woodford is professor of economics at Columbia University and a research associate of NBER.

We would like to thank Jean Boivin, Rick Mishkin, Ed Nelson, and Lars Svensson for helpful discussions, Brad Strum for research assistance, and the National Science Foundation for research support through a grant to the NBER.

desirability of "flexible" inflation targeting, by which it is meant[1] that the target criterion involves not only the projected path of the inflation rate but one or more other variables, such as a measure of the output gap, as well.

We here consider the question of what sort of additional variables ought to matter—and with what weights, and what dynamic structure—in a target criterion that is intended to implement optimal policy. We wish to use economic theory to address questions such as which measure of inflation is most appropriately targeted (an index of goods prices only, or wage inflation as well?), which sort of output gap, if any, should justify short-run departures of projected inflation from the long-run target rate (a departure of real gross domestic product [GDP] from a smooth trend path, or from a "natural rate" that varies in response to a variety of disturbances?), and how large a modification of the acceptable inflation projection should result from a given size of projected output gap. We also consider how far in the future the inflation and output projections should extend upon which the current interest rate decision is based, and the degree to which an optimal target criterion should be *history dependent*—that is, should depend on recent conditions and not simply on the projected paths of inflation and other target variables from now on.

In a recent paper (Giannoni and Woodford 2002a), we expound a general approach to the design of an optimal target criterion. We show, for a fairly general class of linear-quadratic policy problems, how it is possible to choose a target criterion that will satisfy several desiderata. First, the target criterion has the property that insofar as the central bank is expected to ensure that it holds at all times, this expectation will imply the existence of a determinate rational-expectations equilibrium. Second, that equilibrium will be optimal, from the point of view of a specified quadratic loss function, among all possible rational-expectations equilibria, given one's model of the monetary transmission mechanism.[2] Thus the policy rule implements the optimal state-contingent evolution of the economy, in the sense of giving it a reason to occur if the private sector is convinced of the

1. Svensson discusses two alternative specifications of an inflation-targeting policy rule, one of which (a "general targeting rule") involves specification of a loss function that the central bank should use to evaluate alternative paths for the economy, and the other of which (a "specific targeting rule") involves specification of a target criterion. We are here concerned solely with policy prescriptions of the latter sort. On the implementation of optimal policy through a "general targeting rule," see Svensson and Woodford (chap. 2 in this volume).

2. Technically, the state-contingent evolution that is implemented by commitment to the policy rule is optimal from a "timeless perspective" of the kind proposed in Woodford (1999a), which means that it would have been chosen as part of an optimal commitment at a date sufficiently far in the past for the policymaker to fully internalize the implications of the anticipation of the specified policy actions, as well as their effects at the time that they are taken. This modification of the concept of optimality typically used in Ramsey-style analyses of optimal policy commitments allows a time-invariant policy rule to be judged optimal and eliminates the time inconsistency of optimal policy. See Giannoni and Woodford (2002a) and Svensson and Woodford (chap. 2 in this volume) for further discussion.

central bank's commitment to the rule and fully understands its implications.

Third, the rule is robustly optimal, in the sense that the same target criterion brings about an optimal state-contingent evolution of the economy regardless of the assumed statistical properties of the exogenous disturbances, despite the fact that the target criterion makes no explicit reference to the particular types of disturbances that may occur (except insofar as these may be involved in the definition of the target variables—the variables appearing in the loss function that defines the stabilization objectives). This robustness greatly increases the practical interest in the computation of a target criterion that is intended to implement optimal state-contingent responses to disturbances, for actual economies are affected by an innumerable variety of types of disturbances, and central banks always have a great deal of specific information about the ones that have most recently occurred. The demand that the target criterion be robustly optimal also allows us to obtain much sharper conclusions as to the form of an optimal target criterion. For while there would be a very large number of alternative relations among the paths of inflation and other variables that are equally consistent with the optimal state-contingent evolution in the case of a particular type of assumed disturbances, only relations of a very special sort continue to describe the optimal state-contingent evolution even if one changes the assumed character of the exogenous disturbances affecting the economy.

Our general characterization in Giannoni and Woodford (2002a) is in terms of a fairly abstract notation, involving eigenvectors and matrix lag polynomials. Here we offer examples of the specific character of the optimally flexible inflation targets that can be derived using that theory. Our results are of two sorts. First, we illustrate the implications of the theory in the context of a series of simple models that incorporate important features of realistic models of the monetary transmission mechanism. Such features include wage and price stickiness, inflation inertia, habit persistence, and predeterminedness of pricing and spending decisions. In the models considered, there is a tension between two or more of the central bank's stabilization objectives, which cannot simultaneously be achieved in full; in the simplest case, this is a tension between inflation and output-gap stabilization, but we also consider models in which it is reasonable to seek to stabilize interest rates or wage inflation as well. These results in the context of very simple models are intended to give insight into the way in which the character of the optimal target criterion should depend on one's model of the economy, and they should be of interest even to readers who are not persuaded of the empirical realism of our estimated model.

Second, we apply the theory to a small quantitative model of the U.S. monetary transmission mechanism, the numerical parameters of which are fit to vector autoregression (VAR) estimates of the impulse responses of several aggregate variables to identified monetary policy shocks. While the model remains an extremely simple one, this exercise makes an attempt to judge the likely quantitative significance of the types of effects that have previously been discussed in more general terms. It also offers a tentative evaluation of the extent to which U.S. policy over the past two decades has differed from what an optimal inflation-targeting regime would have called for.

3.1   Model Specification and Optimal Targets

Here we offer a few simple examples of the way in which the optimal target criterion will depend on the details of one's model of the monetary transmission mechanism. (The optimal target criterion also depends, of course, on one's assumed stabilization objectives. But here we shall take the view that the appropriate stabilization objectives follow from one's assumptions about the way in which policy affects the economy, although the welfare-theoretic stabilization objectives implied by our various simple models are here simply asserted rather than derived.) The examples that we select illustrate the consequences of features that are often present in quantitative optimizing models of the monetary transmission mechanism. They are also features of the small quantitative model presented in section 3.2; hence, our analytical results in this section are intended to provide intuition for the numerical results presented for the empirical model in section 3.3.

The analysis of Giannoni and Woodford (2002a) derives a robustly optimal target criterion from the first-order conditions that characterize the optimal state-contingent evolution of the economy. Here we illustrate this method by directly applying it to our simple examples, without any need to recapitulate the general theory.

3.1.1   An Inflation-Output Stabilization Trade-Off

We first consider the central issue addressed in previous literature on flexible inflation targeting, which is the extent to which a departure from complete (and immediate) stabilization of inflation is justifiable in the case of real disturbances that prevent joint stabilization of both inflation and the (welfare-relevant) output gap.[3] We illustrate how this question would be answered in the case of a simple optimizing model of the monetary transmission mechanism that allows for the existence of such "cost-push shocks" (to use the language of Clarida, Galí, and Gertler 1999).

As is well known, a discrete-time version of the optimizing model of staggered price-setting proposed by Calvo (1983) results in a log-linear aggregate supply relation of the form

---

3. Possible sources of disturbances of this sort are discussed in Giannoni (2000), Steinsson (2003), and Woodford (2003, chap. 6).

(1)
$$\pi_t = \kappa x_t + \beta E_t \pi_{t+1} + u_t,$$

sometimes called the "New Keynesian Phillips curve" (after Roberts 1995).[4] Here π_t denotes the inflation rate (rate of change of a general index of goods prices), x_t the output gap (the deviation of log real GDP from a time-varying "natural rate," defined so that stabilization of the output gap is part of the welfare-theoretic stabilization objective[5]), and the disturbance term u_t is a "cost-push shock," collecting all of the exogenous shifts in the equilibrium relation between inflation and output that do not correspond to shifts in the welfare-relevant "natural rate" of output. In addition, $0 < \beta < 1$ is the discount factor of the representative household, and $\kappa > 0$ is a function of a number of features of the underlying structure, including both the average frequency of price adjustment and the degree to which Ball and Romer's (1990) "real rigidities" are important.

We shall assume that the objective of monetary policy is to minimize the expected value of a loss function of the form

(2)
$$W = E_0 \left\{ \sum_{t=0}^{\infty} \beta^t L_t \right\},$$

where the discount factor β is the same as in equation (1), and the loss each period is given by

(3)
$$L_t = \pi_t^2 + \lambda(x_t - x^*)^2,$$

for a certain relative weight $\lambda > 0$ and optimal level of the output gap $x^* > 0$. Under the same microfoundations as justify the structural relation (1), one can show (Woodford 2003, chap. 6) that a quadratic approximation to the expected utility of the representative household is a decreasing function of equation (2), with

(4)
$$\lambda = \frac{\kappa}{\theta}$$

(where $\theta > 1$ is the elasticity of substitution between alternative differentiated goods) and x^* a function of both the degree of market power and the size of tax distortions. However, we here offer an analysis of the optimal

4. See Woodford (2003, chap. 3) for a derivation in the context of an explicit intertemporal general equilibrium model of the transmission mechanism. Equation (1) represents merely a log-linear approximation to the exact equilibrium relation between inflation and output implied by this pricing model; however, under circumstances discussed in Woodford (2003, chap. 6), such an approximation suffices for a log-linear approximate characterization of the optimal responses of inflation and output to small enough disturbances. Similar remarks apply to the other log-linear models presented below.

5. See Woodford (2003, chaps. 3 and 6) for discussion of how this variable responds to a variety of types of real disturbances. Under conditions discussed in chapter 6, the "natural rate" referred to here corresponds to the equilibrium level of output in the case that all wages and prices were completely flexible. However, our results in this section apply to a broader class of model specifications, under an appropriate definition of the "output gap."

target criterion in the case of any loss function of the form of equation (3), regardless of whether the weights and target values are the ones that can be justified on welfare-theoretic grounds or not. (In fact, a quadratic loss function of this form is frequently assumed in the literature on monetary policy evaluation and is often supposed to represent the primary stabilization objectives of actual inflation-targeting central banks in positive characterizations of the consequences of inflation targeting.)

The presence of disturbances of the kind represented by u_t in equation (1) creates a tension between the two stabilization goals reflected in equation (3) of inflation stabilization on the one hand and output-gap stabilization (around the value x^*) on the other; under an optimal policy, the paths of both variables will be affected by cost-push shocks. The optimal responses can be found by computing the state-contingent paths $\{\pi_t, x_t\}$ that minimize equation (2) with loss function (3) subject to the sequence of constraints in equation (1).[6] The Lagrangian for this problem, looking forward from any date t_0, is of the form

$$(5) \quad \mathcal{L}_{t_0} = E_{t_0} \sum_{t=t_0}^{\infty} \beta^{t-t_0} \left\{ \frac{1}{2} [\pi_t^2 + \lambda_x(x_t - x^*)^2] + \varphi_t[\pi_t - \kappa x_t - \beta \pi_{t+1}] \right\},$$

where φ_t is a Lagrange multiplier associated with constraint (1) on the possible inflation-output pairs in period t. In writing the constraint term associated with the period-t aggregate-supply relation, it does not matter that we substitute π_{t+1} for $E_t\pi_{t+1}$, for it is only the conditional expectation of the term at date t_0 that matters in equation (5), and the law of iterated expectations implies that

$$E_{t_0}[\varphi_t E_t\pi_{t+1}] = E_{t_0}[E_t(\varphi_t\pi_{t+1})] = E_{t_0}[\varphi_t\pi_{t+1}]$$

for any $t \geq t_0$.

Differentiating equation (5) with respect to the levels of inflation and output each period, we obtain a pair of first-order conditions

$$(6) \quad\quad\quad\quad\quad \pi_t + \varphi_t - \varphi_{t-1} = 0,$$

$$(7) \quad\quad\quad\quad\quad \lambda(x_t - x^*) - \kappa\varphi_t = 0,$$

for each period $t \geq t_0$. These conditions, together with the structural relation in equation (1), have a unique nonexplosive solution[7] for the infla-

6. Note that the aggregate-demand side of the model does not matter, as long as a nominal interest rate path exists that is consistent with any inflation and output paths that may be selected. This is true if, for example, the relation between interest rates and private expenditure is of the form of equation (15) assumed below, and the required path of nominal interest rates is always nonnegative. We assume here that the nonnegativity constraint never binds, which will be true, under the assumptions of the model, in the case of any small enough real disturbances $\{u_t, r_t^n\}$.

7. Obtaining a unique solution requires the specification of an initial value for the Lagrange multiplier φ_{t_0-1}. See Woodford (2003, chap. 7) for the discussion of alternative possible choices of this initial condition and their significance. Here we note simply that regardless of the value chosen for φ_{t_0-1}, the optimal responses to cost-push shocks in period t_0 and later are the same.

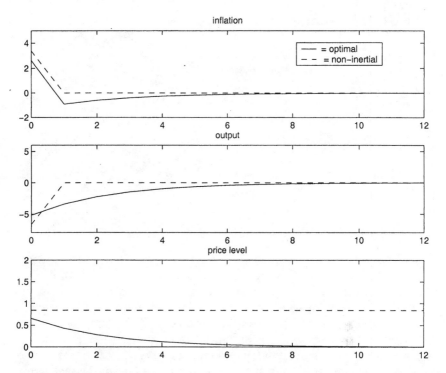

Fig. 3.1 Optimal responses to a positive cost-push shock under commitment, in the case of Calvo pricing

tion rate, the output gap, and the Lagrange multiplier (a unique solution in which the paths of these variables are bounded if the shocks u_t are bounded), and this solution (which therefore satisfies the transversality condition) indicates the optimal state-contingent evolution of inflation and output.

As an example, figure 3.1 plots the impulse responses to a positive cost-push shock, in the simple case that the cost-push shock is purely transitory, and unforecastable before the period in which it occurs (so that $E_t u_{t+j} = 0$ for all $j \geq 1$). Here the assumed values of β, κ, and λ are those given in table 3.1,[8] and the shock in period zero is of size $u_0 = 1$; the periods represent quarters, and the inflation rate is plotted as an annualized rate, meaning

8. These parameter values are based on the estimates of Rotemberg and Woodford (1997) for a slightly more complex variant of the model used here and in section 3.1.3. The coefficient λ here corresponds to λ_x in the table. Note also that the value of .003 for that coefficient refers to a loss function in which π_t represents the *quarterly* change in the log price level. If we write the loss function in terms of an annualized inflation rate, $4\pi_t$, as is conventional in numerical work, then the relative weight on the output-gap stabilization term would actually be $16\lambda_x$, or about .048. Of course, this is still quite low compared the relative weights often assumed in the *ad hoc* stabilization objectives used in the literature on the evaluation of monetary policy rules.

Table 3.1   Calibrated parameter values for the examples in section 3.1

	Value
Structural parameters	
β	0.99
κ	0.024
θ^{-1}	0.13
σ^{-1}	0.16
Shock processes	
ρ_u	0
ρ_r	0.35
Loss function	
λ_x	0.003
λ_i	0.236

that what is plotted is actually $4\pi_t$. As one might expect, in an optimal equilibrium inflation is allowed to increase somewhat in response to a cost-push shock, so that the output gap need not fall as much as would be required to prevent any increase in the inflation rate. Perhaps less intuitively, the figure also shows that under an optimal commitment monetary policy remains tight even after the disturbance has dissipated, so that the output gap returns to zero only much more gradually. As a result of this, while inflation overshoots its long-run target value at the time of the shock, it is held *below* its long-run target value for a time following the shock, so that the unexpected increase in prices is subsequently undone. In fact, as the bottom panel of the figure shows, under an optimal commitment the price level eventually returns to exactly the same path that it would have been expected to follow if the shock had not occurred.

This simple example illustrates a very general feature of optimal policy once one takes account of forward-looking private-sector behavior: optimal policy is almost always *history dependent.* That is, it depends on the economy's recent history and not simply on the set of possible state-contingent paths for the target variables (here, inflation and the output gap) that are possible from now on. (In the example shown in the figure, the set of possible rational-expectations equilibrium paths for inflation and output from period t onward depends only on the value of u_t, but under an optimal policy the actually realized inflation rate and output gap depend on past disturbances as well.) This is because a commitment to respond later to past conditions can shift expectations at the earlier date in a way that helps to achieve the central bank's stabilization objectives. In the present example, if price setters are forward looking, the anticipation that a current increase in the general price level will predictably be "undone" soon gives suppliers a reason not to increase their own prices currently as much as they otherwise would. This leads to smaller equilibrium deviations from the long-run inflation target at the time of the cost-push shock, without requiring such a large change in the output gap as would be required to stabilize inflation to the same degree without a change in expectations regarding future inflation. (The impulse responses under the best possible equilibrium that does not involve history dependence are shown by the dashed lines in the figure.[9] Note that a larger initial output contraction is required, even though both the initial price increase and the long-run price increase caused by the shock are greater.)

It follows that no *purely forward-looking* target criterion—one that involves only the projected paths of the target variables from the present time onward, like the criterion that is officially used by the Bank of England—can possibly determine an equilibrium with the optimal responses to disturbances. Instead, a history-dependent target criterion is necessary, as stressed by Svensson and Woodford (chap. 2 in this volume).

A target criterion that works is easily derived from the first-order conditions (6)–(7). Eliminating the Lagrange multiplier, one is left with a linear relation

$$(8) \qquad \pi_t + \phi(x_t - x_{t-1}) = 0,$$

with a coefficient $\phi = \lambda/\kappa > 0$, that the state-contingent evolution of inflation and the output gap must satisfy. Note that this relation must hold in an optimal equilibrium regardless of the assumed statistical properties of the disturbances. One can also show that a commitment to ensure that equation (8) holds each period from some date t_0 onward implies the existence of a determinate rational-expectations equilibrium,[10] given any initial output gap x_{t_0-1}. In this equilibrium, inflation and output evolve according to the optimal state-contingent evolution characterized above.

This is the optimal target criterion that we are looking for: it indicates that deviations of the projected inflation rate π_t from the long-run inflation target (here equal to zero) should be accepted that are proportional to the degree to which the output gap is projected to decline over the same period that prices are projected to rise. Note that this criterion is history dependent, because the acceptability of a given projection (π_t, x_t) depends on the recent past level of the output gap; it is this feature of the criterion that will result in the output gap's returning only gradually to its normal level following a transitory cost-push shock, as shown in figure 3.1.

How much of a projected change in the output gap is needed to justify a

---

9. See Woodford (2003, chap. 7) for derivation of this "optimal non-inertial plan." In the example shown in figure 3.1, this optimal non-inertial policy corresponds to the Markov equilibrium resulting from discretionary optimization by the central bank. That equivalence would not obtain, however, in the case of serially correlated disturbances.

10. The characteristic equation that determines whether the system of equations consisting of (1) and (8) has a unique nonexplosive solution is the same as for the system of equations solved above for the optimal state-contingent evolution.

given degree of departure from the long-run inflation target? If λ is assigned the value that it takes in the welfare-theoretic loss function, then $\phi = \theta^{-1}$, where θ is the elasticity of demand faced by the typical firm. The calibrated value for this parameter given in table 3.1 (based on the estimates of Rotemberg and Woodford 1997) implies that $\phi = .13$. If we express the target criterion in terms of the annualized inflation rate $(4\pi_t)$ rather than the quarterly rate of price change, the relative weight on the projected quarterly change in the output gap will instead be 4ϕ, or about 0.51. Hence, a projection of a decline in real GDP of 2 percentage points relative to the natural rate of output over the coming quarter would justify an increase in the projected (annualized) rate of inflation of slightly more than 1 percentage point.

3.1.2   Inflation Inertia

A feature of the New Keynesian aggregate-supply relation (1) that has come in for substantial criticism in the empirical literature is the fact that past inflation rates play no role in the determination of current equilibrium inflation. Instead, empirical models of the kind used in central banks for policy evaluation often imply that the path of the output gap required in order to achieve a particular path for the inflation rate from now onward depends on what rate of inflation has already been recently experienced, and this aspect of one's model is of obvious importance for the question of how rapidly one should expect that it is optimal to return inflation to its normal level, or even to undo past unexpected price-level increases, following a cost-push shock.

A simple way of incorporating inflation inertia of the kind that central-bank models often assume into an optimizing model of pricing behavior is to assume, as Christiano, Eichenbaum, and Evans (2001) propose, that individual prices are indexed to an aggregate price index during the intervals between reoptimizations of the individual prices, and that the aggregate price index becomes available for this purpose only with a one-period lag. When the Calvo model of staggered price-setting is modified in this way, the aggregate-supply relation (1) takes the more general form[11]

(9) $$\pi_t - \gamma\pi_{t-1} = \kappa x_t + \beta E_t[\pi_{t+1} - \gamma\pi_t] + u_t,$$

where the coefficient $0 \leq \gamma \leq 1$ indicates the degree of automatic indexation to the aggregate price index. In the limiting case of complete indexation ($\gamma = 1$), the case assumed by Christiano et al. and the case found to best fit U.S. data in our own estimation results below, this relation is essentially identical to the aggregate-supply relation proposed by Fuhrer and Moore (1995), which has been widely used in empirical work.

The welfare-theoretic stabilization objective corresponding to this alternative structural model is of the form of equation (2) with the period loss function (3) replaced by

---

11. See Woodford (2003, chap. 3) for a derivation from explicit microeconomic foundations.

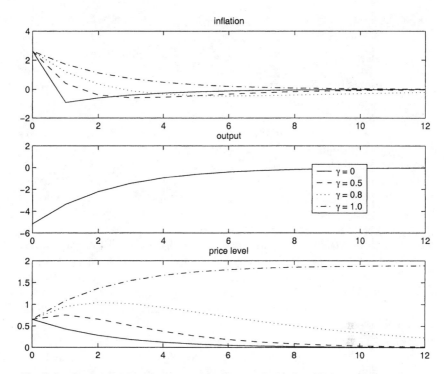

Fig. 3.2   Optimal responses to a positive cost-push shock under commitment, for alternative degrees of inflation inertia

(10) $$L_t = (\pi_t - \gamma\pi_{t-1})^2 + \lambda(x_t - x^*)^2,$$

where $\lambda > 0$ is again given by equation (4), and $x^* > 0$ is similarly the same function of underlying microeconomic distortions as before.[12] (The reason for the change is that with the automatic indexation, the degree to which the prices of firms that reoptimize their prices and those that do not are different depends on the degree to which the current overall inflation rate π_t differs from the rate at which the automatically adjusted prices are increasing—i.e., from $\gamma\pi_{t-1}$.) If we consider the problem of minimizing equation (2) with loss function (10) subject to the sequence of constraints in equation (9), the problem has the same form as in the previous section, except with π_t everywhere replaced by the quasi-differenced inflation rate

(11) $$\pi_t^{qd} \equiv \pi_t - \gamma\pi_{t-1}.$$

The solution is therefore also the same, with this substitution.

Figure 3.2 shows the impulse responses of inflation, the output gap, and the price level to the same kind of disturbance as in figure 3.1, under opti-

---

12. See Woodford (2003, chap. 6) for derivation of this loss function as an approximation to expected utility.

mal policy for economies with alternative values of the indexation parameter γ. (The values assumed for β, κ, and λ are again as in table 3.1.) Once again, under an optimal commitment, the initial unexpected increase in prices is eventually undone, as long as $\gamma < 1$, and this once again means that inflation eventually undershoots its long-run level for a time. However, for any large enough value of γ, inflation remains greater than its long-run level for a time even after the disturbance has ceased, and only later undershoots its long-run level; the larger is γ, the longer this period of above-average inflation persists. In the limiting case that $\gamma = 1$, the undershooting never occurs; inflation is simply gradually brought back to the long-run target level.[13] In this last case, a temporary disturbance causes a permanent change in the price level, even under optimal policy. However, the *inflation rate* is eventually restored to its previously anticipated long-run level under an optimal commitment, even though the rate of inflation (as opposed to the rate of *acceleration* of inflation) is not welfare relevant in this model. (Note that the optimal responses shown in figure 3.2 for the case $\gamma = 1$ correspond fairly well to the conventional wisdom of inflation-targeting central banks, but our theoretical analysis allows us to compute an optimal rate at which inflation should be projected to return to its long-run target value following a disturbance.)

As in the previous section, we can derive a target criterion that implements the optimal responses to disturbances regardless of the assumed statistical properties of the disturbances. This optimal target criterion is obtained by replacing π_t in equation (8) by π_t^{qd}, yielding

$$(12) \qquad \pi_t - \gamma\pi_{t-1} + \phi(x_t - x_{t-1}) = 0,$$

where $\phi > 0$ is the same function of model parameters as before. This indicates that the acceptable inflation projection for the current period should depend not only on the projected change in the output gap, but also (insofar as $\gamma > 0$) on the recent past rate of inflation: a higher existing inflation rate justifies a higher projected near-term inflation rate, in the case of any given output-gap projection.

In the special case that $\gamma = 1$, the optimal target criterion adjusts the current inflation target one-for-one with increases in the existing rate of inflation—the target criterion actually involves only the rate of acceleration of inflation. But this does not mean that disturbances are allowed to permanently shift the inflation rate to a new level, as shown in figure 3.2. In fact, in the case of full indexation, an alternative target criterion that also leads to the optimal equilibrium responses to cost-push shocks is the simpler criterion

13. Note that the impulse response of inflation (for $\gamma = 1$) in panel A of figure 3.2 is the same as the impulse response of the price level (under optimal policy) in panel C of figure 3.1. The scales are different because the inflation rate plotted is an annualized rate, $4\pi_t$, rather than π_t.

(13) $$\pi_t + \phi x_t = \overline{\pi},$$

where again $\phi > 0$ is the same coefficient as in equation (12) and the value of the long-run inflation target $\overline{\pi}$ is arbitrary (but not changing over time). Note that equation (12) is just a first-differenced form of equation (13), and a commitment to ensure that equation (12) holds in each period $t \geq t_0$ is equivalent to a commitment to ensure that equation (13) holds, for a particular choice of $\overline{\pi}$, namely $\overline{\pi} = \pi_{t_0-1} + \phi x_{t_0-1}$. But the choice of $\overline{\pi}$ has no effect on either the determinacy of equilibrium or the equilibrium responses of inflation and output to real disturbances (only on the long-run average inflation rate), and so any target criterion of the form of equation (13) implements the optimal responses to disturbances.[14] Note that this optimal target criterion is similar in form to the kind that Svensson (1999) suggests as a description of the behavior of actual inflation-targeting central banks, except that the inflation and output-gap projections in equation (13) are not so far in the future (they refer only to the coming quarter) as in the procedures of actual inflation targeters.

The result that the long-run inflation target associated with an optimal target criterion is indeterminate depends, of course, on the fact that we have assumed a model in which no distortions depend on the inflation rate, as opposed to its rate of change. This is logically possible but unlikely to be true in reality. (Distortions that depend on the level of nominal interest rates, considered in the next section, would be one example of a realistic complication that would break this result, even in the case of full indexation.) Because the model considered here with $\gamma = 1$ does not determine any particular optimal long-run inflation target (it need *not* vary with the initially existing inflation rate, for example), even a small perturbation of these assumptions is likely to determine an optimal long-run inflation target, and this will generally be independent of the initially existing rate of inflation. (The monetary frictions considered in the next subsection provide an example of this.)

It is worth noting that even though the optimal dynamic responses shown in figure 3.2 for the case of large γ confirm the conventional wisdom of inflation-targeting central bankers with regard the desirability of a gradual return of the inflation rate to its long-run target level following a cost-push shock, the optimal target criterion for this model does *not* involve a "medium-term" inflation forecast rather than a shorter-run projection.

---

14. Any such policy rule is also optimal from a timeless perspective, under the definition given in Giannoni and Woodford (2002a). Note that alternative rules that result in equilibria that differ only in a transitory, deterministic component of the path of each of the target variables can each be considered optimal in this sense. This ambiguity as to the initial behavior of the target variables cannot be resolved if our concept of optimal policy is to be time consistent. In the present case, ambiguity about the required initial behavior of the target variable, inflation acceleration, implies ambiguity about the required long-run average level of the inflation rate, although there is no ambiguity about how inflation should respond to shocks.

Even in the case that we suppose that the central bank will often have advance information about disturbances that will shift the aggregate-supply relation only a year or more in the future, the robust description of optimal policy is one that indicates how short-run output-gap projections should modify the acceptable short-run inflation projection, rather than one that checks only that some more distant inflation forecast is still on track. Of course, a commitment to the achievement of the target criterion in equation (12) each period does imply that the projection of inflation several quarters in the future should never depart much from the long-run inflation target, but the latter stipulation is not an equally useful guide to what should actually be done with interest rates at a given point in time.

3.1.3   An Interest Rate Stabilization Objective

The policy problems considered above assume that central banks care only about the paths of inflation and the output gap and not about the behavior of nominal interest rates that may be required to bring about a given evolution of inflation and output that is consistent with the aggregate-supply relation. However, actual central banks generally appear to care about reducing the volatility of nominal interest rates as well (Goodfriend 1991). Such a concern can also be justified in terms of microeconomic foundations that are consistent with the kind of aggregate-supply relations assumed above, as discussed in Woodford (2003, chap. 6).

For example, the transaction frictions that account for money demand imply a distortion that should be an increasing function of the nominal interest rate, as stressed by Friedman (1969); the deadweight loss resulting from a positive opportunity cost of holding money should also be a convex function of the interest rate, at least for interest rates close enough to the optimal one (the interest rate paid on base money). Alternatively, the existence of a zero lower bound on nominal interest rates can make it desirable to accept somewhat greater variability of inflation and the output gap for the sake of reducing the required variability of nominal interest rates, given that the smaller range of variation in the nominal interest rate allows the average nominal interest rate (and hence the average inflation rate) to be lower. A quadratic penalty for deviations of the nominal interest rate from a target level may then be justified as a proxy for a constraint that links the feasible average level of nominal interest rates to the variability of the nominal interest rate.

For any of these reasons, we may be interested in a policy that minimizes a loss function of the form

$$(14) \qquad L_t = \pi_t^2 + \lambda_x(x_t - x^*)^2 + \lambda_i(i_t - i^*)^2,$$

where $\lambda_x > 0$ is the same function of underlying parameters as λ in equation (3), i_t is a short-term nominal interest rate, $\lambda_i > 0$ for one of the reasons discussed above, and i^* is the level around which the nominal interest rate would ideally be stabilized. In this case, the aggregate-supply relation is not the only relevant constraint in our optimal policy problem; it also matters what interest rate path is required in order to induce a given evolution of aggregate demand.

In a simple optimizing model that has been used in many recent analyses of optimal monetary policy (e.g., McCallum and Nelson 1999; Clarida, Galí, and Gertler 1999; and Woodford 1999b), the aggregate-supply relation (1) is combined with an intertemporal Euler equation for the timing of private expenditure of the form

(15) $$x_t = E_t x_{t+1} - \sigma(i_t - E_t \pi_{t+1} - r_t^n),$$

where $\sigma > 0$ represents the intertemporal elasticity of substitution and r_t^n exogenous variation in Wicksell's "natural rate of interest." Real disturbances that cause the natural rate of interest to vary are now another reason why (if $\lambda_i > 0$) it will be impossible for the central bank to completely stabilize all of its target variables simultaneously, and hence for transitory variations in the inflation rate to be optimal, even in the absence of cost-push shocks.

This leads us to consider the problem of finding the state-contingent evolution of inflation, output, and interest rates to minimize the expected discounted value of equation (14) subject to the constraints of equations (1) and (15). A similar Lagrangian method as in section 3.1.1 leads to first-order conditions of the form

(16) $$\pi_t - \beta^{-1}\sigma\varphi_{1t-1} + \varphi_{2t} - \varphi_{2t-1} = 0,$$

(17) $$\lambda_x(x_t - x^*) + \varphi_{1t} - \beta^{-1}\varphi_{1t-1} - \kappa\varphi_{2t} = 0,$$

(18) $$\lambda_i(i_t - i^*) + \sigma\varphi_{1t} = 0,$$

where φ_{1t} is the multiplier associated with constraint (15) and φ_{2t} the one associated with constraint (1). We can once again solve this system of equations for unique bounded paths for the endogenous variables in the case of any bounded processes for the exogenous disturbances $\{r_t^n, u_t\}$. The implied optimal responses to an exogenous increase in the natural rate of interest are shown in figure 3.3. Here the model parameters are calibrated as in table 3.1, and the natural rate of interest is assumed to be a first-order autoregressive process with serial correlation coefficient $\rho_r = 0.35$.[15]

A notable feature of figure 3.3 is that once again optimal policy must be history dependent, for the optimal responses to the disturbance are more persistent than the disturbance itself. As discussed in Woodford (1999b), optimal interest rate policy is *inertial,* in the sense that interest rates are

---

15. The real disturbances that cause the natural rate of interest to vary are assumed to create no variation in the cost-push term u_t; that is, they shift the equilibrium relation between inflation and output only through possible shifts in the natural rate of output. A variety of examples of real disturbances with this property are discussed in Woodford (2003, chap. 6).

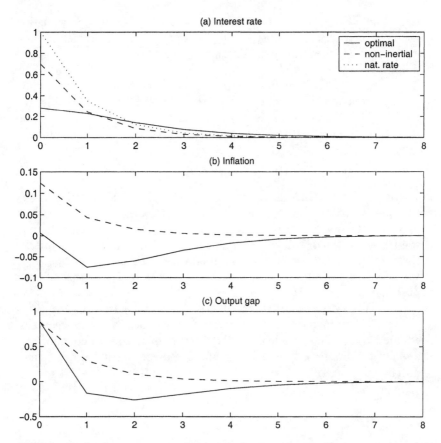

Fig. 3.3   Optimal responses to an increase in the natural rate of interest

both raised only gradually in response to an increase in the natural rate of interest and then are returned to their normal level more gradually than the natural rate itself as well. (The impulse response of the natural rate is shown by the dotted line in panel a of the figure.) Because spending responds to expected future interest rates and not only current short rates, it is possible to achieve a given degree of stabilization of demand (relative to the natural rate) in response to disturbances with less volatility of short-term interest rates if short rates are moved in a more inertial fashion. (The optimal responses among those achievable using a purely forward-looking target criterion are shown, for purposes of comparison, by the dashed lines in the figure.)

A history-dependent target criterion that can bring about the desired impulse responses, again regardless of the statistical properties of the disturbances r_t^n and u_t (including any assumptions about the degree of correlation between these disturbances), can be derived once more from the first-order conditions (16)–(18). Using the last two equations to substitute for the two Lagrange multipliers in the first equation, we are left with a linear relation of the form

(19) $$A(L)(i_t - i^*) = \phi_\pi \pi_t + \phi_x(x_t - x_{t-1})$$

that must be satisfied each period under an optimal policy. Here the coefficients of the lag polynomial are

$$A(L) \equiv 1 - \left(1 + \frac{\kappa\sigma}{\beta}\right)L - \beta^{-1}L(1 - L),$$

and the inflation and output response coefficients are

(20) $$\phi_\pi = \frac{\kappa\sigma}{\lambda_i} > 0, \qquad \phi_x = \frac{\sigma\lambda_x}{\lambda_i} > 0.$$

One can furthermore show that not only is this a necessary feature of an optimal equilibrium, but it also suffices to characterize it, in the sense that the system consisting of equation (19) together with the structural equations (1) and (15) has a unique nonexplosive solution, in which the equilibrium responses to shocks are optimal.[16]

Requirement (19) can be interpreted as an inertial Taylor rule, as discussed in Giannoni and Woodford (2003). However, this requirement can also be equivalently expressed in a forward-integrated form, that more directly generalizes the optimal target criterion derived in section 3.1.1. It is easily seen that our sign assumptions on the model parameters imply that $A(L)$ can be factored as

$$A(L) \equiv (1 - \lambda_1 L)(1 - \lambda_2 L),$$

where $0 < \lambda_1 < 1 < \lambda_2$. It then follows that equation (19) is equivalent to

(21) $$(1 - \lambda_1 L)(i_{t-1} - i^*) = -\lambda_2^{-1}E_t[(1 - \lambda_2^{-1}L^{-1})^{-1}(\phi_\pi \pi_t + \phi_x \Delta x_t)],$$

in the sense that bounded stochastic processes $\{i_t, \pi_t, x_t\}$ satisfy equation (19) for all $t \geq t_0$ if and only if they satisfy (21) for all $t \geq t_0$.[17] Hence a commitment to ensure that equation (21) is satisfied at all times implies a determinate rational-expectations equilibrium in which the responses to shocks are optimal. This conclusion is once again independent of any assumption about the statistical properties of the disturbances, so that equation (21) is a robustly optimal target criterion.

This optimal target criterion can be expressed in the form

(22) $$F_t(\pi) + \phi F_t(x) = \theta_x x_{t-1} - \theta_i(i_{t-1} - i^*) - \theta_\Delta \Delta i_{t-1},$$

---

16. See Giannoni and Woodford (2003), proposition 1.
17. See Giannoni and Woodford (2002b), proposition 7.

where for each of the variables $z = \pi, x$ we use the notation $F_t(z)$ for a conditional forecast

$$F_t(z) \equiv \sum_{j=0}^{\infty} \alpha_{z,j} E_t z_{t+j}$$

involving weights $\{\alpha_{z,j}\}$ that sum to one. Thus, the criterion specifies a time-varying target value for a weighted average of an inflation forecast and an output-gap forecast, where each of these forecasts is in fact a weighted average of forecasts at various horizons, rather than a projection for a specific future date. The coefficients of this representation of optimal policy are given by

$$\phi = \theta_x = (1 - \lambda_2^{-1}) \frac{\lambda_x}{\kappa} > 0,$$

$$\theta_i = \lambda_2 (1 - \lambda_1)(1 - \lambda_2^{-1}) \frac{\lambda_i}{\kappa\sigma} > 0,$$

$$\theta_\Delta = \lambda_1 \lambda_2 (1 - \lambda_2^{-1}) \frac{\lambda_i}{\kappa\sigma} > 0,$$

while the optimal weights in the conditional forecasts are

$$\alpha_{\pi,j} = \alpha_{x,j} = (1 - \lambda_2^{-1})\lambda_2^{-j}.$$

Thus the optimal conditional forecast is one that places positive weight on the projection for each future period, beginning with the current period, with weights that decline exponentially as the horizon increases. The mean distance in the future of the projections that are relevant to the target criterion is equal to

$$\sum_{j=0}^{\infty} \alpha_{z,j} j = (\lambda_2 - 1)^{-1}$$

for both the inflation and output-gap forecasts.

In the case of the calibrated parameter values in table 3.1, the rate at which these weights decay per quarter is $\lambda_2^{-1} = .68$, so that the mean forecast horizon in the optimal target criterion is 2.1 quarters. Thus, while the optimal target criterion in this case involves projections of inflation and output beyond the current quarter, the forecast horizon remains quite short compared to the actual practice of inflation-forecast-targeting central banks. For these same parameter values, the optimal relative weight on the output-gap forecast is $\phi = .04$,[18] indicating that the target criterion is largely an inflation target. The remaining optimal coefficients are $\theta_x = .04$, $\theta_i = .24$, and $\theta_\Delta = .51$, indicating a substantial degree of history depend-

---

18. If we write the target criterion in terms of a forecast for the annualized inflation rate $(4\pi_t)$, the relative weight on the output-gap forecast will instead be 4ϕ, or about .15.

ence of the optimal flexible inflation target. The fact that $\theta_x = \phi$ indicates that it is the forecasted increase in the output gap *relative* to the previous quarter's level, rather than the absolute level of the gap, that should modify the inflation target, just as in section 3.1.1. The signs of θ_i and θ_Δ imply that policy will be made tighter (in the sense of demanding a lower modified inflation forecast) when interest rates have been high and/or increasing in the recent past; this is a way of committing to interest rate inertia of the kind shown in figure 3.3.

Note that in the limiting case in which $\lambda_i = 0$, this target criterion reduces to equation (8). In that limit, θ_i, θ_Δ and the decay factor λ_2^{-1} become equal to zero, while ϕ and θ_x have a well-defined (common) positive limit. Thus in this limiting case, the optimal targeting rule is one in which the inflation target must be modified in proportion to the projected change in the output gap, but it is no longer also dependent on lagged interest rates, and the relevant inflation and output-gap projections do not involve periods beyond the current one. This will also be nearly true in the case of small enough positive values of λ_i.

We may similarly introduce an interest rate stabilization objective in the case of the model with inflation inertia considered in section 3.1.2. In this case, the loss function (10) is generalized to

$$(23) \qquad L_t = (\pi_t - \gamma\pi_{t-1})^2 + \lambda_x(x_t - x^*)^2 + \lambda_i(i_t - i^*)^2,$$

for some $\lambda_i > 0$ and some desired interest rate i^*. In this generalization of the problem just considered, the first-order condition (16) becomes instead

$$(24) \qquad \pi_t^{qd} - \beta\gamma E_t\pi_{t+1}^{qd} - \beta^{-1}\sigma\varphi_{1t-1} - \beta\gamma E_t\varphi_{2,t+1} + (1 + \beta\gamma)\varphi_{2t} - \varphi_{2t-1} = 0,$$

where π_t^{qd} is again defined in equation (11). Conditions (17)–(18) remain as before.[19]

Again using the latter two equations to eliminate the Lagrange multipliers, we obtain a relation of the form

$$(25) \qquad E_t[A(L)(i_{t+1} - i^*)] = -E_t[(1 - \beta\gamma L^{-1})q_t]$$

for the optimal evolution of the target variables. Here $A(L)$ is a cubic lag polynomial

$$(26) \quad A(L) \equiv \beta\gamma - (1 + \gamma + \beta\gamma)L + (1 + \gamma + \beta^{-1}(1 + \kappa\sigma))L^2 - \beta^{-1}L^3,$$

while q_t is a function of the projected paths of the target variables, defined by

---

19. One easily sees that in the case that $\gamma = 1$, the only long-run average inflation rate consistent with these conditions is $\bar{\pi} = i^* - \bar{r}$, where $\bar{r}$ is the unconditional mean of the natural rate of interest. This is true for any $\lambda_i > 0$, no matter how small. Hence, even a slight preference for lower interest rate variability suffices to break the indeterminacy of the optimal long-run inflation target obtained for the case $\gamma = 1$ in section 1.2.

$$q_t \equiv \frac{\kappa\sigma}{\lambda_i}\left[\pi_t^{qd} + \frac{\lambda_x}{\kappa}\Delta x_t\right].$$

The lag polynomial $A(L)$ can be factored as $A(L) = (1 - \lambda_1 L)L^2 B(L^{-1})$, where $B(L^{-1})$ is a quadratic polynomial, and under our sign assumptions one can further show[20] that $0 < \lambda_1 < 1$, while both roots of $B(L)$ are outside the unit circle. Relation (25) is then equivalent[21] to a relation of the form

(27) $$(1 - \lambda_1 L)(i_{t-1} - i^*) = -E_t[B(L^{-1})^{-1}(1 - \beta\gamma L^{-1})q_t],$$

which generalizes equation (21) to the case $\gamma \neq 0$.

This provides us with a robustly optimal target criterion that can be expressed in the form

(28) $$F_t(\pi) + \phi F_t(x) = \theta_\pi \pi_{t-1} + \theta_x x_{t-1} - \theta_i(i_{t-1} - i^*) - \theta_\Delta \Delta i_{t-1},$$

generalizing equation (22). Under our sign assumptions, one can show[22] that

$$\phi = \theta_x > 0,$$
$$0 < \theta_\pi \leq 1,$$

and

$$\theta_i, \theta_\Delta > 0.$$

Furthermore, for fixed values of the other parameters, as $\gamma \to 0$, θ_π approaches zero and the other parameters approach the nonzero values associated with the target criterion (22). Instead, as $\gamma \to 1$, θ_π approaches 1, so that the target criterion involves only the projected change in the rate of inflation relative to its already existing level, just as we found in section 3.1.2 when there was assumed to be no interest rate stabilization objective.

The effects of increasing γ on the coefficients of the optimal target criterion (28) is illustrated in figure 3.4, where the coefficients are plotted against γ, assuming the same calibrated values for the other parameters as before. It is interesting to note that each of the coefficients indicating history dependence (θ_π, θ_x, θ_i, and θ_Δ) increases with γ (except perhaps when γ is near one). Thus if there is substantial inflation inertia, it is even more important for the inflation-forecast target to vary with changes in recent economic conditions. It is also worth noting that the degree to which the inflation target should be modified in response to changes in the output-gap projection (indicated by the coefficient ϕ) increases with γ. While our conclusion for the case $\gamma = 0$ above ($\phi = .04$) might have suggested that this

20. See Giannoni and Woodford (2003), proposition 2.
21. See Giannoni and Woodford (2002b), proposition 11.
22. See Giannoni and Woodford (2002b), proposition 12.

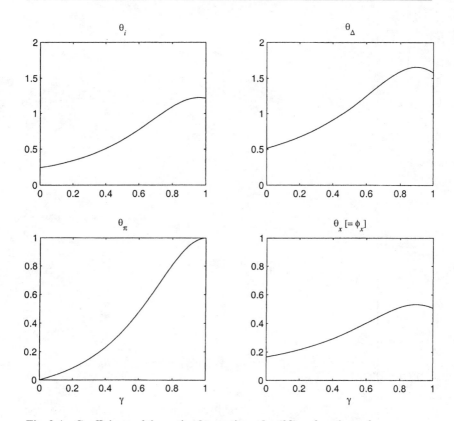

Fig. 3.4   Coefficients of the optimal targeting rules (28) as functions of γ

sort of modification of the inflation target is not too important, we find that a substantially larger response is justified if γ is large. The optimal coefficient is φ = 0.13, as in sections 3.1.1 and 3.1.2, if γ = 1; and once again this corresponds to a weight of 0.51 if the inflation target is expressed as an annualized rate.

The panels of figure 3.5 correspondingly show the relative weights $\alpha_{z,j}/\alpha_{z,0}$ on the forecasts at different horizons in the optimal target criterion (28), for each of several alternative values of γ. As above, the inclusion of an interest-rate stabilization objective makes the optimal target criterion more forward looking than was the case in section 3.1.2. Indeed, we now find, at least for high enough values of γ, that the optimal target criterion places nonnegligible weight on forecasts more than a year in the future. But it is not necessarily true that a greater degree of inflation inertia justifies a target criterion with a longer forecast horizon. Increases in γ increase the optimal weights on the current-quarter projections of both inflation and the output gap (normalizing the weights to sum to one), and instead make the weights on the projections for quarters more than two quarters in

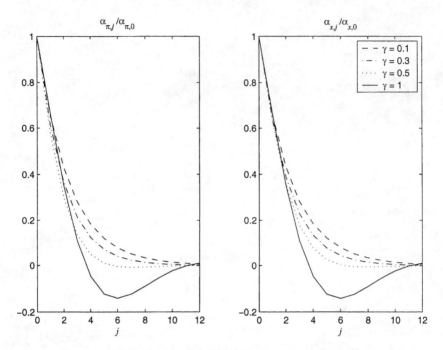

Fig. 3.5   Relative weights on forecasts at different horizons in the optimal criterion (28)

the future *less* positive. At least for low values of γ (in which case the weights are all nonnegative), this makes the optimal target criterion *less* forward looking.

For higher values of γ, increases in γ do increase the absolute value of the weights on forecasts for dates one to two years in the future (these become more negative). But even in this case, the existence of inflation inertia does not justify the kind of response to longer-horizon forecasts that is typical of inflation-targeting central banks. An increase in the forecast level of inflation and/or the output gap during the second year of a bank's current projection should justify a *loosening* of current policy, in the sense of a policy intended to *raise* projected inflation and/or the output gap in the next few quarters. This is because in the model with large γ, welfare losses result from inflation variation rather than high inflation as such; a forecast of higher inflation a year from now is then a reason to accept somewhat higher inflation in the nearer term than one otherwise would.

3.1.4   Wages and Prices Both Sticky

A number of studies have found that the joint dynamics of real and nominal variables are best explained by a model in which wages as well as prices are sticky (e.g., Amato and Laubach 2003; Christiano, Eichenbaum, and

Evans 2001; Smets and Wouters, 2002; Altig et al., 2002; and Woodford, 2003, chap. 3). This is often modeled in the way suggested by Erceg, Henderson, and Levin (2000), with monopolistic competition among the suppliers of different types of labor, and staggered wage setting analogous to the Calvo (1983) model of price setting. The structural equations of the supply side of this model can be written in the form

(29) $$\pi_t = \kappa_p(x_t + u_t) + \xi_p(w_t - w_t^n) + \beta E_t \pi_{t+1},$$

(30) $$\pi_t^w = \kappa_w(x_t + u_t) + \xi_w(w_t^n - w_t) + \beta E_t \pi_{t+1}^w,$$

together with the identity

(31) $$w_t = w_{t-1} + \pi_t^w - \pi_t,$$

generalizing the single equation (1) for the flexible-wage model. Here π_t^w represents nominal wage inflation, w_t is the log real wage, w_t^n represents exogenous variation in the "natural real wage," and the coefficients $\xi_p, \xi_w, \kappa_p,$ κ_w are all positive. The coefficient ξ_p indicates the sensitivity of goods-price inflation to changes in the average gap between marginal cost and current prices; it is smaller the stickier are prices. Similarly, ξ_w indicates the sensitivity of wage inflation to changes in the average gap between households' "supply wage" (the marginal rate of substitution between labor supply and consumption) and current wages, and measures the degree to which wages are sticky.[23]

We note furthermore that $\kappa_p \equiv \xi_p \omega_p$ and $\kappa_w \equiv \xi_w(\omega_w + \sigma^{-1})$, where $\omega_p >$ 0 measures the elasticity of marginal cost with respect to the quantity supplied, at a given wage; $\omega_w > 0$ measures the elasticity of the supply wage with respect to quantity produced, holding fixed households' marginal utility of income; and $\sigma > 0$ is the same intertemporal elasticity of substitution as in equation (15). In the limit of perfectly flexible wages, ξ_w is unboundedly large, and equation (30) reduces to the contemporaneous relation $w_t - w_t^n = (\omega_w + \sigma^{-1})(x_t + u_t)$. Using this to substitute for w_t in equation (29), the latter relation then reduces to equation (1), where

(32) $$\kappa \equiv \xi_p(\omega_p + \omega_w + \sigma^{-1})$$

and the cost-push shock u_t has been rescaled.

Given the proposed microeconomic foundations for these relations, Erceg, Henderson, and Levin (2000) show that the appropriate welfare-theoretic stabilization objective is a discounted criterion of the form of equation (2), with a period loss function of the form

(33) $$L_t = \lambda_p \pi_t^2 + \lambda_w \pi_t^{w2} + \lambda_x(x_t - x^*)^2.$$

---

23. For further discussion of these coefficients, and explicit formulas for them in terms of the frequency of wage and price adjustment, see section 3.2 below.

Here the relative weights on the various stabilization objectives are given by

(34) $\lambda_p = \dfrac{\theta_p \xi_p^{-1}}{\theta_p \xi_p^{-1} + \theta_w \phi^{-1} \xi_w^{-1}} > 0, \qquad \lambda_w = \dfrac{\theta_w \phi^{-1} \xi_w^{-1}}{\theta_p \xi_p^{-1} + \theta_w \phi^{-1} \xi_w^{-1}} > 0,$

(35) $$\lambda_x = \lambda_p \frac{\kappa}{\theta_p} > 0,$$

as functions of the underlying model parameters. Note that we have normalized the weights so that $\lambda_p + \lambda_w = 1$, and that equation (35) generalizes the previous expression (4) for the flexible-wage case.

Here we again abstract from the motives for interest rate stabilization discussed in the previous section. As a result, we need not specify the demand side of the model. We then wish to consider policies that minimize the criterion defined by equations (2) and (33), subject to the constraints (29)–(31).

The Lagrangian method illustrated above now yields a system of first-order conditions

(36) $$\lambda_p \pi_t + \varphi_{pt} - \varphi_{p,t-1} + \upsilon_t = 0,$$

(37) $$\lambda_w \pi_t^w + \varphi_{wt} - \varphi_{w,t-1} - \upsilon_t = 0,$$

(38) $$\lambda_x (x_t - x^*) - \kappa_p \varphi_{pt} - \kappa_w \varphi_{wt} = 0,$$

(39) $$\upsilon_t = \xi_p \varphi_{pt} - \xi_w \varphi_{wt} + \beta E_t \upsilon_{t+1},$$

where $\varphi_{pt}, \varphi_{wt}, \upsilon_t$ are the Lagrange multipliers associated with constraints (29), (30), and (31) respectively. We can again use three of the equations to eliminate the three Lagrange multipliers, obtaining a target criterion of the form

(40) $(\kappa_w - \kappa_p) \pi_t^{\text{asym}} + (\xi_p + \xi_w) q_t$

$\qquad + (\kappa_w - \kappa_p)\{ E_t[\beta q_{t+1} - q_t] - E_{t-1}[\beta q_t - q_{t-1}] \} = 0,$

where

$$\pi_t^{\text{asym}} \equiv \lambda_p \xi_p \pi_t - \lambda_w \xi_w \pi_t^w$$

is a measure of the asymmetry between price and wage inflation,

$$\pi_t^{\text{sym}} \equiv \frac{\lambda_p \kappa_p \pi_t + \lambda_w \kappa_w \pi_t^w}{\lambda_p \kappa_p + \lambda_w \kappa_w}$$

is a (weighted) average of the rates of price and wage inflation, and

(41) $$q_t \equiv (\lambda_p \kappa_p + \lambda_w \kappa_w) \left[\pi_t^{\text{sym}} + \frac{\lambda_x}{\lambda_p \kappa_p + \lambda_w \kappa_w} (x_t - x_{t-1}) \right].$$

In the special case that $\kappa_w = \kappa_p = \kappa > 0$, which empirical studies such as that of Amato and Laubach (2003) find to be not far from the truth,[24] the optimal target criterion (40) reduces simply to $q_t = 0$, or

$$(42) \qquad \pi_t^{\text{sym}} + \phi(x_t - x_{t-1}) = 0,$$

with $\phi = \lambda_x/\kappa$ as in section 3.1.1.[25] More generally, the optimal target criterion is more complex, and slightly more forward looking (as a result of the inertia in the real-wage dynamics when both wages and prices are sticky[26]). But it still takes the form of an output-adjusted inflation target, involving the projected paths of both price and wage inflation; and since all terms except the first one in equation (40) are equal to zero under a commitment to ensure that $q_t = 0$ at all times, the target criterion (42) continues to provide a fairly good approximation to optimal policy even when κ_w is not exactly equal to κ_p.

This is of the same form as the optimal target criterion (8) for the case in which only prices are sticky, with the exception that the index of goods price inflation π_t is now replaced by an index π_t^{sym} that takes account of both price and wage inflation. Of course, the weight that should be placed on wages in the inflation target depends on the relative weight on wage stabilization in the loss function (33). If one assumes a "traditional" stabilization objective of the form of equation (3), so that $\lambda_w = 0$, then equation (42) is again identical to equation (8). However, one can show that expected utility maximization corresponds to minimization of a discounted loss criterion in which the relative weight on wage-inflation stabilization depends on the relative stickiness of wages and prices, as discussed by Erceg, Henderson, and Levin (2000).[27]

3.1.5   Habit Persistence

In the simple models thus far, the intertemporal IS relation (15) implies that aggregate demand is determined as a purely forward-looking function of the expected path of real interest rates and exogenous disturbances. Many empirical models of the monetary transmission mechanism instead

---

24. See the discussion in Woodford (2003, chap. 3). In this case, the structural equations (29)–(30) imply that the real wage will be unaffected by monetary policy, instead evolving as a function of the real disturbances alone. Empirical studies often find that the estimated response of the real wage to an identified monetary policy shock is quite weak, and not significantly different from zero. Indeed, it is not significantly different from zero in our own analysis in section 3.2, although the point estimates for the impulse response function suggest that wages are not as sticky as prices.

25. Here we assume a normalization of the loss function weights in equation (33) in which $\lambda_p + \lambda_w = 1$, corresponding to the normalization in equation (3).

26. This only affects the optimal target criterion, of course, to the extent that the evolution of the real wage is endogenous, which requires that $\kappa_w \neq \kappa_p$.

27. See also Woodford (2003, chap. 6), which modifies the derivation of Erceg, Henderson, and Levin to take account of the discounting of utility.

imply that the current level of aggregate real expenditure should depend positively on the recent past level of expenditure, so that aggregate demand should change only gradually even in the case of an abrupt change in the path of interest rates. A simple way of introducing this is to assume that private expenditure exhibits "habit persistence" of the sort assumed in the case of consumption expenditure by authors such as Fuhrer (2000), Edge (2000), Christiano, Eichenbaum, and Evans (2001), Smets and Wouters (2002), and Altig et al. (2002).

Here, as in the models above, we model all interest-sensitive private expenditure as if it were nondurable consumption; that is, we abstract from the effects of variations in private expenditure on the evolution of productive capacity.[28] Hence, we assume habit persistence in the level of aggregate private expenditure, and not solely in consumption, as in the models of Amato and Laubach (2001) and Boivin and Giannoni (2003). This might seem odd, given that we do not really interpret the C_t in our model as referring mainly to consumption expenditure. But quantitative models that treat consumption and investment spending separately often find that the dynamics of investment spending are also best captured by specifications of adjustment costs that imply inertia in the rate of investment spending (e.g., Edge 2000; Christiano, Eichenbaum, and Evans 2001; Altig et al. 2002; Basu and Kimball 2002). The "habit persistence" assumed here should be understood as a proxy for adjustment costs in investment expenditure of that sort, and not solely (or even primarily) as a description of household preferences with regard to personal consumption.[29]

Following Boivin and Giannoni (2003), let us suppose that the utility flow of any household h in period t depends not only on its real expenditure C_t^h in that period, but also on that household's level of expenditure in the previous period.[30] Specifically, we assume that the utility flow from expenditure is given by a function of the form

$$u(C_t^h - \eta C_{t-1}^h; \xi_t),$$

where ξ_t is a vector of exogenous taste shocks, $u(\cdot; \xi)$ is an increasing, concave function for each value of the exogenous disturbances, and $0 \leq \eta \leq 1$ measures the degree of habit persistence. (Our previous model corresponds to the limiting case $\eta = 0$ of this one.) The household's budget constraint remains as before.

In this extension of our model, the marginal utility for the representative household of additional real income in period t is no longer equal to the marginal utility of consumption in that period, but rather to

---

28. See McCallum and Nelson (1999) and Woodford (2003, chap. 4) for further discussion of this simplification.

29. For further discussion, see Woodford (2003, chap. 5, sec. 1.2).

30. Note that the consumption "habit" is assumed here to depend on the household's own past level of expenditure and not on that of other households.

(43) $\lambda_t = u_c(C_t - \eta C_{t-1}; \xi_t) - \beta\eta E_t[u_c(C_{t+1} - \eta C_t; \xi_{t+1})].$

The marginal utility of income in different periods continues to be linked to the expected return on financial assets in the usual way, so that equilibrium requires that

(44) $$\lambda_t = \beta E_t\left[\lambda_{t+1}(1 + i_t)\frac{P_t}{P_{t+1}}\right].$$

Using equation (43) to substitute for λ in equation (44), we obtain a generalization of the usual Euler equation for the intertemporal allocation of aggregate expenditure given expected rates of return.

Log-linearization of this Euler equation yields a generalization of our previous IS relation (15), of the form

(45) $$\tilde{x}_t = E_t\tilde{x}_{t+1} - \varphi^{-1}(i_t - E_t\pi_{t+1} - r_t^n),$$

where

$$\tilde{x}_t \equiv (x_t - \eta x_{t-1}) - \beta\eta E_t(x_{t+1} - \eta x_t),$$

$$\varphi^{-1} \equiv (1 - \beta\eta)\sigma > 0,$$

and $\sigma \equiv -u_c/(\overline{Y}u_{cc})$ as before. Here x_t is again the log gap between actual output and the flexible-price equilibrium level of output in the absence of markup fluctuations, and r_t^n is again the flexible-price equilibrium real interest rate in the absence of markup fluctuations—that is, the real interest rate associated with an equilibrium in which $x_t = 0$ at all times. Note that when $\eta = 0$, φ reduces to σ^{-1}, $\tilde{x}_t$ reduces to x_t, and equation (45) reduces to equation (15). In the general case, the log marginal utility of real income is negatively related to $\tilde{x}_t$, rather than to x_t, which is why $\tilde{x}_t$ appears in the generalized IS relation (45).

This modification of preferences changes the form of the aggregate-supply relation (1) as well. (For simplicity, we here consider only the case of a model with flexible wages and Calvo pricing.) In the derivation of equation (1), we have assumed that the log marginal utility of real income (which affects real supply costs owing to its effect on real wage demands) can be replaced by a linear function of x_t, but just as in the case of the IS relation, this now must be written as a linear function of $\tilde{x}_t$ instead. We then obtain an aggregate-supply relation of the form

(46) $$\pi_t = \xi_p(\omega x_t + \varphi\tilde{x}_t) + \beta E_t\pi_{t+1} + u_t,$$

where $\xi_p > 0$ is the same coefficient as in equation (29) and $\omega \equiv \omega_p + \omega_w > 0$. The relation can equivalently be rewritten in the form

(47) $$\pi_t = \kappa[(x_t - \delta x_{t-1}) - \beta\delta E_t(x_{t+1} - \delta x_t)] + \beta E_t\pi_{t+1} + u_t,$$

where $0 \le \delta \le \eta$ is the smaller root of the quadratic equation

(48) $$\eta\varphi(1 + \beta\delta^2) = [\omega + \varphi(1 + \beta\eta^2)]\delta,$$

and[31]

(49) $$\kappa \equiv \frac{\xi_p \eta \varphi}{\delta} > 0.$$

Again taking a second-order Taylor series expansion of the expected utility of the representative household,[32] we again obtain a discounted criterion of the form of equation (2), but now with a period loss function of the form

(50) $$L_t = \pi_t^2 + \lambda(x_t - \delta x_{t-1} - \hat{x}^*)^2,$$

generalizing equation (3). Here λ is again defined as in equation (4), the parameters κ, δ are the same as in the aggregate-supply relation (47), and the size of $\hat{x}^* > 0$ depends once more on both the degree of market power and the size of tax distortions. As in the analysis of Amato and Laubach (2001), habit persistence implies that the period loss function should depend on the lagged output gap as well as the present gap. However, we note that both the inflationary pressures indicated in equation (47) and the deadweight losses measured by equation (50) depend on the quasi-differenced output gap $x_t - \delta x_{t-1}$, where δ is the smaller root of equation (48). And while δ is an increasing function of η, it may be much smaller than it; if ω is large relative to φ, then δ may be quite small even in the presence of substantial habit persistence. This is the case that our estimates below suggest is empirically realistic: while the best empirical fit is obtained for the extreme value $\eta = 1$, the implied value of δ is only 0.14.

An optimal target criterion is easily derived, even in the presence of habit persistence, in the case that there are no transactions frictions, nor any other grounds for an interest rate stabilization objective. In this case an optimal policy seeks to minimize the discounted sum of losses in equation (50) subject to the sequence of constraints in equation (47). The same Lagrangian method as above yields first-order conditions

(51) $$\pi_t + \varphi_t - \varphi_{t-1} = 0,$$

(52) $$\lambda(x_t - \delta x_{t-1} - \hat{x}^*) - \kappa\varphi_t + \delta\kappa\varphi_{t-1} = 0,$$

generalizing equations (6) and (7). An optimal target criterion is again obtained by eliminating the Lagrange multiplier. In the case that $\delta < 1$, as is necessarily true (even in the extreme case where $\eta = 1$) given $\omega > 0$, equa-

---

31. In the limiting case in which $\eta = 0$, $\delta = 0$, while δ/η approaches the well-defined limit $\varphi(\omega + \varphi)$, so that $\kappa = \xi_p(\omega + \varphi) = \xi_p(\omega + \sigma^{-1})$. Thus in this limit equation (47) reduces to equation (1), where κ is defined as in equation (32).

32. For details of the calculation, see the derivation in the appendix for the full model, incorporating habit persistence, that is introduced in section 3.2.

tion (52) implies that a time-invariant way of identifying the Lagrange multiplier is

$$\varphi_t = \frac{\lambda}{\kappa}(x_t - x^*),$$

where $x^* \equiv \hat{x}^*/(1 - \delta)$. Substituting this into equation (51), we obtain

(53) $$\pi_t + \frac{\lambda_x}{\kappa}(x_t - x_{t-1}) = 0.$$

Thus the optimal target criterion is exactly the same as in our baseline model and is unaffected by the estimated value of η. The estimated degree of habit persistence does matter for the central bank's judgment about which inflation or output paths are feasible, and also about the interest rate path that will be necessary in order to achieve them. But it has no consequences for the target criterion that should be used to judge whether a given inflation or output projection is acceptable.

The degree of habit persistence does matter for the optimal target criterion in the case of an interest rate stabilization objective. Suppose that the loss function (50) is generalized to the form

(54) $$L_t = \pi_t^2 + \lambda_x(x_t - \delta x_{t-1} - \hat{x}^*)^2 + \lambda_i(i_t - i^*)^2,$$

where $\lambda_i > 0$ for any of the reasons discussed in section 3.1.3. In this case the relevant constraints on possible equilibrium paths of the target variables include both equations (45) and (47) each period. In the resulting system of first-order conditions, equations (16) and (18) are again exactly as in section 3.1.3, but equation (17) generalizes to

(55) $$\lambda_x E_t[(1 - \beta\delta L^{-1})^{-1}(1 - \delta L)(x_t - x^*)]$$
$$+ E_t[B(L)\varphi_{1,t+1}] - \kappa E_t[(1 - \beta\delta L^{-1})^{-1}(1 - \delta L)\varphi_{2t}] = 0,$$

where

$$B(L) \equiv (1 - \beta^{-1}L)(1 - \eta L)(L - \beta\eta).$$

Using two of these relations to eliminate the Lagrange multipliers from the other, we obtain a target criterion of the form

(56) $$(1 - \delta L)[\phi_\pi \pi_t + \phi_x(x_t - x_{t-1})] =$$
$$(1 - L)E_t[(1 - \beta\delta L^{-1})^{-1}B(L)i_{t+1}] - \frac{\kappa}{\beta\varphi}(1 - \delta L)(i_{t-1} - i^*),$$

generalizing equation (19), where the definitions of ϕ_π and ϕ_x are as in equation (20) but with φ replacing σ^{-1} in the previous expressions. Here we see that the presence of habit persistence introduces additional dynamics into the form of the optimal target criterion. Nonetheless, it is interesting to note that once again the optimal target criterion involves only the rate of change of the output gap, rather than its absolute level, even when the utility-based stabilization objective instead indicates a concern to stabilize the value of $x_t - \delta x_{t-1}$.

3.2   A Small Quantitative Model of the U.S. Economy

We now turn to the question of the likely quantitative importance of the various considerations discussed in section 3.1 in the actual conduct of monetary policy. In order to do this, we first estimate the numerical parameters of a model that, while still very stylized, is intended to capture important features of the monetary transmission mechanism in the U.S. economy. We present an updated version of the analysis in Rotemberg and Woodford (1997), incorporating a number of additional complications—habit persistence, wage stickiness, and inflation inertia—that have been argued in the subsequent empirical literature to afford important improvements in the realism of this sort of optimizing model of the transmission mechanism, as discussed in section 3.1. The model that we use is similar to the one estimated by Boivin and Giannoni (2003), extended to allow for sticky wages.

Our approach to estimation of the model parameters follows the lines proposed in Rotemberg and Woodford (1997) and also used in Boivin and Giannoni (2003). First, we estimate an unconstrained vector autoregression (VAR) model of a small number of U.S. aggregate time series. This VAR is used (along with weak identifying assumptions) both to identify the coefficients of the Federal Reserve's reaction function in the historical period, and to estimate the impulse responses of our variables to an identified monetary policy shock under that historical policy. In a second step, we develop a simple optimizing model that can replicate the effects of identified monetary policy shocks, as implied by the VAR. We estimate the structural parameters of the model by minimizing the weighted distance between the estimated VAR impulse responses to a monetary policy shock and the model's predicted responses to the same shock. We are then able to recover the historical sequence of structural disturbances and to estimate a law of motion for them, which we use for certain exercises in section 3.3. However, for purposes of the sort of characterization of optimal policy offered here (as opposed to those proposed by Rotemberg and Woodford [1997, 1999]), our conclusions about the character of the historical disturbance processes are much less important than our conclusions about the coefficients of the structural relations that relate the endogenous variables to one another.

In a third step, discussed in section 3.3, we derive a welfare-theoretic loss function for the evaluation of alternative monetary policy rules, by computing a second-order approximation to the expected utility of the representative household in our model. We then proceed along the lines of Giannoni and Woodford (2002a,b) to derive a robustly optimal inflation-targeting rule for monetary policy.

3.2.1   The Effects of Monetary Disturbances

Here we briefly present the VAR that we use to estimate the actual monetary policy rule as well as the effects of monetary policy disturbances. We assume that the recent U.S. monetary policy can be described by the following feedback rule for the federal funds rate

$$
(57) \quad i_t = \bar{\imath} + \sum_{k=1}^{n_i} \phi_{ik}(i_{t-k} - \bar{\imath}) + \sum_{k=0}^{n_w} \phi_{wk}\hat{w}_{t-k} + \sum_{k=0}^{n_\pi} \phi_{\pi k}(\pi_{t-k} - \bar{\pi})
$$
$$
+ \sum_{k=0}^{n_y} \phi_{yk}\hat{Y}_{t-k} + \varepsilon_t,
$$

where i_t is the federal funds rate in period t, π_t denotes the rate of inflation between periods $t - 1$ and t, $\hat{w}_t$ is the deviation of the log real wage from trend at date t, $\hat{Y}_t$ is the deviation of log real GDP from trend, and $\bar{\imath}, \bar{\pi}$ are long-run average values of the respective variables.[33] The disturbances ε_t represent monetary policy "shocks" and are assumed to be serially uncorrelated. Estimated policy rules often omit real wages, but we include them in equation (57) for generality; the VAR that we use below to estimate impulse responses is then completely unrestricted (except as to number of lags).

To identify the monetary policy shocks and estimate the coefficients in equation (57) we assume as in the studies of Bernanke and Blinder (1992), Rotemberg and Woodford (1997), Bernanke and Mihov (1998), and Christiano, Eichenbaum, and Evans (2001), among others, that a monetary policy shock at date t has no effect on inflation, output, or the real wage in that period. It follows that equation (57) can be estimated by ordinary least squares (OLS) and that the residuals of the estimated equation will represent a historical sequence of monetary policy shocks.

We model the dynamics of the vector $\mathbf{Z}_t = [i_t, \hat{w}_{t+1}, \pi_{t+1}, \hat{Y}_{t+1}]'$ by a structural VAR of with three lags. This can then be written in companion form as

$$
(58) \quad\quad\quad\quad T\overline{\mathbf{Z}}_t = \mathbf{a} + A\overline{\mathbf{Z}}_{t-1} + \bar{e}_t,
$$

where $\overline{\mathbf{Z}}_t \equiv [\mathbf{Z}_t', \mathbf{Z}_{t-1}', \mathbf{Z}_{t-2}']'$ and T is a lower triangular matrix with ones on the diagonal and nonzero off-diagonal elements only in the first four rows, the first four rows of the vector $\mathbf{a}$ contain constants, and A contains estimated coefficients from the VAR in the first four rows and an identity ma-

---

33. Specifically, $\hat{Y}_t$ is the log of real GDP minus a linear trend. Inflation is computed as the quarterly growth of the GDP deflator (chain-type), annualized. The interest rate i_t is the quarterly average of the federal funds rate, annualized. The real wage is the log of wages and salaries in the compensation of employees published by the Bureau of Economic Analysis, divided by the GDP deflator; a linear trend is then subtracted from the log real wage to obtain $\hat{w}_t$.

Table 3.2   Estimated monetary policy rule (1980:1–2002:2)

	Estimates
ϕ_{i1}	0.572
	(0.104)
ϕ_{i2}	−0.085
	(0.127)
ϕ_{i3}	0.192
	(0.090)
ϕ_{w0}	0.365
	(0.202)
ϕ_{w1}	−0.008
	(0.302)
ϕ_{w2}	−0.406
	(0.191)
$\phi_{\pi 0}$	0.071
	(0.098)
$\phi_{\pi 1}$	0.146
	(0.115)
$\phi_{\pi 2}$	0.472
	(0.115)
ϕ_{y0}	0.333
	(0.176)
ϕ_{y1}	−0.038
	(0.241)
ϕ_{y2}	−0.118
	(0.169)
R^2	0.956
DW	2.033

Note: Standard errors are in parentheses.

trix in the lower rows. The first row of the estimated system (58) corresponds to the estimated monetary policy rule (57).

To estimate the VAR, we consider quarterly U.S. data on the sample period 1980:1–2002:2. As in Rotemberg and Woodford (1997) and Amato and Laubach (2003), we begin the sample in the first quarter of 1980 because several empirical studies have identified a significant change in monetary policy around that period (see, e.g., Clarida, Galí, and Gertler 2000; Boivin 2003; Boivin and Giannoni 2003; Cogley and Sargent 2001, 2002).[34]

Table 3.2 reports the coefficients of the estimated policy rule. While these coefficients are difficult to interpret as such, we note that the estimated rule

34. Some studies suggest that monetary policy has changed again around the mid-1980s. However, Boivin and Giannoni (2003), following the approach proposed by Bernanke, Boivin, and Eliasz (2004), show that impulse response functions to monetary policy disturbances in a factor-augmented VAR are similar to the ones reported here, when estimated on both the 1980–2002 and 1984–2002 sample periods.

implies that the interest rate would eventually increase by 2.14 percentage points in the long run, in response to a 1 percentage point permanent increase in inflation, and that it would increase by 0.55 percentage point in response to a 1 percent permanent increase in output. These are similar long-run response coefficients to those obtained by authors such as Taylor (1993, 1999), Judd and Rudebusch (1998), and Clarida, Galí, and Gertler (2000). The estimated real-wage response coefficients at different lags are close to cancelling; the estimated reaction function is quite similar to one in which the central bank responds only to the rate of real-wage growth rather than to the level of real wages. The response to real wage growth is strongly positive, indicating that increases in wages lead to a stronger and more immediate increase in nominal interest rates than do increases in prices of the same magnitude. While wages are not often included as an explanatory variable in estimated federal reaction functions, our results here suggest that wage growth is also an important explanatory variable.

Figure 3.6 shows the estimated impulse response functions of output, the real wage, inflation, and the interest rate. Here the dashed lines indicate 90 percent confidence intervals, obtained using Kilian's (1998) bootstrap procedure. Because of our identifying assumption, output, inflation, and

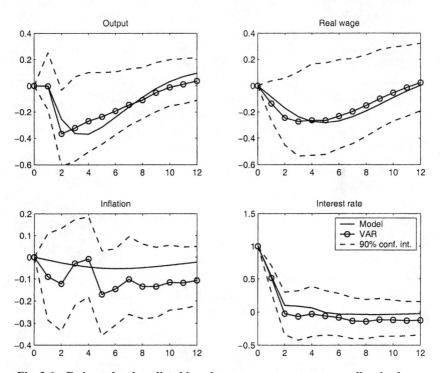

Fig. 3.6   Estimated and predicted impulse responses to a monetary policy shock

the real wage remain unchanged in the period of the shock. In the quarter following the shock, output still barely moves, while inflation and the real wage start declining. Output falls substantially in the second quarter after the shock and then returns progressively to its initial level. In contrast, inflation and the real wage both reach their lowest levels only five quarters after the shock.

3.2.2   A Quantitative Model of the Transmission Mechanism

We now describe a simple optimizing model that we use to explain the effects of monetary policy on output, inflation, the real wage, and interest rates. While the model is still very stylized, it contains several ingredients that allow it to replicate important features of the impulse response functions estimated using our VAR. We assume that there exists a continuum of households indexed by h and distributed uniformly on the [0, 1] interval. Each household h seeks, at date t, to maximize a lifetime expected utility of the form

$$(59) \qquad E_t \left\{ \sum_{T=t}^{\infty} \beta^{T-t} [u(C_T^h - \eta C_{T-1}^h; \xi_T) - \upsilon(H_T^h; \xi_T)] \right\},$$

where $\beta \in (0, 1)$ is the household's discount factor (assumed to be equal for each household), C_t^h is a Dixit and Stiglitz (1977) index of the household's consumption of each of the differentiated goods supplied at time t, P_t is the corresponding price index, and H_t^h is the amount of labor (of type h) that household h supplies at date t. Here we assume that each household specializes in the supply of one type of labor and that each type of labor is supplied by an equal number of households. The parameter $0 \leq \eta \leq 1$ represents the degree of habit formation, as in section 3.1.5. The stationary vector ξ_t represents exogenous disturbances to preferences. For each value of ξ, the function $u(\cdot; \xi)$ is assumed to be increasing and concave, while $\upsilon(\cdot; \xi)$ is increasing and convex.

Optimal Consumption Decisions

While the optimal allocation consumption at date t is chosen at date t and is determined by the usual Dixit-Stiglitz demand relations, we assume as in Rotemberg and Woodford (1997) that households must choose their index of consumption C_t^h at date $t - 2$. Equivalently, we assume that C_t^h is determined at the beginning of period $t - 1$ (i.e., before the monetary policy shock in $t - 1$ is known). We assume that financial markets are complete so that risks are efficiently shared. As a result, each household faces a single intertemporal budget constraint.

The first-order conditions for optimal timing of consumption by the representative household require that

(60) $E_{t-2}\{u_c(C_t - \eta C_{t-1}; \xi_t) - \beta \eta u_c(C_{t+1} - \eta C_t; \xi_{t+1})\} = E_{t-2}\{\lambda_t\}$

for each date $t \geq 2$ and each possible state at date $t - 2$, generalizing equation (43), where again λ_t denotes the representative household's marginal utility of real income at date t.[35] The marginal utilities of income at different dates and in different states must furthermore satisfy

(61) $$\frac{\lambda_t Q_{t,T}}{P_t} = \frac{\beta^{T-t}\lambda_T}{P_T}$$

for any possible state at any date $T \geq t$, where $Q_{t,T}$ is the stochastic discount factor that defines the market valuations of alternative random income streams. Noting that the riskless one-period nominal interest rate i_t must satisfy $(1 + i_t)^{-1} = E_t Q_{t,t+1}$, we obtain once again equation (44) as an equilibrium relation linking interest rates to the evolution of the marginal utility of income. We assume furthermore that the government purchases a Dixit-Stiglitz aggregate G_t, determined at date $t - 1$, of all goods in the economy, so that aggregate demand Y_t satisfies $Y_t = C_t + G_t$.

We make use of log-linear approximations of these relationships about a steady state equilibrium in which there is no inflation. Log-linearization of equation (44) yields

(62) $$\hat{\lambda}_t = E_t[\hat{\lambda}_{t+1} + \hat{\imath}_t - \pi_{t+1}],$$

where $\hat{\lambda}_t \equiv \log(\lambda_t/\bar{\lambda})$, $\hat{\imath}_t \equiv \log(1 + i_t/1 + \bar{\imath})$, and $\pi_t \equiv \log(P_t/P_{t-1})$. Using this, and log-linearizing equation (60), we obtain an equation of the form

(63) $$\tilde{Y}_t = \tilde{g}_t + E_{t-2}(\tilde{Y}_{t+1} - \tilde{g}_{t+1}) - \varphi^{-1}E_{t-2}(\hat{\imath}_t - \pi_{t+1})$$
$$- \beta\eta(E_t\hat{Y}_{t+1} - E_{t-2}\hat{Y}_{t+1}),$$

where φ is defined as in equation (45), $\tilde{g}_t$ represents exogenous demand shocks including preference shocks and fluctuations in government expenditure, and $\tilde{Y}_t \equiv (\hat{Y}_t - \eta\hat{Y}_{t-1}) - \beta\eta(E_t\hat{Y}_{t+1} - \eta\hat{Y}_t)$, $\hat{Y}_t \equiv \log(Y_t/\bar{Y})$. Equation (63) generalizes the intertemporal IS relation (45).

For our welfare analysis, it is convenient to rewrite this relation in terms of the output gap

$$x_t \equiv \hat{Y}_t - \hat{Y}_t^n,$$

where $\hat{Y}_t^n$ indicates log deviations in the natural rate of output, by which we mean the equilibrium level of output under flexible prices, flexible wages, constant levels of distorting taxes and of desired markups in the labor and

35. Because the problem is the same for each household h (the initial level of wealth is assumed to differ for any two households in a way that compensates for any difference in their expected labor incomes, and complete financial markets allow complete pooling of idiosyncratic labor income risk thereafter), all households choose identical state-contingent plans for consumption.

product markets, and with wages, prices, and spending decisions predetermined by only one period.[36]

Expressing equation (63) in terms of the output gap, we obtain

$$(64) \qquad E_{t-2}\tilde{x}_t = E_{t-2}\tilde{x}_{t+1} - \varphi^{-1}E_{t-2}(\hat{\imath}_t - \pi_{t+1} - \hat{r}_t^n),$$

where $\tilde{x}_t \equiv (x_t - \eta x_{t-1}) - \beta\eta(E_t x_{t+1} - \eta x_t)$ and $\hat{r}_t^n$ is an exogenous variable that represents the deviation from steady state of the natural rate of interest—that is, the equilibrium real rate of interest in the ideal situation defined above. The actual output gap relates furthermore to the expected output gap through

$$(65) \qquad \tilde{x}_t = E_{t-2}\tilde{x}_t + (\tilde{g}_t - \tilde{Y}_t^n) - E_{t-2}(\tilde{g}_t - \tilde{Y}_t^n)$$
$$- \beta\eta[E_t(x_{t+1} + \hat{Y}_{t+1}^n) - E_{t-2}(x_{t+1} + \hat{Y}_{t+1}^n)].$$

Optimal Wage and Price Setting

As in Erceg, Henderson, and Levin (2000), Amato and Laubach (2003), and Woodford (2003, chap. 3), we assume that there is a single economy-wide labor market. The producers of all goods hire the same kinds of labor and face the same wages. Firm z is a monopolistic supplier of good z, which it produces according to the production function

$$y_t(z) = A_t F(\overline{K}, H_t(z)) \equiv A_t f(H_t(z)),$$

where $f' > 0, f'' < 0$, the variable $A_t > 0$ is an exogenous technology factor, and capital is assumed to be fixed so that labor is the only variable input. The labor used to produce each good z is a constant elasticity of substitution (CES) aggregate

$$(66) \qquad H_t(z) \equiv \left[\int_0^1 H_t^h(z)^{(\theta_w-1)/\theta_w} dh \right]^{\theta_w/(\theta_w-1)}$$

for some elasticity of substitution $\theta_w > 1$, where $H_t^h(z)$ is the labor of type h that is hired to produce a given good z. The demand for labor of type h by firm z is again of the Dixit-Stiglitz form $H_t^h(z) = H_t(z)(w_t(h)/W_t)^{-\theta_w}$, where $w_t(h)$ is the nominal wage of labor of type h, and W_t is a wage index.

---

36. Up to the log-linear approximation used in our estimation of the model, $\hat{Y}_t^n$ defined in this way is just the conditional expectation at date $t-1$ of the log deviation of the equilibrium level of output when none of these variables are predetermined at all. Because wages and prices are both predetermined a period in advance, it is only the component of the output gap that is forecastable a period in advance that matters in any event for these equations. It is similarly only the variation in the forecastable component of the output gap that need be considered when evaluating welfare under alternative policies, since the unforecastable component of the output gap (defined relative to a concept of the "natural rate" that is not predetermined) would in any event be both exogenous and uncorrelated with the forecastable component. It then simplifies notation to *define* the output gap as the gap between actual output and the *forecastable component* of the natural rate. In this way, x_t becomes a predetermined state variable.

We assume that the wage for each type of labor is set by the supplier of that type, who is in a situation of monopolistic competition and who is ready to supply as many hours of work as may be demanded at that wage. We assume that each wage is reoptimized with a fixed probability $1 - \alpha_w$ each period. However, as in Woodford (2003, chap. 3), if a wage is not reoptimized, it is adjusted according to the indexation rule

$$\log w_t(h) = \log w_{t-1}(h) + \gamma_w \pi_{t-1}$$

for some $0 \leq \gamma_w \leq 1$. A worker of type h who chooses a new wage $w_t(h)$ at date t expects to have a wage $w_t(h)(P_{T-1}/P_{t-1})^{\gamma_w}$ with probability α_w^{T-t} at any date $T \geq t$. We assume furthermore that the newly chosen wage that comes into effect in period t, w_t^*, is chosen at the end of period $t - 1$ (i.e., on the basis of information available at date $t - 1$).

As shown in Woodford (2003, chap. 3), this setup yields as a first-order approximation, a wage inflation equation of the form

$$(67) \quad (\pi_t^w - \gamma_w \pi_{t-1}) = \xi_w E_{t-1}(\omega_w x_t + \varphi \tilde{x}_t) - \xi_w E_{t-1} \mu_t + \xi_w E_{t-1}(w_t^n - w_t)$$
$$+ \beta E_{t-1}(\pi_{t+1}^w - \gamma_w \pi_t),$$

generalizing equation (30) to allow for indexation to the lagged price index, habit persistence, and predetermined wage-setting and spending decisions. Here π_t^w denotes nominal wage inflation, w_t is the log real wage, and w_t^n is an exogenous variable representing the log of the "natural real wage"— that is, the equilibrium real wage when both wages and prices are fully flexible and consumption is not predetermined. The parameter

$$(68) \quad \xi_w \equiv \frac{(1 - \alpha_w)(1 - \alpha_w \beta)}{\alpha_w(1 + \nu\theta_w)} > 0$$

is a function of the degree of wage stickiness, the elasticity of marginal disutility of labor supply at the steady state, $\nu \equiv v_{hh}\overline{H}/v_h$, and the elasticity of substitution for different types of labor. The parameter $\omega_w \equiv \nu\phi > 0$ indicates the degree to which higher economic activity increases workers' desired wages for given prices. (Once again, $\phi \equiv f/(\overline{H}f') > 0$ is the elasticity of the required labor input with respect to output variations.)

Integrating equation (67) forward, we note that nominal wages at date t tend to increase (above lag inflation) when expected future positive output gaps are positive and when real wages are expected to be below their natural rate. The variable $\mu_t \equiv \hat{\lambda}_t - \varphi E_t(\tilde{g}_t - \tilde{Y}_t)$, which corresponds to the discrepancy between the (log) marginal utility of real income and the (log) marginal utility of consumption, satisfies

$$(69) \quad E_{t-1}\mu_t = E_{t-1}(\hat{\imath}_t - \pi_{t+1}) + \varphi E_{t-1}[(\tilde{g}_{t+1} - \tilde{g}_t) - (\tilde{Y}_{t+1} - \tilde{Y}_t)].$$

The presence of $E_{t-1}\mu_t$ in equation (67) indicates a moderating effect on nominal wage inflation of an expectation at date $t - 1$ of real rates of return between t and $t + 1$ that are higher then those that were anticipated at $t - 2$—that is, at the time that consumption decisions were made for period t. In fact, unexpectedly high real rates of return increase the value of income in period t and thus lower average wage demands.

Similarly, we assume that the suppliers of goods are in monopolistic competition and that each price is reoptimized with a fixed probability $1 - \alpha_p$ each period. However, as in Woodford (2003, chap. 3), if a price is not reoptimized, it is again adjusted according to the indexation rule

$$\log p_t(z) = \log p_{t-1}(z) + \gamma_p \pi_{t-1}$$

for some $0 \leq \gamma_p \leq 1$. Again following the development in Woodford (2003, chap. 3), we can show that optimal pricing decisions result in an aggregate supply relation of the form

$$(70) \quad \pi_t - \gamma_p \pi_{t-1} = \xi_p \omega_p E_{t-1} x_t + \xi_p E_{t-1}(w_t - w_t^n) + \beta E_{t-1}(\pi_{t+1} - \gamma_p \pi_t),$$

generalizing equation (29) to allow for indexation to the lagged price index and predetermination of pricing decisions. Here

$$(71) \quad \xi_p \equiv \frac{(1 - \alpha_p)(1 - \alpha_p \beta)}{\alpha_p(1 + \omega_p \theta_p)} > 0$$

is a function of the degree of price stickiness, the elasticity of substitution for different goods $\theta_p > 1$, and $\omega_p > 0$ which measures the degree to which higher economic activity increases producers' prices for given wages. Integrating equation (70) forward, we observe that inflation tends to increase (relative to past inflation) when agents expect positive future output gaps and/or expect that real wages will be above their natural rate.

Finally, the evolution of the real wage is linked to wage inflation and price inflation through the identity (31). Our structural model can then be summarized by a demand block of equations (64) and (65) and a supply block consisting of equations (67)–(70) together with equation (31). We finally close the model with an equation such as (57) that characterizes the behavior of the central bank. These equations then allow us to determine the equilibrium evolution of the variables of interest: π_t, π_t^w, x_t, $\hat{\imath}_t$, and w_t.

3.2.3 Estimated Parameter Values

We turn now to the estimation of the parameters of the structural model just set out. As mentioned above, we are looking for structural parameters that allow the model to describe as well as possible the transmission mechanism of monetary policy. Following Rotemberg and Woodford (1997), we choose the structural parameters that minimize the distance between the estimated VAR impulse response functions to a monetary policy shock and the model's predicted response to the same shock. As discussed in Amato and Laubach (2003), Boivin and Giannoni (2003), and Christiano, Eichenbaum, and Evans (2001), this is quite generally an estimation procedure that allows for statistical inference on the model's estimated structural parameters. Note also that the model that we consider is constructed so as to be consistent with the identifying assumptions made for the estimation of the VAR impulse response functions. In particular, both the model and the VAR have the feature that output, inflation, and the real wage respond to unexpected changes in the interest rate with a lag of at least one quarter. In addition, to the extent that we estimate the structural parameters on the basis of impulse responses to monetary shocks, our estimation method has the advantage of providing parameter estimates that are robust to potential misspecifications of the remaining shock processes in the model. This is because in order to compute the impulse responses we do not need to specify the stochastic process of the shocks such as $\tilde{g}_t$, $\hat{Y}_t^n$, $\hat{\omega}_t^n$, $\hat{r}_t^n$.

As in the studies mentioned above, we set $\beta = 0.99$ so that β^{-1} corresponds approximately to the steady-state real gross rate of interest, which is about 1.01. In addition, we calibrate the elasticity $\omega_p \equiv -f''\overline{Y}/(f')^2$ to 0.33 as in Rotemberg and Woodford (1997). This would be implied by a Cobb-Douglas production function in which the elasticity of output with respect to hours is 0.75. Such a production function would yield a share of wages in the value of output of $0.75/\mu_p$ where $\mu_p \equiv \theta_p/(\theta_p - 1)$ is the average gross markup of prices over marginal cost due to market power in the goods markets. (This means a labor share of 0.74, given the markup estimate reported below.)

We estimate the vector of the remaining seven structural parameters $\upsilon \equiv [\varphi, \eta, \xi_p, \xi_w, \omega_w, \gamma_p, \gamma_w]'$ by minimizing the distance

$$D(\upsilon) = [\mathbf{f}_V - \mathbf{f}_M(\hat{\phi}, \upsilon)]'\mathbf{V}[\mathbf{f}_V - \mathbf{f}_M(\hat{\phi}, \upsilon)]$$

where $\mathbf{f}_V$ is a vector that contains the VAR-based impulse response functions of output, inflation, the real wage, and the interest rate to an unexpected monetary policy shock, and $\mathbf{f}_M(\hat{\phi}, \upsilon)$ is vector containing the corresponding impulse response functions generated by the model, for a given vector of structural parameters υ and the vector of policy rule coefficients $\hat{\phi}$ estimated in section 3.2.1. In fact, to the extent that we estimated consistently the policy rule of the form of equation (57) when estimating the VAR, we do not need to estimate again its coefficients at this stage. The positive definite weighting matrix $\mathbf{V}$ that we use in our estimation is a diagonal matrix, with the inverse of the variance of the estimate of each impulse response as the corresponding diagonal element. This allows us to weight the various impulse responses according to the degrees of precision with which each is estimated.[37] We estimate the structural parameters by match-

---

37. The use of the inverse of the complete variance-covariance matrix of impulse responses as a weighting matrix would be more attractive, as this would yield efficient estimates. But such a weighting matrix appears to hinder the stability of the minimization algorithm. The matrix that we propose has the advantage of reducing the weight on responses about which we are less sure, in addition to making our results independent of the units in which we happen to measure the various series.

ing model-based and VAR-based impulse responses of output, inflation, the real wage, and the interest rate on quarters zero to 12 following an unexpected monetary policy shock. For consistency with the model, we constrain all parameters to be positive and impose an upper bound at 1 on η, γ_p and γ_w.

The estimated parameter values are shown in table 3.3. Standard errors are in parentheses; an asterisk next to the reported standard error indicates that the standard error may not be reliable as the estimated parameter lies on the boundary of the allowed parameter space. Here we report estimates

Table 3.3   **Estimated structural parameters for the baseline case and restricted models**

	Baseline	No habit $\eta = 0$	No indexation $\gamma_p = \gamma_w = 0$	Flexible wages $\xi_w^{-1} = 0$
Estimated parameters				
$\psi \equiv \dfrac{\varphi^{-1}}{1 + \beta\eta^2}$	0.6715 (0.3330)	4.3144 (1.0253)	1.5026 (0.4221)	0.7564 (0.2823)
$\tilde{\eta} \equiv \dfrac{\eta}{1 + \beta\eta^2}$	0.5025 (0.0692)*	0 (—)	0.5025 (0.1121)*	0.5025 (0.0515)*
ξ_p	0.0020 (0.0009)	0.0015 (0.0005)	0.0072 (0.0039)	0.0015 (0.0012)
ξ_w	0.0042 (0.1343)	0.0042 (0.0612)	0.0046 (0.0310)	$+\infty$ (—)
ω_w	19.551 (595.1)	19.991 (269.5)	19.072 (122.6)	0.5642 (0.1253)
γ_p	1 (0.3800)*	1 (0.3484)*	0 (—)	1 (0.5374)*
γ_w	1 (10.908)*	1 (12.4613)*	0 (—)	0 (—)
Implied parameters				
φ	0.7483	0.2318	0.3344	0.6643
η	1	0	1	1
$\kappa_p \equiv \xi_p \omega_p$	0.0007	0.0005	0.0024	0.0004
$\omega \equiv \omega_p + \omega_w$	19.884	20.325	19.405	0.8975
$\nu \equiv \dfrac{\omega_w}{\phi}$	14.663	14.994	14.304	0.4231
$\mu_p \equiv \dfrac{\theta_p}{\theta_p - 1}$	1.0039	1.0027	1.0143	1.0029
$\mu_w \equiv \dfrac{\theta_w}{\theta_w - 1}$	1.5361	1.5731	1.6113	n.a.
Objective function value	13.110	15.886	16.580	18.837
Wald test (p-value)	n.a.	0.000	0.000	0.000

Notes: Standard errors in parentheses. Asterisk indicates that standard error lies on boundary of parameter space and may be unreliable. n.a. = not available.

Table 3.4   **Additional calibrated parameter values**

	Value
β	0.99
ω_p	1/3
α_p	2/3
α_w	2/3
ϕ	4/3

(with standard errors) for parameters $\psi \equiv \varphi^{-1}/(1 + \beta\eta^2)$ and $\tilde{\eta} \equiv \eta/(1 + \beta\eta^2)$ rather than for φ and η, as the former nonlinear transformations of these parameters can be estimated with greater precision.[38] The values of φ and η implied by these estimates are shown in the second part of the table, along with the implied values for other model parameters, making use of the calibrated parameter values reported in table 3.4.

While some of the model parameters cannot be estimated at all precisely, as indicated by the large standard errors, our estimation results are consistent with our theory insofar as we estimate positive values for the response coefficients φ, ξ_p, ξ_w, and ω_w in our structural equations. The values of ψ, measuring the interest sensitivity of aggregate expenditure,[39] and ξ_p, measuring the response of inflation to the real-wage gap, are both significantly positive, although the estimates of ξ_w and ω_w are instead quite imprecise. We also find small enough standard errors on the estimates of $\tilde{\eta}$, measuring the degree of habit persistence, and γ_p, measuring the degree of indexation of prices, to allow some inference about the magnitudes of those parameters (for example, both are significantly positive), while the value of γ_w is very imprecisely estimated. In general, the parameters of our wage equation are poorly estimated, while both our IS relation and our inflation equation are much better estimated.[40]

The second through fourth columns of table 3.3 report the corresponding estimates, using the same method, of various restricted versions of our model. In column (2), we assume zero habit persistence, as in the models of Rotemberg and Woodford (1997) and Amato and Laubach (2003); in column (3), no inflation inertia (i.e., no indexation of either wages or prices to

---

38. Here ψ is estimated to be significantly positive, implying a significant effect of interest rates on aggregate demand, while the corresponding standard error for an estimate of φ would not allow us to judge that the latter coefficient was significantly positive. Similarly, $\tilde{\eta}$ is estimated to be significantly positive, implying habit persistence, even though the corresponding standard error for the estimated value of η is much greater than one.

39. The parameter ψ is called by Boivin and Giannoni (2003) the "pseudo-elasticity of substitution"; it measures the elasticity of expected output growth with respect to changes in the expected real rate of return, holding constant output growth in other periods.

40. A Matlab program, available on our webpages, allows readers to check the extent to which our numerical characterization of optimal policy would be different in the case of alternative parameter values.

the lagged price index), also like the two models just mentioned; and in column (4), flexible wages, as in the models of Rotemberg and Woodford (1997) and Boivin and Giannoni (2003).[41] In each case, the objective function value is reported for the restricted model—that is, the weighted distance $D(\upsilon)$ defined above. The p-values reported on the last line refer to Wald tests of the null hypothesis that the restricted model is correct. In the last column, the parameter γ_w is set to zero as it is not identified in the case of flexible wages. We see that each of these restrictions assumed in earlier studies can be individually rejected, although the assumption of flexible wages is the one that would reduce the model's ability to fit the estimated impulse response functions to the greatest extent.[42] Hence each of the complications introduced here is found to be justified: in this respect, our findings agree with those of Christiano, Eichenbaum, and Evans (2001), Altig et al. (2002), and Smets and Wouters (2002), although these authors all also introduce additional complications in order to explain a larger set of time series.

It is striking to note that the model fits the impulse responses best when the degree of inflation indexing (γ_p) and wage indexing to inflation (γ_w) reach their upper bound at 1. This corresponds to the assumption of full wage and price indexing made by Christiano, Eichenbaum, and Evans (2001). A value of $\gamma_p = 1$ is also roughly consistent with the weight on lagged inflation in the "hybrid" aggregate-supply relation estimated by Galí and Gertler (1999) and results in an aggregate-supply relation quite similar to the one proposed by Fuhrer and Moore (1995).

The relatively small values of ξ_p and ξ_w suggest that changes in the output gap and the real wage gap have a relatively small impact on price and wage inflation. However, the estimated value of ω_w suggests that a 1 percent increase in economic activity increases workers' desired wages by nearly 20 percent, for given prices. The estimate of φ corresponds to an elasticity of intertemporal substitution (adjusted by the degree of habit formation) of $\varphi^{-1} = 1.3$. While authors such as Fuhrer (2000) and Christiano, Eichenbaum, and Evans (2001), among others, have estimated substantial degrees of habit formation, our estimate lies at the upper bound of 1.

While the estimated parameter values for η, γ_p, and γ_w are significantly smaller when we estimate our model using impulse response functions over

41. The restricted model considered in column (4) corresponds to the model of Boivin and Giannoni, although their method of estimation is different in that they do not fit estimated impulse responses of the real wage along with those of the other three variables, and their model assumes a different form of monetary policy rule. They also calibrate the value of $\omega = \omega_w + \omega_p$, rather than only specifying a calibrated value for ω_p, and they assume a value of ω much smaller than our estimate. Nonetheless, the estimates for the other parameters reported in column (4) are similar to those obtained by Boivin and Giannoni, providing further evidence regarding the robustness of our conclusions here.

42. The implied impulse response functions are compared to the estimated ones in the case of each of the restricted models in the technical appendix to this paper (see http://www.nber .org/data-appendix/giannoni04/).

the first six quarters or less following the monetary shock, all parameter estimates are very similar to those reported in table 3.2, when we use impulse response functions that extend longer than six quarters.[43] This suggests that in order to adequately capture the degree of persistence in the endogenous variables we need to perform our estimation using long enough responses.

Assuming, as in Rotemberg and Woodford (1997), that $\alpha_p = 2/3$,[44] and similarly that $\alpha_w = 2/3$, together with the other parameter values already mentioned above, it is possible to infer the elasticities of substitution θ_p and θ_w from the estimated values of ξ_p and ξ_w respectively, using the definitions (68) and (71). The values of these elasticities implied by our estimates imply a gross markup of prices over marginal costs of only $\mu_p = \theta_p/(\theta_p - 1) = 1.004$ in the goods market, but a considerably higher gross markup of $\mu_w = \theta_w/(\theta_w - 1) = 1.54$ in the labor market. The fact that these implied markups are greater than 1 (i.e., that the implied elasticities of substitution are greater than 1) again indicates consistency of our estimates with our theoretical model.

Finally, our estimated value for ω_w can be used to derive an implied value of v, the inverse of the Frisch elasticity of labor supply, using the definition $\omega_w = v\phi$ and a calibrated value for ϕ, the inverse of the elasticity of output with respect to the labor input. (The calibrated value of ϕ reported in table 3.4 is implied by the same Cobb-Douglas production function as was used to calibrate the value of ω_p, discussed above.) The Frisch elasticity of labor supply implied by our estimates is thus only on the order of 0.07, less than one one-hundredth of the value implied by the estimates of Rotemberg and Woodford (1997), and much more consistent with many estimates in the empirical literature on labor supply. Because of the assumption of sticky wages, our model is able to account for nonnegligible effects of a monetary disturbance on real activity without assuming that voluntary labor supply (under flexible wages) would be highly elastic. (Note that under the restriction of flexible wages, we would obtain estimates implying an elasticity of labor supply greater than 2.) While the values of these implied parameters do not matter for the ability of our model to fit the estimated impulse responses, they do matter for our welfare analysis below.

The solid lines in figure 3.6 indicate the impulse response functions generated by our estimated model. Overall, it appears that the model is able to replicate quite well the impulse responses estimated by the VAR (circled lines), and the impulse responses remain consistently within the 90 percent confidence intervals. The model replicates in particular the estimated hump-shaped output and real-wage responses. While it does not capture

---

43. Again, see the technical appendix for details.

44. Rotemberg and Woodford (1997) base this calibration on Blinder's (1994) survey evidence that prices are maintained constant for an average of nine months, so that $1/(1 - \alpha_p)$ equals three quarters.

the oscillations in the inflation response implied by the VAR, we note that this response is estimated quite imprecisely.

3.3   Optimal Policy for the Estimated Model

Now that we have an estimated structural model that allows us to account for at least certain aspects of the responses of output and of price and wage inflation to monetary disturbances, we turn to the characterization of optimal policy in the context of this model.

3.3.1   A Welfare-Theoretic Stabilization Objective

An advantage of having developed a structural model based on optimizing behavior is that it provides a natural objective for the monetary policy, namely, maximization of the expected utility of the representative household. Following the method of Woodford (2003, chap. 6), we can express a second-order Taylor series approximation to this objective as a quadratic function of (wage and price) inflation, the output gap, and the nominal interest rate. The way in which various aspects of our model specification affect the appropriate welfare-theoretic stabilization objective in simple cases has already been discussed in section 3.1.

In the technical appendix to this paper (see www.nber.org/data/), we show that for the model developed in section 3.2, the corresponding welfare-theoretic loss function, abstracting from any grounds for concern with interest-rate stabilization, is given by

$$(72) \quad E_0 \sum_{t=0}^{\infty} \beta^t [\lambda_p (\pi_t - \gamma_p \pi_{t-1})^2 + \lambda_w (\pi_t^w - \gamma_w \pi_{t-1})^2 + \lambda_x (x_t - \delta x_{t-1} - \hat{x}^*)^2].$$

In this expression, the weights λ_p, $\lambda_w > 0$ are again defined as in equation (34); the weight $\lambda_x > 0$ is again defined as in equation (35), but using now the definition (49) for κ in the latter expression; the coefficient $0 \leq \delta \leq \eta$ is again the smaller root of equation (48); and $\hat{x}^* > 0$ is the same function of the microeconomic distortions affecting the efficiency of the steady-state output level as in equation (50).

This result combines features of several simpler cases discussed in section 3.1. Deadweight loss depends on squared deviations of both price and wage inflation (separately) from the rates that would minimize relative-price and relative-wage distortions, given that both wages and prices are sticky, as in equation (33). Due to the indexation of both prices and wages to a lagged price index, the loss-minimizing rates of wage and price inflation each period are determined by the lagged inflation rate and the indexation coefficients in each case, as in equation (10). And finally, the presence of habit persistence implies that deadweight loss depends not on squared deviations of the output gap from a constant value but rather on squared deviations of $x_t - \delta x_{t-1}$ from a constant value, as in equation (50).

Table 3.5   Loss-function coefficients implied by our parameter estimates

λ_p	λ_w	$16\lambda_x$	δ
0.9960	0.0040	0.0026	0.035

The numerical coefficients of the welfare-theoretic loss function implied by the estimated parameter values reported in table 3.3 (for the baseline model) are reported in table 3.5. Interestingly, our estimated model implies that it is optimal for the central bank to put a much larger weight on the stabilization of goods-price inflation than on the stabilization of wage inflation or of the output gap. Moreover, despite the fact that we estimate a very high degree of habit formation, which implies that household utility depends on the rate of change of real expenditure rather than its level, the central bank's loss function does not involve the variability of the change in the output gap. Instead, it involves the variability of the level of the output gap relative to a small fraction of the lagged output gap.

These conclusions depend, of course, on our parameter estimates. It may seem surprising that the weight on wage inflation stabilization is so small, given that our estimates do not imply that wages are substantially more flexible than prices (for example, ξ_w is larger than ξ_p, but not by a large factor). The conclusion that λ_w is nonetheless very much smaller than λ_p reflects mainly the fact that our estimates imply a value for θ_p that is much larger than $\phi^{-1}\theta_w$. This in turn results from the fact that the estimated value of ω_w is much larger than the calibrated value of ω_p.[45] Because it is not plausible to assume a technology for which ω_p could be nearly as large as the estimated value of ω_w, we are led to assume a value of θ_p substantially larger than $\phi^{-1}\theta_w$. The result that λ_p greatly exceeds λ_w then follows, using equation (34).

The conclusion that λ_x is small follows, using equation (35), from the small value of κ_p and large value of θ_p implied by our parameter estimates. Since $\kappa_p \equiv \xi_p\omega_p$ and the value of θ_p is inferred from the value of ξ_p using equation (71), both of these conclusions depend crucially on the small estimated value for ξ_p. Essentially, the observed insensitivity of inflation to variations in output allows us to infer underlying microeconomic parameters that imply that variations in the output gap cause relatively modest distortions—this is the only way, in the context of our other assumptions, to explain the fact that inflation is not more strongly affected (i.e., that the Phillips curve is not steeper).

45. If ξ_p and ξ_w were assigned equal values, then under our assumption of equal values for α_p and α_w, (68) and (71) would imply equal values for $\omega_p\theta_p$ and $\omega_w\phi^{-1}\theta_w$. (Here we recall that $\omega_w \equiv \nu\phi$.) The implied value of θ_p is then larger than $\phi^{-1}\omega_w$ by exactly the same factor as ω_w is larger than ω_p. In fact, our estimated value for ξ_p is smaller than our estimate for ξ_w, and this further increases the relative size of the implied value of θ_p.

Finally, the conclusion that δ is small (despite the fact that $\eta = 1$) follows, using equation (48), from the fact that the value of ω implied by our estimates is large relative to the estimated value of φ. Essentially, the observed sensitivity of wages to variations in real activity on the one hand (implying a large value for ω_w) and the sensitivity of aggregate expenditure to interest rate changes on the other (implying that φ cannot be too large) indicate preferences under which variations in the level of real activity will create greater distortions than variations in the rate of growth of real activity. Even when $\eta = 1$, the level of output matters to the representative household because of its consequences for the amount that the household must work; if the marginal disutility of output supply increases sharply with the level of real activity (as implied by a large value of ω), it will still be relatively more important to stabilize the level of real activity than its rate of change.[46]

3.3.2   An Optimal Target Criterion

The method illustrated in section 3.1 for the derivation of optimal target criteria under alternative assumptions can be applied as well in the case of the empirical model described in section 3.2. Details of the relevant calculations are included in the technical appendix to this paper; here we simply present the quantitative implications of our estimated parameter values.

A first observation about optimal policy in our estimated model follows from the fact that wages, prices, and output are all predetermined for one quarter or longer in the model. It follows that in our structural equations, any variations in the short-term nominal interest rate i_t that are not forecastable a quarter earlier are irrelevant to the determination of wages, prices, or output. Hence this component of interest rate policy cannot be relevant for welfare except through its consequences for the expected discounted value of the $\lambda_i(i_t - i^*)^2$ term that must be added to equation (72) if we take account of monetary frictions. But this last term is obviously minimized (in the case of any $\lambda_i > 0$) by a policy under which the nominal interest rate is completely forecastable a quarter in advance. Even in the case that $\lambda_i = 0$, there is no harm to any other stabilization objectives in eliminating unforecastable interest rate variations; and so it seems plausible to assumes at least some tiny concern with interest rate stabilization, so that it is optimal to suppress such variation in the interest rate.[47]

---

46. As discussed in section 3.1.3 above, it may also be desirable to reduce the variability of nominal interest rates; in this case, the loss function (72) should include an additional term, proportional to the squared deviation of the nominal interest rate from an optimal value. We do not take up this possible extension of the analysis here.

47. For example, even if we assume that monetary frictions are of negligible quantitative significance, we may reasonably assume that the economy is a "cashless limiting economy" of the kind discussed in Woodford (1998), rather than a genuinely cashless economy. In this case, there should in fact exist tiny monetary frictions that suffice to entail a preference for a completely forecastable nominal interest rate in the absence of any offsetting benefit from variations in response to current shocks.

Hence

(73)
$$i_t = E_{t-1} i_t$$

is a requirement for optimal policy. This can be understood to say that all interest rate changes should be signaled by the central well in advance of the date at which they take effect. The instrument that the central bank must adjust in period t in order to ensure that its period-t target criterion will be projected to be satisfied is then not the period-t interest rate i_t but rather the bank's precommitted value $E_t i_{t+1}$ for the level of short-term nominal interest rates in the following period.[48] We turn now to the property that the bank's projections regarding period-t endogenous variables should be made to satisfy through an appropriate commitment of this kind.

To simplify, we shall restrict attention to the case of a model in which $\gamma_p = \gamma_w = 1$, as assumed by Christiano, Eichenbaum, and Evans (2001), and as indicated by our estimates in section 3.2. In the appendix, we show that the first-order conditions for an optimal state-contingent evolution of the endogenous variables can be manipulated, after the fashion illustrated in section 3.1, to yield a characterization of optimal policy in terms of the projected paths of the target variables alone. However, in the present case, unlike the simpler ones discussed in section 3.1, the most convenient representation of these conditions is not in terms of a single target criterion, but two distinct ones. First of all, optimality requires that projections in any period t satisfy a condition of the form[49]

(74)
$$F_t(\pi_{+1}) + \phi_w[F_t(w_{+1}) - w_t] = \bar{\pi}_t.$$

Here for each of the variables $z = \pi, w$, the expression $F_t(z + 1)$ refers to a weighted average of forecasts of the variable z at various future horizons, conditional on information at date t,

(75)
$$F_t(z_{+1}) = \sum_{j=1}^{\infty} \alpha_{zj} E_t z_{t+j},$$

where the weights $\{\alpha_{zj}\}$ sum to one. Thus the coefficient ϕ_w is actually the sum of the weights on real-wage forecasts at different horizons j. We observe that the target criterion can be thought of as a wage-adjusted inflation target. In addition to the correction for the projected growth of real

48. See further discussion in Svensson and Woodford (chap. 2 in this volume).
49. The target criterion could equivalently be expressed in the form $\phi_p F_t(\pi_{+1}) + \phi_w F_t(\pi_{+1}^w) = \bar{\pi}_t$, in which case the target criterion would refer solely to projected inflation of different sorts (both price and wage inflation). This would be a representation analogous to the one given in section 3.1.4 above and would make clear that only the projected future paths of target variables (variables that enter the loss function) matter. We feel, however, that the representation proposed here allows a more convenient numerical summary of the content of the target criterion, by collecting the central bank's projections regarding the future level of nominal quantities in a single variable, the projected future price level.

wages in the future, the acceptable rate of projected future inflation also varies due to time variation in the target $\overline{\pi}_t$. Optimality further requires that $\overline{\pi}_t$ be a function only of information available at date $t-1$, and hence that

(76) $\overline{\pi}_t \equiv E_{t-1}[F_t(\pi_{+1}) + \phi_w(F_t(w_{+1}) - w_t)].$

In general, this optimal target will not be constant over time.

In addition to the above requirement (which amounts to the condition that the left-hand side of equation [74] be forecastable a quarter in advance), optimality also requires that projections at date t satisfy another condition as well, of the form

(77) $F_t^*(\pi_{+1}) + \phi_w^* F_t^*(w_{+1}) + \phi_x^* F_t^*(x_{+1}) = \pi_t^*,$

where the expressions $F_t^*(z_{+1})$ are again weighted averages of forecasts at different horizons (but with relative weights α_{zj}^* that may be different in this case), and π_t^* is another time-varying target value, once again a predetermined variable. In this case the criterion specifies a target for a wage- and output-adjusted inflation projection.[50]

$$\pi_t^* \equiv (1 - \theta_\pi^*)\pi^* + \theta_\pi^* F_{t-1}^1(\pi_{+1}) + \theta_w^* F_{t-1}^1(w_{+1}) + \theta_x^* F_{t-1}^1(x_{+1}),$$

where the expressions $F_t^1(z_{+1})$ are still other weighted averages of forecasts at different horizons, with relative weights α_{zj}^1 that again sum to one, and π^* is an arbitrary constant.[51] Here, as with equation (76), the optimal target value depends on the previous quarter's forecasts of the economy's subsequent evolution; this is a further example of the history dependence of optimal target criteria, already observed in simpler cases in section 3.1.

The optimal target criteria in equations (74)–(76) and (77)–(78) generalize, for the estimated model, the simple criterion in equation (13) obtained in the case of inflation inertia, $\gamma = 1$, flexible wage, no habit persistence and no delays. To make this comparison more apparent, and to get some intuition about the two optimal target criteria, it is useful to consider the special case in which wages are flexible. As we show in the technical appendix, the short-run optimal target criterion of equations (74)–(76) reduces in this case to

$$\pi_{t+1} = E_{t-1}\pi_{t+1}$$

---

50. As with equation (74), we could equivalently express this criterion in terms of a linear function of projections for price inflation, wage inflation, and the output gap.

51. Note that in the model considered here, as in section 3.1.2 when $\gamma = 1$, there is no welfare significance to any absolute inflation rate, only to changes in the rate of inflation and to wage growth relative to prices. There is therefore no particular inflation rate that could be justified as optimal from a timeless perspective. For purposes of comparison between historical policy and the optimal criterion, discussed below, we assume that steady-state inflation and the steady-state real wage are equal to the long-run values estimated (by the VAR) under historical policy.

so that the central bank needs make inflation fully predictable two periods in advance under optimal policy. The long-run optimal target criterion (77)–(78) reduces in turn to a criterion of the form

$$E_t[(\pi_{t+2} - \delta\pi_{t+1}) + \phi(x_{t+2} - \delta x_{t+1})] = (1 - \delta)\pi^*,$$

where δ is again the parameter that appears in the loss function and $\phi = \theta_p^{-1}$, i.e., the inverse of the elasticity of demand faced by the typical firm.

As in section 3.1.2, a commitment to ensure that equations (77) and (78) hold in each period $t \geq t_0$ for a particular value of the constant π^* is equivalent to a commitment to ensure that a first-differenced form of these equations holds in each period.[52] Such a first-differenced form would have the advantage that it could be expressed entirely in terms of projections of the *first differences* of the three variables—the inflation rate, the real wage, and the output gap—with no dependence on the *absolute levels* of any of the variables. The target criterion of equations (77) and (78), instead, has the advantage of being simpler, as it only involves a comparison of projections made in the current period with certain other projections in the previous period.

It may be wondered how we can specify optimal policy in terms of two distinct target criteria involving different linear combinations of projections, when the central bank has only one instrument at its disposal. The key to this is to observe that the target criterion specified by equations (74)–(76) restricts only the *surprise* components of the quarter t projections—that is, the way in which they may differ from the projections that were made in quarter $t - 1$ for the same variables. Hence it is only the *surprise* component of the central bank's interest-rate decision—the difference between the $E_t i_{t+1}$ announced in quarter t and $E_{t-1} i_{t+1}$—that can be determined by this criterion for optimal policy. The evolution of the (two-period-ahead) predetermined component of policy, $E_{t-2} i_t$, can instead be chosen so as to ensure that the second target criterion, specified by equations (77) and (78), is satisfied each period.

We may thus imagine the implementation of the optimal targeting rule to occur in the following way.[53] First, in each quarter t, the central bank intervenes in the money markets (through open-market operations, re-purchases, standing facilities in the interbank market for central-bank balances, etc.) so as to implement the interest rate target i_t announced in

---

52. We suppress the details of this alternative optimal targeting rule here. The first-differenced formulation is the one described in Woodford (2003, chap. 8). The calculations reported there are further explained in a note that is available on our web pages.

53. Because our empirical model is quarterly, it is simplest to discuss the policy process as if a policy decision is also made once per quarter, even though in reality most central banks reconsider their operating targets for overnight interest rates somewhat more frequently than this. Our discussion should not be taken to imply that it is optimal for the policy committee to meet only once per quarter; this would follow from our analysis only if (as in our model) all other markets were also open only once per quarter.

quarter $t - 1$. Second, as part of the quarter-t decision cycle, the bank must choose an operating target i_{t+1} to announce for the following quarter. This is chosen in order to imply a projected evolution of (wage and price) inflation from quarter $t + 1$ onward that satisfies the target criterion (74), where $\overline{\pi}_t$ is a target value that had been determined in quarter $t - 1$. Third, it is also necessary, as part of the quarter-t decision cycle, for the central bank to choose the target $\overline{\pi}_{t+1}$ for the following quarter. This is chosen so as to ensure that future policy will be conducted in a way that allows the bank to project (conditional on its current information) that the target criterion of equations (77) and (78) should be satisfied. In practice, this means that the central bank should use its model of the transmission mechanism to determine the future evolution of the economy under the assumption that equations (77) and (78) will hold in all future periods; this forecast then determines the target value $\overline{\pi}_{t+1}$ using equation (76).[54]

Algebraic expressions for each of the coefficients in the optimal target criteria, as functions of the underlying model parameters, are given in the appendix. Here we discuss only the numerical coefficients implied by our estimated parameter values. In the case of the short-term criterion (74), the coefficient ϕ_w is equal to 0.565.[55] Thus, if unexpected developments in quarter t are projected to imply a higher future level of real wages than had previously been anticipated, policy must ensure that projected future price inflation is correspondingly reduced. This is because of a desire to stabilize (nominal) wage inflation as well as price inflation, and under circumstances of expected real wage growth, inflation must be curbed in order for nominal wage growth to not be even higher.

The relative weights that this criterion places on projections at different future horizons are shown in figure 3.7. The two panels plot the coefficients $\alpha_{\pi j}$, α_{wj} respectively, as functions of the horizon j. Note that the quarter for which the projections receive greatest weight is one quarter in the future, in each case. However, while the real-wage projection that matters is primarily the projected growth in real wages between the present quarter and the next one, substantial weight is also placed on projected inflation farther in the future; in fact, the mean lead $\Sigma_j \alpha_{\pi j} j$ is between ten and eleven quarters in the future in the case of the inflation projection $F_t(\pi_{+1})$. Thus the short-run target criterion is a (time-varying) target for the average rate of inflation that is projected over the next several years, adjusted to take account of expected wage growth, mainly over the coming quarter. Roughly speaking, optimal policy requires the central bank to choose $E_t i_{t+1}$ in quarter t so

54. See Svensson and Woodford (chap. 2 in this volume) for further discussion of the sort of calculations involved in a forecast-targeting decision procedure.
55. Here and below, we present the coefficients for a target criterion where the inflation rate is measured in annualized percentage points, rather than as a quarterly rate of change as in the model of section 3.2. When the variables are defined as in the model, the coefficients multiplying the real-wage and output-gap terms are only one-quarter as large as those given here and below.

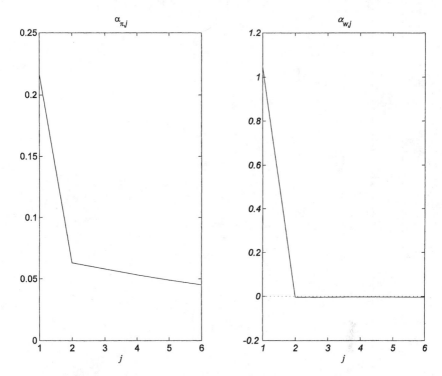

Fig. 3.7   Relative weights on projections at different horizons in the short-run target criterion (3.3)

Note: The horizontal axis indicates the horizon j in quarters.

as to head off any change in the projected average inflation rate over the next several years that is due to any developments not anticipated in quarter $t-1$ (and hence reflected in the current target $\overline{\pi}_{t-1}$). This is a criterion in the spirit of inflation-forecast targeting as currently practiced at central banks such as the Bank of England, except that projected wage growth matters as well as price inflation and the target shifts over time.

In the case of the long-term criterion (77), instead, the numerical coefficients of the target criterion are given by

$$\phi_w^* = 0.258, \qquad \phi_x^* = 0.135.$$

In this case, output-gap projections matter as well; a higher projected future output gap will require a reduction in the projected future rate of inflation, just as will a higher projected future real wage. The numerical size of the weight placed on the output-gap projection may appear modest; but as we shall see in the next section, the degree of variability of output-gap projections in practice are likely to make this a quite significant correction to the path of the target criterion.

The relative weights on forecasts at different horizons in this criterion

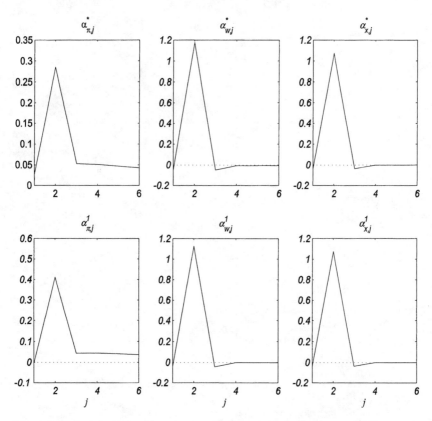

Fig. 3.8   Relative weights on projections at different horizons in the long-run target criterion

Note: Panels in the first row indicate the projections in equation (77), while the second row indicates the projections from the previous quarter that define the target value π_t^*.

are plotted in the panels in the first row of figure 3.8. We observe that in the case of this criterion, the projections that mainly matter are those for two quarters in the future; the criterion is nearly independent of projections regarding the quarter after the current one. Hence, it makes sense to think of this criterion as the one that should determine the policy that the central bank plans on in periods two or more quarters in the future (and hence its choice in quarter t of the target $\overline{\pi}_{t+1}$ to constrain its choice in the following period of $E_{t+1} i_{t+2}$), but not as a primary determinant of whether the bank's intended policy in period $t + 1$ is on track.

Finally, the coefficients of the rule (78) determining the target value for the long-term criterion are given by

$$\theta_\pi^* = 0.580, \qquad \theta_w^* = 0.252, \qquad \theta_x^* = 0.125.$$

The weights in the projections (conditional on information in the previous quarter) at various horizons are plotted in the second row of figure 3.8. Here too, it is primarily projections for two quarters in the future that matter in each case. Roughly speaking, then, the target value for the wage- and output-adjusted inflation projection two quarters in the future is high when a similar adjusted inflation projection (again for a time two quarters in the future) was high in the previous quarter.

Thus we find that forecasting exercises, in which the central bank projects the evolution of both inflation and real variables many years into the future under alternative hypothetical policies on its own part, play a central role in a natural approach to the implementation of optimal policy. A forecast of inflation several years into the future is required in each (quarterly) decision cycle in order to check whether the intended interest rate operating target for the following quarter is consistent with the criterion (74). In addition, the time-varying medium-term inflation target, $\bar{\pi}_t$ must be chosen each period on the basis of yet another forecasting exercise. While the long-run target criterion (77) primarily involves projections for a time only two quarters in the future, the choice of $\bar{\pi}_{t+1}$ requires that the central bank solve for a projected path of the economy in which criterion (77) is satisfied not only in the current period but in all future periods as well. Hence, this exercise as well requires the construction of projected paths for inflation and real variables extending many years into the future. The relevant paths, however, will not be constant–interest rate projections (of the kind currently published by the Bank of England) but rather projections of the economy's future evolution given how policy is expected to evolve. Indeed, the projections are used to select constraints upon the bank's own actions in future decision cycles (by choosing both the interest rate operating target $E_t i_{t+1}$ and the adjusted inflation target $\bar{\pi}_{t+1}$ in period t).

3.3.3 A Comparison with Actual U.S. Policy

An interesting question about this policy rule is the extent to which it would prescribe policy different from that which the Federal Reserve has actually pursued during our sample period. A simple way of considering this is to ask to what extent, under actual policy, projections of the evolution of inflation and output have satisfied the optimal target criteria stated above. Answering this question requires, of course, that we estimate what the projected future paths of the target variables should have been at various past dates. However, our VAR characterization of the data over our sample period provides one way of generating such projections. Here we propose to appraise how close actual policy has been to being optimal by asking to what extent projections based on the VAR would have satisfied the target criterion.

In our characterization of optimal policy above, there are actually three criteria that must be satisfied each period—one relating to the component

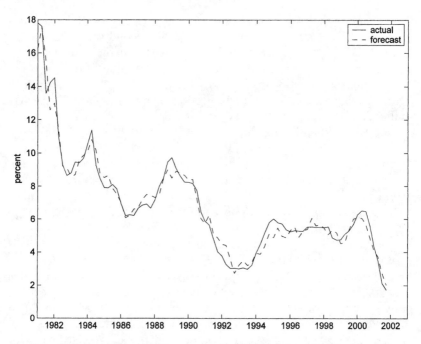

Fig. 3.9   Actual and forecastable variation in the U.S. federal funds rate

of interest rate policy that cannot be forecasted even a quarter in advance, one relating to the component of policy that is forecastable a quarter in advance but not earlier, and one relating to the component of policy that can be anticipated two quarters in advance. The first criterion, that the evolution of interest rates satisfy criterion (73) each period, is simplest to check, as long as we are willing to assume that our VAR forecasts fully capture public information in a given quarter. Figure 3.9 shows a plot of the actual (quarterly average) path of the federal funds rate over our sample period, together with the VAR forecast using the previous quarter's information set.[56] This allows a test of the degree to which condition (73) has been satisfied in practice. We find that under actual U.S. policy, variation in the U.S. federal funds rate has been largely predictable; the gap between the two series in figure 3.9 has a standard deviation of only 65 basis points.[57] This

56. Note that, here and below, the "quarter-t information set" is taken to include π_{t+1}, w_{t+1}, and $\hat{Y}_{t+1}$, as well as all variables dated t or earlier, on the ground that prices, wages, and output are all predetermined variables according to our model. See Rotemberg and Woodford (1997) for further discussion.

57. Of course, we are judging the forecastability of the funds rate using a VAR that has been fitted to this data set, rather than considering the out-of-sample forecasting ability of a regression model estimated using only data prior to the quarter for which the funds rate is being forecasted. We are also including variables in the quarter-t information set the values of which are not announced in quarter t (indeed, not even during quarter $t + 1$, although the

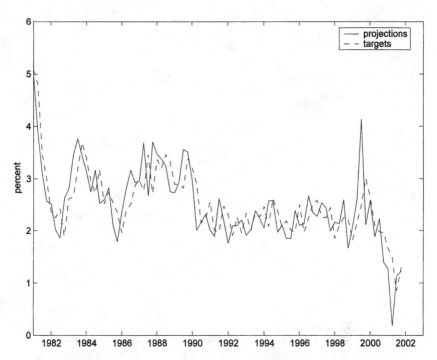

Fig. 3.10   Testing whether actual U.S. policy has satisfied the short-run target criterion: The adjusted inflation projection (74) compared with the optimal target given by equation (76)

means that the identified monetary policy shocks, according to the VAR analysis discussed in section 3.2, have been relatively small. This is what one should expect, in a period in which the conduct of monetary policy has been fairly sensible.

The next condition for optimality that we consider is the short-term target criterion (74)–(76). Figure 3.10 shows a plot of the historical path of the wage-adjusted inflation projection that is targeted under this criterion, using the VAR forecasts to form this projection each quarter, together with the path for the target value $\bar{\pi}_t$ given by equation (76), also using the VAR forecasts for the projections in the previous quarter. Figure 3.11 decomposes the variation in both the adjusted inflation projection (74) and the time-varying target $\bar{\pi}_t$ into the parts that are due to variation in the inflation projections (at various horizons) on the one hand and the parts that

measurements are made during that quarter), which also exaggerates the information actually available in quarter t. But it must also be recognized that decision makers have access to a great deal of information in quarter t that is not included in our data set and that might well allow better forecasting of the funds rate than is possible on the basis of only the variables included in our VAR.

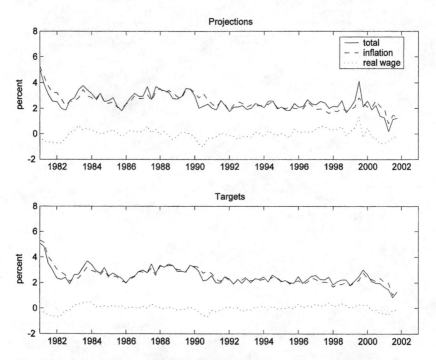

Fig. 3.11   Decomposition of the variation in the short-run target criterion into parts due to variation in inflation projections and real wage projections, respectively

are due to variation in the real-wage projections. We observe that a substantial part of the quarter-to-quarter variation in the adjusted inflation projection is in fact due, over this historical period, to variation in the real-wage projection,[58] although variation in the real-wage projection a quarter earlier appears to be less important as a source of variation in the optimal target value.

Once again, the data are fairly consistent with this criterion for optimal policy. While the wage-adjusted inflation projection has varied (according to the VAR) over a range of a few percentage points, these variations have been fairly forecastable based on the previous quarter's information set, as required by the target criterion. The gap between the projection and the target value has a standard deviation of only 48 basis points over this sample.

Of course, passing this test requires only that wage and price inflation, like the federal funds rate, be highly forecastable a quarter in advance. It may accordingly be felt that it is the inertial character of wage and price in-

58. We have not attempted to quantify the share since the two components are not orthogonal.

flation that is confirmed by figure 3.10, rather than something that depends much on monetary policy. It should also be noted that the "target" series plotted in the figure only indicates how the right-hand side of equation (76) has varied over the sample period, under actual U.S. monetary policy, rather than the way in which the target $\bar{\pi}_t$ *would have* evolved under optimal monetary policy, given that the inflation projections that determine this target would have been different under a different sort of monetary policy. This latter sort of exercise would require that we solve for the counterfactual equilibrium paths of the endogenous variables under optimal policy, given the historical sequence of exogenous shocks, as undertaken by Rotemberg and Woodford (1997). We do not attempt such an exercise here.

Testing the extent to which the historical data have satisfied the long-run target criterion (77)–(78) is more complicated, because it requires the construction of projections for the path of the output gap. The output gap is not directly observed, and our approach to the estimation of the model in section 3.2 does not require us to commit ourselves to an empirical proxy for the gap, despite the appearance of this variable in the model structural equations. In order to estimate the model parameters needed for our calculations thus far, we had only to be able to compute the predicted impulse responses of prices, wages, output, and interest rates to a monetary disturbance. For this purpose, we could rely on the fact that, according to our model, the output gap should equal $\hat{Y}_t$ (detrended log output) minus a term that is unaffected by monetary disturbances; there was no need to identify the time variation in that latter term. Yet in order to evaluate the long-run target criterion at each date, we need to be able to do so.

One possible approach is to use our estimated structural equations to infer the historical sequence of disturbances from the residuals of the structural equations, using VAR forecasts of the endogenous variables as proxies for the expectation terms in these equations, as do Rotemberg and Woodford (1997). This approach can be used, however, only under strong assumptions of debatable validity. The "natural rate of output" process that we are able to infer from the residuals of our structural equations corresponds to the equilibrium level of output under complete wage and price flexibility.[59] But this may or may not be the concept of exogenously given potential output that should be used to define the welfare-relevant "output gap" that appears in the loss function (72).

Under certain assumptions that are made precise in the appendix (and that have been tacitly maintained thus far in our exposition), the "output

---

59. To be precise, it corresponds to the component of this variable that is forecastable a quarter in advance. This is all that can be reconstructed from the paths of the endogenous variables, given that wages, prices, and output are all predetermined according to our model, but this is also what is relevant for the construction of the variable x_t that appears in our loss function (72) and, hence, the target criterion stated in the previous section.

gap" that appears in the structural equations (57) and (60) as a source of inflationary pressure—without any additional cost-push shock term of the kind routinely included in the models of section 3.1—is exactly the same variable as the distortion measure appearing in equation (72). Yet this need not be true in general; time variation in distorting taxes or in the degree of market power in either labor markets or goods markets, for example, will result in a time-varying wedge between the flexible-wage-and-price equilibrium level of output and the efficient level of output, with the result that the relevant output gap for the two purposes ceases to be the same.[60] We can allow for this extension of our framework by letting the gap between actual output and the flexible-wage-and-price equilibrium output be denoted $x_t + u_t$, as in equations (29)–(30) above, where x_t is the welfare-relevant output-gap concept (the variable that appears in the welfare-theoretic loss function), while u_t is a cost-push disturbance term.

In the case of the extended model, the method of Rotemberg and Woodford allows us to construct an empirical proxy for the evolution of the series $x_t + u_t$, as this is what appears in the wage- and price-setting equations. However, the projections that are required for checking whether the target criterion is satisfied are projections for x_t, the variable that appears in the loss function (72). Further assumptions must be made in order to infer what the projected variations in the welfare-relevant output gap should have been. These assumptions are not testable within the context of the model and the small set of time series used here.

One simple, though extreme, assumption, would be that the welfare-relevant concept of potential output is a smooth trend, so that cyclical variation in $\hat{Y}_t^n$ should be almost entirely attributed to transitory variation in the cost-push term u_t.[61] In this case, it should be more accurate to identify the welfare-relevant output gap with $\hat{Y}_t$, detrended output, than with the series $x_t + u_t$ inferred from the residuals of the structural equations. Under this assumption, we can construct our output-gap projections using the VAR alone, without any need to reconstruct disturbances using the equation residuals.

We first consider the conformity of historical policy with the optimal target criteria when detrended output is considered an adequate proxy for the output gap. In figure 3.12, we plot the historical series for the wage- and output-adjusted inflation projection that is targeted under the long-term criterion (77) over our sample period, using the VAR forecasts for inflation, the real wage, and detrended output, and the numerical weights given in section 3.3.2. (Since the constant π^* in equation [78] is arbitrary, we assume a long-run inflation target equal to 2.39 percent per annum, which

---

60. See Giannoni (2000) or Woodford (2003, chap. 6) for further discussion in the context of simpler models.

61. This view is implicit in the output-gap measures commonly used in the literature on empirical central-bank reaction functions.

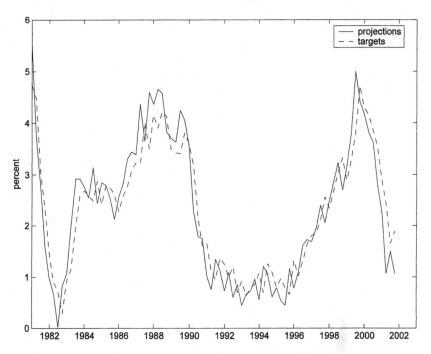

Fig. 3.12   Testing whether actual U.S. policy has satisfied the long-run target criterion: The adjusted inflation projection (77) compared with the optimal target given by equation (78)

corresponds to the long-run value average inflation rate under historical policy, as implied by our estimated VAR.) Figure 3.13 similarly decomposes both the projection and its optimal target value into their components due to variation over time in inflation projections, real-wage projections, and output projections. Note that when the output gap is measured in this way, the projected change in the output gap over a two-quarter horizon is modest enough that terms of this kind are not responsible for too much of the variation from quarter to quarter in either the adjusted inflation projection or in its optimal target value. Instead, the target criterion is largely a function of the inflation and real-wage projections (or alternatively, projected price and wage inflation).

This alternative (longer-run) adjusted inflation projection has also been relatively stable over our historical sample, and once again the gap between the target and the current projection has never been large; the standard deviation of target misses in the case of this criterion is only 52 basis points. However, target misses under this criterion have been somewhat persistent, with a quarterly autocorrelation of 0.19. Thus we can identify periods in which policy was consistently too loose or too tight for quarters at a time, according to this criterion, although federal policy never violated the cri-

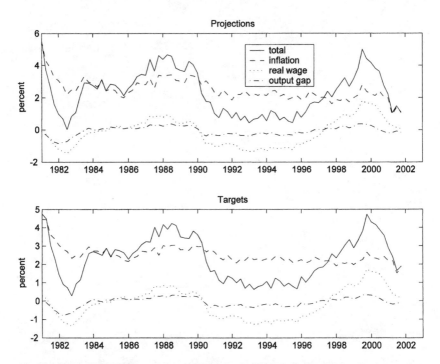

Fig. 3.13   Decomposition of the variation in the long-run target criterion into parts due to variation in inflation, real-wage, and output projections, respectively

terion to too great an extent. Figure 3.14 plots the extent to which the adjusted inflation projection exceeded the target in each quarter (the dashed line in the figure), together with a smoothed version of the same series that makes the average tendency of U.S. policy clearer.[62] One observes that policy was consistently too tight (the adjusted inflation projection was too low) under this criterion in the period 1981–82, too loose in much of the period 1983–89, a bit too tight again in the period 1990–95, somewhat too loose in the late 1990s, and finally again consistently too tight in the last nine quarters of our sample. However, in none of these periods did the adjusted inflation projection differ consistently from the inflation projection for several quarters by an amount greater than half a percentage point in either direction.

If, instead, we use the residuals from our structural equations to infer the evolution of the output gap, the plots corresponding to figures 3.12 and 3.13 instead look like those shown in figures 3.15 and 3.16. In this case, historical paths of both the adjusted inflation projection and its optimal tar-

---

62. In the figure, the solid line is a two-sided moving average of the dashed line, equal to 1/3 the discrepancy in that quarter, 2/9 of the discrepancy in both the preceding and following quarters, and 1/9 of the discrepancy both two quarters earlier and two quarters later.

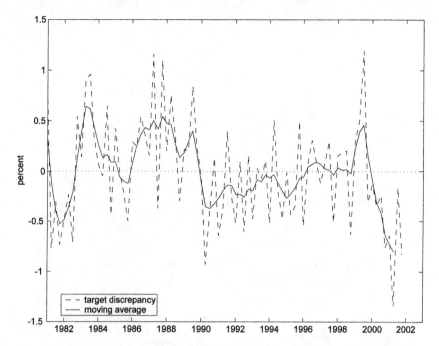

Fig. 3.14   The extent to which the adjusted inflation projection exceeded the optimal target at various times

Note: The dashed line shows the quarterly discrepancy, the solid line a moving average.

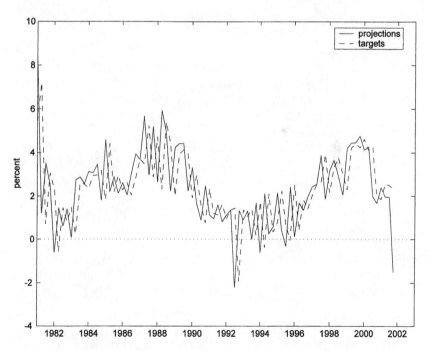

Fig. 3.15   Alternative version of figure 3.12, using equation residuals to infer the variation in the natural rate of output

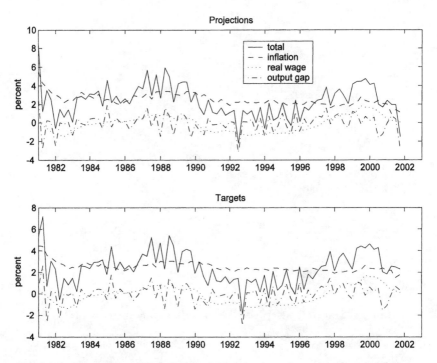

Fig. 3.16   Alternative version of figure 3.13, using equation residuals to infer the variation in the natural rate of output

get value are more volatile. The change is due to the greater (and much more transitory) volatility of the output gap process that is inferred in this manner. As shown in figure 3.16, in this case the quarter-to-quarter variation in projected growth of the output gap is an important factor resulting in variation in the adjusted inflation projection and in the target value. Of course, the high volatility of (and high-frequency variation in) this series may well suggest that it reflects mainly specification error in the structural equations of our wage-price block, rather than actual variation in the welfare-relevant output gap.[63]

In this case, the gap between the adjusted inflation projection and its optimal target value (plotted in figure 3.17) is also found to be fairly large in many individual quarters. The standard deviation of the discrepancy using this measure of the output gap is nearly 1.80 percentage points. However, the target misses are extremely transitory in this case; their autocorrelation is actually negative (−0.53), indicating that a target overshoot one quarter

63. The fact that our model does relatively poorly at matching the dynamics of the estimated response of inflation, as shown in figure 3.6, does not give us much confidence in this regard.

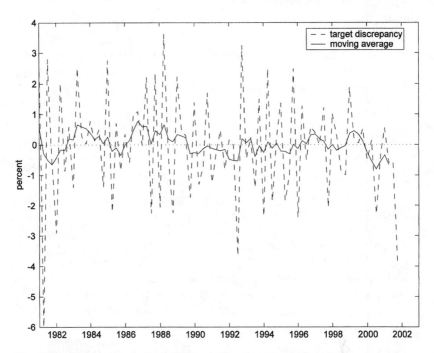

Fig. 3.17   Alternative version of figure 3.14, using equation residuals to infer the variation in the natural rate of output

tends to have its sign reversed in the next quarter. Except again at the end of our sample, there are no periods of time over which policy can be identified as having been consistently too tight or too loose for several quarters in succession. However, if we smooth the discrepancy series in the same way as in figure 3.14 (again shown by the solid line in the figure), we obtain very similar conclusions as before regarding the periods in which (and the degree to which) U.S. policy should be judged to have been too tight or too loose on average.

Overall, a comparison between U.S. time series over the past twenty years and the criteria for optimal policy discussed in the previous section do not indicate any gross discrepancy. However, this may simply mean that the diagnostics proposed here are not very useful as a way of diagnosing deviations from optimal policy in the historical record. We have plotted only the time variation in the optimal target criteria that would be implied by the variation in lagged projections that *has* occurred, given the actual evolution of the U.S. time series, rather than attempting to determine the variation in the target values that *would have* occurred under optimal policy, given the historical disturbance processes. These two ways of judging the historical time series might yield quite different pictures. Our optimal target criteria demand that certain adjusted inflation projections not be too different than similar projections have been in the quarter before; this will result in plots of projections and target values that look fairly similar, regardless of the paths of the U.S. time series, as long as each of our four variables has been relatively smooth (as is the case). Nonetheless, inflation and other variables might have wandered for years at some distance from the levels that they would have had under fully optimal responses to the historical disturbances.

3.4 Conclusions

We have shown that it is possible to derive robustly optimal monetary policy rule for optimizing models of the monetary transmission mechanism that incorporate a number of common features of recent empirical models: staggered wage- and price-setting; inflation inertia resulting from automatic indexation of wages and prices to a lagged price index; predetermined wage-setting, pricing, and spending decisions; and habit persistence in the level of real private expenditure. In this way, we have sought to show that the approach to the design of optimal policy rules proposed by Giannoni and Woodford (2002a) can be applied to models of practical interest.

In each of the cases that we have discussed, the optimal policy rule is a modified inflation-forecast targeting rule. The optimal rule differs from a simple (or "strict") inflation target in that projections of the future paths of variables other than goods-price inflation also receive some weight in the target criterion—in particular, wage inflation, a measure of the output gap, and nominal interest rates. Nonetheless, according to our numerical analysis in the case of an estimated model of the U.S. monetary transmission mechanism, the weight on the inflation projection (in each of the two target criteria involved in our characterization of optimal policy for that model) is strong enough that it makes sense to speak of optimal policy as a (flexible) inflation-forecast-targeting procedure.

In our examples, the optimal rule also differs from a simple inflation target (and even from many simple examples of "flexible inflation targeting" rules discussed in the literature) in that the optimal target value for the modified inflation forecast should vary over time, depending on current and recent past macroeconomic conditions. We have illustrated the possible degree of history dependence of an optimal inflation target by showing how our two optimal target criteria would have varied in the United States over the past two decades, given our VAR characterization of the U.S. time series and the parameters of our estimated structural model. Even when we use detrended output as our proxy for the output gap (which results in a less volatile output-gap series than the one implied by the residuals of our structural equations), and even over the relatively uneventful period 1984–2000, our analysis implies that the optimal target criterion has varied from quarter to quarter over a range of several percentage points.

Finally, we have shown, in the context of our empirical model, that an optimal policy may be too complex in structure to be conveniently described by a single target criterion. Our estimated model of the U.S. monetary transmission mechanism implies that optimal policy must satisfy three distinct criteria: one that governs the way that interest rates in a given quarter should respond to unexpected developments during that quarter; one that governs the way in which the central bank's commitment regarding interest rates in that quarter, announced the quarter before, should respond to unexpected developments in the quarter when the commitment is made; and still a third criterion that determines the component of interest rate policy that can be anticipated two quarters in advance. Nonetheless, the decision procedure takes the form of an inflation-forecast-targeting procedure, in which (a) the instrument used to ensure satisfaction of the target criterion is the central bank's commitment regarding its interest rate operating target for the following quarter, and (b) the inflation target each quarter is itself the product of a policy decision in the previous quarter, also aimed at ensuring that a certain adjusted inflation projection satisfies a target criterion.

Our optimal target criteria are a good bit more complex than the sort used by actual inflation-targeting central banks, which typically specify a time-invariant inflation target and a particular horizon at which it is to be reached (for example, RPIX inflation of 2.5 percent at a horizon of eight quarters in the future, in the case of the Bank of England). Our advocacy of a more complex form of targeting rule is not meant to deny the desirability of having a medium-term inflation target that remains the same even if the actual inflation rate may depart from it temporarily. In the examples that we have considered, optimal policy almost always involves a well-defined long-run inflation target, to which the inflation rate should be expected to return after each disturbance, and it is surely desirable for a central bank to be explicit about this aspect of its policy commitment, in order to anchor the public's medium-term inflation expectations.

Rather, we wish to suggest that it is *insufficient* to specify no more of a policy commitment than this. The mere fact that a central bank wishes to see inflation return to a rate of 2.5 percent at a horizon two years in the future is not sufficient to say which of the various possible transition paths that reach that endpoint should be preferred. There will always be a range of possible scenarios consistent with the terminal condition: for example, looser policy this year to be compensated for by tighter policy next year, or alternatively the reverse.

In practice, the Bank of England, like many other forecast-targeting banks, deals with this problem by demanding that a *constant–interest rate* forecast satisfy the terminal condition. That is, the current level of overnight interest rates is held to be justified if a projection under the assumption that that level of interest rates will be maintained implies that RPIX inflation should equal 2.5 percent eight quarters in the future. However, this implies no commitment to actually maintain interest rates at the current level over that period, or even that interest rates are currently expected to remain at that level on average. (It is frequently the case that the published constant–interest rate projection would itself imply that interest rates will need to be changed over the coming year, in order for the target criterion to be satisfied by a constant–interest rate projection under the conditions that are forecasted to obtain by then.) It is thus hard to see how basing policy decisions on a forecast-targeting exercise of this particular kind can be expected to serve the goals of making monetary policy more transparent or improving the degree to which policy is correctly anticipated by the private sector.

The conceptually superior approach, surely, is to base policy on a projection that is computed under the assumption that policy will be made in accordance with the targeting rule in the future as well,[64] so that the projection that is used to justify current policy will correspond to the bank's own best forecast of how it should act in the future, as in the case of the projections used to justify policy decisions by the Reserve Bank of New Zealand. It will, of course, be necessary to stress that the bank's only commitment is to the *rule* embodied in this projection, not to the particular time path of interest rates indicated as most likely. But given the use of "fan charts" to show that a variety of possible future scenarios can be envisioned, depending on how various types of uncertainty happen to be resolved, it is not clear why it should not be possible to talk about probability distributions for future interest rates along with those for inflation and real activity without giving rise to the appearance of a more specific commitment than is intended.

Once this is done, however, it becomes necessary to specify a target criterion that can determine the appropriate short-run dynamics for the economy, and not simply a terminal condition for a date some years in the future. Such a criterion will accordingly place substantial weight on projections of the target variables over the coming year, as in the case of the optimal target criteria derived in this chapter. It will also have to take a stand as to the kinds of projected departures of real variables from their long-run average values that justify short-run departures of the inflation projection from its long-run target value; it will no longer suffice simply to specify what the (unchanging) long-run inflation target is. None of the inflation-targeting central banks actually believe that it is desirable to keep inflation as close as possible to the long-run target value at all times; this is

---

64. See Svensson and Woodford (chap. 2 in this volume) for further discussion of what this would mean in practice.

why forecast-targeting procedures only seek to ensure that inflation is projected to return to the target value after many quarters.[65] But by formulating no explicit doctrine as to the way in which one should choose among
alternative transition paths to that medium-term goal, they avoid having to
clarify the nature of acceptable trade-offs among competing stabilization
goals.[66]

A coherent approach—and, in particular, one that could be justified as
seeking to implement the conditions for optimal policy discussed in this
chapter—would instead have to make explicit the kind of projections for
output and other real variables that should justify a modification of the
short-run inflation target, and the degree to which they should affect it. In
all likelihood, the inflation-targeting banks have shied away from such ex-
plicitness out of a suspicion that the types of circumstances that might reasonably justify short-term departures from the inflation target are too various to be catalogued. But the theory developed here has sought to show
that it is possible to state *short-run* target criteria (criteria that apply to the
shortest horizon at which current policy decisions can still have an effect)
that will be *robustly* optimal, meaning that the same criterion continues to
determine the correct degree of short-run departure from the long-run inflation target regardless of the nature of the disturbance that may have occurred.

Much work remains to be done, of course, before a quantitative characterization of optimal policy of the kind that we offer in section 3.3 could be
used in practical policy deliberations. One of the most obvious issues requiring further study concerns the way in which a central bank should take
account of uncertainty about the correct model of the transmission mechanism, as well as uncertainty in its evaluation of current macroeconomic
conditions. Uncertainty about the current state of the economy is relatively
straightforward to deal with, at least in principle. One can allow for partial
information on the part of the central bank in characterizing the optimal
equilibrium responses to shocks, using methods similar to those employed
here, and derive an optimal target criterion that is valid in the presence of
partial information (Svensson and Woodford 2003, 2004; Giannoni and
Woodford 2002b). Because of the principle of certainty equivalence in linear-quadratic policy problems of this kind (discussed in detail by Svensson
and Woodford 2003, 2004), the optimal target criterion (once correctly expressed) involves coefficients that are independent of the degree of uncer-

65. On this point, see, for example, Bernanke et al. (1999) or Svensson (1999).
66. The fact that a real GDP projection is always included with the projection for RPIX inflation in the introduction to the Bank of England's *Inflation Report*—and in fact is always
discussed *first*—suggests that some attention is paid to the projected path of output in deciding upon the appropriateness of the current level of interest rates. But the Bank's official target criterion, involving only the constant–interest rate projection of RPIX inflation at the
eight-quarter horizon, does not make explicit the way in which the output projection should
be taken into account.

tainty in central-bank estimates of the current state of the economy; however, the target may involve variables that are not directly observed by the central bank and that must instead be estimated using a Kalman filter.

Dealing with uncertainty about the numerical values of structural parameters (to say nothing of more fundamental doubts about model specification) is a much harder problem, for which few general guidelines exist at present. Giannoni (2001, 2002) illustrates one approach to the problem, for the case of uncertainty about the numerical values of the elasticities κ and σ in a model similar to our baseline model (but in which an interest rate stabilization objective is assumed). For the particular kind of parameter uncertainty considered, Giannoni finds that a concern for robustness (in the sense of guarding against bad outcomes in the least favorable case) should lead a central bank to choose a Taylor-style interest rate rule with stronger response coefficients than it would choose on the basis of its preferred estimates of the model parameters; this means allowing *less* variability of inflation in equilibrium, at the cost of greater variability in nominal interest rates. This suggests that a concern for robustness might justify targeting rules that are even closer to strict inflation targeting than the optimal rules obtained in this paper; the question is surely one that deserves further analysis.

References

Altig, David, Lawrence J. Christiano, Martin S. Eichenbaum, and Jesper Linde. 2002. Technology shocks and aggregate fluctuations. Cleveland, Ohio: Federal Reserve Bank of Cleveland. Unpublished manuscript.

Amato, Jeffrey D., and Thomas Laubach. 2001. Implications of habit formation for optimal monetary policy. Finance and Economics Discussion Series Paper no. 2001-58. Washington, D.C.: Federal Reserve Board, August.

———. 2003. Estimation and control of an optimization-based model with sticky wages and prices. *Journal of Economic Dynamics and Control* 27 (May): 1181–1215.

Ball, Laurence, and David Romer. 1990. Real rigidities and the non-neutrality of money. *Review of Economic Studies* 57:183–203.

Basu, Susanto, and Miles S. Kimball. 2002. Investment planning costs and the effects of fiscal and monetary policy. University of Michigan, Department of Economics. Manuscript, November.

Bernanke, Ben S., and Alan S. Blinder. 1992. The federal funds rate and the transmission of monetary policy. *American Economic Review* 82:901–21.

Bernanke, Ben S., Thomas Laubach, Frederic S. Mishkin, and Adam S. Posen. 1999. *Inflation targeting*. Princeton, N.J.: Princeton University Press.

Bernanke, Ben S., Jean Boivin, and Piotr Eliasz. 2004. Measuring the effects of monetary policy: A factor-augmented vector autoregressive FAVAR approach. NBER Working Paper no. 10220. Cambridge, Mass.: National Bureau of Economic Research, January.

Bernanke, Ben S., and Ilian Mihov. 1998. Measuring monetary policy. *Quarterly Journal of Economics* 113 (3): 869–902.

Blinder, Alan S. 1994. On sticky prices: Academic theories meet the real world. In *Monetary policy,* ed. N. G. Mankiw, 117–50. Chicago: University of Chicago Press.

Boivin, Jean. 2003. Has U.S. monetary policy changed? Evidence from drifting co-efficients and real-time data. Unpublished Manuscript. Columbia University, Graduate School of Business.

Boivin, Jean, and Marc P. Giannoni. 2003. Has monetary policy become more effective? NBER Working Paper no. 9459. Cambridge, Mass.: National Bureau of Economic Research, January.

Calvo, Guillermo A. 1983. Staggered prices in a utility-maximizing framework. *Journal of Monetary Economics* 12 (3): 383–98.

Christiano, Lawrence J., Martin S. Eichenbaum, and Charles L. Evans. 2001. Nominal rigidities and the dynamic effects of a shock to monetary policy. NBER Working Paper no. 8403. Cambridge, Mass.: National Bureau of Economic Research, July.

Clarida, Richard, Jordi Galí, and Mark Gertler. 1999. The science of monetary policy: A new Keynesian perspective. *Journal of Economic Literature* 37:1661–707.

———. 2000. Monetary policy rules and macroeconomic stability: Evidence and some theory. *Quarterly Journal of Economics* 115:147–80.

Cogley, Timothy, and Thomas Sargent. 2001. Evolving post–World War II U.S. inflation dynamics. *NBER macroeconomics annual 2001,* ed. Ben S. Bernanke and Kenneth Rogoff, 331–73. Cambridge: MIT Press.

———. 2002. Drifts and volatilities: Monetary policies and outcomes in the post–WWII U.S. University of California, Davis, Department of Economics, and New York University, Department of Economics. Manuscript, August.

Dixit, Avinash K., and Joseph E. Stiglitz. 1977. Monopolistic competition and optimum product diversity. *American Economic Review* 67:297–308.

Edge, Rochelle. 2000. Time-to-build, time-to-plan, habit-persistence, and the liquidity effect. International Finance Discussion Paper no. 2000-673. Washington, D.C.

Erceg, Christopher J., Dale W. Henderson, and Andrew T. Levin. 2000. Optimal monetary policy with staggered wage and price contracts. *Journal of Monetary Economics* 46:281–313.

Friedman, Milton. 1969. The optimum quantity of money. In *The optimum quantity of money and other essays.* Chicago: Aldine.

Fuhrer, Jeffrey C. 2000. Habit formation in consumption and its implications for monetary-policy models. *American Economic Review* 90 (3): 367–90.

Fuhrer, Jeffrey C., and Geoffrey R. Moore. 1995. Inflation persistence. *Quarterly Journal of Economics* 110 (1): 127–59.

Galí, Jordi, and Mark Gertler. 1999. Inflation dynamics: A structural econometric analysis. *Journal of Monetary Economics* 44:195–222.

Giannoni, Marc P. 2000. Optimal interest-rate rules in a forward-looking model, and inflation stabilization versus price-level stabilization. Princeton University, Department of Economics. Unpublished manuscript.

———. 2001. Robust optimal monetary policy in a forward-looking model with parameter and shock uncertainty. Federal Reserve Bank of New York. Unpublished manuscript.

———. 2002. Does model uncertainty justify caution? Robust optimal monetary policy in a forward-looking model. *Macroeconomic Dynamics* 6 (1): 111–44.

Giannoni, Marc P., and Michael Woodford. 2002a. Optimal interest-rate rules: I.

General theory. NBER Working Paper no. 9419. Cambridge, Mass.: National Bureau of Economic Research, December.

———. 2002b. Optimal interest-rate rules: II. Applications. NBER Working Paper no. 9420. Cambridge, Mass.: National Bureau of Economic Research, December.

———. 2003. How forward-looking is optimal monetary policy? *Journal of Money, Credit, and Banking* 35 (6): 1425–69 (part II).

Goodfriend, Marvin. 1991. Interest rate smoothing in the conduct of monetary policy. *Carnegie-Rochester Conference Series on Public Policy* 34:7–30.

Judd, John F., and Glenn D. Rudebusch. 1998. Taylor's rule and the Fed: 1970–1997. *Federal Reserve Bank of San Francisco Economic Review* 1998 (3): 3–16.

Kilian, Lutz. 1998. Small-sample confidence intervals for impulse response functions. *Review of Economics and Statistics* 80 (2): 218–30.

King, Mervyn. 1997. Changes in UK monetary policy: Rules and discretion in practice. *Journal of Monetary Economics* 39:81–97.

McCallum, Bennett T., and Edward Nelson. 1999. Performance of operational policy rules in an estimated semi-classical structural model. In *Monetary policy rules,* ed. J. B. Taylor, 15–56. Chicago: University of Chicago Press.

Roberts, John M. 1995. New Keynesian economics and the Phillips curve. *Journal of Money, Credit and Banking* 27 (4): 975–84.

Rotemberg, Julio J., and Michael Woodford. 1997. An optimization-based econometric framework for the evaluation of monetary policy. In *NBER macroeconomics annual,* ed. Ben S. Bernanke and Kenneth Rogoff, 297–346. Cambridge: MIT Press.

———. 1999. Interest-rate rules in an estimated sticky-price model. In *Monetary policy rules,* ed. J. B. Taylor, 57–119. Chicago: University of Chicago Press.

Smets, Frank, and Raf Wouters. 2002. Sources of business cycle fluctuations in the U.S.: A Bayesian DSGE approach. Seminar presentation. Princeton University, 1 November.

Steinsson, Jon. 2003. Optimal monetary policy in an economy with inflation persistence. *Journal of Monetary Economics* 50:1425–56.

Svensson, Lars E. O. 1999. Inflation targeting as a monetary policy rule. *Journal of Monetary Economics* 43:607–54.

Svensson, Lars E. O., and Michael Woodford. 2003. Indicator variables for optimal policy. *Journal of Monetary Economics* 50:691–720.

———. 2004. Indicator variables for optimal policy under asymmetric information. *Journal of Economic Dynamics and Control* 28:661–90.

Taylor, John B. 1993. Discretion versus policy rules in practice. *Carnegie-Rochester Conference Series on Public Policy* 39:195–214.

———, ed. 1999. *Monetary policy rules.* Chicago: University of Chicago Press.

Vickers, John. 1998. Inflation targeting in practice: The UK experience. *Bank of England Quarterly Bulletin* 38:368–75.

Woodford, Michael. 1998. Doing without money: Controlling inflation in a post-monetary world. *Review of Economic Dynamics* 1:173–219.

———. 1999a. Commentary: How should monetary policy be conducted in an era of price stability? In *New challenges for monetary policy,* 277–316. Kansas City, Mo.: Federal Reserve Bank of Kansas City.

———. 1999b. Optimal monetary policy inertia. NBER Working Paper no. 7261. Cambridge, Mass.: National Bureau of Economic Research, August.

———. 2003. *Interest and prices: Foundations of a theory of monetary policy.* Princeton, N.J.: Princeton University Press.

Comment   Edward Nelson

General Remarks

The contribution to this volume by Marc Giannoni and Michael Woodford is of a very important, wide-ranging, and innovative nature. Building on their earlier work,[1] the authors estimate a New Keynesian model featuring a significant amount of dynamics from the specification of preferences, the indexation structure, and wage stickiness. They derive the aggregate welfare function that is consistent with their model and compare actual U.S. inflation outcomes with the recommended inflation path that arises from the model.

Giannoni and Woodford's main finding is that the optimal inflation target—that is, the period-by-period rate of quarterly inflation consistent with the maximum attainable value of households' intertemporal utility function—varies sharply over time, with values ranging over several percent under several different assumptions about the shock processes. And this finding occurs despite seemingly small weights on terms beside inflation variability in the model's welfare function.

Giannoni and Woodford's finding illustrates that trade-offs between inflation stability and other policy goals matter very much in their model. These trade-offs come from the generalizations that the authors contemplate of a basic New Keynesian model with price stickiness and few sources of intrinsic dynamics. As Woodford (2003, chap. 6) has shown, this basic model provides a rationalization for an approximately quadratic loss function that penalizes variations in inflation and in output relative to potential—Giannoni and Woodford's initial loss function (3). Giannoni and Woodford's modifications to the basic model, suggested by other recent work with optimizing models for monetary policy, include habit formation in preferences over consumption, nominal wage stickiness, automatic indexation of nominal wages and prices, and a time-varying wedge between the socially desirable output level and the level of potential output. In keeping with results reported in other papers, each modification has an effect on the implied social welfare function. Habit formation puts volatility in the quasi-difference, rather than in the level, of the output gap into the period loss function; wage stickiness makes nominal wage growth variability welfare-relevant; indexation means that fluctuations in the quasi-difference of inflation and wage growth, rather than the level fluctuations, matter for

Edward Nelson is a research officer at the Federal Reserve Bank of St. Louis.

The views expressed here should not be interpreted as those of the Bank of England or the Monetary Policy Committee.

1. For example, Boivin and Giannoni (2003), Giannoni and Woodford (2002a,b), Rotemberg and Woodford (1997), and Woodford (2003).

utility; and distortions to potential GDP have the effect of making some deviations in output relative to potential optimal.

Not all these modifications to the social welfare function produce sizable fluctuations in the optimal inflation target. As Giannoni and Woodford note (section 3.1.5), habit formation by itself has no material effect on the first-order condition for optimal policy, because the habit-formation parameters cancel after substitution. Indexation of nominal prices does have a substantial effect, because—with the price-indexation parameter estimated to be at the boundary of its parameter space—the period loss function now penalizes the variability of the first difference of price inflation rather than the level of inflation. But, as Giannoni and Woodford observe, this actually takes the policy implications of the model closer to inflation targeting in practice, since the model then recommends that the price level be permitted to exhibit nonstationary behavior.

These considerations suggest that the principal sources of the time variation in the optimal inflation target come from (a) nominal wage stickiness (including wage indexation), and the consequent trade-off between inflation and nominal wage-growth volatility; and (b) the trade-off between stabilizing inflation and stabilizing the welfare-relevant output gap.

I will suggest in the remainder of this comment that these two factors imply a less severe trade-off than the authors' findings suggest. This more benign outlook arises from considering two separate issues. The first issue involves a free lunch: I will suggest that observed nominal wage rigidity may give an exaggerated picture of the trade-off faced by welfare-maximizing policymakers. Consequently, there is not a compelling reason to give up stability in price inflation in order to moderate wage-growth volatility. The second issue does not imply a free lunch: given the setting of other policy instruments, greater stability of price inflation may well, as the authors suggest, come at a cost of larger swings of output around its socially desirable level. Nevertheless, I argue that a strategy of targeting price inflation alone may be a sensible one for a central bank even in the presence of this trade-off.

The Trade-Off between Inflation and Wage-Growth Volatility

The possibility that stickiness in nominal wages creates a distortion, for which the monetary policy remedy is to stabilize nominal wage fluctuations, was recognized explicitly by Friedman (1967, n. 11) and formalized in a dynamic general equilibrium context by Erceg, Henderson, and Levin (2000). The latter paper established that, in conditions of staggered contracts for both nominal prices and nominal wages, optimal monetary policy involves a trade-off between stabilization of price inflation and nominal wage growth. Thus, wage stickiness considerably complicates the welfare-maximization problem for monetary policy. It is therefore vital to establish that the nominal wage behavior observed in practice corresponds to the kind of wage stickiness that monetary policy should be concerned about.

Giannoni and Woodford's parameter estimates are consistent with wage and not just price stickiness being empirically important. These estimates are obtained by achieving as close a match as possible for the model with vector autoregression impulse responses to a monetary policy shock in the U.S. data, for four variables including the real wage. This procedure could exaggerate the trade-off situation in an environment that, following Mankiw (1987) and Goodfriend and King (2001), I consider to be empirically relevant: namely, one where observed nominal wages display considerable rigidity, yet output and inflation behavior are consistent with a sticky-price, flexible-wage model.

To be concrete, let us neglect the complications of decision lags, indexation, and habit formation, and consider simply the basic sticky-price New Keynesian model considered early in Giannoni and Woodford's paper—namely, their equations (1) and (15). In this standard sticky-price model, the predicted behavior of real unit labor costs is that they are proportional to the output gap:

$$(1) \qquad w_t - p_t - n_t = g(y_t - y_t^*), \qquad g > 0.$$

With a production function of the form $y_t = \alpha n_t + a_t$ (a_t being a technology shock), this relationship implies that real wages are a function of current output

$$(2) \qquad w_t - p_t = hy_t + \varepsilon_t,$$

where $h = (1/\alpha) + g$, and ε_t is an exogenous real shock that can be held constant when contemplating the effects of a monetary policy shock.

In the alternative to this baseline that I want to entertain, observed real wages are a noisy mixture of their lagged value and output:

$$(3) \qquad w_t - p_t = (1 - \mu)hy_t + \mu(w_{t-1} - p_{t-1}) + e_{wt}, \qquad 0 < \mu < 1.$$

One rationalization for equation (3) is that, as conjectured by Mankiw and Goodfriend-King, observed wages are not a satisfactory indicator of current labor-market conditions. Equation (3) can also be viewed as holding in a more general situation in which, although inflation is driven by real marginal cost, measurement error in wages renders observed real unit labor costs an imperfect and sluggish indicator of true marginal cost, where the latter is strictly proportional to the output gap. The positive weight on current output[2] in equation (3) delivers the property that real unit labor costs and true marginal cost are positively correlated, and so it is consistent

---

2. Actually this weight is on the current output *gap*, but potential GDP has been included in the composite disturbance e_{wt} in equation (3).

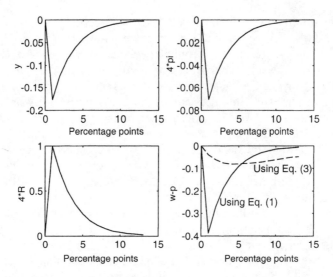

Fig. 3C.1   Responses to unit shock to policy rule

with Sbordone's (2002) finding that the expected path of observed real unit labor costs explains inflation behavior well.

In a sticky-price model, completed by a standard Taylor rule with smoothing,[3] the output, inflation, and nominal interest rate responses to a monetary policy shock will necessarily be the same whether wage equation (1) or (3) is used, as figure 3C.1 shows.[4] But the figure also confirms that if observed real labor costs follow equation (3), real wages will exhibit an inertial response to monetary policy shocks that will appear to confirm the importance of wage stickiness. It is important to bear in mind that the real-wage response constitutes approximately one-quarter of the criterion function that determines Giannoni and Woodford's parameter estimates. Once the wage-stickiness parameter is estimated to be sizable, the volatility of nominal wage growth (or of its first difference) enters Giannoni and Woodford's utility-based welfare function and the associated trade-off calculations. But in the example given here, the inertial observed real-wage response to the policy shock is solely responsible for the estimated wage stickiness; output and inflation responses are consistent with a purely sticky-price story, and wage variability does not appear in the true social welfare function.

Nor, under certain conditions, do departures of actual output and infla-

---

3. I use the estimated specification of Rudebusch (2002, 1164): $4R_t = (1 - \rho_R)(1.53[\Sigma_{i=0}^3 \pi_{t-i}]$ $+ 0.93y_t) + \rho_R 4R_{t-1} + e_{Rt}$, where $\rho_R = 0.73$. This rule is shocked in period 1.

4. I set the interest elasticity of aggregate demand to 0.20 and the output-gap coefficient in the Phillips curve to 0.10. Equations (1) and (3) are parameterized as follows: $h = 2.2$, $\mu = 0.9$.

tion responses from the patterns predicted by a flexible-wage, sticky-price model imply that wage stickiness is of genuine policy significance. Consider a situation where real wages follow a pattern like equation (3), while real wages enter the monetary policy reaction function as they do in Giannoni and Woodford's equation (57). Then matching the persistence of observed real wages will be important in obtaining a good fit of the model with the data responses for the interest rate, output, and inflation. But this improvement in fit will not reflect any importance of wage stickiness in the structure of the Phillips curve or the welfare function; the improved fit comes in effect from a better match to the policy rule in force during the estimation period.

An initial glance at the authors' table 3.3 might lead to the conclusion that the hypothesis that prices are the sole source of nominal stickiness is strongly rejected. For example, the flexible-wage restriction does more damage to the objective function value than other restrictions that are contemplated in the table, such as the no-habit and no-indexation settings. This finding does amount to a strong rejection of the joint hypothesis of sticky prices *and* of wages being allocative and observed without error. But it is not necessarily inconsistent with the hypothesis that prices are the sole source of nominal rigidity that are relevant for inflation dynamics and welfare, with observed nominal wage rigidity reflecting a measurement error of the form implicit in equation (3). Under the latter hypothesis, improvements in fit from modeling wages as sticky are to be expected, for the reasons outlined above. And there is an important feature of the Giannoni-Woodford estimates that seems to me highly consistent with the hypothesis that price stickiness is the only inflation-relevant and welfare-relevant form of nominal rigidity. This feature is that several key parameters, notably φ (governing the interest elasticity of aggregate demand), η (the habit formation parameter), and κ_p (the elasticity of inflation with respect to the output gap), are virtually identical to their unrestricted values when the restriction of flexible wages is imposed (see the "implied parameters" in the final column of Giannoni and Woodford's table 3.3). If wage stickiness played a decisive role in the structure of the model, and so in the intrinsic dynamics of output and inflation behavior, one would expect these parameter estimates to be highly sensitive to the assumption made about wages. In fact, they do not exhibit such a sensitivity, which lends support to the proposition that separate terms involving real wages or wage growth are not required in the Phillips curve or in the social welfare function. The behavior of nominal wages, in other words, does not justify trading off stability in price inflation against stability in nominal wage growth.

The Trade-Off between Inflation and Output-Gap Volatility

If the trade-off between stability in inflation and nominal wage growth is put aside, the key trade-off in Giannoni and Woodford's model is between variability in inflation and variability in output relative to its socially desirable value. This real deviation, denoted x_t, is labeled the "output gap" in the paper, but it is important to stress that this is a slightly different output-gap concept from that used in Phillips-curve analysis. The latter, which I will call the "inflation-relevant output gap," corresponds to $x_t + u_t$ in Giannoni and Woodford's paper, and represents the percentage difference between (detrended levels of) output and potential output. With (detrended log) potential output (i.e., the level of output prevailing in the absence of any nominal rigidity) denoted by y_t^*, the following relationship holds between output concepts, the inflation-relevant output gap $x_t + u_t$, and what Giannoni and Woodford call the "welfare-relevant output gap," x_t:

$$(4) \qquad y_t - y_t^* = (y_t - y_t^E) + (y_t^E - y_t^*) = x_t + u_t,$$

where y_t^E is the detrended value of the efficient log-level of output. Giannoni and Woodford therefore rationalize a trade-off between inflation and output-gap variability with the u_t term, representing "real disturbances that prevent joint stabilization of both inflation and the (welfare-relevant) output gap." As in Giannoni (2000), these shocks correspond to variations over time in the inefficiencies that the economy faces—for example, changes in the degree of monopoly power exercised by firms or in the level of distorting tax rates. They thus affect potential output y_t^*, and so they tend to produce shifts in the inflation rate—since it is $x_t + u_t$, rather than x_t alone, that appears in the Phillips curve. If monetary policy is, as in Giannoni and Woodford's analysis, dictated by maximization of household intertemporal utility, then the impact on output of inefficient movements in potential output should not be accommodated, other things being equal. Since variability in both x_t and π_t appear in households' welfare function, the conduct of optimal monetary policy amounts to partial accommodation of the u_t shocks in order to contain the variability in inflation.

One of the key conditions describing optimal policy in Giannoni and Woodford's setup is that projections of endogenous variables under optimal policy satisfy their equation (77), reproduced here:

$$(5) \qquad F_t^*(\pi) + \phi_w^*[F_t^*(w)] + \phi_x^*[F_t^*(x)] = \pi_t^*.$$

If, as argued in the previous section, the term involving wages in this condition can be ignored, the expression can be alternatively written as

$$(6) \qquad \sum_{k=1}^{\infty} \alpha_k^{\pi^*} E_t \pi_{t+k} + \phi_x^* \left(\sum_{k=1}^{\infty} \alpha_k^{x^*} E_t x_{t+k} \right) = \pi_t^*.$$

With $\pi_t \equiv \pi_t^{qd} + \gamma_p \pi_{t-1}$,

$$(7) \qquad \sum_{k=1}^{\infty} \alpha_k^{\pi^*} E_t(\pi_{t+k}^{qd} + \gamma_p \pi_{t+k-1}) + \phi_x^* \left(\sum_{k=1}^{\infty} \alpha_k^{x^*} E_t x_{t+k} \right) = \pi_t^{qd^*} + \gamma_p \pi_{t-1}^*.$$

And with the Phillips curve (omitting wage terms) implying the relationship $\pi_t^{qd} = \varepsilon_p \omega_p \Sigma_{i=0}^{\infty} \beta^i E_{t-1}(x_{t+i} + u_{t+i})$, condition (7) may be cast as

$$\left\{ \sum_{k=1}^{\infty} b_k E_t(x_{t+k} + u_{t+k}) \right\} + c_1 \pi_{t-1} + \phi_x^* \left(\sum_{k=1}^{\infty} \alpha_k^{x^*} E_t x_{t+k} \right)$$
$$= \left\{ \sum_{i=0}^{\infty} d_i E_t(x_{t+i} + u_{t+i}) \right\} + f_1 \pi_{t-1},$$

where the b_k, c_1, d_i, and f_1 coefficients are functions of the coefficients in equation (7) and the Phillips-curve parameters. A policy that made inflation zero every period ($\pi_t = 0 \ \forall \ t$, implying that the inflation-relevant output gap follows $x_t + u_t = 0 \ \forall \ t$) would be optimal only if all fluctuations in potential output y_t^* were efficient (i.e., $u_t \equiv 0 \ \forall \ t$), which is not the case in this model, *or* if the objective function is modified to make replication of flexible-price equilibrium a goal (i.e., replacing x_t in the period loss function with $x_t + u_t$).

Let us consider the merits of making such a modification to the objective function. It *would* represent a departure from the spirit of assigning to monetary policy the goal of maximizing social welfare. But it would be a departure only in a limited sense: by instructing the central bank that it should not engineer deviations of GDP from potential, even when the latter is distorted relative to the social optimum.

In Rotemberg and Woodford (1997) and in many of the cases in Woodford (2003), fluctuations in y_t^* are efficient, but the steady-state level of potential output is generally inefficient. These studies assume that a subsidy is provided by the government that eliminates the inefficiency of the steady-state potential output level. While this subsidy is often treated as a convenient assumption, it can be given a normative interpretation as reflecting an optimal assignment of policy instruments. Indeed, Rotemberg and Woodford (1998, 52) offered just such a normative interpretation, arguing that "monetary policy is not an appropriate instrument with which to seek to affect the long-run average level of real economic activity, given the existence of other instruments." This perspective is closely related to the resolution of the inflation-bias issue proposed by King (1996, 61), whereby "the central bank does not use monetary policy as a substitute for microeconomic structural reforms" and is embedded in Svensson's (1999) "flexible inflation targeting" concept. So far, this argument applies to the mean level of output, but there is a clear dynamic analogue to this policy prescription. Specifically, for stabilization policy, the above principle entails trying to limit variability in the inflation-relevant output gap, $x_t + u_t$, rather than variation in x_t alone.

From such a perspective, monetary policy is a natural instrument for eliminating the real distortions (i.e., deviations of y_t from y_t^*) that arise from nominal stickiness, and for pursuing a mean inflation rate that is consistent with insulating the economy from the most serious effects of violations of superneutrality (e.g., downward pressure on potential output arising from the interaction of high inflation and nonindexed tax scales). But the achievement of minimum price inflation and gap variability is conditional on the real shocks and on the steady-state magnitudes that determine the flexible-price values of output and other real variables. Such an arrangement amounts to a prescription for a "neutral" monetary policy, in the terminology of Goodfriend and King (1997). Movement of output closer to its social optimum is then the task of other policy instruments, which achieve this aim through policies designed to reduce the variance of u_t to zero. If this view about instrument delegation is accepted, the trade-off problem of monetary policy is eased. There is no conflict between minimizing variability in inflation and in the inflation-relevant output gap, and so the sharp fluctuations in the inflation target exhibited in Giannoni and Woodford's section 3.3.3 are no longer called for.

Conclusions

As I noted at the outset, Giannoni and Woodford have produced an important, wide-ranging, and innovative paper. Its findings on the optimal inflation target for the United States will be a benchmark for future work, and applications to inflation-targeting countries can provide a welfare evaluation of the constant inflation targets typically followed in practice. In my comments here, I have argued that the trade-off problem—and so the sources of desirable variations in inflation—may be exaggerated by Giannoni and Woodford's emphasis on the importance of wage stickiness for inflation dynamics and optimal policy, and by their assigning to monetary policymakers the duty of offsetting inefficiencies arising from tax and competition arrangements. If, as I have suggested, the nominal wage rigidity observed in practice does not have welfare consequences, and the output-gap concepts that appear in the Phillips curve and in monetary policymakers' objective function coincide, then there is a stronger case for a constant inflation target.

References

Boivin, Jean, and Marc P. Giannoni. 2003. Has monetary policy become more effective? NBER Working Paper no. 9459. Cambridge, Mass.: National Bureau of Economic Research.

Erceg, Christopher J., Dale W. Henderson, and Andrew T. Levin. 2000. Optimal monetary policy with staggered wage and price contracts. *Journal of Monetary Economics* 46:281–313.

Friedman, Milton. 1967. The monetary theory and policy of Henry Simons. *Journal of Law and Economics* 10:1–13.

Giannoni, Marc P. 2000. Optimal interest-rate rules in a forward-looking model, and inflation stabilization versus price-level stabilization. Princeton University, Department of Economics. Unpublished manuscript.

Giannoni, Marc P., and Michael Woodford. 2002a. Optimal interest-rate rules: I. General theory. NBER Working Paper no. 9419. Cambridge, Mass.: National Bureau of Economic Research.

———. 2002b. Optimal interest-rate rules: II. Applications. NBER Working Paper no. 9420. Cambridge, Mass.: National Bureau of Economic Research.

Goodfriend, Marvin, and Robert G. King. 1997. The new neoclassical synthesis and the role of monetary policy. In *NBER macroeconomics annual* 12, ed. Ben S. Bernanke and Julio J. Rotemberg, 231–83. Cambridge: MIT Press.

———. 2001. The case for price stability. NBER Working Paper no. 8423. Cambridge, Mass.: National Bureau of Economic Research.

King, Mervyn A. 1996. How should central banks reduce inflation?—Conceptual issues. In *Achieving price stability,* 53–91. Kansas City, Mo.: Federal Reserve Bank of Kansas City.

Mankiw, N. Gregory. 1987. Comment on "The new Keynesian microfoundations." In *NBER macroeconomics annual* 2, ed. Stanley Fischer, 105–10. Cambridge: MIT Press.

Rotemberg, Julio J., and Michael Woodford. 1997. An optimization-based econometric framework for the evaluation of monetary policy. In *NBER macroeconomics annual* 12, ed. Ben S. Bernanke and Julio J. Rotemberg, 297–346. Cambridge: MIT Press.

———. 1998. An optimization-based econometric framework for the evaluation of monetary policy: Expanded version. NBER Technical Working Paper no. 233. Cambridge, Mass.: National Bureau of Economic Research.

Rudebusch, Glenn D. 2002. Term structure evidence on interest rate smoothing and monetary policy inertia. *Journal of Monetary Economics* 49:1161–87.

Sbordone, Argia M. 2002. Prices and unit labor costs: A new test of price stickiness. *Journal of Monetary Economics* 49:265–92.

Svensson, Lars E. O. 1999. Inflation targeting as a monetary policy rule. *Journal of Monetary Economics* 43:607–54.

Woodford, Michael. 2003. *Interest and prices: Foundations of a theory of monetary policy.* Princeton, N.J.: Princeton University Press.

Discussion Summary

Olivier Blanchard commended the paper's concern for performing the analysis within a model that had plausible empirical properties, but expressed skepticism about several features of the model introduced to achieve better empirical performance, notably the use of indexation in price setting and of habit formation in consumption. If these features were indeed a wrong representation of the structure of the economy, then the welfare analysis based on the model would be misleading.

Glenn Rudebusch suggested that the distinction between the new classical and New Keynesian Phillips curve, namely the timing of inflation expectations, might not be an important issue. Although the model used in the analysis was parameterized as a quarterly model, the relevant expectation was probably a four-quarter-ahead expectations of inflation, which was not very sensitive to the timing.

Marvin Goodfriend expressed concern about the degree of inflation control that the model assumed the central bank had. This feature relied on the assumption that the public was able to observe all shocks with precision. It would be important to account in the analysis for the possibility that the public might mistake movements in observed inflation for a change in the central bank's inflation target.

Donald Kohn questioned the feasibility of the central bank's committing one quarter ahead to an inflation target and not altering the previously announced target for the current period regardless of the nature of incoming information.

Laurence Ball expressed skepticism about the strategy of refining optimization-based models by including frictions that would bring them closer to the data. In the case of the Phillips curve, the specification used in the present paper would imply still counterfactual inflation volatility, while the inflation inertia implied by the presence of lagged inflation would make the model vulnerable to the Lucas critique.

Marc Giannoni responded by stressing that the target criterion remains remarkably similar to the one of the basic model when additional features such as habit formation, inflation indexation, and wages stickiness are introduced into the model. Moreover, adding more structure to the model would not necessarily complicate the target criterion as long as the number of variables in the target criterion does not increase, facilitating communication with the public. He also emphasized the robustness property of the proposed rule with respect to the sources and processes of the stochastic shocks.

In response to the skepticism expressed about the model, *Michael Woodford* emphasized that the paper did not attempt to recommend a specific rule but rather attempted to provide a disciplined way of translating assumptions about the structure of the economy into a target criterion, and thus into prescriptions of what the policy setting should be.

4

Inflation Targeting, Price-Path Targeting, and Output Variability

Stephen G. Cecchetti and Junhan Kim

4.1 Introduction

The 1990s were amazing in many ways. Not only did the internet and cellular phones come into widespread use, but overall economic conditions improved nearly everywhere we look. Growth was higher, inflation was lower, and both were more stable. In the United States, for example, inflation fell from 6 percent at the beginning of the decade to less than 2 percent by the end. Meanwhile real growth rose from less than 3 percent to over 4 percent. Volatility declined, too. The American case is the most dramatic instance of what has really been a worldwide trend.[1] And while these improvements in economic performance could have been the consequence of the world being calmer, Cecchetti, Flores-Lagunes, and Krause (2002) argue that roughly three-quarters of it can be explained by better monetary policy. That is, central bankers did a better job of stabilizing inflation at low levels while keeping growth high.

Making better monetary policy is not just a problem of finding competent central bankers. In fact, there is a history of central bankers who tried to do their jobs but were thwarted by politicians. Over the years we have

Stephen G. Cecchetti is professor of international economics and finance at Brandeis University and a research associate of the National Bureau of Economic Research. Junhan Kim is an economist at the Bank of Korea.

We wish to thank our discussant Greg Mankiw, as well as Edwin Truman and Mark Wynne for providing us with data, and Bill Gavin, Stefan Krause, Lianfa Li, Roisin O'Sullivan, and the conference participants, especially Lars Svensson, for helpful suggestions. The views expressed herein are those of the authors and not necessarily those of the Bank of Korea.

1. Cecchetti and Ehrmann (2002) compare the 1985–89 period with 1993–97 for a set of twenty-three industrialized and emerging-market countries and find that annual inflation fell by an average of 5 percentage points, annual growth rose by an average of 1 percentage point, and both were significantly more stable.

learned that the institutional environment is at least as important as the people in ensuring good policy outcomes. Without a well-designed central bank, the people in charge don't have a chance. Today, we have a good sense of what best practice is in the design of central banks. First, it is crucial that monetary policymakers are independent of short-term political influences. Second, these independent central bankers must be held accountable through mechanisms that involve public announcement of objectives. Inflation targeting is the most common formulation of the sort of policy regime in place today.[2] The primary element of inflation targeting is a public commitment to price stability in the form of a medium-term numerical inflation target.

With the success of inflation targeting has come a discussion of potential refinements. One issue is whether the central bank should adopt a target for inflation or a target for the path of the price level. With an inflation target, the central bank simply tries to ensure that period-by-period inflation remains close to the target. When inflation turns out to be above or below the target, the miss is forgotten. Bygones are bygones, so there is a form of base drift in the (log) price level. Price-path targeting, or "price-level targeting" as it is often called, is different as it implies that when the price level is above or below the target path, the objective of policy is to return it to the present target path.[3] This means that if prices move above the target path, then policy will need to bring them back down.[4] But which one is better? Should central banks be instructed to target inflation or target the price path?

Svensson (1999) is the first person to take on this question. He starts by assuming that society cares about inflation. The social objective is to minimize the expected present discounted value of the weighted average of squared deviations of inflation and output from their targets. He then posits that the central bank can be bound to meet a particular objective but not to respond to shocks in a specific way. That is, the central bank will always have discretion in adjusting its instrument, but it can be held accountable for its objective. This sort of discretion, what we might refer to as "instrument discretion," implies that if we were to instruct central bankers to minimize the true social loss function, there would be a bias. The exact form of the bias depends on the structure of the economy, but in most cases there is a bias toward stabilizing output.[5] One solution to this problem is to instruct the central bank to minimize a loss function that deviates

---

2. For a brief synopsis of what inflation targeting entails see Mishkin (forthcoming).

3. We adopt the terminology "price-path" targeting rather than the traditional "price-level" targeting to emphasize that the target path can have a positive slope and so a period of inflation need not be countered with one of deflation.

4. Mervyn King (1999) argues that in practice there is little difference between inflation targeting and price-path targeting. The reason is that politicians will hold central bankers accountable for meeting inflation targets over sufficiently long horizons so that it will look like a price-path target. We will take this up in more detail below.

5. For a discussion see Clark, Goodhart, and Huang (1999).

from society's. Rogoff (1985) suggested appointing central bankers that are more avid inflation hawks than the public at large.

In this context, Svensson shows that in countries where output is sufficiently persistent, performance can be improved by instructing policymakers to target the price path, even though society cares about inflation.[6] To understand why output persistence is central to the result, note that the more persistent output is, the longer output stays away from equilibrium following a disturbance. Now consider the possibility of a policy response. Monetary policy responds to shocks by inducing a price-level surprise, immediately creating a conflict between the output and inflation stability objectives. And the more persistent output is, the longer-lasting the shocks and the more important it will be to respond aggressively to them. If the goal is to stabilize prices, then these aggressive responses will have to be undone quickly, which ends up lowering the volatility of inflation.

There are several issues that arise in considering this result. First, Svensson compares inflation targeting with price-path targeting in order to emphasize the contrast between the two. But there is really a continuum of intermediate possibilities that weight the two. Batini and Yates (2003) have labeled these "hybrid-targeting" regimes. We begin by showing that for a given degree of output persistence, there is an optimal hybrid-targeting policy that is a weighted average of inflation and price-path targeting. But second, and more important, the focus on output persistence means that the choice is an empirical one. What is the optimal regime for a given country? Beyond this, there is the question of whether it is worth trying to move to the optimal regime. Clarity is and should be prized in central banking.

In fact, an optimal hybrid target sacrifices simplicity for optimality. It is much more difficult to explain a hybrid than it would be to explain either of the extreme alternatives. However, as King (1999) has suggested, one of the key policy choices is the horizon over which central bankers are evaluated. That is, are they asked to maintain inflation at or near the target level on average every two, three, five, or even ten years? Put another way, central bankers will have a horizon over which they are expected to bring the price level back to its desired path. Under this interpretation, hybrid targeting becomes a statement about the *optimal horizon* over which the price level is brought back to the desired path; it may not be that hard to convince people that they should give the central bank some time to fight back unwanted price shocks.

Even so, the idea that central bankers should, for strategic reasons, be told to do something that explicitly deviates from what society truly cares about will trouble many people. Should we go to the effort of explaining that we are instructing the central bank to do one thing, while we care

---

6. More recent papers by Dittmar and Gavin (2000) and Vestin (2000) confirm this result.

about another, because we know that they can't be trusted? Again, this is an empirical question. How much do we lose by just telling monetary policymakers to target the thing that society cares about?

To address these issues, we examine a set of twenty-three countries and find that for nearly all of them some form of hybrid-targeting regime would be optimal—at least in principle. But we go on to show that adopting such an optimal regime has only very modest benefits (as measured by the percentage reduction in the social loss) when compared with strict inflation targeting. In other words, once you look at the numbers closely it is hard to see the benefit of starting to engage in what would surely be a very difficult public dialogue. Our conclusion is that we should hold central bankers accountable for meeting our social loss function, not some contrived one that might incrementally improve macroeconomic performance.

The remainder of this paper is organized as follows. First, we set out the theoretical problem and derive the optimal hybrid-targeting regime, and we show that this can be interpreted as the optimal horizon. We also show the relationship between output persistence and the weight on price stability. We also present a set of empirical results and compare the loss between an optimal-targeting regime and inflation or price-path targeting. The final section concludes.

4.2   Hybrid Targeting

The theoretical exercise is straightforward. Society cares about a weighted average of inflation and output deviations from their target paths. If it were possible to bind policymakers to react to shocks in a particular way, then it would be optimal to give them society's objective and then hold them accountable for adjusting their policy instrument in the way prescribed by the reaction function that minimizes this social objective. But such commitment is impossible (and may not even be desirable). Instead, the central bank can be held accountable for minimizing a loss function under discretion. What should that loss function be?

To answer this question, we proceed in two steps. First, we derive the central bank's policy reaction function, or instrument rule, under discretion for a family of loss functions that admits a wide variety of targeting regimes. Second, given the solution we find the targeting regime that minimizes the social loss. This is the optimal hybrid.

4.2.1   The Central Banker's Problem

The policymaker solves a standard optimal control problem, choosing the path of the price level that minimizes a quadratic loss function subject to the constraints imposed by the linear structure of the economy. We assume that the central bank minimizes

(1)
$$L^{CB} = E\left\{\sum_t \beta^t [\lambda(p_t - p_t^*)^2 + (1 - \lambda)(y_t - y_t^*)^2]\right\},$$

where L^{CB} is the central bank's loss, E is the expectation operator, p_t is the (log) actual price level, p^* is the desired price level, y_t is the (log) actual output, y^* is desired (or potential) output level, λ is the degree to which the central bank prefers price stability to output stability, and β is the time discount factor. Equation (1) is sufficiently general to admit inflation targeting, price-path targeting, and everything in between. Targeting regimes differ depending on how the target, p_t^*, is defined. The simplest cases are inflation targeting, where

(2)
$$p_t^*(\text{IT}) = p_{t-1} + \pi^*,$$

and price-path targeting, where

(3)
$$p_t^*(\text{PPT}) = p_{t-1}^* + \pi^*.$$

In both cases the inflation target is π^*. But under inflation targeting, given by equation (2), the target is an increment over the past period's realized price level, whatever it turned out to be. By contrast, under price-path targeting, the current target is an increment over the past period's *target*.

Hybrid targeting is a weighted average of inflation and price-path targeting. That is,

(4)
$$p_t^*(\text{Hybrid}) = \eta(p_{t-1} + \pi^*) + (1 - \eta)(p_{t-1}^* + \pi^*)$$
$$= \eta p_{t-1} + (1 - \eta)p_{t-1}^* + \pi^*,$$

where η is the weight on inflation targeting. Notice that $\eta = 1$ and $\eta = 0$ are the special cases, inflation and price-path targeting, respectively. Substituting equation (4) into the loss function (1), and normalizing various constants and initial conditions to zero, we get

(5)
$$L^{CB} = E\left\{\sum_t \beta[\lambda(p_t - \eta p_{t-1})^2 + (1 - \lambda)y_t^2]\right\}.$$

Normalization implies that y is now the output gap and that the price path is now measured as the deviation from the inflation objective π^*.

Following Svensson (1999) and others, we assume that the dynamics of the economy are adequately described by a neoclassical Phillips Curve.[7] That is,

---

7. We choose the neoclassical Phillips curve because of its theoretical tractability. There are a number of alternatives, including the now common New Keynesian Phillips curve in which the output gap depends on expected future prices rather than current ones, and the aggregate supply formulation derived by Mankiw and Reis (2001) in their work on sticky information. While it would be feasible to examine these alternatives numerically, the more conventional Phillips curve allows us to derive a wider range of conclusions.

(6)
$$y_t = \rho y_{t-1} + \alpha(p_t - p_t^e) + \varepsilon_t,$$

where p_t^e is the expectation of p at time t, ρ and α are constants, and ε is an independently and identically distributed (i.i.d.) shock with variance σ_ε^2. For the points that we wish to make here, this closed-economy model is sufficient. In the empirical section, we expand the analysis to an open-economy version that includes import prices as well.

The job of the central bank is to choose a path for the price level p_t that minimizes the loss (5) subject to equation (6).[8] Assuming rational expectations, we can use the techniques described in Svensson (1999) to first derive the first-order conditions, guess the solution, and then use the method of undetermined coefficients.[9] The first-order conditions include the output equation (6) and

(7)
$$p_t - \eta p_{t-1} = -\frac{\alpha(1 - \lambda)(1 - a\rho\beta)}{\lambda[1 - \rho\beta(\rho - b\alpha)](1 - \eta\rho\beta)}\, y_t.$$

Equation (7) embodies the trade-off between output and prices in the loss function. It tells us the extent to which prices react to output shocks along an optimal path. Under rational expectations, we know that the solution for the price level must be of the form

(8)
$$p_t = a p_{t-1} + b y_{t-1} + c\varepsilon_t.$$

We can solve this for

$$a = \eta$$

$$b = \frac{-(1 - \rho^2\beta) + \sqrt{(1 - \beta\rho^2)^2 - 4\rho^2\alpha^2\beta\dfrac{1 - \lambda}{\lambda}}}{2\rho\beta\alpha}$$

$$c = -\frac{D}{1 + \alpha D},$$

$$\text{where } D = \frac{\alpha(1 - \lambda)}{\lambda[1 - \rho\beta(\rho - b\alpha)]}.$$

Setting η equal to either zero or 1, this solution collapses to the one in Svensson (1999).

This formulation allows us to write the laws of motion for output and prices, and these are

(9)
$$y_t = \rho y_{t-1} + (1 + \alpha c)\varepsilon_t$$

8. By adding an aggregate-demand curve relating the price level to the interest rate, we could shift the problem to one in which the central bank does not choose prices directly. This increase in complexity changes none of our results.
9. See also Söderlind (1999).

(10) $$p_t = \eta p_{t-1} + b y_{t-1} + c \varepsilon_t.$$

That is, output depends on lagged output, while prices depend on both lagged prices and lagged output.

As others have noted, for a solution to the central banker's problem to exist, the coefficient on lagged output in the price equation, b, must have a real value. That is, a solution exists if and only if

(11) $$\frac{1 - \lambda}{\lambda} \le \frac{(1 - \beta \rho^2)^2}{4 \rho^2 \alpha^2 \beta}.$$

Parkin (2000) points out that this condition is somewhat restrictive, since only large values of λ are consistent with high persistence in output (ρ close to one). This means that if λ is low and ρ is high, there is no solution. The reason is that under these circumstances the optimal response to stabilize output requires very high, even infinite, volatility of the price level (or inflation).[10] Fortunately, most estimates that we know of suggest that central banks place much higher weight on inflation than they do on output volatility. For example, Cecchetti and Ehrmann (2002) estimate λ's for a number of countries, and most of them are 3/4 or higher. So we view this problem as unlikely to occur in practice.

4.2.2 Society's Problem

With a complete characterization of the central bank's problem in hand, we can now turn to society's problem: what value of η should monetary policymakers be instructed to use? To figure this out, all we need to do is find the value of η that minimizes the social loss function, taking account of the central banker's behavior. Recall that we assume society minimizes a weighted average of inflation and output variability. We can write this as

(12) $$L^S = \lambda \sigma_\pi^2 + (1 - \lambda) \sigma_y^2.$$

For now we look only at the case in which λ is the same for society and the central bank. Using the previous results, we can write this as

(13) $$L^S = \left[D^2 \frac{2\lambda(1 - \rho)}{(1 + \eta)(1 - \rho\eta)} + (1 - \lambda) \right] \left[\frac{1}{1 - \rho^2} \left(\frac{c}{D} \right)^2 \right] \sigma_\varepsilon^2.$$

Taking the derivative with respect to η (noting that D is not a function of η and assuming that the condition [11] holds) yields the optimal hybrid-targeting regime:

(14) $$\eta^* = \frac{1 - \rho}{2\rho}.$$

---

10. As we show in the appendix, this is a problem that only arises under discretion. If the central bank can be forced to commit to an instrument rule, then the problem always has a solution.

The result tells us that as ρ approaches 1, so that the shocks to output are extremely persistent, η^* goes to zero. As ρ shrinks, η^* grows, but we assume that it can never exceed 1. Importantly, the expression is consistent with Svensson's result. He shows that if one is restricted to choosing $\eta = 0$ or $\eta = 1$, then the threshold is at $\rho = 0.5$.

Before proceeding, we note that under commitment, where society can bind policymakers not just to an objective function but to an instrument rule as well, the best thing to do is to give the central bank society's loss function. That is not at all surprising. What is surprising is that if society's loss is in terms of the *price path* rather than inflation—that is, L^S is a function of σ_p^2 rather than σ_π^2—then the discretionary solution is the same as the commitment solution.[11]

4.2.3   Stabilization Bias

So far, we have been concerned with the benefits to be obtained from giving the central bank a hybrid target. But in addition to choosing η^*, society has the option of giving the central bank a λ that deviates from its own. The incentive for doing this comes from the fact that, left to their own devices, central bankers may choose to stabilize output more than is socially optimal. Avoiding this stabilization bias requires setting λ^{CB} above λ^S.

To see how this works, we return to equation (13) and note first that λ here represents social preferences and that D (defined in the previous section) is a function of the central bank's λ. Using this, we can rewrite the expression for the social loss as

$$(15) \qquad L^S = \left[D(\lambda^{CB})^2 \frac{2(1 - \rho)\lambda^s}{(1 + \eta)(1 - \rho\eta)} + (1 - \lambda^s) \right]$$
$$\cdot \left\{ \frac{1}{1 - \rho^2} \left[\frac{1}{1 + \alpha D(\lambda^{CB})} \right]^2 \right\} \sigma_\varepsilon^2.$$

This change has no impact on the degree of optimal hybrid targeting. η^* was not a function of λ before, and it is not now. But minimizing equation (15) requires not only finding η^* but also figuring out what λ^{CB} should be as well. The first-order condition for this second choice is given by

$$\frac{\alpha(1 - \lambda^{CB})}{\lambda^{CB}} f(\rho) = \frac{\alpha(1 - \lambda^s)}{\lambda^s},$$

where $f(\cdot)$ is an increasing function of ρ. So with given λ^s, as ρ rises, λ^{CB} rises as well.

Figure 4.1 plots the relationship between output persistence and λ^{CB}

---

11. If inflation's primary cost is that it makes long-term planning difficult, then this may be the case we should all be focusing on. See the appendix for details.

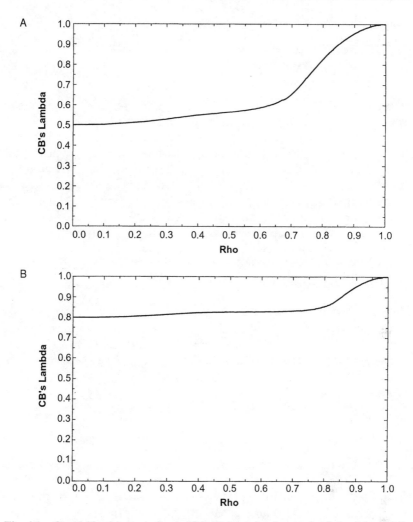

Fig. 4.1   Central bank's λ: *A*, Central bank's lambda when society's lambda = 0.5;
***B*, Central bank's lambda when society's lambda = 0.8**

when λ^s is 0.5 and 0.8. Throughout we assume that η is set at the optimal level, η^* in equation (14). The result is clear: the more persistent output is, the more conservative the central bank should be. And as the output approaches a random walk, the closer λ^{CB} gets to 1.

This is a good place to make another important point. In the last section we noted that there are times when the discretionary solution to the central banker's problem does not exist. Looking back at the restriction (11) required for existence, we see that there is always a solution when λ is big enough. So, if we are concerned that ρ may be high, we can avoid potential difficulties by instructing the central banker to care almost exclusively about inflation.

4.3 Empirical Results

We now see that the optimal hybrid-targeting regime—the degree to which the central bank should target inflation relative to targeting the path of the price level—depends on how persistent output is. This leads us to ask the following questions: how persistent is output, and how close is the actual behavior of prices to what it would be under an optimal-targeting regime? The task of this section is to bring data to bear on these questions.

We do this in three steps. First, we estimate an empirical analog of the closed-economy model we studied in section 4.2. Second, since a number of countries we consider are small open economies, we introduce external factors into the estimation. Finally, we posit a social loss function in order to do welfare comparisons and measure the gains from adopting an optimal hybrid target.

4.3.1   Closed Economy

Our strategy is the following. Using quarterly data on consumer prices and industrial production, we estimate equations (9) and (10).[12] (The data are all described in the appendix.) Taking account of the serial correlation in output, we use the following specifications:

$$(16) \qquad y_t = \rho y_{t-1} + \sum_{i=1}^{4} \gamma_i \Delta y_{t-i} + e_{1t}$$

$$(17) \qquad p_t = \eta p_{t-1} + b_1 y_{t-1} + b_2 y_{t-2} + b_3 y_{t-3} + b_4 y_{t-4} + e_{2t},$$

where y is computed as the deviation of log output from Hodrick-Prescott (HP) filtered output, and p measures the deviation of the log price level from a measure of the target. During the periods when countries were employing inflation targets, we used the target itself for this computation.[13] In the absence of an inflation target, we used a Hodrick-Prescott filter.

The results for both the full sample (1980s and 1990s) and just the last decade are reported in tables 4.1 and 4.2. Estimates range widely.[14] The first table shows estimates of ρ, together with standard errors. The important thing to notice is that ρ ranges from a low of 0.29 to a high of 0.82 and that

---

12. We note that our exact results are not invariant to the choice of the frequency of the data.

13. For the cases in which we have data for an explicit inflation target, we compute the price-path target as $p_t^* = \log(CPI_{t-1}) + \pi^*$, where π^* is the annual inflation target. Details are in the appendix.

14. All estimates throughout the paper are median-bias corrected using the empirical distributions that are also used to compute the standard errors.

Table 4.1   **Output persistence: The closed-economy case**

Country	Full sample		1990s	
	$\hat{\rho}$	Standard error	$\hat{\rho}$	Standard error
Australia	0.64	0.10	0.49	0.18
Austria	0.76	0.19	0.66	0.36
Canada	0.73	0.06	0.74	0.09
Chile	0.57	0.21	0.47	0.43
Denmark	0.56	0.14	0.31	0.23
Finland	0.78	0.07	0.65	0.13
France	0.61	0.15	0.61	0.15
Germany	0.70	0.10	0.61	0.17
Ireland	0.56	0.12	0.50	0.19
Israel	0.56	0.09	0.29	0.15
Italy	0.71	0.10	0.63	0.15
Japan	0.78	0.05	0.69	0.09
Korea	0.58	0.10	0.60	0.13
Mexico	0.64	0.10	0.69	0.15
The Netherlands	0.64	0.15	0.68	0.23
New Zealand	0.58	0.10	0.58	0.15
Norway	0.43	0.16	0.55	0.19
Portugal	0.76	0.08	0.69	0.14
Spain	0.72	0.07	0.70	0.11
Sweden	0.71	0.09	0.60	0.13
Switzerland	0.33	0.22	0.35	0.33
United Kingdom	0.80	0.07	0.78	0.08
United States	0.76	0.04	0.82	0.06

Notes: Estimates $\hat{\rho}$ are small sample bias-corrected autocorrelation coefficients from fourth-order autoregression using industrial production, equation (16). All data are quarterly data, seasonally adjusted and filtered using a Hodrick-Prescott filter. The full sample is 1980 Q1 to 2001 Q4 for non-euro-area countries. For countries in EMU, the sample ends in 1998 Q4. Standard errors are constructed from nonparametric bootstrap with 3,000 replications.

it is unstable across time periods. Both the range and instability have important implications for policy, so we will return to them later.[15]

Table 4.2 reports our estimates of the optimal hybrid-targeting regime, $\hat{\eta}^*$, as well as the estimate that is implied by the actual behavior of prices in each country, $\tilde{\eta}$. Our estimates of ρ suggest that a number of countries should be putting significant weight on the price path, $\hat{\eta}^* \ll 1$, but virtually all of them exhibit behavior that is closer to inflation targeting, $\tilde{\eta} \approx 1$. Given these estimates, we test whether $\tilde{\eta} = \eta^*$, and the answer is no. The p-value is reported in columns (3) and (6) of table 4.2.[16]

15. While we report results for a Hodrick-Prescott (HP) filter with parameter set to the standard 1600, experimentation in the range from 800 to 3200 leaves the character of our results unchanged.

16. Using a nonparametric bootstrap, we compute the empirical distribution of $\hat{\eta}^*$ and then report the p-value for $\tilde{\eta}$ in that distribution.

Table 4.2   **The optimal hybrid-targeting regime: The closed-economy case**

| | Full sample | | | 1990s | | |
Country	$\hat{\eta}^*$	$\tilde{\eta}$	p-value testing $\tilde{\eta} = \eta^*$	$\hat{\eta}^*$	$\tilde{\eta}$	p-value testing $\tilde{\eta} = \eta^*$
Australia	0.29	0.81	0.01	0.50	0.69	0.33
Austria	0.15	0.68	0.07	0.25	0.46	0.26
Canada	0.18	0.94	0.00	0.18	0.88	0.00
Chile	0.36	0.72	0.22	0.31	0.64	0.31
Denmark	0.39	0.67	0.17	1.00	0.24	0.14
Finland	0.14	0.91	0.00	0.26	0.84	0.03
France	0.31	0.80	0.08	0.32	0.80	0.08
Germany	0.21	0.83	0.00	0.32	0.67	0.15
Ireland	0.39	0.81	0.09	0.49	0.63	0.37
Israel	0.39	0.90	0.03	1.00	0.79	0.26
Italy	0.21	0.94	0.00	0.29	1.00	0.05
Japan	0.14	0.75	0.00	0.23	0.70	0.01
Korea	0.35	0.90	0.02	0.34	0.56	0.19
Mexico	0.28	0.86	0.01	0.23	0.83	0.05
The Netherlands	0.28	0.88	0.06	0.24	0.60	0.17
New Zealand	0.36	0.93	0.03	0.36	0.54	0.25
Norway	0.64	0.77	0.39	0.38	0.56	0.32
Portugal	0.16	0.88	0.00	0.23	0.83	0.04
Spain	0.19	0.80	0.00	0.22	0.92	0.01
Sweden	0.21	0.84	0.00	0.33	0.53	0.21
Switzerland	1.00	0.89	0.44	0.89	0.87	0.36
United Kingdom	0.12	0.76	0.00	0.14	0.44	0.01
United States	0.16	1.00	0.00	0.11	0.91	0.00

Source: Data sources are all described in the appendix.

Notes: Estimates of $\hat{\eta}^*$ are constructed using the $\hat{\rho}$ in table 4.1. Estimates of $\tilde{\eta}$ are the coefficient on the lag of prices from equation (17). The p-values for the tests are constructed using a nonparametric bootstrap with 3,000 replications.

4.3.2   Open Economy

To take account of the fact that countries like Israel, Belgium, and Ireland are small and open, we introduce external factors into our analysis. Following Svensson (2000), we introduce import prices into the Phillips curve (6):

(18) $$y_t = \rho y_{t-1} + \alpha(p_t - p_t^e) + \phi_y p_t^F + \varepsilon_t,$$

where p_t^F is the foreign price level denominated in domestic currency. With this modification, all of the results in section 4.2 go through, and we can rewrite empirical specification equations (9) and (10) as

(19) $$y_t = \rho y_{t-1} + \sum_{i=1}^{4} \gamma_i \Delta y_{t-i} + \phi_y p_t^F + e_{1t}$$

(20) $$p_t = \eta p_{t-1} + b_1 y_{t-1} + b_2 y_{t-2} + b_3 y_{t-3} + b_4 y_{t-4} + \phi_p p_t^F + e_{2t}.$$

Table 4.3   **Output persistence: The open-economy case**

Country	Full sample		1990s	
	$\hat{\rho}$	Standard error	$\hat{\rho}$	Standard error
Australia	0.66	(0.09)	0.58	(0.19)
Austria	0.84	(0.23)	0.63	(0.50)
Canada	0.75	(0.06)	0.73	(0.11)
Chile	0.61	(0.07)	n.a.	n.a.
Denmark	0.61	(0.15)	0.13	(0.31)
Finland	0.79	(0.05)	0.78	(0.14)
France	n.a.	n.a.	0.61	(0.17)
Germany	0.73	(0.11)	0.69	(0.20)
Ireland	0.48	(0.14)	0.60	(0.22)
Israel	0.56	(0.09)	0.15	(0.17)
Italy	0.73	(0.09)	0.63	(0.13)
Japan	0.73	(0.04)	0.59	(0.09)
Korea	0.67	(0.11)	0.60	(0.12)
Mexico	0.67	(0.11)	0.53	(0.21)
The Netherlands	0.65	(0.17)	0.59	(0.29)
New Zealand	0.59	(0.10)	0.64	(0.16)
Norway	0.46	(0.16)	0.67	(0.21)
Portugal	0.78	(0.08)	0.75	(0.18)
Spain	0.73	(0.05)	0.74	(0.09)
Sweden	0.74	(0.10)	0.65	(0.16)
Switzerland	0.32	(0.24)	0.18	(0.43)
United Kingdom	0.81	(0.07)	0.79	(0.04)
United States	0.78	(0.03)	0.84	(0.04)

Source: See appendix and notes to table 4.1 for data sources.
Note: n.a. = not available.

Table 4.3 reports estimates of output persistence, ρ, after accounting for these external factors. The results are very similar to those in table 4.1. The correlation between these two sets of estimates is 0.96 for the full sample and 0.89 for the 1990s, and the mean absolute difference between the estimates is 0.03 and 0.075, respectively. Looking at the estimates of the various measures of η in table 4.4, our conclusions from the closed-economy analysis remain. In virtually every case, our estimate of the optimal hybrid target has η well below 1, closer to price-path targeting than inflation targeting, but the actual behavior of prices in these countries suggests something close to inflation targeting.

It is interesting to relate all of these results to what King (1999) referred to as an evaluation horizon for central bankers. He suggested that in practice an inflation-targeting central bank will be evaluated on whether it met its target on average over some number of years. The evaluation horizon is related to the hybrid regime. The longer the period over which inflation is averaged, the closer the regime is to price-path targeting. Using this intu-

Table 4.4   Optimal hybrid-targeting regime: The open-economy case

Country	Full sample			1990s		
	$\hat{\eta}^*$	$\tilde{\eta}$	p-value testing $\tilde{\eta} = \eta^*$	$\hat{\eta}^*$	$\tilde{\eta}$	p-value testing $\tilde{\eta} = \eta^*$
Australia	0.26	0.82	0.01	0.37	0.70	0.20
Austria	0.09	0.52	0.09	0.29	0.38	0.32
Canada	0.17	0.95	0.00	0.19	0.90	0.00
Chile	0.20	0.57	0.17	n.a.	n.a.	n.a.
Denmark	0.31	0.52	0.20	1.00	0.30	0.37
Finland	0.13	0.89	0.00	0.14	0.83	0.01
France	n.a.	n.a.	n.a.	0.33	0.67	0.17
Germany	0.19	0.72	0.01	0.21	0.75	0.09
Ireland	0.53	0.78	0.27	0.32	0.71	0.20
Israel	0.39	0.90	0.02	1.00	0.80	0.23
Italy	0.19	0.83	0.01	0.25	0.90	0.07
Japan	0.18	0.71	0.00	0.35	0.70	0.06
Korea	0.26	0.86	0.02	0.29	0.48	0.26
Mexico	0.26	0.88	0.01	0.42	0.88	0.20
The Netherlands	0.26	0.83	0.10	0.30	0.60	0.27
New Zealand	0.34	0.99	0.01	0.28	0.50	0.19
Norway	0.56	0.77	0.32	0.24	0.62	0.16
Portugal	0.14	0.85	0.00	0.16	0.85	0.04
Spain	0.18	0.78	0.00	0.17	0.90	0.01
Sweden	0.19	0.80	0.00	0.26	0.53	0.16
Switzerland	1.00	0.86	0.48	1.00	0.87	0.34
United Kingdom	0.11	0.76	0.00	0.13	0.44	0.00
United States	0.14	0.91	0.00	0.10	0.63	0.00

Source: See appendix and notes to text table 4.2.

Note: n.a. = not available.

ition, we can construct approximate measures of the horizon as $(1/\eta)$. For many countries we find that η^* is between 0.2 and 0.3, implying a horizon of between three and four quarters. To get a number that is usable in practice, we need to add another four to six quarters, the length of time that it takes for policy changes to have an impact on prices and output. The implication is that the evaluation horizon should be in the range of two to three years.

Before continuing, note that we recomputed all of the results for both the closed- and open-economy versions of our model substituting core consumer prices for the headline measures used in sections 4.3.1 and 4.3.2. Tables analogous to 4.2 and 4.4 are in the appendix. Overall, we find that the change in the price measure makes very little difference. Estimates of $\tilde{\eta}$ from the price equation are highly correlated between the two sets of matching results. For the full sample, the correlation for the seventeen countries for which we have data is 0.79 for the closed-economy model and 0.83 when import prices are included.

4.3.3 Loss Comparison

Simply computing the optimal value for η, the degree of a hybrid regime, is only the first step. What we really want to know is whether adopting the optimal hybrid makes any difference to welfare. Given the fact that estimates of η are fairly imprecise, this question is particularly important. To address it, we construct estimates of the social loss, L^S, for different targeting regimes and compare them. Computing the loss requires that we choose a series of parameters. Before turning to the data, it is useful to look at some simulations. Using the theoretical results, we can estimate the extent of the welfare gain that comes from going from an inflation-targeting regime to an optimal one. That is, we compare $L^S(\eta = 1)$ with $L^S(\eta = \eta^*)$ for various values of the parameters of the model. Note that throughout this exercise we assume that the preference parameter λ is the same for society and the central bank.

While it would be interesting to look across a wide range of values for the preference parameter λ, output persistence ρ, and the slope coefficient α, the condition (11) places restrictions on the relationship among these. So instead we look at a representative example. First, the restriction has a few simple properties: (a) given α, the higher ρ the higher the minimum λ; and (b) given ρ, the higher α the higher the minimum λ. What that means is that the more persistent output and the flatter the aggregate supply curve—that is, the inverse of α in equation (6)—the higher the preference for inflation stability has to be for there to be a solution to the central bank's problem. To understand how restrictive this is, we have done a few simple calculations. Setting the discount factor $\beta = 0.99$, we see that for $\alpha = 0.5$ and $\rho = 0.7$, λ must be greater than 0.65. As α decreases, the range of permissible values grows. So when $\alpha = 0.3$, λ can be as low as 0.4 for $\rho = 0.7$. This creates a potential problem for the choice of α. While we would like to work with relatively low values, we choose $\alpha = 0.5$. This is the choice made by Dittmar, Gavin, and Kydland (1999), who use estimates in Rudebusch and Svensson (1999) as justification.

Using these parameter values, we examine the improvement in the social loss for each country for two changes: (a) moving from strict inflation targeting to the optimal hybrid regimes, that is, $L^S(\eta^*)/L^S(\eta = 1)$; and (b) shifting from a strict price-path targeting regime to the optimal hybrid, $L^S(\eta^*)/L^S(\eta = 0)$. Throughout we assume that the preference parameter $\lambda = 0.8$ and the discount rate $\beta = 0.99$. The results are somewhat sensitive to the choice of λ but not to the choice of β. Looking at table 4.5, we see that there is an important pattern. In no case does a move from price-path targeting to the optimal hybrid bring a sizable welfare gain. The same is not true of a move from inflation targeting. That is, the first and third columns include numbers that are far below 1—for example, 0.82 for Canada and 0.87 for Germany—while the second and fourth columns contain none.

Table 4.5   Loss comparison

	Full sample		1990s	
Country	$L^S(\eta^*)/L^S(\eta=1)$	$L^S(\eta^*)/L^S(\eta=0)$	$L^S(\eta^*)/L^S(\eta=1)$	$L^S(\eta^*)/L^S(\eta=0)$
Australia	0.94	0.99	0.97	0.99
Austria	0.71*	0.71*	0.95	1.00
Canada	0.82	1.00	0.86	1.00
Chile	0.91	0.99	0.71*	0.71*
Denmark	0.96	0.99	1.00	0.96
Finland	0.71*	0.71*	0.72	1.00
France	0.96	0.99	0.96	0.99
Germany	0.87	1.00	0.91	0.99
Ireland	0.99	0.99	0.96	0.99
Israel	0.98	0.99	1.00	0.96
Italy	0.87	1.00	0.94	0.99
Japan	0.85	1.00	0.97	0.99
Korea	0.93	0.99	0.95	0.99
Mexico	0.93	0.99	0.98	0.99
The Netherlands	0.96	0.99	0.97	0.99
New Zealand	0.96	0.99	0.95	0.99
Norway	0.99	0.99	0.93	0.99
Portugal	0.71	1.00	0.80	1.00
Spain	0.86	1.00	0.84	1.00
Sweden	0.86	1.00	0.94	0.99
Switzerland	1.00	0.97	1.00	0.98
United Kingdom	0.71*	0.71*	0.71*	0.71*
United States	0.71*	0.71*	0.71*	0.71*

Notes: Computations use $\alpha = 0.5$ and $\lambda = 0.8$, as well as the estimated value of ρ reported in table 4.1. Asterisks indicate values of (α, λ, ρ) for which restriction (11) is not met, and so the loss cannot be computed. The reported value is the minimum for which it can be computed.

It is worth examining this result in more detail. Figure 4.2 plots the two ratios $L^S(\eta^*)/L^S(\eta = 0)$ and $L^S(\eta^*)/L^S(\eta = 1)$ for a range of values for ρ and λ, assuming $\alpha = 0.5$ and $\beta = 0.99$. Taken together, these give us a striking picture of the potential benefits from adopting various regimes. First, note from panel A that even if ρ is very small, and so the optimal regime is close to one of pure inflation targeting, the loss from adopting price-path targeting is small. Only when λ is set to 2/3, a relatively low value, and when output has virtually no persistence does a move from price-path targeting to the optimal hybrid imply a welfare gain of as much as 10 percent.

This is in stark contrast to panel B of figure 4.2, where we see the consequences of shifting from a pure inflation-targeting regime to the optimal hybrid. As output persistence rises above 0.6, the ratio of the losses starts to decrease very quickly. (Note that the lines end at the point where restriction [11] is no longer met.) That is, the gain from moving from inflation targeting to the optimal hybrid can be very large. To use Svensson's

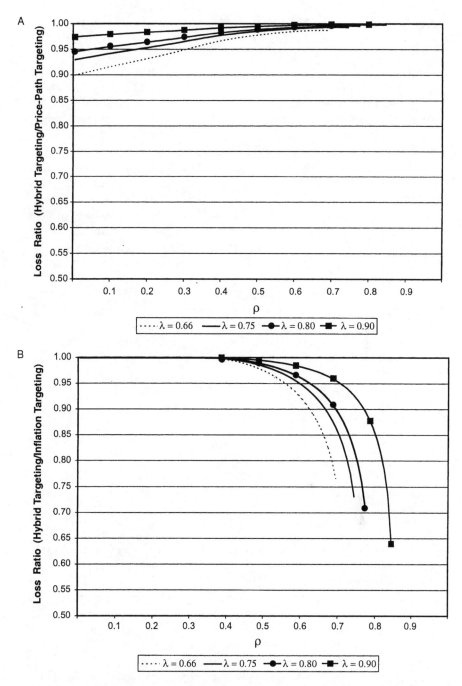

Fig. 4.2   Loss comparing targeting regimes with optimal targeting: *A,* Comparing price-path targeting to the optimal hybrid regime (α = 0.5); *B,* Comparing inflation targeting to the optimal hybrid regime (α = 0.5)

terminology, there is a "free lunch," and it can be big. And since we are unsure how big ρ really is, it is likely prudent to move to price-path targeting.

4.4 Conclusion

We have examined whether a country is well advised to target inflation, target the price path, or do something in between. The issue turns on the persistence of output deviations from their trend. With high persistence, which is what we tend to observe, our theoretical results suggest that countries are best off if they adopt a hybrid target that is close to price-path targeting. But such a policy regime would be difficult to adopt for two reasons. First, there is the technical one. The exact targeting procedure depends on the estimation of both the output trend and output persistence, both of which are going to be measured with substantial error. Second, the success or failure of any monetary policy regime rests critically on the ability of central bankers to communicate what they are doing to the public. Explaining a hybrid target would be challenging for even the best central bankers.

Taking these problems into account, we examine the welfare loss from adopting pure inflation or price-path targeting rather than the optimal hybrid. Our conclusion is that price-path targeting is less risky, in that the maximum social loss from being wrong—choosing price-path targeting when something else is better—is much smaller than if one chooses inflation targeting.

Appendix

Data Description

All data are quarterly beginning in quarter 1 (Q1) of 1980. For European Monetary Union (EMU) countries, data are through 1998 Q4. For non-EMU countries, data are through 2001 Q4.

1. Prices: Consumer Price Index (CPI) from the International Monetary Fund (IMF) International Financial Statistics.
2. Output: Industrial Production from the IMF International Financial Statistics (IFS), except for Portugal and Ireland, which are entirely from the Organization for Economic Cooperation and Development (OECD); New Zealand is from the OECD for 2000 Q3 on; Italy is from OECD for 2001 Q1 on; and Chile is manufacturing production only.
3. Core consumer prices: From the OECD.
4. Import prices: The import price index from the IMF International Financial Statistics, except for Spain, New Zealand, the Netherlands, Canada, France, Ireland, Israel, Italy (where the unit value of imports

from IFS is used), Mexico (Import Price Index from Haver Analytics), Austria (which uses the German CPI), and Portugal (an equally weighted average of the CPIs for the United Kingdom, Spain, France, and Germany).

5. Inflation targets are computed from the Inflation Targeting Country Fact Sheets" by Frank Gaenssmantel of the Institute of International Economics, courtesy of Edwin Truman.

The inflation targets are listed in table 4A.1. The target p_t^* is computed as follows:

(A1) $\qquad p_t^* = p_{t-1} + \pi^*$

(A2) $\qquad p_t = \log(\text{CPI}_t) - p_t^* \qquad\qquad$ when there is p_t^*

(A3) $\qquad p_t = \log(\text{CPI}_t) - \text{HPtrend}_t \qquad$ otherwise,

where π^* is the annual inflation target in table 4A.1, divided by four. When the target is a range, the midpoint is used.

The Commitment Case

Our solutions in the text assume that the central bank operates under discretion. Discretion means that policymakers reoptimize the loss function every period after observing the state variable y_{t-1} and the shock ε_t. The alternative to this is commitment, in which the central bank optimizes once and commits to an instrument rule once and for all.

To find the commitment solution we take the derivative of the central bank's loss in equation (5) with respect to p_t and p_t^e, subject to the constraint imposed by the Phillips curve in equation (6). The resulting policy rule, the equivalent to equation (8), is

(A4) $\qquad\qquad\qquad\qquad p_t = \eta p_{t-1} + \tilde{c}\varepsilon_t,$

where

$$\tilde{c} = -\frac{\tilde{D}}{1 + \alpha\tilde{D}} \quad \text{and} \quad \tilde{D} = \frac{\alpha(1 - \lambda)}{\lambda(1 - \rho^2\beta)}.$$

This is exactly the same as the case under discretion considered in section 4.2.1, except that $b = 0$. That is, under commitment the optimal response is to react only to the past price level and the shock, not to y_{t-1}. Recall, moreover, that the condition for a solution to exist under discretion, shown in equation (11), arises in computing b, and so it is not present here.

Continuing with the problem under commitment, society's loss, the equivalent to equation (13), is now

(A5) $\qquad\qquad\qquad\qquad \tilde{L}^S = \left[\frac{2\lambda\tilde{c}^2}{1 + \eta} + \frac{1 - \lambda}{1 - \rho^2}\left(\frac{\tilde{c}}{\tilde{D}}\right)^2 \right]\sigma_\varepsilon^2.$

Table 4A.1   Annual inflation target

Country	Period	Inflation target (%)
Australia	1993 Q1–2001 Q4	2.5
Austria	1993 Q1–2001 Q4	2.0
Canada	1992 Q1–1994 Q4	4.0
	1995 Q1–2001 Q4	3.0
Chile	1991 Q1–1991 Q4	18.0
	1992 Q1–1992 Q4	17.5
	1993 Q1–1993 Q4	11.0
	1994 Q1–1994 Q4	10.0
	1995 Q1–1995 Q4	8.0
	1996 Q1–1996 Q4	7.0
	1997 Q1–1997 Q4	6.0
	1998 Q1–1998 Q4	5.0
	1999 Q1–1999 Q4	4.3
	2000 Q1–2000 Q4	3.5
	2001 Q1–2001 Q4	3.0
Finland	1993 Q1–2001 Q4	2.0
Israel	1992 Q1–1992 Q4	14.5
	1993 Q1–1993 Q4	10.0
	1994 Q1–1994 Q4	8.0
	1995 Q1–1995 Q4	9.5
	1996 Q1–1996 Q4	9.0
	1997 Q1–1997 Q4	8.5
	1998 Q1–1999 Q4	4.0
	2000 Q1–2000 Q4	3.5
	2001 Q1–2001 Q4	3.0
Korea	1999 Q1–1999 Q4	3.75
	2000 Q1–2000 Q4	2.5
	2001 Q1–2001 Q4	3.0
Mexico	1995 Q1–1995 Q4	19.0
	1996 Q1–1996 Q4	20.5
	1997 Q1–1997 Q4	15.0
	1998 Q1–1998 Q4	12.0
	1999 Q1–1999 Q4	13.0
	2000 Q1–2000 Q4	10.0
	2001 Q1–2001 Q4	6.5
New Zealand	1992 Q1–1996 Q4	1.0
	1997 Q1–2001 Q4	1.5
Norway	2001 Q1–2001 Q4	2.5
United Kingdom	1992 Q1–2001 Q4	2.5

Source: Gaenssmantel (2002).

The η that minimizes this loss is trivially 1, which implies inflation targeting. Under commitment, it is optimal to simply give the central bank society's loss function.

When Society Prefers Price-Path Targeting

What if society's preferences are in terms of the path of the price level rather than an inflation target? In this case, the central bank's problem is the same as the one in section 4.2.1. It is the social loss, equation (12), that changes. Assuming society cares about the price path implies that the social loss function is

(A6)
$$L^S = \lambda\sigma_p^2 + (1 - \lambda)\sigma_y^2.$$

Substituting in the solution for the central bank's problem, this becomes

(A7)
$$L^S = \left[\lambda D^2\left(\frac{1}{1 - \eta^2}\right)\left(\frac{1 + \eta\rho}{1 - \eta\rho}\right) + (1 - \lambda)\right]\sigma_y^2.$$

Equation (A7) is the equivalent to text equation (13). The optimal η that minimizes this loss is zero. So, if society cares about the price path, then the central bank should be told to care about it, too.

Substituting Core for Headline Consumer Prices

The following tables are from substituting measures of the core CPI for the headline CPI in the computations of section 4.3. Table 4A.2 is the analog to text table 4.2, and table 4A.3 is the analog to text table 4.4. Note that

Table 4A.2   Optimal hybrid-targeting regime: Closed economy with core CPI

	Full sample			1990s		
Country	$\hat{\eta}^*$	$\tilde{\eta}$	p-value testing $\tilde{\eta} = \eta^*$	$\hat{\eta}^*$	$\tilde{\eta}$	p-value testing $\tilde{\eta} = \eta^*$
Australia	n.a.	n.a.	n.a.	0.50	0.70	0.32
Austria	0.15	0.44	0.14	0.25	0.27	0.41
Canada	0.18	0.93	0.00	0.18	0.87	0.00
Chile	n.a.	n.a.	n.a.	n.a.	n.a.	n.a.
Denmark	0.39	0.56	0.25	1.00	0.21	0.12
Finland	0.14	0.91	0.00	0.26	0.73	0.05
France	0.31	0.92	0.06	0.32	0.92	0.06
Germany	0.21	0.90	0.00	0.32	0.81	0.11
Ireland	0.39	0.81	0.08	0.49	0.67	0.33
Israel	n.a.	n.a.	n.a.	n.a.	n.a.	n.a.
Italy	0.21	0.94	0.00	0.29	1.03	0.04
Japan	0.14	0.39	0.00	0.23	0.47	0.04
Korea	n.a.	n.a.	n.a.	0.34	0.63	0.16
Mexico	0.28	0.91	0.01	0.23	0.84	0.05
The Netherlands	0.28	0.79	0.07	0.24	0.52	0.20
New Zealand	0.36	0.81	0.03	0.36	0.54	0.26
Norway	n.a.	n.a.	n.a.	0.38	0.63	0.28
Portugal	n.a.	n.a.	n.a.	0.23	0.79	0.04
Spain	0.19	0.79	0.00	0.22	0.83	0.01
Sweden	0.21	0.78	0.00	0.33	0.46	0.27
Switzerland	1.00	1.02	0.39	1.00	0.93	0.34
United Kingdom	0.12	0.70	0.00	0.14	0.35	0.02
United States	0.16	0.97	0.00	0.11	0.68	0.00

Source: See appendix and notes to text table 4.2.
Note: n.a. = not available.

Table 4A.3   Optimal hybrid-targeting regime: Open economy with core CPI

Country	Full sample			1990s		
	$\hat{\eta}^*$	$\tilde{\eta}$	p-value testing $\tilde{\eta} = \eta^*$	$\hat{\eta}^*$	$\tilde{\eta}$	p-value testing $\tilde{\eta} = \eta^*$
Australia	n.a.	n.a.	n.a.	0.37	0.72	0.21
Austria	0.09	0.26	0.23	0.29	0.17	0.45
Canada	0.17	0.94	0.00	0.19	0.88	0.00
Chile	n.a.	n.a.	n.a.	n.a.	n.a.	n.a.
Denmark	0.31	0.44	0.29	1.00	0.05	0.35
Finland	0.13	0.91	0.00	0.14	0.70	0.01
France	n.a.	n.a.	n.a.	0.33	0.93	0.08
Germany	0.19	0.87	0.00	0.21	0.86	0.07
Ireland	0.53	0.79	0.24	0.32	0.58	0.25
Israel	n.a.	n.a.	n.a.	n.a.	n.a.	n.a.
Italy	0.19	0.83	0.01	0.25	0.93	0.02
Japan	0.18	0.37	0.01	0.35	0.45	0.26
Korea	n.a.	n.a.	n.a.	0.29	0.62	0.15
Mexico	0.26	0.95	0.01	0.42	0.89	0.20
The Netherlands	0.26	0.79	0.09	0.30	0.42	0.37
New Zealand	0.34	0.82	0.02	0.28	0.51	0.19
Norway	n.a.	n.a.	n.a.	0.24	0.69	0.14
Portugal	n.a.	n.a.	n.a.	0.16	0.75	0.05
Spain	0.18	0.79	0.00	0.17	0.77	0.00
Sweden	0.19	0.76	0.00	0.26	0.46	0.21
Switzerland	1.00	1.02	0.41	1.00	0.94	0.33
United Kingdom	0.11	0.71	0.00	0.13	0.34	0.01
United States	0.14	0.94	0.00	0.10	0.69	0.00

Source: See appendix and notes to text table 4.4.
Note: n.a. = not available.

since the output equations (16) and (19) do not include the price level, the estimates of ρ and η^* are unchanged, and so the corresponding columns in the tables are identical. Comparing these results to those in the text, we conclude that substituting core for headline prices changes little.

References

Batini, Nicoletta, and Anthony Yates. 2003. Hybrid inflation and price level targeting. *Journal of Money, Credit and Banking* 35 (3): 283–300.
Cecchetti, Stephen G., and Michael Ehrmann. 2002. Does inflation targeting increase output volatility? An international comparison of policymakers' preferences and outcomes. In *Monetary Policy: Rules and Transmission Mechanisms,* Proceedings of the fourth annual conference of the Central Bank of Chile, ed. Norman Loayza and Klaus Schmidt-Hebbel, 247–74. Santiago, Chile: Central Bank of Chile.

Cecchetti, Stephen G., Alfonso Flores-Lagunes, and Stefan Krause. 2002. Has monetary policy become more efficient? Brandeis University, International Business School, University of Arizona, Department of Economics, and Emory University, Department of Economics. Unpublished manuscript.

Clark, Peter B., Charles A. E. Goodhart, and Haizhou Huang. 1999. Optimal monetary policy rules in a rational expectations model of the Phillips curve. *Journal of Monetary Economics* 43:497–520.

Dittmar, Robert, and William T. Gavin. 2000. What do New Keynesian Phillips curves imply for price-level targeting? *Economic Review of the Federal Reserve Bank of St. Louis* 82 (April): 21–30.

Dittmar, Robert, William T. Gavin, and Finn Kydland. 1999. The inflation-output variability trade-off and price-level targeting. *Economic Review of the Federal Reserve Bank of St. Louis* 81 (1): 23–39.

Gaenssmantel, Frank. 2002. Inflation targeting country fact sheets. Institute of International Economics. Mimeograph.

King, Mervyn. 1999. Challenges for monetary policy: New and old. In *New challenges for monetary policy,* proceedings of the Federal Reserve Bank of Kansas City symposium, 11–57. Kansas City, Mo.: Federal Reserve Bank of Kansas City.

Mankiw, N. Gregory, and Ricardo Reis. 2001. Sticky information vs. sticky prices: A proposal to replace the New Keynesian Phillips curve. NBER Working Paper no. 8290. Cambridge, Mass.: National Bureau of Economic Research, May.

Mishkin, Frederic S. Forthcoming. Inflation targeting. In *Encyclopedia of macroeconomics,* ed. Howard Vane and Brian Snowdon. London: Edward Elgar.

Parkin, Michael. 2000. A note on inflation targeting versus price level targeting. University of Western Ontario, Department of Economics. Mimeograph.

Rogoff, Kenneth. 1985. The optimal degree of commitment to an intermediate monetary target. *Quarterly Journal of Economics* 100:1169–90.

Rudebusch, Glenn D., and Lars E. O. Svensson. 1999. Policy rules for inflation targeting. In *Monetary policy rules,* ed. John B. Taylor, 203–46. Chicago: University of Chicago Press.

Söderlind, Paul. 1999. Solution and estimation of RE macromodels with optimal policy. *European Economic Review* 43:813–23.

Svensson, Lars E. O. 1999. Price level targeting vs. inflation targeting. *Journal of Money, Credit and Banking* 31 (August): 277–95.

———. 2000. Open-economy inflation targeting. *Journal of International Economics* 50 (February): 155–83.

Vestin, David. 2000. Price level targeting vs. inflation targeting in a forward-looking model. Working Paper no. 106. Stockholm, Sweden: Sveriges Riksbank, May.

Comment   N. Gregory Mankiw

I like the starting point of this paper—the question of whether inflation targeting or price-level targeting is the better policy for a central bank to adopt. Like the authors, I think this is an important and still open question

N. Gregory Mankiw is currently chairman of the Council of Economic Advisers, Allie S. Freed Professor of Economics at Harvard University, and a research associate of the National Bureau of Economic Research.

in the analysis of monetary policy. And I agree with the paper's conclusion that, given our current understanding of the issue, price-level targeting is probably the better of the two alternatives. (For my approach to this issue, see Ball, Mankiw, and Reis 2003.)

The job of discussant, however, is like that of Mark Antony—not to praise the authors but to bury them. So even though there is a lot in this paper that I agree with, in my comments I will emphasize the points of disagreement. Going from the starting point (which I like) to the conclusion (with which I concur), this paper takes a few wrong turns along the way. Sometimes these wrong turns follow in the footsteps of the literature; other times the authors strike out in a mistaken direction all on their own.

Fortunately, one wrong turn the authors avoided is the use of an implausible model of inflation-output dynamics, although they make the mistake of apologizing for this fact. In a footnote, they say that they use a neoclassical Phillips curve for its tractability, suggesting that they would have preferred to use a New Keynesian Phillips curve. In my view, this gets things exactly backward. I think that every paper in this conference that uses the New Keynesian Phillips curve should apologize. Let me suggest the following footnote for those papers: "We use the New Keynesian Phillips curve even though its predictions about monetary policy are inconsistent with what most empirical studies find and with what every central banker knows to be true. We use this model because we think it is neat, and because that's what everybody else is doing."

Another way in which the authors' views differ from mine is in their acceptance of the Svenssonian approach to the analysis of monetary policy. As I understand it, the Svenssonian approach is based on the idea that two wrongs make a right, as least if the wrongs are well chosen. That is, society has a problem because monetary policy is made by discretion and thus suffers from time inconsistency. We can fix this problem, however, by assigning the central bank an objective function that differs from the true social welfare function. The Svensson insight is that the wrong of having an incorrect objective function can offset the wrong of having discretionary policy. This is a classic second-best type of analysis.

What puzzles me about this approach is the question of implementation. That is, how are we supposed to give the central bank this new objective function?

One possibility is that the central bank takes direction from a higher authority, such as Congress. In this case, why would the higher authority direct the central bank to have the wrong objective function? It seems more natural to direct the central bank to follow the optimal rule based on the true social welfare function. This is roughly McCallum's "just do it" viewpoint, and it is similar to the approach envisioned by Woodford's "timeless" perspective on monetary policy analysis. It is not at all obvious to me why one type of direction from a higher authority to a central bank is more feasible than the other. That is, if the higher authority can assign an objective function to the central bank, it should be able to assign the central bank the constraint of being time consistent.

There is, however, another way to think about implementing the Svenssonian objective function. When we appoint central bankers, we can look around the population of candidates and pick someone who happened to think that the true social welfare function was the one that Svensson derives as the right one for a central bank to maximize. This central banker would be wrong, but he would be wrong in a useful way. This is akin to Rogoff's analysis of why we might want central bankers to be more conservative, in the sense of more inflation averse, than the general public.

This approach to implementation also strikes me as a bit odd. If a potential central banker is misguided about the social welfare function, why would that be the case? Most likely, he has the wrong model of the economy. The Svensson-Rogoff assumption is that the central banker has the right model but the wrong social welfare function. My experience is that people who are confused about one thing are often confused about other things as well. Looking for public servants who are confused in just the right way to offset the problems of discretionary policy does not seem like a winning strategy.

These comments, however, are aimed more at the broader literature than at this particular paper. Let me now put these larger concerns aside and turn to some issues that are more specific to this paper.

The empirical heart of this paper concerns the persistence of output. In Svensson's model, the desirability of inflation or price-level targeting depends on the autoregressive parameter in the output equation. The more persistent output shocks are, the more attractive price-level targeting becomes. An autoregressive parameter of 0.5 is a crucial cutoff.

This raises a natural question: how long is a period in the model? That is, what frequency of data should we use to implement the model? If output is AR(1) with parameter 0.8 in quarterly data, it is AR(1) with parameter 0.41 ($=0.8^4$) in annual data. We would reach a different conclusion about policy if we applied the model at an annual rather than a quarterly frequency. The Cecchetti-Kim paper uses quarterly data, but it does not explain why this is the right choice.

There is, however, something in the model that can be used to pin down the choice of data frequency: the timing of expectations. The Phillips curve in this model is based on one-period-ahead expectations of the price level. The paper does not tell us precisely how this equation is motivated, but one common approach is Fischerian labor contracts predetermining the nominal wage. In this case, the relevant issue is how far in advance wages are set. If wages are set one year ahead, rather than one quarter, applying the model at an annual frequency would make more sense. In this case, the estimated autoregressive parameters would be much lower than those presented in the paper. By using higher-frequency data, the authors build in a bias toward their conclusion of price-level targeting.

Another nuts-and-bolts empirical issue that is crucial for this paper is the classic topic of detrending. Cecchetti and Kim look at persistence in quarterly output detrended with the Hodrick-Prescott (HP) filter. But an arbitrary parameter in this filter governs how much of the low-frequency movement in the data is filtered out. Their results in table 4.1 tell us that shocks to U.S. GDP have a half-life of about three quarters. I suspect that this result is more an artifact of the filter than a fact about the data. If they altered the smoothing parameter in the HP filter, they would be likely to get very different estimates for this key autoregressive parameter.

A central issue in this model is the length of time with which monetary shocks influence output. If we knew the answer to this question, we could use it to calibrate the autoregressive parameter and judge whether the parameter is bigger or smaller than 1/2, the key cutoff. If I am right that we should be thinking at an annual frequency, because labor contracts are annual more often than quarterly, then the key question is this: does a monetary shock's effect on output dissipate by more or less than 50 percent if measured a year after the shock? I don't know the answer, but I doubt we can learn it from running univariate autoregressions using HP filtered output.

In closing, let me briefly address the big question of whether price-level targeting really would be a good monetary policy. There are now a lot of academic studies suggesting that it would be a good policy for a variety of reasons. My experience from talking to central bankers, however, is that they are often horrified at the idea. They have trouble imagining that a period of higher-than-target inflation should be followed by a period of lower-than-target inflation.

The reason they are horrified by this prospect, I think, is that in their hearts they don't really believe the Lucas critique. They tend to view the world through the lens of an expectations-augmented Phillips curve with adaptive expectations. If that model were truly structural, then price-level targeting would not be very attractive. Academics, however, are more likely to view that reduced form as an artifact of the monetary regime we have had over the past several decades. The reduced-form Phillips curve would look very different if a central bank adopted price-level targeting.

We academics, however, should be careful to maintain a bit of humility when we engage in this policy debate. We have to admit that our understanding of inflation-output dynamics is still primitive. Until we reach a consensus about the right model about the Phillips curve, we cannot be confident about the effect of any alternative monetary policy, especially proposals as radical as price-level targeting.

Reference

Ball, Laurence, N. Gregory Mankiw, and Ricardo Reis. 2003. Monetary policy for inattentive economies. NBER Working Paper no. 9491. Cambridge, Mass.: National Bureau of Economic Research.

Discussion Summary

In response to Gregory Mankiw's comments, *Lars Svensson* defended the relevance and importance of delegating an objective other than social welfare to the central bank. Social welfare is obviously too complex and multidimensional an objective to be operational for monetary policy, and assigning it to monetary policy is counterproductive, as monetary history has clearly shown. A large part of successful monetary policy reforms in many countries has instead consisted of assigning, by legislation or government instructions, simple and verifiable objectives for central banks, such as price stability or flexible inflation targeting, with (for instance) the understanding that the explicit or implicit output target is the natural output level rather than the socially optimal output level. This has resulted in better outcomes from a social welfare point of view. Other economic policy than monetary policy is then assigned to raise the natural output level toward the optimal level.

George Evans suggested that the New Keynesian Phillips curve was attractive because it is forward-looking, an assumption that policymakers would find plausible.

Bennett McCallum argued that the assumption that central bankers act in a discretionary manner was at odds with the assumption that they would be willing to minimize a delegated loss function that was different from their own. Concerning price-level targeting, in his earlier work on targeting the level of nominal GDP versus targeting nominal GDP growth, he had found beneficial effects of using growth but giving some small weight also to the level and hence inducing trend stationarity of nominal GDP.

Michael Woodford agreed with Gregory Mankiw that the assignment of an objective to the central bank was a problematic way of avoiding the losses caused by discretionary optimization. He argued, however, that price-level targeting was valuable independent of whether it was implemented by delegation of a loss function or in some other way—for example, because it was easily interpretable and robust across different model specifications.

Mervyn King expressed the view that price-level targeting would be too costly if the Phillips curve was backward looking, and that therefore the private sector's expectations formation was a key issue to judge whether price-level targeting was desirable. He also argued that price-level targeting may give the impression that the central bank was too much engaged in fine-tuning the economy, unless the horizon chosen over which to return the price level to its target was sufficiently long.

John Berry expressed the concern that the choice of the target path for the price level had to take into consideration measurement error in the price index in terms of which the target was formulated.

Stephen Cecchetti replied that he agreed that the delegation of an objective function was an idea that in practice would be difficult to implement.

Imperfect Knowledge, Inflation Expectations, and Monetary Policy

Athanasios Orphanides and John C. Williams

5.1 Introduction

Rational expectations provide an elegant and powerful framework that has come to dominate thinking about the dynamic structure of the economy and econometric policy evaluation over the past thirty years. This success has spurred further examination of the strong information assumptions implicit in many of its applications. Thomas Sargent (1993) concludes that "rational expectations models impute much *more* knowledge to the agents within the model . . . than is possessed by an econometrician, who faces estimation and inference problems that the agents in the model have somehow solved" (3, emphasis in original).[1] Researchers have

Athanasios Orphanides is an adviser in the division of monetary affairs of the Federal Reserve Board. John C. Williams is a senior vice president and advisor at the Federal Reserve Bank of San Francisco.

We would like to thank Roger Craine, George Evans, Stan Fischer, Mark Gertler, John Leahy, Bill Poole, Tom Sargent, Lars Svensson, and participants at meetings of the Econometric Society, the Society of Computational Economics, the University of Cyprus, the Federal Reserve Banks of San Francisco and Richmond, the National Bureau of Economic Research (NBER) Monetary Economics Program, and the NBER Universities Research Conference on Macroeconomic Policy in a Dynamic Uncertain Economy for useful comments and discussions on earlier drafts. We thank Adam Litwin for research assistance and Judith Goff for editorial assistance. The opinions expressed are those of the authors and do not necessarily reflect views of the Board of Governors of the Federal Reserve System or the Federal Reserve Bank of San Francisco.

1. Missing from such models, as Benjamin Friedman (1979) points out, "is a clear outline of the way in which economic agents derive the knowledge which they then use to formulate expectations." To be sure, this does not constitute a criticism of the traditional use of the concept of "rationality" as reflecting the optimal use of information in the formation of expectations, taking into account an agent's objectives and resource constraints. The difficulty is that in Muth's (1961) original formulation, rational expectations are not optimizing in that sense. Thus, the issue is not that the rational-expectations concept reflects too much rationality but

proposed refinements to rational expectations that respect the principle that agents use information efficiently in forming expectations, but nonetheless recognize the limits to and costs of information processing and cognitive constraints that influence the expectations-formation process (Sargent 1999; Evans and Honkapohja 2001; Sims 2003).

In this study, we allow for a form of imperfect knowledge in which economic agents rely on an adaptive learning technology to form expectations. This form of learning represents a relatively modest deviation from rational expectations that nests the latter as a limiting case. We show that the resulting process of perpetual learning introduces an additional layer of interaction between monetary policy and economic outcomes that has important implications for macroeconomic dynamics and for monetary policy design. As we illustrate, monetary policies that would be efficient under rational expectations can perform poorly when knowledge is imperfect. In particular, with imperfect knowledge, policies that fail to maintain tight control over inflation are prone to episodes in which the public's expectations of inflation become uncoupled from the policy objective. The presence of this imperfection makes stabilization policy more difficult than would appear under rational expectations and highlights the value of effectively communicating a central bank's inflation objective and of continued vigilance against inflation in anchoring inflation expectations and fostering macroeconomic stability.

In this paper, we investigate the macroeconomic implications of a process of "perpetual learning." Our work builds on the extensive literature relating rational expectations to learning and the adaptive formation of expectations (Bray 1982; Bray and Savin 1984; Marcet and Sargent 1989; Woodford 1990; Bullard and Mitra 2002). A key finding in this literature is that under certain conditions an economy with learning converges to the rational-expectations equilibrium (Townsend 1978; Bray 1982, 1983; Blume and Easley 1982). However, until agents have accumulated sufficient knowledge about the economy, economic outcomes during the transition depend on the adaptive learning process (Lucas 1986). Moreover, in a changing economic environment, agents are constantly learning, and their beliefs converge not to a fixed rational-expectations equilibrium but to an ergodic distribution around it (Sargent 1999; Evans and Honkapohja 2001).[2]

---

rather that it imposes too little rationality in the expectations formation process. For example, as Sims (2003) has pointed out, optimal information processing subject to a finite cognitive capacity may result in fundamentally different processes for the formation of expectations from those implied by rational expectations. To acknowledge this terminological tension, Simon (1978) suggested that a less misleading term for Muth's concept would be "model consistent" expectations (2).

2. Our work also draws on some other strands of the literature related to learning, estimation, and policy design. One such strand has examined the formation of inflation expectations when the policymaker's objective may be unknown or uncertain—for example, during a transition following a shift in policy regime (Taylor 1975; Bomfim et al. 1997; Erceg and Levin 2003; Koz-

As a laboratory for our experiment, we employ a simple linear model of the U.S. economy with characteristics similar to more elaborate models frequently used to study optimal monetary policy. We assume that economic agents know the correct structure of the economy and form expectations accordingly. But, rather than endowing them with complete knowledge of the parameters of these functions—as would be required by imposing the rational-expectations assumption—we posit that economic agents rely on finite memory least squares estimation to update these parameter estimates. This setting conveniently nests rational expectations as the limiting case corresponding to infinite memory least squares estimation and allows varying degrees of imperfection in expectations formation to be characterized by variation in a single model parameter.

We find that even marginal deviations from rational expectations in the direction of imperfect knowledge can have economically important effects on the stochastic behavior of our economy and policy evaluation. An interesting feature of the model is that the interaction of learning and control creates rich nonlinear dynamics that can potentially explain both the shifting parameter structure of linear reduced-form characterizations of the economy and the appearance of shifting policy objectives or inflation targets. For example, sequences of policy errors or inflationary shocks, such as were experienced during the 1970s, could give rise to stagflationary episodes that do not arise under rational expectations with perfect knowledge.

Indeed, the critical role of the formation of inflation expectations for understanding the successes and failures of monetary policy is a dimension of policy that has often been cited by policymakers over the past two decades but that has received much less attention in formal econometric policy evaluations. An important example is the contrast between the stubborn persistence of inflation expectations during the 1970s, when policy placed relatively greater attention on countercyclical concerns, and the much-improved stability in both inflation and inflation expectations following the renewed emphasis on price stability in 1979. In explaining the rationale for this shift in emphasis in 1979, Federal Reserve Chairman Volcker highlighted the importance of learning in shaping the inflation expectations formation process.[3]

---

icki and Tinsley 2001; Tetlow and von zur Muehlen 2001). Another strand has considered how policymaker uncertainty about the structure of the economy influences policy choices and economic dynamics (Balvers and Cosimano 1994; Wieland 1998; Sargent 1999; and others). Finally, our work relates to explorations of alternative approaches for modeling aggregate inflation expectations, such as Ball (2000), Carroll (2003), and Mankiw and Reis (2002).

3. Indeed, we would argue that the shift in emphasis toward greater focus on inflation was itself influenced by the recognition of the importance of facilitating the formation of stable inflation expectations—which had been insufficiently appreciated earlier during the 1970s. See Orphanides (2004) for a more detailed description of the policy discussion at the time and the nature of the improvement in monetary policy since 1979. See also Christiano and Gust (2000) and Sargent (1999) for alternative explanations of the rise in inflation during the 1960s and 1970s.

It is not necessary to recite all the details of the long series of events that have culminated in the serious inflationary environment that we are now experiencing. An entire generation of young adults has grown up since the mid-1960's knowing only inflation, indeed an inflation that has seemed to accelerate inexorably. In the circumstances, it is hardly surprising that many citizens have begun to wonder whether it is realistic to anticipate a return to general price stability, and have begun to change their behavior accordingly. Inflation feeds in part on itself, so part of the job of returning to a more stable and more productive economy must be to break the grip of inflationary expectations. (Volcker 1979, 888)

This historical episode is a clear example of inflation expectations becoming uncoupled from the intended policy objective and illustrates the point that the design of monetary policy must account for the influence of policy on expectations.

We find that policies designed to be efficient under rational expectations can perform very poorly when knowledge is imperfect. This deterioration in performance is particularly severe when policymakers put a high weight on stabilizing real economic activity relative to price stability. Our analysis yields two conclusions for the conduct of monetary policy when knowledge is imperfect. First, policies that emphasize tight inflation control can facilitate learning and provide better guidance for the formation of inflation expectations. Second, effective communication of an explicit numerical inflation target can help focus inflation expectations and thereby reduce the costs associated with imperfect knowledge. Policies that combine vigilance against inflation with an explicit numerical inflation target mitigate the negative influence of imperfect knowledge on economic stabilization and yield superior macroeconomic performance. Thus, our findings provide analytical support for monetary policy frameworks that emphasize the primacy of price stability as an operational policy objective—for example, the inflation-targeting approach discussed by Bernanke and Mishkin (1997) and adopted by several central banks over the past decade or so.

5.2   The Model Economy

We consider a stylized model that gives rise to a nontrivial inflation-output variability trade-off and in which a simple one-parameter policy rule represents optimal monetary policy under rational expectations.[4] In this section, we describe the model specification for inflation and output and the central bank's optimization problem; in the next two sections, we take up the formation of expectations by private agents.

---

4. Since its introduction by Taylor (1979), the practice of analyzing monetary policy rules using such an inflation-output variability trade-off has been adopted in a large number of academic and policy studies.

Inflation is determined by a modified Lucas supply function that allows for some intrinsic inflation persistence,

$$(1) \qquad \pi_{t+1} = \phi\pi_{t+1}^e + (1 - \phi)\pi_t + \alpha y_{t+1} + e_{t+1}, \qquad e \sim \text{i.i.d.}(0, \sigma_e^2),$$

where π denotes the inflation rate, π^e is the private agents' expected inflation rate based on time t information, i.i.d. indicates "independently and identically distributed," y is the output gap, $\phi \in (0, 1)$, $\alpha > 0$, and e is a serially uncorrelated innovation. As discussed by Clark, Goodhart, and Huang (1999) and Lengwiler and Orphanides (2002), this specification incorporates an important role for inflation expectations for determining inflation outcomes while also allowing for some inflation persistence that is necessary for the model to yield a nontrivial inflation-output gap variability trade-off.[5]

We assume that the policymaker can set policy during period t so as to determine the intended level of the output gap for period $t + 1$, x_t, subject to a control error, u_{t+1},

$$(2) \qquad\qquad y_{t+1} = x_t + u_{t+1} \qquad u \sim \text{i.i.d.}(0, \sigma_u^2).$$

This is equivalent to assuming that the intended output gap for period $t + 1$ is determined by the real rate gap set during period t, $x_t = -\xi(r_t - r^*)$, where r is the short-term real interest rate and r^* is the equilibrium real rate.[6] As will become clear, with this assumption the model has the property that under perfect knowledge both the optimal policy rule and the optimal inflation-forecast rule can be written in terms of a single state variable, the lagged inflation rate. This facilitates our analysis. Inflation expectations are fundamentally anchored by monetary policy, while output expectations are anchored by views of aggregate supply that are presumably less influenced by monetary policy. For this reason, we focus on the interaction between monetary policy and inflation expectations.

The central bank's objective is to design a policy rule that minimizes the loss, denoted by $\mathscr{L}$, equal to the weighted average of the asymptotic variances of the output gap and of deviations of inflation from the target rate,

$$(3) \qquad\qquad \mathscr{L} = (1 - \omega)\text{Var}(y) + \omega\text{Var}(\pi - \pi^*),$$

where $\text{Var}(z)$ denotes the unconditional variance of variable z, and $\omega \in (0, 1]$ is the relative weight on inflation stabilization. This completes the description of the structure of the model economy, with the exception of the expectations formation process that we examine in detail below.

---

5. We have also examined the "New Keynesian" variant of the Phillips curve studied by Galí and Gertler (1999) and others, which also allows for some intrinsic inflation inertia. As we report in section 5.6, our main findings are not sensitive to this alternative.

6. Note, however, that this abstracts from the important complications associated with the real-time measurement of the output gap and the equilibrium real interest rate for formulating the policy rule. See Orphanides (2003a), Laubach and Williams (2003), and Orphanides and Williams (2002) for analyses of these issues.

5.3   The Perfect-Knowledge Benchmark

We begin by considering the "textbook" case of rational expectations with perfect knowledge in which private agents know both the structure of the economy and the central bank's policy. In this case, expectations are rational in that they are consistent with the true data-generating process of the economy (the model). In the next section, we use the resulting equilibrium solution as a "perfect-knowledge" benchmark against which we compare outcomes under imperfect knowledge, in which case agents do not know the structural parameters of the model but instead must form expectations based on estimated forecasting models.

Under the assumption of perfect knowledge, both the evolution of the economy and optimal monetary policy can be expressed in terms of two variables, the current inflation rate and its target level. These variables determine the formation of expectations and the policy choice, which, together with serially uncorrelated shocks, determine output and inflation in period $t + 1$. Specifically, we can write the monetary policy rule in terms of the inflation gap,

$$(4) \qquad x_t = -\theta(\pi_t - \pi^*),$$

where $\theta > 0$ measures the responsiveness of the intended output gap to the inflation gap.

Given this monetary policy rule, inflation expectations are

$$(5) \qquad \pi_{t+1}^e = \frac{\alpha\theta}{1 - \phi}\pi^* + \frac{1 - \phi - \alpha\theta}{1 - \phi}\pi_t.$$

Inflation expectations depend on the current level of inflation, the inflation target, and the parameter θ measuring the central bank's responsiveness to the inflation gap. Substituting this expression for expected inflation into equation (1) yields the rational-expectations solution for inflation for a given monetary policy,

$$(6) \qquad \pi_{t+1} = \frac{\alpha\theta}{1 - \phi}\pi^* + \left(1 - \frac{\alpha\theta}{1 - \phi}\right)\pi_t + e_{t+1} + \alpha u_{t+1}.$$

One noteworthy feature of this solution is that the first-order autocorrelation of the inflation rate, given by $1 - ([\alpha\theta]/[1 - \phi])$, is decreasing in θ and is invariant to the value of π^*. Note that the rational-expectations solution can also be written in terms of the "inflation expectations gap"—the difference between inflation expectations for period $t + 1$ from the inflation target, $\pi_{t+1}^e - \pi^*$,

$$(7) \qquad \pi_{t+1}^e - \pi^* = \frac{1 - \phi - \alpha\theta}{1 - \phi}(\pi_t - \pi^*).$$

Equations (4) and (5) close the perfect-knowledge benchmark model.

5.3.1   Optimal Monetary Policy under Perfect Knowledge

For the economy with perfect knowledge, the optimal monetary policy, θ^P, can be obtained in closed form and is given by[7]

$$(8) \quad \theta^P = \frac{\omega}{2(1-\omega)} \left(-\frac{\alpha}{1-\phi} + \sqrt{\left(\frac{\alpha}{1-\phi}\right)^2 + \frac{4(1-\omega)}{\omega}} \right) \text{ for } 0 < \omega < 1.$$

In the limit, when ω equals unity (that is, when the policymaker is not at all concerned with output stability), the policymaker sets the real interest rate so that inflation is expected to return to its target in the next period. The optimal policy in the case $\omega = 1$ is given by $\theta^P = (1-\phi)/\alpha$, and the irreducible variance of inflation, owing to unpredictable output and inflation innovations, equals $\sigma_e^2 + \alpha^2 \sigma_u^2$. More generally, the optimal value of θ depends positively on the ratio $(1-\phi)/\alpha$, and the parameters α and ϕ enter only in terms of this ratio. In particular, the optimal policy response is larger the greater the degree of intrinsic inertia in inflation, measured by $1-\phi$.

The greater the central bank's weight on inflation stabilization, the greater is the responsiveness to the inflation gap and the smaller the first-order autocorrelation in inflation. Differentiating equation (8) shows that the policy responsiveness to the inflation gap is increasing in ω, the weight the central bank places on inflation stabilization. As a result, the autocorrelation of inflation is decreasing in ω, with a limiting value approaching unity when ω approaches zero, and zero when ω equals 1. That is, if the central bank cares only about output stabilization, the inflation rate becomes a random walk, while if the central bank cares only about inflation stabilization, the inflation rate displays no serial correlation. And, as noted, this model yields a nontrivial monotonic trade-off between the variability of inflation and the output gap for all values of $\omega \in (0, 1]$. These results are illustrated in figure 5.1. Panel A of the figure shows the variability trade-off described by optimal policies for values of ω between zero and 1. Panel B plots the optimal values of θ against ω.

5.4   Imperfect Knowledge

As the perfect-knowledge solution shows, private inflation forecasts depend on knowledge of the structural model parameters and of policymaker

---

7. The optimal policy can be described in terms of the Euler equation that relates the intended output gap to the inflation rate and the intended output gap expected in the next period:

$$x_t = E_{t-1}\left(x_{t+1} - \frac{\omega}{1-\omega} \frac{\alpha}{1-\phi} \pi_{t+1} \right).$$

Under the assumption of serially uncorrelated shocks, the solution simplifies to the expression given in the text.

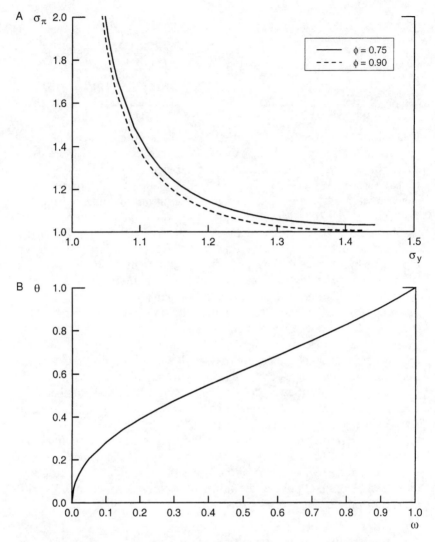

Fig. 5.1 *A,* **Efficient policy frontier with perfect knowledge;** *B,* **Optimal policy response to inflation**

Notes: The top panel shows the efficient policy frontier corresponding to optimal policies for different values of the relative preference for inflation stabilization ω, for the two specified parameterizations of α and φ. The bottom panel shows the optimal response to inflation corresponding to the alternative weights ω which are identical for the two parameterizations.

preferences. In addition, these parameters influence the expectations formation function nonlinearly. We now relax the assumption that private agents have perfect knowledge of all structural parameters and policymaker preferences. Instead, we posit that agents must somehow infer the information necessary for forming expectations by observing historical data, in essence acting like econometricians who know the correct specification of the economy but are uncertain about the parameters of the model.

In particular, we assume that private agents update the coefficients of their model for forecasting inflation using least squares learning with finite memory. We focus on least squares learning because of its desirable convergence properties, straightforward implementation, and close correspondence to what real-world forecasters actually do.[8] Estimation with finite memory reflects agents' concern for changes in the structural parameters of the economy. To focus our attention on the role of imperfections in the expectations formation process itself, however, we deliberately abstract from the introduction of the actual uncertainty in the structure of the economy which would justify such concerns in equilibrium. Further, we do not model the policymaker's knowledge or learning but instead focus on the implications of policy based on simple time-invariant rules of the form given in equation (4) that do not require explicit treatment of the policymaker's learning problem.[9]

We model perpetual learning by assuming that agents use a constant gain in their recursive least squares formula that places greater weight on more recent observations, as in Sargent (1999) and Evans and Honkapohja (2001). This algorithm is equivalent to applying weighted least squares where the weights decline geometrically with the distance in time between the observation being weighted and the most recent observation. This approach is closely related to the use of fixed sample lengths or rolling-window regressions to estimate a forecasting model (Friedman 1979). In terms of the mean "age" of the data used, a rolling-regression window of

---

8. This method of adaptive learning is closely related to optimal filtering, where the structural parameters are assumed to follow random walks. Of course, if private agents know the complete structure of the model—including the laws of motion for inflation, output, the unobserved states, and the distributions of the innovations to these processes—then they could compute efficient inflation forecasts that could outperform those based on recursive least squares. However, uncertainty regarding the precise structure of the time variation in the model parameters is likely to reduce the real efficiency gains from a method optimized to a particular model specification relative to a simple method such as least squares learning. Further, once we begin to ponder how economic agents could realistically model and account for such uncertainty precisely, we quickly recognize the significance of respecting (or the absurdity of ignoring) the cognitive and computational limits of economic agents.

9. We also abstract from two other elements that may further complicate policy design: the possibilities that policymakers may rely on a misspecified model or a misspecified information set for computing agents' expectations; see Levin, Wieland, and Williams (2003) and Orphanides (2003a), respectively, for a discussion of these two issues.

length l is equivalent to a constant gain κ of $2/l$. The advantage of the constant gain least squares algorithm over rolling regressions is that the evolution of the former system is fully described by a small set of variables, while the latter requires one to keep track of a large number of variables.

5.4.1   Least Squares Learning with Finite Memory

Under perfect knowledge, the predictable component of next period's inflation rate is a linear function of the inflation target and the current inflation rate, where the coefficients on the two variables are functions of the policy parameter θ and the other structural parameters of the model, as shown in equation (5). In addition, the optimal value of θ is itself a nonlinear function of the central bank's weight on inflation stabilization and the other model structural parameters. Given this simple structure, the least squares regression of inflation on a constant and lagged inflation,

$$(9) \qquad \pi_i = c_{0,t} + c_{1,t}\pi_{i-1} + v_t,$$

yields consistent estimates of the coefficients describing the law of motion for inflation (Marcet and Sargent 1988; Evans and Honkapohja 2001). Agents then use these results to form their inflation expectations.[10]

To fix notation, let $\mathbf{X}_i$ and $\mathbf{c}_i$ be the 2×1 vectors $\mathbf{X}_i = (1, \pi_{i-1})'$ and $\mathbf{c}_i = (c_{0,i}, c_{1,i})'$. Using data through period t, the least squares regression parameters for equation (9) can be written in recursive form:

$$(10) \qquad c_t = c_{t-1} + \kappa_t R_t^{-1} X_t(\pi_t - X_t' c_{t-1}),$$

$$(11) \qquad R_t = R_{t-1} + \kappa_t(X_t X_t' - R_{t-1}),$$

where κ_t is the gain. With least squares learning with infinite memory, $\kappa_t = 1/t$, so as t increases, κ_t converges to zero. As a result, as the data accumulate this mechanism converges to the correct expectations functions and the economy converges to the perfect-knowledge benchmark solution. As noted above, to formalize perpetual learning—as would be required in the presence of structural change—we replace the decreasing gain in the infinite-memory recursion with a small constant gain, $\kappa > 0$.[11]

With imperfect knowledge, expectations are based on the perceived law of motion of the inflation process, governed by the perpetual-learning algorithm described above. The model under imperfect knowledge consists

---

10. Note that here we assume that agents employ a reduced form of the expectations formation function that is correctly specified under rational expectations with perfect knowledge. However, agents may be uncertain of the correct form and estimate a more general specification: for example, a linear regression with additional lags of inflation, which nests equation (9). In section 5.6, we also discuss results from such an example.

11. In terms of forecasting performance, the "optimal" choice of κ depends on the relative variances of the transitory and permanent shocks, as in the relationship between the Kalman gain and the signal-to-noise ratio in the case of the Kalman filter. Here, we do not explicitly attempt to calibrate κ in this way but instead examine the effects for a range of values of κ.

of the structural equation for inflation (1), the output-gap equation (2), the monetary policy rule (4), and the one-step-ahead forecast for inflation, given by

(12) $$\pi_{t+1}^e = c_{0,t} + c_{1,t}\pi_t,$$

where $c_{0,t}$ and $c_{1,t}$ are updated according to equations (10) and (11).

We emphasize that in the limit of perfect knowledge (that is, as $\kappa \to 0$), the expectations function above converges to rational expectations and the stochastic coefficients for the intercept and slope collapse to

$$c_0^P = \frac{\alpha\theta\pi^*}{1 - \phi},$$

$$c_1^P = \frac{1 - \phi - \alpha\theta}{1 - \phi}.$$

Thus, this modeling approach accommodates the Lucas critique in the sense that expectations formation is endogenous and adjusts to changes in policy or structure (as reflected here by changes in the parameters θ, π^*, α, and ϕ). In essence, our model is one of "noisy rational expectations." As we show below, although expectations are imperfectly rational, in that agents need to estimate the reduced-form equations they employ to form expectations, they are nearly rational, in that the forecasts are close to being efficient.

5.5   Perpetual Learning in Action

We use model simulations to illustrate how learning affects the dynamics of inflation expectations, inflation, and output in the model economy. First, we examine the behavior of the estimated coefficients of the inflation-forecast equation and evaluate the performance of inflation forecasts. We then consider the dynamic response of the economy to shocks similar to those experienced during the 1970s in the United States. Specifically, we compare the outcomes under perfect knowledge and imperfect knowledge with least squares learning that correspond to three alternative monetary policy rules to illustrate the additional layer of dynamic interaction introduced by the imperfections in the formation of inflation expectations.

In calibrating the model for the simulations, each period corresponds to about half a year. We consider values of κ of 0.025, 0.05, and 0.075, which roughly correspond to using forty, twenty, or thirteen years of data, respectively, in the context of rolling regressions. We consider two values for ϕ, the parameter that measures the influence of inflation expectations on inflation. As a baseline case, we set ϕ to 0.75, which implies a significant role for intrinsic inflation inertia, consistent with the contracting models of Buiter and Jewitt (1981), Fuhrer and Moore (1995), and Brayton et al.

(1997).[12] In the alternative specification, we allow for a greater role for expectations and correspondingly give less weight to inflation inertia by setting $\phi = 0.9$, consistent with the findings of Galí and Gertler (1999) and others. To ease comparisons between the two values of ϕ, we set α so that the optimal policy under perfect knowledge is identical in the two cases. Specifically, for $\phi = 0.75$, we set $\alpha = 0.25$, and for $\phi = 0.9$, we set $\alpha = 0.1$. In all cases, we assume $\sigma_e = \sigma_u = 1$.

The three alternative policies we consider correspond to the values of θ, $\{0.1, 0.6, 1.0\}$, which represent the optimal policies under perfect knowledge for policymakers whose preferences reflect a relative weight on inflation, ω, of 0.01, 0.5, and 1, respectively. Hence, $\theta = 0.1$ corresponds to an "inflation dove" policymaker who is primarily concerned about output stabilization, $\theta = 0.6$ corresponds to a policymaker with "balanced preferences" who weighs inflation and output stabilization equally, and $\theta = 1$ corresponds to an "inflation hawk" policymaker who cares exclusively about inflation.

5.5.1   The Performance of Least Squares Inflation Forecasts

Even absent shocks to the structure of the economy, the process of least squares learning generates time variation in the formation of inflation expectations and thereby in the processes of inflation and output. The magnitude of this time variation is increasing in κ—which is equivalent to using shorter samples (and thus less information from the historical data) in rolling regressions. Table 5.1 reports summary statistics of the estimates of agents' inflation-forecasting models based on stochastic simulations of the model economy for the two calibrations we consider. As seen in the table, the unconditional standard deviations of the estimates increase with κ. This dependence of the variation in the estimates on the rate of learning is portrayed in figure 5.2, which shows the steady-state distributions of the estimates of c_0 and c_1 for the case of $\phi = 0.75$. For comparison, the vertical lines in each panel indicate the values of c_0 and c_1 in the corresponding perfect-knowledge benchmark.

The median values of the coefficient estimates are nearly identical to the values implied by the perfect-knowledge benchmark; however, the mean estimates of c_1 are biased downward slightly. Although not shown in the table, the mean and median values of c_0 are nearly zero, consistent with the assumed inflation target of zero. There is contemporaneous correlation between estimates of c_0, and c_1 is nearly zero. Each of these estimates, however, is highly serially correlated, with first-order autocorrelations just below unity. This serial correlation falls only slightly as κ increases.

Note that a more aggressive policy response to inflation reduces the vari-

---

12. Other researchers suggest an even smaller role for expectations relative to intrinsic inertia; see Fuhrer (1997), Roberts (2001), and Rudd and Whelan (2001).

Table 5.1   **Least squares learning, by value of κ**

	RE	$\phi = 0.75, \alpha = 0.25$			$\phi = 0.90, \alpha = 0.10$		
	0	0.025	0.050	0.075	0.025	0.050	0.075
$\theta = 0.1$							
Mean c_1	0.90	0.86	0.83	0.81	0.88	0.89	0.93
Median c_1	0.90	0.89	0.88	0.88	0.95	0.97	0.98
SD c_0	0.00	0.37	0.67	1.01	0.79	2.06	4.92
SD c_1	0.00	0.12	0.17	0.21	0.18	0.23	0.20
$\theta = 0.6$							
Mean c_1	0.40	0.37	0.34	0.32	0.37	0.35	0.33
Median c_1	0.40	0.38	0.37	0.36	0.40	0.41	0.42
SD c_0	0.00	0.25	0.38	0.50	0.40	0.66	0.91
SD c_1	0.00	0.20	0.28	0.33	0.31	0.42	0.50
$\theta = 1.0$							
Mean c_1	0.00	−0.02	−0.04	−0.05	−0.03	−0.03	−0.04
Median c_1	0.00	−0.02	−0.04	−0.05	−0.03	−0.04	−0.06
SD c_0	0.00	0.24	0.35	0.44	0.37	0.58	0.74
SD c_1	0.00	0.21	0.29	0.35	0.33	0.44	0.51

Notes: RE = rational expectations. SD = standard deviation.

ation in the estimated intercept, c_0, but increases the magnitude of fluctuations in the coefficient on the lagged inflation rate, c_1. In the case of $\theta = 1$, the distribution of estimates of c_1 is nearly symmetrical around zero. For $\theta = 0.1$ and 0.6, the distribution of estimates of c_1 is skewed to the left, reflecting the accumulation of mass around unity, but the absence of much mass above 1.1.

Finite-memory least squares forecasts perform very well in this model economy. As shown in table 5.2, the mean-squared error of agents' one-step-ahead inflation forecasts is only slightly above the theoretical minimum given in the first line of the table (labeled "Perfect knowledge").[13] Only when both inflation displays very little intrinsic inertia and the policymaker places very little weight on inflation stabilization does the performance of finite-memory least squares forecasts break down. Not surprisingly, given that we assume that the structure of the economy is fixed, agents' forecasting performance deteriorates somewhat as κ increases. Nonetheless, finite-memory least squares estimates perform better than those with infinite memory (based on the full sample), and the difference in performance is more pronounced the greater the role of inflation expectations in determining inflation. In an economy where inflation is determined by the forecasts of other agents who use finite-memory least squares, it is

---

13. This is consistent with earlier findings regarding least squares estimation. Anderson and Taylor (1976), for example, emphasize that least squares forecasts can be accurate even when consistent estimates of individual parameter estimates are much harder to obtain.

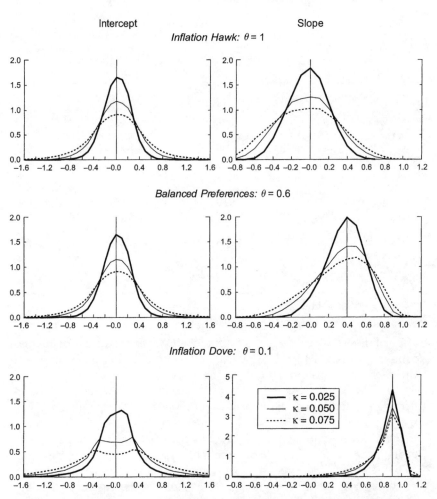

Fig. 5.2   Estimated expectations function parameters ($\phi = 0.75$, $\alpha = 0.25$)

Notes: The intercept and slope refer to the coefficients c_0 and c_1, respectively, in the agents' forecasting equation (9). The plots show the steady-state distributions of the estimates of c_0 and c_1 for different values of κ and θ.

better to follow suit rather than to use estimates that would have better forecast properties under perfect knowledge (Evans and Ramey 2001).

With imperfect knowledge, the private agents' ability to forecast inflation depends on the monetary policy in place, with forecast errors on average smaller when policy responds more aggressively to inflation. This effect is more pronounced the greater the role of inflation expectations in determining inflation. The marginal benefit from tighter inflation control on the ability of private agents to forecast accurately is greatest when the policymaker places relatively little weight on inflation stabilization. In this

Table 5.2   Forecasting performance: Mean-squared error, by value of κ

Forecast method	$\phi = 0.75, \alpha = 0.25$			$\phi = 0.90, \alpha = 0.10$		
	0.025	0.050	0.075	0.025	0.050	0.075
Perfect knowledge	1.03	1.03	1.03	1.01	1.01	1.01
$\theta = 0.1$						
LS (finite memory)	1.04	1.05	1.06	1.03	1.19	1.57
LS (infinite memory)	1.05	1.06	1.09	1.08	1.72	3.49
Long-lag Phillips curve	1.05	1.06	1.07	1.06	1.08	1.11
$\theta = 0.6$						
LS (finite memory)	1.04	1.04	1.05	1.01	1.01	1.02
LS (infinite memory)	1.06	1.09	1.12	1.10	1.20	1.31
Long-lag Phillips curve	1.05	1.07	1.08	1.07	1.11	1.17
$\theta = 1.0$						
LS (finite memory)	1.04	1.04	1.05	1.01	1.01	1.02
LS (infinite memory)	1.06	1.10	1.14	1.12	1.28	1.51
Long-lag Phillips curve	1.05	1.07	1.08	1.07	1.12	1.18

Note: LS = least squares.

case, inflation is highly serially correlated, and the estimates of c_1 are frequently in the vicinity of unity. Evidently, the ability to forecast inflation deteriorates when inflation is nearly a random walk. As seen by comparing the cases of θ of 0.6 and 1.0, the marginal benefit of tight inflation control disappears once the first-order autocorrelation of inflation is well below 1.

Finally, even though only one lag of inflation appears in the equations for inflation and inflation expectations, it is possible to improve on infinite-memory least squares forecasts by including additional lags of inflation in the estimated forecasting equation. This result is similar to that found in empirical studies of inflation, where relatively long lags of inflation help predict inflation (Staiger, Stock, and Watson 1997; Stock and Watson 1999; Brayton, Roberts, and Williams 1999). Evidently, in an economy where agents use adaptive learning, multiperiod lags of inflation are a reasonable proxy for inflation expectations. This result may also help explain the finding that survey-based inflation expectations do not appear to be "rational" using standard tests (Roberts 1997, 1998). With adaptive learning, inflation-forecast errors are correlated with data in the agents' information set; the standard test for forecast efficiency applies only to stable economic environments in which agents' estimates of the forecast model have converged to the true values.

5.5.2   Least Squares Learning and Inflation Persistence

The time variation in inflation expectations resulting from perpetual learning induces greater serial correlation in inflation. As shown in table 5.3, the first-order unconditional autocorrelation of inflation increases with κ. The first column shows the autocorrelations for inflation under per-

Table 5.3   Inflation persistence: First-order autocorrelation, by value of κ

		$\phi = 0.75, \alpha = 0.25$			$\phi = 0.90, \alpha = 0.10$		
θ	0	0.025	0.050	0.075	0.025	0.050	0.075
0.1	0.90	0.97	0.98	0.99	1.00	1.00	1.00
0.6	0.40	0.47	0.54	0.60	0.61	0.78	0.88
1.0	0.00	0.02	0.06	0.08	0.07	0.18	0.25

fect knowledge ($\kappa = 0$); note that these figures are identical across the two specifications of ϕ and α. In the case of the "inflation dove" policymaker ($\theta = 0.1$), the existence of learning raises the first-order autocorrelation from 0.9 to very nearly unity. For the policymaker with moderate preferences ($\theta = 0.6$), increasing κ from 0 to 0.075 causes the autocorrelation of inflation to rise from 0.40 to 0.60 when $\phi = 0.75$, or to 0.88 when $\phi = 0.9$.

Thus, in a model with a relatively small amount of intrinsic inflation persistence, the autocorrelation of inflation can be very high, even with a monetary policy that places significant weight on inflation stabilization. Even for the "inflation hawk" policymaker whose policy under perfect knowledge results in no serial persistence in inflation, the perpetual learning generates a significant amount of positive serial correlation in inflation. As we discuss below, the rise in inflation persistence associated with perpetual learning in turn affects the optimal design of monetary policy.

5.5.3   The Economy Following Inflationary Shocks

Next, we consider the dynamic response of the model to a sequence of unanticipated shocks, similar in spirit to those that arose in the 1970s. The responses of inflation expectations and inflation do not depend on the "source" of the shocks—that is, on whether we assume the shocks are due to policy errors or to other disturbances.[14] The configuration of shocks we have in mind would not be expected to occur frequently, of course. It is, however, instructive in that it illustrates how in these infrequent episodes the evolution of inflation expectations with learning could dramatically deviate from the perfect-knowledge benchmark under some policies. Inflation expectations in these episodes can become uncoupled from the policymakers' objectives, resulting in a period of stagflation that cannot occur under the perfect-knowledge benchmark.

---

14. The policy error we have in mind is the systematic misperception of the economy's noninflationary potential supply following an unobserved shift in potential output growth or an increase in the natural rate of unemployment, as apparently experienced in the 1970s. (See, for example, Orphanides and Williams [2002] and Orphanides 2003b.) Because such changes can only be perceived with the passage of time, they yield errors that are recognized to be serially correlated only in retrospect. In our model, the effect of such errors on inflation dynamics is isomorphic to that of an exogenous serially correlated inflation shock.

Note that under least squares learning, the model responses depend nonlinearly on the initial values of the states c and R. In the following, we report the average response from 1,000 simulations, each of which starts from initial conditions drawn from the relevant steady-state distribution. The shock is 2 percentage points in period one, and it declines in magnitude from periods two through eight. In period nine and beyond there is no shock. For these experiments we assume the baseline values for ϕ and α, and set $\kappa = 0.05$.

With perfect knowledge, the series of inflationary shocks causes a temporary rise in inflation and a decline in the output gap, as shown by the dashed lines in figure 5.3. The speed at which inflation is brought back to target depends on the monetary policy response, with the more aggressive policy yielding a relatively sharp but short decline in output and a rapid return of inflation to target. With the inflation hawk or moderate policymaker, the peak increase in inflation is no more than 2.5 percentage points, and inflation returns to its target within ten periods. With the inflation dove policymaker, the modest policy response avoids the sharp decline in output, but inflation is allowed to rise to a level about 4.5 percentage points above target, and the return to target is more gradual, with inflation still remaining 1 percentage point above target after twenty periods.

Imperfect knowledge with learning amplifies and prolongs the response of inflation and output to the shocks, especially when the central bank places significant weight on output stabilization. The solid lines in the figure show the responses of inflation and output under imperfect knowledge for the three policy rules. The inflation hawk's aggressive response to inflation effectively keeps inflation from drifting away from target, and the responses of inflation and output differ only modestly from those under perfect knowledge. In the case of balanced preferences, the magnitude of the peak responses of inflation and the output gap is a bit larger than under perfect knowledge, but the persistence of these gaps is markedly higher. The outcomes under the inflation dove, however, are dramatically different. The inflation dove attempts to finesse a gradual reduction in inflation without incurring a large decline in output, but the timid response to rising inflation causes the perceived process for inflation to become uncoupled from the policymaker's objectives. Stagflation results, with the inflation rate stuck over 8 percentage points above target, while output remains well below potential.

The striking differences in the responses to the shocks under imperfect knowledge are a product of the interaction between learning, the policy rule, and inflation expectations. The lines in figure 5.4 show the responses of the public's estimates of the intercept and the slope parameter of the inflation-forecasting equation under imperfect knowledge. Under the inflation hawk policymaker, inflation expectations are well anchored to the policy objective. The serially correlated inflationary shocks cause some

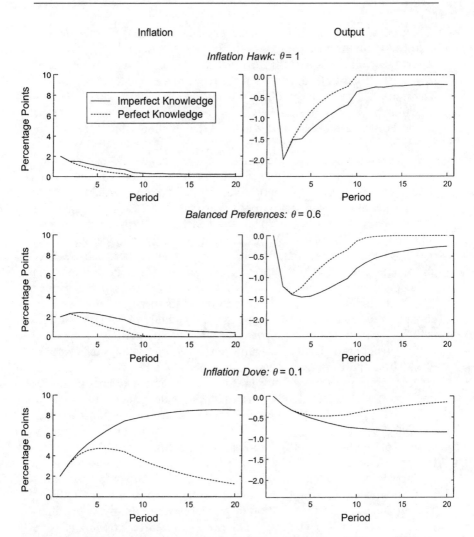

Fig. 5.3   Evolution of economy following inflation shocks ($\phi = 0.75$, $\alpha = 0.25$)

Notes: The plots show the mean responses of the inflation rate and the output gap to a series of inflationary shocks.

increase in both estimates, but the implied increase in the inflation target peaks at only 0.3 percentage point (not shown in the figure). Even for the moderate policymaker who accommodates some of the inflationary shock for a time, the perceived inflation target rises by just half of a percentage point. In contrast, under the inflation dove policymaker, the estimated persistence of inflation, already very high owing to the policymaker's desire to minimize output fluctuations while responding to inflation shocks, rises steadily, approaching unity. With inflation temporarily perceived to be a

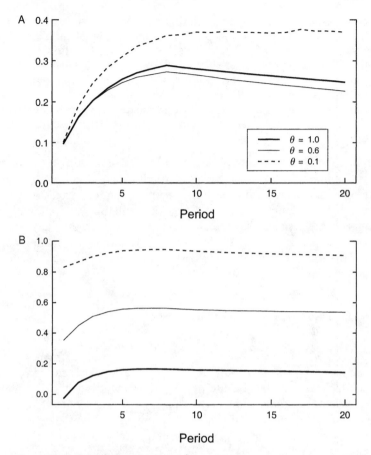

Fig. 5.4   *A,* **Estimated intercept following inflation shocks ($\phi = 0.75$, $\alpha = 0.25$);** *B,* **Estimated slope following inflation shocks**

Notes: The intercept and slope refer to the coefficients c_0 and c_1, respectively, in the agents' forecasting equation (9). The plots show the mean responses of the coefficients c_0 and c_1 to a series of inflationary shocks.

near-random walk with positive drift, agents expect inflation to continue to rise. The policymaker's attempts to constrain inflation are too weak to counteract this adverse-expectations process, and the public's perception of the inflation target rises by 5 percentage points. Despite the best of intents, the gradual disinflation prescription that would be optimal with perfect knowledge yields stagflation—the simultaneous occurrence of persistently high inflation and low output.

Interestingly, the inflation dove simulation appears to capture some key characteristics of the U.S. economy at the end of the 1970s, and it accords well with Chairman Volcker's assessment of the economic situation at the time:

Moreover, inflationary expectations are now deeply embedded in public attitudes, as reflected in the practices and policies of individuals and economic institutions. After years of false starts in the effort against inflation, there is widespread skepticism about the prospects for success. Overcoming this legacy of doubt is a critical challenge that must be met in shaping—and in carrying out—all our policies.

Changing both expectations and actual price performance will be difficult. But it is essential if our economic future is to be secure. (Volcker 1981, 293)

In contrast to this dismal experience, the model simulations suggest that the rise in inflation—and the corresponding costs of disinflation—would have been much smaller if policy had responded more aggressively to the inflationary developments of the 1970s. Although this was apparently not recognized at the time, Chairman Volcker's analysis suggests that the stagflationary experience of the 1970s played a role in the subsequent recognition of the value of continued vigilance against inflation in anchoring inflation expectations.

5.6   Imperfect Knowledge and Monetary Policy

5.6.1   Naive Application of the Rational-Expectations Policy

We now turn to the design of efficient monetary policy under imperfect knowledge. We start by considering the experiment in which the policymaker sets policy under the assumption that private agents have perfect knowledge when, in fact, they have only imperfect knowledge and base their expectations on the perpetual-learning mechanism described above. That is, policy follows equation (4) with the response parameter, θ, computed using equation (8).

Figure 5.5 compares the variability pseudo-frontier corresponding to this equilibrium to the frontier from the perfect-knowledge benchmark. Panel A shows the outcomes in terms of inflation and output-gap variability with the baseline parameterization, $\phi = 0.75$. Panel B shows the results of the same experiment with the more forward-looking specification for inflation, $\phi = 0.9$. In each case, we show the imperfect-knowledge equilibria corresponding to three different values of κ.

With imperfect knowledge, the perpetual-learning mechanism introduces random errors in expectations formation—that is, deviations of expectations from the values that would correspond to the same realization of inflation and the same policy rule. These errors are costly for stabilization and are responsible for the deterioration in performance shown in figure 5.5.

This deterioration in performance is especially pronounced for the policymaker who places relatively low weight on inflation stabilization. As

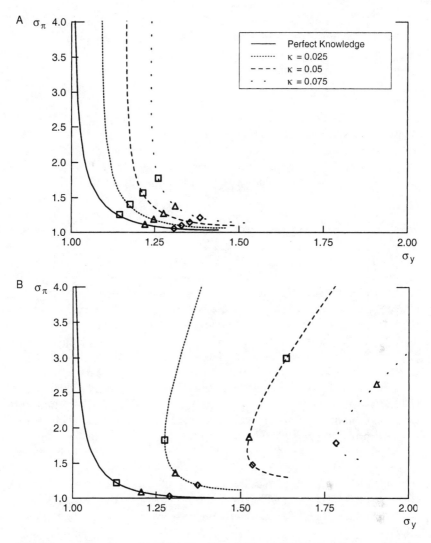

Fig. 5.5   *A,* **Outcomes with RE policy (φ = 0.75, α = 0.25);** *B,* **Outcomes with RE policy (φ = 0.9, α = 0.1)**

Notes: Each panel shows the efficient frontier with perfect knowledge and corresponding outcomes when the RE-optimal policies are adopted while, in fact, knowledge is imperfect. The square, triangle, and diamond correspond to preference weights ω = {0.25, 0.5, 0.75}, respectively.

seen in the simulations of the inflationary shocks reported above, for such policies the time variation in the estimated autocorrelation of inflation in the vicinity of unity associated with learning can be especially costly. Furthermore, the deterioration in performance relative to the case of the perfect-knowledge benchmark is larger the greater is the role of expectations in determining inflation. With the higher value for ϕ, if a policymaker's preference for inflation stabilization is too low, the resulting outcomes under imperfect knowledge are strictly dominated by the outcomes corresponding to the naïve policy equilibrium for higher values of ω.

5.6.2 Efficient Simple Rule

Next we examine imperfect-knowledge equilibria when the policymaker is aware of the imperfection in expectations formation and adjusts policy accordingly. To allow for a straightforward comparison with the perfect-knowledge benchmark, we concentrate on the efficient choice of the responsiveness of policy to inflation, θ^S, in the simple linear rule

$$x_t = -\theta^S(\pi_t - \pi^*),$$

which has the same form as the optimal rule under the perfect-knowledge benchmark.[15]

The efficient policy response with imperfect knowledge is to be more vigilant against inflation deviations from the policymaker's target relative to the optimal response under perfect knowledge. Figure 5.6 shows the efficient choices for θ under imperfect knowledge for the two model parameterizations; the optimal policy under perfect knowledge—which is the same for the two parameterizations considered—is shown again for comparison. As before, we present results for three different values of κ: our baseline $\kappa = 0.05$ and also a smaller and a larger value. The increase in the efficient value of θ is especially pronounced when the policymaker places relatively little weight on inflation stabilization—that is, when inflation would exhibit high serial correlation under perfect knowledge. Under imperfect knowledge, it is efficient for a policymaker to bias the response to inflation upward relative to that implied by perfect knowledge. This effect is especially pronounced with the more forward-looking inflation process. Consider, for instance, the baseline case $\kappa = 0.05$. In the parameterization with $\phi = 0.9$, it is never efficient to set θ below 0.6, the value that one would choose under balanced preferences ($\omega = 0.5$) under perfect knowledge.

Accounting for imperfect knowledge can significantly improve stabilization performance relative to outcomes obtained when the policymaker naively adopts policies that are efficient under perfect knowledge. Figure 5.7 compares the loss to the policymaker with perfect and imperfect knowledge for different preferences ω. Panel A shows the outcomes for the

15. In Orphanides and Williams (2003), we explore policies that respond directly to private expectations of inflation, in addition to actual inflation. These rules are not fully optimal; with imperfect knowledge, the fully optimal policy would be a nonlinear function of all the states of the system, including the elements of c and R. However, implementation of such policies would assume the policymaker's full knowledge of the structure of the economy—an assumption we find untenable in practice.

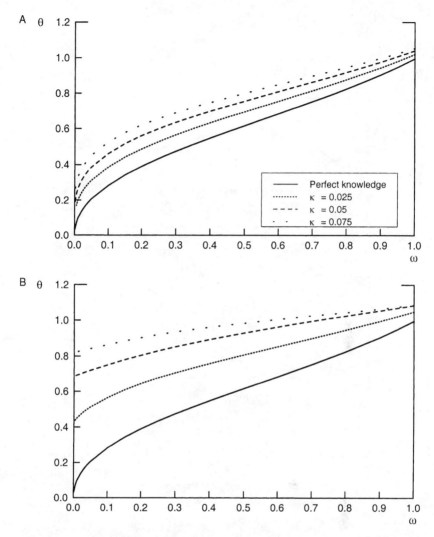

Fig. 5.6 *A*, Efficient policy response to inflation ($\phi = 0.75$, $\alpha = 0.25$); *B*, Efficient policy response to inflation ($\phi = 0.9$, $\alpha = 0.1$)

Notes: The solid line in each panel shows the optimal value of θ under perfect knowledge for alternative values of the relative preference for inflation stabilization ω. Remaining lines show the efficient one-parameter policy under imperfect knowledge.

baseline parameterization, $\phi = 0.75$, $\alpha = 0.25$; panel B reports the outcomes for the alternative parameterization of inflation, $\phi = 0.9$, $\alpha = 0.1$. In both panels, the results we show for imperfect knowledge correspond to our benchmark case, $\kappa = 0.05$. The payoff to reoptimizing θ is largest for policymakers who place a large weight on output stabilization, with the gain huge in the case of $\phi = 0.9$. In contrast, the benefits from reoptimiza-

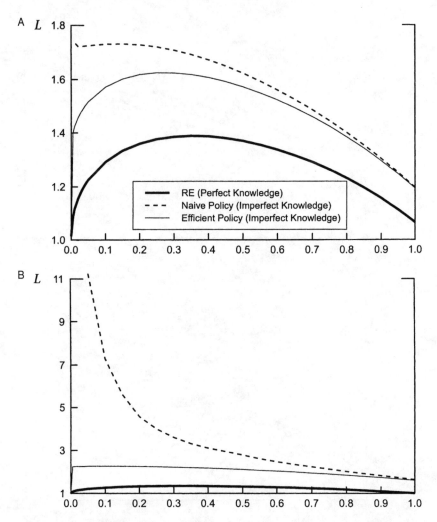

Fig. 5.7 *A,* **Policymaker loss ($\phi = 0.75$, $\alpha = 0.25$); *B,* Policymaker loss ($\phi = 0.9$, $\alpha = 0.1$)**

Notes: The two panels show the loss corresponding to alternative values of the relative preference for inflation stabilization ω for different assumptions regarding knowledge and different model parameterizations. The thick-solid line shows the case of perfect knowledge. The dashed line shows the outcomes assuming the policymaker chooses θ assuming perfect knowledge when knowledge is in fact imperfect. The thin-solid line shows the outcomes for the efficient one-parameter policy under imperfect knowledge.

tion are trivial for policymakers who are primarily concerned with inflation stabilization regardless of ϕ.

The key finding that the public's imperfect knowledge raises the efficient policy response to inflation is not unique to the model considered here and carries over to models with alternative specifications. In particular, we find the same result when the equation for inflation is replaced with the "New Keynesian" variant studied by Galí and Gertler (1999; see also Gaspar and Smets 2002). Moreover, we find that qualitatively similar results obtain if agents include additional lags of inflation in their forecasting models.

5.6.3   Dissecting the Benefits of Vigilance

In order to gain insight into the interaction of imperfections in the formation of expectations and efficient policy, we consider a simple example where the parameters of the inflation-forecast model vary according to an exogenous stochastic process.

From equation (5), recall that expectations formation is driven by the stochastic coefficient expectations function:

$$(13) \qquad \pi^e_{t+1} = c_{0,t} + c_{1,t}\pi_t.$$

For the present purposes, let $c_{0,t}$ and $c_{1,t}$ vary relative to their perfect-knowledge benchmark values; that is, $c_{0,t} = c_0^P + v_{0,t}$ and , $c_{1,t} = c_1^P + v_{1,t}$, where $v_{0,t}$ and $v_{1,t}$ are independent zero-mean normal distributions with variances σ_0^2 and σ_1^2.

Substituting expectations into the Phillips curve and rearranging terms results in the following reduced-form characterization of the dynamics of inflation in terms of the control variable x:

$$(14) \qquad \pi_{t+1} = (1 + \phi v_{1,t})\pi_t + \frac{\alpha}{1 - \phi}x_t + \alpha u_{t+1} + e_{t+1} + \phi u_{0,t}.$$

In this case, the optimal policy with stochastic coefficients has the same linear structure as the optimal policy with fixed coefficients and perfect knowledge, and the optimal policy response is monotonically increasing in the variance σ_1^2.[16]

Although informative, the simple case examined above ignores the important effect of the serial correlation in v_0 and v_1 that obtains under imperfect knowledge. The efficient choice of θ cannot be written in closed form in the case of serially correlated processes for v_0 and v_1, but a set of stochastic simulations is informative. Consider the efficient choice of θ for our benchmark economy with balanced preferences, $\omega = 0.5$. Under perfect

---

16. See Turnovsky (1977) and Craine (1979) for early applications of the well-known optimal control results for this case. For our model, specifically, the optimal response can be written as

$$\theta = \frac{\alpha(1 - \phi)s}{(1 - \phi)(1 - \omega) + \alpha^2 s},$$

where s is the positive root of the quadratic equation $0 = \omega(1 - \omega)(1 - \phi)^2 + (\omega\alpha^2 + [1 - \omega][1 - \phi]^2\phi^2\sigma_1^2)s + (\phi^2\sigma_1^2 - 1)\alpha^2 s^2$.

While the optimal policy response to inflation deviations from target, θ, is independent of σ_0^2, the variance of the $v_{0,t}$, differentiation reveals that it is increasing in σ_1^2), the variance of $v_{1,t}$. As $\sigma_1^2 \to 0$, of course, this solution collapses to the optimal policy with perfect knowledge.

knowledge, the optimal choice of θ is approximately 0.6. Instead, simulations assuming an exogenous autoregressive process for either c_0 or c_1 with a variance and autocorrelation matching our economy with imperfect knowledge suggest an efficient choice of θ approximately equal to 0.7—regardless of whether the variation is due to c_0 or to c_1. For comparison, with the endogenous variation in the parameters in the economy with learning, the efficient choice of θ is 0.75.

As noted earlier, for a fixed policy choice of policy responsiveness in the policy rule, θ, the uncertainty in the process of expectations formation with imperfect knowledge raises the persistence of the inflation process relative to the perfect-knowledge case. This can be seen by comparing the thick-solid and dashed lines in the two panels of figure 5.8, which plot the persistence of inflation when policy follows the rational-expectations (RE) optimal rule and agents have perfect and imperfect knowledge (with κ = 0.05), respectively. This increase in inflation persistence complicates stabilization efforts as it raises, on average, the output costs associated with restoring price stability when inflation deviates from its target.

The key benefit of adopting greater vigilance against inflation deviations from the policymaker's target in the presence of imperfect knowledge comes from reducing this excess serial persistence of inflation. More aggressive policies reduce the persistence of inflation, thus facilitating its control. The resulting efficient choice of reduction in inflation persistence is reflected by the thin-solid lines in figure 5.8.

5.7   Learning with a Known Inflation Target

Throughout the preceding discussion and analysis, we have implicitly assumed that agents do not rely on explicit knowledge regarding the policymaker's objectives in forming expectations. Arguably, this assumption best describes situations where a central bank does not successfully communicate to the public an explicit numerical inflation target and, perhaps, a clear weighting of its price and economic stability objectives. Since the adoption and clear communication of an explicit numerical inflation target is one of the key characteristics of inflation-targeting regimes, it is of interest to explore the implications of this dimension of inflation targeting in our model. To do so, we consider the case where the policymaker explicitly communicates the ultimate inflation target to the public; that is, we assume that the public exactly knows the value of π^* and explicitly incorporates this information in forming inflation expectations. Of course, even in an explicit inflation-targeting regime, the public may remain somewhat uncertain regarding the policymaker's inflation target, π^*, so that this assumption of a perfectly known inflation target may not be obtainable in practice and may be seen as an illustrative limiting case.

The assumption of a known numerical inflation target simplifies the

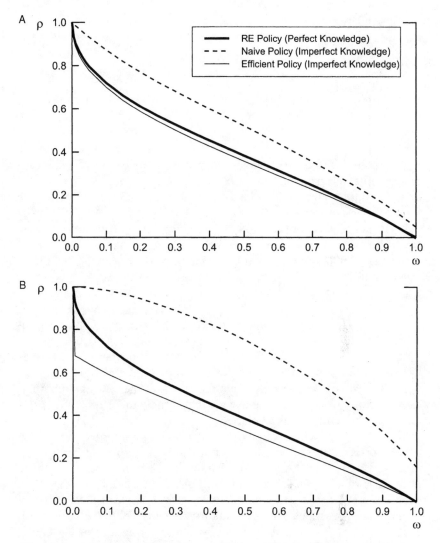

Fig. 5.8 *A,* Inflation persistence ($\phi = 0.75$, $\alpha = 0.25$); *B,* Inflation persistence ($\phi = 0.9$, $\alpha = 0.1$)

Notes: The figure shows the population first-order autocorrelation of inflation corresponding to policies based on alternative inflation stabilization weights ω. For each value of ω, the thick-solid line shows the inflation persistence in the benchmark case of rational expectations with perfect knowledge. The dashed line shows the corresponding persistence when policy follows the RE-optimal solution but knowledge is imperfect. The thin-solid line shows the persistence associated with the efficient one-parameter rule with imperfect knowledge.

public's inflation forecasting problem. From equations (7) and (8), the reduced-form equation for inflation under rational expectations is given by

(15) $$\pi_{t+1} - \pi^* = \left(1 - \frac{\alpha\theta}{1 - \phi}\right)(\pi_t - \pi^*) + e_{t+1} + \alpha u_{t+1}.$$

With a known inflation target, the inflation-forecasting model consistent with rational expectations is simply

(16) $$\pi_i - \pi^* = c_{1,t}(\pi_{i-1} - \pi^*) + v_i.$$

Note that in this forecasting equation only the slope parameter, c_1, is estimated; thus, in terms of the forecasting equation, the assumption of a known inflation target corresponds to a zero restriction on c_0 (when the forecasting regression is written in terms of deviations of inflation from its target). As in the case of an unknown inflation target, constant-gain versions of equations (10) and (11) can be used to model the evolution of the formation of inflation expectations in this case. The one-step-ahead forecast of inflation is given by

(17) $$\pi_{t+1}^e = \pi^* + c_{1,t}(\pi_t - \pi^*),$$

and again, in the limit of perfect knowledge (that is, as $\kappa \to 0$), the expectations function above converges to rational expectations with the slope coefficient $c_1^P = (1 - \phi - \alpha)/(1 - \phi)$. This formulation captures a key rationale for adopting an explicit inflation-targeting regime: to reduce the public's uncertainty and possible confusion about the central bank's precise inflation objective and thereby to anchor the public's inflation expectations to the central bank's objective.[17]

Eliminating uncertainty about the inflation target improves macroeconomic performance, in terms of both inflation and output stability. The thin-solid lines in panel A of figure 5.9 trace the RE-policy pseudo-frontiers in the case of a known inflation target. For comparison, the dashed lines show the pseudo-frontiers assuming that the inflation target is not known by the public (this repeats the curves shown in figure 5.5 for our benchmark case, $\kappa = 0.05$). Recall that the pseudo-frontier is obtained by evaluating the performance of the economy under imperfect knowledge for the set of policies for $\omega \in (0,1]$ given by equation (8) that would be optimal under perfect knowledge. As seen in the figure, economic outcomes are clearly more favorable when the inflation target is assumed to be perfectly known

---

17. The adoption of inflation targeting may affect the private formation of expectations in other ways than by tying down the ultimate inflation objective. For instance, Svensson (2002) argues that inflation-targeting central banks should also make explicit their preference weighting, ω, which in principle could further reduce the public's uncertainty about policy objectives. However, given the remaining uncertainty about model parameters (α and ϕ in our model), the uncertainty about the value of c_1 is not eliminated in this case. The extent to which this uncertainty may be reduced is left to further research.

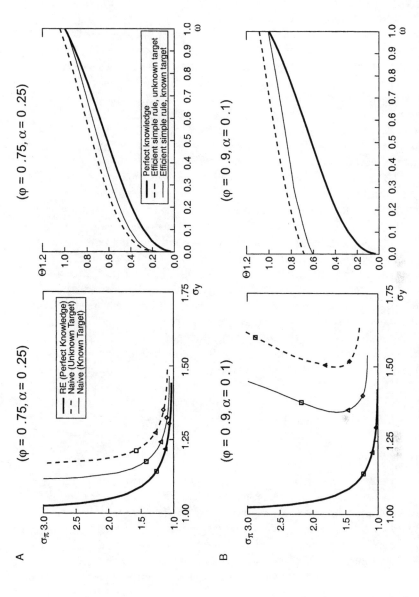

Fig. 5.9 Comparing policies with a known and unknown inflation target: *A*, Outcomes with RE policy; *B*, Efficient response to inflation

Notes: The thin-solid lines indicate economic outcomes (top panel) and efficient policy responses (bottom panel) with perpetual learning when the policy-maker's inflation target is assumed to be perfectly known. The thick-solid and dashed lines correspond, respectively, to the perfect-knowledge benchmark and the case of perpetual learning with an unknown inflation target. See also the notes to figures 5.5 and 5.6.

than otherwise. Still, the resulting pseudo-frontiers lie well to the northeast of those that would obtain under perfect knowledge. Evidently, imperfect knowledge of the dynamic process for inflation alone has large costs in terms of performance, especially when expectations are very important for determining inflation outcomes, represented by the case of $\phi = 0.9$.

The basic finding that, relative to the perfect-knowledge benchmark, policy should be more vigilant against inflation under imperfect knowledge also obtains in the case of a known inflation target. Panel B of figure 5.9 shows the optimal values of θ for the three cases we consider: perfect knowledge, imperfect knowledge with known π^*, and imperfect knowledge with unknown π^*. When π^* is known, the optimal choice of θ is slightly lower than when π^* is unknown. Even with a known inflation target, however, it remains optimal to be more vigilant against inflation relative to the perfect-knowledge case. An exception is the extreme case of $\omega = 1$ when the optimal value of θ is exactly unity, the same value that obtains under perfect knowledge.[18]

A striking result, seen most clearly in the case of $\phi = 0.9$, is that the optimal value of θ is relatively insensitive over a large range of values for the stabilization preference weight, ω, whether the inflation is known or unknown. By contrast, under perfect knowledge, the optimal value of θ is quite sensitive to ω. An implication of this finding is that with imperfect knowledge there is relatively little "cost" associated with policies designed as if inflation were the central bank's primary objective, even when policymakers place substantial value in reducing output variability in fact. By contrast, as shown above, the costs of optimizing policies that incorrectly place a large weight on output stability under the assumption of perfect knowledge can be quite large. This asymmetry suggests that the practice of concentrating attention primarily on price stability in the formulation of monetary policy may be seen as a robust strategy for achieving *both* a high degree of price stability *and* a high degree of economic stability.

5.8   Conclusion

We examine the effects of a relatively modest deviation from rational expectations resulting from perpetual learning on the part of economic agents with imperfect knowledge. The presence of imperfections in the formation of expectations makes the monetary policy problem considerably more difficult than would appear under rational expectations. Using a simple linear model, we show that although inflation expectations are nearly efficient, imperfect knowledge raises the persistence of inflation and

---

18. In this limiting case, estimates of c_1 are symmetrically distributed around zero. Hence, in terms of a simple rule of the form given by equation (4), there is no gain from overresponding, relative to the case of perfect knowledge, to actual inflation.

distorts the policymaker's trade-off between inflation and output stabilization. As a result, policies that appear efficient under rational expectations can result in economic outcomes significantly worse than would be expected by analysis based on the assumption of perfect knowledge. The costs of failing to account for the presence of imperfect knowledge are particularly pronounced for policymakers who place a relatively greater value on stabilizing output: a strategy emphasizing tight inflation control can yield superior economic performance, in terms of both inflation and output stability, than can policies that appear efficient under rational expectations. More generally, policies emphasizing tight inflation control reduce the persistence of inflation and the incidence of large deviations of expectations from the policy objective, thereby mitigating the influence of imperfect knowledge on the economy. In addition, tighter control of inflation makes the economy less prone to costly stagflationary episodes.

The adoption and effective communication of an explicit numerical inflation target also mitigate the influence of imperfect knowledge on the economy. Communication of an inflation target may greatly improve attainable macroeconomic outcomes and afford greater economic stability relative to the outcomes that are attainable when the public perceives the policymaker's ultimate inflation objective less clearly. These results highlight the potential value of communicating a central bank's inflation objective and of continued vigilance against inflation in anchoring inflation expectations and fostering macroeconomic stability.

References

Anderson, T. W., and John B. Taylor. 1976. Some experimental results on the statistical properties of least squares estimates in control problems. *Econometrica* 44 (6): 1289–1302.

Ball, Laurence. 2000. Near-rationality and inflation in two monetary regimes. NBER Working Paper no. 7988. Cambridge, Mass.: National Bureau of Economic Research, October.

Balvers, Ronald J., and Thomas F. Cosimano. 1994. Inflation variability and gradualist monetary policy. *The Review of Economic Studies* 61 (4): 721–38.

Bernanke, Ben S., and Frederic S. Mishkin. 1997. Inflation targeting: A new framework for monetary policy. *Journal of Economic Perspectives* 11 (2): 97–116.

Blume, Lawrence E., and David Easley. 1982. Learning to be rational. *Journal of Economic Theory* 26 (2): 340–51.

Bomfim, Antulio, Robert Tetlow, Peter von zur Muehlen, and John Williams. 1997. Expectations, learning and the costs of disinflation: Experiments using the FRB/US model. *Topics in Monetary Policy Modelling* 4 (July): 222–43.

Bray, Margaret M. 1982. Learning, estimation, and the stability of rational expectations. *Journal of Economic Theory* 26 (2): 318–39.

———. 1983. Convergence to rational expectations equilibrium. In *Individual fore-*

casting and aggregate outcomes, ed. Roman Frydman and Edmund S. Phelps, 123–32. Cambridge: Cambridge University Press.

Bray, Margaret M., and Nathan E. Savin. 1984. Rational expectations equilibria, learning, and model specification. *Econometrica* 54 (5): 1129–60.

Brayton, Flint, Eileen Mauskopf, David Reifschneider, Peter Tinsley, and John Williams. 1997. The role of expectations in the FRB/US macroeconomic model. *Federal Reserve Bulletin* 83 (4): 227–45.

Brayton, Flint, John M. Roberts, and John C. Williams. 1999. What's happened to the Phillips curve? Federal Reserve Board Finance and Economics Discussion Series Working Paper no. 1999-49. Washington, D.C.: Federal Reserve Board, September.

Buiter, Willem H., and Ian Jewitt. 1981. Staggered wage setting with real wage relativities: Variations on a theme by Taylor. *The Manchester School* 49 (3): 211–28.

Bullard, James B., and Kaushik Mitra. 2002. Learning about monetary policy rules. *Journal of Monetary Economics* 49 (6): 1105–29.

Carroll, Christopher D. 2003. Macroeconomic expectations of households and professional forecasters. *Quarterly Journal of Economics* 118 (1): 269–98.

Christiano, Lawrence J., and Christopher Gust. 2000. The expectations trap hypothesis. In *Money, monetary policy and transmission mechanisms,* 347–83. Ottawa: Bank of Canada.

Clark, Peter, Charles A. E. Goodhart, and Haizhou Huang. 1999. Optimal monetary policy rules in a rational expectations model of the Phillips curve. *Journal of Monetary Economics* 43 (2): 497–520.

Craine, Roger. 1979. Optimal monetary policy with uncertainty. *Journal of Economic Dynamics and Control* 1 (1): 59–83.

Erceg, Christopher J., and Andrew T. Levin. 2003. Imperfect credibility and inflation persistence. *Journal of Monetary Economics* 50 (4): 915–44.

Evans, George, and Seppo Honkapohja. 2001. *Learning and expectations in macroeconomics.* Princeton: Princeton University Press.

Evans, George, and Garey Ramey. 2001. Adaptive expectations, underparameterization and the Lucas critique. University of Oregon, Department of Economics. Mimeograph, May.

Friedman, Benjamin M. 1979. Optimal expectations and the extreme information assumptions of "rational expectations" macromodels. *Journal of Monetary Economics* 5 (1): 23–41.

Fuhrer, Jeffrey C. 1997. The (un)importance of forward-looking behavior in price specifications. *Journal of Money, Credit and Banking* 29 (3): 338–50.

Fuhrer, Jeffrey C., and George Moore. 1995. Inflation persistence. *Quarterly Journal of Economics* 110 (1): 127–59.

Galí, Jordi, and Mark Gertler. 1999. Inflation dynamics: A structural economic analysis. *Journal of Monetary Economics* 44 (2): 195–222.

Gaspar, Vitor, and Frank Smets. 2002. Monetary policy, price stability and output gap stabilisation. *International Finance* 5 (2): 193–211.

Kozicki, Sharon, and Peter A. Tinsley. 2001. What do you expect? Imperfect policy credibility and tests of the expectations hypothesis. Federal Reserve Bank of Kansas City Working Paper no. 01-02. April.

Laubach, Thomas, and John C. Williams. 2003. Measuring the natural rate of interest. *Review of Economics and Statistics* 85 (4): 1063–70.

Lengwiler, Yvan, and Athanasios Orphanides. 2002. Optimal discretion. *Scandinavian Journal of Economics* 104 (2): 261–76.

Levin, Andrew, Volker Wieland, and John Williams. 2003. The performance of forecast-based monetary policy rules under model uncertainty. *American Economic Review* 93 (3): 622–45.

Lucas, Robert E., Jr. 1986. Adaptive behavior and economic theory. *Journal of Business* 59 (4): S401–S426.

Mankiw, N. Gregory, and Ricardo Reis. 2002. Sticky information versus sticky prices: A proposal to replace the New Keynesian Phillips curve. *Quarterly Journal of Economics* 117 (4): 1295–1328.

Marcet, Albert, and Thomas Sargent. 1988. The fate of systems with "adaptive" expectations. *American Economic Review* 78 (2): 168–72.

———. 1989. Convergence of least squares learning mechanisms in self referential linear stochastic models. *Journal of Economic Theory* 48 (2): 337–68.

Muth, John F. 1961. Rational expectations and the theory of price movements. *Econometrica* 29:315–35.

Orphanides, Athanasios. 2003a. Monetary policy evaluation with noisy information. *Journal of Monetary Economics* 50 (3): 605–31.

———. 2003b. The quest for prosperity without inflation. *Journal of Monetary Economics* 50 (3): 633–63.

———. 2004. Monetary policy rules, macroeconomic stability and inflation: A view from the trenches. *Journal of Money, Credit and Banking* 36 (2): 151–75.

Orphanides, Athanasios, and John C. Williams. 2002. Monetary policy rules with unknown natural rates. *Brookings Papers on Economic Activity,* Issue no. 2:63–145.

———. 2003. Inflation scares and forecast-based monetary policy. Board of Governors of the Federal Reserve System and Federal Reserve Bank of San Francisco. Mimeograph, March.

Roberts, John M. 1997. Is inflation sticky? *Journal of Monetary Economics* 39 (2): 173–96.

———. 1998. Inflation expectations and the transmission of monetary policy. Federal Reserve Board Finance and Economics Series Discussion Paper no. 1998-43. Washington, D.C.: Federal Reserve Board, October.

———. 2001. How well does the New Keynesian sticky-price model fit the data? Federal Reserve Board Finance and Economics Series Discussion Paper no. 2001-13. Washington, D.C.: Federal Reserve Board, February.

Rudd, Jeremy, and Karl Whelan. 2001. New tests of the New-Keynesian Phillips curve. Federal Reserve Board Finance and Economics Series Discussion Paper no. 2001-30. Washington, D.C.: Federal Reserve Board, July.

Sargent, Thomas J. 1993. *Bounded Rationality in Macroeconomics.* Oxford and New York: Oxford University Press, Clarendon Press.

———. 1999. *The conquest of American inflation.* Princeton: Princeton University Press.

Simon, Herbert A. 1978. Rationality as process and as product of thought. *American Economic Review* 68 (2): 1–16.

Sims, Christopher. 2003. Implications of rational inattention. *Journal of Monetary Economics* 50 (3): 665–90.

Staiger, Douglas, James H. Stock, and Mark W. Watson. 1997. How precise are estimates of the natural rate of unemployment? In *Reducing inflation: Motivation and strategy,* ed. Christina D. Romer and David H. Romer, 195–242. Chicago: University of Chicago Press.

Stock, James H., and Mark W. Watson. 1999. Forecasting inflation. *Journal of Monetary Economics* 44 (2): 293–335.

Svensson, Lars. 2002. Monetary policy and real stabilization. In *Rethinking stabilization policy,* 261–312. Kansas City: Federal Reserve Bank of Kansas City.

Taylor, John B. 1975. Monetary policy during a transition to rational expectations. *Journal of Political Economy* 83 (5): 1009–21.

———. 1979. Estimation and control of a macroeconomic model with rational expectations. *Econometrica* 47 (5): 1267–86.

Tetlow, Robert J., and Peter von zur Muehlen. 2001. Simplicity versus optimality: The choice of monetary policy rules when agents must learn. *Journal of Economic Dynamics and Control* 25 (1–2): 245–79.

Townsend, Robert M. 1978. Market anticipations, rational expectations, and Bayesian analysis. *International Economic Review* 19 (2): 481–94.

Turnovsky, Stephen. 1977. *Macroeconomic analysis and stabilization policies.* Cambridge: Cambridge University Press.

Volcker, Paul. 1979. Statement before the Joint Economic Committee of the U.S. Congress. October 17, 1979. Reprinted in *Federal Reserve Bulletin* 65 (11): 888–90.

———. 1981. Statement before the Committee on the Budget, U.S. House of Representatives. March 27, 1981. Reprinted in *Federal Reserve Bulletin* 67 (4): 293–6.

Wieland, Volker. 1998. Monetary policy and uncertainty about the natural unemployment rate. Board of Governors of the Federal Reserve System Finance and Economics Series Discussion Paper no. 98-22. Washington, D.C.: Federal Reserve Board, April.

Woodford, Michael. 1990. Learning to believe in sunspots. *Econometrica* 58 (2): 277–307.

Comment   George W. Evans

Introduction

This is a very nice paper. The main points are important, the structure is simple and clear, and I find the key arguments persuasive. In my comments I am going to begin by summarizing the heart of the Orphanides-Williams argument. Then I will locate their paper within the rapidly growing literature on learning and monetary policy. Finally I will return to their paper and offer a number of specific comments on natural extensions or alternative approaches.

Summary of the Argument

Orphanides and Williams (OW) work with a simple two-equation macro model. The first equation is an augmented Phillips curve with inertia:

$$\pi_{t+1} = \phi\pi_{t+1}^e + (1 - \phi)\pi_t + \alpha y_{t+1} + e_{t+1},$$

where π_{t+1} is the rate of inflation between period t and period $t + 1$, π_{t+1}^e is the rate of inflation over this period expected at time t, y_{t+1} is the level of the output gap in $t + 1$, and e_{t+1} is a white noise inflation shock. The second equation is an aggregate-demand relation that embodies a lagged policy effect,

George W. Evans is John B. Hamacher Professor of Economics at the University of Oregon.

$$y_{t+1} = x_t + u_{t+1},$$

where x_t is set by monetary policy at t and u_{t+1} is white noise. Through monetary policy it is assumed that policymakers are able one period ahead to control aggregate output up to the unpredictable random disturbance u_{t+1}.

The combination of this aggregate-demand equation and the neoclassical (as opposed to neo-Keynesian) inflation equation yields a particularly tractable model for studying the effects of private agents' learning. In particular, the timing assumptions are carefully crafted to yield simplicity.

Policymakers choose the x_t process to minimize

$$(1 - \omega)Ey_t^2 + \omega E(\pi_t - \pi^*)^2.$$

This is a standard quadratic loss function. We can think of ω as reflecting policymakers' preferences, which may (or may not) be derived from the preferences of the representative agent.

Optimal Policy under Rational Expectations

Under rational expectations (RE), optimal policy takes the form of the feedback rule

$$x_t = -\theta^P(\pi_t - \pi^*),$$

where $\theta^P = \theta^P(\omega, \alpha/[1 - \phi])$. This leads to an efficiency frontier, described by a familiar trade-off between σ_π and σ_y, shown in their figure 5.1.

For this choice of feedback parameter, in the rational-expectations equilibrium (REE) inflation follows the process

$$\pi_t = c_0^P + c_1^P \pi_{t-1} + \text{noise}_t$$

$$E_t\pi_{t+1} = c_0^P + c_1^P\pi_t,$$

where c_0^P, c_1^P depend on $\theta^P\alpha/(1 - \phi)$. Here noise$_t$ is white noise. The superscript P refers to "perfect knowledge," which OW use as a synonym for RE.

Thus, under RE the problem is quite straightforward. How "aggressive" policy should be with respect to deviations of inflation from target depends in a natural way on the structural parameters ϕ, α and policymaker preferences as described by ω.

Least Squares Learning

Now we make the crucial step of backing away from RE. Instead of assuming that agents are endowed a priori with RE, we model the agents as forecasting in the same way that an econometrician might: by assuming a simple time series model for the variable of interest, and by estimating its parameters and using it to forecast. Specifically, suppose that private agents believe that inflation follows an AR(1) process, as it does in an REE, but that they do not know c_0^P, c_1^P. Instead they estimate the parameters of

$$\pi_t = c_0 + c_1 \pi_{t-1} + v_t$$

by a least squares–type regression, and at time t forecast

$$\pi_{t+1}^e = c_{0,t} + c_{1,t} \pi_t.$$

Over time the estimates $c_{0,t}$, $c_{1,t}$ are updated as new data become available. We consider two cases for this updating.

Infinite Memory—"Decreasing Gain"

First we suppose that agents literally do least squares using all the data. We assume that policymakers do not explicitly take account of private agent learning and follow the feedback rule with $\theta = \theta^P$. Then, with "infinite memory" (no discounting of observations), one can show (e.g., Evans and Honkapohja 2001)

$$c_{0,t}, c_{1,t} \to c_0^P, c_1^P \text{ w.p.} 1,$$

so that asymptotically we get the optimal REE.

Technically the most convenient way to set up least squares learning by private agents is using the recursive least squares (RLS) algorithm.[1] In this algorithm the agents carry their parameter estimates (and an estimate of the second moment matrix of the regressors) into the next period. Updated estimates next period are then generated recursively using the most recent data point. Because each data point is counted equally by least squares, the "gain" κ_t (i.e., the effective weight placed on the last data point) is given by $\kappa_t = 1/t$ (i.e., by the inverse of the sample size). In the learning literature this is called the "decreasing gain" case, because $\kappa_t \to 0$ as $t \to \infty$.

I remark that convergence to the REE is not obvious. This is because the model is "self-referential": that is, the evolution of the data depends on expectations and hence on the estimated coefficients, and these in turn are updated using the data generated. Convergence to REE does take place because the equilibrium in this model satisfies the "E-stability" conditions that govern stability in such a system.

Finite Memory—"Constant Gain"

OW make a small but significant change to the standard least squares updating formula. Instead of assuming that all observations count equally, they discount or downweight past data. In terms of the RLS algorithm, this is accomplished technically by setting the gain, the weight on the most recent observation used to update estimates, to a small constant (i.e., setting $\kappa_t = \kappa$; e.g., 0.05).

Why would it be natural for agents to use a constant rather than de-

---

1. The technique of formulating learning as a recursive algorithm, and then applying stochastic approximation tools to analyze convergence, was introduced by Marcet and Sargent (1989).

creasing gain? The main rationale for this procedure is that it allows estimates to remain alert to structural shifts. As economists, and as econometricians, we tend to believe that structural changes occasionally occur, and we might therefore assume that private agents also recognize and allow for this. Although in principle one might attempt to model the process of structural change, this typically unduly strains the amount of knowledge we have about the economic structure. A reasonable alternative is to adjust parameter estimators to reflect the fact that recent observations convey more accurate information on the economy's law of motion than do past data, and "constant gain" estimators are one very natural way of accomplishing this downweighting of past data.[2]

Implications of Constant-Gain Least Squares

With constant-gain procedures, estimates no longer fully converge to the REE. The estimators $c_{0,t}$, $c_{1,t}$ converge instead to a stochastic process. Because of this, OW use the term "perpetual learning" to refer to the constant gain case.

If the gain parameter κ is very small, then estimators will be close to the REE values for most of the time with high probability, and output and inflation will be near their REE paths. Nonetheless, small plausible values like $\kappa = 0.05$ can lead to very different outcomes in the calibrations OW consider. In particular, they find the following:

1. The standard deviations of $c_{0,t}$ and $c_{1,t}$ are large even though forecast performance remains good.

2. There is a substantial increase in the persistence of inflation, compared to the REE.

3. Most strikingly, the policy frontier shifts out very substantially and in a nonmonotonic way (see their figure 5.5).

Policy Implications

Under perpetual learning if policymakers keep to the same class of rules

$$x_t = -\theta^S(\pi_t - \pi^*),$$

then they should choose a different θ. Here the notation θ^S is meant to indicate that we restrict policymakers to choose from the same "simple" class of policy rules. There are four main implications for policy in the context of constant-gain (perpetual) learning by private agents.

---

2. Two remarks are in order. First, an alternative rationale for constant gain is that it can be an equilibrium in learning rules, even if structural change is not present; see section 14.4 of Evans and Honkapohja (2001). Second, there are other ways of allowing for structural change: for example, through time-varying gain sequences or explicit models of structural variation.

1. Naive policy choice can be strictly inefficient. This is illustrated in the second panel of their figure 5.5. By "naive" policy is meant the policy that assumes RE (perfect knowledge) on the part of agents, when in fact the agents are following perpetual learning with $\kappa > 0$. In particular, there are cases in which increasing θ^S would decrease the standard deviations of *both* inflation and output.

2. In general, policy should be more hawkish; that is, under perpetual learning the monetary authorities should pick a larger θ^S than if agents had RE.

3. Following a sequence of unanticipated inflation shocks, inflation doves (i.e., policymakers with low θ reflecting a low ω) can do very poorly. This is illustrated in OW's figure 5.3.

4. If the inflation target π^* is known to private agents, so that they need estimate only the slope parameter c_1, then the policy frontier is more favorable than when it is not known. This is illustrated in the first panel of their figure 5.9.

I will return to a discussion of these and other specific results after discussing learning and monetary policy in a more general setting.

Learning in Monetary Policy

Recently, considerable research has begun to focus on the implications for monetary policy when explicit account is taken of the literature on adaptive/econometric learning in macroeconomics.[3]

I will give a selective overview of this recent research and locate OW within this context. Then I will return to a discussion of OW. There are four main issues I will use to group my general remarks: (a) the theoretical roles played by learning, (b) the question of who or what group of agents is learning, (c) the particular implications of constant-gain learning, and (d) some further (personal) thoughts on rationality.

Roles for Learning

There are three main types of result that can be delivered by incorporating learning into a monetary policy model.

Stability under Private Agent Learning

An REE need not necessarily be stable under private agent learning. It is logically possible that if agents follow least squares learning (with the

---

3. For example, two recent workshops or conferences have considered this topic, one at the Cleveland Federal Reserve Bank, in February 2001, on "Learning and Model Misspecification," and a second at the Atlanta Federal Reserve Bank, in March 2003, on "Monetary Policy and Learning."

usual decreasing gain) then the system fails to converge to an REE, even if their parameter estimates are initially close to the REE.

This theoretical possibility of instability turns out to be a genuine concern for monetary policy in New Keynesian or New Phillips curve models (as is the related but distinct issue of indeterminacy). Bullard and Mitra (2002) show that stability under private agent learning should not be taken for granted if policymakers follow Taylor-type rules. Depending on the specific formulation of the rule, instability can arise for certain choices of parameter settings. Evans and Honkapohja (2002, 2003a, 2003c) examine this issue in the context of optimal monetary policy. They show that stability under learning is a pervasive problem when the interest rate rule is formulated as a reaction to fundamental shocks, but it can be overcome when the rule reacts appropriately to private expectations. Recent work by Preston (2003) has considered this issue in the context of long-horizon agents.

Selection Criterion

In some models the phenomenon of indeterminacy (i.e., multiple REE) arises. In this setting, learning can provide a natural way of choosing between equilibria. A particular question of interest is the following. It is known that when a steady state of a linear model is indeterminate there exist "sunspot" equilibria—that is, REE in which the solution is driven by extraneous noise. Such solutions, with economic fluctuations driven in a self-fulfilling way by extrinsic random variables, would usually be considered an unintended and undesirable by-product of economic policy. A particular question of interest, in cases of multiple equilibria, is whether the sunspot equilibria can be stable under learning.

It has been known for some time that it is possible in some cases for sunspot equilibria to be stable under learning. This was initially demonstrated by Woodford (1990) in the context of the overlapping-generations model of money. In general, whether a sunspot equilibrium is stable under learning depends on the model and the particular solution (see chap. 12 of Evans and Honkapohja 2001). There has been recent interest in whether stable sunspot solutions can arise in more realistic monetary models. In particular, Evans, Honkapohja, and Marimon (2003) look at when this can occur in cash-in-advance models, and Honkapohja and Mitra (forthcoming), Carlstrom and Fuerst (2004), and Evans and McGough (forthcoming) examine the issue for New Keynesian models.

Non-REE Learning Dynamics

Finally, we move to the possibility that the economy under learning generates solutions that in some way go beyond RE. Here it appears useful to group results into two broad categories. One possibility is that learning converges to a "restricted-perceptions equilibrium." This arises if agents are endowed with an econometric model that is misspecified asymptotically, as discussed in chapter 13 of Evans and Honkapohja (2001). For example, agents may omit some variables that help forecast the variables of interest, or their forecasting model may fail to capture nonlinearities that are present.

Somewhat more radically, learning may generate "persistent learning dynamics" (see chap. 14 of Evans and Honkapohja 2001) as a result of local instability of an REE under learning (as in Bullard 1994) or due to a learning rule that fails to fully converge to REE parameter values (as in constant-gain learning rules). The OW paper falls into this last class: private agents use a learning rule in which parameter estimates never quite converge to REE values. This "perpetual learning" then turns out to have major policy implications, even when the deviation from REE might be thought not too large.

Who Is Learning?

The earliest literature on learning focused on private agents (i.e. households and firms). In dynamic macroeconomic models private agents, in order to make optimal decisions, must make forecasts of relevant future variables. Clearly the expectations of households and firms do matter enormously for the actual evolution of the economy. The RE revolution made the crucial advance of defining and analyzing what it means for expectations to be consistent with the economic structure and optimizing agents. However, this has had the potential disadvantage of demoting private expectations as an independent force. Consequently it was natural that the initial focus of the learning literature was on private agent learning. The OW paper follows the primary strand of the literature in this respect.

However, policymakers also need to form expectations and make forecasts, and they too are not endowed with full knowledge of the economic structure or fully rational forecast functions. Some recent research has begun to tackle this issue. Most notably, Thomas Sargent's (1999) book on the disinflation in the 1990s emphasized learning by policymakers about a (misspecified) Phillips curve trade-off. Sargent's model incorporates a tantalizing combination of misspecification, learning, and optimal policy formulation.

Obviously it is possible to allow for separate learning by private agents and policymakers. In fact, Sargent (1999) actually allows for this in some cases, although much of his analysis, and that of Cho, Williams, and Sargent (2002), focuses on learning by policymakers with RE assumed for private agents. Simultaneous learning by policymakers is also analyzed in Honkapohja and Mitra (2002) and discussed in Evans and Honkapohja (2003c).

There is an additional asymmetry that should be noted. Both private agents and policymakers need to make forecasts of future aggregate variables, but in addition, implementation of optimal policy may require simultaneous estimation of structural parameters. This issue is considered in Evans and Honkapohja (2003a, 2003c).

Constant-Gain Learning

As already emphasized, the use of constant-gain (or "perpetual") learning plays a central role in OW. In general, constant-gain learning can lead to a number of phenomena. First, the work of Sargent (1999), Cho, Williams, and Sargent (2002), Williams (2002), and Bullard and Cho (2002) emphasizes the possibility of "escapes"—that is, occasional big deviations from a unique REE. This is a surprising finding: for significant periods of time learning dynamics can drive the economy away from the REE, but in a predictable direction.

When there are multiple REE, escapes can take a different form. The most widely examined case is the case of multiple distinct REE steady states. Here escapes take the form of periodic shifts between the different steady states as a result of large random shocks interacting with the learning dynamics. This phenomenon is seen in chapter 14 of Evans and Honkapohja (2001), the hyperinflation model of Marcet and Nicolini (2003c), the exchange rate model of Kasa (2004) and the liquidity trap model of Evans and Honkapohja (2003b).

Finally, it turns out that, even in a quite standard model with a unique REE and without the more exotic effects just described, constant-gain learning has significant implications for optimal policy. This is the important new finding that is demonstrated in the current paper by OW.

Some Further Thoughts on Rationality

In constructing economic models we have three kinds of agents: (a) private agents, (b) policymakers, and (c) economists (us). In the bad old days of adaptive expectations, private agents made systematic mistakes, but we the economists were very smart. We told policymakers what to do, so they were smart too.

The RE revolution changed all this. Now private agents became smart, and policymakers (and earlier economists) were mistaken, as shown by the Lucas critique. As theorists we were again smart (because we understood how private agents really formed expectations), but as econometricians we were not quite so smart. This is because as econometricians we had to estimate parameters that were known with certainty by the private agents and theorists.

The adaptive-learning viewpoint has the enormous advantage over these earlier approaches that it (potentially) achieves greater cognitive consistency between these three kinds of agents. In particular, private agents are modeled as behaving like econometricians—that is, like economists in our forecasting role. Of course, as theorists we still typically analyze models with a specified structure that is effectively known only to us, but at least it can be consistently treated as unknown to private agents, policymakers, and econometricians. Furthermore, the degree of smartness of each group is a matter of choice or judgement for us as theorists.

An important aspect of this "bounded rationality" approach is that many features of RE do carry over to the adaptive-learning approach. For example, the Lucas critique can apply under bounded rationality, as emphasized in Evans and Ramey (2003). The Lucas critique will often arise if agents attempt to forecast in an optimal way, even if they are not perfectly rational in the sense of "rational expectations."

Back to Orphanides and Williams

Returning now to the OW paper, let me make some specific critical comments and suggest some extensions.

1. *The inflation shocks experiment.* My first point concerns the inflation shocks scenario shown in OW's figure 5.3. OW examine a sequence of unanticipated positive inflation shocks starting with $e_1 = 2$ percent and declining to zero over nine (semiannual) periods. My main point is that this is more like a structural shift, and that the effects are the same as a decrease in potential output over four years. This raises several questions that would need to be explicitly addressed in a full treatment of this issue.

Suppose, for example, that e_{t+1} is partly predictable, as seems appropriate for a structural shift, and that the loss function is

$$L = E_0\left\{\sum_{t=0}^{\infty}[(1 - \omega)(y_t - y_t^*)^2 + \omega(\pi_t - \pi^*)^2]\right\}.$$

Depending on the source of the shock, policymakers may want to lower their output target y_t^* (to $y_t^* = -\alpha^{-1}e_t$). Even if policymakers continue to set $y_t^* = 0$, policy should take into account expected $e_{t+1} > 0$.

This is perhaps a setup in which it would be particularly fruitful also to incorporate policymaker learning.

2. *Bias toward "hawkishness."* OW show that policymakers should be more hawkish. The intuition for this result is fairly intuitive. A more hawkish (high θ) policy helps to keep inflation expectations π_{t+1}^e "in line" (i.e., closer to RE values). This gives policy an additional role, besides stabilizing y and π, and this additional role means that under perpetual learning it is optimal for policymakers to be more hawkish than they would be, for given policymaker preferences, under RE.

This observation leads naturally to the question of how robust this result is. In particular, in New Keynesian models y_{t+1}^e also matters. The structure in such models is

$$y_t = -\varphi(i_t - \pi_{t+1}^e) + y_{t+1}^e + g_t$$

$$\pi_t = \lambda y_t + \beta\pi_{t+1}^e + \gamma\pi_{t-1} + u_t.$$

Will the presence of y_{t+1}^e in the "IS" curve (the first equation) make the direction of bias for the policymaker ambiguous? The answer is not clear a priori and would need to be explicitly analyzed.

3. *Choice of gain parameter κ.* The value of κ is taken as given and not explained. This is quite standard in the constant-gain learning literature. In one respect this is convenient, since it can then be treated as a parameter to be estimated empirically.

However, one can think about the issue further from a theoretical viewpoint. The most typical rationale for introducing constant gain, as indicated above, is that it is a way of allowing for structural shifts. The choice of κ can then be thought of as providing a balance between tracking and filtering: high values of κ allow the estimator to better track structural change, but with the disadvantage of yielding noisier estimators.

One possibility would then be to explicitly introduce structural shifts into the model and find the optimal value of κ. This type of exercise is done in chapter 14 of Evans and Honkapohja (2001) and in Evans and Ramey (2003). In OW this would add complexity and is unlikely to matter. However, the issue of the optimal choice of gain is likely to become important in future work.

4. *Smarter agents.* Using the bounded rationality approach one can always ask: should the agents be smarter? less smart? This is always a matter of judgment. There are several possible ways in which the private agents in OW could be "smarter." For example, private agents could be modeled as estimating an AR(p) instead of an AR(1). Indeed, one could consider the possibility that the agents choose the lag length p in the same way as an applied econometrician. Similarly, agents might consider forecasting based on a vector autoregression (VAR), perhaps using one of the standard statistics to choose the order of the VAR.

It seems likely that the qualitative results would be unaffected, but it would be of interest to know how the detailed results depend on such specification issues. It might appear unsatisfactory, compared to the lack of ambiguity in the RE approach, to be faced with questions about lag length and model specification. But this is really a strength of the adaptive-learning framework. Econometricians dealing with forecasting and estimation problems inevitably face precisely such issues in practice. It seems absurd to assume that private agents and policymakers have clear-cut answers to problems that in effect remain research issues for us as econometricians.

Conclusions

This is an important paper. Theoretically, Orphanides and Williams provide a new reason for studying adaptive learning, based on optimal policy when agents follow "perpetual learning" rules. From an applied viewpoint, the paper suggests another factor that can generate stagflation, and it provides policy recommendations that are intuitive and plausible. I hope (and confidently anticipate) that the authors (and others) will do more work along these lines.

References

Bullard, J. 1994. Learning equilibria. *Journal of Economic Theory* 64:468–85.
Bullard, J., and I.-K. Cho. 2002. Escapist policy rules. Federal Reserve Bank of St. Louis Working Paper no. 2002-0023.
Bullard, J., and K. Mitra. 2002. Learning about monetary policy rules. *Journal of Monetary Economics* 49:1105–29.
Carlstrom, C. T., and T. S. Fuerst. 2004. Learning and the central bank. *Journal of Monetary Economics* 51:327–38.
Cho, I.-K., N. Williams, and T. J. Sargent. 2002. Escaping Nash inflation. *Review of Economic Studies* 69:1–40.
Evans, G. W., and S. Honkapohja. 2001. *Learning and expectations in macroeconomics.* Princeton, N.J.: Princeton University Press.
———. 2002. Monetary policy, expectations and commitment. Working Paper no. 2002-11. University of Oregon, Department of Economics.
———. 2003a. Expectations and the stability problem for optimal monetary policies. *Review of Economic Studies* 70:807–24.
———. 2003b. Policy interaction, expectations and the liquidity trap. Working Paper no. 2003-33. University of Oregon, Department of Economics.
———. 2003c. Adaptive learning and monetary policy design. *Journal of Money, Credit and Banking* 35:1045–72.
Evans, G. W., S. Honkapohja, and R. Marimon. 2003. Stable sunspot equilibria in a cash-in-advance economy. Working Paper no. 2001-5 (revised March 2003). University of Oregon, Department of Economics.
Evans, G. W., and B. McGough. Forthcoming. Monetary policy, indeterminacy and learning. *Journal of Economic Dynamics and Control.*
Evans, G. W., and G. Ramey. 2003. Adaptive expectations, underparameterization and the Lucas critique. Working Paper no. 2003-2 (revised June 2003). University of Oregon, Department of Economics.
Honkapohja, S., and K. Mitra. 2002. Performance of monetary policy with internal central bank forecasting. European Central Bank Working Paper no. 127.
———. Forthcoming. Are non-fundamental equilibria learnable in models of monetary policy? *Journal of Monetary Economics.*
Kasa, K. 2004. Learning, large deviations, and recurrent currency crises. *International Economic Review* 45:141–73.
Marcet, A., and J. P. Nicolini. 2003. Recurrent hyperinflations and learning. *American Economic Review* 93:1476–98.
Marcet, A., and T. J. Sargent. 1989. Convergence of least-squares learning mechanisms in self-referential linear stochastic models. *Journal of Economic Theory* 48:337–68.

Preston, B. 2003. Learning about monetary policy rules when long-horizon forecasts matter. Federal Reserve Bank of Atlanta Working Paper no. 2003-18.

Sargent, T. J. 1999. *The conquest of American inflation.* Princeton, N.J.: Princeton University Press.

Williams, N. 2002. Escape dynamics in learning models. Princeton University. Department of Economics. Mimeograph.

Woodford, M. 1990. Learning to believe in sunspots. *Econometrica* 58:277–307.

Discussion Summary

Lars Svensson remarked that the Orphanides-Williams model provides an important argument for announcing an inflation target: namely, that this simplifies private-sector learning, stabilizes inflation expectations, and thereby allows the central bank to respond less aggressively to inflation than it would have to do otherwise. This should have some bearing on the Federal Reserve's decision on an inflation target. He also suggested that, in addition to the simpler linear policies presented in the paper, the authors should also compute the optimal, nonlinear policies.

Ricardo Caballero commented on the arbitrariness of the particular model of learning used in the paper, and suggested that it would be more convincing to consider forms of learning in which the degree of learning depended upon the magnitude of observed shocks.

Olivier Blanchard pointed out that the aggressive policy responses to inflation are driven by the assumptions about the source of model uncertainty and might be overturned in a setting in which uncertainty about output was more important. In the current U.S. situation, for example, there was greater uncertainty about growth going forward than about inflation.

Frank Smets asked whether the form of adaptive learning used in the paper provided a rationale for price-level targeting.

Donald Kohn argued that output stabilization had an important role to play for agents' ability to learn about permanent income. Moreover, he suggested considering a situation in which both the central bank and private agents were learning, which would allow for private agents' and policymakers' inflation expectations to be different, a situation that had been important between 1994 and 2001.

John Berry stressed that how agents interpreted policy outcomes depended importantly on communication between policymakers and the public. The wage-price controls of 1972, for example, were judged by the press as a failure despite the fact that inflation was merely a few tenths of a percentage point above the announced target rate of 2.5 percent. Based on this experience, he asked whether there was an appropriate role for ambiguity in communications with the public.

Mark Gertler questioned whether the restrictions placed on agents' information sets played an important role in the results, and suggested allowing agents to use lags of both inflation and the output gap in their forecasting rules.

Gregory Mankiw pointed out that the particular value of the gain chosen by the authors was a suspicious free parameter, and he argued that it would be more convincing to derive the optimal gain from explicit modeling of the source of uncertainty, which would lead back to rational expectations.

Christopher Sims argued that the results under learning depended critically on the specific form of the equation that agents are learning about. In the present case, an important question was whether agents had to learn about the intercept or the slope of the Phillips curve, and at which rates they were updating their estimates of either of these parameters.

John Williams responded that their results remained robust even when agents used several lags of both inflation and the output gap in their inflation forecasts, due to the high degree of inflation persistence generated by the model. He argued that, while the precise value of the gain used in learning could be determined inside the model, a constant-gain formula for learning was both realistic and robust. Adding uncertainty about the future output gap was a topic of work in progress, but it should not overturn the results presented in their paper because of the important role played by the persistence of inflation in deriving inflation forecasts.

II

Critical Perspectives

6

Does Inflation Targeting Matter?

Laurence Ball and Niamh Sheridan

The performance of inflation-targeting regimes has been quite good. Inflation-targeting countries seem to have significantly reduced both the rate of inflation and inflation expectations beyond that which would likely have occurred in the absence of inflation targets. (Mishkin 1999, 595)

[The U.K. data show] that not only has inflation been lower since inflation targeting was introduced, but that, as measured by its standard deviation, it has also been more stable than in recent decades. Moreover, inflation has been less persistent—in the sense that shocks to inflation die away more quickly—under inflation targeting than for most of the past century. (King 2002, 2).

[O]ne of the main benefits of inflation targets is that they may help to "lock in" earlier disinflationary gains, particularly in the face of one-time inflationary shocks. We saw this effect, for example, following the exits of the United Kingdom and Sweden from the European Exchange Rate Mechanism and after Canada's 1991 imposition of the Goods and Services Tax. In each case, the re-igniting of inflation seems to have been avoided by the announcement of inflation targets that helped to anchor the public's inflation expectations and to give an explicit plan for and direction to monetary policy. (Bernanke et al. 1999, 288).

Laurence Ball is professor of economics at Johns Hopkins University and a research associate of the National Bureau of Economic Research (NBER). Niamh Sheridan is an economist at the International Monetary Fund (IMF).

We are grateful for research assistance from Witold Czubala, Gergana Danailova-Trainor, and Migiwa Tanaka, and for suggestions from Andrew Feltenstein, Mark Gertler, and participants at the NBER Inflation Targeting Conference, January 2003. The views presented are those of the authors and do not necessarily reflect the views of the IMF or IMF policy.

6.1   Introduction

Economists have long sought the ideal framework for monetary policy. Since the early 1990s, many have come to believe they have finally found the right approach: inflation targeting. Proponents of this policy cite many benefits. Inflation targeting solves the dynamic consistency problem that produces high average inflation. It reduces inflation variability, and if "flexible" it can stabilize output as well (Svensson 1997). Targeting locks in expectations of low inflation, which reduces the inflationary impact of macroeconomic shocks. For these reasons, many economists advocate inflation targeting for the Federal Reserve and the European Central Bank.

This paper attempts to measure the effects of inflation targeting on macroeconomic performance. We examine twenty Organization for Economic Cooperation and Development (OECD) countries, seven that adopted inflation targeting during the 1990s and thirteen that did not. Not surprisingly, economic performance varies greatly across individual countries, both targeters and nontargeters. On average, however, there is no evidence that inflation targeting improves performance as measured by the behavior of inflation, output, or interest rates.

If we examine inflation-targeting countries alone, we see that their performance improved on average between the period before targeting and the targeting period. For example, inflation fell and became more stable, and output growth also stabilized. However, countries that did *not* adopt inflation targeting also experienced improvements around the same times as targeters. This finding suggests that better performance resulted from something other than targeting.

For some performance measures, both inflation targeters and nontargeters improve over time, but the improvements are larger for targeters. For example, average inflation fell for both groups between the pretargeting and targeting periods, but the average for targeters went from above that of nontargeters to roughly the same. Similar findings have led authors such as Neumann and von Hagen (2002) to argue that inflation targeting promotes "convergence": it helps poorly performing countries catch up with countries that are already doing well. Our results, however, do not support even this modest claim of benefits from targeting. For many measures of performance, we find strong evidence of generic regression to the mean. Just as short people on average have children who are taller than they are, countries with unusually high and unstable inflation tend to see these problems diminish, regardless of whether they adopt inflation targeting. Once we control for this effect, the apparent benefits of targeting disappear.

The rest of this paper comprises eight sections. Section 6.2 describes the countries and sample periods that we study, and section 6.3 describes our methodology for measuring the effects of inflation targeting.

Sections 6.4 and 6.5 present our results concerning inflation and output growth. We estimate the effects of inflation targeting on these variables' average levels, variability, and persistence. There are occasional hints that targeting has beneficial effects and occasional hints of adverse effects, but overall it appears that targeting does not matter.

Section 6.6 turns to the behavior of interest rates and presents two main findings. First, inflation targeting has no effect on the level of long-term interest rates, contrary to what one would expect if targeting reduces inflation expectations. Second, targeting does not affect the variability of the short-term interest rates controlled by policymakers. At least by this crude measure, central banks respond neither more nor less aggressively to economic fluctuations under inflation targeting.

Section 6.7 investigates the effects of targeting on several bivariate relations: the slope of the output-inflation trade-off, the inflationary effect of supply shocks (specifically, changes in commodity prices), and the effect of inflation movements on expectations (as measured by OECD inflation forecasts). Here the results are imprecise, as it is difficult to estimate these relations over the short periods for which we have observed inflation targeting. However, the results suggest again that targeting has no important effects.

Section 6.8 compares our results to previous cross-country studies of inflation targeting. Finally, section 6.9 interprets our results. To be clear, we do not present a case *against* inflation targeting. We do not find that targeting does anything harmful, and we can imagine future circumstances in which it might be beneficial. Our results suggest, however, that no major benefits have occurred so far.

6.2 The Sample

This section describes the countries in our sample and the inflation-targeting and non-targeting periods that we examine.

6.2.1 Targeters and Nontargeters

We examine major developed, moderate-inflation economies. Specifically, we start with all members of the OECD as of 1990 (thus excluding the emerging-market economies that have joined since then). We delete countries that lacked an independent currency before the Euro (Luxembourg) or have experienced annual inflation over 20 percent since 1984 (Greece, Iceland, and Turkey). We are left with twenty countries, which are listed in table 6.1. Previous macroeconomic studies using the same sample of countries include Layard, Nickell, and Jackman (1991) and Ball (1997).

Seven of the countries in our sample adopted inflation targeting before 1999: Australia, Canada, Finland, Spain, Sweden, the United Kingdom,

Table 6.1   Starting dates for inflation targeting and constant inflation targeting periods

Country	Inflation targeting	Constant inflation targeting	Rationale for choice of starting dates
Australia	Q4 1994	Q4 1994	In September 1994, the Governor of the Reserve Bank of Australia announced that "underlying inflation of 2 to 3 percent is a reasonable goal for monetary policy." See Bernanke et al. (1999, 218–220) for further discussion.
Canada	Q1 1992	Q1 1994	The first target range was announced by the Bank of Canada in February 1991: 2 to 4 percent over 1992 (i.e. December 1991 to December 1992). In December 1993, a range of 1 to 3 percent was established for 1994, and the range has remained constant since then.
Finland	Q1 1994	Q1 1994	In February 1993, the Bank of Finland stated its intention to "stabilize the rate of inflation permanently at the level of 2% by 1995." It appears that they were referring to year-over-year inflation measured at the start of 1995; thus the period covered by the first target begins at the start of 1994.
New Zealand	Q3 1990	Q1 1993	A target of 3–5 percent over 1990 was announced in April 1990. A target of 0–2 percent for 1993 was announced in February 1991. The target range has remained roughly unchanged since then (but see footnote 2 in the text).
Spain	Q2 1995	Q1 1994	The first target, announced in December 1994, was for year-over-year inflation of 3.5–4 percent "by early 1996."
Sweden	Q1 1995	Q1 1995	The Riksbank announced in January 1993 that it aimed "to limit the annual increase in the consumer price index from 1995 onwards to 2 percent." This target applied to inflation over all of 1995, not to year-over-year inflation at the start of 1995 (Svensson 1995).
United Kingdom	Q1 1993	Q1 1993	In October 1992, the Bank of England announced a 2.5 percent target, beginning immediately.
Non-IT countries	Q3 1993	Q1 1994	The starting dates were computed as averages of the starting dates for inflation targeting or constant inflation targeting countries.

Note: Spain is an inflation targeter but not a constant inflation targeter. Q1 1994 is the start date of the constant-targeting period for nonconstant targeters.

and New Zealand. For each country, we define the beginning of targeting as the first full quarter in which a specific inflation target or target range was in effect, and the target had been announced publicly at some earlier time. This definition of targeting is more stringent than that of previous authors, such as Bernanke et al. (1999) and Scheater, Stone, and Zelmer

(2000). These authors often date the start of targeting at the point when targets were first announced, even if they were implemented with a delay. In other cases, targeting is said to begin when the central bank retrospectively said it did, even though it was not announced at the time. Our view is that many of the intended effects of targeting, such as those working through expectations, depend on agents knowing that they are currently in a targeting regime.

As an example of our dating, consider Sweden. Sweden announced its shift to inflation targeting during 1993, so Bernanke et al. (1999) and Scheater, Stone, and Zelmer (2000) date the regime from then. However, the first announced target was 2 percent for inflation over the twelve months to December 1995. We choose the first quarter of this period, 1995:1, as the beginning of the targeting regime. Table 6.1 gives the starting dates of targeting for the other countries along with brief explanations for our choices. The starting dates range from 1990:3 for New Zealand to 1995: 2 for Spain.

The targeting period lasts through 2001 for all countries except Finland and Spain, where it lasts through 1998 because of the advent of the Euro. For each country, we compare the targeting period to two pretargeting periods, a longer one that begins in 1960 and a shorter one that begins in 1985. The last quarter of the pretargeting period is the last full quarter before targeting began (either the quarter before the start of the targeting period or two quarters before, depending on whether targeting began at the start of a quarter or in the middle).

Throughout, we compare the seven inflation targeters to the other thirteen countries in the sample. Two of these countries have adopted inflation targeting recently: Switzerland in 1999 and Norway in 2000. We exclude these countries' brief targeting periods from our sample and treat Switzerland and Norway as nontargeters. Following our approach for targeters, we compare pretargeting periods starting in 1960 and 1985 to posttargeting periods. For the nontargeters, we define the posttargeting period as starting at the mean of the start dates for targeters, which is 1993:3. The posttargeting period ends in 1998 for Euro countries and 2001 for non-Euro countries besides Norway and Switzerland. Table 6.2 gives details of our dating.

Of the thirteen nontargeting countries, eight joined the Euro in 1999. Previously, these countries were part of the European Monetary System (EMS), so their monetary policies focused on fixing exchange rates and meeting convergence criteria. Two of the nontargeters, Germany and Switzerland (one also in the EMS), followed policies based on money-supply targets. The remaining four countries did not follow any announced rule—they pursued the policy of "just do it" (Mishkin 1999). In the results we report, we lump all nontargeting countries together and compare them to targeters. We have checked, however, whether there are systematic

Table 6.2   Sample periods

Country	Sample 1	Sample 2	Sample 3	Sample 4	Sample 5	Sample 6
Australia	1960:1	1985:1	1994:4	1960:1	1985:1	1994:4
	1994:2	1994:2	2001:4	1994:2	1994:2	2001:4
Canada	1960:1	1985:1	1992:1	1960:1	1985:1	1994:1
	1991:4	1991:4	2001:4	1993:3	1993:3	2001:4
Finland	1960:1	1985:1	1994:1	1960:1	1985:1	1994:1
	1993:4	1993:4	1998:4	1993:4	1993:4	1998:4
New Zealand	1960:1	1985:1	1990:3	1960:1	1985:1	1993:1
	1990:1	1990:1	2001:4	1992:4	1992:4	2001:4
Spain	1960:1	1985:1	1995:2	1960:1	1985:1	1994:1
	1995:1	1995:1	1998:4	1993:3	1993:3	1998:4
Sweden	1960:1	1985:1	1995:1	1960:1	1985:1	1995:1
	1994:4	1994:4	2001:4	1994:4	1994:4	2001:4
United Kingdom	1960:1	1985:1	1993:1	1960:1	1985:1	1993:1
	1992:3	1992:3	2001:4	1992:3	1992:3	2001:4
United States, Japan,	1960:1	1985:1	1993:3	1960:1	1985:1	1994:1
Denmark	1993:2	1993:2	2001:4	1993:3	1993:3	2001:4
Austria, Belgium, France,	1960:1	1985:1	1993:3	1960:1	1985:1	1994:1
Germany, Ireland, Italy,	1993:2	1993:2	1998:4	1993:3	1993:3	1998:4
Netherlands, Portugal						
Norway	1960:1	1985:1	1993:3	1960:1	1985:1	1994:1
	1993:2	1993:2	2000:4	1993:3	1993:3	2000:4
Switzerland	1960:1	1985:1	1993:3	1960:1	1985:1	1994:1
	1993:2	1993:2	1999:4	1993:3	1993:3	1999:4

Notes: First number in column indicates start of sample. Second number in column indicates end of sample.

differences in performance among the nontargeting groups, and fail to find any. We have also performed our comparisons of targeters and nontargeters excluding all Euro countries (which leaves five targeters and five nontargeters). This produces no noteworthy changes in results.[1]

6.2.2   Constant Targeting

In addition to studying inflation-targeting periods, we examine periods in which countries are *constant* inflation targeters, meaning they have an unchanging target or target range. In some countries the target is always constant, but in others the constant-targeting period is preceded by a transitional period in which the target exceeds its final level. We examine constant-targeting periods because some benefits of targeting might not arise if the target changes. For example, proponents of targeting argue that it re-

1. In addition, we tried adding a Euro dummy to all of our cross-country regressions. This variable is usually insignificant. The only exception is that Euro countries experienced larger falls in the standard deviation of output growth between the pre- and posttargeting periods. Including the Euro dummy never changes our findings about the effects of inflation targeting.

duces the persistence of inflation movements, but a changing target causes permanent changes in inflation.[2]

Throughout this paper, we compare inflation targeters (IT) to non-targeters (NIT), and constant-inflation targeters (CIT) to non-constant-inflation targeters (NCIT). Spain is an inflation targeter, but its target fell throughout its targeting period; when we split countries into CIT and NCIT, we put Spain in the second group. For both CIT and NCIT countries, we examine periods before and after the start of constant targeting. The start date of the posttargeting period for NCIT countries is the average start date for constant targeting in CIT countries.

Table 6.2 lists sample periods for each of the twenty countries. We call the two pre-inflation-targeting periods, those starting in 1960 and 1985, samples 1 and 2, respectively. Sample 3 is the posttargeting period. Samples 4 and 5 are pre-constant-targeting periods, and sample 6 is the post-constant-targeting period. While the distinction between IT and CIT is important in principle, our findings about economic performance in the pre- and posttargeting periods are similar in the two cases.

6.3   Methodology

We want to determine how inflation targeting (or constant targeting) affects dimensions of economic performance such as inflation, output growth, and interest rates. We examine each aspect of performance in turn, using a consistent methodology to measure the effects of targeting. Here we describe the methodology.

Suppose we are interested in how targeting affects a variable X—for example, X might be the average level of inflation or the variance of output growth. We first calculate X for each of our twenty countries in each of our six sample periods. Then, for each period, we calculate the average value of X for inflation targeters and nontargeters (or, for samples 4 through 6, constant targeters and nonconstant targeters). These averages show whether X differs systematically across periods or across targeters and nontargeters.

As we have mentioned, many measures of economic performance improved on average between the pre-inflation-targeting and posttargeting periods. In most major economies, the period since the early 1990s has seen low and stable inflation and stable output growth. If we examine inflation-targeting countries alone, there are clear economic improvements that one might be tempted to attribute to targeting. However, to learn the

---

2. For New Zealand, we date the constant-targeting period from 1993:1 to the end of the sample even though the target range was widened from 0–2 percent to 0–3 percent in 1997. The half-point change in the midpoint was smaller (and of the opposite sign) than the target changes during transitional periods in other countries. In our judgment the 1997 episode was not a substantial change in policy.

true effects of targeting, we must compare improvements in targeting countries to improvements in nontargeting countries.

As a first pass at this comparison, we use a standard "differences in differences" approach. For our sample of twenty countries, we run the regression

$$(1) \qquad\qquad X_{post} - X_{pre} = a_0 + a_1 D + e,$$

where X_{post} is a country's value of X in the posttargeting period, X_{pre} is the value in the pretargeting period, and D is a dummy variable equal to 1 if the country is a targeter. We run several versions of this regression corresponding to different start dates for the pretargeting period (1960 or 1985) and whether targeting means IT or CIT. The coefficient a_1 is meant to measure the effect of targeting on the variable X.

This regression can be misleading, however. For some versions of the variable X, the initial value, X_{pre}, is substantially different on average for inflation targeters and nontargeters. For example, average inflation in the pretargeting period is higher for targeters. This fact is not surprising: a switch to targeting was most attractive to countries with poor performances under their previous policies. However, a problem arises because of regression to the mean. Poor performers in the pretargeting period tend to improve more than good performers simply because initial performance depends partly on transitory factors. If inflation targeters are poor initial performers, they will improve more than nontargeters, even if targeting does not affect performance. The coefficient on the targeting dummy can be significant, producing a spurious conclusion that targeting matters.

As an analogy, consider the behavior of Major League batting averages. Suppose a crackpot sports consultant suggests that a hitter will perform better if he sleeps next to his bat at night. In reality, this idea does not work. Most .300 hitters merely chuckle at the consultant, but .220 hitters are desperate enough to try anything, and start taking their bats to bed. Because of regression to the mean, the low-average hitters who sleep with their bats will tend to improve more than the high-average hitters who leave their bats in their lockers. If the sports consultant regresses the change in a player's average on a bat-in-bed dummy, he will find a significant effect. He will claim incorrectly that the evidence supports his theory.[3]

For readers who prefer math to baseball, the appendix to this paper formalizes our argument. We assume that the variable X depends on a country effect, a period effect, a country-period effect, and possibly an inflation-targeting dummy. The presence of the country-period effect generates regression to the mean. If X_{pre} is correlated with the targeting dummy, as happens in practice, then regression (1) produces a biased estimate of the dummy coefficient.

---

3. Baseball statistics exhibit substantial regression to the mean. This fact explains the well-known "sophomore slump": the tendency of players with strong rookie years to do less well during their second years (e.g., Gilovich 1984).

Fortunately, there is a simple way to eliminate this bias: add the initial value of X to the differences regression. That is, we run

$$(2) \qquad X_{post} - X_{pre} = a_0 + a_1 D + a_2 X_{pre} + e.$$

Including X_{pre} controls for regression to the mean. The coefficient on the dummy now shows whether targeting affects a country's change in performance for a given initial performance. If a_1 is significant, then a targeter with poor initial performance improves more than a nontargeter with equally poor initial performance. This difference implies a true effect of targeting.

Once again, the appendix formalizes our argument. Under the assumptions we make there, regression (2) produces an unbiased estimate of the dummy coefficient.

6.4   Inflation

In a recent speech, the next governor of the Bank of England posed the question "Ten Years of the Inflation Target: What Has It Achieved?" As quoted at the start of this paper, he suggests that targeting has reduced the average level, variability, and persistence of U.K. inflation. In contrast, we find little evidence in cross-country data that targeting has any of these effects.

6.4.1   Average Inflation

Table 6.3 presents our results concerning the average level of inflation. Inflation is measured by the annualized percentage change in consumer prices from the IMF's *International Financial Statistics* (IFS). In panel A of the table, we show average inflation in each of our twenty countries and six sample periods. For each period, we also show the averages across targeting and nontargeting countries. Panel B reports our estimates of equations (1) and (2) above.

Not surprisingly, there is considerable cross-country variation in average inflation. In sample 2, for example (1985 to start of inflation targeting), average inflation ranges from double digits in New Zealand and Portugal to less than 2 percent in Japan and the Netherlands. In almost every country, average inflation is lower in the targeting periods (samples 3 and 6) than in the pretargeting periods. The cross-country variation is smaller in the targeting periods, as all inflation rates are under 4 percent.

Turning to cross-country averages, we see that the IT group had higher inflation than the NIT group before targeting was introduced. (Here and elsewhere, the comparison between the CIT and NCIT groups is similar.) For the shorter pretargeting sample, average inflation is 5.8 percent for IT countries and 3.7 percent for NIT. In the targeting period, by contrast, average inflation is close to 1.9 percent for both groups. On average, targeters converged to the lower inflation levels of nontargeters.

Table 6.3   **Mean inflation rate (annualized)**

	Sample 1	Sample 2	Sample 3	Sample 4	Sample 5	Sample 6
			Panel A			
Australia	6.23	5.38	2.62	6.23	5.38	2.62
Canada	5.35	4.37	1.62	5.16	3.83	1.58
New Zealand	8.62	10.23	1.94	8.08	7.48	2.00
Sweden	6.41	5.38	1.01	6.41	5.38	1.01
United Kingdom	7.54	5.50	2.43	7.54	5.50	2.43
Finland	6.90	4.07	1.08	6.90	4.07	1.08
Spain	9.16	5.93	2.49	9.35	6.12	3.06
United States	4.82	3.72	2.47	4.80	3.66	2.47
Japan	5.16	1.63	0.12	5.15	1.68	0.09
Denmark	6.50	3.23	2.21	6.47	3.19	2.23
Austria	4.30	2.72	1.77	4.29	2.72	1.64
Belgium	4.64	2.53	1.65	4.63	2.53	1.55
France	6.11	3.05	1.37	6.08	3.01	1.33
Germany	3.40	2.24	1.65	3.40	2.25	1.59
Ireland	7.85	3.13	2.11	7.82	3.13	2.05
Italy	8.43	5.72	3.29	8.40	5.69	3.18
The Netherlands	4.41	1.58	2.19	4.40	1.64	2.12
Portugal	11.99	10.64	3.54	11.96	10.54	2.94
Norway	6.26	4.93	2.20	6.22	4.81	2.28
Switzerland	3.89	3.26	0.84	3.87	3.22	0.79
Averages						
IT	7.17	5.84	1.88			
NIT	5.98	3.72	1.95			
CIT				6.72	5.27	1.78
NCIT				6.20	3.87	1.95

Dependent variable: Change in mean inflation between samples	Equation 1				Equation 2			
	(3)−(1)	(3)−(2)	(6)−(4)	(6)−(5)	(3)−(1)	(3)−(2)	(6)−(4)	(6)−(5)
			Panel B					
Constant	−4.03	−1.77	−4.25	−1.92	0.42	1.12	0.52	1.01
	(0.46)	(0.52)	(0.47)	(0.46)	(0.49)	(0.32)	(0.50)	(0.33)
Inflation targeting dummy	−1.26	−2.19	−0.68	−1.57	−0.38	−0.55	−0.29	−0.51
	(0.78)	(0.88)	(0.86)	(0.84)	(0.33)	(0.35)	(0.33)	(0.34)
Initial value					−0.74	−0.78	−0.77	−0.76
					(0.08)	(0.07)	(0.07)	(0.07)
Adjusted R^2	0.08	0.21	−0.02	0.12	0.85	0.90	0.85	0.87

Note: Standard errors are in parentheses.

This convergence result is echoed in the first part of panel B, where we regress the change in average inflation on the targeting dummy. For the shorter pretargeting sample, the coefficient on the dummy is −2.2: average inflation fell by 2.2 points more in targeters than in nontargeters. This coefficient is the same as the difference-in-differences of means between samples 2 and 3. The regression reveals that this inflation-targeting effect is statistically significant ($t = 2.5$).

Inflation targeting is important if it really reduces average inflation by more than 2 percentage points. However, most of this apparent effect is illusory: it reflects the facts that targeters had high initial inflation and that there is regression to the mean. Panel B shows that regression to the mean is strong: when initial inflation is included in the inflation-change equation, its coefficient is -0.78. Controlling for this effect, the estimated effect of targeting is only -0.55, and its statistical significance is weak ($t = 1.57$, p-value $= 0.14$). Looking ahead, however, we will see that this result is one of our more positive findings about inflation targeting!

Note how much of the variation in inflation changes is explained by initial inflation: including this variable raises the R-squares from 0.2 or below to 0.9. Figure 6.1 illustrates this point by plotting the change in inflation from sample 2 to sample 3 against the level in sample 2. Figure 6.1 shows a tight relationship, confirming the strong role of regression to the mean. The targeting countries tend to have high initial inflation and large decreases, but the decrease for a given initial level looks similar for targeters and nontargeters.

6.4.2   Inflation Variability

Tables 6.4 and 6.5 examine the variability of inflation, using the same format as the average-inflation table. Table 6.4 presents standard deviations of quarterly inflation, and table 6.5 presents standard deviations of "trend inflation," defined as a nine-quarter moving average. We examine

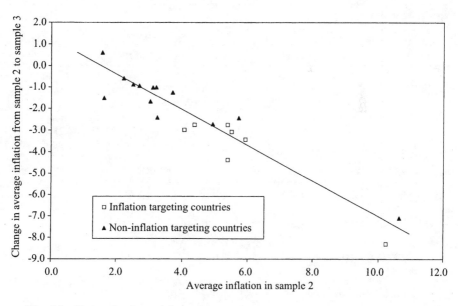

Fig. 6.1   Regression toward the mean

Table 6.4   **Standard deviation of inflation rate**

	Sample 1	Sample 2	Sample 3	Sample 4	Sample 5	Sample 6
			Panel A			
Australia	4.62	3.51	3.01	4.62	3.51	3.01
Canada	3.34	1.75	1.59	3.35	1.93	1.75
New Zealand	5.83	7.42	1.70	5.88	7.21	1.78
Sweden	3.99	3.62	1.57	3.99	3.62	1.57
United Kingdom	5.70	2.80	1.34	5.70	2.80	1.34
Finland	4.51	1.87	1.16	4.51	1.87	1.16
Spain	5.80	2.00	1.38	5.85	2.07	1.64
United States	3.27	1.64	0.94	3.26	1.65	0.96
Japan	5.00	1.76	1.73	4.98	1.76	1.65
Denmark	4.77	2.14	0.68	4.77	2.12	0.70
Austria	2.70	1.36	1.18	2.69	1.34	1.15
Belgium	3.31	1.54	1.20	3.31	1.51	1.23
France	3.77	1.15	0.81	3.78	1.15	0.84
Germany	2.32	2.85	1.02	2.31	2.81	1.05
Ireland	6.52	1.54	1.04	6.50	1.52	1.06
Italy	6.08	1.55	1.60	6.06	1.54	1.64
The Netherlands	3.40	1.71	0.75	3.39	1.72	0.71
Portugal	9.21	3.86	2.50	9.18	3.84	1.52
Norway	3.84	2.52	1.24	3.85	2.57	1.24
Switzerland	2.73	2.61	0.89	2.72	2.57	0.89
Averages						
IT	4.83	3.28	1.68			
NIT	4.38	2.02	1.20			
CIT				4.67	3.49	1.77
NCIT				4.48	2.01	1.16

Dependent variable: Change in standard deviation of inflation between samples	Equation 1				Equation 2			
	(3) – (1)	(3) – (2)	(6) – (4)	(6) – (5)	(3) – (1)	(3) – (2)	(6) – (4)	(6) – (5)
			Panel B					
Constant	−3.18	−0.82	−3.31	−0.85	0.50	0.92	0.79	1.01
	(0.41)	(0.34)	(0.43)	(0.32)	(0.32)	(0.24)	(0.30)	(0.22)
Inflation targeting dummy	0.03	−0.78	0.41	−0.87	0.41	0.31	0.59	0.50
	(0.70)	(0.58)	(0.78)	(0.59)	(0.23)	(0.27)	(0.21)	(0.26)
Initial value					−0.84	−0.86	−0.92	−0.93
					(0.07)	(0.10)	(0.06)	(0.09)
Adjusted R^2	−0.06	0.04	−0.04	0.06	0.89	0.83	0.92	0.92

Note: Standard errors are in parentheses.

trend inflation because targeters might stabilize this variable even if they cannot smooth out higher-frequency inflation shocks.[4]

There is no evidence whatsoever that inflation targeting reduces inflation

---

4. In analyzing trend inflation, we include a quarter in a sample only if all quarters that contribute to the nine-quarter average are in the sample.

Table 6.5   Standard deviation of trend inflation rate (9-quarter moving average)

	Sample 1	Sample 2	Sample 3	Sample 4	Sample 5	Sample 6
			Panel A			
Australia	3.80	2.76	1.37	3.80	2.76	1.37
Canada	2.89	0.44	0.53	2.88	0.92	0.53
New Zealand	4.43	3.55	0.83	4.48	4.20	0.92
Sweden	2.63	2.04	0.57	2.63	2.04	0.57
United Kingdom	4.59	1.69	0.34	4.59	1.69	0.34
Finland	3.54	1.26	0.28	3.54	1.26	0.28
Spain	4.66	0.79	0.42	4.65	0.67	0.92
United States	2.81	0.81	0.44	2.81	0.82	0.45
Japan	3.71	1.06	0.68	3.70	1.04	0.70
Denmark	2.85	0.95	0.27	2.87	0.99	0.27
Austria	1.78	0.82	0.49	1.78	0.83	0.41
Belgium	2.72	0.78	0.21	2.71	0.77	0.21
France	3.35	0.32	0.37	3.36	0.35	0.39
Germany	1.67	1.33	0.25	1.67	1.42	0.18
Ireland	5.20	0.41	0.31	5.20	0.43	0.25
Italy	5.35	0.54	1.10	5.34	0.56	1.06
The Netherlands	2.55	1.30	0.14	2.54	1.31	0.13
Portugal	7.21	1.37	0.72	7.19	1.47	0.50
Norway	2.51	1.92	0.33	2.53	1.96	0.33
Switzerland	1.92	1.68	0.41	1.91	1.65	0.39
Averages						
IT	3.79	1.79	0.62			
NIT	3.36	1.02	0.44			
CIT				3.65	2.14	0.67
NCIT				3.45	1.02	0.44

Dependent variable: Change in standard deviation of trend inflation between samples	Equation 1				Equation 2			
	(3)–(1)	(3)–(2)	(6)–(4)	(6)–(5)	(3)–(1)	(3)–(2)	(6)–(4)	(6)–(5)
			Panel B					
Constant	−2.92	−0.58	−3.00	−0.58	0.16	0.30	0.14	0.33
	(0.37)	(0.20)	(0.36)	(0.20)	(0.18)	(0.13)	(0.19)	(0.13)
Inflation targeting dummy	−0.25	−0.58	0.02	−0.90	0.15	0.08	0.21	0.10
	(0.62)	(0.33)	(0.65)	(0.36)	(0.14)	(0.16)	(0.15)	(0.19)
Initial value					−0.92	−0.87	−0.91	−0.89
					(0.05)	(0.09)	(0.05)	(0.10)
Adjusted R^2	−0.05	0.10	−0.06	0.22	0.95	0.84	0.95	0.85

Note: Standard errors are in parentheses.

variability. The standard deviations of inflation and trend inflation fall for all groups of countries during the targeting period. At all times, the standard deviations are lower for nontargeters than for targeters. Equation (1) suggests that targeters experience larger falls in standard deviations, but this result disappears when equation (2) controls for regression to the mean.

In fact, table 6.4 suggests that, controlling for regression to the mean, inflation targeting *raises* the standard deviation of inflation. This effect is sometimes statistically significant. Nonetheless, this perverse result is likely a fluke (given the number of regressions we run, our tests should produce some Type 1 errors). Our robust finding is that inflation targeting has no beneficial effects.

6.4.3   Inflation Persistence

Finally, we examine the persistence of inflation movements. For each country and sample period, we estimate a fourth-order autoregressive model (AR[4]) for quarterly inflation. Then, for each period, we average each AR coefficient across targeting and nontargeting countries. Using these average coefficients, we compute impulse response functions showing the effects of inflation shocks on future inflation.

Figure 6.2 presents some of our results. We use solid lines for the impulse response functions in targeting countries and dashed lines for nontargeters. For each group, we present results for the long pretargeting periods (samples 1 and 4) and the targeting periods (samples 3 and 6). We omit responses for the short pretargeting samples, which always lie between the responses that we show.

Figure 6.2 shows that inflation persistence has decreased over time—inflation has become more "anchored." In the pretargeting periods, a unit inflation shock in quarter t raises inflation at $t + 1$ by more than 0.4 points, and this effect dies out slowly. For the targeting period, the effect is around 0.2 at $t + 1$, and it disappears in a few quarters. Crucially, this pattern holds for both targeting and nontargeting countries. Once again, there is no evidence that targeting affects inflation behavior.[5]

6.5   Output Growth

We now ask whether inflation targeting affects output behavior. We examine the mean and standard deviation of real output growth, using the same methods we applied to inflation behavior. We use annual output data, as reliable quarterly data are not available for all countries in our sample. For each country, we include a year in a given sample period only if all four quarters of the year belong to the sample under our quarterly dating.

---

5. Note that the impulse responses for targeters in samples 3 and 6 are negative at some lags. We have checked the statistical significance of the negative responses with Monte Carlo experiments, following Sheridan (2001). The only response that is significantly negative is the response for CIT countries in period $t + 4$. We are inclined to dismiss the negative responses as a fluke, because they are not plausible theoretically.

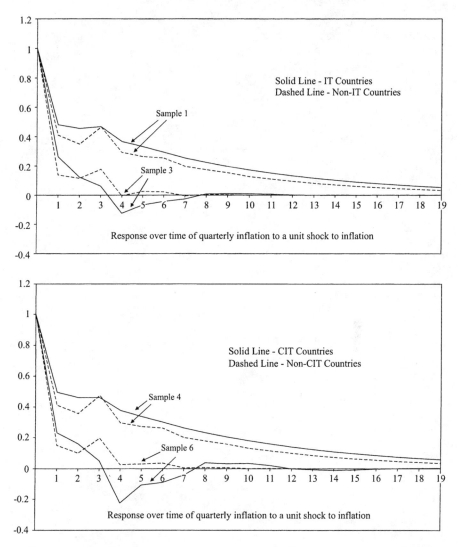

Fig. 6.2   Inflation persistence

6.5.1   Average Growth

There is no obvious theoretical reason that inflation targeting should affect average output growth. (It might if it affected inflation behavior and inflation affects growth, but see our negative findings about inflation.) Nonetheless, Mishkin (1999, 597) suggests that a

conservative conclusion is that, once low inflation is achieved, inflation targeting is not harmful to the real economy. Given the strong economic growth after disinflation was achieved in many countries that have adopted inflation targets, New Zealand being one outstanding example, a case can be made that inflation targeting promotes real economic growth in addition to controlling inflation.

Here we examine this idea, with inconclusive results.

Table 6.6 presents our results about average growth rates. Average

Table 6.6   Mean annual growth rates

	Sample 1	Sample 2	Sample 3	Sample 4	Sample 5	Sample 6
			Panel A			
Australia	3.65	3.09	4.59	3.65	3.09	4.59
Canada	4.04	2.52	3.06	3.94	2.30	3.44
New Zealand	3.05	2.72	2.79	2.76	1.68	3.42
Sweden	2.51	1.18	2.82	2.51	1.18	2.82
United Kingdom	2.40	2.69	2.94	2.40	2.69	2.94
Finland	3.15	1.00	4.68	3.15	1.00	4.68
Spain	4.22	2.91	3.25	4.45	3.51	2.94
United States	3.40	2.84	3.39	3.40	2.84	3.39
Japan	5.67	4.12	1.17	5.67	4.12	1.17
Denmark	2.10	1.46	2.81	2.10	1.46	2.81
Austria	3.38	2.87	2.13	3.38	2.87	2.13
Belgium	3.32	2.56	2.54	3.32	2.56	2.54
France	3.64	2.55	2.02	3.64	2.55	2.02
Germany	3.44	4.31	1.62	3.44	4.31	1.62
Ireland	4.17	4.36	8.50	4.17	4.36	8.50
Italy	3.91	2.43	2.01	3.91	2.43	2.01
The Netherlands	3.99	2.90	3.19	3.99	2.90	3.19
Portugal	4.10	4.41	3.08	4.10	4.41	3.08
Norway	3.48	2.50	3.50	3.48	2.50	3.50
Switzerland	2.55	2.01	1.18	2.55	2.01	1.18
Averages						
IT	3.29	2.30	3.45			
NIT	3.63	3.02	2.86			
CIT				3.07	1.99	3.65
NCIT				3.69	3.06	2.86

Dependent variable: Change in mean annual growth rate between samples	Equation 1				Equation 2			
	(3)−(1)	(3)−(2)	(6)−(4)	(6)−(5)	(3)−(1)	(3)−(2)	(6)−(4)	(6)−(5)
			Panel B					
Constant	−0.77	−0.17	−0.82	−0.19	2.04	1.64	1.78	1.40
	(0.47)	(0.46)	(0.44)	(0.43)	(1.79)	(1.31)	(1.83)	(1.31)
Inflation targeting dummy	0.93	1.31	1.40	1.85	0.67	0.88	0.97	1.30
	(0.80)	(0.77)	(0.81)	(0.78)	(0.78)	(0.81)	(0.84)	(0.88)
Initial value					−0.77	−0.60	−0.71	−0.52
					(0.48)	(0.41)	(0.48)	(0.41)
Adjusted R^2	0.02	0.09	0.10	0.20	0.10	0.15	0.15	0.23

Note: Standard errors are in parentheses.

growth increased in inflation-targeting countries after targeting began, and it decreased slightly in nontargeting countries. When we control for regression to the mean, our point estimates imply that targeting raises average growth by a substantial amount: from 0.7 to 1.3 percentage points, depending on the specification. However, all the *t*-statistics are below 1.5, and three of four are below 1.2. Thus the point estimates do not mean much.

Our estimates are imprecise because growth rates vary greatly across individual countries. In our short samples, average growth depends on economies' cyclical positions when the samples start and end as well as growth in potential output. We need to observe inflation targeting over longer periods to see whether it affects average growth.

6.5.2   Output Variability

Some economists argue that "flexible" inflation targeting stabilizes output as well as inflation. Others, such as Cecchetti and Ehrmann (1999), suggest that targeting makes output more variable. Once again, we find that targeting simply does not matter.

Table 6.7 presents results about the standard deviation of annual output growth. These results mostly echo our findings about the standard deviation of inflation. In the short pretargeting periods and the targeting periods, output is more stable for nontargeting countries than for targeters. For both groups, output becomes more stable during the targeting period. When we control for regression to the mean, our estimates suggest that targeting raises output variability, but this effect is not statistically significant.

6.6   Interest Rates

We next examine the level of long-term interest rates, which should reflect inflation expectations, and the variability of short-term rates, which might indicate the activism of monetary policy.

6.6.1   Average Long-Term Rates

We have seen that inflation targeters and nontargeters have experienced similar reductions in inflation since the early 1990s. Targeting proponents argue, however, that targeting locks in low inflation permanently, while adverse events might reignite inflation under "just do it" policies. If the public believes this argument, then targeting should reduce both expected inflation and inflation uncertainty. As discussed by King (2002), both effects should reduce long-term interest rates.

We look for this effect in OECD data on ten-year government bond rates. The data are annual, so we date our sample periods by years, as in our work on output behavior. The data start in 1970, so we begin samples 1 and 4 in that year rather than 1960.

Table 6.8 presents our results, which are highly reminiscent of our infla-

Table 6.7   **Standard deviation of annual growth rate**

	Sample 1	Sample 2	Sample 3	Sample 4	Sample 5	Sample 6
			Panel A			
Australia	2.24	1.91	1.73	2.24	1.91	1.73
Canada	2.50	2.60	1.46	2.53	2.48	1.32
New Zealand	2.82	3.50	2.28	2.85	3.06	1.93
Sweden	2.27	2.10	1.36	2.27	2.10	1.36
United Kingdom	2.17	2.33	0.77	2.17	2.33	0.77
Finland	3.23	3.95	1.09	3.23	3.95	1.09
Spain	3.13	2.08	0.73	3.05	1.66	0.68
United States	2.38	1.51	1.38	2.38	1.51	1.38
Japan	4.00	1.74	1.28	4.00	1.74	1.28
Denmark	2.31	1.50	1.26	2.31	1.50	1.26
Austria	2.23	1.17	0.74	2.23	1.17	0.74
Belgium	2.11	1.13	0.93	2.11	1.13	0.93
France	1.98	1.28	0.88	1.98	1.28	0.88
Germany	2.79	3.84	0.58	2.79	3.84	0.58
Ireland	2.08	1.86	1.92	2.08	1.86	1.92
Italy	2.91	1.01	0.66	2.91	1.01	0.66
The Netherlands	5.53	1.09	0.54	5.53	1.09	0.54
Portugal	3.59	1.98	0.47	3.59	1.98	0.47
Norway	1.85	1.66	1.70	1.85	1.66	1.70
Switzerland	2.77	1.92	0.84	2.77	1.92	0.84
Averages						
IT	2.54	2.73	1.45			
NIT	2.81	1.67	1.01			
CIT				2.55	2.64	1.37
NCIT				2.83	1.67	0.99

Dependent variable: Change in standard deviation of growth rate between samples	Equation 1				Equation 2			
	(3)−(1)	(3)−(2)	(6)−(4)	(6)−(5)	(3)−(1)	(3)−(2)	(6)−(4)	(6)−(5)
			Panel B					
Constant	−1.80	−0.65	−1.84	−0.68	1.59	0.95	1.53	1.08
	(0.32)	(0.24)	(0.30)	(0.23)	(0.38)	(0.30)	(0.34)	(0.28)
Inflation targeting dummy	0.52	−0.64	0.66	−0.60	0.29	0.30	0.32	0.43
	(0.54)	(0.41)	(0.55)	(0.43)	(0.22)	(0.28)	(0.21)	(0.26)
Initial value					−1.20	−0.96	−1.19	−1.06
					(0.13)	(0.16)	(0.11)	(0.15)
Adjusted R^2	0.00	0.07	0.02	0.05	0.83	0.69	0.86	0.75

Note: Standard errors are in parentheses.

tion and output results. If we define better performance by lower interest rates, then nontargeters always do better than targeters. Both groups improved during the targeting period; the improvement is somewhat larger for targeters, but the effect of targeting disappears when we control for regression to the mean.

Table 6.8   **Long-term interest rates**

	Sample 1	Sample 2	Sample 3	Sample 4	Sample 5	Sample 6
			Panel A			
Australia	10.78	11.83	6.82	10.78	11.83	6.82
Canada	8.72	10.19	7.04	8.72	10.02	6.72
New Zealand	10.70	15.15	7.44	10.65	13.34	7.04
Sweden	9.22	10.99	6.48	9.22	10.99	6.48
United Kingdom	9.86	10.35	6.62	9.86	10.35	6.62
Finland	9.46	10.65	7.13	9.46	10.65	7.13
Spain	11.78	12.24	6.66	11.90	12.77	8.25
United States	7.61	8.43	6.05	7.61	8.43	6.05
Japan	7.01	5.65	2.45	7.01	5.65	2.45
Denmark	12.06	10.17	6.28	12.06	10.17	6.28
Austria	8.12	7.66	6.18	8.12	7.66	6.18
Belgium	8.51	9.05	6.33	8.51	9.05	6.33
France	9.44	9.68	6.26	9.44	9.68	6.26
Germany	7.60	7.32	6.03	7.60	7.32	6.03
Ireland	10.34	10.34	6.90	10.34	10.34	6.90
Italy	10.42	12.45	8.77	10.42	12.45	8.77
The Netherlands	7.43	7.43	6.02	7.43	7.43	6.02
Portugal	15.69	21.23	8.35	15.69	21.23	8.35
Norway	8.56	11.65	6.38	8.56	11.65	6.38
Switzerland	4.67	5.16	3.82	4.67	5.16	3.82
Averages						
IT	10.07	11.63	6.88			
NIT	9.04	9.71	6.14			
CIT				9.78	11.19	6.80
NCIT				9.24	9.93	6.29

Dependent variable: Change in mean long-term interest rate between samples	Equation 1				Equation 2			
	(3)−(1)	(3)−(2)	(6)−(4)	(6)−(5)	(3)−(1)	(3)−(2)	(6)−(4)	(6)−(5)
			Panel B					
Constant	−2.89	−3.57	−2.95	−3.64	2.57	3.38	2.23	3.23
	(0.47)	(0.73)	(0.44)	(0.69)	(0.98)	(0.67)	(0.96)	(0.70)
Inflation targeting dummy	−0.30	−1.18	−0.03	−0.76	0.33	0.20	0.27	0.12
	(0.80)	(1.24)	(0.80)	(1.25)	(0.49)	(0.45)	(0.49)	(0.47)
Initial value					−0.60	−0.72	−0.56	−0.69
					(0.10)	(0.06)	(0.10)	(0.07)
Adjusted R^2	−0.05	−0.01	−0.06	−0.03	0.63	0.88	0.61	0.86

Note: Standard errors are in parentheses.

6.6.2   The Variability of Short-Term Interest Rates

In addition to examining economic outcomes, we would like to know whether inflation-targeting central banks move their policy instruments differently from nontargeters. In principle, one can address this issue by estimating reaction functions for short-term interest rates (i.e., Taylor rules).

In practice, it appears difficult to get meaningful estimates of these equations with the short samples at hand. We therefore examine a cruder measure of policy behavior, the standard deviation of short-term rates. Differences in policy rules should affect this statistic. For example, if inflation targeters respond more strongly to inflation movements, then short-term rates should become more volatile (unless targeting stabilizes inflation, an effect we fail to find).[6]

We examine the volatility of short-term rates at the quarterly frequency. Our data are interbank rates from the IFS (line 60b). We examine only the shorter of our pretargeting samples, the ones starting in 1985, because consistent data are not available before then. For once, we throw out a few troublesome outliers. For all countries, we delete the three quarters of the exchange rate mechanism (ERM) crisis, 1992:3 through 1993:1, when interest rates jumped to very high levels.

The results, given in table 6.9, follow the pattern we have seen again and again. Interest rate volatility is lower for nontargeters than for targeters and falls over time for both groups. The decrease appears larger for targeters if we ignore regression to the mean, but not if we control for it.

6.7   Bivariate Results

So far we have examined the univariate behavior of inflation, output, and interest rates. In principle, we would like to look more deeply at whether inflation targeting changes the structure of the economy. For our short samples, however, it is impractical to estimate sophisticated structural equations. Here we take one step beyond our univariate analysis by examining several bivariate relations.

6.7.1   Methodology

For each country and sample period, we run three regressions:

$$(3) \qquad\qquad \Delta\pi = a(y - y^*),$$

$$(4) \qquad\qquad \Delta\pi = K_0 + b(\Delta p^{\text{com}} - \pi^{\text{US}}),$$

$$(5) \qquad\qquad \pi^{\text{fore}} = K_1 + c\pi(-1),$$

where y^* is the trend level of output (measured by the Hodrick-Prescott filter with smoothing parameter 100); p^{com} is an index of commodity prices in U.S. dollars, from the IFS; π^{US} is U.S. inflation; and π^{fore} is an OECD forecast of inflation. All the data are annual.

---

6. Neumann and von Hagen (2002) and Kuttner and Posen (1999) estimate Taylor rules for inflation targeters. For a critique, see Mishkin's (2002) discussion of Neumann and von Hagen (2002).

Table 6.9   **Standard deviation of short-term interest rates**

	Sample 2	Sample 3	Sample 5	Sample 6
		Panel A		
Australia	4.15	1.07	4.15	1.07
Canada	1.87	1.21	2.35	1.20
New Zealand	5.24	2.35	5.85	1.79
Sweden	2.21	1.86	2.21	1.86
United Kingdom	2.10	0.85	2.10	0.85
Finland	2.26	1.10	2.26	1.10
Spain	2.59	1.97	1.99	1.82
United States	1.63	1.04	1.75	0.93
Japan	1.62	0.89	1.64	0.75
Denmark	1.01	1.70	1.03	1.14
Austria	1.94	1.11	1.91	0.78
Belgium	1.62	1.62	1.61	1.05
France	1.05	1.60	1.04	1.38
Germany	2.08	1.20	2.06	0.91
Ireland	2.00	0.77	2.08	0.76
Italy	1.51	1.93	1.59	2.00
The Netherlands	1.68	1.17	1.66	0.92
Portugal	2.77	2.54	2.79	2.38
Norway	1.73	1.27	1.97	1.30
Switzerland	2.55	1.27	2.51	1.10
Averages				
IT	2.92	1.49		
NIT	1.79	1.39		
CIT			3.15	1.31
NCIT			1.83	1.23

Dependent variable: Change in standard deviation of the short term interest rate	Equation 1		Equation 2	
	(3) – (2)	(6) – (5)	(3) – (2)	(6) – (5)
	Panel B			
Constant	–0.39	–0.60	1.04	0.96
	(0.23)	(0.24)	(0.28)	(0.26)
Inflation targeting dummy	–1.04	–1.24	–0.13	–0.11
	(0.39)	(0.44)	(0.28)	(0.28)
Initial value			–0.80	–0.85
			(0.14)	(0.12)
Adjusted R^2	0.28	0.31	0.76	0.82

Note: Standard errors are in parentheses.

Equation (3) can be interpreted as an accelerationist Phillips curve: it shows how the output gap affects the change in inflation. Equation (4) measures the inflationary effect of a change in the relative price of commodities, which we interpret as a "supply shock." The change in the relative price is the change in the U.S. dollar price minus U.S. inflation. Finally, equation (5) shows how expected inflation responds to movements in past inflation. We measure expectations with OECD forecasts, which are produced in consistent ways for all countries.[7]

Previous authors suggest that inflation targeting should affect the coefficients a, b, and c in these equations. For example, Bernanke et al. (1999) argue that targeting "anchors" inflation expectations, so c should fall. They also argue that targeting reduces the effects of supply chocks, so b should fall (see the quote at the start of this paper). The effects on a, the Phillips curve slope, are debatable. This coefficient might fall if inflation becomes more anchored. On the other hand, Corbo, Landerretche, and Schmidt-Hebbel (2002) argue that targeting reduces the cost of disinflation, which suggests a rise in a.

We are interested in the averages of a, b, and c for targeting and nontargeting countries. When we estimate these coefficients for individual countries, the standard errors vary greatly. Since there is more noise in some estimated coefficients than in others, a simple average is an inefficient estimator of the true average coefficient. We therefore compute weighted averages, with weights inversely proportional to the variances of the coefficient estimates. Similarly, we estimate our differences regression by weighted least squares, with weights inversely proportional to the standard deviations of the estimated changes in coefficients. We do not add estimates of initial coefficients to the right-hand sides of our regressions, because the measurement error in the coefficients would create bias.[8]

6.7.2 Results

Table 6.10 presents our bivariate results. For the final time, we find that economic behavior has changed over time, but the changes are similar for inflation targeters and nontargeters.

There are two significant changes over time: expectations respond less to inflation movements, and inflation responds less to commodity prices. Both results suggest a greater anchoring of inflation. Strikingly, the commodity-price coefficients fall by an order of magnitude. For example, the average coefficient in sample 1 (1960 to the start of IT) is 0.05 for nontargeters.

7. Some details: We exclude a constant term from equation (3) because $y - y^*$ has a zero mean and we want to rule out a deterministic trend in inflation. In equation (4), the change in relative commodity prices is the same for all countries. We have also estimated equation (4) with $y - y^*$ included, which can be interpreted as a Phillips curve augmented with supply shocks. Our results about the coefficient on the change in commodity prices do not change. In addition, we obtain similar results when we replace the change in commodity prices with the change in the relative price of oil. In equation (5), $\pi(-1)$ is inflation in year -1 as estimated by the OECD in December of that year, when they make forecasts for the following year.

8. In principle, the optimal estimators of the group means and equation (1) use weights that depend on both the variances of the coefficient estimates and the variances of true coefficients across countries in a group. Using the residuals from our cross-country regressions, we have estimated the variances of true coefficients, and we find they are small. We therefore set these variances to zero and derive the optimal weights based on the variances of coefficient estimates. These weights are the ones described in the text.

Table 6.10   **Multivariate results**

Panel A: Phillips-Curve coefficients

Weighted averages	Sample 1	Sample 2	Sample 3	Sample 4	Sample 5	Sample 6
IT	0.35	0.10	0.18			
NIT	0.27	0.25	0.17			
CIT				0.37	0.18	0.14
NCIT				0.27	0.25	0.18

Dependent variable: Change in estimated coefficient between samples	Equation 1 (weighted least squares)			
	(3) − (1)	(3) − (2)	(6) − (4)	(6) − (5)
Constant	−0.12	−0.07	−0.11	−0.05
	(0.07)	(0.09)	(0.07)	(0.07)
Inflation targeting dummy	0.13	0.20	0.00	0.07
	(0.12)	(0.12)	(0.13)	(0.11)

Panel B: Effect of commodity-price changes on inflation

Weighted averages	Sample 1	Sample 2	Sample 3	Sample 4	Sample 5	Sample 6
IT	0.044	0.036	0.005			
NIT	0.054	0.068	0.006			
CIT				0.049	0.082	0.014
NCIT				0.053	0.065	0.006

Dependent variable: Change in estimated coefficient between samples	Equation 1 (weighted least squares)			
	(3) − (1)	(3) − (2)	(6) − (4)	(6) − (5)
Constant	−0.048	−0.050	−0.047	−0.048
	(0.010)	(0.014)	(0.009)	(0.013)
Inflation targeting dummy	0.006	−0.012	0.012	−0.027
	(0.024)	(0.031)	(0.024)	(0.034)

Panel C: Response of expected inflation to inflation

Weighted averages	Sample 1	Sample 2	Sample 3	Sample 4	Sample 5	Sample 6
IT	0.83	0.71	0.43			
NIT	0.83	0.71	0.66			
CIT				0.82	0.63	0.45
NCIT				0.83	0.71	0.63

Dependent variable: Change in estimated coefficient between samples	Equation 1 (weighted least squares)			
	(3) − (1)	(3) − (2)	(6) − (4)	(6) − (5)
Constant	−0.23	−0.10	−0.25	−0.12
	(0.04)	(0.06)	(0.04)	(0.06)
Inflation targeting dummy	−0.15	−0.13	−0.10	−0.05
	(0.10)	(0.14)	(0.11)	(0.15)

Note: Standard errors are in parentheses.

This means that a 10 percent rise in the relative price of commodities raises inflation by 0.5 of a percentage point. For the IT period (sample 3), the coefficient is 0.006.

In contrast, there is no evidence that inflation targeting affects the coefficients that we consider. In the twelve regressions in table 6.10, the targeting dummy is never significant at the 10 percent level.

6.8   Comparison to Other Studies

The closest study to ours is that of Neumann and von Hagen (2002). Their paper and ours have the same title. Part of their paper, like this one, compares the volatility of inflation, output, and interest rates across time periods and groups of countries. But Neumann and von Hagen's conclusion differs from ours: "Taken together, the evidence confirms the claim that IT matters" (144).

Our study differs from Neumann and von Hagen (2002) in many details, but the crucial difference may be our treatment of regression to the mean. After the sentence quoted above, they continue: "Adopting this policy has permitted IT countries to reduce inflation to low levels and curb the volatility of inflation and interest rates; in so doing, these banks have been able to approach the stability achieved by the Bundesbank" (Neumann and von Hagen's main example of a non–inflation targeter). We, too, find that targeters have caught up with nontargeters along some dimensions, but this convergence was not caused by targeting.

A number of other studies report evidence that inflation targeting matters. For example, researchers report that targeting steepens the Phillips curve (Clifton, Hyginus, and Wong 2001); that it dampens movements in expected inflation (Sheridan 2001); and that it increases the predictability of inflation (Corbo, Landerretche, and Schmidt-Hebbel 2002).[9] Some of these results may again reflect regression to the mean rather than a true effect of targeting. This possibility is suggested by Corbo, Landerretche, and Schmidt-Hebbel's (2002, 263) conclusion that "Inflation targeters have consistently reduced inflation forecast errors (based on country VAR models) toward the low levels prevalent in non-targeting industrial countries."

It is difficult to compare our results directly to previous work, as the methodologies are quite different. We believe, however, that our results cast doubt on earlier findings that inflation targeting affects economic behavior. It seems unlikely that targeting would affect the relationships studied by previous authors and yet, as we find, have no effects on the means or standard deviations of inflation, output, or interest rates.

9. See also Johnson (2002) and the literature review in Neumann and von Hagen (2002).

6.9 Conclusion

We find no evidence that inflation targeting improves a country's economic performance. How should one interpret this result?

One possibility is that targeting and nontargeting countries pursue similar interest rate policies. Research suggests that the policies needed to implement inflation targeting are similar to the Taylor rules that fit the United States and other nontargeters (e.g., Svensson 1997; Ball 1999). Indeed, observers have suggested that the United States is a "covert inflation targeter" (Mankiw 2001). This view is supported by our finding of similar interest rate volatility for targeters and nontargeters. If targeting does not change the behavior of policy instruments, it is not shocking that economic outcomes do not change either. This result suggests, however, that the formal and institutional aspects of targeting—the public announcements of targets, the inflation reports, the enhanced independence of central banks—are not important. Nothing in the data suggests that covert targeters would benefit from adopting explicit targets.

Our results do not provide an argument *against* inflation targeting, for we have not found that it does any harm. In addition, there may be benefits that we do not measure. First, aspects of inflation targeting may be desirable for political rather than economic reasons. Bernanke et al. (1999, 333) argue that targeting produces more open policy making, making "the role of the central bank more consistent with the principles of a democratic society."

Second, inflation targeting might improve economic performance in the future. The economic environment has been fairly tranquil during the inflation-targeting era, and so many central banks have not been tested severely. Perhaps future policymakers will face 1970s-sized supply shocks, or strong political pressures for inflationary policies. At that point, we may see that inflation targeters handle these challenges better than policymakers who "just do it."

Thus, a paper that replicates this study in twenty-five or fifty years may find ample evidence that targeting improves performance. The evidence is not there, however, in the data through 2001.

Appendix

Consider the problem of estimating the effect of inflation targeting on X, some measure of economic performance. For concreteness, we will sometimes refer to X as "average inflation." We present a simple statistical model of the determinants of X in different countries and periods. In our model, regression (1) in the text, the differences estimator, produces a biased estimate of the effect of targeting if the targeting dummy is correlated with the pretargeting level of X. Adding the pretargeting X, as in regression (2), eliminates the bias.

Let X_{it} be the value of X in country i and period t. The t subscript takes on two values, "pre" and "post." We assume that X_{it} is given by

$$(A1) \qquad X_{it} = k + a_1 Q_{it} + \mu_i + \eta_t + v_{it},$$

where μ_i is a country-specific effect, η_t is a period-specific effect, v_{it} is an error term specific to country i in period t, and Q_{it} is a dummy equal to 1 if country i targets inflation in period t. For all countries, $Q_{i,\text{pre}}$ equals zero and $Q_{i,\text{post}}$ equals D_i, the targeting dummy in the text.

In equation (A1), the Q_{it} term captures the possible effect of inflation targeting. We would like to estimate its coefficient, a_1. The other terms are a conventional decomposition of the error term in a panel regression. By construction, the idiosyncratic shock v_{it} is uncorrelated with μ_i and η_t, and $v_{i,\text{pre}}$ and $v_{i,\text{post}}$ are uncorrelated with each other.

Differencing equation (A1) over time yields

$$(A2) \qquad X_{i,\text{post}} - X_{i,\text{pre}} = (\eta_{\text{post}} - \eta_{\text{pre}}) + a_1 D_i + (v_{i,\text{post}} - v_{i,\text{pre}}),$$

where we use the fact that $Q_{i,\text{post}} - Q_{i,\text{pre}} = D_i$. Thus, in cross-country data, the change in X depends on a constant $(\eta_{\text{post}} - \eta_{\text{pre}})$, the targeting dummy, and a composite error term. We can interpret regression (1), the differences estimator in the text, as an ordinary least squares (OLS) estimator of equation (A2).

Suppose that countries with higher initial inflation, $X_{i,\text{pre}}$, are more likely to adopt inflation targeting. The error $v_{i,\text{pre}}$ is one component of $X_{i,\text{pre}}$, so a higher $v_{i,\text{pre}}$ makes targeting more likely: $v_{i,\text{pre}}$ is positively correlated with the dummy D_i. The error in (A2) includes $-v_{i,\text{pre}}$, so the dummy is negatively correlated with the error. This correlation implies that the OLS estimate of the dummy coefficient, a_1, is biased downward. Consequently, regression (1) is likely to find that targeting reduces inflation even if there is no true effect.

Now consider what happens when we add the initial level of X to our regression. We can rewrite equation (A2) as

$$(A3) \quad X_{i,\text{post}} - X_{i,\text{pre}} = (\eta_{\text{post}} - \eta_{\text{pre}}) + a_1 D_i + a_2 X_{i,\text{pre}} + (v_{i,\text{post}} - v_{i,\text{pre}}),$$

where the true value of a_2 is zero. We interpret regression (2) in the text as an OLS estimator of this equation. We now sketch a proof that the estimate of a_1 is unbiased even if $X_{i,\text{pre}}$ affects the likelihood of targeting.

Rather than viewing $v_{i,\text{pre}}$ as part of the error term in (A3), let us interpret it as a variable that is left out when we regress the change in X_i on the constant, D_i, and $X_{i,\text{pre}}$. If $v_{i,\text{pre}}$ were measured and included in the regression, then OLS would be unbiased, because all right-side variables would be uncorrelated with the remaining error $v_{i,\text{post}}$. We can therefore use standard results to determine the biases that arise when $v_{i,\text{pre}}$ is left out (Maddala 1989, 122). Specifically, the bias in the OLS estimate of a_1 is proportional to the expected coefficient on D_i in an auxiliary regression of $v_{i,\text{pre}}$ on a constant, D_i and $X_{i,\text{pre}}$. One can show that this expected coefficient is zero, implying zero bias. Intuitively, $v_{i,\text{pre}}$ is correlated with D_i, but this correlation works through the effect of $v_{i,\text{pre}}$ on $X_{i,\text{pre}}$. When one controls for $X_{i,\text{pre}}$ in the auxiliary regression, there is no relation between $v_{i,\text{pre}}$ and D_i.

References

Ball, Laurence. 1997. Disinflation and the NAIRU. In *Reducing inflation: Motivation and strategy,* ed. Christina D. Romer and David H. Romer, 167–85. Chicago: University of Chicago Press.

———. 1999. Efficient rules for monetary policy. *International Finance* 2 (1): 63–83.

Bernanke, Ben S., Thomas Laubach, Frederic S. Mishkin, and Adam S. Posen. 1999. *Inflation targeting: Lessons from the international experience.* Princeton, N.J.: Princeton University Press.

Cecchetti, Stephen G., and Michael Ehrmann. 1999. Does inflation targeting increase output volatility? An international comparison of policymakers' preferences and outcomes. NBER Working Paper no. 7426. Cambridge, Mass.: National Bureau of Economic Research, December.

Clifton, Eric V., Leon Hyginus, and Chorng-Huey Wong. 2001. Inflation targeting and the unemployment-inflation trade-off. IMF Working Paper no. WP/01/166. Washington, D.C.: International Monetary Fund.

Corbo, Vittorio, Oscar Landerretche, and Klaus Schmidt-Hebbel. 2002. Does inflation targeting make a difference? In *Inflation targeting: Design, performance, challenges,* ed. Norman Loayza and Raimundo Saito, 221–70. Santiago, Chile: Central Bank of Chile.

Gilovich, Thomas. 1984. Judgemental biases in the world of sports. In *Cognitive sport psychology,* ed. William F. Straub and Jean M. Williams, 31–41. New York: Sport Science Associates.

Johnson, David R. 2002. The effect of inflation targeting on the behavior of expected inflation: Evidence from an 11 country panel. *Journal of Monetary Economics* 49:1521–38.

King, Mervyn. 2002. *The inflation target ten years on.* Speech delivered to the London School of Economics. 19 November, London, England.

Kuttner, Kenneth N., and Adam S. Posen. 1999. Does talk matter after all? Inflation targeting and central bank behavior. Federal Reserve Bank of New York Staff Reports no. 88. New York: Federal Reserve Bank of New York, October.

Layard, Richard, Stephen Nickell, and Richard Jackman. 1991. *Unemployment: macroeconomic performance and the labour market.* New York: Oxford University Press.

Maddala, G. S. 1989. *Introduction to econometrics.* New York: Maxwell Macmillan International Editions.

Mankiw, N. Gregory. 2001. U.S. monetary policy during the 1990s. NBER Working Paper no. 8471. Cambridge, Mass.: National Bureau of Economic Research, September.

Mishkin, Frederic S. 1999. International experiences with different monetary policy regimes. *Journal of Monetary Economics* 43:579–605.

———. 2002. Does inflation targeting matter? Commentary. *Federal Reserve Bank of St. Louis Review* 84 (4): 149–53.

Neumann, Manfred J. M., and Jurgen von Hagen. 2002. Does inflation targeting matter? *Federal Reserve Bank of St. Louis Review* 84 (4): 127–48.

Scheater, Andrea, Mark R. Stone, and Mark Zelmer. 2000. Adopting inflation targeting: Practical issues for emerging market countries. IMF Occasional Paper no. 202. Washington, D.C.: International Monetary Fund.

Sheridan, Niamh. 2001. *Inflation dynamics.* Ph.D. diss. Johns Hopkins University, Baltimore, Md.

Svensson, Lars E. O. 1995. The Swedish experience of an inflation target. In *Inflation targets,* ed. Leonardo Leiderman and Lars E. O. Svensson, 69–89. London: Centre for Economic Policy Research.

———. 1997. Inflation forecast targeting: Implementing and monitoring inflation targets. *European Economic Review* 41:1111–46.

Comment   Mark Gertler

Introduction

This is an interesting and provocative paper. I enjoyed reading it. The authors make two main arguments:

1. The existing evidence in favor of inflation targeting is open to identification problems.

2. After taking into account this identification problem, the evidence suggests that inflation targeting has been irrelevant.

On the first point I completely agree. On the second point, however, I disagree. I do not think the authors' empirical framework is sharp enough to disentangle the effects.

The essence of the authors' argument is that the endogeneity of inflation targeting makes the existing evidence difficult to interpret. I will argue that this same endogeneity problem potentially clouds the interpretation of their empirical tests. In particular, to the extent that there is not much exogenous variation in the choice to adopt inflation targeting, it may be very difficult to identify the effects, particularly in a small sample.

A second major issue involves the classification scheme. The authors divide the countries into targeters and nontargeters. I will argue that many of the nontargeters (if not just about all), however, adopted monetary policies that were very similar in practice to formal inflation targeting. This lack of

Mark Gertler is Henry and Lucy Moses Professor of Economics and Chairman of the Economics Department at New York University and a research associate of the National Bureau of Economic Research.

sharpness in the classification scheme further complicates the task of disentangling the contribution of inflation targeting.

Below I elaborate on each of these points.

The Empirical Framework

The authors begin with a data set that consists of various economic indicators for most of the OECD countries over the period 1960 to the present. They then consider the following two econometric specifications:

(1)
$$X_{post} - X_{pre} = a_0 + a_1 D + u$$

(2)
$$X_{post} - X_{pre} = a_0 + a_1 D + a_2 X_{pre} + v,$$

where X_{post} is variable X (say, inflation) in the second part of the sample and
X_{pre} is the variable in the first part. In addition, D is a dummy that takes on
a value of unity if the country adopted a formal inflation target in the second part of the sample (no countries adopted in the first part). Finally, u
and v are error terms.

Equation (1) is the specification that much of the existing literature has
considered. Under this specification, estimates of the coefficient a_1 are typically significant for the kinds of variables considered. For example, if X is
inflation, a_1 is typically negative and statistically significant. The temptation in the literature has been to conclude that countries that adopted formal inflation targets experienced a significantly larger drop than countries
that did not: that is, inflation targeting has made a difference.

As the authors correctly point out, however, this interpretation is problematic if (as one might think) the decision to adopt inflation targeting is
endogenous. It is possible, for example, that high inflation in the early part
of the sample induced countries to adopt inflation targeting. Indeed, countries that adopted inflation targeting did tend to have higher-than-average
inflation in the first part of the sample. This potential endogeneity leaves
open the possibility that inflation targeting did not have a true causal effect
on a inflation. Rather, the drop in inflation could simply have been the result of what the authors call "regression to the mean" factors, with inflation targeting being merely a veil.

A sharper way to see the problem is as one of specification bias. It could
be the case that estimate of a_1 is negative because the inflation-targeting
dummy is negatively correlated with the error term u and not because D is
truly causal. This negative correlation arises if (a) high inflation induces inflation targeting and (b) the drop in inflation merely reflects regression-to-
the-mean factors, as the authors suggest.

The authors propose to correct for the specification bias by adding X_{pre}
to the right-hand side, as in equation (2). When they do so, they find that
coefficient a_2 is significantly negative but that a_1 now does not significantly
differ from zero. That is, after controlling for initial inflation, the inflation-

targeting dummy no longer has any explanatory power. The authors interpret this result as suggesting that inflation targeting does not matter.

I think the evidence is not sharp enough to draw any firm conclusion. The alternative interpretation is also consistent with the evidence: countries that experienced high inflation early on subsequently adopted inflation targeting as a consequence. Inflation targeting, in turn, facilitated the disinflation. Under this scenario (where the decision to adopt inflation targeting is completely endogenous), the impact of inflation targeting is embedded in the reduced-form coefficient a_2. The causal variable remains X_{pre}. However, inflation targeting is part of the propagation mechanism, which accounts for how countries with early high inflation experienced a larger drop in inflation in the second part of the sample.

Here one can make an analogy with the identified vector autoregression (VAR) literature. We know from this work that just because nonmonetary shocks account for most of the variation in output, one cannot conclude that monetary policy is not important. It could be that the response of the economy to these nonmonetary shocks is quite sensitive to the endogenous response of monetary policy. Similarly, the endogenous response of inflation targeting to high inflation within the OECD countries might have shaped the dynamic response of inflation. Given the nature of the evidence the authors present, it is difficult to sort out these competing explanations.

To the extent that there is some exogenous variation in decisions to adopt inflation targeting, the authors' empirical framework could in principle identify the effects of inflation targeting. Over the cross section of countries the authors consider, however, the correlation between initial inflation and the decision to adopt targeting appears very strong. That is, initial inflation seems to be a good indicator of whether a country adopts. Even if there is some residual exogenous variation in the adoption decision, however, it is not clear that the sample size is sufficiently large to identify the impact of this variation. That is, multicollinearity is likely an issue.

The Classification Scheme

The other key issue, as I noted earlier, is that the authors' classification scheme may not be sufficiently sharp. In principle, one can only assess the effects of inflation targeting by having a clear alternative monetary policy regime as a benchmark. That is, to draw conclusions about inflation targeting, one must ask what it is being compared to.

In this regard, it is not clear that the non-inflation-targeting countries in the sample followed monetary policies that were clearly distinct from those of the inflation-targeting countries. Many of the nontargeters belong to the European Monetary Union, which has adopted a hybrid of inflation targeting that involves explicit objectives for both inflation and money growth. In addition, while some nontargeting central banks, such as the Federal Reserve, may not have formal numerical objectives for inflation, it

Table 6C.1   Countries in classification scheme

Inflation targeters		Nontargeters	
Non-euro	Euro	Non-euro	Euro
Australia	Finland	United States	Austria
Canada	Spain	Japan	Belgium
New Zealand		Denmark	France
Sweden		Norway	Germany
United Kingdom		Switzerland	Ireland
			Italy
			The Netherlands
			Portugal

could be argued that they implicitly targeted inflation by managing interest rates in a way that is indistinguishable from what a formal inflation-
targeting central bank might choose. Accordingly, given the fuzziness of
the classification scheme, it is perhaps not surprising that it is difficult to
disentangle any impact of inflation targeting. More formally, measurement
error in D_t provides an additional reason why estimates of a_1 may be insignificant, even if inflation targeting really does matter.

It is useful to take a closer look at the classification. In table 6C.1, I divide the countries into the targeting and nontargeting groups. Within each
group I divide the countries into the Euro and non-Euro members.

The sample consists of seven targeters and thirteen nontargeters. However, more than half of the nontargeters (eight) belong to the European
Monetary Union (EMU), as do two of the targeters. Because EMU has followed a policy that is very close in spirit to inflation targeting, it is not clear
that it is desirable to have these countries in the control group.

What about the non-Euro nontargeters? As I alluded to earlier, there is
evidence to suggest that the United States under Volcker and Greenspan
has acted like an implicit inflation targeter. Denmark has been on the verge
of joining the EMU and has thus pursued a monetary policy that has been
very close in spirit. Switzerland in fact follows a system of inflation and
monetary targeting that is similar in practice to that of the EMU. It is not
clear that Japan should be in the group, either: this country has had a drop
in inflation that has been arguably too large. Since this country has experienced deflation, inflation targeting would have produced a more modest
drop in inflation than what occurred. Including Japan thus seems to muck
up the empirical predictions.

This leaves Norway. A (perhaps unfair) characterization of the authors'
econometric framework is that they are trying to achieve identification by
exploiting the differences between Norway and Sweden. In figures 6C.1
and 6C.2, I plot consumer price inflation and the call money rate for Sweden and Norway over the period 1972 to the present. In each case, the two

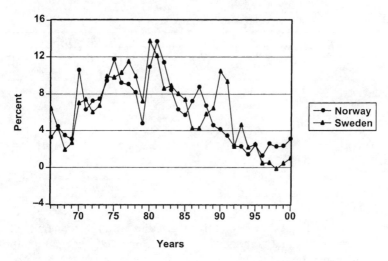

Fig. 6C.1   Inflation

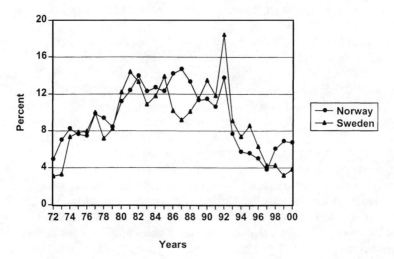

Fig. 6C.2   Call money rate

series move closely together: in this respect, Norway looks a lot like Sweden, although the classification puts them in different groups. What is going on? Even though Norway is not officially a targeter, it appears to have
tied its monetary policy to a country that does inflation target (i.e., Sweden). It has done so by stabilizing its currency relative to the Swedish currency. In doing so, it may have reaped the benefits from inflation targeting,
even though it is not officially categorized as an inflation targeter. The authors' classification scheme is not robust to this possibility.

Concluding Remarks

In sum, I do not think the authors have made the case that inflation targeting has been irrelevant (although they have certainly made the case that the evidence that it has mattered is also not definitive).

I do agree, however, that the adoption of formal inflation targets would have made little difference to the performance of the U.S. economy over the past twenty years. As I noted earlier, the conventional wisdom is that the Federal Reserve has behaved as an implicit inflation targeter. By establishing reputations for being focused on inflation stability, Volcker and Greenspan effectively achieved all the benefits that one might have otherwise obtained from having formal inflation targets. I think proponents of inflation targeting have this view. The case made for adopting formal targets in the United States is not that this system would improved past performance, but rather that it will help future performance by preserving the gains in credibility for Greenspan's successor. This makes sense to me. But is there clear evidence of this potential benefit in the data? Here the authors have some grounds for splashing a bit of rain on the parade. In the end, though, we can all agree: time will tell.

Discussion Summary

Ed Nelson pointed out that the paper's focus on averages across inflation-targeting and non-inflation-targeting countries entailed a loss of information, and that in particular the countries classified as non–inflation targeters had followed very different policies.

Stephen Cecchetti argued that cross-country comparisons of inflation and output variability did not answer the question of whether inflation targeting had helped to move the efficient policy frontier inward toward the origin. Instead, the results presented in the paper suggested that inflation-targeting countries located themselves at a different point on their output-inflation variability frontier from non-inflation-targeting countries.

Gregory Mankiw conjectured that the primary effect of inflation targeting had been to change the conversation between the central bank and the public. If so, it would be difficult for any cross-country study to draw a clear distinction between inflation targeters and non–inflation targeters, as countries without an explicit inflation target might focus in their public statements on the same issues as inflation targeters.

Donald Kohn pointed out that adoption of an inflation target had often occurred in combination with an increase in the central bank's independence, making it difficult to distinguish between the effects of one or the other.

Martin Feldstein suggested that the coefficient estimates on the lagged performance measure would be biased upward if the equation residual was serially correlated, thus inflating the explanatory power of the lagged dependent variable.

Michael Bordo argued that the regime change in the 1980s and 1990s was an increased emphasis on inflation control, which was not confined to inflation-targeting countries, and that beyond this regime change, inflation targeting was a second-order issue.

Jose De Gregorio expressed the view that the effect of commodity price changes on domestic inflation depended more on the exchange rate regime in place than on the presence or absence of an inflation target, creating an endogeneity problem for the study. He also pointed out that several inflation-targeting countries disinflated before adopting an inflation target.

Frederic Mishkin emphasized the lack of proper identification of the effects of inflation targeting in the paper. He also argued that the classification of countries into inflation targeters and non–inflation targeters compounded the identification problem. If, by analogy, one wanted to assess the success of monetary targeting in Germany, it would be inappropriate to treat those countries whose exchange rate to the deutsche mark had been fixed for decades as independent observations.

Christopher Sims pointed out that the reduction in the point estimates of the coefficients on the inflation-targeting dummy in the dynamic specifications may be deceptive, and that the quantitative implications may be very similar to those of the inflation-targeting dummies in the static equations.

Laurence Ball replied that there was no evidence that the adoption of an inflation target helped countries with initially high inflation rates to disinflate. On the question of the proper classification of countries, the authors had tried many different classifications without being able to find a significant effect of inflation targeting.

7

Limits to Inflation Targeting

Christopher A. Sims

7.1 The Two Faces of Inflation Targeting

Economists should recognize that they have a history of proposing simple "nominal anchor" prescriptions for monetary policy that have eventually proved not to be very useful. If economists satisfy a demand for spurious technocratic solutions to the political and institutional pathologies that generate destructive episodes of deflation or inflation, they can do harm by diverting attention from the sources of the problem. Such nostrums can also be harmful, usually with a delay, by failing to work and thereby undermining the credibility of monetary policy. A cynical view might be that inflation targeting has become attractive less because of advances in our discipline than because of the demand for a replacement for the gold standard, monetarism, and exchange rate anchors.

There is some reason to hope, though, that inflation targeting is a "better nostrum." This anchor is something that people do in fact care about, rather than an "intermediate target." It is therefore likely to remain credible that the central bank is committed to its inflation target even though periods when its policies are having difficulties. This anchor is widely recognized not to be directly and immediately under the central bank's control. Inflation targeting therefore requires that the central bank explain how its current actions relate to its view of the future course of the economy and that it be explicit about how precisely it can control inflation.

But there are in fact bounds, set by fiscal policy broadly conceived, on the central bank's control over inflation. It may lose control of a deflation. Benhabib, Schmitt-Grohé, and Uribe (2001; hereafter BSU) show that an

Christopher A. Sims is professor of economics at Princeton University, and a research associate of the National Bureau of Economic Research.

interest rate rule that satisfies the "Taylor principle," because of the zero lower bound on nominal rates, can lead inevitably to a deflationary spiral.[1] They did not emphasize that the result depends on a decidedly peculiar-looking fiscal policy. Peculiar though it is, we see historical examples of something close to such a policy. To understand how such a policy can arise, it may help to step outside the framework of models that treat the central bank and the treasury as a unified entity with a single budget constraint.

The central bank may be faced with a fiscal policy that fails to make primary surpluses respond to the level of debt and thereby undoes any effort by the bank to restrict the volume of outstanding nominal liabilities. Loyo (2000) shows how a failure of fiscal backing for monetary policy can leave interest rate increases powerless to restrain inflation, and he applies his model to interpreting Brazilian experience. Even when what are usually thought of as appropriate fiscal policies prevail, there are generally competitive equilibria in which spiraling inflation leads to the disappearance of real balances. Such equilibria can be suppressed by "backup" policies that put a floor on the value of money, via either taxation or reserve holdings. But it is not automatic that such backup policies are credible.

As a theoretical possibility, moreover, the lack of a credible fiscal policy may open the door to equilibria in which accelerating inflation leads to demonetization of the economy, even when policies are also consistent with stable equilibria. This theoretical possibility may influence central bank thinking, even though it has rarely if ever been observed.

7.2   Deflationary Traps via "Ricardian" Fiscal Policy

In this section and the next we consider two models, both highly simplified, that display in stark form the nature of fiscal bounds on the ability to control the price level. There is no claim here of originality. The basic idea of the deflationary model is in the work of BSU, and the interest rate rule model is a variant of one worked out in Sims (2000). And these models in turn draw on early work on the fiscal theory. The point of displaying these models here is to provide some reminders of the ways control over the price level can fail and of how the failures depend on fiscal policy.

The first model we consider is not an inflation-targeting model in any sense. The BSU models it parallels consider interest rate policy rules that have, in much of the literature, been taken to guarantee a determinate price level. The BSU models therefore can be interpreted as showing that making interest rates respond to inflation in a way that would widely be thought

---

1. "Inevitably" is arguably too strong a word here. They find indeterminacy. But in a stochastic world, indeterminacy reappears at every moment, and any random perturbation of a nicely behaved equilibrium is likely to lead to the deflationary trap.

of as guaranteeing that inflation stays close to target can instead leave the economy open to a deflationary spiral. The model we present here strips away nonneutralities, and even bonds and interest rates, to show that the type of *fiscal* policy BSU consider will produce their sort of result even without an interest rate rule. The pathology they display is likely to be possible whenever policy in effect provides a tax backing for money, as if monetary liabilities were interest bearing.

The model has many identical agents, choosing time paths for their consumption C and money holdings M. They receive an endowment income of Y each period and pay lump sum taxes τ. They have time-separable logarithmic utility functions in C. They value money because increased real balances reduce transactions costs.

Agents:

(1)
$$\max_{\{C_t, M_t\}} E\left[\int_0^\infty e^{\beta t} \log C_t\, dt\right] \quad \text{s.t.}$$

(2)
$$C(1 + \gamma V) + \frac{\dot{M}}{P} = Y - \tau$$

(3)
$$V = \frac{PC}{M}.$$

Government:

(4)
$$\text{policy:} \quad \tau = -\phi_0 + \phi_1 \frac{M}{P}$$

(5)
$$\text{government budget constraint:} \quad \frac{\dot{M}}{P} = -\tau.$$

The first-order conditions of the representative agent are

(6)
$$\partial C: \quad \frac{1}{C} = \lambda(1 + 2\gamma V)$$

(7)
$$\partial M: \quad \frac{\lambda}{P}\left(-\frac{\dot{\lambda}}{\lambda} + \frac{\dot{P}}{P} + \beta\right) = \frac{\lambda}{P}\gamma V^2.$$

In continuous-time rational-expectations models like this one it is particularly important to keep track of what the model defines as being able to "jump" and what it constrains not to jump. Often this is done by listing variables that can jump and that cannot, but not every model is properly characterized this way. It is quite possible for certain functions of variables in the model to be constrained not to jump, whereas all the arguments of the functions individually are not so constrained. In this paper we use the convention that all equations representing constraints hold not only for all $t \geq 0$ but also in a neighborhood of $t = 0$. First-order conditions, on the other hand, apply only for $t \geq 0$. Thus if a constraint equation contains a single dotted variable (e.g., the $\dot{M}$ in equations [2] or [5]), the dotted variable, because its derivative must exist in a neighborhood of $t = 0$, is implied to have time paths continuous at $t = 0$.[2] An equation that is a constraint and contains multiple dotted variables does not constrain each individual dotted variable to have an absolutely continuous path. In a linear equation, it will be only the linear combination whose derivative appears in the constraint that is constrained to be absolutely continuous. On the other hand, a variable like P in this model, which appears "dotted" only as the highest-order derivative in first-order conditions, is constrained only to have a *right* derivative, with a possible discontinuity in its level at $t = 0$.

Some algebraic manipulation allows us to derive from the first-order conditions and the model constraints the following differential equation in V:

$$(8) \qquad \frac{\dot{V}(1 + 4\gamma V)}{V(1 + 2\gamma V)} = \gamma V^2 \left(1 - \frac{\phi_0}{Y}\right) - \frac{\phi_0 V}{Y} + \phi_1 - \beta,$$

which, because its derivation uses first-order conditions, holds only for positive t, so that V is allowed to be discontinuous at $t = 0$.

If we assume Y to be constant and impose the fairly reasonable conditions that $\phi_0 < Y$ and $\phi_1 > \beta$, but $\phi_1 - \beta$ small, then this equation in V has two steady states, a smaller one that is approximately $(\phi_1 - \beta)Y/\phi_0$ and a larger one. The smaller is stable and the larger is unstable.

In this model the definition of V and the social resource constraint $C(1 + 2\gamma V) = Y$ together imply a monotone increasing relation between PY/M and V for positive V. Thus we can conclude that every initial value of P below some critical value is consistent with equilibrium, each implying a different initial V, and all these possible initial Vs imply the same limiting behavior—convergence of V to the lower steady-state value. At this lower steady state for V, if $\phi_1 > \beta$ and $\phi_1 - \beta$ is small, we have that

$$(9) \qquad \frac{\dot{M}}{M} = \frac{\dot{P}}{P} \doteq -\beta$$

to first-order accuracy in $\phi_1 - \beta$. Thus we have the same kind of behavior found by BSU: indeterminacy of the price level and convergence, from a wide range of initial values, to the same equilibrium of steady deflation.

It is not difficult to understand why this policy results in indeterminacy—the policy authority has committed to back the real value of money balances with taxes *regardless of how large this real value might be*. The policy therefore implies no nominal "anchor." Prices can fall to arbitrarily low levels, boosting real balances to arbitrarily high levels, and even though no

---

2. The derivative itself does not have to be continuous at $t = 0$. What is required is that M be absolutely continuous with a derivative defined except on a set of measure zero and with the time path of M the integral of its time derivative.

one has a transactions use for the additional real balances, the tax backing and resulting deflation make holding the real balances attractive.

Above the upper steady state, the price level explodes rapidly upward and velocity also rises rapidly. In fact, velocity converges to infinity in finite time. There is no violation of transversality or of feasibility conditions in these explosive equilibria.

In this model, simple, apparently realistic policies will eliminate the indeterminacy. For example, if the government replaces its "tax-backed money" rule (4) with a commitment to hold M constant, the differential equation in V (8) is replaced by

$$(10) \qquad \dot{V} = \frac{(\gamma V^2 - \beta)V(1 + 2\gamma V)}{1 + 4\gamma V}.$$

This equation has a unique, unstable steady state. Initial conditions with $V < \sqrt{\beta/\gamma}$ imply V converging to zero, but this entails here that $M/P \to \infty$. Since agents in this equilibrium have bounded consumption paths, their accumulation of arbitrarily large real money balances violates transversality, so these deflationary paths are not equilibria.

With either constant-M or Ricardian policy, the inflationary paths that start with V above its steady-state value are equilibria. They can be eliminated by an apparently simple policy, a commitment to back a minimal value for money with taxation. It is well known, though, that there have in fact been historical episodes of hyperinflation in which, far from using taxes to put a floor on the value of money, fiscal authorities have persisted in running primary deficits as inflation has accelerated to extreme levels. Furthermore, as we will discuss at more length below, some institutional frameworks aimed at ensuring "independence" of the central bank undermine the credibility of any claim to provide a tax-backed floor to the value of money.

With the Ricardian policy, real money balances grow very large on the paths toward the lower steady state and, in the case where $\phi_1 = \beta$, grow without bound in equilibrium. The growth does not violate individual optimizing behavior, however, because the foreseen steady rise in taxes makes individuals see themselves as dependent on the deflationary real return on their money balances to maintain intertemporal budget balance. The usual argument that arbitrarily high real wealth with bounded consumption violates transversality fails because the real-balance wealth is offset by the discounted present value of future taxes.

Since in this abstract model the consequences of backing money with a Ricardian fiscal rule are undesirable, and since better policies are easily available, one might ask why we need pay any attention to these results. The Ricardian policy looks crazy because the model assumes homogeneous, freely marketable, nominal government debt or money. This makes it easy for the government to dilute the claims of existing asset holders by new borrowing, without obviously targeting a narrow and organized constituency. It also makes it easy for asset holders, were the real current market value of their holdings of government liabilities to grow while their future tax liabilities apparently did not, to try to turn their increased wealth into current purchases.

In Japan today, and probably also the United States in the 1930s, deflation has its strongest effect in increasing nonmarketable, heterogeneous government liabilities. Tomita (2002) explains the variety of ways in which Japan's explicit debt is less easily marketed, more concentrated in the hands of banks and government agencies, and less homogeneous than government debt in the United States or Europe. And it is widely understood that both in the United States in the 1930s and in present-day Japan, the existence of large institutions with negative net worth that grows more negative with declining prices creates implicit, nonmarketable government liabilities, via potential claims to bailouts, as prices decline. When price declines create perceptions of claims on future tax revenues via bailouts as fast as or faster than they increase the value of marketable nominal securities in the hands of the public, they can fail to produce any strong positive wealth effects.

Another route by which deflationary equilibria might arise is via central bank balance sheet illusion.[3] We have seen in the United States just a few years ago a discussion of the consequences for the Federal Reserve balance sheet of the vanishing of the U.S. public debt. In simple macroeconomic models, the balance sheets of the central bank and the treasury are consolidated, so that the public debt has vanished when only debt held by the central bank remains. But in the recent policy discussions it was assumed that the Fed might need to turn to holding private securities as backing for monetary reserves. That is, it was assumed that the treasury would continue to tax to run surpluses to retire the debt held by the Fed. This is exactly the assumption of BSU's Ricardian fiscal policy, although BSU require further that as deflation proceeds the treasury will continually replenish the central bank balance sheet by further purchases of private assets as the real value of high-powered money increases.

In the case of the U.S. Federal Reserve, it may seem unreasonable that the treasury should see debt held by the Federal Reserve as a liability requiring tax backing or that the Federal Reserve should ever perceive a need to ask for treasury replenishment of its balance sheet. The Federal Reserve has a nearly perfectly hedged balance sheet, with most of its assets nominal U.S. government bonds and its liabilities mostly high-powered money. Even if it did somehow develop substantial negative net worth, why would

---

3. The discussion of balance sheet illusion here and the model below of inflation stabilization with reserves draws on the discussion in Sims (2000).

this be a problem? Its high-powered money liabilities carry no explicit promise that they are redeemable, so there are no creditors whose demands could make negative net worth a problem.

But there are other structures for central bank balance sheets. The most common direction of deviation is toward holding large amounts of reserves in the form of securities that are not denominated in domestic currency and hence leave the central bank less than perfectly hedged. A good example is the European System of Central Banks, which holds most of its assets in non-Euro securities. This clearly introduces balance sheet risk and the possibility of the bank's arriving at a situation of negative net worth. While it is true that there is no explicit promise to redeem high-powered money, we shall see that for a bank that must rely on reserves rather than fiscal resources, any attempt to commit to stabilizing the price level or inflation will make net worth a concern. This fact may both limit the bank's ability to dampen fluctuations in inflation and contribute to inappropriate Ricardian policy behavior in a deflationary environment.

7.3   Stabilizing Inflation, with Reserves or Tax Backing

Here we return to modeling both bonds and money, so that we can discuss policy in terms of an interest rate rule, as has recently been standard practice. We also introduce a foreign currency–denominated asset, so that we can consider a central bank with reserves only and no access to a backup taxing power.

In Sims (2000) I considered a model like this one, but with a central bank that tries to control the price level. That model made the point, which is perhaps nearly obvious, that when the central bank tries to enforce an upper bound on the price level, it must either limit its goals when its net worth is negative (or might become negative) or else have access to fiscal backing that would restore net worth whenever necessary. The outstanding high-powered money, while carrying no explicit promise of redemption, acquires an implicit redemption value when there is a commitment to a bound on the price level. A central bank that relies on the value of its reserves to back its money issue cannot guarantee a value for the currency stock outstanding that exceeds the value of its reserves. If it tries to do so, it is likely to face a run. A bank that uses an interest rate rule that aims at control of the price level does not avoid the problem. To implement its interest rate rule, the bank will have to stand ready to supply bonds for high-powered money. Disturbances to the economy—for example, to the real interest rate—can require time paths for reserves that are not feasible without replenishment of the balance sheet by fiscal actions. The likelihood of this happening is greater the more seriously underwater is the central bank balance sheet and the more tightly the bank attempts to control the price level.

Here we consider a policy authority that uses interest rate rules. Because in this model there is no tax backing of non-interest-bearing money, the model does not have the indeterminacy and deflationary equilibria of the BSU model. Nonetheless it retains the "inflationary demonetization" equilibria, which can be avoided only with tax backing or reserves.

We suppose an economy with a representative agent maximizing

$$(11) \qquad \int_0^\infty e^{-\beta t} \log C_t \, dt$$

with respect to the time paths of C, F_p, B, and M, subject to the constraint

$$(12) \qquad C[1 + \psi(v)] + \dot{F}_p + \frac{\dot{M} + \dot{B}}{P} = Y + \rho F_p + \frac{rB}{P} + \tau.$$

Here C is consumption, $v = PC/M$ is velocity of money, F_p is private holdings of the real asset, B is nominal government debt, M is money (non-interest-bearing currency), Y is an exogenous endowment stream, and τ is transfer payments from the government. The real and nominal interest rates are, respectively, ρ and r.

The first-order conditions for the private agent are

$$(13) \qquad \partial B: \quad \frac{\lambda}{P}\left(-\frac{\dot{\lambda}}{\lambda} + \beta + \frac{\dot{P}}{P}\right) = \frac{r\lambda}{P}$$

$$(14) \qquad \partial F: \quad -\dot{\lambda} + \beta\lambda = \rho\lambda$$

$$(15) \qquad \partial M: \quad \frac{\lambda}{P}\left(-\frac{\dot{\lambda}}{\lambda} + \beta + \frac{\dot{P}}{P}\right) = \frac{\lambda}{P}\psi' v^2$$

$$(16) \qquad \partial C: \quad C^{-1} = \lambda(1 + \psi + \psi' v).$$

These equations can be reduced to

$$(17) \qquad r = \rho + \frac{\dot{P}}{P}$$

$$(18) \qquad r = \psi' v^2$$

$$(19) \qquad \rho - \beta = \frac{\dot{C}}{C} + \frac{(2\psi' + \psi'' v)\dot{v}}{1 + \psi + \psi' v}.$$

As usual, the equations derived from first-order conditions hold only for $t \geq 0$, while the constraint (12) holds continuously. The only variable forced to be continuous at $t = 0$ by this single private constraint is the artificial construct "cumulative real asset purchases by the private sector, valued at acquisition cost"—that is,

$$\int_{-T}^t \left(\dot{F}_P(t) + \frac{\dot{M}_t + \dot{B}_t}{P_t} \right) dt.$$

So instantaneous, discontinuous portfolio adjustments, swapping among M, B, and F_P, are not ruled out. Instantaneous changes in wealth can occur, but only via jumps in P that revalue bond and money holdings. Instantaneous jumps in wealth via purchases or sales of assets are not possible, because they would have to draw on savings or dissavings, and consumption and income flow at finite rates.

The consolidated government budget constraint is

$$(20) \qquad \dot{F}_G = \rho F_G - r\frac{B}{P} + \frac{\dot{M} + \dot{B}}{P} - \tau,$$

where F_G is government holdings of the reserve asset. Substituting equation (20) in the private budget constraint gives us the social resource constraint

$$(21) \qquad C \cdot (1 + \psi) + \dot{F} = \rho F + Y,$$

where $F = F_P + F_G$ is total holdings of the reserve asset, by both private individuals and the government.

Assuming the central bank is the only government holder of the reserve asset and that government bonds are not held by the central bank, we get as the central bank's budge constraint

$$(22) \qquad \dot{F}_G = \rho F_G + \frac{\dot{M}}{P} - \tau_B.$$

It is natural to assume that in normal times, when seigniorage $\rho F_B + \dot{M}/P$ is positive, the bank will transfer sufficient revenues to the treasury or the public that its reserves remain aligned with outstanding money balances. When seigniorage revenue becomes negative, we assume that τ_B is set to zero. It may seem that it would be better policy to prevent net worth from deteriorating by allowing τ_B to go negative, but here we are trying to model a central bank whose "independence" entails not being dependent on the legislature for funding bailouts when net worth goes negative.

Now suppose that the monetary authority adopts an interest rate rule that reacts to inflation, setting

$$(23) \qquad \dot{r} = \theta_0 + \theta_1 \frac{\dot{P}}{P} - \theta_2 r.$$

Note that this policy rule makes r react to inflation with a delay, although the delay will be small if θ_2 is large. This equation does not imply that r and P must have continuous time paths. It allows discontinuous jumps Δr in r so long as they are matched by corresponding jumps $\Delta \log P/\theta_1$ in $\log P$.

Using equation (17) to eliminate $\dot{P}/P$ in equation (23), we arrive at

$$(24) \qquad \dot{r} = \theta_0 + (\theta_1 - \theta_2)r - \theta_1\rho.$$

If $\theta_1 > \theta_2$, the unique stable solution to this equation is

(25)
$$r = \theta_1 \int_{s=0}^{\infty} e^{-(\theta_1 - \theta_2)s} \rho_{t+s} ds - \frac{\theta_0}{\theta_1 - \theta_2}$$

(26)
$$\frac{\dot{P}}{P} = -\rho + \theta_1 \int_{s=0}^{\infty} e^{-(\theta_1 - \theta_2)s} \rho_{t+s} ds - \frac{\theta_0}{\theta_2 - \theta_1}.$$

Note that despite the interest rate smoothing policy, r must move immediately in response to jumps in ρ that are expected to have any persistence. This entails v jumping in response to shifts in ρ. Here P jumps up when ρ does, but $d \log P/d\rho$ is less than $-d \log C/d\rho$. M must therefore decrease to allow the equilibrium jump in velocity. The interest rate–setting bank must therefore be concerned with having reserves on hand to meet sudden shifts in real rates.

The differential equation (24) in r has unstable solutions in addition to the stable ones. The solutions that explode downward are unsustainable. They force r, and hence v, to zero in finite time. But this can occur only via M/P going to infinity, and in this setup, with tax backing only for bonds, the upward explosion in M/P violates transversality: agents will try to spend the high real balances, cutting off the deflation.

The solutions that make $\dot{P}/P$ explode upward have no such internal cut-off mechanism, however. Although they imply that the economy converges to a barter equilibrium, no market mechanism along the path to this outcome provides incentives to stop the explosion. If such paths do not occur, it has to be because of a backstop commitment, based on taxation or reserves.

A bank backed by a fiscal authority that can credibly increase its primary surplus to provide resources to redeem money at some fixed-ceiling price level can cut off the explosive paths. Of course, as we have already pointed out, fiscal authorities have historically continued to run primary deficits during high inflations, so that no such backstop commitment was credible. (Where such a commitment were credible, the model implies that the inflation would never get underway.)

A bank relying on reserves can set a fixed ceiling to the price level at any point where its reserves are adequate to redeem the entire stock of money. But if it follows the policy rule in equation (23), there is no guarantee that it can always be in this positive net worth position. It earns a return ρ on its reserves, while the value of its liabilities M/P either remains constant or grows at the rate of deflation. As long as there are no surprise jumps in the price level (or, what is equivalent in this abstract model, the exchange rate between reserve assets and domestic currency), the return on non-interest-bearing money will be less than that on nominal bonds, and the bonds earn the same real return as reserves. Therefore a bank that has reserves whose value matches its liabilities always earns positive *expected* seigniorage if it is undertaking no open-market operations.

However, if rising inflation requires rapid shrinkage of nominal money balances in order to implement the policy rule, seigniorage can turn negative. Along an unstable path, in which inflation accelerates and interest rates rise, the bank will of course be undertaking contractionary open-market operations. Whether these force it into negative seigniorage depends on the nature of the demand for money. If money is "essential," in the sense that as velocity increases the public is willing to pay ever-increasing opportunity costs to avoid further small decreases in real balances, then large rises in the interest rate can be accomplished with small rates of contraction in money balances, and seigniorage may remain robustly positive. If instead demand for real balances falls rapidly when interest rates reach high levels, then increasingly high rates of contraction in M may be required for given amounts of increase in r. This can result in large negative values of seigniorage and hence in disappearance of reserves while nonzero money balances remain outstanding.

To illustrate these points, we consider a version of the model in which the transactions technology has the specific form

$$(27) \qquad\qquad \psi(v) = \frac{\gamma v}{1 + \phi v}.$$

This gives equation (18) the specific form

$$(28) \qquad\qquad r = \frac{\gamma v^2}{(1 + \phi v)^2}.$$

This implies that if ϕ is positive, there is an upper bound on the nominal interest rate, beyond which demand for real balances is totally extinguished. Also, with $\phi > 0$ there is an upper bound on the fraction of income that can be absorbed by transactions costs. With $\phi = 0$ nominal interest rates are unbounded above and transactions costs can absorb a fraction of income arbitrarily close to 1.

We consider a scenario in which the economy begins in a steady state with zero inflation, real and nominal interest rates both constant at 2 percent per year. The policy rule has $\theta_0 = .02$, $\theta_1 = 1.2$, and $\theta_2 = 1$. We consider an unanticipated drop in the real interest rate ρ to a new level, 1.8 percent per year. A new stable equilibrium requires that the nominal interest rate drop to 0.8 percent, with a corresponding drop of 1 percent in the price level. The result will be a new equilibrium that again has a constant interest rate but now has steady deflation at 1 percent per year, lower velocity, higher real balances, and slightly higher consumption.

Suppose that instead the price level does not drop far enough, so that the nominal interest rate falls only to 1 percent. Because the price level is above the level consistent with a stable solution of the system, it sets the economy on a path of rising nominal interest rates. Consider the case where $\gamma = .02$, $\phi = .3$. This implies that in noninflationary steady state transactions costs

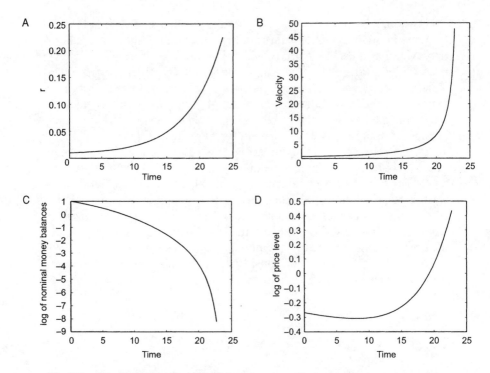

Fig. 7.1   Consequences of an insufficient response of p to a ρ drop

consume 2 percent of income and that there is an upper bound on the nominal interest rate, beyond which demand for money disappears, at 22 percent. The time paths for interest rates, velocity, the log of nominal money balances, and the log of the price level, are shown in panels A through D of figure 7.1.

Whether or not a central bank reliant on reserves can extinguish this explosive path depends on its initial net worth position and its policy on distributing or accumulating seigniorage revenue. Assuming it accumulates all of its seigniorage revenue results in time paths for $F_G P/M$ as shown in figure 7.2. If its initial net worth is negative but it has assets worth 90 percent of its outstanding real balances at the initial date, then accumulating its seigniorage in the initial period allows it to achieve positive net worth, at which point it could cut off the inflation by announcing it will redeem money for the reserve asset at a fixed rate of exchange. But if its initial net worth is much below this, it never achieves positive net worth, and indeed its reserves hit zero before the date at which real balances disappear. Obviously this makes it impossible for the bank to continue implementing its interest rate policy rule with open-market operations. The likely outcome

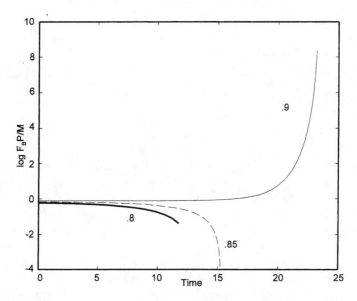

Fig. 7.2   Ratio of reserve to real balances outstanding under three assumptions about initial $F_G P/M$

would be an immediate jump to the barter equilibrium, and if this were foreseen, the jump would occur at the initial date.

That such scenarios are possible legitimizes attention to its balance sheet by a central bank that does not have reliable fiscal backing. The radical approach to central bank independence in the setup of the European Central Bank (ECB)—cutting all explicit connections with fiscal authorities and ruling out the holding of government debt as assets—has resulted in both an unhedged balance sheet and the absence of any explicit institutional structure for the ECB to use in case it were to need balance sheet replenishment. The Bank of Japan appears to be concerned that it would lose its recent gains in independence from the Ministry of Finance were it to arrive at a need for balance sheet replenishment. Records of monetary policy discussions in the United States in the 1930s show that there was concern about the "soundness" of assets being discounted by the Federal Reserve.

But in a deflationary environment, when the interest rate has hit its zero lower bound, the effective policy measures available to a central bank all carry balance sheet risk. This is obviously true of purchases of illiquid bank loans or of long-term government bonds whose current value will fall if deflation ends and interest rates rise. Even the "foolproof way" of Svensson (2001), which prescribes massive purchases of foreign currency–denominated bonds, because of the inherent volatility of exchange rates, creates substantial balance sheet risk for the central bank.

Our conclusion is that a central bank can lose control of the price level during a liquidity trap episode because of timidity induced by balance sheet worries. These balance sheet worries are justified, if there truly is no fiscal backing for the bank, because of the opposite possibility, that a bank with negative net worth and no fiscal backing can lose control of the price level in an explosive inflation.

In our discussion of this model to this point, we have not paid any attention to fiscal policy. This can be justified only by assuming a passive fiscal policy that keeps real debt under control regardless of the path of inflation. Suppose instead, as in the scenario Loyo considers, the fiscal authority does not make the primary surplus respond to the level of the real debt. As an extreme case, suppose it sets the primary surplus to be constant. Then in this, as in many previous models of this type, going back at least to Sargent and Wallace (1981), there is no equilibrium with active monetary policy ($\phi_1/\phi_2 > 1$).

Some economists believe that there is an asymmetry here, that when these incompatible monetary and fiscal policies are asserted, a firmly committed monetary authority can always prevail over any attempt by the fiscal authority to commit to an incompatible policy. But this is not true. It cannot even be discussed coherently in a conventional macro model with a unified budget constraint for the central bank and the treasury. If we introduce separate budget constraints for the central bank and the treasury, so that each can be imagined to possibly go bankrupt independently, we see that there is no formal asymmetry. If anything, the asymmetry is the other way. Central banks have died while the legislature that created them survived, but are there any examples of the reverse? And the lack of central, rational direction of the fiscal policy process in democratic countries probably makes it easier, not harder, for the fiscal authority to commit to a policy in the face of a threat (from the CB) that it could lead to disaster.

7.4   Pros and Cons of Inflation Targeting

It is plausible that the CB wants to bring inflation or deflation under control, even when it has recently been having trouble doing so. This may be less true of more artificial targets like M growth or the exchange rate. The credibility of a commitment to inflation targeting may therefore be somewhat more stable. Because monetary policy can affect inflation only with a substantial delay, inflation-targeting central banks in practice produce explicit projections, generally quarterly, for a time horizon of about two years into the future. This entails their explaining, at least to some extent, how current policy actions are related to future objectives. This allows greater public understanding of policy, and thereby greater credibility. The delay means that there are generally many ways to get inflation into the target range over the policy horizon. This creates room for other objectives to affect policy choices, thereby further improving the alignment between the public rationale for policy choices and the actual interests of the polity.

Since there are conditions under which an inflation-targeting commitment, as a central bank policy, has a high probability of proving unsustainable, it should not be recommended in those conditions. It can easily lead to disaster, or to an apparent initial success that magnifies a later disaster, when the necessary fiscal backup to monetary policy is not available. It would not be a good idea in Argentina today, and it may yet prove to have been a mistake, or at least unsustainable, in Brazil. It can worsen the situation for a central bank that is at the zero bound on its policy rate and thus has no tools to influence inflation. A projection for a desirable path for inflation (or deflation) that cannot be backed up with an explanation of how current central bank actions are expected to lead to the desired path will undermine central bank credibility. Inflation targeting is therefore not in itself a policy prescription for the Bank of Japan.

7.5   How to Improve It

The main virtue of an influence-targeting regime is that it leads to increased transparency as to the objectives of the central bank and as to how the bank believes its current actions contribute to achieving those objectives. These aspects of the regime ought to be pursued even where (the United States?) the inflation target itself meets resistance. In fact, I would argue that if here, in contrast to other countries, the "inflation-targeting" label is a hindrance to getting the Federal Reserve Board to be more explicit about its projections of the path of the economy and about how its actions are expected to affect that path, it would be a good idea to abandon the campaign for inflation targeting.

We could extend the virtues of inflation targeting by accompanying inflation-report projections of inflation, output, and so on with projected time paths of the policy rate. We could improve central bank models so that they become capable of providing realistic probability bands on projections and can be invoked in explaining central bank policy choices to the public.

It would be a good idea to make explicit the conditional nature of the commitment to an inflation target. It is already well accepted that some kinds of "shocks" can push the economy away from the inflation target temporarily. When these occur, an inflation-targeting bank explains the source of the shock and explains its plans to bring inflation back into the target range over time. This enhances credibility, compared to taking drastic policy actions to get quickly back into the target range at the cost of a potential backlash from the political system.

Fiscal policy ought to be treated as a potential source of shocks. Ideally, where fiscal policy that undermines central bank control of inflation is a real possibility, this be should be accounted for, discussed in inflation reports, and reflected in central bank projections. Such proposals meet stiff resistance. They can be seen as threatening the current conventions of central bank "independence," which depend on keeping a firm distinction between fiscal policy, where political considerations are considered inevitable, and monetary policy, which is seen as a technical matter, ideally completely insulated from politics. (Recently Fed Staff, in conversation, cited the danger that Fed projections of fiscal variables would become public as a reason to maintain the five-year secrecy rule for Fed *Green Book* and model forecasts.)

Where there is little prospect of fiscal policy becoming a constraint on monetary policy, or of fiscal policy becoming the only instrument available for controlling the price level, detailed fiscal projections would not be important. But where there is such a prospect, the central bank is likely to be the leading candidate for an institution that can analyze the policy options for controlling inflation. As the designated steward of the inflation rate it could make a contribution by conducting and disseminating such analysis, even when it has reached the point where its own policy levers are not effective.

7.6 Conclusion

Inflation targeting is in most countries an improvement in the monetary policy regime. But the improvement comes from its being a step toward goal and model transparency. Inflation targeting is a dubious recommendation in precisely those economies where advice from economists about controlling inflation is most needed. If we separate the transparency aspects of inflation targeting from its nominal-anchor-nostrum aspect, we may come up with a more widely applicable policy recommendation. The central bank should probably everywhere be charged with making projections of inflation, laying out policy actions that could stabilize inflation, and either taking those actions or explaining why it cannot and who could.

References

Benhabib, Jess, Stephanie Schmitt-Grohé, and Martin Uribe. 2001. The perils of Taylor rules. *Journal of Economic Theory* 96:40–69.
Loyo, Eduardo. 2000. Tight money paradox on the loose: A fiscalist hyperinflation. Harvard University, John F. Kennedy School of Government. Technical report.
Sargent, Thomas J., and Neil Wallace. 1981. Some unpleasant monetarist arithmetic. *Quarterly Review of the Minneapolis Federal Reserve Bank* 5 (3): 1–17.
Sims, Christopher A. 2000. Fiscal aspects of central bank independence. Princeton

University, Department of Economics. Technical report. Available at http://www.Princeton.edu/~sims.

Svensson, Lars E. O. 2001. The zero bound in an open economy: A foolproof way of escaping from a liquidity trap. *Monetary and Economic Studies* 19 (S-1): 277–312.

Tomita, Toshiki. 2002. The need for redefining Japan's government debt management policy. NRI paper no. 42. Tokyo: Nomura Research Institute.

Comment   Stephanie Schmitt-Grohé

When I was invited to discuss Christopher Sims's contribution to the Inflation Targeting Conference, one of the reasons I looked very much forward to preparing the discussion—besides the fact that a Sims paper is typically a very rewarding read—was that I hoped to finally learn what exactly inflation targeting is and what exactly an inflation-targeting central bank is supposed to do. However, I soon realized that this would not happen. I have come to the conclusion that inflation targeting is a nebulous monetary policy prescription. This concept is not as clearly defined as I had hoped for, and it certainly cannot easily be tied to very precise instructions for the central bank on how to behave. Chris Sims, though, I should note, is more willing to come forward with a definition of inflation targeting than others who write on the topic. His definition of inflation targeting is "simply any commitment by the central bank to control the time path of the inflation rate or the price level, at least in the long run." In my opinion, this definition could be one of any monetary policy rather than that of inflation targeting in particular. This is because undoubtedly, any central bank strives to control the time path of inflation or the price level. With this in mind, one can then interpret the limits of inflation targeting that are presented in the Sims paper as limits that any monetary policymaker, and not just an inflation targeter, will face. Thus, the concerns raised in the Sims paper will apply very generally, making them only the more relevant.

The Sims paper analyzes two economies in which there are limits to inflation targeting. In one case inflation targeting may open the door to unintended deflation, and in the other case inflation targeting may open the door to a speculative inflation. The logical next question the paper asks is how those speculative in- and deflations can be avoided. Contrary to the existing related literature, the Sims analysis treats the central bank and the fiscal authority as independent entities, each with its own budget con-

Stephanie Schmitt-Grohé is professor of economics at Duke University and a research associate of the National Bureau of Economic Research.

I would like to thank Martín Uribe for comments.

straint. The main contribution of the paper is to show that a central bank that lacks fiscal backing from the treasury may be more limited in its ability to achieve its goals regarding inflation than a central bank that enjoys the full financial support of the fiscal authority.

The Sims paper effectively communicates through insightful discussions that central bank independence may interfere with a central bank's ability to fight off self-fulfilling in- and deflations. The most formal presentation of this idea is given for an economy that tries to control inflation through an inertial interest rate feedback rule (see section 7.3). First, in this section it is shown that, contrary to the intentions of the central bank, the interest rate feedback rule may allow for speculative inflations. Then the paper shows that the usual remedy against speculative inflations, namely fractional reserve backing, may not work if the central bank does not have access to revenues created by the taxing power of the fiscal authority.

In what follows, I present a short review of the existing literature on limits to price-level or inflation control and on how to rule out speculative in- and deflations. I then ask whether those strategies will also work under the assumption of central bank independence. I show that for the economy studied in greatest detail in the Sims paper, the one of section 7.3, it is possible to rule out speculative inflations despite the fact that the central bank is independent. What is needed, should the economy embark on a speculative inflation, is a commitment by the central bank to switch to a monetary policy that first builds central bank net worth and then pegs the price level.

Can the Central Bank Alone Control the Path of Inflation?

Given fiscal policy, one can in general distinguish three cases. In the first case, the inflation path targeted by the central bank is necessarily unsustainable under all conceivable ways of conducting monetary policy; that is, it creates too little seigniorage revenue to make fiscal policy sustainable. In the second case, the inflation path targeted by the central bank can in principle be supported as an equilibrium outcome. But some monetary policies will imply that the inflation path is not attained and instead the economy must converge either to a self-fulfilling inflation or to a self-fulfilling deflation with probability one. For example, Loyo (1999) argues that the combination of an active interest rate feedback rule and a non-Ricardian fiscal policy led Brazil to hyperinflation in the mid-1980s. In the third scenario, it could also be the case that some monetary policies will imply that the targeted inflation path is only one of several price paths that are consistent with the monetary fiscal regime. Here again there are two cases. Besides the target rate of inflation, equilibria exist with self-fulfilling inflations and deflations. For examples see the work of Brock (1974, 1975), Obstfeld and Rogoff (1983), Woodford (1994, 2003), and Benhabib, Schmitt-Grohé, and

Uribe (2001b). The second possibility is that besides the target path of inflation there exist other bounded equilibria. Those can be of two types. One type is perfect-foresight equilibria converging to the steady state. Typically, not just a single one of those exists, but a continuum. To name but a few, examples are contained in the work of Woodford (1994); Leeper (1991); Clarida, Galí, and Gertler (2000); and Benhabib, Schmitt-Grohé, and Uribe (2001a). Another class of bounded equilibria that may exist is equilibria converging to a cycle, as shown in Benhabib, Schmitt-Grohé, and Uribe (2001a, b, 2003), or chaotic equilibria (Benhabib, Schmitt-Grohé, and Uribe, 2002b). Finally, it could be the case that the monetary policy will imply that the targeted path of inflation is the only equilibrium outcome. This scenario is the one that is desired, but as the above discussion demonstrates, this will not always be the case.

What Monetary Strategies Have Been Proposed to Rule Out Speculative Inflations or Deflations?

In the existing literature two strategies have been proposed to rule out self-fulfilling inflations. One strategy is to impose restrictions on preferences that imply that money is essential in the sense that utility would converge to negative infinity when real balances approach zero. This route has been studied (and criticized as economically unreasonable) in Brock (1974, 1975), Gray (1984), and Obstfeld and Rogoff (1983). The model analyzed in the Sims paper does not make this assumption. Rather, it makes the more plausible assumption that once liquidity becomes too expensive agents are willing to regress to barter and not use money at all. The second strategy, which is typically regarded as more compelling, for it does not rely on questionable assumptions about the nature of preferences, is to switch to a price-level peg (see Wallace [1981] and Obstfeld and Rogoff [1983]). It is the effectiveness of this second strategy that the Sims paper studies in detail in the case that the central bank lacks financial backing from the fiscal authority.

Similarly, the existing literature contains routes on how to rule out self-fulfilling deflations relying on preference specifications and on monetary policy switches. One possible route is the adoption of a price-level peg. For this strategy to work, the central bank must be willing to purchase, for example, foreign exchange at a fixed price with money. Svensson (2001) has labeled this strategy of avoiding unintended deflations the "foolproof way" and has recommended it as a promising strategy for Japan to escape its deflationary trap. An alternative route to escaping the liquidity trap has been proposed by Benhabib, Schmitt-Grohé, and Uribe (2002a). They show that the switch to a positive money growth rate peg, if accompanied by the right fiscal policy, will prevent an economy from falling into a deflationary spiral.

Would Those Antispeculative Strategies Also Work When the Central Bank Is Independent of the Fiscal Authority?

The Svensson (2001) foolproof way of avoiding a self-fulfilling liquidity trap requires that the central bank stand ready to buy (in principle, unlimited quantities of) assets in exchange for currency. From a balance sheet point of view, this strategy should provide few problems. It requires the central bank to buy financial assets with money. Since the central bank has access to unlimited amounts of money, this strategy is clearly feasible even in the absence of resource transfers from the fiscal authority. In the Sims paper, it is argued that this strategy may not be adopted because the central bank does not want to make its balance sheet longer. The reason given why a central bank may object to making its balance sheet longer is that it would make it more prone to variations in net worth stemming from variations in the real value of central bank assets. The Sims paper cites in particular the exchange rate risk associated with purchases of foreign currency–denominated bonds.

However, if the foolproof way of avoiding speculative deflations is effective, it means that prices will never start falling to begin with and the central bank will never have to actually implement the price-level peg. In this case the balance sheet considerations should play no role. Second, suppose an economy is already in a liquidity trap and contemplates the implementation of a price-level peg to prevent further declines in prices. In the self-fulfilling deflation, prices and nominal balances are declining at about the same rate (ignoring growth for the moment). But if a price-level peg is implemented, then real balances should fall (because inflation will increase from a negative quantity to zero), and with the price level pegged this means that nominal money balances must fall, leading to outflows of central bank reserves rather than inflows. That is, the balance sheet of the central bank will become shorter and not longer. (This is the famous balance-of-payments crisis argument.) The central bank may even set the price-level peg at exactly that level that will imply that nominal money balances are unchanged. To be able to achieve this, it will have to announce that the price level is pegged at a higher level than the price level in place immediately before the switch to the price-level peg. In this case, central bank independence will again not stand in the way of the quest for price stability.

Benhabib, Schmitt-Grohé, and Uribe (2002a) show that the central bank can rule out self-fulfilling deflations by switching policy to a (positive) money growth rate peg. As will become clear from the discussion in the next section, this strategy can be successful even if the net worth of the central bank is initially negative and the central bank is independent.

The central argument in the Sims paper is that a price-level peg may not rule out self-fulfilling inflations under central bank independence. Specifically, it is argued that a self-fulfilling inflation may not be averted if the central bank has negative net worth. However, this result hinges critically on the particular specification of monetary policy in the Sims analysis, where it is assumed that the central bank follows an inertial interest rate feedback rule. In the example studied in section 7.3 of the Sims paper, when the economy demonetizes—that is, when real balances converge to zero—nominal balances are actually declining. So it is a case of a self-fulfilling inflation with shrinking nominal balances. In most existing historical examples of economies in which accelerating inflation led to demonetization of the economy, the opposite was observed. The accelerating inflation occurs in an environment in which nominal money balances are increasing, albeit at a slower rate than prices.

This feature of the Sims analysis is important. For only if $\dot{M} < 0$ is net worth of the central bank shrinking along the hyperinflationary path. To see this, let $w(t)$ denote the ratio of central bank assets to central bank liabilities—that is, in the notation of the Sims paper $w(t) = P(t)F_G(t)/M(t)$. It follows that $\dot{w}/w = \pi + \dot{F}_G/F_G - \dot{M}/M$. Using the central bank's budget constraint, equation (22) in the Sims paper, and assuming that the central bank makes no transfers to the fiscal authority, $\tau_B = 0$, it follows that $\dot{w}/w = (\pi + \rho) + \dot{M}/M(1/w - 1)$. Suppose that initially the central bank's net worth is negative, so that $0 < w < 1$. Then, in a self-fulfilling inflation, the balance sheet of the central bank is deteriorating only if nominal money balances are falling.[1] This seems to suggest that in cases in which in a self-fulfilling hyperinflation nominal money balances are increasing central bank independence may not be an obstacle to ruling out self-fulfilling hyperinflations.

In the section that follows, I present an example of a self-fulfilling hyperinflation in which along the hyperinflationary path nominal money balances are increasing and argue that in this case one can rule out those inflationary paths through fractional reserve backing even in the case that the central bank is independent. The reason is that if nominal money balances are increasing on the way to a speculative inflation, the central bank accumulates real resources. At some point it must then be the case that the net worth of the central bank becomes nonnegative. That is, we must have that at some point $PF^G/M \geq 1$. At that exact instance, the central bank could switch to a pure price-level peg. This price-level peg will be sustainable because the central bank could, if need be, redeem the entire stock of money for reserves.

An Example of Ruling Out Speculative Inflations under Central Bank Independence

The Household

The household's problem is almost the same as the one described in section 7.3 of the Sims paper. The main difference is that it is assumed that

---

1. Note that $\pi + \rho$ denotes the nominal interest rate, which in equilibrium must be nonnegative.

time is discrete, whereas in the Sims paper time is continuous. Without loss of generality, one can assume that households can only hold two types of asset—money and foreign bonds—rather than three, as is assumed in the Sims paper. Under this assumption the household's budget constraint can be written as[2]

$$\max \sum_{t=0}^{\infty} \beta^t \ln c_t$$

subject to

(1) $$\frac{M_{t-1}}{P_t} + (1 + \rho_{t-1})F^P_{t-1} + y_t + \tau_t = c_t[1 + \psi(v_t)] + \frac{M_t}{P_t} + F^P_t$$

(2) $$v_t = \frac{P_t c_t}{M_t}$$

(3) $$\lim_{j \to \infty} \left(\prod_{s=t}^{j-1} \frac{1}{1 + \rho_{t+s}} \right) \left[\frac{M_{t+j-1}}{P_{t+j}} + (1 + \rho_{t+j-1})F^P_{t+j-1} \right] \geq 0.$$

The household takes P_t, ρ_t, y_t, and τ_t as exogenously given. The initial conditions of the household are M_{-1} and $(1 + \rho_{-1})F^P_{-1}$.

The Lagrangian of the household's maximization problem can then be written as

$$\mathcal{L} = \sum_{t=0}^{\infty} \beta^t \left\{ \ln c_t + \lambda_t \left[-c_t \left(1 + \psi \left[\frac{c_t}{M_t} \right] \right) - \frac{M_t}{P_t} \right. \right.$$
$$\left. \left. - F^P_t + \frac{M_{t-1}}{P_t} + (1 + \rho_{t-1})F^P_{t-1} + y_t + \tau_t \right] \right\}.$$

The first-order conditions are equations (1), (2), and (3) holding with equality and

(4) $$\frac{1}{c_t} = \lambda_t[1 + \psi(v_t) + v_t\psi'(v_t)]$$

(5) $$1 - v_t^2\psi'(v_t) = \beta \frac{\lambda_{t+1}}{\lambda_t} \frac{P_t}{P_{t+1}}$$

(6) $$\lambda_t = (1 + \rho_t)\beta\lambda_{t+1}$$

The Fiscal Authority

We assume that the fiscal authority does not issue bonds and simply rebates any seigniorage income it receives from the central bank to private households—that is,

---

2. The notation follows that of the Sims paper.

(7) $$\tau_t = \tau_t^B.$$

This assumption about the nature of fiscal policy is consistent with the treatment of fiscal policy in the Sims paper. The Sims paper, however, is less specific and simply states that "a passive fiscal policy keeps real debt under control regardless of the path of inflation."[3]

The Monetary Authority

At the end of period t, the central bank has real assets in the amount of F_t^G. Following the Sims paper, I assume that its period-by-period budget constraint is given by

(8) $$F_t^G = (1 + \rho_{t-1})F_{t-1}^G + \frac{M_t - M_{t-1}}{P_t} - \tau_t^B.$$

Central bank independence is interpreted in the Sims paper to mean that τ_t^B must be nonnegative; that is, the central bank cannot get backing for its liabilities in the form of transfers from the fiscal authority.[4] For simplicity, I will assume further that

(9) $$\tau_t^B = 0.$$

Equilibrium

A perfect-foresight equilibrium is a set of sequences $\{c_t, v_t, M_t, P_t, F_t^G, F_t^P, \lambda_t, \tau_t, \tau_t^B\}$ given exogenous $\{y_t, \rho_t\}$ and the initial values of M_{-1}, $(1 + \rho_{-1})F_{-1}^G$, and $(1 + \rho_{-1})F_{-1}^P$ satisfying equations (1)–(9), with equation (3) holding with equality, and one additional equation describing monetary policy.

To characterize the equilibrium dynamics, use equation (4) to eliminate λ_t from equation (5) to obtain

$$1 - v_t^2\psi'(v_t) = \beta \frac{1 + \psi(v_t) + v_t\psi'(v_t)}{1 + \psi(v_{t+1}) + v_{t+1}\psi'(v_{t+1})} \frac{c_t P_t}{c_{t+1} P_{t+1}}.$$

Using equation (2) this expression can be rewritten as

(10) $$1 - v_t^2\psi'(v_t) = \beta \frac{1 + \psi(v_t) + v_t\psi'(v_t)}{1 + \psi(v_{t+1}) + v_{t+1}\psi'(v_{t+1})} \frac{v_t}{v_{t+1}} \frac{M_t}{M_{t+1}}.$$

3. Central bank independence and non-Ricardian fiscal policy can give rise to default by the fiscal authority. See Uribe (2002) for a characterization of the equilibrium behavior of default under central bank independence and alternative non-Ricardian policy regimes.

4. A slightly different interpretation of central bank independence is that the central bank chooses τ_t^B subject to the constraint that it has to be nonnegative. For if the fiscal authority could determine the magnitude of τ_t^B, then the fiscal authority would effectively gain control over net worth of the central bank and could, for example, finance fiscal deficits with reserves. For the arguments that follow, it is important that the central bank, and not the fiscal authority, control the size of τ_t^B.

Consider now the case that the central bank follows a money growth rate peg by setting $M(0)$ and then letting M_t evolve according to the rule

(11)
$$M_{t+1} = \mu M_t; \qquad \mu > 1,$$

where μ denotes the gross growth rate of the money supply. For this monetary policy specification, equation (10) is a first-order difference equation in one endogenous variable, v_t. The steady state of that equation solves

$$1 - v^{*2}\psi'(v^*) = \beta\mu^{-1},$$

where v^* denotes the steady-state value of consumption velocity. For the particular functional form of $\psi(v)$ assumed in the Sims paper—that is, $\psi(v) = \gamma v/(1 + \phi v)$—we have

$$v^* = \frac{\sqrt{1 - \beta\mu^{-1}}}{\sqrt{\gamma} - \phi\sqrt{1 - \beta\mu^{-1}}}.$$

The existence of a steady state in which velocity is positive requires that $\gamma/\phi^2 > 1 - \beta\mu^{-1}$. One can show that if a steady state exists, it is unique. Next I wish to show that for any $v(0) > v^*$, equation (10) implies that as long as the money growth rate peg is in place $v_{t+1} > v_t$. To see this, rewrite equation (10) as

$$[1 + \psi(v_{t+1}) + v_{t+1}\psi'(v_{t+1})]v_{t+1} = \frac{\beta}{\mu[1 - v_t^2\psi'(v_t)]}[1 + \psi(v_t) + v_t\psi'(v_t)]v_t.$$

Let $G(v_t) = [1 + \psi(v_t) + v_t\psi'(v_t)]v_t$ and $F(v_t) = \beta/\{\mu[1 - v_t^2\psi'(v_t)]\}[1 + \psi(v_t) + v_t\psi'(v_t)]v_t$. Note that both $G(\cdot)$ and $F(\cdot)$ are increasing in v. Clearly, at $v = v^*$, $G(v) = F(v)$. However, for $v > v^*$, $F(v) > G(v)$ because $\beta/(\mu[1-v_t^2\psi'\{v_t\}] > 1$. Thus, in order for v_t to satisfy equilibrium condition (10) in the case that $v_0 > v^*$, it must be the case that v_t is increasing over time. If this explosive path for v can be supported as an equilibrium outcome, then speculative inflations are possible in this economy. For simplicity, we assume that $\beta(1 + \rho_t) = 1$ for all t. It follows from equation (4) that $\lambda_t = \lambda_0$ for all $t \geq 0$. By equation (4) the time path for consumption is then given by $c_t = 1/\lambda_0/(1 + \psi[v_t] + v_t\psi'[v_t])$ for all t. From this relation and the definition of velocity it follows that $P_0 = v_0 M_0\lambda_0(1 + \psi[v_0] + v_0\psi'[v_0])$. Iterating equation (1) forward and using equation (1) one obtains a present discounted value constraint of the form $\Sigma_{t=0}^\infty q_t(y_t + \tau_t - [1 + \psi(v_t)]c_t - M_t/P_t[R_{t+1} - 1]/R_{t+1}) + M_{-1}/P_0 + (1 + \rho)F_{-1}^P = 0$, where $q_t \equiv \Pi_{s=0}^{t-1}(1\,\rho_s)^{-1}$ and $R_{t+1} \equiv (1 + \rho_t)P_{t+1}/P_t = 1/(1 - v_t^2\psi'[v_t])$. Using the definition of velocity to eliminate M_t/P_t and equation (4), we can rearrange this expression to get $\Sigma_{t=0}^\infty q_t(y_t + \tau_t - [1 + \psi\{v_t\}]/[1 + \psi\{v_t\} + v_t\psi'\{v_t\}]/\lambda_0 - 1/[1 + \psi\{v_t\} + v_t\psi'\{v_t\}]/\lambda_0/v_t[R_{t+1} - 1]/R_{t+1}) + M_{-1}/v_0/M_0/(1 + \psi[v_0] + v_0\psi'[v_0])/y_0 + (1 + \rho)F_{-1}^P = 0$. Given a time path for v_t, this expression uniquely determines λ_0. Finally, note that because nominal money balances are not shrinking ($\mu \geq 1$) over time, central bank net wealth is increasing; that is, $P_{t+1} F_{t+1}^G/M_{t+1} > P_t F_t^G/M_t$.

The arguments just presented establish that a self-fulfilling inflation can be supported as an equilibrium outcome. The consequence of this result is that the central bank would not have control over inflation. This is because any $v_0 \geq v^*$ constitutes a perfect-foresight equilibrium. The existence of self-fulfilling inflations in economies in which monetary policy takes the form of a money growth rate peg is a well-known result; see, for example, Brock (1974, 1975), Obstfeld and Rogoff (1983), and Woodford (1994). Equally well known are ways to rule such speculative inflations out. In particular, Wallace (1981) and Obstfeld and Rogoff have suggested using fractional backing as a way to rule out speculative inflations. Under a policy of fractional backing the central bank commits to adopt a price-level target at some price level $\overline{P}$ should the price level pass a certain threshold. For this threat to be credible it must be the case that, at the moment the price-level target is implemented, the central bank has sufficient reserves on hand to exchange the entire money stock in circulation at the preannounced price; that is, we need that $\overline{P}F_{t-1}^G \geq M_{t-1}$, where t is the first period in which the price-level peg is in place. In standard analysis the fiscal and monetary authority are treated as a unit with a single consolidated budget constraint. In this case, the solvency requirement of the central bank is of no concern, for the central bank is implicitly guaranteed support from the fiscal authority (in the form of tax revenue) to redeem money for real assets should there be a need.

Our concern here is how we can rule a self-fulfilling inflation in this model even if the central bank is independent. Suppose that the central bank announces that it will follow a money growth rate peg with $\mu > 1$ and that should $v_0 > v^*$, then the money growth rate peg would only stay in place until $P_t F_t^G \geq M_t$. Let T denote the first period in which $P_t F_t^G \geq M_t$; then the central bank will keep the money growth rate peg until period T, and from period $T + 1$ on, it will follow a price-level peg of the form $P_t = P_T$ for all $t > T$. Then we know from equation (5) that $1 - v_T^2 \psi'(v_T) = \beta$, which implies that $v_T < v^*$. At the same time, with $v_0 > v^*$ equilibrium condition (31) can only be satisfied if $v_T > v_{T-1} > v_{T-2} > \ldots > v_0 > v^*$. But both of those conditions can never be satisfied at the same time. Therefore, $v_0 > v^*$ cannot be supported as a perfect-foresight equilibrium. It follows that fractional backing is capable of ruling out a self-fulfilling inflation even in the case in which the central bank starts out with negative net worth and never receives an injection of resources from the fiscal authority.

Finally, suppose that a central bank wishes to follow an interest rate feedback rule like the one studied in the Sims paper. One possible strategy to rule out self-fulfilling inflations in this case is to commit to switching to a money growth rate peg should central bank net worth fall too low, and in addition threaten to switch monetary policy yet again to a price-level target once the net worth of the central bank is sufficiently large.

The reason why fractional reserve backing does not work in the economy presented in section 7.3 of the Sims paper is that under the interest rate policy, net worth of the central bank may be falling along the self-fulfilling hyperinflation (see figure 7.2 of the Sims paper). Specifically, the analysis of the Sims paper shows that if a central bank starts with sufficiently negative net worth, it will never be able to reach solvency when the economy falls into a speculative inflation, and hence the central bank will never be able to announce a credible price-level peg. However, under a positive money growth rate peg, even under a self-fulfilling inflation, nominal money balances increase over time, and therefore the net worth of the central bank, $P_t F_t^G / M_t$, improves with time.

References

Benhabib, Jess, Stephanie Schmitt-Grohé, and Martín Uribe. 2001a. Monetary policy and multiple equilibria. *American Economic Review* 91 (March): 167–86.
———. 2001b. The perils of Taylor rules. *Journal of Economic Theory* 96 (February): 40–69.
———. 2002b. Chaotic interest rate rules. *American Economic Review Papers and Proceedings* 92 (May): 72–78.
———. 2002a. Avoiding liquidity traps. *Journal of Political Economy* 110 (June): 535–63.
———. 2003. Backward-looking interest-rate rules, interest rate smoothing, and macroeconomic instability. *Journal of Money, Credit and Banking* 35 (December): 1379–1412.
Brock, William. 1974. Money and growth: The case of long-run perfect foresight. *International Economic Review* 15 (October): 750–77.
———. 1975. A simple perfect foresight monetary model. *Journal of Monetary Economics* 1 (April): 133–50.
Clarida, Richard, Jordi Galí, and Mark Gertler. 2000. Monetary policy rules and macroeconomic stability: Evidence and some theory. *Quarterly Journal of Economics* 115 (February): 147–80.
Gray, Jo Anna. 1984. Dynamic instability in rational expectations models: An attempt to clarify. *International Economic Review* 25 (February): 93–122.
Leeper, Eric. 1991. Equilibria and active and passive monetary and fiscal policies. *Journal of Monetary Economics* 27 (February): 129–47.
Loyo, Eduardo. 1999. Tight money paradox on the loose: A fiscalist hyperinflation. Harvard University, John F. Kennedy School of Government. Manuscript, June.
Obstfeld, Maurice, and Kenneth Rogoff. 1983. Speculative hyperinflations in maximizing models: Can we rule them out? *Journal of Political Economy* 91: 675–87.
Svensson, Lars. 2001. The zero bound in an open economy: A foolproof way of escaping from a liquidity trap. *Monetary and Economic Studies* 19:277–312.
Uribe, Martín. 2002. A fiscal theory of sovereign risk. NBER Working Paper no. 9221. Cambridge, Mass.: National Bureau of Economic Research, September.
Wallace, Neil. 1981. A hybrid fiat-commodity monetary system. Journal of Economic Theory 25 (December): 421–30.
Woodford, Michael. 1994. Monetary policy and price-level determinacy in a cash-in-advance economy. *Economic Theory* 4:345–80.
———. 2003. Price-level determination under interest-rate rules. In *Interest and prices: Foundations of a theory of monetary policy,* 61–138. Princeton, N.J.: Princeton University Press.

Discussion Summary

Frederic Mishkin suggested that risks to financial stability imposed as important limits on monetary policy as did fiscal stability. In recent work with Guillermo Calvo, the authors argued that in emerging economies problems related to financial and fiscal policies were of a larger order of magnitude compared to problems related to monetary policy. Another example was the recent experience of Brazil, where depreciation in response to political uncertainty forced the inflation target to be raised. He agreed with Sims on the important role that the central bank's balance sheet had to play, and pointed out that the Bank of Japan had explained in this regard its reluctance to pursue more expansionary monetary policies.

Masaaki Shirakawa pointed out that in the current situation in Japan, with nominal interest rates even at long maturities near zero, the distinction between bonds and money becomes blurred, meaning that distinction between monetary policy and fiscal policy is also becoming blurred. At the moment, the amount of Japan government bonds held by the Bank of Japan was about 60 percent of the monetary base, which according to conventional measures could raise questions about the soundness of the Bank of Japan's balance sheet. The Bank of Japan had already engaged in substantial quantitative easing, expanding the size of its balance sheet from 15 percent of GDP four years ago to about 26 percent now. A related question was whether the Bank of Japan should take on different forms of risk by purchasing assets other than JGBs. For the Bank of Japan to engage in some form of fiscal policy, it would probably need some kind of commitment from the government to guarantee its solvency, if the general public questioned the ability of a central bank whose capital position is impaired to pursue adequate monetary policy.

Bennett McCallum questioned the view that transparency was the main advantage of inflation targeting, and argued that from the mid-1970s until the start of EMU the Bundesbank had been both the most successful central bank in terms of inflation control and one of the least transparent.

Christopher Sims responded that central banks usually faced legal restrictions on trading money for real assets, which pointed to the need for monetary-fiscal coordination in preventing deflationary spirals. This pointed to further need to rethink the boundaries between fiscal and monetary policy, and the proper role of central bank independence.

Inflation Targeting in
the United States?

Marvin Goodfriend

8.1 Introduction

In what sense can monetary policy as currently practiced by the Federal Reserve (Fed) be characterized as inflation targeting? And what, if any, features of an inflation-targeting policy regime should the Fed adopt more formally? These are the questions implicit in the title of this paper. U.S. macroeconomic performance has improved greatly since the early 1980s. The 1980s and 1990s saw two of the longest expansions in U.S. history and two of the mildest contractions in 1990–01 and 2001. The paper argues that this success can be attributed in large part to inflation-targeting policy procedures that the Fed has adopted gradually and implicitly over the last two decades. Much of the paper is devoted to explaining the origins of the Fed's implicit commitment to inflation targeting. Understanding the historical record suggests that some form of inflation targeting is likely to remain at the core of Fed monetary policy indefinitely.

Explicit inflation targeting is characterized by the announcement of an official target for the inflation rate and by an acknowledgment that low inflation is a priority for monetary policy. Inflation targeting also involves enhanced transparency of the procedures and objectives of monetary policy,

Marvin Goodfriend is senior vice president and policy advisor at the Federal Reserve Bank of Richmond.

This chapter benefited from seminars at the Federal Reserve Board and the Federal Reserve Bank of Richmond, and from discussions with B. Bernanke, A. Broaddus, R. Ferguson, B. Hetzel, R. King, D. Kohn, J. Lacker, B. McCallum, A. Meltzer, R. Mishkin, A. Orphanides, D. Small, S. Williamson, and A. Wolman. The views expressed are the author's alone and not necessarily those of the Federal Reserve Bank of Richmond or the Federal Reserve System.

and increased accountability of the central bank for attaining those objectives.[1]

To a large extent the explicit adoption of inflation targeting would merely continue the approach to monetary policy developed under Chairmen Volcker and Greenspan. Nevertheless, it seems worthwhile to consider whether more explicit inflation-targeting procedures could help the Fed sustain good monetary policy in the future.[2] Detailed, explicit, and transparent inflation-targeting procedures have been adopted by numerous central banks abroad to build and secure credibility for low inflation.[3] The main objection to some sort of explicit, public commitment to inflation targeting is the concern that inflation targeting would focus the Fed too narrowly on inflation at the expense of output and employment. Moreover, the Fed has achieved price stability and arrived at monetary policy procedures that resemble inflation targeting by "just doing it." So one might argue that the Fed has little need to adopt inflation targeting formally. Admittedly, the priority for low inflation is "in the water" at the Fed these days, but on the other hand "bottling" it for the future might not be a bad idea.

The Fed has been extraordinarily fortunate in having two remarkable chairmen since the late 1970s who skillfully helped to turn monetary policy from a source of instability into a major stabilizing force for the macroeconomy. It is well to remember how uniquely qualified they were to lead the Fed. Each had decades of professional experience observing the business cycle before becoming chairman—Volcker at the New York Fed and Greenspan as a private business economist in New York. Each had an extensive knowledge of financial markets and market participants from having worked in New York (see, e.g., Martin 2000 and Woodward 2000). Each had prior experience in Washington—Volcker at the Treasury and Greenspan at the Council of Economic Advisors. And both were trained economists. Moreover, both men personally experienced and understood as professionals the disruptive consequences of inflation. It will be difficult to find a successor to lead the Fed with all these qualifications who can navigate the appointments process successfully (see e.g., Stevenson 2002).

---

1. See Bernanke and Mishkin (1997) and Meyer (2001) for discussions of explicit inflation-targeting policy procedures.

2. Federal Open Market Committee (1995, 1996) contains early debates on inflation targeting. Saxton (1997, 2002) makes the case for inflation targeting. McCallum (2000) argues that the United States should formalize its monetary standard by committing to a low long-run target for inflation. A consensus among well-known monetary economists supporting a priority for low long-run inflation is evident in Federal Reserve Bank of Kansas City (1996).

3. See Bernanke et al. (1999), Blejer et al. (2000), Haldane (1995), King (1997), Kohn (2000), Liederman and Svensson (1995), Loayza and Soto (2002), McCallum (1997), Neumann and von Hagen (2002), Schmitt-Hebbel and Tapia (2002), Sterne (1999), and Svensson (2001).

A second, more fundamental reason to consider the adoption of explicit inflation targeting is simply that in a democracy a central bank should be fully accountable for the monetary policy that it pursues (see Blinder 1996). Adopting inflation-targeting procedures explicitly would improve the transparency of the policy process and the ability of Congress to hold the Fed accountable for monetary policy. For both of these reasons it is important to distill the essence of the implicit inflation-targeting procedures developed under Volcker and Greenspan and to consider how inflation targeting could be institutionalized to help the Fed sustain its improved performance after Chairman Greenspan retires.

The paper addresses these objectives in four parts. Section 8.2 describes the origins of the case for price stability in the United States by reviewing postwar monetary policy as practiced by the Fed and enumerating the problems created by failing to make price stability a priority. In particular, section 8.2 discusses the inflationary go/stop era and the Volcker disinflation, and describes the ways in which monetary policy as conducted in the Greenspan era can be characterized as implicit inflation targeting. Section 8.3 considers arguments for and against making low long-run inflation a priority, and whether a quantitative inflation target is a good idea. Section 8.4 considers inflation targeting in the short run, including complications involved in managing departures of inflation from its long-run target, the feasibility and desirability of strictly targeting a constant inflation objective in the short run, and the relationship of inflation targeting to countercyclical stabilization policy. Finally, section 8.5 suggests how to make the Fed's inflation-targeting procedures explicit in order to secure the commitment to low inflation, enhance transparency, and improve the Fed's accountability for attaining its monetary policy objectives. A brief summary concludes the paper.

8.2   Origins of the Case for Price Stability in the United States

In order to appreciate fully the rationale for inflation targeting as implicitly practiced in the United States today and why inflation targeting will likely remain at the core of Fed monetary policy in the future, one must understand the origins of the case for price stability in the United States. These are found in three distinct subperiods of postwar U.S. monetary history: the period of inflationary go/stop policy from the late 1950s to the late 1970s, the Volcker disinflation from 1979 to 1987, and the subsequent achievement of credibility for low inflation under Greenspan. The go/stop period illustrates the consequences of failing to make low inflation a priority for monetary policy. The Volcker period illustrates the difficulty in restoring credibility for low inflation after it has been compromised. And the Greenspan era illustrates how and why the Fed has come to target low inflation implicitly in recent years. Each subperiod is discussed in turn below.[4]

8.2.1   Inflationary Go/Stop Monetary Policy

The inflationary tendency evident during the period of go/stop monetary policy derived initially from a desire not to repeat the disastrous deflation of the 1930s. The disruptive potential of inflation was consistently underestimated, and each increase in inflation was tolerated in the belief that it would soon die down. Moreover, go/stop policy reflected the Fed's inclination to be responsive to the shifting balance of concerns between inflation and unemployment. In the "go" phase of the policy cycle inflation became a major concern only after it clearly moved above its previous trend; hence, the Fed did not tighten policy early enough to preempt inflationary outbursts before they became a problem. By the time the public became concerned about rising inflation, pricing decisions already embodied higher inflation expectations. At that point the Fed would *need a recession* to bring inflation and inflation expectations back down, and an aggressive increase in short-term interest rates would initiate the "stop" phase of the policy cycle. At best, there was only a relatively narrow window of public support for the Fed to raise interest rates. That window opened when rising inflation was widely judged to be a problem and closed after tighter monetary policy caused the unemployment rate to begin to rise. Thus, the Fed found it difficult to reverse rising inflation, and the trend rate of inflation tended to ratchet up with each go/stop policy cycle (see, e.g., Romer and Romer 1989).

Another reason for the rising inflation trend was that deliberately expansionary monetary policy in the go phase of the policy cycle came to be anticipated by workers and firms. Workers learned to take advantage of tight labor markets to make higher wage demands, and firms took advantage of tight product markets to pass along higher costs in higher prices. Increasingly aggressive wage and price behavior tended to neutralize the favorable effects of stimulative monetary policy. The Fed persisted in trying to pursue what it regarded as a reasonable balance between inflation and unemployment objectives. But in practice it became ever more expansionary on average in the pursuit of low unemployment, which produced correspondingly higher inflation and inflation expectations. As a result, lenders demanded ever-higher inflation premia in bond rates. In the absence of an anchor for inflation, inflation expectations and bond rates moved higher and fluctuated widely, which destabilized the economy and complicated countercyclical stabilization policy enormously.

In retrospect, the central problem for most of the postwar period up to

---

4. Goodfriend (1997) provides a longer-term historical perspective on the evolution of monetary theory and policy.

the Volcker disinflation beginning in 1979 was that the Fed tended to justify its periodic inflation-fighting actions against an implicit objective for low unemployment. In doing so, the Fed made monetary policy a source of instability and wound up worsening both inflation *and* unemployment. Eventually the Fed recognized that it would be better to justify its actions to stimulate employment against a commitment to low inflation.

8.2.2   The Volcker Disinflation: 1979–87

The case for price stability as we know it today was strengthened by the extraordinary difficulties encountered in dealing with inflation during the period of the Volcker disinflation from 1979 to 1987. In particular, the Fed experienced the adverse consequences of a near total collapse of credibility for low inflation, and learned how difficult it is to pursue interest rate policy to restore credibility for low inflation once that credibility has been thoroughly compromised. Although the challenges confronting the Fed during the Volcker disinflation were far larger than those today, their nature is similar and still relevant. This section considers, in turn, four features of this tumultuous period: the breakdown of mutual understanding between the Fed and the public, the loss of flexibility to use interest rate policy to stabilize the output gap, the nature of the cost of restoring low inflation, and the inflation scare problem.

The Breakdown of Mutual Understanding between the Fed and the Public

By the time that Volcker became Fed chairman in 1979, the sharp increase in the level and volatility of inflation and inflation expectations born of the previous decade's go/stop monetary policy made it exceptionally difficult for the Fed to contribute constructively to macroeconomic stabilization. The Fed continued to make monetary policy by managing short-term nominal interest rates. But the effect of interest rate policy on the economy is determined by its effect on *real* interest rates—nominal rates minus inflation expectations. Stabilization policy became more difficult, in part, because relatively large adjustments in the real rate were necessary to stabilize the economy. Moreover, the Fed found it increasingly difficult to judge the public's inflation expectations and to gauge how its own policy actions might influence those expectations. Hence, the Fed could not judge how a given nominal interest rate policy action would translate into an adjustment in real interest rates. In short, there was a breakdown of mutual understanding between the Fed and the public: the public could no longer discern the Fed's policy intentions, and the Fed could not predict how the economy would respond to its policy actions. Consequently, the opportunity for policy mistakes was greatly enlarged, and macroeconomic stabilization policy became increasingly difficult.

As a result, the Volcker Fed came to appreciate what the Fed had taken for granted previously—that monetary policy must be conducted so as to preserve a mutual understanding between the public and the Fed. In particular, the Volcker Fed realized that price stability must be the cornerstone of that mutual understanding. In large part the subsequent disinflation can be seen as an effort to rebuild that mutual understanding in order to rehabilitate countercyclical stabilization policy.

Loss of Flexibility to Use Interest Rate Policy to Stabilize Output Relative to Potential

When the Fed's credibility for low inflation is in question, the Fed loses the *flexibility* to use interest rate policy to stabilize output relative to its potential. Obviously, when the Fed needs an output gap to restrain inflation and stabilize inflation expectations, it cannot also use interest rate policy to narrow that output gap. The behavior of interest rate policy in the brief recession of 1980 makes this point well.

The Volcker Fed raised the nominal federal funds rate target sharply from around 11 percent in September of 1979 to around 17 percent in April 1980 in its initial effort to bring down inflation. About half of that 6 percentage point increase occurred in the fall of 1979. January 1980 later turned out to be a National Bureau of Economic Research (NBER) business cycle peak, and evidence of a weakening economy caused the Fed to pause in its aggressive tightening between late 1979 and March 1980. But with the federal funds rate held steady, the thirty-year (long) bond rate jumped by around 2 percentage points between December and February despite the weakening in the economy. A number of factors contributed to the unprecedented increase in inflation expectations evident in the sharp rise in the bond rate: the ongoing increase in oil prices, the unprecedented rise in the price of gold, and the Soviet invasion of Afghanistan. In addition, the Fed's hesitation to tighten further probably created doubts about its willingness to bear the output costs necessary to reduce inflation. In any case, faced with this evidence of a further increase in inflation expectations, the Fed was forced to react with an enormous 3 percentage point increase in the nominal funds rate in March. The short recession that occurred in the first half of 1980 probably resulted from this aggressive policy tightening in conjunction with the imposition of credit controls in March (see Schreft 1990).

Thus, interest rate policy helped to precipitate the 1980 recession as it would precipitate the 1981–82 recession, and for the same reasons. The difference is that in 1980 the Fed cut the federal funds rate sharply by around 8 percentage points between April and July to act against the downturn, and the recession ended quickly with around 8 percent real gross domestic product (GDP) growth in the fourth quarter (4Q) of 1980. However, inflation remained high in 1980. The lesson of 1980 was that the Fed could not restore credibility for low inflation if it continued to utilize interest rate policy to stabilize the output gap.

The Cost of Restoring Credibility for Low Inflation

The Volcker disinflation made particularly clear why it is so costly to re-store credibility for low inflation once it has been compromised. Consider the striking disinflation that occurred in 1981. In early 1981 the Fed main-tained the nominal federal funds rate at 19 percent. As measured by per-sonal consumption expenditures (PCE) inflation, which was around 10 percent in Q1 1981, real short-term interest rates were then a very high 9 percent. Not surprisingly, the aggressive policy tightening began to take hold by midyear. The NBER business cycle peak was reached in July, and real GDP growth fell at a 6 percent annual rate in Q4 1981 and at a 5 per-cent annual rate in Q1 1982. The Fed brought the nominal federal funds rate down from 19 percent in the summer to the 14 percent range at the end of the year, where it remained until the summer of 1982, when it was re-duced further to around 10 percent.

The 5 percentage point funds rate reduction through the end of 1981 was large in nominal terms. But PCE inflation also fell by about 5 percentage points by early 1982 to the 5 percent range. To the extent that short-term inflation expectations followed the decline in actual inflation during 1981, the Fed maintained an extraordinarily high 9 percent real funds rate *dur-ing* the recession! Amazingly, the Volcker Fed maintained a 9 percent real short rate even as the recession worsened and the unemployment rate rose from around 7 percent in July 1981 toward a peak of nearly 10 percent at the recession trough in November 1982.

Why did interest rate policy remain so extraordinarily tight even after the sharp break in inflation in 1981? One reason is that the behavior of long bond rates suggested that the Fed's credibility for low inflation continued to deteriorate. In fact, the long bond rate actually *rose* by about 3 percent-age points from January 1981 to more than 14 percent in October, even as the economy weakened. And although the rate showed some tendency to decline thereafter, it remained in the 13 to 14 percent range until it began to come down more persistently in the summer of 1982. Only after this ev-idence emerged in the bond market, that the Fed was finally beginning to acquire credibility for low inflation, did the Fed ease policy decisively in August 1982. This policy easing paved the way for an end to the recession. Inflation stabilized at around 4 percent. And real GDP grew by a spectac-ular 6.7 percent in 1983 and 4.5 percent in 1984.

The Volcker Fed disinflation of 1981 is an extreme illustration of the point mentioned in section 8.2.2 that, in practice, the Fed *needs a recession* to restore credibility for low inflation after it has been compromised. The reason is this: if a disinflation is fully credible, then wage and price inflation can slow immediately without much effect on real interest rates or output (see Ball 1994). If, however, as in 1981, a disinflation is not immediately credible, then wage and price inflation continue as before. If the Fed persists in tightening monetary policy anyway, real interest rates rise, aggregate demand moves below potential output, employment falls, and the output gap thus created causes wage and price inflation to slow gradually. Postwar U.S. monetary history makes it abundantly clear that disinflation is costly in practice because credibility for low inflation is hard to acquire after it has been lost. Moreover, the Fed's commitment to low inflation is only as credible as the public's support for it. And that support usually remains in question until a disinflation is nearly complete.

The Inflation Scare Problem

The Fed's credibility problems during the Volcker era showed up as "inflation scares," sharply rising long-term bond rates reflecting rising long-term inflation expectations.[5] Inflation scares presented the Fed with a costly dilemma because ignoring them would encourage even more doubt about the central bank's commitment to low inflation. Yet raising real short rates to restore credibility for low inflation risked precipitating a recession. There were four striking examples of inflation scares in the bond rate during the Volcker era. As discussed above, the Fed's response to the first two scares in 1980 and 1981 precipitated recessions in those years.

The third inflation scare occurred in 1983–84. By then, inflation was running at around 4 percent, and, for the most part, it held in that range during this episode. Nonetheless, an inflation scare in the bond market raised the long rate from the 10 percent range in the summer of 1983 to its peak the following summer in the 13 percent range—only about 1 percentage point short of its 1981 peak even though inflation was over 6 percentage points lower in 1983 than in early 1981! The Fed reacted by moving the nominal funds rate up from the 8 percent range to the 11 percent range. Inflation remained low, so the tightening took the real short-term interest rate up by about 3 percentage points to around 7 percent briefly in mid-1984 before the inflation scare subsided and the bond rate began to come down. In this case, the high real short rate needed to contain the scare succeeded in bringing real GDP growth down to a sustainable 2 to 3 percent range in the second half of 1984. This episode was important because it demonstrated that a well-timed and well-calibrated series of preemptive interest rate policy actions could defuse an inflation scare without creating a recession. The 6 percentage point drop in the bond rate from its June 1984 peak to the 7 percent range in early 1986 indicates that the Fed acquired enormous additional credibility for low inflation during this period, in large part no doubt due to the aggressive inflation-fighting actions taken in 1983–84.

5. See Goodfriend (1993). Ireland (1996a) uses the modern theory of interest to show that movements in long bond rates reliably signal changes in expected inflation. Gurkaynak, Sack, and Swanson (2003) present evidence that the apparent "excess sensitivity" of long bond rates to macrodata largely reflects fluctuations in inflation expectations.

Remarkably, even after the Volcker Fed had demonstrated its determination to act against inflation for almost a decade, there was yet another inflation scare when the bond rate rose by 2 percentage points from March to October 1987. Surprisingly, the Fed reacted little to this scare. In part, this may have reflected real growth weaker than in 1983–84. The scare may have occurred in part because Volcker was near the end of his term as chairman and there was doubt about whether the Fed under Volcker's successor would continue to place a high priority on low inflation. In any case, the 1987 scare is particularly striking evidence of the fragility of the credibility of the Fed's commitment to low inflation, possibly connected to the transition from one Fed chairman to another.

8.2.3   The Greenspan Era: 1987 to the Present

When Alan Greenspan succeeded Paul Volcker as Fed chairman in the summer of 1987 the inflation scare needed immediate attention. However, the October 1987 stock market crash forced the Fed to *ease* monetary policy and put off raising interest rates until the spring of 1988. Judging by the behavior of the long bond rate, which did not return to its early 1987 levels until 1992, it took the Greenspan Fed about five years to overcome the 1987 inflation scare.

The discussion of the Greenspan era below is in four parts. It begins by emphasizing the difficulty of reversing even a relatively minor loss of credibility for low inflation. It then describes the preemptive interest rate policy actions in 1994 that achieved virtual price stability and the benefits, thereafter, of having achieved full credibility for low inflation. One can see in the behavior of the Greenspan Fed the emergence of an implicit inflation-targeting policy regime. The section concludes by pointing out five aspects of inflation targeting practiced implicitly by the Greenspan Fed.

Reversing a Minor Loss of Credibility for Low Inflation

As a result of the 1987 inflation scare and the policy easing that followed the October 1987 crash, PCE inflation *rose* by over 2 percentage points from around 3 percent in 1986 to around 5.5 percent in 1990. In response, the Fed raised the funds rate by over 3 percentage points to a peak of nearly 10 percent from the spring of 1988 to the spring of 1989 in an effort to reverse the rise in inflation and inflation expectations. As a result of those policy actions and the Gulf War recession, inflation began to recede in 1991. However, the unemployment rate rose by about 1 percentage point during the 1990–91 recession and rose further to nearly 8 percent in June 1992 during the "jobless recovery" that followed. Here is another instance where, having been insufficiently preemptive in containing inflation (in 1987 and 1988), monetary policy was obliged to be more restrictive than otherwise. With its credibility for low inflation compromised earlier, the Greenspan Fed lowered the federal funds rate tentatively and haltingly from a peak around 8 percent at the start of the recession in mid-1990 to 3 percent in the fall of 1992. By September 1992, the bond rate had returned to the 7 percent range, inflation had come down to around 3 percent, and the real federal funds rate was therefore near zero.

The zero real short rate was in place for eighteen months from September 1992 to February 1994. During that time the unemployment rate came down to 6.6 percent, the bond rate fell to the 6 percent range, and the inflation rate fell slightly. It appeared that the Fed had acquired an additional degree of credibility for low inflation. To secure that credibility, however, the Fed would need to preempt rising inflation by raising real short rates as the economy strengthened further in 1994. At a minimum, the Fed would have to move real short rates up from zero to a range historically consistent with sustainable growth without inflation. In part, preemptive policy was motivated by yet another inflation scare in the bond market. The more than 2 percentage point increase in the bond rate from late 1993 to November 1994 indicated that the Fed's credibility for low inflation still was not secure.

Preemptive Interest Rate Policy in 1994

The series of policy actions that lifted the real funds rate by 3 percentage points from February 1994 to February 1995 marked the Greenspan Fed's first preemptive actions against inflation. Like the Volcker Fed's 1983–84 actions, the Greenspan Fed's 1994 preemptive policy held the line on inflation without creating unemployment. After falling to the mid–5 percent range during 1994, the unemployment rate moved up only slightly in April 1995 and then began to fall again. The 1994 tightening proved once more that well-timed preemptive interest rate policy actions are nothing to be feared. By January 1996 the bond rate was down to around 6 percent, and there was widespread talk of the "death of inflation" (see Bootle 1996).

The successful preemptive policy action in 1994 brought the economy to virtual price stability. Inflation and inflation expectations were anchored more firmly than ever before. Inflation has remained low ever since, and long bond rates have remained in the 5 to 6 percent range with little evidence of inflation scares. Remarkably, price stability was maintained even though the economy grew in the 4 percent range annually from 1996 through 1999, and the unemployment rate briefly fell below 4 percent for a while. Unquestionably, rising productivity growth during the period helped to hold down inflation, but the fact that the economy achieved this growth without much of an increase in inflation or an inflation scare further reinforced the Greenspan Fed's credibility for low inflation.[6]

6. Goodfriend (2002b) discusses the consequences of rising productivity growth and credible price stability in the second half of the 1990s for inflation and monetary policy.

Benefits of Full Credibility for Low Inflation

Three closely related benefits of full credibility for low inflation have been apparent in the second half of the Greenspan era. First, credibility helped the economy to operate well beyond the levels that might have created inflation and inflation scares in the past. Second, when in 1999 and 2000 the Fed set out to slow the growth of real aggregate demand to a more sustainable rate, it raised real short rates to the 5 percent range, somewhat below the range of real short rates it had targeted in previous periods of policy restraint. As in 1994, less real rate restraint was necessary in 2000 because the Fed did not have to restore low inflation or its credibility for low inflation after they had been compromised. Having attained price stability, the Fed did not need *a recession* to bring inflation and inflation expectations down. The Fed's objective in 2000 was *only* to bring aggregate demand back into line with potential output so that the expansion would not end with an outbreak of inflation, an inflation scare, or an unsustainable real boom and bust.

Third, when the expansion *did* end in an unsustainable boom and bust, the fact that inflation and inflation expectations were well anchored enabled the Greenspan Fed to cut the nominal federal funds rate aggressively from 6.5 percent to 1.75 percent in 2001 to cushion the fall in aggregate demand and employment.[7] Amazingly, the Fed was able to cut the real federal funds rate by 4 or 5 percentage points to around zero without a hint of an inflation scare. Since the Fed did not *need* a recession in 2001, it had the *flexibility* to cut the real funds rate aggressively to prevent one.

8.2.4 Implicit Inflation Targeting Practiced by the Greenspan Fed

When one considers the Greenspan era as a whole, it would appear that the Greenspan Fed adopted, gradually and implicitly, an approach to monetary policy that can be characterized as inflation targeting. To begin, the Greenspan Fed must have appreciated something like the case for price stability described above as it developed in the years of go/stop policy and during the Volcker disinflation. Moreover, Chairman Greenspan testified in 1989 in favor of a qualitative zero-inflation objective for the Fed, defined as a situation in which "the expected rate of change of the general level of prices ceases to be a factor in individual and business decisionmaking" (see Greenspan 1990, 6). Thus, it is reasonable to think that the Greenspan Fed set out to achieve low enough inflation to make that definition of price stability a reality. This is the *first* sense in which it

---

7. Some economists argue that monetary policy should have acted more aggressively against the extreme asset price increases in the late 1990s. See Bernanke and Gertler (1999) and Goodfriend (2003) for reasons why interest rate policy should not react directly to asset prices.

is plausible to think that the Greenspan Fed has adopted an implicit form of inflation targeting.

However, the Greenspan Fed clearly has not focused singlemindedly on achieving low inflation. Had it done so, it surely could have restored low inflation and the credibility for low inflation lost in 1987–88 sooner than it did. However, given the initial credibility problems, attempting to act against inflation too aggressively could have come at too great a cost in lost employment and output. It was plausible to think that the relatively small slippage in inflation and credibility for low inflation that occurred in the late 1980s could be contained eventually without an aggressive monetary tightening. Such reasoning probably contributed to the decision to pursue a mildly restrictive interest rate policy to build back credibility for low inflation gradually. In other words, the Greenspan Fed displayed great patience in overcoming the effects on inflation and Fed credibility of the unfortunate initial conditions (the 1987 inflation scare and stock market crash) that it started with.

Moreover, the Greenspan Fed did not proceed to push the inflation rate down deliberately to price stability after 1992 in a way that might have been costly in terms of employment and output. Instead, preemptive policy was utilized in 1994 to reinforce the transition to price stability. The Fed held real short rates near zero for a year and a half until the economy showed strength in 1994 and then acted to preempt what might have been a cyclical increase in inflation. Holding the line on inflation proved to be a virtually costless way of moving the economy to price stability and fully securing the Fed's credibility for low inflation.

The manner in which the Greenspan Fed moved to restore credibility for low inflation before 1992 and pushed to price stability after 1992 demonstrates a *second* sense in which it may be said to have targeted inflation implicitly. It is clear that the Greenspan Fed practiced a form of *flexible* inflation targeting in its pursuit of price stability.

Arguably, it is plausible to think that the Fed has finally achieved price stability in the sense that a measure of inflation favored by the Fed, core PCE inflation, has remained in the 1 to 2 percent range since the mid-1990s (see Federal Open Market Committee 1996, 11). It is difficult to imagine circumstances that would cause the Greenspan Fed to *deliberately* target core PCE inflation *above* 2 percent in either the long run or the short run. This is the third sense in which it may be said that the Greenspan Fed has adopted an implicit form of inflation targeting. Likewise, it is hard to imagine any circumstances in which the Greenspan Fed would *deliberately* target core PCE inflation below 1 percent. There is no reason to take the inflation rate lower than that, given the risk of deflation and the problems associated with the zero bound on nominal interest rates. This is the fourth sense in which it may be said that the Greenspan Fed has adopted an implicit form of inflation targeting.

Finally, it is clear that the Greenspan Fed practices inflation targeting in large part to enhance the flexibility of interest rate policy to stabilize the output gap over the business cycle. For instance, the discussion above explained how the Greenspan Fed exploited its full credibility for low inflation to lower short-term interest rates flexibly to cushion the 2001 recession. In this sense, inflation targeting as practiced by the Greenspan Fed involves a *fifth* characteristic: constrained countercyclical stabilization policy. In other words, the Greenspan Fed appears willing to pursue aggressive countercyclical interest rate policy as long as inflation and inflation expectations remain anchored in or near the long-run target range.

8.3   Should Low Long-Run Inflation Be a Priority?

Since the record shows that the Greenspan Fed has pursued inflation targeting implicitly, we now ask what features of those implicit inflation-targeting procedures should be made explicit. We use the case for inflation targeting developed in section 8.2 to help answer that question. In this section we consider only whether the Fed should make low *long-run* inflation a priority. We begin with arguments supporting a priority for price stability. Then we consider opposing arguments and counterarguments. Finally we consider the case for a quantitative long-run inflation target.

8.3.1   Arguments Supporting a Long-Run Priority for Price Stability

A priority for low long-run inflation derives not so much from a belief in its intrinsic value relative to other goals such as full employment and economic growth, but from theory and evidence suggesting that monetary policy encourages employment and growth in the long run mostly by controlling inflation (see, e.g., Feldstein 1997 and Federal Reserve Bank of Kansas City 1996). Moreover, the U.S. monetary policy record outlined in section 8.2 suggests that the *flexibility* to pursue short-run stabilization policy has been enhanced by a credible commitment to low inflation. Arguably, that credibility would be strengthened if the Fed announced publicly a priority for low long-run inflation.[8]

Further, in 1994 the Fed began to announce its current federal funds rate target publicly for the first time. The Fed became more forthcoming about its policy instrument in part because Congress and the public expressed an interest in greater transparency in monetary policy. For instance, all twelve reserve bank presidents were invited to explain their views on monetary policy before the Senate banking committee in March 1993 and again before the House banking committee in October of that year. This increased trans-

---

8. Fed officials have spoken repeatedly over the years about the benefits of low inflation and the Fed's commitment to price stability. However, the Fed has not asserted a priority for low long-run inflation.

parency of the Fed's policy instrument, the federal funds rate, has enhanced the understanding of monetary policy and facilitated a public debate about Fed policy. A healthy debate about whether the Fed's policy actions are appropriate to achieve its objectives is to be expected. But the current situation is one in which the Fed has not clarified its priority for low inflation as well as it might. Thus, a debate about Fed policy actions in the current institutional environment can become a debate about the Fed's policy objectives.

The combination of instrument transparency with ambiguity about the priority for low inflation creates problems for monetary policy. For instance, the visibility of the Fed's aggressive preemptive tightening against inflation in 1994 attracted much criticism in part because the priority the Fed placed on low inflation had not been clarified, understood, and accepted by Congress and the public. The criticism from Congress and elsewhere at the time was seen by many as a threat to price stability and probably contributed to the severity of the inflation scare that raised the long bond rate by over 2 percentage points in 1994. Especially now that price stability has been achieved and the transition costs are behind us, the Fed's commitment to long-run price stability could be clarified to minimize the risk that a debate about Fed policy actions could create inflation scares in the future.[9]

8.3.2   Opposing Arguments and Counterarguments

The most fundamental argument against making low *long-run* inflation a priority is that it might unduly constrain interest rate policy from stabilizing output relative to its potential in the *short run*. The concern is that, in practice, the Fed might become more timid in using interest rate policy flexibly to stabilize real economic activity over the business cycle for fear of the inflationary consequences. That being said, the policy record outlined above shows that the Fed's power to stabilize the output gap over the business cycle was considerably *enhanced* as inflation and inflation expectations became more firmly anchored. Nevertheless, the above argument must be taken seriously.

The second argument against formally adopting a priority for low long-run inflation is that there is little to be gained, since the Fed has achieved and maintained low inflation by "just doing it." The Greenspan Fed appears to have acquired near-full credibility for low inflation without a formal priority for low inflation. And there is every reason to think that the Greenspan Fed can continue to pursue inflation targeting implicitly and successfully. This argument seems to take it for granted that the Fed needs no institutional help in carrying on after Chairman Greenspan retires.

---

9. Gurkaynak, Sack, and Swanson (2003) present evidence indicating that the Bank of England's credible commitment to an inflation target helped to anchor long-term inflation expectations and bond rates in the United Kingdom.

The third argument admits that a legislative mandate for low long-run inflation would be helpful but stresses that it would be awkward, inappropriate, and potentially counterproductive for the Fed to announce a priority for low long-run inflation unilaterally. To be sure, the Fed is an independent central bank in the sense that its interest rate policy actions are not subject to further evaluation by other authorities. And Congress did not object to the Volcker disinflation and the Greenspan Fed transition to price stability. Yet the Fed is supposed to take direction on its goals from Congress. The current understanding between the Fed and Congress would appear to amount to a "don't ask, don't tell" equilibrium: Congress doesn't ask the Fed whether it places a priority on low long-run inflation, and the Fed does not say whether it has such a priority.[10] Both the Fed and Congress appear to be satisfied with "don't ask, don't tell," so apparently the status quo is satisfactory.

The problem with this argument is that waiting for Congress to endorse formally a priority for low long-run inflation poses some risks. Currently, a large fraction of the public has had firsthand experience with inflation and naturally supports the view that it must be contained. But as the Fed succeeds over time in maintaining low inflation, that collective memory will fade, and Congress will be less likely to mandate a priority for price stability than it may be today. If the Greenspan Fed, in its capacity as the repository of central-banking expertise in the United States, believes that monetary policy would benefit from a legislatively mandated priority for low long-run inflation, then it could *ask* Congress for one. The time is right to do so. Because price stability has been achieved, transition costs are no longer an obstacle. More important, the public has great confidence in the Greenspan Fed, and future Feds will have less personal experience with and appreciation of the reasons why monetary policy would benefit from such a mandate. Institutionalizing that knowledge and experience in a mandate will go a long way toward insuring that future generations do not repeat the inflationary mistakes of the past.

8.3.3   The Case for a Quantitative Long-Run Inflation Target

The above discussion made the case that low long-run inflation should be a priority for monetary policy. In principle, that priority could be specified in either a qualitative or a quantitative way. If a priority for low inflation is largely about anchoring inflation expectations, then arguably much of the benefit could be derived by specifying the priority in qualitative language using Chairman Greenspan's definition of price stability. For instance, such a commitment could be stated as a priority for maintaining

---

10. Federal Open Market Committee (FOMC; 1996, 64, 67, 72) indicates the consensus within the FOMC on the desirability of a 2 percent long-run objective for a CPI measure of inflation.

monetary conditions in which "the expected rate of change of the general level of prices ceases to be a factor in individual and business decision making." The discussion above suggests that explicitly adopting even a qualitative priority for low long-run inflation would be a major step forward for monetary policy.

There are a number of reasons, however, why a priority for low long-run inflation could be stated usefully in quantitative terms. The Fed could choose the measure of inflation to target from any number of candidate measures that have been exceptionally stable since the mid-1990s. Moreover, Fed staff routinely use for internal policy simulations a quantitative working definition of low inflation that constitutes price stability. Arguably, that working definition is the FOMC's de facto quantitative long-run inflation target, and it would serve naturally as a quantitative long-run inflation target for external purposes as well. It makes sense to put a quantitative lower bound on inflation to protect against deflation and the problem of the zero bound on nominal interest rates. Announcing an explicit lower bound on inflation would make the public more confident that the Fed will not allow the United States to fall into a Japanese-style deflation, zero-bound trap. That, in turn, would protect against potentially destabilizing *deflation* scares, to which the Fed would have to respond by pushing the nominal funds rate closer to zero. If it makes sense for the Fed to announce an explicit lower bound on its long-run inflation target to protect against deflation, then it also makes sense to announce an explicit *upper* bound to emphasize that the Fed intends to hold the line on inflation as well. Finally, a quantitative long-run inflation target would serve as a better benchmark against which to judge departures from price stability in the short run.

A target *range* would have advantages over a *point* inflation target. A target range would give the Fed a "safe harbor" within which it would not have to explain or respond to movements in inflation very much. Only when inflation moved outside the range would the Fed be expected to explain how policy would return inflation to the range. Without a range, the Fed might find it difficult to switch rhetorically from relatively little concern about inflation to greater concern when inflation moved up or down on a sustained basis. Specifying a quantitative range would not tie the Fed's hands in practice. What it would do is put the burden of proof on the Fed to explain how it intends to return inflation to its target. And that would be a valuable disciplining device.

A range of 1 to 2 percent for core PCE inflation monthly over twelve or twenty-four months earlier would be a reasonable quantitative long-run target. The Fed is apparently comfortable using the core PCE price index to measure inflation (see Federal Open Market Committee 1996, 11). Core PCE inflation has ranged between 1 and 2 percent since 1997. Given this observed stability, a 1 percentage point range should provide enough lee-way for routine short-run fluctuations of inflation. Finally, core PCE infla-tion would provide a more stable measure than overall PCE inflation against which to judge departures from price stability in the short run.

The main reasons for the Fed not to adopt a quantitative inflation target are fourfold. First, the Fed may not be quite sure yet what measure of in-flation and target range to adopt. Second, as discussed above, there is no pressing need to adopt a quantitative inflation target. Finally, the Fed's credibility for low inflation may actually be jeopardized if, for whatever reason, it cannot keep inflation within its long-run quantitative target range. Fourth, adopting a quantitative inflation target may generate pres-sure to adopt a quantitative target for the unemployment rate, which would create problems for monetary policy of the sort encountered during the go/stop period reviewed in section 8.2.1.

8.4   Inflation Targeting in the Short Run

This section considers inflation targeting in the short run. It begins by outlining complications that the Fed must confront in managing depar-tures of inflation from the long-run target range. It then suggests strongly that it is both feasible and desirable for the Fed to keep inflation within its long-run inflation target even in the short run. The section closes by point-ing out that strict inflation targeting is compatible with stabilizing output at its potential over the business cycle in a reasonable benchmark macro-model.

This discussion does not deny that inflation could be pushed outside of the target range in the short run. The analysis asserts only that it is likely to take an exceptional event to destabilize inflation when the Fed purpose-fully pursues price stability. Undoubtedly, bad luck or bad judgment could create excessively inflationary or deflationary conditions. If that were to happen, then presumably the Fed would return inflation to the target range flexibility, much as the Greenspan Fed restored credibility for low inflation in the late 1980s and early 1990s.

8.4.1   Managing Departures of Inflation from the Long-Run Target

If inflation moves outside its long-run target range, for whatever reason, the Fed must choose a path for its interest rate policy instrument that bal-ances the speed with which inflation is returned to target against the cost in lost output relative to potential. The Fed must decide how *fast* to rebuild credibility for its long-run inflation objective. As a formal matter, the deci-sion would depend on the following factors: (a) the mechanism by which interest rate policy is assumed to be transmitted to aggregate demand in the macromodel used by the Fed; (b) the specification of the relationships among aggregate demand, the output gap, and the inflation-generating process in that macromodel; (c) the relative weights placed on the output gap and inflation stabilization in the Fed's (implicit) loss function, or (d) the length of time that the Fed arbitrarily allows for returning its conditional inflation forecast to the long-run target; and (e) any conditional information on current shocks and adjustments to the model or the loss function weights due to special circumstances or evolving economic conditions. In sum, the policy response would depend on all information available to the Fed affecting the conditional inflation forecast and the output-gap forecast (see Svensson 1999 and Galí 2001).

The complexity of the elements listed above shows how difficult it is for the Fed to manage inflation once it moves outside its long-run target range. Arguably, the inflation-generating process is the weakest part of the macromodel. Among other things the cost, in terms of lost output relative to potential, of returning inflation to its long-run range depends on the credibility of the Fed's commitment to do so. The historical record discussed in section 8.2 suggests that such credibility is sensitive to the Fed's actions *themselves* in the context of other aspects of the political economy in a way that is difficult to model. In any particular case the Fed must *judge* the extent to which drawing out the return of inflation to its long-run target might be counterproductive by reducing the credibility of its intention to bring inflation all the way back down. That consideration must be balanced against attempting to bring inflation down before the credibility for doing so has been built up. An error in either direction would increase the output cost of restoring price stability.

Another problem arises because the Fed may tend to overstate the extent to which inflation has an inherent tendency to persist after it has been shocked. U.S. inflation has exhibited a high degree of persistence in the past (see Fuhrer and Moore 1995 and Goodfriend and King 2001, 75–81). The Fed tolerated outbursts of inflation in the go phase of the policy cycle and showed only a limited inclination to risk recession to reverse those outbursts but a willingness to allow "opportunistic" shocks to reduce inflation. Thus, both positive and negative inflation shocks tended to be propagated through time.[11] Firms would quickly build a shock to inflation into inflation expectations and incorporate those expectations into their own price-setting behavior. By underestimating its own role in creating inflation persistence in the past, the Fed may be too quick to accommodate and propagate deviations of inflation from its long-run target in the present (see Cecchetti 1995 and Cogley and Sargent 2001).

It is optimal for the monetary authority to vary its short-run inflation target deliberately in response to some shocks in some macromodels. How-

11. The empirical findings reported in Atkeson and Ohanian (2001) reflect this behavior.

ever, that optimal variation depends sensitively on the details of the macro-model and on the size and type of shocks hitting the economy. Given our uncertainty about the structure of the economy, the difficulty in promptly and accurately identifying the shocks hitting the economy, and the complications discussed above, attempting to *fine-tune* the inflation target in the short run is more likely to be counterproductive than not (see Orphanides and Williams 2002 and Schmitt-Grohé and Uribe 2002). In any case, the historical record suggests that the Fed's ability to deliberately and systematically manipulate inflation in response to shocks is very limited. Moreover, such attempted manipulation would open the door to inflation scares. For all these reasons the presumption must be that it is inadvisable for the Fed to attempt to vary the short-run inflation target deliberately over time.

8.4.2   Precluding Inflation from Moving Outside the Long-Run Range

As a practical matter, the Fed can adhere closely to its long-run inflation target only if interest rate policy can *preclude* shocks from moving inflation outside the long-run target range. Is it plausible that the Fed can do so? The answer would appear to be yes, especially for a core inflation index that excludes highly flexible commodity and food prices. As mentioned above, evidence from the mid-1990s to the present suggests that inflation will remain stable over the business cycle when the Fed makes price stability a priority.

Theory suggests why the Fed has been able to stabilize inflation so well and is likely to continue to do so in the future. Credibility for stable prices is self-enforcing to a great extent. Forward-looking, sticky-price firms are less likely to pass cost shocks through to prices if firms expect the Fed to take policy actions promptly to conform aggregate demand to potential output in order to relieve the cost pressures (see Taylor 2000). Moreover, credible price stability gives the Fed greater leeway to cut short-term interest rates in response to a financial market crisis or to stabilize the output gap without creating inflation or an inflation scare in bond markets. Thus, the Fed was able to cut the federal funds rate target by 75 basis points in 1998–99 in aftermath of the Russian debt default, and then by 475 basis points when the economy turned down in 2001, without much effect on inflation or inflation expectations in either case. Because the Fed is known to have such leeway to act aggressively and preemptively against recessions, firms are less likely to pass *deflationary* cost shocks through to prices as well.

8.4.3   Strict Inflation Targeting and Countercyclical Stabilization Policy

According to the argument above, strictly targeting core inflation within its long-run range has much to recommend it. The strength of that argument derived in part from the fact that doing otherwise would require the

Fed to take a stand on theoretical and empirical inflation dynamics, about which there is much uncertainty. This section supplements the case by pointing out that strict inflation targeting is entirely consistent with stabilizing output at its potential over the business cycle in a reasonable benchmark macromodel. In other words, strict inflation targeting can be regarded as the anchor for *constrained countercyclical stabilization policy* along the lines of the description in section 8.2.4 of inflation targeting as practiced by the Greenspan Fed. From this perspective, even those who care mainly about output and employment can support strict inflation targeting.

This point is clear with respect to a shock to aggregate demand. For instance, a positive shock that moves aggregate demand above potential output would increase labor demand and put upward pressure on wages. That cost pressure would be passed to sticky (core) prices in the absence of a tightening of monetary policy. However, by raising short-term interest rates, the Fed could bring aggregate demand back into line with potential output, move employment back down, eliminate the upward pressure on wages, and hold the line on inflation. In other words, interest rate policy can stabilize simultaneously both inflation and the output gap in the face of a shock to aggregate demand.

What about a shock to aggregate supply, such as a temporary increase in the price of oil? The question is: can the interest rate policy actions that stabilize core inflation against an oil price shock also be construed as stabilizing output relative to its potential? The higher price of oil would raise the cost of production for sticky-price firms, and again that cost pressure could be passed to sticky (core) prices in the absence of a tightening of monetary policy. To stabilize sticky (core) price inflation the Fed would have to raise real short rates and depress aggregate demand enough to *reduce* employment and wages in order to *offset* the effect of higher oil prices on production costs. In effect, price stability could be maintained by making aggregate demand conform to the temporary reduction in potential output. From this perspective, the answer to the question above could be yes.

In fact, in a benchmark macromodel with sticky prices and effectively flexible wages, interest rate policy that stabilizes sticky (core) prices automatically makes output conform to its time-varying potential.[12] The reason is twofold: (a) strict inflation targeting neutralizes fluctuations in employment and output that would otherwise occur due to sticky prices, and (b) effective wage flexibility assures that output fluctuates with its potential defined as the outcome of an imperfectly competitive real business

---

12. See Goodfriend and King (1997, 2001) and Goodfriend (2002a) for a discussion of the benchmark new neoclassical synthesis model in which strict inflation targeting also stabilizes the output gap. Goodfriend (2002a), Ireland (1996b), and Woodford (2001) show why strict inflation targeting maximizes welfare in related models.

cycle model with a constant markup and perfectly flexible wages and prices.

Of course, there is some question about the extent to which actual wages are effectively flexible. Nominal wages exhibit about the same temporary rigidity as nominal prices (see Taylor 1999). To the extent that nominal wages are temporarily rigid, the Fed might have to push employment and output below potential as defined above in order to relieve cost pressures and stabilize core inflation against an oil price shock. Pushing employment down further would reduce labor costs by raising the marginal physical product of labor. In this case, however, the Fed would face a short-run trade-off between inflation and output relative to its potential.

That being said, there are two reasons why such a trade-off may be of relatively little concern in practice. First, an inflation target of 1 to 2 percent with trend productivity growth of around 2 percent would yield average nominal wage growth in the 3 to 4 percent range. Such high nominal wage growth should keep the economy safely away from situations in which significant downward nominal wage rigidity, as opposed to slower nominal wage growth, is required to stabilize inflation and the output gap. Second, wages may be effectively flexible in the context of the long-term implicit and explicit contracts that characterize most employment relationships. It would be inefficient for either firms or workers to allow temporary nominal wage rigidity to upset the terms of otherwise efficient long-term employment relationships. In particular, one might expect future wage adjustments to undo any effects of temporary nominal wage stickiness, so that wages would be effectively flexible. Such behavior would neutralize the allocative consequences of sticky nominal wages (see Barro 1977 and Hall 1999).

8.5 How to Make Inflation Targeting Explicit in the United States

At the core of the case for inflation targeting is the idea that monetary policy encourages economic growth and stabilizes output at its potential over the business cycle in large part by anchoring inflation and inflation expectations. The need to influence expectations puts a premium on a central bank's credibility, commitment to goals, and perceived independence and competence to achieve its objectives. Currently, these foundations are secure in the United States because the public has confidence in the Greenspan Fed. If price stability is to be sustained, however, the operating procedures of the Greenspan Fed must be credibly transferred to its successor. Over the long run, the Fed's credibility must be based on an understanding of how inflation targeting works rather than being based in the leadership of the Fed. Making the Fed's inflation-targeting procedures explicit would help to achieve these ends by securing the Fed's commitment to low inflation and improving the transparency and accountability of the

Fed for attaining its monetary policy objectives (see Broaddus 2001 and Ferguson 2002).

Based on the discussion above, it seems fair to say that, consistent with theory and U.S. experience, and in line with practices that have been adopted abroad, low inflation *is* a priority for Fed monetary policy in the following sense: in the *long run* there are no circumstances in which sustained inflation should ever be much higher or lower than it is today. A public *acknowledgment* by the Fed of this would be a useful starting point for making the Fed's inflation-targeting procedures explicit. The priority for long-run price stability would simply reflect *best-practice* monetary policy as the Fed, other central banks, and the economics profession have come to understand it. Hence, the Fed could assert that priority on its own initiative without direction from Congress. In fact, the Fed has an *obligation* to inform Congress to that effect without any expectation of a response in order to help the oversight committees understand better how to evaluate monetary policy. The Fed Chairman could add that as a practical matter there is little reason for the Fed *deliberately* to allow inflation to deviate from price stability in the *short run* either, since price stability best facilitates maximum sustainable employment, growth, and output stabilization relative to potential.

A unilateral acknowledgement of this sort would be worthwhile in its own right. Openly clarifying the priority for price stability would reinforce the Fed's commitment to low inflation and enhance the credibility of that commitment. It would balance the recently increased transparency of the Fed's interest rate instrument with greater transparency of its low-inflation goal. And it would act to defuse further the idea that secrecy has any role to play in monetary policy (see Goodfriend 1986). In this regard, the Fed could go further and publicly acknowledge its quantitative working definition of long-run price stability. If a 1 to 2 percent range for core PCE inflation is it, then the Fed could acknowledge that it intends to keep core PCE inflation *in or near* that range indefinitely.

An acknowledgement of either a quantitative or a qualitative priority for low long-run inflation would open the door for the oversight committees in Congress to *recognize* a priority for low long-run inflation. By accepting that priority, the oversight committees could then hold the Fed accountable for maintaining low inflation. Presumably, the Fed would welcome being held accountable by Congress because that would secure further its commitment to low inflation. Congress, of course, might be concerned that holding the Fed accountable for low *long-run* inflation would skew Fed policy in the *short run* toward price stability at the expense of stabilizing output relative to its potential. The reality, though, is that it is not feasible to hold the Fed accountable for employment or output objectives because in the long run these are determined *independently* of monetary policy. This is the lesson of the inflationary go/stop period discussed in section 8.2.1.

There is a chicken-and-egg problem here. Without a mechanism by which the Fed's reasoning about short-run policy can be assessed more fully, Congress may be reluctant to recognize a priority for low long-run inflation. And without some assurance that Congress accepts a priority for low long-run inflation, the Fed may be reluctant to be more transparent about how it strikes a balance between inflation and output in the short run.

This conundrum suggests the following possibility: in exchange for a congressional acceptance of a priority for low long-run inflation, the Fed could consider participating in a public *monetary policy forum* where the FOMC (through its chairman and other representatives) would subject its current assessment of the economy and thinking about recent policy actions to questions from invited academic and business economists who are expert in monetary policy. The discussion would be disciplined by a congressional directive to utilize monetary policy flexibly to stabilize output at its potential over the business cycle *subject* to inflation remaining in or near its long-run target range.

The policy forum could be held publicly for one full day, twice a year, a month before the Fed's regular monetary policy reports to Congress in order to unearth key policy issues and better inform the congressional oversight hearings. Invited participants would be drawn from the community of professional Fed watchers, economic forecasters, and academic monetary economists. The forum could be arranged and participants invited by the Fed itself or by a private nonprofit sponsor. It would be held independently of Congress, although representatives from Congress would be welcome to attend. By enabling Congress to observe a professional exchange of views on monetary policy, the forum would give Congress more insight into the thinking of the FOMC.

To achieve balance in the questions and comments, the invited participants should be grouped according to whether they think that policy is too easy, about right, or too tight, and equal time should be given to all points of view. The opportunity for the FOMC to address comments and questions from all perspectives would enable the Fed to build public understanding as well as confidence in its own policy position. The Fed's thinking on the economy and current policy could be summarized in an "Inflation Report" prepared and distributed in advance of the forum. The forum would provide the Fed with regular opportunities to respond to professional comments on its assessments of the economy without appearing defensive or self-congratulatory. The forum would also provide the Fed with a convenient and efficient means of acquiring regular professional advice and council on monetary policy. Finally, the forum would help to educate economists, the press, and the financial markets so that eventually the public's confidence in monetary policy could be based on a deeper understanding of how inflation targeting works to optimize the economy's performance.

8.6 Conclusion

The paper began by tracing the origins of the case for inflation targeting in postwar U.S. monetary history from the inflationary go/stop period, through the Volcker disinflation, to the period of price stability in the Greenspan era. This historical review made clear why the Fed has made price stability a priority as never before in its history and why low inflation will remain a priority indefinitely. In particular, the historical review served three purposes. First, it showed why price stability improves monetary policy. Second, it showed how the Greenspan Fed practices inflation targeting implicitly. Third, it showed why the Fed should continue to utilize the inflation-targeting procedures developed and employed implicitly by the Greenspan Fed after Chairman Greenspan retires.

In the second half of the paper consideration was given to whether the Fed's implicit inflation-targeting procedures should be made explicit, how tightly inflation should be targeted in the short run, and how the Fed's inflation targeting procedures *could* be made explicit. The main findings were these: (a) low long-run inflation should be an explicit priority for monetary policy; (b) as a practical matter it is not desirable for the Fed to vary its inflation target in the short run; and (c) strict inflation targeting can be efficient constrained countercyclical stabilization policy. The Fed should publicly acknowledge its implicit priority for low long-run inflation so that Congress could publicly accept that priority and agree to hold the Fed accountable for attaining it. In return, representatives of the FOMC should consider participating in a monetary policy forum to better inform the congressional oversight committees and the public about current monetary policy.

References

Atkeson, A., and L. E. Ohanian. 2001. Are Phillips curves useful for forecasting inflation? *Federal Reserve Bank of Minneapolis Quarterly Review* 25:2–11.
Ball, L. 1994. Credible disinflation with staggered price-setting. *American Economic Review* 84:282–89.
Barro, R. 1977. Long-term contracting, sticky prices, and monetary policy. *Journal of Monetary Economics* 3 (July): 305–16.
Bernanke, B. S., and M. Gertler. 1999. Monetary policy and asset price volatility. In *New challenges for monetary policy: A symposium,* 77–128. Kansas City, Mo.: Federal Reserve Bank of Kansas City.
Bernanke, B. S., and F. S. Mishkin. 1997. Inflation targeting: A new framework for monetary policy? *Journal of Economic Perspectives* 11:97–116.
Bernanke, B. S., T. Laubach, F. S. Mishkin, and A. S. Posen. 1999. *Inflation targeting: Lessons from the international experience.* Princeton, N.J.: Princeton University Press.

Blejer, M. L., A. Ize, A. Leone, and S. Werlang. 2000. *Inflation targeting in practice: Strategic and operational issues and application to emerging market economies.* Washington, D.C.: International Monetary Fund.

Blinder, Alan S. 1996. Central banking in a democracy. *Federal Reserve Bank of Richmond Economic Quarterly* 82:1–14.

Bootle, R. 1996. *The death of inflation.* London: Nicholas Brealey Publishing.

Broaddus, J. Alfred, Jr. 2001. Transparency in the practice of monetary policy. *Federal Reserve Bank of Richmond Economic Quarterly* 87:1–9.

Cecchetti, Stephen G. 1995. Inflation indicators and inflation policy. In *NBER macroeconomics annual 1995,* ed. B. Bernanke and J. Rotemberg, 189–219. Cambridge: MIT Press.

Cogley, T., and T. J. Sargent. 2001. The evolution of postwar U.S. inflation dynamics. In *NBER macroeconomics annual 2001,* ed. B. Bernanke and K. Rogoff, 331–73. Cambridge: MIT Press.

Federal Open Market Committee. 1995. *Transcript,* January 31–February 1:39–59.

———. 1996. *Transcript,* July 2–3.

Federal Reserve Bank of Kansas City. 1996. Achieving Price Stability: A Symposium. 29–31 August, Federal Reserve Bank of Kansas City.

Feldstein, M. 1997. The costs and benefits of going from low inflation to price stability. In *Reducing inflation: Motivation and strategy,* ed. C. Romer and D. Romer, 123–66. Chicago: University of Chicago Press.

Ferguson, R. 2002. Why central banks should talk. Remarks at Graduate Institute of International Studies. 8 January, Geneva, Switzerland.

Fuhrer, J., and G. Moore. 1995. Inflation persistence. *Quarterly Journal of Economics* 110:127–59.

Galí, J. 2001. Targeting inflation in an economy with staggered price setting. Paper presented at Ten Years of Inflation Targeting: Design, Performance, Challenges. 30 November–1 December, Santiago, Chile, Central Bank of Chile.

Goodfriend, M. 1986. Monetary mystique: Secrecy and central banking. *Journal of Monetary Economics* 17:63–92.

———. 1993. Interest rate policy and the inflation scare problem: 1979–1992. *Federal Reserve Bank of Richmond Economic Quarterly* 79:1–24.

———. 1997. Monetary policy comes of age: A 20th century odyssey. *Federal Reserve Bank of Richmond Economic Quarterly* 83:1–22.

———. 2002a. Monetary policy in the new neoclassical synthesis: A primer. *International Finance* 5:165–92.

———. 2002b. The phases of U.S. monetary policy: 1987 to 2001. *Federal Reserve Bank of Richmond Economic Quarterly* 88:1–17.

———. 2003. Interest rate policy should not react directly to asset prices. In *Asset price bubbles: Implications for monetary, regulatory, and international policies,* ed. W. C. Hunter, G. G. Kaufman, and M. Pomerleano, 445–57. Cambridge: MIT Press.

Goodfriend, M., and R. G. King. 1997. The new neoclassical synthesis and the role of monetary policy. In *NBER macroeconomic annual 1997,* ed. B. S. Bernanke and J. J. Rotemberg, 231–83. Cambridge: MIT Press.

———. 2001. The case for price stability. In *Why price stability?,* ed. A. G. Herrero, V. Gaspar, L. Hoogduin, J. Morgan, and B. Winnkler, 53–94. Frankfurt, Germany: European Central Bank.

Greenspan, A. 1990. Statement before the U.S. Congress, House of Representatives, Subcommittee on Domestic Monetary Policy of the Committee on Banking, Finance and Urban Affairs. Zero Inflation hearing. 101 Cong. 1 Sess. Washington, D.C.: Government Printing Office.

Gurkaynak, R. S., B. Sack, and E. Swanson. 2003. The excess sensitivity of long-term interest rates: Evidence and implications for macroeconomic models. Finance and Economics Discussion Series no. 2003-50. Washington, D.C.: Federal Reserve Board, February.

Haldane, A. G. ed. 1995. *Targeting inflation.* London: Bank of England.

Hall, R. E. 1999. Labor market frictions and employment fluctuations. In *Handbook of macroeconomics,* ed. J. B. Taylor and M. Woodford, 1137–70. Amsterdam: Elsevier Science.

Ireland, P. 1996a. Long-term interest rates and inflation: A Fisherian approach. *Federal Reserve Bank of Richmond Economic Quarterly* 82:21–36.

———. 1996b. The role of countercyclical monetary policy. *Journal of Political Economy* 104:704–24.

King, M. 1997. The inflation target five years on. Lecture delivered at the London School of Economics. 29 October.

Kohn, D. 2000. *Report to the non-executive directors of the court of the Bank of England on monetary policy processes and the work of monetary analysis.* Washington, D.C.: Board of Governors of the Federal Reserve System. Manuscript.

Leiderman, L., and L. E. O. Svensson, eds. 1995. *Inflation targets.* London: Centre for Economic Policy Research.

Loayza, N., and R. Soto, eds. 2002. *Inflation targeting: Design, performance, challenges.* Santiago, Chile: Central Bank of Chile.

Martin, J. 2000. *Greenspan: The man behind money.* Cambridge, Mass.: Perseus Publishing.

McCallum, B. 1997. Inflation targeting in Canada, New Zealand, Sweden, the United Kingdom, and in general. In *Towards more effective monetary policy,* ed. I. Kuroda, 211–41. New York: St. Martin's Press.

———. 2000. *The United States deserves a monetary standard.* Washington, D.C.: Shadow Open Market Committee. Manuscript.

Meyer, L. H. 2001. Inflation targets and inflation targeting. *Federal Reserve Bank of St. Louis Review* 83:1–13.

Neumann, M. J. M., and J. von Hagen. 2002. Does inflation targeting matter? Center for European Integration Studies Working Paper no. B 01. Bonn, Germany: Center for European Integration Studies.

Orphanides, A., and J. C. Williams. 2002. Imperfect knowledge, inflation expectations, and monetary policy. Washington, D.C.: Board of Governors of the Federal Reserve System. Manuscript, May.

Romer, C. D., and D. H. Romer. 1989. Does monetary policy matter? A new test in the spirit of Friedman and Schwartz. In *NBER macroeconomics annual 1989,* ed. O. J. Blanchard and S. Fisher, 121–69. Cambridge: MIT Press.

Saxton, J. 1997. A response to criticisms of price stability. Washington, D.C.: Joint Economic Committee. Manuscript.

———. 2002. Inflation targeting goals for the Federal Reserve. Joint Economic Committee. Manuscript.

Schmitt-Grohé, S., and M. Uribe. 2002. Optimal fiscal and monetary policy under sticky prices. NBER Working Paper no. 9220. Cambridge, Mass.: National Bureau of Economic Research.

Schmitt-Hebbel, K., and M. Tapia. 2002. Monetary policy implementation and results in twenty inflation-targeting countries. Central Bank of Chile Working Paper no. 166. Santiago, Chile: Central Bank of Chile.

Schreft, S. L. 1990. Credit controls: 1980. *Federal Reserve Bank of Richmond Economic Review* 76:25–55.

Sterne, G. 1999. The use of explicit targets for monetary policy: Practical experiences of 91 economies in the 1990s. *Bank of England Quarterly Bulletin* 39:272–81.

Stevenson, R. W. 2002. Oh so quietly: Fed ponders what follows Greenspan. *New York Times,* October 3, sec. C1 and C6.

Svensson, L. E. O. 1999. Inflation targeting as a monetary policy rule. *Journal of Monetary Economics* 43:607–54.

———. 2001. Independent review of the operation of monetary policy in New Zealand: Report to the minister of finance. Stockholm University, Institute for International Economic Studies. Manuscript.

Taylor, J. B. 2000. Low inflation, pass through, and the pricing power of firms. *European Economic Review* 44:1389–1408.

———. 1999. Staggered price and wage setting in macroeconomics. In *Handbook of Macroeconomics,* ed. J. B. Taylor and M. Woodford, 1009–50. Amsterdam: Elsevier Science B. V.

Woodford, M. 2001. Inflation stabilization and welfare. NBER Working Paper no. 8071. Cambridge, Mass.: National Bureau of Economic Research.

Woodward, B. 2000. *Maestro: Greenspan's fed and the American boom.* New York: Simon & Schuster.

Comment   Donald L. Kohn

Introduction

Marvin Goodfriend answers the question in his title with a "yes" and, in the process, has provided us with an excellent foundation for a discussion of inflation targeting in the United States. I completely agree with the fundamental premise that low inflation is an indispensable long-run focus of the central bank. Low and stable rates of inflation allow economies to function more effectively, and having inflation expectations anchored facilitates countercyclical monetary policy and improves the trade-off between output and inflation that policymakers face. For the most part, in a regime of flexible exchange rates, the trend of prices over the long run should be under the control of the central bank, and exercising that control to achieve something approximating price stability over time is the way the central bank can best contribute to the long-run prosperity of its economy.

Marvin builds his case in the first part of his paper by recounting the experience of the United States over the last thirty years or so. I have no quarrel with the overall arc of his story.[1] The rise of inflation from the mid-1960s through the 1970s was highly damaging to the performance of the U.S.

Donald L. Kohn is a member of the Board of Governors of the Federal Reserve System.

The views in this comment are the author's own and do not necessarily represent the views of other members of the Federal Open Market Committee, the Board, or its staff. Brian Sack of the Board's staff contributed importantly to this comment.

1. However, I do take issue with his descriptions of several episodes over the period. In particular, see my critique of his discussion of the 1986–90 period.

economy and could have been stopped and reversed much earlier than it was by a determined monetary policy better focused on price stability. The restoration of price stability has taken time and entailed considerable cost to output in the 1979–82 period and, perhaps, some constraint on policy flexibility thereafter. A number of factors have contributed to the reestablishment of price stability, but surely an essential ingredient has been the attention that the Federal Reserve has paid to long-run trends in inflation and inflation expectations since 1979. We are better off now that price stability has been restored and economic agents expect inflation to stay low and stable. Moreover, this stability has been accomplished in the context of a highly successful policy strategy that, by anticipating emerging imbalances and actively leaning against shocks to the financial sector and the real economy, has contributed to two extraordinarily long expansions since 1980.

Marvin argues that to extend this successful policy record the United States should adopt an explicit, numerical target range for inflation and the Federal Reserve should strive to keep inflation in or near that range.[2] However, in my opinion, adopting such an inflation target would not be an effective means for locking in past policy practices. I do not believe that inflation targeting, in any meaningful sense of that term, describes what the Federal Reserve has been doing over the last twenty years, or even in recent years, when Marvin claims that policy has evolved into "implicit" inflation targeting. Instead, the success of U.S. monetary policy has in large part derived from its ability to adapt to changing conditions—a flexibility that likely has benefited from the absence of an inflation target. Nonetheless, the U.S. economy has enjoyed most of the benefits ascribed to inflation targeting in terms of anchoring inflation expectations as well as inflation itself. It is the focus on long-term price stability that has fostered these benefits, and I believe that this focus will not be at risk with a change in personnel at the Federal Reserve. Considering these points, I am skeptical that for the United States the potential benefits of changing to a regime of inflation targeting would outweigh its possible costs. Let me develop my argument.

The Federal Reserve Has Not Been Practicing Inflation Targeting.

One difficulty in assessing whether the United States has been practicing inflation targeting is in defining the term. For more than twenty years, the Federal Reserve has conducted policy with one eye on fostering long-run price stability over time. The law specifies price stability as one of the Federal Reserve's long-term objectives; its importance to economic performance has been supported by theory and experience, and hence achieving

---

2. He does not recommend "inflation-forecast targeting," in which the central bank, to achieve an inflation target, aims at the intermediate objective of an explicit, published, inflation forecast. Consequently, I have not commented on this aspect of many inflation-targeting frameworks.

this objective has been a key influence, together with promoting maximum sustainable output, on monetary policy actions. The Federal Reserve has stated publicly many times that it considers long-run price stability both its unique responsibility and the way it can contribute to maximum growth and employment over time.[3]

Although some might view this policy approach as inflation targeting, this would be a very weak definition. I believe that inflation targeting, as commonly understood and recommended, involves more substance and constraint than this allegiance to achieving price stability over the long run.

As Marvin's discussion suggests, there are two key elements in inflation targeting. First is the announcement of an explicit, numerical, inflation target. The numerical goal is important because putting a number on the objective gives it weight and importance and a focus for accountability—it becomes an explicit yardstick against which to measure performance.

The second element is a priority for price stability in monetary policy. Such a priority usually implies a presumption that the central bank should act to keep inflation at the target (or in the range) within some time horizon—that is, that the central bank would not deliberately allow inflation to deviate from the target and would return it to the target promptly if shocks pushed it away.

I recognize that flexible inflation-targeting frameworks can be derived from structures that minimize the variability of output around potential as well as inflation around its target. But inflation targeting is not usually framed that way in practice. In inflation-targeting countries, either the central bank law or the agreement between the central bank and the government usually is stated so that inflation is expected to be held at the target. To be sure, inflation targeting has not meant that countries have ignored output fluctuations. In many circumstances, especially in response to demand shocks, no conflict exists between stabilizing inflation around its objective and stabilizing output around potential. And some deviations from target, of course, are inevitable and permitted; indeed, inflation targeting has become more flexible over time in many countries. But in practice, the presumption still is that the numerical goal will be hit consistently, with the burden of proof on any deviations—and that presumption must be part of the

3. In this regard, the Federal Reserve has been very clear on many occasions about its emphasis on achieving long-run price stability. For example, in his monetary policy testimony of July 1992, Chairman Greenspan said, "As I have often noted to this committee, the most important contribution the Federal Reserve can make to encouraging the highest sustainable growth the U.S. economy can deliver over time is to provide a backdrop of reasonably stable prices on average for business and household decisionmaking" (Greenspan, 1992, 675–76). Nearly every monetary policy testimony (and many reports) for the past fifteen years contains similar sentiments and reasoning. Consequently, I do not agree with Marvin's characterization of the Federal Reserve's communication of the importance or priority it places on its long-run price stability objective as "don't ask, don't tell"; the Federal Reserve has in fact been telling the Congress and the public that price stability is its most important long-run responsibility and intention.

mind-set of the policymaker; in most inflation-targeting countries the periodic reports of the central banks are called inflation reports, not inflation and output variability reports. The attitude of policymakers is understandable. Inflation targeting is usually accompanied by elements of accountability linked directly to the inflation target—and to that target alone—and that shapes much of the transparency associated with this framework.

The Federal Reserve is not an inflation targeter in the obvious sense that it has not had an announced inflation target. Nonetheless, it is interesting to ask whether the Federal Reserve has been an "implicit inflation targeter," as Marvin and others have asserted. That is, has Federal Reserve policy been consistent with the second aspect of the definition above—a priority for placing inflation at its "implicit" target and keeping it there? In my judgment, it has not. This is clearest for policy between 1983 and the mid-1990s, as Marvin acknowledges. Over this period, inflation remained above most definitions of price stability, and the Federal Reserve was not actively seeking to reduce it. This can be seen by the FOMC's forecasts for inflation reported in the semiannual Monetary Policy Report to the Congress, shown in figure 8C.1. Inflation forecasts for the subsequent year were mostly at or above those for the current year, even though inflation was running well in excess of any reasonable notion of price stability. An inflation-targeting central bank presumably would have been setting policy so that inflation forecasts were moving toward the "implicit" price stability target. The Federal Reserve leaned against potential upticks in inflation, but it had no commitment to achieving price stability in a particular time frame; the priority seemed to be on realizing "maximum sustainable growth" as long as inflation was not rising from moderate levels.

Since the mid-1990s, inflation has been low and stable as measured by the core PCE chain price index—within the range that Marvin has designated as price stability. However, the level and stability of core PCE inflation since 1997 are as much a consequence of unexpected developments as of deliberate policy choices. Importantly, the speedup in productivity growth, even after it was detected, seemed to have greater disinflationary force than anticipated; the broad-based strength of the dollar and the weakness in global commodity prices that accompanied the East Asian crisis that began in 1997 put substantial downward pressure on prices in the United States, and, more recently, the recession and resulting output gap have provided another unexpected source of disinflation. Notably, as can be seen in figure 8C.1, in 1997, 1998, and 1999, the FOMC was projecting an increase in inflation the following year from levels already to the high side of Marvin's implicit target.[4] And in 2000 and 2001, the FOMC's projections of total PCE inflation for the year ahead exceeded the 2 percent

---

4. The level comparisons to Marvin's target in those years are admittedly ambiguous. Until 2000, the FOMC was projecting total Consumer Price Index (CPI) inflation, not core PCE price movements.

Inflation Forecasts

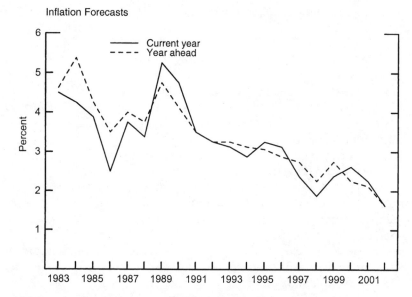

Fig. 8C.1   FOMC forecasts from Monetary Policy Report

Notes: Measures shown are the midpoint of the range of the central tendency projections reported in the Monetary Policy Report in July of each year. The solid line shows the forecast for inflation in that calendar year; the dashed line shows the forecast made at that time for inflation in the subsequent calendar year. The inflation variable is based on the GNP deflator from 1983 to 1988, the CPI from 1989 to 1999, and the PCE chain-type price index after 1999.

upper end of Marvin's range (see fig. 8C.1). Still, the FOMC took no action to bring inflation down; tightening from mid-1999 through mid-2000 was seen as necessary to forestall a sustained acceleration in prices. It was not until July 2002 that the FOMC projected inflation to remain within the range Marvin takes to be its implicit target.[5]

In addition, at a few key junctures in the past five years, the Federal Reserve exercised a more flexible monetary policy than inflation targeting probably would have suggested or allowed. The first occurred in reaction to the "seizing up" of financial markets that followed the Russian debt default in the late summer of 1998. Although forecasts were marked down at this time, the easing was faster and larger than would have been suggested by Taylor-type rules based on our past pattern of behavior and incorporating an implicit inflation target. In effect, to protect against the potential for a really bad outcome for markets and economic activity, the policymakers raised the most likely outcome for inflation—or at least skewed the risks toward the possibility that inflation would pick up. Similarly, in 2001,

5. Of course, the FOMC might have had higher (implicit) targets than Marvin is suggesting, but a policy regime in which one cannot discern the implicit inflation target over several years is probably not inflation targeting.

easing was unusually aggressive, even before September 11, as the extent of the demand shock gradually revealed itself. To be sure, when one looks back, the outcomes in both instances in terms of stable inflation were not any different from what inflation targeting would have sought. At issue, however, is whether the FOMC would have responded so aggressively to these shocks if it had been constrained by an inflation target. It is a matter of how the central bank is likely to weigh the risks and rewards of various courses of action—where it takes its chances. My sense is that, given the stress on hitting inflation objectives, the pressures of an inflation target would have constrained flexibility that in the end turned out to be useful.

Marvin argues that such flexibility is not critical. His argument is that, in an RBC model with flexible wages, policymakers face no trade-off between stabilizing inflation and the output gap, which obviously bolsters the case for inflation targeting. Unfortunately, though, in thinking about appropriate policy frameworks, we have to leave the comfort of his model for the real world. I think it would be naïve to assume that circumstances would not arise in which the central bank faced short-term choices between inflation stability and economic or financial stability.

The U.S. Economy Has Realized the Benefits of Inflation Targeting for Anchoring Inflation and Inflation Expectations without Its Constraints.

Inflation targeting would benefit the United States if it would help tie down inflation expectations or reduce errors in private-sector inflation forecasts. The former would give the central bank more scope to lean against economic imbalances and result in a more favorable trade-off between changes in inflation and in the output gap than otherwise. Better forecasts would produce more efficient allocation of resources as private agents made decisions about spending and saving, and it would reduce arbitrary redistributions of wealth from inflation surprises.

In general, however, the empirical evidence does not support a conclusion that shifting to inflation targeting would produce such benefits for the United States.[6] In some countries, the adoption of inflation targeting (and the granting of central bank independence, which often occurs at the same time) has helped to reduce inflation expectations. But the countries that have taken this step are often those with a history of high and variable inflation, and it has tended to bring their inflation experience more closely into line with other countries. Since the late 1970s, inflation and inflation expectations have come down in inflation-targeting and non-inflation-targeting countries alike. Studies do not tend to show that inflation-targeting countries have gained an advantage relative to other countries in anchoring inflation expectations and reducing sacrifice ratios or in reduc-

6. See, for example, Bernanke et al. (1999) and Ball and Sheridan (chap. 6 in this volume). All empirical work on this subject is handicapped by the relatively recent advent of inflation targeting and, as a consequence, the paucity of episodes in which to differentiate behaviors in targeting and nontargeting economies.

ing the variance of inflation-forecast errors. Apparently, credibility and predictability flow primarily from achieving low inflation, not from the presence of an announced target. As a consequence, inflation expectations seem to be as well anchored and as accurate in the United States as they are in inflation-targeting countries, despite the absence of a numerical inflation target or specification of "price stability" here.

To investigate further whether inflation targeting helps tie down longer-term inflation expectations, I took a closer look at the sensitivity of some measures of such expectations to economic developments in the United States and several other countries. One such proxy is the survey by Consensus Economics, which records the forecasts of economists and other market commentators over various horizons. To measure how firmly long-term inflation expectations are held, I looked at the extent to which long-term forecasts react to changes in short-term forecasts. The three columns of table 8C.1 give the variation in short- and long-term forecasts and the ratio of the two. Column (2) clearly shows that long-term forecasts have varied no more—and perhaps slightly less—in the United States than in inflation-targeting countries, and column (3) indicates that they are also no more sensitive to variations in short-term forecasts in the United States. Apparently, long-term inflation expectations are as well anchored against short-term inflation variations in the United States as in inflation-targeting countries; variations in short-term inflation forecasts do not appear to pass through to long-term forecasts in any of these countries, whatever the policy regime.

Figure 8C.2 shows another proxy for changes in inflation expectations—

Table 8C.1   **Variation in inflation expectations (in hundredths of percentage points)**

	Average absolute $\Delta\pi^e$		
	Current year (1)	5 to 10 years ahead (2)	Ratio (2)/(1) (3)
United States			
1990–1995	45	10	0.22
1996–2002	39	9	0.24
United Kingdom			
1990–1995	98	20	0.21
1996–2002	21	15	0.70
Canada			
1990–1995	88	23	0.26
1996–2002	47	15	0.32
Germany			
1990–1995	33	10	0.31
1996–2002	36	13	0.35
Sweden			
1990–1995	n.a.	n.a.	n.a.
1996–2002	51	15	0.29

Notes: Table reports semiannual survey measures of inflation expectations from Consensus economics; n.a. = not available.

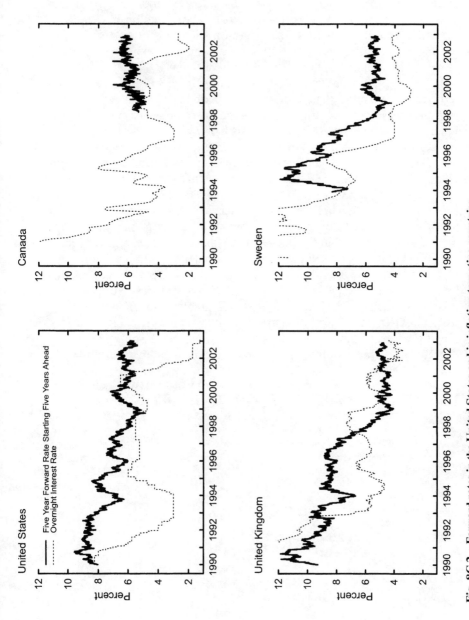

Fig. 8C.2   Forward rates in the United States and in inflation-targeting countries

Note: Overnight interest rate is the intended federal funds rate for the United States and the monthly average of a market interest rate for all other countries.

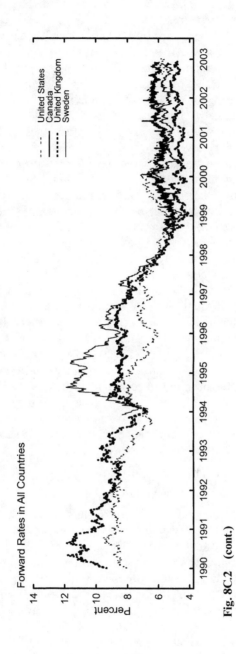

Forward Rates in All Countries

Fig. 8C.2   (cont.)

movements in long-term forward rates derived from the government securities yield curve. These are of particular interest since they are related to the "inflation scares" identified by Marvin, which he defined by sizable increases in long-term interest rates. However, long-term rates are influenced to some extent by anticipated near-term movements in short-term rates, which may not be related to longer-term inflation expectations, and so the use of a long-term *forward* rate in this context is preferred. Even so, these rates, like those used by Marvin, can vary with changes in longer-term expected real rates, resulting for example from changes in the longer-term prospects for fiscal policy or the trend rate of growth in productivity. Thus, these measures are, at best, a rough proxy of inflation expectations.[7]

Since 1990, long-term forward rates in the United States have risen substantially on two occasions—in 1994 and in 1999. Marvin identifies the former as an inflation scare but, for unexplained reasons, not the latter, although the change in the forward rate is no smaller in the second case. In 1994, forward rates rose in all the countries shown. However, inflation targeting was just beginning in Sweden and the United Kingdom and was not well established or, arguably, credible.

In 1999, forward rates also rose in the United States in response to strong economic growth and high levels of resource utilization. But they increased as much in Canada and Sweden, both inflation targeters. The exception is the United Kingdom, whose forward rates have been quite stable in recent years. The behavior of forward rates in 2001 is also instructive. The Federal Reserve eased aggressively—more so than other central banks and more so than might have been expected based on its past pattern of actions. Nonetheless, forward rates behaved similarly in all the countries shown. Judging from this proxy, even without an explicit inflation target, the Federal Reserve could strongly counter a perceived demand shock without significant adverse consequences for expectations.

An Inflation-Targeting Framework Is Not Necessary to Lock In Low Inflation in the Future.

So far I have argued that inflation targeting would not simply replicate existing policy practices, it would not buy credibility or clarity about future inflation prospects, and it would likely reduce the flexibility that has so importantly contributed to the success of U.S. monetary policy. One could still argue that inflation targeting might be worthwhile, though, if its added constraints on central-bank actions were needed to forestall a tendency to backslide toward higher inflation in the future. However, a number of features in the policy environment in the United States already provide considerable protection against such a development.

---

7. This comparison is also handicapped by the paucity of countries for which yield curves are sufficiently detailed to derive forward rates.

First, the importance of long-run price stability and its appropriateness as an essential long-run goal of monetary policy are widely recognized and acknowledged. Certainly, this objective for the central bank and the limits of its ability to affect long-term trends in income and employment are agreed on within the academic and central-banking communities.

More important, the key role of price stability is also recognized and supported by the public and its elected representatives. Price stability has been a legislated long-term goal of the Federal Reserve since 1977; notably, it was retained in 1978 when the Humphrey-Hawkins Act was passed, despite that legislation's overall emphasis on high employment. The contrast between the economic difficulties of the 1970s and the successes of the 1980s and 1990s has probably contributed to public understanding and support for low inflation. Even when politicians call for easier monetary policy, they usually frame their recommendation in the context that such a policy would still be consistent with keeping inflation low.

Second, the Federal Reserve Act has established an institutional structure for making monetary policy that militates against forgetting or ignoring the lessons of theory and experience or the requirements of the law. Policy is made by a large and diverse committee within a central bank that has substantial insulation from short-term political pressures. In addition, owing to the length of governors' terms and the nature of the Reserve Bank presidents' positions, there has been considerable continuity in the makeup of the FOMC over the years, which has been echoed on the staff level as well. To be sure, the FOMC has tended to operate by consensus under the leadership of the chairman, who exerts a strong influence on the nature of the consensus. But it is a committee, and deference to a new chairman is not likely to be as strong as it has become for the existing chairman, given his record of extraordinary judgment and success over the years. Indeed, a leader whose recommendations seem to be leading to higher inflation would be likely to lose influence rapidly.

Marvin foreshadows and supports his argument that inflation targeting is needed to sustain good inflation performance across leadership shifts by raising the possibility that the "inflation scare" of 1987 was linked to the change in chairmen that year and emphasizing how long the subsequent rise in inflation and inflation expectations took to unwind. Inflation and inflation expectations did rise in 1987, reversing a decline in 1986. Oil and import prices escalated rapidly, likely triggering memories of similar circumstances in the 1970s, and import prices were expected to continue to increase for some time as the dollar corrected its earlier overvaluation. In addition, strong demand was boosting capital and labor utilization rates (see Council of Economic Advisors 1988, 26–28). Consequently, a number of reasons existed for a rise in inflation expectations that were not linked to the leadership change. Moreover, as Marvin notes, inflation expectations had increased a few years earlier and were to do so again in 1989 and 1994, when leadership change was not in the wind. The rise in underlying inflation and inflation expectations was far smaller and less persistent in the late 1980s than Marvin implies. He cites a jump of more than 2 percentage points from 1986 to 1990 in *total* PCE inflation, but this increase was greatly influenced by movements in oil prices, which fell in 1986 and spiked higher in 1990 because of the invasion of Kuwait. The acceleration in *core* PCE inflation, the measure Marvin recommends be targeted, was one-fourth as much—from 3.93 to 4.39 percent—from 1986 to 1990. The ten-year CPI forecasts of Blue Chip respondents rose from 4 percent in 1986 to 4.5 percent in 1987 but by the beginning of 1990 had reversed that uptick.

Of course, erosion of the weight that the Federal Reserve has placed on long-term price stability is not impossible and would have adverse consequences for inflation and economic performance. Inflation targeting with an explicit political mandate to give long-term price stability priority would make erosion much less likely. But it is not very likely in any event, and I would be hesitant to incur the constraints of inflation targeting until they seemed more necessary.

Even If I Favored Inflation Targeting, I Still Would Have Serious Reservations about the Way Marvin Seems to Propose It Be Implemented.

Marvin notes several levels on which the Federal Reserve could "make inflation targeting explicit," differing by their specificity and whether they would hold in the short run as well as in the long run. They range from declaring that inflation in the long run should never vary much on a sustained basis from recent levels to announcing a specific numerical target range for core PCE inflation of 1 to 2 percent and setting policy so that realized inflation would be expected to remain in that range almost always.

To implement explicit targeting, he argues that the Federal Reserve could obtain "congressional acceptance" of a priority for low long-term inflation by offering in exchange to participate in policy forums that would allow outside commentators to voice their opinions and interact with Federal Reserve officials. However, this trade is not likely to have great appeal to congressional skeptics, since they already have the authority to get testimony and analysis from outside observers and critics of monetary policy. Indeed, such hearings used to be a regular feature in the weeks leading up to semiannual monetary policy hearings.

More fundamental is the issue of "congressional acceptance." Marvin does not specify what he means by this, which is problematic because it could encompass a variety of interactions between the central bank and the legislature. In my view, because the Federal Reserve, appropriately, has limited "goal independence," it has little scope for announcing a numerical inflation target that would tend to constrain its actions without explicit authorization and direction from new legislation.

The place of an independent central bank in a democratic society is finely balanced. In exchange for insulation from political pressures, the central bank agrees to strive for the objectives it has been given by the elected representatives. The Federal Reserve has already exercised considerable discretion in interpreting its "dual mandate" of price stability and maximum employment in ways it has made clear in its testimonies and reports. In the absence of legislation, going appreciably further in the direction of prioritizing price stability, as would be implied by a numerical target that was expected to be achieved most of the time, would be potentially damaging to the democratic balance and would risk a backlash. Congress has had several opportunities over the past fifteen years to consider bills proposed by legislators to make price stability the primary goal of the Federal Reserve, and it has not passed them or even given them serious consideration. This statement does not necessarily imply that Congress would oppose such a step if it were asked again—especially if the Federal Reserve were strongly behind the proposal. But it does reinforce the view that it should be asked, and actions to adopt and give priority to numerical inflation targets should await explicit legislative authorization. Moreover, acting without specific authorization would abrogate one of the important advantages of inflation targeting as practiced in most countries—it requires the elected representatives to discuss and reach a conclusion on just what they can and should expect from the central bank.

This point does not mean that there are no steps the Federal Reserve might consider taking within its current mandate to clarify its views on price stability. One such step might be similar to the first level in Marvin's list—discussing in a general way how recent inflation rates relate to the central bank's view of price stability. A more specific approach would be to announce a numerical range of a particular index that might be expected to prevail over the long run, but with no change in the Federal Reserve's relative priorities on price stability and growth (see, e.g., Meyer 2001). To avoid the constraints of inflation targeting, the Federal Reserve would need to be clear that the range did not constitute a firm or presumptive target for inflation over the short or intermediate term and that the range could change in response to shifting assessments of the costs and benefits of particular inflation rates, to improvements in measurement techniques, and to readings from other price indexes that seemed to be conveying different information about underlying price trends.

However, I have some concerns about even such a "soft" inflation target. Placing any number on an inflation objective—however much it would be surrounded with caveats—has the potential to constrain policy in some circumstances in which it would not be desirable to do so. That is, the quantification itself might tend to create a presumption that deviations from the long-run goal would need to be resisted more than would be consistent with the policy flexibility exercised over the past twenty years. And I would be hesitant to proceed down this path without some kind of explicit congressional acceptance. Congress might in fact perceive that the weight on its legislated goals had been changed, without its approval. If, partly as a consequence, it demanded that the Federal Reserve also quantify "maximum employment" or "maximum sustainable growth" and give weight to those specifications, policy could be adversely affected. As we have seen so graphically in the last several years, assessments of the level and growth of potential GDP must be revised frequently, and of course these variables are not under the control of the central bank. As I noted earlier, markets seem no less certain of the path for inflation in the United States than in many of those countries with numerical inflation targets, and so the gains from putting numbers on "price stability" are likely to be limited.

References

Bernanke, B. S., T. Laubach, F. S. Mishkin, and A. S. Posen. 1999. *Inflation targeting: Lessons from the international experience.* Princeton, N.J.: Princeton University Press.
Council of Economic Advisors. 1988. *Economic report of the president.* Washington, D.C.: Government Printing Office.
Greenspan, Alan. 1992. Statement before the Committee on Banking, Housing and Urban Affairs, U.S. Senate, July 21, 1992. *Federal Reserve Bulletin* 78 (September): 673–78.
Meyer, L. H. 2001. Inflation targets and inflation targeting. *Federal Reserve Bank of St. Louis Review* 83:1–13.

Discussion Summary

Laurence Meyer suggested as a framework for thinking about Goodfriend's and Kohn's positions a two-by-two matrix with implicit versus explicit numerical inflation target in the columns, and dual versus hierarchical mandate as rows. The common interpretation of inflation targeting would thus be the bottom right element—an explicit inflation target with a hierarchical mandate. Meyer had instead suggested in the past the upper right element—an explicit inflation target with a dual mandate that would preserve the flexibility to respond to output fluctuations as well. Kohn seemed to suggest that this was impossible to do.

Lars Svensson proposed that, even without announcing an inflation target, the Federal Reserve could publish inflation reports with inflation forecasts up to three years ahead, which would allow the public to infer what rate of inflation it was aiming for.

Frederic Mishkin disagreed with the view that the Federal Reserve's response to events in 1998 and 2001 would have been different had there been an explicit inflation target. He suggested that in situations of this kind the

Fed should mention in its statements deflationary risks instead of using language related to economic weakness. His main concern was to ensure that a nominal anchor was in place by the time that the current chairman left office, but a unilateral announcement by the Federal Reserve of an inflation target risked an undesirable reaction of Congress.

Mervyn King emphasized the responsibility of central banks to communicate to the wider public the importance of price stability as an objective for monetary policy, and the constraints that this objective imposes on the conduct of monetary policy. An argument for an inflation target was that it made explicit these constraints.

Stephen Cecchetti suggested that policy making by committee such as the FOMC would be improved by having agreed-upon objectives. Once the objectives had been agreed upon, they should be communicated to the public for both transparency and accountability. It was incumbent on those who took exception to inflation targeting to produce alternative objectives.

John Berry questioned whether, given the approval in Congress of the Fed's conduct, there was any support in Congress for changing the Federal Reserve's objectives. Neither were recent administrations involving themselves in a debate about the objectives for monetary policy. He also suggested that there was little support for an announced numerical target for inflation within the FOMC.

Martin Feldstein pointed out that both Paul Volcker and Alan Greenspan had mentioned in public speeches practical definitions of price stability, and that the inflation expectations derived from long-term interest rates suggested that market participants believed the Fed was committed to price stability in the long run.

Athanasios Orphanides expressed concern about the degree of flexibility inherent in the Fed's current operating regime. He pointed out that Arthur Burns had been a chairman with as excellent qualifications as the chairmen after him, and yet mistakes were made that led to the great inflation. It was therefore important to search for refinements to the current procedures that would prevent a repetition of past policy mistakes, and inflation targeting might be such a refinement.

Laurence Ball proposed to combine inflation targeting with the concern for flexibility expressed in Kohn's comments by having an extended list of caveats, such as financial crises, similar to the current practice of the Reserve Bank of New Zealand, such that deviations from an inflation target are admissible when specific events occur.

Bennett McCallum suggested exploring the possibility of explicit, but not quantitative, targets, such as the definition of price stability used by Alan Greenspan. Performance with respect to such a definition could be measured by looking at long-term inflation expectations.

Ben Bernanke agreed with Meyer's suggestion that a dual mandate was the only sensible choice, albeit one that put a large weight on inflation control. He expressed concern with the lack of communication between the Fed and the public, and he suggested that the Fed could use its resources to provide more information to the public about its outlook for the economy.

In response to Kohn's comments, *Marvin Goodfriend* argued that his proposed policy forum would provide the Fed with flexibility in the short run through improved transparency and public understanding of its policy. In response to Meyer, Goodfriend said that he did favor making the long-run inflation target explicit and encouraging the Fed to target inflation within the long-run range in the short run. But Goodfriend also favored allowing the Fed to take employment into account in the short run if inflation is inside the long-run target range, and even if the Fed is trying to work inflation back inside the range after a shock.

Donald Kohn emphasized that the large number of FOMC members complicated communication with the public enormously. In response to Ball's suggestions, he expressed the view that caveats had a tendency of being ignored, so that the announced numerical target could well assume more importance, and be perceived as more unqualified, than was intended.

Inflation Targeting in Transition Economies
Experience and Prospects

Jiri Jonas and Frederic S. Mishkin

9.1 Introduction

In the second half of the 1990s, several transition countries abandoned fixed exchange rate regimes and instead introduced inflation targeting as framework for the conduct of monetary policy. In this paper, we will analyze the experience of three countries that moved to an inflation-targeting regime: the Czech Republic, Hungary, and Poland.

It is worth studying inflation targeting in these transition countries for two reasons. First, the transition countries are becoming an important part of Europe, and designing the right monetary policy regime for their transition into successful European economies is valuable in its own right. Second, these countries have three unique features that make the study of inflation targeting in these countries particularly interesting: (a) they are new democracies that are in the process of developing new governmental institutions; (b) their economies are undergoing radical restructuring as part of the transition from socialism to capitalism; and (c) they are very likely to enter the European Union (EU) and Economic and Monetary Union (EMU) in the near future. These three unique features are emphasized in our discussion of their inflation-targeting regimes.

In the next section of the paper we discuss the reasons why these coun-

Jiri Jonas is senior advisor in the Office of Executive Director at the International Monetary Fund. Frederic S. Mishkin is the Alfred Lerner Professor of Banking and Financial Institutions in the Graduate School of Business, Columbia University, and a research associate of the National Bureau of Economic Research.

The views expressed in this paper are exclusively those of the authors and not those of the International Monetary Fund, Columbia University, or the National Bureau of Economic Research (NBER). We thank the participants in the Macro Lunch at Columbia University and the NBER Inflation Targeting Conference for their helpful comments.

tries moved to a more flexible exchange rate regime and introduced inflation targeting. In the third section, we examine in more detail the introduction of inflation targeting in the three countries, and in the fourth section, we evaluate the preliminary experience with inflation targeting. In the fifth section, we discuss a number of specific issues for inflation targeting in transition economies: what inflation measure to target, whether to target a point or a range, what should be the time horizon for the inflation target, who should set the inflation target, what should be the response to faster-than-targeted disinflation, how monetary policy should respond to deviations of inflation from the target, how much the floor of the inflation target should be emphasized relative to the ceiling, and what role the exchange rate should play in an inflation-targeting regime. In the sixth section, we discuss the future prospects of inflation targeting in transition economies in connection with the planned adoption of the euro, focusing on inflation targeting within the fluctuation band of exchange rate mechanism 2 (ERM2) regime and on the potential conflict between the inflation target and the exchange rate target. The final section contains concluding remarks.

9.2   From Peg to Float

In economic history books, the 1990s will be probably remembered as a decade when fixed exchange rate regimes lost much of their attraction as nominal anchors for the conduct of monetary policy. As a result of devastating financial crises, many emerging-market countries were forced to abandon fixed exchange rate regimes and replace them with more flexible exchange rate arrangements. Some countries—albeit a significant minority—even opted to introduce more flexible exchange rate regimes in an orderly way, without being forced to exit the peg as a result of financial crisis or market pressure on their currency.

This trend from more fixed to more flexible exchange rate regimes was also observed in the transition economies of Central and Eastern Europe. In the early years of transition, in the aftermath of price liberalization and exchange rate devaluation, many transition economies have used the exchange rate peg as a nominal anchor to achieve a rapid stabilization of price level. However, as with other emerging-market economies, transition economies too have suffered the standard problem of exchange rate–based stabilization programs: while inflation did decline significantly, it did not decline enough to prevent a large real appreciation that ultimately created a balance-of-payment problem and forced the abandonment of the fixed exchange rate. While some countries opted for a hard version of a fixed exchange rate—a currency board arrangement—others introduced managed float: first the Czech Republic in 1997, then the Slovak Republic and Poland in 1998. Hungary did not move to a fully floating currency regime, but in May 2001 it introduced an exchange rate band, allowing the currency to move up and down within this band by 15 percent.

When abandoning the exchange rate pegs, the authorities of these countries had to decide what nominal anchor to use instead of the fixed exchange rate. While the Slovak Republic did not accompany the move to a floating exchange rate by an explicit introduction of new monetary policy framework, the other three countries opted for inflation targeting. Why did the authorities in these countries opt for inflation targeting, and why did they reject alternative policy frameworks? We can learn why by examining the problems of other monetary policy regimes.

One alternative would be to use monetary aggregates as an intermediate target and nominal anchor. However, targeting monetary aggregates does not have much attraction in transition economies.[1] The traditional problem of instability of money demand, and therefore the unstable relationship between the growth of money supply and inflation, could be a particularly serious obstacle to targeting monetary aggregates in transition economies. Economic transition is characterized by a sequence of price shocks, including corrections in administered prices and tax reforms, that make the relationship between money supply and price level very difficult to predict. The instability of money demand and money-price relationship is further exacerbated by far-reaching changes in the financial sector, including deep institutional changes, the emergence of new types of financial assets and players, and so on. Therefore, relying solely on targeting money supply growth could be a quite ineffective approach to conducting monetary policy.

Transition economies could have also applied a discretionary, "just-do-it" approach to monetary policy, as the Federal Reserve in the United States is doing, in which there is no explicit nominal anchor.[2] Given the difficulty of establishing a more stable relationship between some intermediate target and price level, some may think that a less formal approach to monetary policy would be advisable. However, while this approach may work in countries whose central bank has well-established anti-inflationary credibility, and where inflation is low, it is doubtful that it would work well in transition economies. Particularly in the Czech Republic where inflation was relatively high and rising after the fixed exchange rate regime was abandoned, the just-do-it approach to monetary policy was not seen as be-

---

1. Indeed, it is not at all clear that monetary targeting is a viable strategy, even in industrialized countries, because the relationship between monetary aggregates and goal variables such as inflation and nominal spending is typically quite weak. For example, see Estrella and Mishkin (1997).

2. For a description of the just-do-it approach in the United States, see Bernanke et al. (1999). Some transition economies are pursuing a managed float (Romania, the Slovak Republic, Slovenia) or free float (Albania) without a formal inflation-targeting framework in place, although Albania is now introducing full-fledged inflation targeting. It is interesting to compare the development of inflation in these countries that have similarly flexible exchange rate regimes but no formal inflation-targeting regime in place (see section 9.4.3).

ing potentially effective in bringing inflation expectations and actual inflation down. Without anti-inflation credibility, the just-do-it approach would not sufficiently anchor inflation expectations and persuade economic agents that monetary policy would be actually conducted to control inflation.

A third option would be to replace a fixed exchange rate regime with a harder variant of exchange rate peg—that is, by introducing a currency board, or even unilaterally euroizing. This option has the advantage that it provides a nominal anchor that helps keep inflation under control by tying the prices of domestically produced tradable goods to those in the anchor country, and making inflation expectations converge to those prevailing in the anchor country. In addition, it provides an automatic adjustment mechanism that helps mitigate the time-inconsistency problem of monetary policy. Hard pegs also have the advantages of simplicity and clarity, which make them easily understood by the public. However, the hard peg option has the disadvantage that it leaves little scope for the country to conduct its own monetary policy in order to react to domestic or foreign shocks.

For transition countries that wanted to retain some control over domestic monetary policy and so opted to keep a flexible exchange rate, the problems with monetary targeting and the just-do-it approach led them to adopt a fourth option, inflation targeting. Inflation targeting has several advantages over a hard peg, monetary targeting, and the just-do-it approach. In contrast to a hard peg, inflation targeting enables monetary policy to focus on domestic considerations and to respond to shocks of both domestic and foreign origin. Inflation targeting also has the advantage that stability in the relationship between money and inflation is not critical to its success because it does not depend on such a relationship. Inflation targeting, like a hard peg, also has the key advantage that it is easily understood by the public and thus highly transparent. In contrast, monetary targets, although visible, are less likely to be well understood by the public, especially as the relationship between monetary aggregates and inflation becomes less stable and reliable. Because an explicit numerical target for inflation increases the accountability of the central bank relative to a discretionary regime, inflation targeting also has the potential to reduce the likelihood that the central bank will fall into the time-inconsistency trap. Moreover, since the source of time inconsistency is often found in (covert or open) political pressures on the central bank to engage in expansionary monetary policy, inflation targeting has the advantage of focusing the political debate on what a central bank can do on a sustainable basis—that is, control inflation—rather than on what it cannot do through monetary policy—for example, raise output growth, lower unemployment, or increase external competitiveness.

How well were the transition economies prepared for the introduction of inflation targeting? In the literature, a relatively long list of requirements

Table 9.1   Inflation-targeting countries: General government balance (in % of GDP, excluding privatization revenues)

Country	1998	1999	2000	2001
Czech Republic	–2.4	–2.0	–4.2	–5.2
Hungary	–4.8	–3.4	–3.3	–4.7
Poland	–3.2	–3.7	–3.2	–6.0

Source: European Bank for Reconstruction and Development (2002).

has been identified that countries should meet if inflation targeting regime is to operate successfully.[3] These requirements include (a) a strong fiscal position, (b) a well-understood transmission mechanism between monetary policy instruments and inflation, (c) a well-developed financial system, (d) central-bank independence and a clear mandate for price stability, (e) a reasonably well-developed ability to forecast inflation, (f) absence of other nominal anchors than inflation, and (g) transparent and accountable monetary policy.

It is not possible to say whether a country meets these requirements or not: it is more a question of the degree to which these preconditions are met. On the whole, it could be argued that the three transition countries that adopted inflation targeting, the Czech Republic, Hungary, and Poland, met these requirements to a sufficient degree to make inflation targeting feasible and useful.[4]

All three countries have an independent central bank with a clear mandate to pursue price stability. In some cases, this independence and price stability mandate has been strengthened just before the introduction of inflation targeting. There has also been significant progress in making monetary policy decisions more transparent and central banks more accountable, although this is still to some extent a work in progress in some countries. Financial markets in the three analyzed economies are relatively well developed, allowing for a reasonably effective transmission mechanism between monetary policy instruments and inflation.

With respect to fiscal position, partly as a result of explicit recognition of hidden transformation-related costs, fiscal deficits have widened significantly, particularly in the Czech Republic and Hungary (see table 9.1). However, these deficits have not yet posed a direct problem to inflation targeting in the sense of fiscal dominance of monetary policy, because they have been financed by nonmonetary means at relatively favorable terms.[5]

---

3. See Debelle (1997) and Schaechter, Stone, and Zelmer (2000).

4. For a discussion of whether Hungary is ready for inflation targeting, see Siklos and Ábel (2002).

5. Note that one can argue that a strong fiscal position is a requirement for successful conduct of monetary policy under any policy framework, not just inflation targeting. See Eichengreen (1999) and Mishkin and Savastano (2001).

The main reason why large fiscal deficits in accession countries do not trigger adverse market reaction is that they are widely considered to be temporary. In part this reflects the recognition of implicit public-sector liabilities from the past. Moreover, as a result of EU/EMU accession, these countries will adopt an institutional framework (the Stability and Growth Pact, or SGP) that will require them to pursue disciplined fiscal policies. Still, before the constraint of the SGP begins to operate, large fiscal deficits can complicate monetary policy conduct in indirect ways, as we will see in our later discussion of these three countries' experience with inflation targeting.

As for the absence of multiple nominal anchors, this condition is clearly met in the Czech Republic and Poland. These countries have in place a regime of managed floating, and inflation is the only nominal anchor in the economy. In Hungary, the situation is more complicated because of the presence of the exchange rate band. Theoretically, this could be incompatible with the requirement of the single nominal anchor if the band is too narrow. We should note that the existence of the exchange rate fluctuation band is not only an issue of concern to Hungary today; it will be of concern to all transition countries that join the ERM2 system, when they will have to put in place the same fluctuation band. We will discuss the issue of fluctuation band and inflation targeting in the section on monetary policy within the ERM2 system.

Perhaps the most serious objection raised against the adoption of inflation targeting in transition economies is the limited ability to forecast inflation accurately. This is partly the result of the relatively frequent occurrence of shocks to which transition economies are exposed, including price deregulation and catching up with the more advanced economies, and also the result of relatively large degree of openness of these economies. Actual inflation is relatively unstable relative to the long-term inflation trend (Orlowski 2000). Under such circumstances, there are natural limits to central banks' ability to forecast inflation that cannot be quickly and substantially improved by more sophisticated forecasting models. However, inflation-targeting central banks are nevertheless making progress in improving their inflation-forecasting capacity. One approach is to use alternative and less formal methods of gauging future inflation. For example, in 1999 the Czech National Bank introduced a survey of inflation forecasts by market participants to measure inflation expectations.

9.3 Introduction of Inflation Targeting in Individual Countries

We will now turn in more detail to the introduction of inflation targeting in individual countries. We will briefly examine economic developments preceding the introduction of inflation targeting, and the main operational characteristics of the inflation-targeting regimes in the three countries.

9.3.1   The Czech Republic

The Czech Republic was the first transition economy to introduce an inflation-targeting regime, which it did after abandoning the fixed exchange rate regime following currency turbulence in May 1997.[6]

A fixed exchange rate regime played an important role in the macroeconomic stabilization package introduced in 1991. Several months after liberalization of prices and devaluation of currency in 1991, the rate of inflation came down quickly, although not quite to levels prevailing in advanced economies. Inflation remained stuck at around 10 percent, and wages and other nominal variables soon adjusted to this level. Higher domestic inflation and the fixed nominal exchange rate produced a real appreciation, which was not fully validated by higher productivity growth, and after some time, erosion of competitiveness became a concern. The economy began to overheat, political constraints prevented a sufficiently vigorous and flexible use of fiscal policy to mitigate imbalances in the nonpublic sector, and tightening of monetary policy alone could not cope with these rapidly growing imbalances. The mix of tighter monetary policy and continued loose fiscal policy may have only made things worse: it contributed to higher interest rates, which attracted more short-term foreign capital, further fueling the growth of liquidity, keeping inflation high, and widening the current account deficit.

Ultimately, as the external deficit continued to widen despite the visible deceleration of economic growth later in 1996, the situation became unsustainable. It became increasingly obvious that the policy adjustment that was feasible under the existing political constraints would fall short of what was needed to reverse the unsustainable deterioration of current account position. Uncertainties in financial markets, triggered initially by speculative attacks on the Thai baht, only accelerated the flight of foreign investors from koruna assets, which forced the authorities to stop defending a fixed exchange rate. On May 26, 1997, the government and the Czech National Bank (CNB) decided to allow the koruna to float freely.[7]

Like many other emerging-market countries, the Czech Republic did not exit the peg at a time of strong external position, doing so only when it was forced to do so by market pressure. However, unlike other central banks that were ultimately forced to abandon the defense of a fixed parity, the CNB did not wait too long after the pressure on the koruna intensified.

6. For an early analysis of inflation targeting in the Czech Republic see Hrnčíř and Šmidková (1999) and Mahadeva and Šmidková (2000).

7. For a discussion of the Czech exchange rate crisis see Begg (1998). It is noteworthy that, unlike the case of many other emerging-market countries that were forced to abandon the currency peg, the Czech koruna depreciated only moderately, and it subsequently strengthened again. One reason for this limited depreciation was the relatively low degree of dollarization and currency mismatches in the Czech economy and thus the limited effect of the exit from the peg on companies' and banks' balance sheets.

Even though it first tried to fend off the pressure by raising interest rates, it did not waste a large amount of foreign reserves in foreign exchange market intervention. In the week before the decision to float, the CNB's foreign reserves declined by about $2.5 billion, to $10 billion. Given the unsatisfactory experience with interventions as a tool to prevent the exit from a pegged exchange rate regime, this was a correct decision.

Possible inflationary effects of currency depreciation after the exit from the peg, together with the absence of an alternative nominal anchor to guide inflation expectations, created a risk that inflation would increase significantly in the coming months. Therefore, the CNB began to work on a new monetary policy framework, and in the meantime it tried to guide inflation expectations by its public pronouncements. After the koruna (CZK) was allowed to float, the CNB issued a public statement that it expected the average koruna exchange rate to stabilize within months at roughly CZK 17 to 19.50 per 1 deutsche mark (DM) (Czech National Bank 1997). Furthermore, the CNB made it clear that in the future, monetary policy would be unambiguously focused on domestic price-level stability and reduction of potential inflationary effects of the koruna's exchange rate movements (Czech National Bank 1997). The first sentence may seem to have been somewhat at odds with the managed float. The reason for announcing a band in which the CNB expected the CZK/DM exchange rate to settle was to prevent overshooting at a time when there was no other nominal anchor to tie down exchange rate and inflation expectations, and to limit to the extent possible any pass-through of currency depreciation to domestic inflation.

However, the CNB felt that this approach to monetary policy conduct was not satisfactory and could not continue for much longer. Therefore, on December 21, the CNB Bank Board decided that in the future, monetary programs would be formulated on basis of inflation targeting. The stated purpose of inflation targeting was to provide a nominal anchor in the form of an inflation target, to use monetary policy tools directly to achieve the inflation target, and to regularly inform the public about the conduct of monetary policy.[8]

In deciding what measure of inflation to target, the CNB faced a trade-off between transparency and the ability to control inflation, an issue that we will look at in detail later. The CNB opted for a compromise that it considered most appropriate for an economy in transition. For the purpose of inflation targeting, it introduced a new concept, so-called net inflation. Net inflation measures changes in the consumer price index (CPI), excluding the movement in regulated prices, and is further adjusted for the impact on

---

8. The path to inflation targeting for the CNB has many similarities to the path followed by the Bank of England and the Riksbank after the collapse of their exchange rate pegs in 1992. See Bernanke et al. (1999).

the remaining items of changes in indirect taxes or subsidy elimination.[9] Unlike many other inflation-targeting countries, the Czech Republic did not exclude from net inflation changes in the prices of energy and agricultural products. Such an exclusion would have narrowed the targeted price index too much and would have made it too detached from the headline inflation. Instead, the CNB subsequently introduced so-called exceptions to deal with this problem (see below).

In choosing whether to target a range or a single numerical value of inflation, the CNB opted for a range. Initially, in 1998 and 1999, it was targeting a band 1 percentage point wide, but from 2000, it widened the band to 2 percentage points. The CNB's decision about the width of the band was guided mainly by its assessment of the accuracy with which it thought it could hit net inflation targets, as well as the past volatility of net inflation.

At the end of 1998, the CNB made some modifications to its inflation-targeting strategy. First, the CNB introduced the "exceptions" that could justify missing an inflation target. Exceptions refer to exceptional and unpredictable factors that cause actual inflation to deviate from the inflation target and for which the CNB cannot bear responsibility. These factors include the following: significant differences between actual and predicted world prices of commodities; significant differences between actual and predicted exchange rate that do not reflect developments of domestic economic fundamentals and monetary policy; significant changes of conditions in agriculture that affect agriculture producer prices; and natural disasters and other extraordinary events that produce demand-led and cost-pushed price shocks (Czech National Bank 1999, 57).

Second, the CNB decided to take a more active role in affecting inflation expectations. It realized that a much more rapid than originally expected decline in inflation in the second half of 1998, together with large degree of rigidity in nominal variables, could produce undesirable developments in real variables—most importantly, real wages. The CNB therefore initiated an informative meeting with the representatives of trade unions and employees in order to explain what inflation it expected in 1999 and, in this way, to help reduce inflation expectations.[10]

In December 1999, the CNB approved *Long-Term Monetary Strategy,*

---

9. At the end of 1997, the CPI consisted of 754 items, 91 items had regulated price, and net inflation measured the movements of 663 items, which in terms of weights in the consumer basket represented about four-fifths of the total basket.

10. Trade unions agreed that it would not be desirable to aim for higher than zero growth in real wages in 1999. The catch was that trade unions' economic experts projected that inflation in 1999 would reach 10 percent, and trade unions therefore demanded a 10 percent increase in nominal wages, which in their view would be consistent with zero growth in real wages. As inflation in 1999 remained close to 2 percent, 10 percent nominal wage growth resulted in a large increase in real wages. At the end of 1999, when the CNB was again discussing with the representatives of trade unions inflation prospects for 2000, they seemed to have learned from their mistake and expressed more trust in CNB's inflation forecast for 2000.

which specified the long-term inflation target for 2005. The objective was to make the inflation-targeting strategy more forward looking. Importantly, the CNB made an effort to involve the public and the government in discussion of the long-term monetary policy target. No doubt this outreach effort reflected the criticism by some politicians that the process of disinflation was too fast and too costly in 1998 and 1999. The CNB did not wish to announce the quantified long-term target corresponding to price stability and the speed with which this ultimate objective was to be achieved without acquiring the support of the government. The CNB seems to have acknowledged implicitly that the decision on the speed of disinflation is ultimately a political one and that it had to be taken by a body with political mandate.

Another modification of the inflation-targeting framework took place in April 2001. At that time, the CNB decided that the main reasons for favoring net inflation targeting rather than headline inflation targeting had disappeared, and it decided that from 2002 on, it would target headline inflation measured by the CPI.[11] The CNB explained that headline inflation covers more comprehensively price developments in the economy and that it is more relevant for decisions of economic agents. For these reasons, by targeting headline inflation, monetary policy should also be better able to affect inflation expectations. Headline inflation targets for the period 2002–2005 were derived from the trajectory of net inflation specified in the December 1999 *Long-Term Monetary Strategy.* The CNB realized that targeting headline inflation has its risks as well, the most important one being the uncertainty regarding the development of regulated prices and effects of changes in administered prices. For example, the need to achieve a stronger adjustment of fiscal imbalances could require a larger-than-expected increase in administered prices, with consequently larger impact on headline inflation. Another complication could arise from the harmonization of indirect taxes with the EU ahead of the EU entry. But these unexpected effects of changes in regulated prices or administrative measures on headline inflation were included in the exceptions that allowed actual inflation to deviate from the inflation target without necessitating a monetary policy response. After the April 2001 modification, the list of the exceptions included the following:

- Major deviations in world prices of raw materials, energy-producing materials, and other commodities
- Major deviations of the koruna's exchange rate that are not connected with domestic economic fundamentals and domestic monetary policy
- Major changes in the conditions for agricultural production having an impact on agriculture producer prices

11. However, already in 2000, when it announced the net inflation target for end-2001, the CNB also began publishing its projection of headline inflation.

- Natural disasters and other extraordinary events having cost and demand impacts on prices
- Changes in regulated prices whose effects on headline inflation would exceed 1–1.5 percentage points
- Step changes in indirect taxes

The CNB has also announced that the list of exceptions could be further widened in the future to include one-time price shocks resulting from the adoption of EU standards.

9.3.2   Poland

After the Czech Republic, Poland was the second transition country to introduce inflation targeting. Its approach to inflation targeting differs in some important aspects from that of the Czech Republic.

As a part of Poland's big-bang approach to macroeconomic stabilization, the zloty was pegged to a basket of currencies in 1990. But inflation did not decline sufficiently rapidly, and fixed nominal exchange rate resulted in rapid real appreciation and erosion of competitiveness. Therefore, a preannounced crawling peg was introduced in October 1991. Capital account liberalization led in 1994 and 1995 to large capital inflows, which forced the authorities to widen the crawling exchange rate band in May 1995 to ±7 percent. Upward pressure on the currency continued, and in December 1995 the central rate was revalued by 6.4 percent in order to be aligned with the prevailing market rate. In early 1998, the National Bank of Poland (NBP) began to widen the band again: to ±10 percent in February 1998, to ±12.5 percent in October 1998, and finally to ±15 percent in March 1999. At the same time, the rate of crawl was reduced from an initial 1.8 percent per month in 1991 to 0.3 percent per month. The main reason for the gradual widening of the band was the effort of the NBP to be better able to accommodate large capital inflows.

Poland's transition to an inflation-targeting regime began during 1998. As in Hungary, the introduction of inflation targeting was preceded by the amendment of the Act on the NBP. This Act specified that the primary objective of the NBP is to maintain a stable price level and simultaneously support economic policy of the government, provided that this does not constrain the execution of the primary target. The Act also established the Monetary Policy Council (MPC) of the NBP, which replaced the NBP Management Board as the decision-making body. In April 1998, the MPC updated the *Assumptions of Monetary Policy for 1998,* prepared originally by NBP Management Board in September 1997, and confirmed that the 1998 NBP inflation target of 9.5 percent remained unchanged.[12] In June 1998, the MPC defined target for monetary policy in 1999, which was to re-

---

12. This should be interpreted more as a forecast than as a full-fledged inflation target.

duce inflation to 8–8.5 percent and began to work on *Assumptions of Monetary Policy for 1999,* as well as on *Medium-Term Monetary Policy Strategy for 1999–2003.* These documents were approved in September 1998, and at the same time the NBP officially announced the introduction of inflation targeting. The NBP also announced at that time the medium-term inflation target for 2003: reduction of inflation to less than 4 percent. The NBP also indicated that from that time on, annual inflation targets would be announced in *Assumptions of Monetary Policy.*

It should be noted that at the time of announcement to implement inflation targeting, Poland still maintained an exchange rate band, which at the time of announcement was widened from ±10 percent to ±12.5 percent, and later to ±15 percent. Only in April 2000 did Poland abandon the exchange rate band and switch to a managed float.

Poland has decided to target the broad CPI. The NBP explained that the CPI has been used extensively in Poland since the beginning of transition, and that it is deeply rooted in public perceptions as the measure of inflation. The CPI provides accurate information about changes in price levels of consumer goods and services. Application of some measure of core inflation would require eliminating from the targeted index some prices of goods and services that strongly affect public perception of inflation developments. However, the NBP has started preparatory work for calculating the core inflation index, and it did not exclude the possibility that it would start targeting core inflation in the future.[13]

Like the Czech Republic, Poland has chosen to target a band rather than a point. Initially, it chose a quite narrow target range, just one-half of a percentage point, which was subsequently widened to 1.2 points. The NBP explains that before the introduction of inflation targeting, monetary targets in Poland were defined as fixed points, and a wider band could possibly signal to the public a weaker commitment to reducing inflation. It could be argued that under such circumstances a fixed point could be better than a narrow band, as both are unlikely to be hit, and the damage of missing a point could be less serious than the damage of missing a band. However, the NBP did not exclude the possibility that it may widen the band in the future.

Unlike the Czech National Bank, the NBP did not explicitly define exceptions that would allow missing the inflation target without requiring the monetary policy response. However, the NBP subsequently analyzed in depth the process of inflation in Poland and the role of monetary and nonmonetary factors (National Bank of Poland 2001, appendix 2). Specifically, the NBP calculates and analyzes different measures of the core inflation. It explains that even though core inflation rates do not replace the

---

13. See National Bank of Poland (1998). It is noteworthy that the NBP intends to calculate the core inflation itself. Usually, central banks targeting a measure of underlying inflation do not calculate this index. In order to avoid a conflict of interest, they let other agencies, mainly statistical offices, calculate and publish underlying inflation.

headline consumer price index, they provide input for research and analysis and for decisions on monetary policy.

9.3.3 Hungary

The introduction of inflation targeting in the Czech Republic could be characterized as a "big bang" approach. There was a clear break with the past fixed exchange rate regime, and after a few months of technical preparation, a full-fledged inflation-targeting regime was put in place. In contrast, Hungary's introduction of inflation targeting could be characterized as "gradualist," even more so than for Poland.[14]

Like other transition economies, Hungary adopted early in its transition an exchange rate peg of the forint against the basket of currencies. However, the peg was adjusted downward quite often to maintain external competitiveness. The fluctuation band was gradually widened from ± 0.5 percent to ± 2.25 percent, to reduce speculative pressures ahead of the predictable adjustments of the parity. But this mechanism did not prevent large short-term capital inflows in late 1994, and in March 1995, after a devaluation of 8.3 percent, the regime of ad hoc adjustment was replaced with a crawling band. The monthly rate of crawl was initially set at 1.9 percent but was gradually reduced to 0.4 percent after October 1999. This regime succeeded in bringing inflation down from about 30 percent in 1995 to below 10 percent in 1999.

Even at the time when the Czech Republic and Poland were abandoning fixed exchange rate regimes, the Hungarian authorities continued to view this narrow fluctuation band as a useful nominal anchor. The band helped reduce inflation and anchor inflation expectations, while at the same time avoiding excessive real appreciation and erosion of competitiveness. However, like other emerging-market countries with a fixed exchange rate, Hungary too was ultimately forced to deal with the problems caused by large capital inflows. For some time, Hungary was able to avoid pressure on the narrow exchange rate band because of the presence of controls on short-term capital flows. These controls were effective in introducing a wedge between onshore and offshore interest rates, providing some degree of independence to monetary policy. But it was clear that as capital controls were relaxed in line with progression to EU accession a narrow-band regime would become more difficult to sustain.

The problems with the narrow exchange rate band began to intensify in the course of 2000. Inflation, which declined significantly in the period 1995–99, began to creep up again. While this increase in inflation was initially triggered by external shocks, like higher world oil prices, domestic fac-

---

14. Perhaps this is just another example of the gradualist approach of Hungary to economic reforms more generally, unlike the "big bang" or "shock therapy" approach applied in the Czech Republic and Poland.

tors began to play a role as well, including the exchange rate regime. The constraints of the narrow band and increasing capital inflows in 2000 began to make it more difficult for the central bank to simultaneously pursue disinflation and nominal exchange rate stability. Early in 2000, the central bank acted to reduce the pressure on the exchange rate band by cutting interest rates, and it also threatened to introduce capital controls. This strategy worked, and the exchange rate depreciated. However, in a situation of strong economic growth, robust domestic demand, and tight labor markets, reducing interest rates did not help much in fighting inflation, which remained relatively high. Periodically, speculative pressures for appreciation and widening of the band appeared, forcing the central bank to cut interest rates and/or intervene in foreign exchange market. It opted to do mainly the latter, and it sterilized the liquidity created as a result of these interventions.

However, as the sterilization costs were increasing, it was becoming clear that the narrow exchange rate band had outlived its usefulness and that Hungary needed to introduce more exchange rate flexibility if it was to succeed in reducing inflation further.[15] In May 2001, the authorities finally decided to widen the fluctuation band around the forint parity against the euro to ±15 percent.[16] The crawling regime was maintained, with the rate of crawl reduced to 0.2 percent monthly, and remaining controls on short-term capital flows were phased out. In October 2001, the crawling peg was completely abolished.

While a wider exchange rate band should allow the government to attach more priority to fighting inflation, as we will discuss below, a conflict between the inflation target and exchange rate target could still arise and complicate the conduct of monetary policy. However, the change in the monetary policy regime has been somewhat confused. At the time when the authorities decided to widen the fluctuation band, they did not immediately announce a shift to a new monetary policy regime. Even though the new exchange rate band was too wide to serve as a useful nominal anchor, the authorities were moving to inflation targeting only gradually. But on July 13, 2001, the new Act on the National Bank of Hungary (NBH) was enacted by Parliament, which defined the achievement and maintenance of

15. In 2000, inflation ended at 10.1 percent (December to December), much more than the government had projected earlier. In 1999, the government projected that average annual inflation would be 6–7 percent in year 2000. In early 2001, inflation increased further, close to 11 percent. Hungary's ambition to join the EU and adopt the euro as soon as possible had probably contributed to the increasing emphasis on further progress with disinflation that could be accomplished only with a higher degree of nominal exchange rate flexibility, and on the willingness to accept the consequences of a stronger currency for the competitiveness and external balance.

16. Israel also adopted an inflation-targeting regime with a narrow exchange rate band in 1991. Like Hungary, it also found it necessary to widen the exchange rate band, doing so in 1995. Over time, the Israelis have further downplayed the exchange rate in their inflation-targeting regime. For a discussion of Israeli inflation targeting and the role of the exchange rate, see Leiderman and Bufman (2000) and Bernanke et al. (1999).

price stability as the prime objective of the NBH. The Act also sought to reinforce NBH independence, in accordance with the EU requirement.

In its August 2001 Quarterly Inflation report, the NBH explained that for the next couple of years it would be using the inflation-targeting system to achieve a gradual reduction of inflation to a level corresponding to price stability (National Bank of Hungary 2001, 35–36). The NBH objective is to meet the Maastricht criterion on inflation in 2004–2005, so that it can adopt the euro in 2006–2007. Specifically, the NBH states that it will seek to bring inflation down to around 2 percent. In agreement with the government, the NBH set an inflation target of 7 percent for December 2001, 4.5 percent for 2002, and 3.5 percent for 2003 and 2004. In recognition of the fact that the NBH cannot instantly offset unexpected inflationary shocks, it has also established a ±1 percent tolerance band around the announced disinflation path.

The primary instrument that the NBH uses to attain its inflation targets is changes in its benchmark interest rates. The NBH has particularly emphasized the important role of changes in exchange rate on inflation. It argues that in Hungary, the exchange rate channel is the central bank's fastest and most powerful means of influencing domestic prices. (However, we will see later in section 9.5 that this reasoning may be dangerous.) While the exchange rate will not have the same prominent role as during the narrow-band regime, and the NBH will be less able to control its short-term movements, it will continue to play an important role. The NBH has indicated that it will try to influence the exchange rate in order to achieve the desired inflation outcome. In order to achieve the changes in exchange rate, it will use mainly changes in interest rates, while direct intervention in the foreign exchange market will be used only exceptionally, to deal with emergency situations. The NBH recognizes that in the short term, the actual exchange rate could deviate from an exchange rate path that would be consistent with the disinflation path. All in all, exchange rate movements seem to play a much more important role in Hungary than in other inflation-targeting countries. Such explicit emphasis on the role of exchange rate movements in achieving inflation targets as seen in Hungary is quite unique.

The NBH estimates that it takes up to one and a half years for changes in interest rates to have a full impact on inflation. It argues that if it tried to keep inflation in line with the targeted path over the short-term horizon, the result could be excessive volatility of output (and arguably also excessive instrument volatility). Therefore, it will confine policy responses only to deviation of forecasted inflation from targeted inflation over the horizon of one to one and a half years.

The transparency of this new system should be enhanced by the publication of NBH's inflation projections every quarter for the following six quarters. Moreover, the NBH will also publish the considerations that were behind its monetary policy decisions, and its analysis of the achievement of inflation target. The Quarterly Report on Inflation also contains the projection of inflation using a fan chart.

Unlike the CNB, the NBH began to target headline inflation immediately. But there is no discussion in NBH official documents about the reasons for choosing to target headline inflation rather than adjusted or underlying inflation. The NBH also did not specify any exceptions that would justify a deviation of actual inflation from its inflation target, although there is some discussion in its inflation reports about the possible extent of price deregulation and its effects on headline inflation. When announcing the introduction of inflation targeting, the NBH was also silent about the possible conflict between the exchange rate band and the inflation target.

Overall, the impression is that the NBH has focused less on operational aspects of the inflation-targeting regime than has the CNB or even the NBP. Perhaps this reflects the fact that NBH officials still attach importance to the nominal exchange rate band as an important anchor of the economy. They seem to believe that moving the exchange rate within the band will help them to achieve a long-term inflation target that will allow them to qualify for euro adoption. In a sense, this strategy could be understood: why invest heavily in a detailed design for a policy framework that will be removed in a few years anyway after Hungary adopts the euro? The Czech Republic and Poland introduced inflation targeting much earlier, and they may also be less eager to adopt the euro as soon as possible. This means that inflation targeting could be in place for a longer time and that a well-designed inflation-targeting framework may be more necessary.

9.4   Preliminary Experience with Inflation Targeting

In view of the relatively short period during which inflation targeting has been implemented in the transition economies, it is too early to make a definitive judgment about the experience of the operation of this new policy framework. Nevertheless, some preliminary observations can be made. There are two ways in which we can evaluate the experience with inflation targeting in transition economies.

First, we can look at how successful inflation-targeting central banks were in achieving inflation rates close to their inflation targets. Here the answer is "not all that successful." Initially, the CNB significantly undershot its inflation target several times, while the NBP first overshot it and subsequently undershot it. The NBH hit its targets in 2001 and 2002, but its short experience with inflation targeting does not tell us much yet. But even this short-term experience makes one thing clear: namely, the problems of simultaneously targeting inflation and exchange rate in a world of free capital flows.

Second, we can examine the success of inflation targeting in reducing inflation. Looking only at these countries' success in hitting their inflation targets could be too narrow a perspective for assessing the performance of inflation targeting. All central banks in inflation-targeting transition economies have emphasized that the main purpose of the inflation-targeting framework is to allow these countries to bring inflation down to a level that would qualify them for euro adoption. When we evaluate inflation targeting from this perspective, the preliminary experience with this regime should be judged more positively: all three countries are proceeding well with disinflation, and there is a good chance that in a few years they will be able to reach price stability, as defined for the purpose of euro adoption. However, the process of disinflation is not a smooth one, and there are quite large variations in inflation.

Let us now look in more detail at the record of implementation of inflation targeting in the three analyzed countries. First we will discuss the speed of disinflation implied by announced inflation targets, and then we will examine how successful the inflation-targeting countries were in hitting these targets.

9.4.1   Inflation Targets and the Speed of Disinflation

In many advanced economies that pursue inflation targeting, this regime has been introduced only after price stability has been reached (Bernanke et al. 1999). But this was not the case in the transition economies, where, at the time of introduction of inflation targeting, inflation was still running well above the level considered consistent with price stability. Therefore, the authorities in these countries had to make two decisions: (a) to quantify an inflation target that would be compatible with the long-term objective of price stability, and (b) to decide on the time horizon within which this ultimate objective was to be met—that is, to decide on the speed of disinflation.

There is extensive literature discussing how to quantify price stability. In the literature, we can find several arguments why central banks should not quantify price stability as inflation at zero or near zero (in the range of 0–1 percent). One reason relates to downward nominal wage rigidity. If the inflation rate were to approach zero under the condition of downward wage rigidity, it would be difficult to achieve real wage adjustment in response to changed market conditions, such as a negative demand shock. The result could be higher-than-desirable real wages, higher unemployment, and lower economic growth.[17] A second reason relates to the impossibility of reducing nominal interest rates below zero, which means that if inflation is close to zero, real interest rates cannot be pushed below zero when this might be necessary in order to stimulate economic activity.[18] Furthermore,

17. This mechanism is described in Akerlof, Dickens, and Perry (1996), but it is highly controversial because the evidence that low inflation leads to a rise in unemployment is very mixed. In addition, as pointed out in Groshen and Schweitzer (1996, 1999), inflation can not only put "grease" in the labor markets as Akerlof, Dickens, and Perry argue, but also put in "sand" that makes the labor markets less efficient.
18. This argument has been made in Summers (1991).

Table 9.2   **Inflation targets**

Country	Targeted inflation (%)	Period
Czech Republic	1–3 (2–4)[a]	2005
Australia	2–3	Average during a business cycle
Brazil[b]	2–6	2001
Chile	2–4	2001
Poland	< 4	2003
Hungary	Around	2004–2005
Mexico	3	2003
Izrael	3–4	2001
New Zealand	0–3	From 1996
Canada	1–3	From 1995
Euro area	< 2	From 1999
United Kingdom	2.5	From 1996

Source: Schaechder, Stone, and Zelmer (2000); web sites of Banco de México (http://www
.banxico.org.mx/), National Bank of Hungary (http://www.mnb.hu/), and European Central
Bank (http://www.ecb.int/).

[a]1–3 percent is for net inflation, 2–4 percent for headline inflation.

[b]For 2002, the target was subsequently set at 2.5–4.5 percent, but as a result of the debt crisis
and sharp currency depreciation, inflation in 2002 reached 12.5 percent. In response to higher
inflation, the central bank also raised its 2003 and 2004 targets.

a zero inflation target may lead to periods of deflation, which could pro-
mote financial instability and make it harder to conduct monetary policy
because interest rates would no longer provide a useful guide to the stance
of monetary policy (Mishkin and Schmidt-Hebbel 2002).

In the literature, one can observe a convergence of views that an inflation
rate of 1–3 percent corresponds to price stability (see table 9.2). If we look
at how central banks quantify price stability in practice, we see that there
is not much difference between the theoretical conclusions and what the
central banks actually do. This is the case for all economies—developed,
developing, and transition.

However, some have raised the question of whether the specific conditions of transition economies would not justify targeting somewhat higher
inflation than in developed economies. High-growth countries typically experience real exchange rate appreciation by an amount proportional to the
relative difference of traded to nontraded sector productivity growth relative to the rest of the world (the Harrod-Balassa-Samuelson effect). If it is
appropriate for these countries to aim at traded goods inflation similar to
that of industrialized countries in the long run, then trend real appreciation requires a domestic nontraded goods inflation that is somewhat
higher, and so the inflation rate should be slightly higher than would be desirable for average-growth countries. Škreb (1998) notes that in the transition economies it is particularly difficult to measure precisely the improvements in the quality of goods. As a result, actual inflation could be much

lower than measured inflation. Because of these measurement problems, as well as other reasons, Škreb argues that in transition economies inflation in the range of 4–5 percent would correspond to price stability.

Other authors argue, however, that during the convergence with the developed economies, transition economies should be expected to experience a rapid growth of labor productivity from implementation of economic reforms, which should produce lower inflation (Deppler 1998). Clinton (2000) argues that rapid productivity growth in transition economies weakens the traditional arguments in favor of a notably higher-than-zero inflation rate. Given the rapid growth of labor productivity, a decline in nominal wages would rarely be needed.[19] Similarly, given the high real return on capital and high trend toward economic growth, it is not very likely that a situation would arise in which a central bank would have to stimulate an economy in recession with the help of negative real interest rates.

What can be said about the speed of disinflation? Theoretically, disinflation could be too quick, resulting in excessively large (although arguably temporary) loss of output and higher unemployment, or it could be too slow; inflation expectations could become more entrenched at a high level, and this would make it more costly to reduce inflation later.[20] Therefore, it could be argued that there exists an optimal speed of disinflation that would minimize the sacrifice ratio (the ratio of loss of output to disinflation).[21] However, the determination of this optimal speed of disinflation is less a matter of exact science and more a matter of judgment.

In the literature, a number of factors have been identified that affect the sacrifice ratio—that is, the output effect of disinflation. These include the structure of the economy, the degree and the means of indexation of wages and other nominal variables, past history of inflation and stabilization, credibility of monetary policy, the degree of openness of the economy, and so on. Furthermore, as has been shown in the case of other countries, change in inflation is positively correlated with the level of economic activity (Stock and Watson 1999). Given the fact that economic reasoning does not provide a hard conclusion about the optimal speed of disinflation, and in view of the important consequences of the decision about the speed of disinflation for the economy and for different population groups, societies

19. One problem with this argument is that the rapid productivity growth applies economywide, but there could still be firms or industries where productivity growth would be small or negative and where decline in nominal wages would be called for if inflation was close to zero.

20. It could be argued that lower inflation usually means higher output growth, and therefore the sooner lower inflation is reached, the sooner will the economy achieve a higher output growth. But there are also counterarguments. For example, due to a loss of marketable skills, persons that could be seen as temporarily unemployed during the period of rapid disinflation could become permanently unemployed, which results in an additional loss of output.

21. For a discussion of the costs of disinflation see Ball (1994). The author comes to the conclusion that fast disinflation reduces the sacrifice ratio.

pay particular attention to the mechanism through which this decision is reached. By its nature, the decision about the speed of disinflation is not a purely technocratic decision that could be put solely in the hands of professional economists or central bankers. Because different speeds of disinflation will have different consequences for different population groups, this decision is by nature a political one, and thus an argument can be made for entrusting it to a political body that has the political legitimacy to make such political choices. This has implications for the debate on the optimal degree of central bank independence that is discussed in section 9.5.

However, for transition countries in Central and Eastern Europe, the desire to adopt the euro at some point in the future is of more practical relevance for monetary policy than the theoretical arguments about the appropriate quantification of price stability and the optimal speed of disinflation. Eventual euro adoption will depend on the ability to meet the Maastricht criteria, including low inflation, and the decision to adopt the euro at a certain date will thus implicitly contain a decision on how quickly and how far disinflation will have to go.

All three countries that we examine will have to adopt the euro at some point after entering the EU, even though they may choose a different speed with which to do so. But notwithstanding this possible different speed, all three countries are committed to a relatively fast disinflation. Table 9.3 summarizes the speed of disinflation implied by the level of inflation at the time of the introduction of inflation targets and by the long-term inflation objective.

As we can see, the ultimate objective is defined in each country in a different way: as a range in the Czech Republic (both upper and lower band are specified); as a maximum ceiling in Poland (only an upper band is specified), and as a "soft" point target in Hungary (no lower and upper bound are specified, but inflation should meet the Maastricht criterion). This also means that one single inflation rate could meet all these constraints at the same time.

Even though the Czech Republic did not reveal a firm intention to choose the fastest possible strategy to adopt the euro, the CNB still opted for a relatively quick disinflation so that it would be able to meet the Maastricht criterion and eventually move quickly to adopt the euro if it chooses to. Figure 9.1 shows the CNB's actual and targeted inflation. When the inflation-

Table 9.3   The speed of disinflation

Country	End-1997 inflation	Introduction of inflation targeting	Inflation at that time	Direction of inflation	Ultimate objective	Year to be achieved
Czech Republic	10.0	December 97	10.0	Rising	2–4	2005
Hungary	18.4	August 01	8.7	Falling	Around 2	2004–5
Poland	13.2	June 98	12.2	Falling	< 4	2003

Note: All inflation figures refer to CPI.

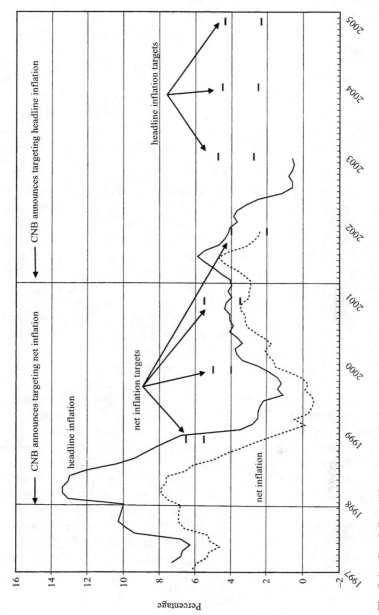

Fig. 9.1   Czech Republic, annual inflation and inflation targets, year-over-year
Source: Czech Statistical Office.

targeting framework was adopted in December 1997, inflation was 10 percent, and it continued to rise, to about 13 percent in early 1998 (in CPI terms; net inflation approached 8 percent). The CNB decided that at the end of 1998 net inflation should decline to 5.5–6.5 percent and, at the end of year 2000, to 3.5–5.5 percent. In December 1999, the CNB quantified its long-term objective of price stability: net inflation in the range of 1–3 percent in 2005, which was subsequently complemented by setting the 2005 CPI target in the range of 2–4 percent. Given the inflation target for the year 2000 in the range of 3.5–5.5 percent, this implied an average annual reduction in net inflation by 0.5 percentage points. The CNB explained that this long-term target would basically imply a continuation of the existing pace of disinflation. However, in December 2002, CPI inflation fell to 0.6 percent, which already brought it well below the long-term target range.

In Poland, the NBP first set a short-term inflation target in June 1998 for end-1999 in the range of 8–8.5 percent (see figure 9.2). At the time of the announcement of the inflation target, inflation was above 12 percent and declining. In September 1999, the NBP also announced the medium-term target of CPI inflation of less than 4 percent at the end of 2003. Subsequently, inflation continued to fall faster that expected, and in March 1999, when it fell to around 6 percent, the NBP modified the end-1999 CPI target to 6.6–7.8 percent. In September 1999, in *Monetary Guidelines for the Year 2000,* the NBP set end-2000 inflation target in the range of 5.4–6.8 percent. However, the process of disinflation in Poland was interrupted, as inflation increased from 5.6 percent in February 1999 to 11.6 percent in July 2000. Therefore, the 2001 inflation target was set higher than in 2000, 6–8 percent, but the targeted inflation range for end-2002 was reduced to 4–6 percent. As inflation at the end of 2001 fell to 3.6 percent, meeting this target would have required another mild pickup in inflation. Instead, inflation in 2002 fell rapidly and in December 2002 reached 0.8 percent, resulting in another significant undershooting of the target. During 2003, inflation in Poland remained below the NBP long-term objective.

Hungary launched official inflation targeting only in mid-2001.[22] At that time, inflation was already declining: from a peak of 10.8 percent in May 2001, it fell to 8.7 percent in August when details of the new inflation-targeting regime were published in the Quarterly Inflation Report (see figure 9.3). For 2001, the inflation target was set in the range of 6–8 percent. For 2002, the inflation target was set at 3.5–5.5 percent, and for 2003 the target was set at 2.5–4.5 percent.[23] The NBH's long-term objective is that

22. The NBH was publishing inflation objectives based on government budgetary projections for 1998, 1999, and 2000 (12–13 percent, 9 percent, and 6–7 percent respectively), but these were not formal inflation targets and there was no formal requirement for the NBH to meet them (see Siklos and Ábel 2002).

23. The long-term inflation target and the 2002 target were announced in the August 2001 Inflation Report, while the 2003 target was announced in the press on December 2001, when the government agreed with the NBH's proposal.

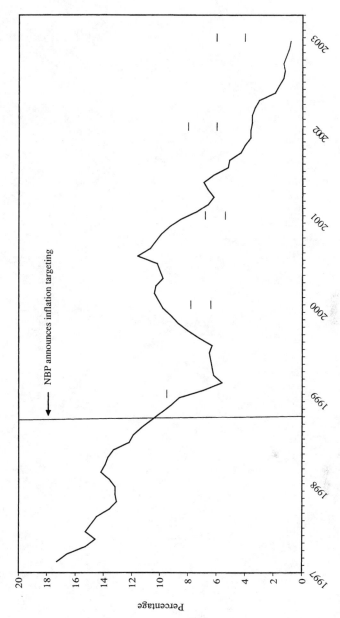

Fig. 9.2 Poland, actual inflation and inflation target, year-over-year

Source: Central Statistical Office Poland.

Note: In June 1998, the NBP defined the end-1999 inflation target. However, the NBP officially announced the introduction of inflation targeting only in September.

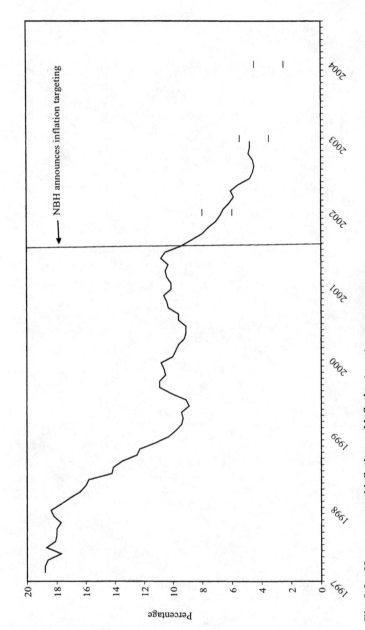

Fig. 9.3　Hungary, actual inflation and inflation targets, year-over-year
Source: Hungarian Central Statistical Office.

Hungary meet the Maastricht criterion on inflation in 2004–2005, which should be possible with inflation even slightly higher than the 2 percent that the NBH seeks to achieve in the long term. Unlike the Czech Republic and Poland, Hungary also specified its long-term inflation target qualitatively, in terms of meeting the Maastricht criterion for inflation, thus underscoring its preference to adopt the euro sooner rather than later. As inflation in late 2003 approached 6 percent, meeting the long-term inflation target would require bringing inflation below present level, in contrast to the Czech Republic and Poland, where inflation is likely to pick up somewhat from present unsustainable low levels.

9.4.2   Hitting and Missing Inflation Targets

In the previous section, we examined experience with inflation targeting from the perspective of disinflation. In this section, we look at how successful the three countries were in meeting their inflation targets. In this respect, we should keep in mind that countries can be quite successful, in the longer term, in bringing inflation down, but if a successful disinflation is accompanied by a significant instability of inflation (as evidenced by repeated large undershooting or overshooting of inflation targets), this can be costly for the economy as well.

There is not yet much we can read from the history of inflation targeting in Hungary because it is so recent (see figure 9.3). The 2001 target was announced only in August 2001, and it therefore was more of a short-term inflation forecast than an actual inflation target. Therefore, the fact that Hungary met this target and the 2002 target does not tell much about the operation of its inflation-targeting framework. The inflation target for 2002 implied a fairly rapid disinflation, alongside the trend started in mid-2001. In 2001 and 2002, disinflation was helped by the appreciation of the forint. However, since the forint has reached the upper end of the fluctuation band and the government seems to resist the revaluation of parity, there is no room for further nominal appreciation that would assist in further disinflation.

Table 9.4 and figures 9.1 and 9.2, which show the history of inflation targeting in the Czech Republic and Poland, tell a very different story. In the Czech Republic, the CNB significantly undershot its inflation targets, particularly in 1998 and 1999, and less in 2000. Net inflation fell to 1.7 percent at the end of 1998 and to 1.5 percent at the end of 1999, well below the CNB's targets. Only in 2001, in the fourth year of inflation targeting, did the CNB succeed in achieving its inflation target, but it undershot its target again in 2002.

As we can see in figure 9.2, in Poland there was an opposite problem, as the NBP significantly overshot its targets in 1999 and 2000. In the course of 1998, inflation in Poland was falling rapidly, and at the end of the year it fell to 8.6 percent, less than the 9.5 percent projected. A more-rapid-than-expected decline in inflation prompted the NBP to reduce early in 1999 its

Table 9.4   Targeted and actual inflation in the Czech Republic and Poland

	Czech Republic (net inflation)		Poland (headline inflation)	
	Target	Actual	Target	Actual
1998	5.5–6.5	1.7	n.a.	8.6
1999	4–5	1.5	6.4–7.8 (8–8.5)[a]	9.8
2000	3.5–5.5	3	5.4–6.8	8.5
2001	2–4	2.4	6–8	3.6
2002	2.75–4.75[b]	0.5	4–6	0.8

Source: Czech National Bank, National bank of Poland, various documents.
Note: n.a. = not applicable.
[a]Initial target in parentheses.
[b]Headline inflation.

target for end-1999, from 8–8.5 percent to 6.4–7.8 percent, a step that in retrospect may seem to have been somewhat premature. If the NBP had maintained its original target, 8–8.5 percent, it would have missed it by only a very small margin. But in the course of 1999, inflation began to increase again, and the 1999 target was missed by a significant margin, as was the 2000 target. Very tight monetary policy and slowing economic activity helped to bring inflation down sharply in 2001, and subsequently the 2001 and 2002 targets were undershot quite sizably.

These repeated large deviations of actual inflation from the inflation target would seem to suggest that inflation targeting was not very successful in the Czech Republic and Poland. But before we make any definitive judgments about the success or failure of inflation targeting in these two countries, it is important to understand the reasons for such significant deviations of actual from targeted inflation. We have to examine more closely both the domestic and the external economic circumstances that prevailed during this period and that affected actual inflation.

At the time when the CNB launched inflation targeting, inflation was rising quite rapidly, but at the same time the economy was already slipping into a prolonged recession. The 1998 and 2000 inflation targets were specified at the time when the CNB (and other public and private forecasters) expected much stronger economic growth than actually materialized.[24] However, with the onset of a major banking crisis in 1997–98, economic activity fell and contributed to a much faster disinflation than was envisaged by the CNB's inflation targets.[25] Moreover, the 1997–98 financial crises and

---

24. For example, the May 1998 *World Economic Outlook* projected real GDP growth in 1998 of 2.2 percent. This forecast was quite accurate, but with an opposite sign. Actual growth was –2.2 percent.

25. Of course, the hotly debated question was whether and to what extent the CNB's excessively tight monetary itself contributed to slower-than-projected growth.

weak global economic activity contributed to falling commodity prices, including energy prices.[26] The CNB calculations suggest that these external factors had a sizeable effect on net inflation: in 1998, these factors reduced net inflation by 2–3 percentage points (Čapek 1999, 9). In the absence of these shocks, net inflation at the end of 1998 would probably have been close to the bottom of the target range. There were also other structural shocks that contributed to lower-than-projected inflation. Among the more important was the continuing unexpected decline in foodstuff prices in 1998 and 1999. Ex post, the decline in foodstuff prices was ascribed to the struggle of the retail distributors for market share in the Czech market. Weak domestic demand, together with strong koruna and strong competitive pressure in the domestic economy resulting from penetration on the Czech market of foreign distributors, continued to keep inflation low even after the effects of external price shocks began to disappear. In addition, the decision not to exclude energy prices and to exclude adjustment of regulated prices from the targeted price index did not achieve its objective of encouraging the government to pursue a "courageous policy of price deregulation," as the CNB initially hoped.

When inflation targeting was introduced, Poland was facing very different economic circumstances from those of the Czech Republic. First, the implications of global developments for domestic inflation were better known to the NBP at that time and could be incorporated into the inflation target. As in the Czech Republic, inflation in Poland declined significantly during 1998 and 1999, but this decline was less dramatic and did not last as long. Already in the second half of 1999, inflation in Poland had begun to exceed by an increasingly wider margin inflation in the Czech Republic. Relatively rapid growth of domestic demand, increase in import prices, and the monopolistic structure of some industries together resulted in the reversal of disinflation in Poland in the course of 1999. Fiscal policy was also much more expansionary than the NBP had expected, and this expansionary stance further fueled domestic demand.

The NBP responded to these developments with a significant tightening of monetary policy, and it continued to keep monetary conditions very tight even when inflation began to fall sharply later in 2000 and in 2001. This (to some excessively) tight monetary policy also brought economic growth nearly to a halt by the end of 2001, and contributed to increased tension between the NBP and the government, which even led by the end of 2001 to threats of reduction of NBP independence. It appears that the NBP tried to use a tight monetary policy stance as an instrument to force

26. In U.S. dollar terms, oil prices fell by 31.2 percent, while nonfuel commodity prices fell by 14.7 percent in 1998. See International Monetary Fund (1999). It should be noted that this effect of financial crises contributed to an unexpected fall in inflation worldwide. The May 1997 IMF World Economic Outlook projected that in 1998 consumer prices in advanced economies would increase by 2.5 percent, while the actual increase was only 1.5 percent.

the government to strengthen structural fiscal balance, even at the cost of significant undershooting of its inflation target.

Judging by its success in meeting its inflation target, the NBP has not been very successful thus far. In the first two years, inflation targets were overshot, and in the third and fourth years there was significant undershooting. Recent years saw a significant instability of inflation, which fell rapidly from 17.8 percent in the beginning of 1997 to 5.6 percent in February 1999, then rose to 11.6 percent in July 2000, and fell again to 0.8 percent in December 2002. In Poland, external factors may have been of less importance in explaining the failure to meet inflation targets than in the Czech Republic, while the conduct of macroeconomic policy probably mattered more. First, unexpected fiscal expansion, combined with easy monetary policy, contributed to the acceleration of inflation and overshooting of inflation targets; subsequently, sharp tightening of monetary policy, in the absence of further easing of fiscal policy, reduced inflation sharply down and produced a significant undershooting of the target.

9.4.3   Comparison of Inflation and Output Performance of Inflation Targeters with Other Transition Countries

We have seen that hitting inflation targets has not been an easy exercise. However, this may have been unavoidable given the shocks the inflation targeters were subjected to. To assess the success of inflation targeting in transition countries, we have to ask how well the inflation targeters have done relative to the nontargeters.

There are two alternative monetary policy regimes to inflation targeting that transition countries have chosen:

1. Exchange rate peg: a crawling peg for Hungary until August 2001, a standard peg for Latvia (peg to SDR), and a hard peg of the currency board type for Bulgaria, Estonia, and Latvia
2. Float without an inflation target: Slovakia, Slovenia, and Romania[27]

Figures 9.4 and 9.5 compare inflation rates (year over year) in the Czech Republic and Poland with those of the other transition countries. A relevant starting date for comparing the different monetary regimes is December 1998 (marked in the figures), which corresponds to the first date that inflation targets were to be met in the Czech Republic. As we can see in figure 9.4, which has a comparison with the non-inflation-targeting floaters, the Czech Republic and Poland experienced lower levels of inflation for most of the 1999–2002 period than did the non-inflation-targeting floaters. On the other hand, figure 9.5, which has a comparison with the exchange rate

---

27. The currency regimes of these countries are characterized as managed floats. In June 2001, Romania's currency regime was reclassified from a managed float to a crawling band because the central bank intervenes to prevent currency appreciation.

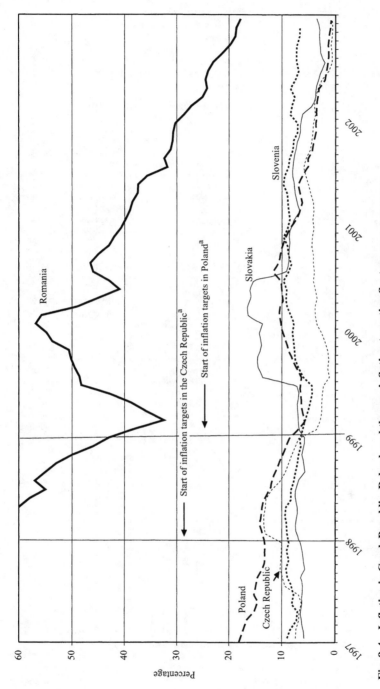

Fig. 9.4   Inflation in Czech Republic, Poland, and the non-inflation-targeting floaters, year-over-year

Source: Czech Statistical Office, Central Statistical Office of Poland, Statistical Office of the Republic of Slovenia, Statistical Office of the Slovak Republic, and National Statistical Office of Romania.

[a]Indicates the date of the first inflation target.

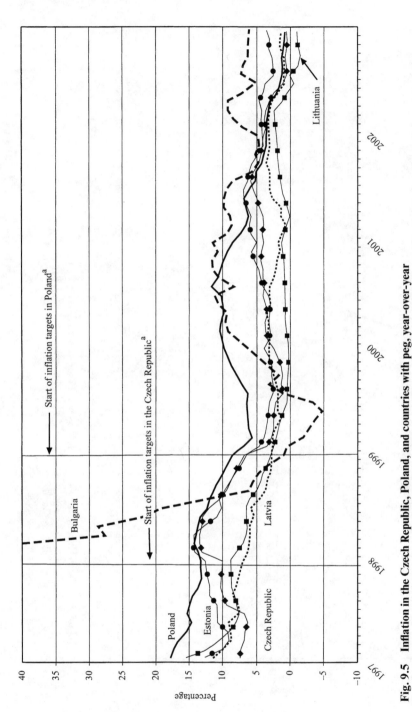

Fig. 9.5   Inflation in the Czech Republic, Poland, and countries with peg, year-over-year

Sources: Czech Statistical Office, Central Statistical Office of Poland, NBP, National Statistical Office of Bulgaria, Statistical Office of Estonia, Statistical Office of the Republic of Slovenia, Statistical Office of the Slovak Republic, Statistics Lithuania, and Central Statistical Bureau of Latvia.

[a]Indicates the date of the first inflation target.

Table 9.5   **Inflation and output growth volatility: 1998–2002**

Country	Inflation volatility	Output volatility
Czech Republic	3.49	2.00
Poland	3.6	1.82
Hungary	3.08	0.72
Estonia	3.08	3.07
Latvia	1.34	2.52
Lithuania	2.18	3.5
Bulgaria	49.7	3.97
Slovakia	3.88	1.39
Slovenia	1.34	0.82
Romania	18.37	4.83

peggers, does not display a clear dominance of inflation targeting over pegging. Hungary, with its soft peg, and Bulgaria, with its currency board, have typically had higher inflation rates than the Czech Republic and Poland; but Lithuania, with its currency board, and Latvia, with its standard peg, have experienced lower inflation rates. Estonia has had inflation rates comparable to those in the Czech Republic, but up until the last half of 2002 had lower inflation than Poland.

Clearly a low level of inflation is only one measure of success of monetary regimes—equally important is the variability of inflation and output. Table 9.5 provides the standard deviation of both inflation and output for the period 1999–2002. Here we see that the Czech Republic and Poland are in the middle of the pack on both criteria. The Czech Republic and Poland have higher standard deviations of inflation than the hard-pegging Baltic countries, while they have lower variability than Hungary, a soft pegger, Bulgaria, a hard pegger, and Slovakia and Romania, non-inflation-targeting floaters. Slovenia, a non-inflation-targeting floater, has equal inflation variability to the Czech Republic but has lower variability than Poland.

Although we should not make too much of the data in figures 9.4 and 9.5 and table 9.5 because they cover such a short period and because these countries have been subjected to different shocks, it is worth noting that in terms of inflation control, inflation targeting does not clearly dominate the other monetary policy regimes chosen by transition countries.

We reach a similar conclusion in terms of output variability as seen by the standard deviations of output growth reported in table 9.5.[28] The Czech Republic and Poland have had lower standard deviations than the hard

28. The mixed results reported here on the performance of inflation-targeting regimes relative to other monetary policy regimes is not very surprising. As argued by Calvo and Mishkin (2003), the choice of monetary policy regime is likely to be less important to the macroeconomic performance of emerging-market and transition countries than deeper institutions.

peggers, Bulgaria and the Baltic states, but have had higher standard deviations than Slovakia and Slovenia, non-inflation-targeting floaters. Hungary, a soft pegger for most of the period, had the lowest standard deviation of output growth of all the countries in the table. However, even less should be made of these comparisons, because real shocks have differed dramatically across the transition countries. For example, as we can see in figure 9.6, the Baltic countries, which have a higher proportion of their trade with Russia as a result of their having been part of the former Soviet Union, suffered very dramatic output declines in 1999 in the aftermath of the Russian financial crisis in the fall of 1998. The contraction of the Russian economy at that time had a far smaller impact on transition countries that were less integrated with Russia and whose trade was mostly with Western Europe.

9.5   Lessons and Problems of Inflation Targeting in Transition Economies

Even though the experience of the implementation of inflation targeting in transition economies is relatively short, it has nevertheless brought out several specific issues, which deserve discussion. First, how should the standard operational aspects of inflation targeting be specified—that is, what price index should be targeted? Should the inflation target be a point or a range? And what should the horizon for the target be? Second, given the fact that transition economies began inflation targeting in a situation of higher inflation than the long-term objective, how should the speed of disinflation be determined, and in a closely related question, how should the government be involved in setting inflation targets? Third, how should monetary policy respond to the deviation of the actual inflation from the targeted disinflation path, and how much should the floor of an inflation target be emphasized relative to the ceiling? Fourth, how should the exchange rate be incorporated into the inflation-targeting framework?

9.5.1   Operational Aspects of Inflation Targeting

What Measure of Inflation to Target?

In deciding what measure of inflation to target, central banks face a trade-off between transparency and the ability to control inflation. The advantage of a broadly defined headline inflation (i.e., the consumer price index) is that it is better understood by the public. However, the problem is that headline movements could reflect factors other than monetary policy measures. A more narrowly defined measure of inflation that excludes possible effects of transitory shocks could be better controlled by a central bank, but at the same time it could be more difficult for the public to assess the conduct of monetary policy on the basis of such measure. Given the emphasis on central banks' accountability and transparency in a regime of

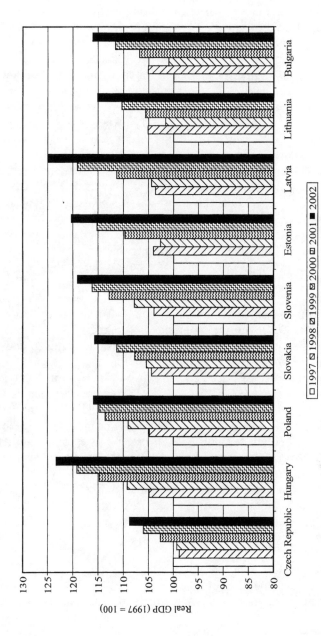

Fig. 9.6 Transition economies: Real GDP (1997 = 100)

Sources: Czech Statistical Office, Central Statistical Office of Poland, National Statistical Office of Bulgaria, Statistical Office of Estonia, Statistical Office of the Republic of Slovenia, Statistical Office of the Slovak Republic, Statistics Lithuania, and Central Statistical Bureau of Latvia.

inflation targeting, this could potentially be a serious handicap, particularly for a central bank that still has to earn its credibility.

The CNB opted for a compromise that it considered most appropriate for an economy in transition. For the purpose of inflation targeting, it introduced a new concept, so-called net inflation, which excluded regulated prices (see section 9.3.1). Specific conditions of economic transition have played an important role in selecting net inflation as the targeted measure of inflation. Unlike in industrial countries, many prices were still regulated in the Czech Republic in late 1997. The CNB knew that substantial changes in these regulated prices, including rents, would be needed before they reached a market-clearing level. As a result, a given monetary policy stance could produce different future paths of headline inflation, depending on the pace of price deregulation or the size of adjustment of administered prices. At the same time, this approach was supposed to avoid a situation in which the government would be hesitant to pursue a faster adjustment of regulated prices out of concern that the inflationary effects of such policy would force the CNB to tighten monetary policy, with adverse effects on economic growth, thus exacerbating the political cost of deregulation. Indeed, the former acting governor of the CNB, Pavel Kysilka, stated that "by targeting net inflation, we have provided a room to the government to pursue a courageous policy of price deregulation" (Kysilka 1998, 10–12). Obviously, a high share of regulated prices in total CPI does not make it easier for the central bank to deal with this trade-off between transparency and ability to control inflation.[29]

Subsequently, the pace of price deregulation and increase in administered prices was less than the CNB had hoped, and so use of the net inflation construct did not produce the desirable outcome the CNB expected. In addition, the net inflation construct turned out to be more volatile than headline inflation, helping to contribute to larger misses of the target. When it decided to target net inflation, the CNB did not exclude the possibility that in the future it could modify the measure of targeted inflation. The problems with the net inflation measure thus led the CNB to abandon it in April 2001, and it subsequently moved to targeting headline inflation as has been discussed in section 9.3.1.

Target a Point or a Range?

As in other aspects of design of the operational framework, there is a trade-off involved in deciding about the width of the band. A wider band increases the chance that monetary policy will be successful in keeping tar-

---

29. The Czech economy is very open, with imports representing about 50 percent of GDP, and changes in import prices of oil and gas have a large impact on domestic prices. However, at the time of the introduction of inflation targeting, the CNB had considered isolating the effects of price deregulation as more important than isolating the effects of terms-of-trade shocks or exchange rate effects.

geted inflation inside. But a too-large band could reduce the ability of inflation targeting to anchor inflation expectations, and it could be of less help in establishing the antiinflationary credibility. Some argue that a band that is narrow enough to anchor inflationary expectations is likely to be frequently missed, and that it is preferable to target a point and explain the deviations of actual inflation from that point target (Bernanke et al. 1999; Mishkin 2001).

In a sense, one can argue that a higher degree of uncertainty in projecting inflation and a correspondingly higher probability that even a target range would be missed makes the issue of point versus range less of an issue than in more advanced inflation-targeting economies. By setting a range, the central bank may indicate what is its estimate of uncertainty of reaching the inflation target. This is how the CNB has explained its decision regarding the width of the targeted range. Missing a target range then carries a larger risk of credibility loss than missing a target point. Targeting a reasonably narrow band (that is, narrow enough so that it provides a sufficient nominal anchor) does not make much sense when the probability that it would be missed is not significantly less than the probability of missing a point.

Time Horizon of Inflation Targeting

Monetary policy affects the economy and particularly inflation with long lags. In industrialized countries, lags from monetary policy to inflation are typically estimated to be on the order of two years. Shorter time horizons, such as one year, can be highly problematic. The first problem with too short a horizon is that it can lead to a controllability problem: too-frequent misses of the inflation target, even when monetary policy is being conducted optimally. The second problem is that it can lead to instrument instability, in which policy instruments are moved around too much in order to try to get inflation to hit its targets over the shorter horizon. A third problem is that too short a horizon implies that not enough weight is put on output fluctuations in the central bank's loss function.[30]

The experience with inflation targeting in New Zealand documented in Bernanke et al. (1999) illustrates these problems. In 1995, the Reserve Bank of New Zealand overshot its one-year-horizon inflation target range, making the governor subject to dismissal under the central-banking law. It was recognized in the Reserve Bank that the overshoot was likely to be short-lived and inflation was likely to fall, indicating that monetary policy had not been overly expansionary. Fortunately, this view was accepted outside the Bank, and the governor, Don Brash, whose performance was excellent, retained his job. Attempting to hit the annual target did, however, have the

---

30. As demonstrated by Svensson (1997), a faster target path of inflation to the long-run inflation goal implies a smaller weight on output variability in the central bank's loss function.

unfortunate consequence of producing excessive swings in the monetary policy instruments, especially the exchange rate. In a small, open economy, like New Zealand, exchange rate movements have a faster impact on inflation than interest rates. Thus, trying to achieve annual inflation targets required heavier reliance on manipulating exchange rates, which led to its having large swings. By trying to hit the short-horizon target, the Reserve Bank also may have induced greater output fluctuations. For example, the Reserve Bank pursued overly tight monetary policy at the end of 1996 with the overnight cash rate going to 10 percent because of fears that inflation would rise above the target range in 1997, and this led to an undesirable decline in output. The Reserve Bank has recognized the problems it had with a too-short target horizon and now emphasizes a horizon of six to eight quarters in their discussions of monetary policy (Sherwin 1999; Drew and Orr 1999). Furthermore, the Policy Target Agreement between the central bank and the government has recently been amended to be more flexible in order to support the longer policy horizon (Reserve Bank of New Zealand 2000).

The solution to avoiding too short a horizon for the inflation target is to set inflation targets for periods two years ahead (or longer). This automatically implies that the central bank will have multiyear inflation targets. The target for the current calendar year will have been set two years previously, while there will also be a target for the following year. With multiyear targets, the target from one year to the next could vary over time. The inflation target would vary in response to shocks to the economy, especially to supply shocks, which might need to be accommodated in order to keep output fluctuations from becoming excessive. Also, putting a weight on output fluctuations in a central bank's objectives, as is sensible, means that the approach of the inflation target to the long-run goal needs to be gradual (Svennson 1997). This also suggests the need for multiyear targets in which the inflation target, even one for two years ahead, may differ from the long-run target if shocks to the economy have driven inflation away from the long-run goal.

Initially, the horizons for inflation targets in the transition countries studied here were short, being on the order of a year, and this may have contributed to the controllability problem and the frequent target misses. Possibly in response to these problems, the CNB was the first to specify a long-term inflation target for a horizon of five years, and the NBH and the NBP have also specified medium-term inflation targets (see table 9.2).

9.5.2   Who Should Set the Inflation Target and Decide the Speed of Disinflation?

In the 1990s, there was a significant shift worldwide toward more independent central banks, partly in response to a better understanding of economic costs of political interference with monetary policy and high inflation. While not all central banks were given complete freedom to set monetary policy targets, most of them gained instrument independence—that is, the freedom to conduct monetary policy without external interference to meet the objective. Among economists, there seems now to be a consensus that central banks should have instrument independence—that is, independence to conduct monetary policy so as to meet the inflation target or other monetary policy objective. There also seems to be a consensus that central banks should not have goal independence—independence to set inflation targets or other monetary policy objectives (Fischer 1994).

From the early stages of economic transition, central banks in all three countries have received a significant degree of de jure independence, not only in the conduct of monetary policy (instrument independence) but also in setting the objectives of monetary policy (goal independence).

In the Czech Republic, the independence of the central bank was anchored in the Constitution, which stated that the government might intervene in the CNB's affairs only for reasons clearly outlined in the Act on CNB. The Act on CNB (No. 6/1993 of Collection of Laws) specified that the primary objective of the CNB is to ensure the stability of the Czech national currency (Article 2) and that the CNB Board should set monetary policy and the instruments for the implementation of these policies (Article 5). Moreover, the Act explicitly states that in providing for its primary objective the CNB shall be independent of any instructions given by the government. The governor, vice-governors, and members of the Board are appointed and recalled by the president (Article 6). The Act was subsequently amended in 2002, and the main objective of the CNB was changed to maintaining price stability, with the standard qualification that without prejudice to its primary objective the CNB shall support economic policies of the government leading to sustainable economic growth. The amended Act also states that "when providing for the primary objective of the CNB and when carrying out their activities, neither the CNB nor the CNB Board shall seek or take instructions from the President of the republics, from Parliament, from the Government, from administrative authorities or from any other body" (Article 9). The appointment of the governor and other CNB officials remains fully the responsibility of the president.

In Hungary, the Act on NBH was passed in October 1991 and reinstated the independence of the NBH. It has been amended several times since. The latest version, from June 2001 (Act LVIII of 2001), states that the primary objective of the NBH shall be to achieve and maintain price stability (Article 3) and that the NBH shall define and implement monetary policy in the interest of maintaining the stability of the national currency (Article 4). Article 6 states that "within the framework provided for by this Act, the NBH shall independently define its monetary policy and the instruments for implementing such policy." Article 38 stipulates that the government may not instruct the NBH in relation to its scope of tasks as set forth in the

Act. The president of the NBH is appointed for a period of six years by the president of the Republic at the proposal of the prime minister. The president of the Republic also appoints vice presidents and other members of the Monetary Council.

The legal position of the NBP is similar. The Act on the NBP of August 29, 1997, stipulates that the basic objective of the NBP shall be to maintain price stability, again with the addition that the NBP shall at the same time support government economic policies, insofar as this does not constrain pursuit of the basic objective (Article 3). The president of the NBP shall be appointed by the Sejm, at the request of the president of the Republic, for a period of six years. The vice presidents and other members of the NBP Management Board are appointed by the president of the Republic at the request of the president of the NBP. The nine members of the Monetary Policy Council (MPC) are appointed in equal numbers by the president of the Republics, the Sejm, and the Senate (Article 13). The responsibility of the MPC is to draw annual monetary policy guidelines and submit them to the Sejm for information (Article 12). Article 21 stipulates that in discharging its responsibilities the NBP shall collaborate with the appropriate bodies of the central government in developing and implementing national economic policy and strive to ensure proper performance of monetary policy guidelines. It should submit monetary policy guidelines to the bodies of the central government and report on the performance of monetary policy.

However, de jure independence does not always imply a de facto independence. While the NBP is not explicitly forbidden by the Act on NBP to seek instructions from the government and other bodies in pursuing its responsibilities, de facto, it decides alone on inflation targets. On the other hand, the NBH is de jure independent and forbidden to seek instruction, but in practice, the governor of the NBH seeks government endorsement for the NBH's monetary policy objectives.

The effort to make central banks legally independent reflected the belief of reformist governments and parliaments that politics should not interfere with the conduct of monetary policy. To a large extent, central-bank legislature in these countries was modeled after the German Bundesbank, which itself—for historical reasons—enjoyed a high degree of independence. In the early years of transition, no one really questioned the high degree of central-bank independence in the transition countries, as governments had to deal with the more urgent tasks of liberalization, privatization, and so on. However, the high degree of central-bank independence eventually became a source of tension.

These tensions appeared first in the Czech Republic. As we have discussed, in the early years of inflation targeting the CNB repeatedly undershot its inflation target, while economic growth turned negative. In many countries, this would probably have been sufficient to create tensions between central bank and government. In the Czech Republic, these tensions were further aggravated by political developments. To a large extent as a result of the poor state of the economy in the aftermath of the currency turbulence of 1997, the main pro-reform party split and new elections were called for mid-1998. In the meantime, a caretaker government was formed and the CNB governor became a caretaker prime minister. When a new government was formed after the election, he returned to the CNB. Inevitably, this drew the CNB further into politics, exactly the opposite of what the high degree of de jure independence was supposed to achieve.

The party that lost the election in 1998 criticized the CNB and the governor for mishandling monetary policy, contributing to economic decline, and thus affecting the outcome of the elections. The CNB was considered to be too independent and unwilling to coordinate monetary policy with the economic policy of the government. The speed of disinflation was considered as excessive, hurting economic growth. This criticism eventually resulted in legislative effort to curb the CNB's independence. When the CNB and the new government introduced jointly to Parliament an amendment to the CNB Act to bring it in line with EU standards, members of the party that lost the 1998 election submitted their own amendment that aimed at significantly reducing the CNB's independence. They proposed for Parliament to supervise and approve the operational budget, salaries of Board members to be cut, monetary policy decisions to be made in consultation with the government, and political parties to have more say in appointing the governor and Board members.

This proposal was strongly criticized by domestic and foreign financial analysts, by the International Monetary Fund, and—most importantly— by the EU and European Central Bank. Central-bank independence is a requirement for both EU and EMU membership, and this argument ultimately carried the most weight because of the planned accession of the Czech Republic into the EU/EMU. In the end, the CNB retained its independence, and with the appointment of new governor in 2000 the relationship with the government improved as well.

Similar tensions between the central bank and the government emerged in Poland during 2000 and 2001. As economic growth began to falter while interest rates remained high, the NBP was blamed by some politicians for having set its monetary policy excessively tight and for contributing to subpar growth performance. Tensions between the government and the NBP accelerated in October 2001, after the new government took office. Contributing to the tensions was the fact that the president of the NBP, Leszek Balcerowicz, was himself a former politician and main author of the cold-turkey stabilization program that was criticized by the center-left politicians who formed the government after the October 2001 elections.

The prime minister and other members of the cabinet have repeatedly attacked the MPC for keeping interest rates too high. The pressure to reduce the NBP's independence rose, and some members of Parliament from the two governing parties drew legal proposals to broaden the NBP's objectives to include economic growth and employment, and to increase the number of members of the MPC. Even though the government did not formally back these proposals, being well aware that this would complicate the EU/EMU accession, it did not mind using them as a tool to put pressure on the NBP to ease monetary policy. Because accession to EU/EMU is an important objective for Poland, it is not likely that these initiatives will succeed.

The Polish experience also illustrates the peril of central-bank effort to use monetary policy as a tool to force the government to pursue a more disciplined fiscal policy. The NBP tried to use tight monetary policy to pressure the government to improve structural fiscal balance, and kept interest rates very high even as inflation was falling below its target and growth came nearly to a halt. But instead of achieving this objective, the NBP only antagonized the government and put its independence under risk.

Even Hungary was not spared tensions between the central bank and the government. Recently, the government put forward a bill that proposed to set up a Supervisory Committee within the NBH. This committee would comprise delegates of political parties and two persons appointed by the minister of finance. Such a committee already existed in the past but was abolished. The NBH argued that such a step would infringe on NBH's operational independence and would go against the EU requirements on central-bank independence. Members of the government have also pressured the NBH to reduce interest rates in order to support growth. They argued that the NBH should not focus too much on inflation.

In Hungary, the reasons for this pressure on the central bank were mainly political and personal. The new NBH president who was appointed in 2001 was a former minister of finance, and from this position he had been exercising pressure on his predecessor. However, the previous NBH president is in close contact with the present prime minister and has used this relationship to put pressure on his successor. More recently, the conflict between the inflation target and exchange rate target has further increased these tensions.

Why do we see these tensions in all three inflation-targeting countries? There are several reasons. First, at the beginning of transition, central banks were given a large degree of both operational and goal independence. In a situation where inflation is still higher than the long-term objective of price stability, this means that central banks are given the freedom to decide on the speed of disinflation. As central bankers tend to be more ambitious with respect to the speed of disinflation than politicians, this creates the potential for tensions. These tensions tend to come into the open once economic growth falters, particularly if this poor growth performance is perceived as contributing to a loss of popularity of the governing party or parties. In our view, this experience suggests the superiority of closer involvement with political authorities in setting monetary policy objectives. Particularly in the difficult period of economic transition, a goal of independence of central banks may complicate rather than facilitate the conduct of monetary policy.

Second, the fact that politicians became central-bank governors, or that central-bank governors stepped into politics, had the unwanted consequence of drawing central banks more into the political arena. Finally, despite significant progress in economic and political reforms, the rule of law still remains less firmly established even in the most advanced transition economies, making politically motivated attacks on central banks more likely.

Public disputes between the central bank and the government of the kind that we have seen in the Czech Republic, Poland, and Hungary are not desirable. They undermine the credibility of the inflation-targeting framework and could increase the costs of future disinflation. As we have already noted, the decision about the speed of disinflation has a different impact on different groups in the society, and there is thus a strong case for such a decision to be made by a politically responsible body like the government. Clearly, it would better serve the credibility of monetary policy if the speed of disinflation were the result of a joint decision by a central bank and the government, although this is obviously not a practice in all inflation-targeting countries.[31] Such a joint decision would have several advantages. Most important, it would be more credible. When a government decides (perhaps jointly with a central bank) on the speed of disinflation, it is explicitly or implicitly committing itself to policies supporting this disinflation objective. The speed of disinflation (co)decided by government would be seen by markets as a political decision that takes into account possible short-term trade-offs, and it would reduce the probability that policies supporting the achievement of targeted disinflation would be challenged on grounds that they do not reflect the preferences of the society and that they are unduly costly.

Even in situations where the ultimate responsibility for deciding on the speed of disinflation would rest with the government, the central bank could still provide important input into this decision by voicing (possibly publicly) its own views about the desirable speed of disinflation. Of course, there is a risk that the government would choose too slow a disinflation. However, it is not clear whether this would impose higher costs on the economy than a unilateral decision by a central bank to pursue a more rapid disinflation that would subsequently be challenged by the government as being too ambitious. Furthermore, a unilateral decision by the

31. Such arrangement need not necessarily imply a formal subordination of the central bank to the government in setting inflation targets. For example, in Australia, the inflation target is set by a central bank alone, and the government subsequently publicly endorses this target.

central bank to pursue rapid disinflation is likely to weaken support for the central bank, as has occurred in the Czech Republic and Poland. This increases the risk of loss of independence and interferes with the ability of the central bank to control inflation in a longer-run context.

The question of who should set inflation targets has a specific aspect in transition economies that are expected soon to adopt the euro. One can argue that when the political decision to adopt the euro is made, it effectively specifies both the disinflation path and the ultimate inflation target. The inflation target is determined by the need to meet the Maastricht criterion concerning maximum permissible inflation, and the speed with which this inflation is to be achieved is determined by the timing of the euro adoption. To the extent that there is a firm political commitment to adopt the euro at a certain date, it becomes to a large extent irrelevant whether the inflation target is set by a central bank or a government. The government does not have much room to be more lenient on inflation than the central bank, because of the possibly large economic and mainly political costs of not meeting the Maastricht criteria.

9.5.3   How Should a Bank Respond to Deviations of Inflation from the Target, and How Much Should the Floor of an Inflation Target Be Emphasized Relative to the Ceiling?

The implementation of inflation targeting in the Czech Republic and Poland has brought out an interesting problem that arises in other inflation-targeting economies as well: how should a bank respond to a significant deviation of inflation from the inflation target? If the inflation rate overshoots the ceiling of the target range, then the logic of inflation targeting clearly requires the central bank to bring the inflation rate back into the target range. However, should an inflation-targeting central bank try to lock in a lower-than-targeted inflation once actual inflation falls below the targeted path if inflation is not yet at the long-run goal? Another way of asking this question is to ask whether a central bank should emphasize the floor of the inflation target as much as the ceiling and thus work as hard to avoid undershoots of the target as overshoots.

As we have noted, the CNB significantly undershot its inflation target in 1998 and 1999, and less so in 2000. Similarly, at the end of 2001, inflation in Poland fell well below the NBP end-2001 target. What should central banks do in such situations? Should they be upset at the undershoot and indicate that this was a serious mistake? Alternatively, would it be appropriate for them to lock in the unexpectedly rapid disinflation of previous two years and focus monetary policy on maintaining price stability from then on?

A case could be made for acting opportunistically and using faster-than-expected disinflation to lock in this windfall benefit of lower inflation (Haldane 1999). This is what Poland has tried to do by adjusting its original end-1999 inflation target after actual inflation early in 1999 began to fall faster than projected. It would seem that when inflation has been reduced to less than the central bank target but still remains above the level of inflation corresponding to price stability, it would make no sense to let inflation go up again only to be forced to reduce it again later. Disinflation, even at a moderate pace, could be costly, and if a country can avoid the need to disinflate in the future, this should spare the economy some loss of output. Whether past faster-than-planned disinflation was a result of luck or mistakenly tight monetary policy may seem not to matter—bygones are bygones, past costs, if any, have been incurred, and let's just avoid any future costs of disinflation.[32]

In practice, central banks have treated the floors of inflation-target ranges in different ways (Clifton 1999). Some treat them as seriously as upper sides of a band and have eased monetary policy to bring inflation back up inside the band (e.g., New Zealand in 1991), while others preferred to consolidate the unexpected rapid disinflation (Israel in 1998).

The recent experience of Poland has shown the risks of trying to lock into inflation that is lower than originally targeted. There are several problems with opportunistic disinflation and with treating the bottom of the band leniently. First, there is a possibility that opportunistic disinflation will not find much sympathy with politicians. Particularly if the disinflation that is faster than originally intended coincides with a significant weakening of economic activity, there will be calls for a relaxation of monetary policy, even if this should mean a return to somewhat higher inflation. The NBP has exacerbated this problem because its inflation target is now stated to be less than 4 percent, suggesting that they are not particularly disturbed by undershooting the inflation target. This may have contributed substantially to the poor relations between the NBP and the government and the decrease in public support for the NBP. The CNB was well aware of the danger from its undershoots of the inflation target and did not even suggest that it could lock in the lower-than-targeted inflation.

Second, if rapid disinflation is a result of temporary external shocks like large declines in the price of commodities, it would be a mistake to assume that monetary policy could lock in such disinflation forever without large future costs. Once these shocks are over, prices of commodities usually do not stay low but rise again as global demand recovers. Monetary policy that would try to prevent an accelerated pace of disinflation in times of declining commodity prices or other positive supply shocks would probably be too expansive. In the same vein, monetary policy would risk being too restrictive if it tried to avoid any acceleration of inflation as positive supply shocks are reversed.[33] Like many other inflation-targeting central banks,

32. Of course, such an argument could be made only if inflation does not fall below the long-term inflation target corresponding to price stability.

33. If a positive price shock was permanent, perhaps as a result of a sudden increase in productivity, it would be appropriate to accommodate the effect of such shocks on inflation.

the CNB has explicitly recognized that monetary policy should not attempt to offset temporary supply shocks that knock disinflation from its projected path.

Third, an opportunistic approach to disinflation could undermine the credibility of an inflation-targeting framework. By setting medium-term inflation targets, central banks attempt to establish a predictable environment that would allow economic agents to plan for the future. Even though there could and will be deviations from the target, credible inflation targeting would lead the agents to expect that a central bank would do its best to return actual inflation to the targeted path. Attempts at opportunistic disinflation could increase the uncertainty, because they would make monetary policy less predictable. For example, economic agents could expect that central banks would adjust an inflation target upward in case of a negative shock as well.

However, a situation may arise where the path of disinflation has been set incorrectly. For example, competitive pressures in the economy due to liberalization, privatization, and a more open trade would produce a faster disinflation for a given monetary policy stance than originally expected. These favorable supply shocks would be likely to cause inflation to undershoot without leading to a decline in output. In this case, maintaining the original disinflation target would require an overly expansionary monetary policy, and it would seem to be more appropriate to accept in such a case a disinflation that is faster than originally intended. This would also likely be politically feasible because the undershoot of the inflation target would not be accompanied by output losses.

9.5.4   Inflation Targets and the Exchange Rate

In the recent literature on inflation targeting, particularly on inflation targeting in emerging-market countries, increased attention has been paid to the open-economy aspect of inflation targeting (Mishkin 2000; Mishkin and Savastano 2001; Eichengreen 2001). It has been recognized that the large degree of openness of some emerging-market economies, in combination with specific characteristics of their financial systems, creates additional challenges for the implementation of inflation targeting. Exchange rate movements directly affect domestic inflation, both as a result of external shocks and as a result of monetary policy measures. The open-economy aspect of inflation targeting plays a prominent role in inflation-targeting transition economies as well.

In the initial stage of transition, all three inflation-targeting countries analyzed in this paper used a fixed exchange rate as a nominal anchor to import price stability and bring domestic inflation quickly down. The currency peg–based stabilization was quite effective, because it allowed them to bring down inflation relatively quickly. The initial monetary overhang was eliminated by a one-time increase in price level rather than by a sustained growth in prices, and thus its elimination did not become embedded in inflation expectations.

However, first Poland, then the Czech Republic, and finally Hungary abandoned the currency peg and moved to more flexible exchange rate arrangements. This has fundamentally changed the operation of monetary policy and the operation of the monetary transmission mechanism.

The importance of the exchange rate channel of monetary policy depends directly on the degree of openness of the economy to trade flows and on the degree of integration into international capital markets. The Czech Republic and Hungary are very open economies with respect to trade flows: the share of exports plus imports in gross domestic product (GDP) exceeds 100 percent. Poland is a more closed economy: the share of exports plus imports reaches "only" about 50 percent. Therefore, exchange rate movements in the Czech Republic and Hungary will have a more important effect on domestic prices and inflation, and thus on inflation targeting. At the same time, all three countries are very open to international capital flows, because in preparation for EU membership they have largely completed capital account liberalization.

There are several reasons why exchange rate movements are important for inflation targeting in transition countries (Svensson 2000). First, exchange rate movements provide an additional transmission channel of monetary policy. While in a closed economy aggregate demand and expectation channels dominate, in open economy the exchange rate channel may be the most important one, particularly in the short run. The exchange rate transmission channel operates both directly and indirectly. Changes in nominal exchange rate directly affect the domestic prices of imported final goods and thus the targeted CPI index.[34] Indirectly, the exchange rate channel operates by affecting domestic demand. Changes in real exchange rate affect domestic and foreign demand for domestic goods, thus enhancing the standard aggregate-demand channel. Second, the exchange rate is one channel through which foreign disturbances could be transmitted into the domestic economy. Third, transition countries also have a particular concern with their exchange rates because they want to become part of the EU and the euro zone. Thus they must eventually fix their exchange rates to the euro as part of their planned entry into the EMU and so naturally care more about the exchange rate at which they will convert their currency into the euro upon accession.

Finally, it should be noted that emerging-market countries and transition economies are usually more vulnerable to large exchange rate move-

---

34. The CPI includes prices of both domestic and imported goods. Consequently, it represents a combined measure of domestic inflation and imported inflation. Domestic inflation is also affected indirectly by changes in prices of imported goods. Changing the price of imported input used for the production of domestic goods would affect costs and—depending on the extent of the pass-through—domestic prices.

ments. The reason is the underdeveloped capital market in domestic currency and the need to borrow in dollars or other foreign currency, except for very short-term borrowing. This results in open foreign exchange positions of banks and/or corporations and thus increased vulnerability of their balance sheets to large exchange rate movements. While large appreciation can make domestic producers uncompetitive (both in foreign and domestic markets), large depreciation could cause substantial damage to firms or banks with large open foreign exchange positions and precipitate a financial crisis of the type described in Mishkin (1996, 1999).

While it is generally recognized that in such open economies as the Czech Republic and Hungary the exchange rate represents both an important channel of monetary transmission and an important channel of transmission of external disturbances, it is less obvious what the implications are for the treatment of the exchange rate in the regime of inflation targeting. We can distinguish two approaches to the exchange rate: an active and a passive approach. In an active approach, the central bank cares about the exchange rate over and above its effects on inflation and actively tries to influence the level of the exchange rate. In a passive approach, a central bank cares about the exchange rate only to the extent that it affects aggregate demand and the inflation rate, and it does not try to directly manipulate the exchange rate, only reacting to changes in exchange rate that would threaten its inflation target.[35]

As we have noted, the Czech Republic and Hungary are particularly open economies, and the exchange rate will therefore have an important effect on inflation and other variables. Poland is less open, and exchange rate movements seem to play a less important role in monetary policy deliberations. It seems that the NBH is pursuing this active approach, to judge from its statements on the role of the exchange rate in affecting inflation outcomes. As Orlowski (2000) argues, in Hungary, the central bank has focused its monetary policy on exchange rate stability, and for this reason changes in the exchange rates have a strong effect on inflation. Such a strong effect was not observed in the Czech Republic and Poland. This may explain the relatively larger emphasis put by the NBH on the exchange rate channel of monetary policy.

The problem is that too much reliance on the exchange rate channel of monetary transmission carries the risk that a central bank would focus excessively on a short-term horizon. In open economies, the exchange rate channel not only is important but operates very fast, because changes in exchange rate directly affect domestic prices of imported final goods, and with longer but still potentially quite short lag prices of domestic goods

35. Again, we can distinguish a more or less active use of this passive approach, depending on the time horizon during which the central bank would try to meet the inflation target by responding to exogenous exchange rate changes.

containing imported inputs. This rapid transmission may induce the infla-tion-targeting central bank into too much of a focus on a short-term hori-zon and into an effort to keep actual inflation in line with the inflation tar-get by orchestrating exchange rate changes. However, excessive use of the exchange rate channel could have undesirable consequences. It could cause a problem óf instrument instability and result in excessive variability of real exchange rate,—and thus in an increased degree of uncertainty in the economy and higher variability of output.[36] In addition, it runs the risk of transforming the exchange rate into a nominal anchor that takes prece-dence over the inflation target. For example, as documented in Bernanke et al. (1999), Israel's intermediate target of an exchange rate around a crawl-ing peg did slow the Bank of Israel's effort to win support for disinflation and lowering of the inflation targets in the early years of its inflation-targeting regime. In addition, an active focus on the exchange rate may in-duce the wrong policy response when a country is faced with real shocks such as a terms-of-trade shock. Two graphic examples of these problems are illustrated by the experiences of New Zealand and Chile in the late 1990s.

The short horizon for the inflation target in New Zealand led the Reserve Bank to focus on the exchange rate as an indicator of the monetary policy stance because of the direct impact of exchange rate movements on infla-tion. By early 1997, the Reserve Bank institutionalized this focus by adopt-ing as its primary indicator of monetary policy a Monetary Conditions In-dex (MCI) similar to that developed by the Bank of Canada. The idea behind the MCI, which is a weighted average of the exchange rate and a short-term interest rate, is that both interest rates and exchange rates on average have offsetting impacts on inflation. When the exchange rate falls, this usually leads to higher inflation in the future, and so interest rates need to rise to offset the upward pressure on inflation. However, the offsetting effects of interest rates and exchange rates on inflation depend on the na-ture of the shocks to the exchange rates. If the exchange rate depreciation comes from portfolio considerations, then it does lead to higher inflation and needs to be offset by an interest rate rise. However, if the reason for the exchange rate depreciation is a real shock, such as a negative terms-of-trade shock, which decreases the demand for a country's exports, then the situation is entirely different. The negative terms-of-trade shock reduces aggregate demand and is thus likely to be deflationary. The correct interest rate response is then a decline in interest rates, not a rise as the MCI sug-gests.

With the negative terms-of-trade shock in 1997, the adoption of the MCI in 1997 led to exactly the wrong monetary policy response to the East

36. This risk seems to be well recognized by the NBH. See National Bank of Hungary (2001, 35–36).

Asian crisis. With depreciation setting in after the crisis began in July 1997 after the devaluation of the Thai baht, the MCI began a sharp decline, indicating that the Reserve Bank needed to raise interest rates, which it did by over 200 basis points. The result was very tight monetary policy, with the overnight cash rate exceeding 9 percent by June of 1998. Because the depreciation was due to a substantial, negative terms-of-trade shock that decreased aggregate demand, the tightening of monetary policy, not surprisingly, led to a severe recession and an undershoot of the inflation target range, with actual deflation occurring in 1999.[37] The Reserve Bank of New Zealand did eventually realize its mistake and reversed course, sharply lowering interest rates beginning in July 1998 after the economy had entered a recession, but by then it was too late. It also recognized the problems with using an MCI as an indicator of monetary policy and abandoned it in 1999. Now the Reserve Bank operates monetary policy in a more conventional way, using the overnight cash rate as its policy instrument, with far less emphasis on the exchange rate in its monetary policy decisions.

Chile's inflation-targeting regime also included a focus on limiting exchange rate fluctuations by having an exchange rate band with a crawling peg that was (loosely) tied to lagged domestic inflation. This focus on the exchange rate induced a serious policy mistake in 1998 because the central bank was afraid it might lose credibility in the face of the financial turmoil if it allowed the exchange rate to depreciate after what had taken place in financial markets after the East Asian crisis and the Russian meltdown. Thus, instead of easing monetary policy in the face of the negative terms-of-trade shock, the central bank raised interest rates sharply and even narrowed its exchange rate band. In hindsight, these decisions were a mistake: the inflation target was undershot and the economy entered a recession for the first time in the 1990s.[38] With this outcome, the central bank came under strong criticism for the first time since it had adopted its inflation-targeting regime in 1990, which weakened support for the independence of the central bank and its inflation-targeting regime. During 1999, the central bank did reverse course, easing monetary policy by lowering interest rates and allowing the peso to decline.

The contrast between the experience of New Zealand and Chile during this period with that of Australia, another small open economy with an in-

---

37. The terms-of-trade shock, however, was not the only negative shock the New Zealand economy faced during that period. Its farm sector experienced a severe drought, which also hurt the economy. Thus, a mistake in monetary policy was not the only source of the recession. Bad luck played a role too. See Drew and Orr (1999) and Brash (2000).

38. Because, given its location in Latin America, Chile's central bank did have to worry more about loss of credibility and also because Chile encountered a sudden stop of capital inflows at the time, the ability of the Chilean central bank to pursue countercyclical policy was more limited than that of the Australian central bank. However, although lowering interest rates in 1998 may not have been as attractive an option, the sharp rise in the policy interest rate in 1998 was clearly a policy mistake.

flation-targeting regime, is striking. Prior to adoption of their inflation-targeting regime in 1994, the Reserve Bank of Australia had adopted a policy of allowing the exchange rate to fluctuate without interference, particularly if the source of the exchange rate change was a real shock, like a terms-of-trade shock. Thus, when faced with the devaluation in Thailand in July 1997, the Reserve Bank recognized that it would face a substantial negative terms-of-trade shock because of the large component of its foreign trade conducted with the Asian region and that it should not fight the depreciation of the Australian dollar that would inevitably result (McFarlane 1999; Stevens 1999). Thus, in contrast to New Zealand, it immediately lowered the overnight cash rate by 50 basis points to 5 percent and kept it near this level until the end of 1998, when it was lowered again by another 25 basis points.

Indeed, the adoption of the inflation-targeting regime probably helped the Reserve Bank of Australia to be even more aggressive in its easing in response to the East Asian crisis and helps explain why its response was so rapid. The Reserve Bank was able to make clear that easing was exactly what inflation targeting called for in order to prevent an undershooting of the target, so that the easing was unlikely to have an adverse effect on inflation expectations. The outcome of the Reserve Bank's policy actions was extremely favorable. In contrast to New Zealand and Chile, real output growth remained strong throughout this period. Furthermore, there were no negative consequences for inflation despite the substantial depreciation of the Australian dollar against the U.S. dollar by close to 20 percent: inflation remained under control, actually falling during this period to end up slightly under the target range of 2 to 3 percent.

While it would not be desirable if a central bank tried to actively manipulate the exchange rate, this does not imply that it should not respond to an exchange rate shock. However, whether it should respond and how it should respond depend on the nature of the shock. As illustrated above, the response to a real shock to the exchange rate such as a change in the terms of trade should be entirely different from the reaction to a portfolio shock.

The relevant question concerning the transition economies is this: what types of shock are they likely to face in the period ahead of the EU/EMU membership? And how vulnerable are they to large exchange rate movements? How much should they be concerned about exchange rate movements for other reasons than the risk that the inflation target will not be met?

Besides the standard shocks that all open emerging-market economies could face, transition economies could face specific external shocks related to the euro adoption: specifically, the convergence play. The convergence play refers to capital inflows to accession countries stimulated by the expected behavior of interest rates and exchange rates ahead of the euro adoption. Countries that have joined the EMU in the past have experienced a sizable decline in the currency risk premium of their debt—that is, the premium to compensate the debt holders for the risk that their currency would lose value. The decline in the currency risk premium resulted in lower interest rates on their debt instruments in local currency, and thus a higher price of these instruments. Increased prices allowed holders of these instruments to realize capital gains. Therefore, investors could reasonably expect that transition countries that have joined the EU will soon adopt the euro as well, and from past experience they could expect a reduction in interest rates on debt instruments issued by these countries that would allow them to reap capital gains. In other words, these investors have incentive to play on the convergence of interest rates to euro area level and invest in fixed-income instruments issued by accession countries. The resulting increase in capital inflows and currency appreciation could be viewed as a pure portfolio shock that would require interest rate reduction. But reducing interest rates could conflict with the inflation target, because it could stimulate domestic demand too much and result in faster increase in domestic prices. On the other hand, if monetary policy does not respond, the large capital inflow could lead to the standard problems of excessive currency appreciation, balance-of-payments problems, and reversal of capital flow resulting in currency depreciation and higher inflation.

Complicating the problem even more is the exposure of accession countries to a second shock—in this case a real shock. It has been well documented that as transition economies catch up with the more developed EU countries, they experience rapid productivity growth, which produces real exchange rate appreciation, either by means of nominal appreciation or by means of higher inflation. In this case, the appreciation of the domestic currency should be seen as an equilibrium phenomenon, which is sustainable and does not require a monetary policy response. In sum, in the period ahead of the EU/EMU membership, accession countries could be exposed to two simultaneous external shocks that would tend to produce exchange rate appreciation but that would call for a different policy response. In practice, it could be difficult to disentangle what part of the currency appreciation is the result of the portfolio shock and what part results from the real shock. Balance-of-payments data on the size and composition of capital flows, and data on productivity growth, should provide some indication of the relative importance of these two types of shocks.

The recent experience of the Czech Republic illustrates yet another problem: currency appreciation caused by a large inflow of foreign direct investment (FDI) as a result of the sale of state-owned enterprises to foreign owners. One can argue that currency appreciation resulting from the inflow of FDI is the typical real shock that does not call for a monetary policy response: the currency appreciates, but FDI inflow results in more investment, better management, and ultimately in higher productivity, which validates the appreciation of the currency. This argument has two problems. First, while currency appreciation will always happen when there is a sale of domestic assets to foreigners for foreign currency, it is less sure that the increase in productivity validating the currency appreciation will follow. For example, a large part of recent sales consisted of utilities where the potential for increasing the competitiveness in export markets is limited. Second, there is a time discrepancy between the timing of the currency appreciation (immediate) and the productivity increase (later). And third, expectation of currency appreciation as a result of sales to foreigners of state-owned assets could itself induce investors to take positions in the domestic currency, in order to benefit from the expected appreciation once the privatization payment materializes. This would produce a currency appreciation even before the privatization-related capital inflow materializes.

All this complicates significantly the task of the inflation-targeting central bank. To the extent that currency appreciation reflects an equilibrium phenomenon, appreciation of the real equilibrium exchange rate, there would be little reason for concern. Such appreciation would not threaten economic growth and external equilibrium, and if inflation is still above the long-term target, it should help the central bank to bring inflation down. But how much should a central bank worry if this real appreciation is too fast and too large? It could result in a widening current account deficit and subsequent large exchange rate depreciation, with negative effects on inflation. And it could cause problems in the corporate sector, because adjustment to a fast and large currency appreciation could be more difficult. The standard prescription for a central bank dealing with large capital inflows and currency appreciation is sterilized intervention: buy foreign currency in the foreign exchange market and neutralize monetary effects of this intervention by selling bonds. Eventually, this intervention could be complemented by interest rate cuts, to reduce the incentive for capital inflows.

But this prescription may be of little help in the circumstances like those in the Czech Republic in 2001–2002. Large capital inflows are mainly in the form of FDI, and not attracted by a large interest rate differential. Reducing interest rates is not going to slow down FDI inflows. These are interest rate insensitive. Sterilized intervention would be possible, but this policy has its own problems. In order to be effective, it would have to be of a very large amount (on the order of several billion dollars) and it may not even be effective at all. Sterilizing such intervention could be quite costly for the central bank.[39]

For these reasons, the CNB has pursued a pragmatic strategy of gradual interest rate reduction, combined with occasional foreign exchange market intervention of limited magnitude. This intervention has been subse-

---

39. Of course, with falling interest rate differential, the costs of sterilization decline as well.

quently sterilized. The CNB recognized that in 2001–2002 currency appreciation reflected mainly the effect of the FDI inflow, and that it was therefore a real shock that the monetary policy had no business of neutralizing. However, the speed of the appreciation could be occasionally too fast, and at that point, the CNB felt that it could slow down the pace of appreciation by intervening, so that the corporate sector would have more time to adjust to the trend appreciation. In late 2002, capital inflows related to the convergence play (the portfolio shock) were not a serious issue for the Czech Republic, partly because the convergence play and the compression of yield spreads had already taken place.[40] Otherwise, the situation would have been even more complicated.

Another reason for not having benign neglect of the exchange rate is emphasized in Mishkin (2000) and Mishkin and Savastano (2001). For the reasons discussed earlier, transition countries with a lot of foreign-denominated debt may not be able to afford large depreciations of their currencies, which can destroy balance sheets and trigger a financial crisis. Central banks in these countries may thus have to smooth "excessive" exchange rate fluctuations, but not attempt to keep the exchange rate from reaching its market-determined level over longer horizons. The stated rationale for exchange rate smoothing would be similar to that for interest rate smoothing, which is practiced by most central banks, even those engaged in inflation targeting: the policy is not aimed at resisting market-determined movements in the exchange rate, but at mitigating potentially destabilizing effects of abrupt changes in exchange rates.

The challenges facing the central bank are somewhat different in Hungary. As was noted, Hungary still maintains an exchange rate band of ±15 percent. In the literature on inflation targeting, it is often emphasized that the absence of a second nominal anchor is one of the prerequisites of successful inflation targeting. Pursuing two nominal objectives could result in a situation where one objective will need to be given preference over the second objective, but without clear guidance as to how such conflict would be resolved, this could make monetary policy less transparent.[41] The question arises: to what extent might the existence of the ±15 percent exchange rate band in Hungary be considered as a second nominal anchor whose attainment could eventually conflict with the inflation target? The answer has turned out to be "a lot."

In mid-February 2002, the exchange rate of the forint hovered some 12–13 percent above parity, quickly approaching the upper part of the band.

---

40. In fact, at the end of 2002, spreads on domestic-currency sovereign bonds compared to the benchmark German bonds were negative for all maturities. See Ceska Sporitelna/Erste bank (2002). Of course, the question is whether such dramatic compression of yield spreads is sustainable.

41. On the experience with inflation targeting in the presence of nominal exchange rate band in Israel, see Leiderman and Bufman (2000).

Partly as a result of uncertainty related to parliamentary election, the currency weakened somewhat during the spring and summer, but it began to appreciate again later in 2002. In January 2003, it approached the upper end of the band, and speculation about the revaluation of parity resulted in a sharp acceleration of capital inflow that forced the NBH to respond by cutting interest rates by 2 percentage points and intervening heavily in the foreign exchange market. The NBH is reported to have bought more than 5 billion euros, increasing international reserves by 50 percent and base money by 70 percent.[42] Even though the NBH subsequently began to sterilize this huge injection of liquidity, market participants now assume that maintaining the exchange rate band will have priority over the inflation target and expect inflation in 2003 to exceed the NBH inflation target.[43]

This conflict between the inflation target and exchange rate target need not be a unique problem for Hungary. Other accession countries could face this problem once they become members of the EU and once they decide to join the ERM2 mechanism that requires them to limit exchange rate fluctuations in exactly the same way as Hungary already does today—that is, to peg the currency against the euro and allow maximum ±15 percent fluctuation around the established parity. Therefore, we now turn to the issue of monetary policy implementation in the period after EU accession and before EMU accession.

9.6   Monetary Policy within the ERM2 System

Participation in the ERM2 mechanism and subsequent adoption of the euro are obligatory for all new EU members (no opt-out clause is available). But the new EU members do not have to join the ERM2 mechanism immediately after the EU entry. Therefore, after joining the EU, the new members will have to decide how quickly to join the ERM2 mechanism and adopt the euro, and whether ERM2 membership would require a modification of the inflation-targeting framework.

How would monetary policy in the accession countries operate under the ERM2 regime, and what would be the main nominal anchor of the economy? Formally, the monetary policy framework after joining the ERM2 mechanism will be similar to the monetary policy framework in Hungary today, where the ±15 percent fluctuation band is already in place. But there will also be important differences. First, the adoption of the euro will be approaching, which could have important implications for capital flows (convergence play) and fiscal policy implementation (the need to meet fiscal criteria). Second, breaching the target band (its lower side)

42. See JPMorgan (2003).
43. Analysts have interpreted this as evidence that the NBH is determined to maintain the currency band even at the cost of temporary higher inflation. See IMF (2002).

would have different consequences for Hungary today and for accession countries operating within the ERM2 regime. Third, unlike Hungary's monetary policy today, the monetary policy and exchange rate of an accession country within the ERM2 regime will be of common interest to all EMU members, and the European Central Bank (ECB) could intervene to help the accession country to keep the exchange rate within the band.

The ERM2 fluctuation band will allow rather large exchange rate movements, too large to provide a sufficiently firm nominal anchor. For this reason, the inflation target will likely need to continue to play the role of nominal anchor, as it did in Spain before its entry into EMU (see Bernanke et al. 1999). Successful operation of inflation targeting after ERM2 entry should be facilitated by the fact that the process of disinflation is likely to be largely completed. Low inflation could reduce, though not fully eliminate, the probability that the inflation target would conflict with the commitment to maintaining the currency within the ERM2. Still, the possibility of a conflict between the inflation target and the ERM2 exchange rate band cannot be fully excluded. But it is important to be clear about the nature of this risk and how it could be mitigated.

Within the ERM2 framework, two situations could arise where monetary and other policies may be constrained by the fact that the exchange rate is approaching the lower or upper side of the band. One possibility is that the exchange rate would approach the upper (appreciated) band, as was happening in Hungary. In order to prevent breaching the permitted fluctuation band, interest rates may need to be reduced to moderate the pressure on the currency. But lower interest rates could interfere with the inflation target, because they could stimulate domestic demand more than the central bank considers prudent and could produce higher inflationary pressures. However, a strongly appreciating currency would also simultaneously act as a mechanism to dampen inflationary pressures, so it is not at all obvious that this conflict with the inflation target would actually become serious.[44] If reducing interest rates would not help, and pressures on the currency to appreciate persisted, another option would be to revalue the central parity.[45] This would reduce the burden of monetary policy and at the same time introduce a one-time deflationary shock.

A different conflict between the inflation target and exchange rate band would arise if there was downward pressure on the currency and if the exchange rate threatened to break through the lower (more depreciated) end of the band. Breaching the ERM2 lower target band would force the coun-

---

44. The direct effect of the appreciated exchange rate on inflation will be felt sooner than the indirect effect of reduced interest rates on aggregate demand and demand-induced acceleration of inflation.

45. For countries in the ERM2 framework, the ECB would also be expected to help a national central bank sustain the currency inside the fluctuation band, of course, to the extent that this does not interfere with the ECB's price stability objective.

try to start the ERM2 two-year test again, so it could be potentially costly. Central banks could react to such a situation by tightening monetary policy and raising interest rates. But this response certainly should not conflict with the inflation target. On the contrary, it should be in line with the inflation-targeting policy if the reason for downward pressure was too relaxed a policy. And tighter monetary policy would also help to mitigate inflationary pressures that may arise from currency depreciation. Tighter monetary policy would also be appropriate in the case when the currency depreciates as a result of a negative portfolio shock. Higher interest rates should help arrest capital outflow by making domestic currency assets more attractive. But the situation could be more complicated when the currency depreciates as a result of negative real shock which at the same time reduced aggregate demand for domestic output (domestic or foreign demand). Maintaining the currency within the fluctuation band could require a tighter policy stance than what would be required if monetary policy were guided only by the inflation target. As a result, actual inflation would become lower than the inflation target, and monetary policy would further weaken demand and economic activity that was already affected adversely by the negative real shock. Under normal circumstances, this would not be desirable. But temporary lower economic activity may be a price worth paying in a situation where the alternative would be to violate the Maastricht criterion of two years of successful operation within the ERM2 system, thus delaying euro adoption.

To some extent, fiscal policy could be used to reconcile eventual conflict between the inflation target and the ERM2 band. First, maintaining a fiscal policy stance that would clearly indicate authorities' determination to meet Maastricht criteria of public debt and fiscal deficit would reduce the risk of downward pressure on the currency as a result of a negative portfolio shock. It would also allow the maintenance of lower interest rates than if fiscal policy were more expansionary, and thus reduce short-term capital inflows. Second, a changing fiscal policy stance could be used as a defense against large exchange rate movements threatening to breach the ERM2 band. Fiscal policy could be tightened even more than what is required by Maastricht criteria in case of downward pressure on the currency that would threaten to break the lower side of the band, or—to the extent that meeting Maastricht criteria is not threatened—it could be relaxed in case of upward pressure on the currency. But in this case, using interest rate policy would be clearly preferable as a first line of defense.

The risk of conflict between the inflation target and exchange rate target will depend importantly on market expectations of the conversion rate of the national currency into the euro. If market participants expect that the current market rate will be also the conversion rate, there will be less risk of such conflict, as the behavior of market participants should actually limit the fluctuation of the actual exchange rate. However, widespread

Table 9.6   Lowest inflation rates in EU countries, 1995–2000

	1995	1996	1997	1998	1999	2000	2001
Country A	0.8	0.6	1.2	0.8	0.5	1.7	1.6
Country B	1.5	1.3	1.3	0.9	0.6	1.9	2.5
Country C	1.7	1.4	1.4	0.9	0.6	2.3	2.5
Average inflation	1.3	1.1	1.3	0.9	0.6	2.0	2.2
Maastrict criterion inflation[a]	2.8	2.6	2.8	2.4	2.1	3.5	3.7

Source: United Nations (2002).

[a]Average inflation in three countries plus 1.5 percentage points. Average inflation rounded up.

market expectation that the future conversion rate will differ significantly from the current exchange rate could result in large and volatile capital flows and swings in actual exchange rate that could severely complicate the simultaneous achievement of the inflation target (sufficiently low inflation to meet the Maastricht criterion) and exchange rate target (keeping the currency within the fluctuation band).

How should inflation targets be set after the countries have joined the EU and eventually the ERM2 mechanism? The obvious answer is to set the inflation target in such way that it will converge to inflation rate estimated to be consistent with the Maastricht criterion. Table 9.6 shows the annual inflation rate in three current EU members with the lowest inflation rate in the period 1995–2001. If we add to the average of inflation in three EU best performers the 1.5 percentage point margin allowed by the Maastricht Treaty, we receive the maximum permissible inflation in the accession countries that would be applied if they were to adopt the euro in that particular year.

If we take the period 1995–2001 as a benchmark, the inflation rate that the accession countries would have to reach in order to meet the Maastricht criterion was in the range of 2.1 to 3.7 percent. In 1998 and 1999, inflation in the EU countries was particularly low, and it would thus seem that reaching the Maastricht objective would have been particularly challenging for accession countries at that time. However, we should note that to some extent exceptionally low inflation in the EU was a part of global tendency of falling inflation, which affected the transition economies as well. To the extent that inflation in the EU and in the transition economies waiting to adopt the euro moves jointly in response to common external shocks like falling commodity prices and weak global economic activity, accompanied by large excess production capacity and weak pricing power of producers, lower permissible inflation does not make it necessarily more difficult (i.e., it does not require a tighter monetary policy) to qualify for euro adoption.

We can also see that the range of maximum permissible inflation of 2.1–

3.7 percent is broadly in line with the long-term inflation targets in the Czech Republic (2–4 percent), Hungary (around 2 percent), and Poland (less than 4 percent).

9.7   Conclusion

In this paper, we have discussed the experience with inflation targeting in the three transition economies—the Czech Republic, Hungary, and Poland. We have examined the circumstances leading to the switch from exchange rate pegs to inflation targeting and the modalities of inflation targeting in each of these countries. The short history of inflation targeting in these three countries does not yet allow us to draw any definitive conclusions about the success or failure of this regime. However, we conclude that inflation targeting in transition economies could be implemented reasonably successfully. While the examined countries have often missed inflation targets by a large margin, they nevertheless progressed well with disinflation. Still, increased uncertainty prevailing in transition economies makes it particularly difficult to predict inflation sufficiently far ahead, as required by the forward-looking nature of the inflation-targeting approach. In view of that, and given the possibility that transition countries will be more frequently hit by shocks that could divert inflation from the targeted path, misses of inflation targets are more likely there than in the more advanced economies.

This does not imply that monetary policy targeting other nominal variables like monetary aggregates would make the task of controlling inflation easier. Even though inflation targeting in transition economies is more difficult than in advanced economies, it could still bring significant benefits. It should be clear, though, that too much focus on hitting inflation targets at any price at all times could produce a significant instability of monetary policy instruments, damaging economic performance. The focus of inflation-targeting central banks should be on the medium-term horizon to ensure that disinflation remains on track and that inflation converges to a level deemed consistent with price stability. Alongside this trajectory, there will inevitably be misses, possibly sizable ones. Thus, the onus is on central banks' ability to clearly communicate to the public what the limits and possibilities of inflation targeting in transition economies are, and if it happens, to explain credibly and openly why inflation targets were missed.

A key lesson from the experience of the inflation-targeting transition countries is that economic performance will improve and support for the central bank will be higher if central banks emphasize avoiding undershoots of the inflation target as much as avoiding overshoots. Undershoots of the inflation targets have resulted in serious economic downturns that have eroded support for the central bank in both the Czech Republic and Poland. Also, economic performance will be enhanced if inflation-targeting central banks in transition countries do not engage in active manipulation of the exchange rate. This seems to be less of an issue in the Czech Republic and Poland, but it is still a live issue in Hungary.

A difficult problem for inflation targeting in transition countries is the often stormy relationship between the central bank and the government. This can be alleviated by having a direct government involvement in the setting of the inflation target and a more active role of the central bank in communicating with both the government and the public. In addition, having technocrats rather than politicians appointed as the head of a central bank may help in depersonalizing the conduct of monetary policy and increase support for the independence of the central bank.

We have also addressed the future perspective of monetary policy in the transition economies. We concluded that even after EU accession, inflation targeting can remain the main pillar of monetary strategy in the three examined accession countries during the time before they adopt the euro. Inflation targets would be guided toward meeting the Maastricht criterion for inflation, which would require maintenance of inflation at the level defined in long-term inflation objectives.

In addition, an important advantage of the inflation-targeting regimes in transition countries is that the central banks in the countries practicing inflation targeting have been learning how to set monetary policy instruments to hit their inflation goals. Since these central banks will have a role in setting monetary policy instruments at the ECB when they adopt the euro, the monetary policy experience that they have acquired by operating an inflation-targeting regime will help them play a more active and positive role in deliberations at the ECB.

References

Akerlof, George, William Dickens, and George Perry. 1996. The macroeconomics of low inflation. *Brookings Papers on Economic Activity,* Issue no. 1:1–76. Washington, D.C.: Brookings Institution.

Ball, Lawrence. 1994. What determines the sacrifice ratio? In *Monetary policy,* ed. N. Gregory Mankiw, 155–82. Chicago: University of Chicago Press.

Begg, David. 1998. Pegging out: Lessons from the Czech exchange rate crisis. *Journal of Comparative Economics* 26:669–90.

Bernanke, B. S., T. Laubach, F. S. Mishkin, and A. S. Posen. 1999. *Inflation targeting: Lessons from the international experience.* Princeton, N.J.: Princeton University Press.

Brash, Donald T. 2000. Inflation targeting in New Zealand, 1988–2000. Speech presented at the Trans-Tasman Business Cycle. 9 February, Melbourne, Australia.

Calvo, Guillermo, and Frederic S. Mishkin. 2003. The mirage of exchange rate regimes for emerging market countries. *Journal of Economic Perspectives* 17 (4): 99–118.

Čapek, Aleš. 1999. Udžet inflaci pod kontrolou bude stále obtížnější. [Keeping inflation under control will be ever more difficult]. *Hospodářské Noviny,* 22 October, 9.
Ceska Sporitelna/Erste Bank. 2002. Macroeconomic and fixed income weekly report. Prague: Ceska Sporitelna/Erste Bank, 16 December.
Clifton, Eric V. 1999. Inflation targeting: What is the meaning of the bottom of the band? *IMF Policy Discussion Paper no. 99/8.* Washington, D.C.: International Monetary Fund.
Clinton, Kevin. 2000. Strategic choices for inflation targeting in the Czech Republic. In *Inflation targeting in transition economies: The case of the Czech Republic,* ed. Warren Coats, 165–84. Prague: Czech National Bank.
Czech National Bank. 1997. Monthly bulletin. Prague: Czech National Bank, May.
———. 1999. Inflation report. Prague: Czech National Bank, January.
Debelle, Guy. 1997. Inflation targeting in practice. *IMF Working Papers no. 97/35.* Washington, D.C.: International Monetary Fund.
Deppler, Michael. 1998. Is reducing inflation costly? In *Moderate inflation: The experience of transition economies,* ed. Carlo Cotarelli and György Szapáry. Washington, D.C.: International Monetary Fund and National Bank of Hungary.
Drew, Aaron, and Adrian Orr. 1999. The Reserve Bank's role in the recent business cycle: Actions and evolution. *Reserve Bank of New Zealand Bulletin* 62 (1).
Eichengreen, Barry. 1999. Solving the currency conundrum. Paper prepared for the Council of Foreign Relations Study Group on Economic and Financial Development. University of California, Berkeley, Department of Economics. Mimeograph.
———. 2001. Can emerging markets float? Should they inflation target? University of California, Berkeley, Department of Economics. Mimeograph.
Estrella, Arturo, and Frederic S. Mishkin. 1997. Is there a role for monetary aggregates in the conduct of monetary policy. *Journal of Monetary Economics* 40 (2): 279–304.
European Bank for Reconstruction and Development. 2002. *Transition report 2002.* London: European Bank for Reconstruction and Development.
Fischer, Stanley. 1994. Modern central banking. In *The future of central banking: The tercentenary symposium of the Bank of England,* ed. Forrest Capie, Charles A. Goodhart, Stanley Fischer, and Norbert Schnadts, 262–308. Cambridge, Cambridge University Press.
Groshen, Erica L., and Mark E. Schweitzer. 1996. The effects of inflation on wage adjustments in firm-level data: Grease or sand? Federal Reserve Bank of New York Staff Report no. 9. New York: Federal Reserve Bank of New York.
Groshen, Erica L., and Mark E. Schweitzer. 1999. Identifying inflation's grease and sand effects in the labor market. In *The costs and benefits of price stability,* ed. Martin Feldstein, 273–308. Chicago: University of Chicago Press.
Haldane, Andrew. 1999. Pursuing price stability: Evidence from the United Kingdom and other inflation-targeters. In *Workshop on inflation targeting,* ed. Andrew P. Fischer, 2–17. Prague: Czech National Bank.
Hrnčíř, M., and K. Šmidková. 1999. The Czech approach to inflation targeting. In *Workshop on Inflation Targeting,* ed. Andrew P. Fischer, 18–38. Prague: Czech National Bank.
International Monetary Fund. 1999. *World economic outlook.* Washington, D.C.: IMF, October.
———. 2002. *Global market monitor.* Washington, D.C.: International Monetary Fund, December 17.
JPMorgan. 2002. *Emerging Europe, Middle East, and Africa weekly.* January 31.

Kysilka, Pavel. 1998. Nezdravý růst dlouho nevydrží. [Unhealthy growth will not be sustainable]. *Ekonom* 4:10–12.

Leiderman, Leonardo, and Gil Bufman. 2000. Inflation targeting under a crawling band: Lessons from Israel. In *Inflation targeting in practice: Strategic and operational issues and application to emerging market economies*, ed. Mario Blejer, Alain Ize, Alfredo M. Leone, and Sergio Werlang, 70–79. Washington, D.C.: International Monetary Fund.

Macfarlane, Ian J. 1999. Statement to Parliamentary Committee. *Reserve Bank of Australia Bulletin* (January): 16–20.

Mahadeva, Lavan, and K. Šmidková. 2000. Inflation targeting in the Czech Republic. In *Monetary frameworks in a global context,* ed. Lavan Mahadeva and Gabriel Sterne, 273–300. London: Bank of England, Centrum for Central Banking Studies.

Mishkin, F. S. 1996. Understanding financial crises: A developing country perspective. In *Annual World Bank conference on development economics,* ed. Michael Bruno and Boris Pleskovic, 29–62. Washington, D.C.: World Bank.

———. 1999. Lessons from the Asian crisis. *Journal of International Money and Finance* 18 (4): 709–23.

———. 2000. Inflation targeting in emerging market countries. *American Economic Review* 90 (2): 105–9.

———. 2001. Issues in inflation targeting. In *Price stability and the long-run target for monetary policy,* 203–22. Ottawa, Canada: Bank of Canada.

Mishkin, F. S., and M. A. Savastano. 2001. Monetary policy strategies for Latin America. *Journal of Development Economics* 66 (2): 415–44.

Mishkin, F. S., and Klaus Schmidt-Hebel. 2002. One decade of inflation targeting in the world: What do we know and what do we need to know? In *Inflation targeting: Design, performance, challenges,* ed. Norman Loayza and Raimundo Soto, 117–219. Santiago, Chile: Central Bank of Chile.

National Bank of Hungary. 2001. *Quarterly report on inflation.* Budapest: National Bank of Hungary, August.

National Bank of Poland. 1998. *Medium-term strategy of monetary policy.* Warsaw: National Bank of Poland.

———. 2001. Inflation report 2000, appendix 2.

Orlowski, Lucjan T. 2000. Direct inflation targeting in central Europe. *Post-Soviet Geography and Economics* 41 (2): 134–54.

Reserve Bank of New Zealand. 2000. Monetary policy statement. Wellington, New Zealand: Reserve Bank of New Zealand, March.

Schaechter, Andrea, M. R. Stone, and M. Zelmer. 2000. Adopting inflation targeting: Practical issues for emerging market countries. IMF Occasional Paper no. 202. Washington, D.C.: International Monetary Fund.

Sherwin, Murray. 1999. Inflation targeting: 10 years on. Speech to New Zealand Association of Economists conference. 1 July, Rotorua, New Zealand.

Siklos, Pierre L., and István Ábel. 2002. Is Hungary ready for inflation targeting? *Economic Systems* (Netherlands) 26 (4): 309–33.

Škreb, Marko. 1998. A note on inflation. In *Moderate inflation,* ed. Carlo Cotarelli and György Szapari, 179–84. Washington, D.C.: International Monetary Fund.

Stevens, Glenn R. 1999. Six years of inflation targeting. *Reserve Bank of Australia Bulletin* (May): 46–61.

Stock, James H., and Mark W. Watson. 1999. Business cycle fluctuations in U.S. macroeconomic time series. In *Handbook of macroeconomics,* ed. J. B. Taylor and M. Woodford, 3–64. Amsterdam: Elsevier.

Summers, Larry. 1991. Panel discussion: Price stability: How should long-term monetary policy be determined? *Journal of Money, Credit and Banking* 23:625–31.

Svensson, Lars E. O. 1997. Inflation forecast targeting: Implementing and monitoring inflation targets. *European Economic Review* 41:1111–46.

———. 2000. Open-economy inflation targeting. *Journal of International Economics* 50:155–83.

United Nations. 2002. *Economic survey of Europe,* no. 1. New York and Geneva: United Nations.

Comment   Olivier Blanchard

The paper by Jonas and Mishkin does a very good job of describing the history, the implementation, and the effects of inflation targeting in Central Europe. The description is rich and informative, showing the inconsistencies and the adjustments in monetary policy over time, the conflicts between monetary and fiscal policy, and the difficulty of achieving inflation targets. The basic conclusion, which is presented with much honesty, is also convincing: inflation targeting has not worked miracles. But it has led to a decline in inflation, at an output cost that does not appear excessively high.

The paper, however, does less good a job of discussing the many issues facing inflation targeters in those countries. It sometimes gives the impression that what remains to be worked out are details of implementation—whether, for example, to have a point or a band for the inflation target, or how to choose the time horizon for inflation targeting. I agree that these are decisions that policymakers must make. But I also believe that there are plenty of hard conceptual issues that have not been solved, and these also need to be tackled, and tackled urgently. This will be the theme of my comments.

Let me start with one remark, however. Many of the criticisms I raise below apply to much of the research on inflation targeting. In this sense, singling out Jonas and Mishkin is unfair. At the same time, many of the unresolved issues are more obvious in countries that are going through large structural changes, such as Central and Eastern European countries. For that reason, it would have been reasonable to expect Jonas and Mishkin to try to tackle some of them. This largely remains to be done.

A Theoretical Detour

At the center of inflation targeting is a proposition that I like to call a "divine coincidence": namely, that, under some reasonable conditions, stabilizing inflation is equivalent to stabilizing output around its natural level.

To be more specific, let me work out a Fischer-type simple example that will serve my needs. Suppose that price and wage setting are given by

Olivier Blanchard is the Class of 1941 Professor of Economics at the Massachusetts Institute of Technology and a research associate of the National Bureau of Economic Research.

$$p = w + \alpha y + e_p$$
$$w = Ep + \beta y + e_w,$$

where p, w, and y are the log of the price level, the nominal wage, and the level of real output, respectively.

The price is an increasing function of the wage, of the level of output, and of a disturbance e_p, which may reflect changes in the relative prices of other inputs, in the markup, or in technology.

The wage is an increasing function of the expected price level, of the level of output (equivalently a decreasing function of the level of unemployment), and of a disturbance e_w, which may reflect shifts in bargaining power, changes in unemployment benefits, and so on.

Suppose that expectations of inflation by wage setters are adaptive and given by

$$Ep = p(-1) + \pi(-1),$$

where π is the rate of inflation.

Define the natural level of output as the level of output that would prevail if there were no nominal rigidities—if w depended on p rather than Ep. Call it y^*. Then y^* is given by

$$y^* = -\frac{1}{\alpha + \beta}(e_p + e_w).$$

Combining all four equations gives the following relation between inflation and output:

$$\pi = \pi(-1) + (\alpha + \beta)(y - y^*)$$

The change in inflation depends on the output gap, the deviation of output from the natural level.

The important point here is the lack of a disturbance term in the relation. In contrast to older specifications with "cost shocks" tacked on to the relation, the relation between inflation and the output gap holds exactly. The reason why: cost shocks are present, but their effect works through the natural level of output, and so through the output gap. Put another way, the output gap is a sufficient statistic for the effect of real activity on inflation.

The model I used to make the point is special in many ways, and so one may wonder how general this proposition is. The lesson from much of the recent research is that it is quite general (see, for example, Woodford 2003 for an exhaustive treatment and discussion). It holds in models with staggered price setting and rational expectations: in those models, inflation depends not on past inflation, as here, but on expected inflation and on the output gap. But, as in the relation above, the relation holds without a disturbance term.

This absence of a disturbance term has a direct and striking implication. Stabilizing inflation—that is, achieving $\pi = \pi(-1) = \overline{\pi}$ (if it can be achieved)—also stabilizes the output gap: that is, it leads to a level of output equal to the natural rate $y_t = y_t^*$. This is what I referred to as the divine coincidence earlier.

This result is, I believe, one of the main reasons for the wide support for inflation targeting by macroeconomists. Those who care about inflation volatility like the stated goal of the policy. Those who care about output stabilization see inflation targeting as a commitment by the central bank to stabilize output around its natural level, to get the economy out of recessions, and to slow the economy down in booms.

The result, however, comes with three important caveats (and here I am preparing the way for the return to Central Europe in the next section):

• "Natural" does not mean first best, but the level of output that would be achieved if we removed nominal rigidities but left all other distortions in the economy.

It follows that, even if it could, the central bank may not want to achieve a level of output equal to the natural level of output every period. Obviously, on average, it has to achieve a level of output equal to the average natural level of output; if it tried to achieve a consistently higher level, then we would be in Barro Gordon mode, inflation would increase, and the policymaker would fail. But it can aim to set output lower than the natural level in some periods, and higher than the natural level of output in others.

Suppose, for example, that the sector most affected by imperfections is also the least cyclical. Then there will be less distortions in booms, more distortions in troughs. It may then make sense to try to achieve a relatively more contractionary policy in booms, a more expansionary one in troughs.

Or suppose that the shocks that affect output also affect the distance of the natural rate of output from the first best. To be more concrete, suppose that increases in the price of oil are associated with increases in distortions and thus a decline in the natural level of output relative to the first best. Then it may make sense to allow actual output to decline less than the natural level of output and thus to allow inflation to increase for some time. (Whether increases in the price of oil are in fact associated with higher or lower distortions is, however, far from clear; if as a first approximation the answer is that distortions are unaffected, then the answer is likely to be to try to achieve a level of output close to the natural level; in other words, keep inflation constant, even after an increase in the price of oil.)

A bit of algebra may help here. Assume, in the model developed above, that the relation of the natural level of output to the first-best level is given by

$$y^* = y^f - a + \eta,$$

where y^f is the first-best level, a is a constant, and η is a disturbance term, with mean 0, reflecting the effect of changes in distortions on the natural rate relative to the first best.

Replacing in the inflation output-gap relation gives

$$\pi = \pi(-1) + (\alpha + \beta)(y - y^f + a) - (\alpha + \beta)\eta.$$

In this case, it is a reasonable guess that optimal monetary policy will be to stabilize the distance of output from first best: that is, $y - y^f + a$. Therefore, to the extent that the economy is affected by changes in distortions, to the extent that η varies, it will indeed face a trade-off between stabilizing inflation and achieving its desired output target.

The important issue is then what lies behind η and how much it varies. Note that η has only a vague relation to what is usually thought of as "cost-push shocks" such as the price of oil. To return to the earlier discussion, a change in the price of oil that does not affect other distortions has no effect on η.

• The assumptions under which the relation between inflation and the output gap hold exactly may not be satisfied. In that case, there will be a disturbance term in the relation between inflation and the output gap.

For example, we know that, if there are both nominal wage and price rigidities, then there is no single rate of inflation, be it price or wage inflation, that will do the job (see, for example, Erceg, Henderson, and Levin 2000). There may be a weighted average of price and wage inflation such that the relation between inflation so defined and the output gap holds exactly. But if the relation is written as a relation between price inflation and the output gap, there will be a disturbance term. And so, in that case, there will be no way to stabilize both inflation and output.

• Achieving the natural level of output may not maximize welfare if it comes at the cost of large distortions in the composition of output. This is likely to be the case if shocks and monetary policy affect different parts of the economy differently.

A parable will make the point. Suppose the West Coast and the East Coast of the United States are separate economies, both with nominal rigidities. Suppose an adverse shock affects demand and output on the West Coast. Suppose monetary policy only affects demand and output on the East Coast. Clearly it would be unwise in this case to try to achieve the natural level of output for the United States as a whole. It would come at the cost of large distortions in the composition of output between the east and the west. In this case, monetary policy should clearly be aimed at what it can actually affect—namely, East Coast output. Or in terms of inflation targeting, monetary policy should aim at stabilizing East Coast inflation, not U.S. inflation (which, in this case, should be allowed to decline, because nothing can and should be done to offset the decrease in inflation on the West Coast).

Replace the East and West Coasts with investment and consumption, or with bank-dependent and non-bank-dependent firms, and so on. The lesson extends straightforwardly. There is nothing that says that stabilizing aggregate output is best if the effects of monetary policy cannot exactly offset the effects of shocks on the composition of output, or put another way, when the cross-sectional effects of the interest rate and the shock are very different.

Back to Transition Economies

Most of us are aware of the issues I just discussed. Anybody who tries to derive optimal rules for monetary policy finds himself confronting them. And, in the most thorough modern treatment of optimal monetary policy to date, Michael Woodford's (2003) book, these issues are discussed at length.

But, when it comes to the policy debate, these issues are largely ignored. Some researchers or policy advocates implicitly invoke the divine coincidence, and argue that decreasing inflation volatility will lead to output-gap stabilization. Others tack a disturbance term to the relation between inflation and the output gap, creating a trade-off between inflation stabilization and output stabilization. But the nature of the disturbance, and its relation to the shocks affecting the economy, is left unspecified. (Rather misleadingly, this disturbance is often called a cost-push shock. As I have argued, it may have little to do with what we usually think of as cost-push shocks: for example, a bad harvest, or an increase in the price of oil).

Ignoring them, however, becomes harder—and almost surely more wrong—when confronted with economies going through major structural changes, such as transition countries:

• These economies started the transition with large distortions, and thus a natural level of output very far from the first-best level of output. Some of these distortions are gone, some are going, and some are still there. Transition economies still have very much of a dual structure: An old state or ex-state sector, composed of large firms, with serious financing and governance problems and often a doubtful future: and a new private sector, which is much more competitive, and is, in large part, the source of growth and also the source of fluctuations.

To the extent, however, that many of the shocks hitting these economies are the result of policies aiming at removing some of these distortions (for example, the liberalization of some prices, or the reduction of agricultural subsidies), this suggests that the distance of the natural rate from the first best is probably changing over time. In other words, many shocks affect both actual output and the natural level of output, but they may not affect very much the first-best level of output. In that environment, it is clearly not best to stabilize the output gap, and by implication it is not necessarily best to stabilize inflation. (If this sounds too abstract, think of the very practical questions addressed in the paper: How should inflation targeting react to increases in prices due to the liberalization of public-sector prices? Should it focus on an index of inflation that excludes them? Should it allow inflation to increase for some time? To answer these questions convincingly, there is no other way than to take the theoretical detour.)

• The inflation process is intrinsically more complex than in richer, more stable, economies. Price liberalization and changes in the evolving structure of labor relations and bargaining are likely to be the source of some of the price and wage movements. Given that these economies are still young market economies, price and wage setting and, by implication, nominal rigidities are probably changing through time. Should central banks ignore all these complications and just target inflation, or should they instead take some of these developments into account?

• Given the segmentation of financial markets and the fragility of many financial intermediaries, the effects of monetary policy are likely to have more asymmetric effects on the economy than in richer, more stable, economies. Sectors that rely more on bank credit will obviously be affected by monetary policy more than the others. Should the central bank ignore these issues in setting its inflation target?

These are hard questions, and central banks had no choice but to proceed without knowing all the answers; but we, as researchers, should not avoid them. To make the discussion more concrete, let me take one example that strikes me as very relevant in the context of transition economies.

Which Inflation Rate to Target?

The paper discusses at some length the issue of what inflation rate the central bank should target. It argues that the trade-off is between transparency (for which the simpler the index, the better) and controllability (for which the more controllable, the more the target is likely to be achieved, the higher the credibility of the central bank is likely to be). These are indeed relevant factors, but I think there are other and more important issues at stake.

To see this, let me extend the model of price and wage setting I introduced earlier. Assume that the price level and the nominal wage follow

$$p = (1 - a)w + aEw + \alpha y + e_p$$
$$w = (1 - b)p + bEp + \beta y + e_w.$$

As before, p, w, and y stand for the log of the price level, the log of the wage, and the log of real output, respectively. There are now potentially both nominal price and wage rigidities. The price level depends on both the actual and the expected nominal wage, the level of activity, and a disturbance term e_p. The wage depends on both the actual and the expected price level, the level of activity, and a disturbance term e_w.

If a is equal to zero, there are no nominal price rigidities; if b is equal to zero, there are no nominal wage rigidities. If both are different from zero, both rigidities are present.

Let me assume adaptive expectations. Again, the reason is to make the algebra more revealing, but nothing important depends on it.

$$Ew = w(-1) + \pi_w(-1)$$

$$Ep = p(-1) + \pi_p(-1)$$

Price setters expect wage inflation to be the same as last period. Wage setters expect price inflation to be the same as last period.

Define the natural level of output as that level of output that would prevail if there were no nominal rigidities:

$$y^* = -\frac{1}{a+b}(e_p + e_w).$$

Then we can combine these relations to get

$$[a\pi_w + b\pi_p] = [a\pi_w(-1) + b\pi_p(-1)] + (\alpha + \beta)(y - y^*).$$

This has four implications.

• If all the nominal rigidities are in wage setting (if $a = 0$) and the central bank wants to stabilize the output gap, it should target price inflation. If instead all the nominal rigidities are in price setting (if $b = 0$), then it should target wage inflation.

If, as is likely, there are nominal rigidities in both price and wage setting, then the central bank should target a combination of price and wage inflation, with weights $a/(a + b)$ on wage inflation and $b/(a + b)$ on price inflation. Targeting either just price inflation or just wage inflation may lead to a very inefficient policy.

The message is simple: which inflation rate to target depends very much on the structural characteristics of the economy. Transparency and controllability are relevant; they may not be as important as the considerations we just discussed.

Lest you thought the issue was of limited empirical relevance, table 9C.1 should disabuse you. It gives the evolution of wage and price inflation in the Czech Republic and Hungary for the years 1997–2002. In 1998, price inflation in the Czech Republic was 10.6 percent, wage inflation 5 percent. In 2000, price inflation was 1.1 percent, wage inflation 7.2 percent. In Hungary, wage inflation in 1999 was 1.8 percent, price inflation 8.4 percent. In such environments, which inflation rate is targeted is likely to make a large difference to real outcomes.

• The second point follows from the first. The right policy, namely here

Table 9C.1   Wage and price inflation in the Czech Republic and Hungary

	1997	1998	1999	2000	2001	2002
Czech Republic						
Wage inflation	7.9	5.0	5.0	7.2	8.1	6.7
Price inflation	8.0	10.6	3.0	1.1	5.3	2.6
Hungary						
Wage inflation	19.5	12.3	1.8	21.6	14.8	13.7
Price inflation	18.5	12.6	8.4	9.7	9.0	8.4

Source: OECD Economic Outlook. Compensation per employee, and GDP deflator.

the right combination of inflation rates to target, requires quite a bit of knowledge about the structural characteristics of the economy.

In the context of the model, it requires knowledge of the degree of nominal rigidity in prices and in wages, as well as the way price and wage setters form expectations. In general, it is clear that the design of inflation targeting requires much more work on the nature of the inflation process. This process may be quite different in transition countries.

• If the central bank wants to achieve a level of output close to the natural level, then the equation above contains a strong message. Once the right weighted average of inflation has been chosen, there is no reason to make exceptions for agricultural prices, the adjustment of public-sector prices, and so on. Maintaining stable inflation will lead output to move, but this movement will reflect movements in the natural rate.

As the paper shows, this policy implication is at variance with practice in most of the Central European countries (and many other countries as well). Many countries exclude a number of prices from the inflation index they target. It is also at variance with our beliefs (at least my beliefs): can it really be that stabilizing inflation in the face of a major increase in the price of oil, or a major depreciation, is really the best policy from the point of view of output and welfare? This leads to the fourth and final point.

• Maybe the reason we do not feel comfortable with this last conclusion is that we do not believe that the fluctuations in the natural rate itself are optimal. If this is the case, then there is really no reason for the central bank to want to achieve a level of output close to the natural rate all the time. Maybe it should try to achieve a path of output smoother than the underlying path of the natural rate.

And, indeed, many of the shocks that have affected Central European economies have come from changes in distortions, the kinds of shock that, we saw earlier, may justify intentional deviations from the natural level of output and thus deviations from the inflation target.

Does this provide a justification for excluding some prices from the index targeted by the central bank? Simple exclusion may be too rough: the logic of our argument is that changes in agricultural prices due to bad weather should be treated differently from changes in agricultural prices due to the removal of subsidies, not that agricultural prices should be simply excluded.

I realize that, even in this example, the answers I have sketched do not lend themselves to easy policy implementation. But the issues cannot be avoided, and we should aim to understand them well enough to be able to translate them into practical advice to central banks. We are not there yet.

References

Erceg, Christopher, Dale Henderson, and Andrew Levin. 2000. Optimal monetary policy with staggered wage and price contracts. *Journal of Monetary Economics* 46:281–313.
Woodford, Michael. 2003. *Interest and prices.* Princeton, N.J.: Princeton University Press.

Discussion Summary

Commenting on Blanchard's discussion, *Gregory Mankiw* pointed out that the literature was distinguishing between productivity and cost-push shocks, with only the former affecting the welfare-optimal level of output. Whether cost-push shocks posed a problem for central banks depended on whether they stabilized output around the welfare-optimal level or the level that would prevail absent nominal rigidities.

Ed Nelson pointed out that in transition economies undergoing many structural changes, not enough was known about the efficient level of output to distinguish between efficient and inefficient output fluctuations. In this context, inflation targeting was a practical way of minimizing damage from inflation to the economy.

Jose De Gregorio emphasized the importance of credibility problems in transition economies and suggested that achieving credibility was more important in the short run than other aspects of the implementation of an inflation target. Moreover, because of structural change in these economies, producing inflation forecasts two years ahead was problematic, and instead in practice central banks in these countries announced their desired inflation rate for the next twelve months.

Jiri Jonas agreed with Blanchard about the importance of the effects of exchange rate fluctuations on the composition of output. In the case of the Czech Republic, large inflows of foreign direct investment in response to the appreciation affected companies and industries very differently, which resulted in considerable pressure on the central bank to avoid further appreciation.

In response to Blanchard's comments, *Frederic Mishkin* emphasized that the most pressing issue for monetary policy in transition economies was to establish a good nominal anchor, which contributed substantially to economic stability. He suggested that, while inflation forecasting was difficult in these economies, it was important for central banks to be prepared to react to, and explain, deviations of inflation from their forecasts.

Inflation Targeting
and Sudden Stops

Ricardo J. Caballero and Arvind Krishnamurthy

10.1   Introduction

Underlying weaknesses in the domestic financial sector and limited integration with world financial markets make emerging market economies vulnerable to "sudden stops" of capital inflows. Without much warning, the capital flows that support a boom may come to a halt, exposing the country to an external crisis.

Monetary policy in this context has often been seen as an additional source of problems rather than as a remedy. Countries with a history of inflation problems have limited central-bank credibility. The currency pressures of the sudden stop test this credibility, so that either the loss of credibility or the attempt to regain it in the middle of the crisis exacerbates the contraction.

However, there is a group of countries for which the problem of high and unstable inflation is no longer present but the problem of sudden stops persists. These countries include Chile, Mexico, and many of the Asian economies. Moreover, looking toward the future, this group is bound to grow, as hopefully Brazil, Turkey, and countries of Eastern Europe establish discipline over seigniorage and fiscal policies.

Many of these advanced emerging economies are now in the process of

Ricardo J. Caballero is the Ford International Professor of Economics at the Massachusetts Institute of Technology and a research associate of the National Bureau of Economic Research. Arvind Krishnamurthy is assistant professor of finance at the Kellogg Graduate School of Management, Northwestern University.

We are grateful to Ben Bernanke, Andrew Hertzberg, and conference participants for their comments. We thank Donna Zerwitz for editorial assistance. Caballero thanks the National Science Foundation for financial support. Krishnamurthy thanks the International Monetary Fund for their hospitality while this paper was being written. All errors are our own.

designing their monetary policy framework. Given the success of "inflation targeting" in a wide range of economies, it seems only natural that this framework be contemplated for these economies as well. In this paper, we study how inflation targeting should be adapted to countries whose primary macroeconomic concern is the presence of sudden stops in capital inflows.

The starting point of our analysis is the observation from Caballero and Krishnamurthy (2002) that, during a sudden stop, monetary policy loses its potency. The principal constraint on output is a shortage of *external* resources. The main effect of domestic money, on the other hand, is on agents' *domestic* borrowing capacity. Thus, the knee-jerk reaction of the central bank to the outflow of capital, of raising domestic interest rates— dubbed "fear of floating" by Calvo and Reinhart (2002)—within our model is the natural consequence of a central bank that is concerned with inflation and output. Raising interest rates reduces the exchange rate depreciation, with limited effects on output beyond the impact of the external constraint. However, while fear of floating may seem optimal from this contemporaneous perspective, it is suboptimal ex ante.

The reason for this suboptimality is that the *anticipation* of the central bank's tight monetary policy during the sudden stop has important effects on the private sector's incentives to insure against sudden-stop events. Insuring against these events means taking prior actions that increase the total dollar assets of the country (decrease the total dollar liabilities of the country) in the sudden-stop event. Since a contractionary monetary policy reduces the domestic scarcity value of dollars, it also lowers the returns to hoarding net dollar assets. Simply put, contracting dollar debt is less costly in an environment where the peso is expected to be supported in the event of a crisis. Thus, the anticipation of a tight monetary policy leaves the economy less insured against the sudden stop.

In this context, expectations shape policy, not in whether inflation is anticipated or unanticipated, but in how the private sector views its rewards to insuring against sudden stops. For incentive reasons, the optimal monetary rule is to expand during external crises, even if the expansion has a limited contemporaneous effect on output.

It should be apparent that time inconsistency is a serious issue in this context. A central bank that cannot commit will ignore the insurance aspect of monetary policy and follow a procyclical, rather than the optimal countercyclical, policy. This bias is made worse by the presence of an expansionary bias a la Barro and Gordon (1983). The reason is that the central bank only sees a benefit from expanding during normal times. As a result, it lowers interest rates during these times, leading to higher inflation (as in Barro and Gordon). When the sudden stop occurs, the central bank has even more reason to defend the exchange rate as it inherits high inflation.

In our framework, since crises are characterized by dollar shortages, there is scope for managing international reserves in order to ease these shortages. Our model provides a natural motivation for both centralized holding of reserves and holding reserves in the form of dollars. However, we show that a central bank that cannot commit will be too aggressive in injecting dollar reserves during a crisis. Moreover, this distortion interacts with the monetary policy problem. A more suboptimal monetary policy will lead to a more severe crisis, and a greater incentive for the central bank to inject reserves.

Given the time inconsistency of the central bank, what should its mandate be? That is, how should the central bank's objectives be modified so that it internalizes the insurance dimension of the sudden-stop problem? We propose modifying inflation targeting so that the central bank follows state-contingent inflation targets, overweights nontradable inflation in the measure of inflation that is targeted, and explicitly weighs reserves holdings in its objectives.

Since the no-commitment central bank loosens during good times and tightens during bad times, we suggest that its mandate should make the inflation target countercyclical (i.e., low during good times and high during sudden stops). In practice, the state contingency may be implemented by making inflation targets contingent on external factors such as commodity prices, U.S. interest rates or U.S. corporate bond spreads, and the Emerging Markets Bond Index Plus (EMBI+).

Tradables experience strong inflationary pressures during crises as the exchange rate depreciates. On other hand, the pass-through to nontradables is more limited. Thus, targeting a measure of inflation that overweights nontradables also will reduce the central bank's incentive to raise interest rates during crises.

Finally, since the central bank injects reserves too aggressively during crises, we suggest that its objectives be modified to place weight on the stock of reserve holdings. Choosing an appropriate weight for reserves will help the central bank to internalize the effect of its exchange interventions on the private sector's insurance incentives.

Our paper is most directly related to the literature on monetary policy in economies with financial frictions (e.g., Bernanke and Blinder 1988; Bernanke, Gertler, and Gilchrist 1999; Christiano, Gust, and Roldos forthcoming; Diamond and Rajan 2001; Gertler, Gilchrist, and Natalucci 2001; Holmstrom and Tirole 1998; Kiyotaki and Moore, 2001; and Lorenzoni, 2001). Unlike most of this literature, we are concerned with monetary policy in emerging markets, so we model the presence of two distinct financial constraints: one between domestic agents and one between domestic agents and foreign investors.[1]

---

1. Of the preceding literature, the Diamond and Rajan paper (2001) is the closest to our analysis in the sense that they also model two distinct constraints: a bank solvency constraint and an aggregate liquidity constraint, in their case.

The recent emerging-markets literature has identified sudden stops of international capital flows as an important part of external crises (see, for example, Calvo 1998 and Calvo and Reinhart 2002). Our model shares this feature. We model the sudden stop as a tightening of international financial constraints. The importance of international financial constraints for emerging markets was first identified in the sovereign debt literature (see, for example, Bulow and Rogoff 1989).

Calvo and Reinhart (2002) offer another perspective on fear of floating. They argue that, since so much of debt in emerging markets is in dollars, a central bank will recognize that the output cost of allowing the exchange rate to depreciate during a crisis is too high, and will therefore raise interest rates. In one sense, the mechanism in our model complements their explanation. An open question in the Calvo and Reinhart model is why firms take on so much dollar debt (i.e., Calvo and Reinhart take stocks of foreign debt as exogenous). We show that stabilizing the exchange rate will reduce the private sector's incentive to insure against sudden stops, and naturally leads to increasing liability dollarization (see Caballero and Krishnamurthy 2003). On the other hand, our central bank stabilizes the exchange rate because it focuses on inflation costs, as opposed to Calvo and Reinhart's output costs. The emphasis on insurance is central to our analysis and links us more closely to Dooley (2000), who also emphasizes insurance effects.

Our monetary policy analysis is conducted in a standard inflation-targeting framework (e.g., King 1994; Svensson 1999; or Woodford 2002). Svensson (2000) has extended the inflation-targeting framework to open economies that fit the usual small-open-economy assumption, in which countries face no international financial constraint. His analysis is most applicable to countries such as Australia or Canada, but less so to the emerging markets that are the focus of this paper.

The next two sections develop a model of monetary policy in an environment of sudden stops. Section 10.4 then studies optimal monetary policy in this environment. Section 10.5 focuses on the central bank's behavior when it cannot commit to its monetary policy choices. Section 10.6 considers two modifications to the central bank's objectives that result in the optimal monetary policy being implemented. Section 10.7 adds international reserves to the model. Section 10.8 concludes.

10.2   A Model of Sudden Stops

In this section we sketch a model of sudden stops. This serves as a prelude to the monetary policy analysis of the next section. The model we outline is developed more rigorously in Caballero and Krishnamurthy (2002).

Firms have assets at time t of A_t. These are domestic assets (i.e., they generate peso revenues), so that their peso value is $A_t(i_t)$, where i_t is the peso interest rate and A_t is a decreasing function.[2]

We assume that firms need dollars for investment. That is, they need dollars in order to import some investment goods that are inputs to production. This is justified by noting that at the margin, firms in developing countries are borrowers in international markets. We are extrapolating this demand, so that firms always have to borrow from abroad.

Moreover, we assume that firms are financially constrained so that the aggregate demand for investment goods can be written as $D(A_t, i_t^d)$. As in most models of financial constraints, the net worth of firms influences their demand. Firms sell their peso assets, worth A_t, along with any other peso funds they are able to borrow, in order to raise dollars for investment goods. The dollars are borrowed at interest rate of i_t^d, which is the price in the demand schedule. D is decreasing in i_t^d and increasing in A_t.

The supply of dollars comes from two sources. First, we assume that domestic lenders have a supply of R_t dollars (small). The rest are capital inflows, CF_t. Thus, in equilibrium,

$$(1) \qquad D(A_t(i_t), i_t^d) = R_t + CF_t.$$

A supplier of dollars earns a return of

$$\frac{\varepsilon_t(1 + i_t)}{\varepsilon_{t+1|t}},$$

where ε_t is the peso-dollar exchange rate. Supplying one dollar yields ε_t pesos today. Invested at the peso interest rate of i_t and converting back into dollars tomorrow at $\varepsilon_{t+1|t}$ yields the above expression.

Supplying one dollar is profitable as long as this return exceeds the international interest rate $(1 + i_t^*)$. Define

$$i_t^d \equiv \frac{\varepsilon_t(1 + i_t)}{\varepsilon_{t+1|t}} - 1.$$

For $i_t^d \geq i_t^*$ there is an excess return on supplying dollars to domestic firms. The spread $i_t^d - i_t^*$ is a liquidity premium.

The usual small-open-economy assumption is that the supply of dollars is perfectly elastic at the price of $i_t^d = i_t^*$. In this case, the equilibrium level

---

2. In the next section we derive a more explicit sticky-price mechanism that justifies using the nominal interest rate as an argument. Note that if *domestic* liabilities are extensively dollarized, then A_t also becomes a decreasing function of the exchange rate. In this case, monetary policy is less effective in influencing the peso value of domestic assets since the expansionary effect of lowering i_t is offset by the depreciation such policy causes. See Caballero and Krishnamurthy (2002) for a discussion of constrained monetary regimes in an environment with sudden stops. On the other hand, dollarization of *external* liabilities can be seen as an endogenous response to the mechanism we discuss in this paper and is described in detail in Caballero and Krishnamurthy (2003).

of investment is simply $D(A_t, i_t^*)$. Fixing the foreign interest rate, a fall in the domestic net worth of firms (say, through an increase in i_t) decreases investment.

The sudden-stop assumption is that there are times when the country is quantity constrained in borrowing from international markets. That is,

$$CF_t \leq L_t,$$

where L_t is the maximum quantity of funds that foreign investors will supply to this country. If this constraint binds, equilibrium is

(2) $$D(A_t, i_t^d) = R_t + L_t \Rightarrow i_t^d > i_t^*$$

Note here that an increase in A_t has no effect on investment. This is because investment is determined by the sudden-stop supply of $L_t + R_t$. Instead the only effect of A_t is on i_t^d.

Defining e_t as the log exchange rate, we can rewrite the *domestic* interest parity condition as

(3) $$e_{t+1|t} - e_t \approx i_t - i_t^d.$$

When $i_t^d = i_t^*$ this is the usual interest parity condition. In that case, fixing $e_{t+1|t}$, a decrease in the peso interest rate of i_t, depreciates the exchange rate. In the sudden-stop case, where $i_t^d > i_t^*$, the current exchange rate is depreciated relative to the future exchange rate by the size of the liquidity premium. In this case, a decrease in i_t has the additional effect of causing the interest parity condition to shift upward, reinforcing the depreciation in the exchange rate.

The model we have outlined embeds two principal ideas. First, there are times when an emerging economy is financially constrained in the international market. In this instance, the supply of dollars is inelastic and the limited supply determines domestic investment and output. The second idea is that the main effect of monetary policy is on the domestic borrowing capacity of firms. In particular, decreasing interest rates during a sudden stop does not attract more capital inflows. It has a potentially very large effect on the exchange rate but limited contemporaneous effect on output. The last part of this statement follows from the right-hand side of equation (2), which is fixed. The earlier part of the statement follows from the left-hand side of the same expression and the fact that A_t rises as i_t falls. Thus i^d must rise to ensure equilibrium; by the interest parity condition, this implies that the exchange rate depreciates to offset not only the reduction in i_t but also the rise in i_t^d.

We denote the sudden-stop state as the V regime. In the V regime, $L_t + R_t$ fully determines investment. Let us imagine shifting to date $t - 1$, to a point in time where private and central bank actions may influence this stock.

Suppose that at date $t - 1$ the economy is not in a sudden stop. The supply of funds it faces is horizontal at i^*_{t-1} (H regime). A domestic agent with some dollars at this date can either lend these funds for domestic investment or can save them in an international bond. By opting to save, the agent will be able to lend the dollar at t and earn an excess return of $i^d_t - i^*_t$. That is, the fact that $i^d_t > i^*_t$ will induce domestic agents to "insure" against the sudden stop (raising R_t).

We have shown elsewhere (see Caballero and Krishnamurthy 2001) that when domestic financial markets are underdeveloped, there is an externality—akin to a free-rider problem—whereby the market value of this benefit, $i^d_t - i^*_t$, is less than its social value. In this circumstance, the private sector will underinsure against sudden stops. This underinsurance may take many forms: for example, borrowing too much, contracting foreign currency–denominated debt, choosing short-term debt maturities, or contracting too few credit lines (see Caballero and Krishnamurthy 2003).

Aside from direct (and costly) regulation of capital inflows and the private sector's insurance decisions, there are two instruments at the central bank's disposal to offset the externality. First, it can increase its own holding of foreign reserves and thereby increase R_t. Our model provides a natural motivation for both centralized holding of reserves and holding them in the form of international liquidity. We will return to this mechanism before concluding the paper. Second, and most important for the purpose of this paper, the central bank can commit to *expanding* monetary policy during the sudden stop. Since lowering i_t during the sudden stop raises i^d_t, this increases the private sector's incentive to self-insure. We develop this idea fully in the next sections.

10.3   Sudden Stops and Monetary Policy

We now extend the preceding model to incorporate monetary policy and private-sector price setting. Our goal is to study optimal monetary policy in an environment of sudden stops.

At date $t - 1$, we assume that the economy is in the H regime. That is, the external supply of funds it faces is elastic at the interest rate of i^*. At date t, the economy either remains in the H regime or transits to the V regime. The probability of remaining in H is q, while that of entering V is $1 - q$. Finally, at date $t + 1$, the crisis episode passes, and the economy is in the H regime. We denote the nominal exchange rate at date $t + 1$ as $\bar{e}$, and fix this to be independent of all events at the prior dates. At prior dates, the exchange rates are e_t and e_{t-1}.

We are mainly interested in what happens at date t. At this date, aggregate demand is given by

$$(4) \qquad\qquad \tilde{y}^d_t = -b(r_t - i^*),$$

where $\tilde{y}_t^d$ is the output gap and i^* is the constant foreign interest rate (only a normalization in this equation). Foreign inflation is equal to zero.

The domestic real interest rate, r_t, is defined by

(5) $$r_t = i_t - \pi_{t+1|t}$$

where i_t is the (peso) nominal interest rate and $\pi_{t+1|t}$ is the expectation of inflation between periods t and $t + 1$, conditional on information at date t.

On the supply side, we assume that the economy is composed of two types of price setters. Slow price setters set their prices to grow at a constant rate of $\overline{\pi}$ over both periods (i.e., from $t - 1$ to t and from t to $t + 1$). They choose this average growth rate to be equal to the expected rate of depreciation of the exchange rate:

(6) $$\overline{\pi} = E_{t-1}\left[\left(\frac{e_t - e_{t-1}}{2}\right) + \left(\frac{e_{t+1} - e_t}{2}\right)\right].$$

Fast price setters index their prices to the exchange rate. Putting these two groups together and assigning positive weights of α and $1 - \alpha$ to the slow and fast price setters, respectively, yields an inflation rate between t and $t + 1$ of

$$\alpha\overline{\pi} + (1 - \alpha)(e_{t+1} - e_t).$$

The expected change in the exchange rate between any two dates satisfies the *domestic* interest parity condition we derived in equation (3),

(7) $$e_{t+1|t} - e_t = i_t - i_t^d.$$

Substituting the interest parity condition into the inflation expression yields

(8) $$\pi_{t+1} \equiv \pi_{t+1|t} = \alpha\overline{\pi} + (1 - \alpha)(i_t - i_t^d).$$

We now rewrite the aggregate-demand equation to account for the inflation term we have derived in equation (8). First note that

$$r_t - i^* = \alpha(i_t - i_t^d - \overline{\pi}) + (i_t^d - i^*).$$

Substituting this into the aggregate-demand expression yields

(9) $$\tilde{y}_t^d = -b(\alpha\tilde{i}_t + \tilde{i}_t^d),$$

where

$$\tilde{i}_t \equiv i_t - i_t^d - \overline{\pi}, \qquad \tilde{i}_t^d \equiv i_t^d - i^*.$$

The aggregate-demand equation, (9), is a simple parameterization of the aggregate demand in the prior section, equation (1). Note that it is decreasing in both the domestic (peso) real interest rate and the domestic interest rate on dollar borrowing.

Equilibrium and policy determine the domestic dollar (i_t^d) and peso (i_t) rates. Beginning with the former, in the H regime domestic dollar rates must be equal to international interest rates because the supply of dollars is perfectly elastic at i_t^*. Thus:

$$\tilde{i}_t^{d,H} = 0.$$

In the V regime, the sudden stop implies that $i^{d,V} > i^*$ (see equation [2]). We impose the sudden-stop constraint directly as a constraint on output:

$$\tilde{y}_t^V = -a_y + a_d \tilde{i}_{t|t-1}^{d,V} \qquad a_y > 0.$$

The first term indicates that output falls below the natural level. The second term reflects the private sector's incentives to insure against the sudden stop. If the private sector anticipates a high value of $\tilde{i}_t^{d,V}$ during the sudden stop, it will be inclined to take precautionary steps. We argued earlier that in emerging markets the private value of precautioning is typically too small relative to its social value (see Caballero and Krishnamurthy 2002 for a model showing this). Thus, in our monetary policy analysis we are concerned with ways in which the central bank can increase the incentive to take precautions.

Finally, we consider the average depreciation of the exchange rate over both periods in order to derive an expression for the $\bar{\pi}$ set by the slow price setters. First note that

$$e_{t+1|t} - e_t = i_t - i_t^d = \tilde{i}_t^\omega + \bar{\pi}.$$

Next, from the interest parity condition at date $t-1$,

$$e_{t|t-1} - e_{t-1} = i_{t-1} - i^*.$$

We need to make an assumption about the central bank's behavior at date $t-1$. We make the simplest one, and assume that it sets the real domestic interest rate equal to the international interest rate (recall that foreign inflation is normalized to zero): $i_{t-1} - \bar{\pi} = i^*$. Note that this policy choice is consistent with attaining a zero output gap if the aggregate-demand relation in equation (9) also applied at date $t-1$.

Substituting the exchange rates back into the expression for $\bar{\pi}$ from equation (6) gives

$$\bar{\pi} = \frac{\bar{\pi}}{2} + \frac{E[\tilde{i}_t^\omega] + \bar{\pi}}{2},$$

which implies that

(11) $$E[\tilde{i}_t^\omega] = 0.$$

Relation (11) is central to what follows. The rate $\tilde{i}^\omega$ is the deviation between the average domestic real interest rate ($i_t^\omega - \bar{\pi}$) and the liquidity-adjusted international interest rate ($i_t^{d,\omega}$). Constraint (11) arises from rational-expectations price setting by the private sector. It tells us that if the central bank chooses a low real interest rate in one of the states, in equilibrium, the real interest rate in the other state must be high.

We can rewrite the expression for π_{t+1} more concisely using the tilde notation as

(12) $$\pi_{t+1} = \overline{\pi} + (1 - \alpha)\tilde{i}_t^\omega.$$

By symmetry with inflation at $t + 1$, the inflation rate between date $t - 1$ and date t is

$$\pi_t = \alpha\overline{\pi} + (1 - \alpha)(e_t - e_{t-1}).$$

Since $e_t = \overline{e} - (\tilde{i}^\omega + \overline{\pi})$ (from interest parity condition and the assumption $e_{t+1} = \overline{e}$) and $\overline{e} - e_{t-1} = 2\overline{\pi}$ (see the definition of $\overline{\pi}$), we find that

(13) $$\pi_t = \overline{\pi} - (1 - \alpha)\tilde{i}_t^\omega.$$

10.4 Optimal Policy

Maximizing social welfare for this economy is achieved by minimizing the expected value, given information at $t - 1$, of the loss function, L:

(14) $$L = \lambda\tilde{y}_t^2 + \pi_t^2 + (1 - \delta)\pi_{t+1}^2,$$

where $0 < \delta < 1$ is a discount rate.

These terms are fairly standard in the inflation-targeting literature. The first term is the cost of output fluctuations around potential output, while the other terms reflect the cost of inflation. The parameter λ determines the relative weight on output gap stabilization.

We now derive the optimal monetary policy when the central bank can commit to its choices of ($\tilde{i}_t^H, \tilde{i}_t^V$) in advance.

The output equation in H follows directly from equation (9), with $\tilde{i}_t^d$ set to zero:

$$\tilde{y}_t^H = -b\alpha\tilde{i}_t^H.$$

In V, we solve for the equilibrium $\tilde{i}_t^{d,V}$. Analogous to equation (2), in the V regime, $\tilde{i}_t^{d,V}$ must be such that y_t from equation (9) is consistent with y_t^V from the external financial constraint (10). That is,

$$-b\tilde{i}_t^{d,V} - b\alpha\tilde{i}_t^V = -a_y + a_d\tilde{i}_{t|t-1}^{d,V}.$$

Since $\tilde{i}_t^{d,V} = \tilde{i}_{t|t-1}^{d,V}$ under rational expectations, we see that the relation between $\tilde{i}_t^{d,V}$ and $\tilde{i}_t^V$ for *anticipated* changes in the latter is

(15) $$\tilde{i}_t^{d,V} = \Psi(a_y - b\alpha\tilde{i}_t^V), \qquad \Psi \equiv \frac{1}{b + a_d}.$$

Note that the external constraint (10) has y_t increasing in $\tilde{i}_t^{d,V}$. Since $\tilde{i}_t^{d,V}$ is decreasing in $\tilde{i}_t^V$, this means that lowering $\tilde{i}_t^V$ has a beneficial effect on output in V. The effect is through an "insurance" channel. By anticipating a lower $\tilde{i}_t^V$ during the sudden stop, the expectation of $\tilde{i}_t^{d,V}$ rises. That is, the return to insuring against the sudden stop increases, and this relaxes the aggregate financial constraint. On the other hand, the usual aggregate-demand effect of lowering interest rates—the contemporaneous effect of $\tilde{i}_t^V$ on y—is absent in the V regime. Ex post, since $\tilde{y}_t^V$ is fixed at date t, the positive effect on aggregate demand of a reduction in $\tilde{i}_t^V$ is fully offset by the negative effect of the corresponding rise in $\tilde{i}_t^{d,V}$.

When state-contingent monetary policy is fully anticipated, output in V is

$$\tilde{y}_t^V = -\Psi b(a_y + \alpha a_d \tilde{i}_t^V).$$

We assume throughout that $\tilde{y}_t^V < 0$, so that increasing $\tilde{y}_t^V$ lowers the objective in equation (14).[3]

The objective for the central bank is

$$\min_{(\tilde{i}_t^H, \tilde{i}_t^V, \overline{\pi})} qL^H + (1 - q)L^V,$$

where

$$L^V = \lambda(b\Psi)^2(a_y + \alpha a_d \tilde{i}_t^V)^2 + [\overline{\pi} - (1 - \alpha)\tilde{i}_t^V]^2 + (1 - \delta)[\overline{\pi} + (1 - \alpha)\tilde{i}_t^V]^2$$

and

$$L^H = \lambda(b\alpha\tilde{i}_t^H)^2 + [\overline{\pi} - (1 - \alpha)\tilde{i}_t^H]^2 + (1 - \delta)[\overline{\pi} + (1 - \alpha)\tilde{i}_t^H]^2$$

subject to the rational expectations constraint that

$$E[\tilde{i}_t^\omega] = 0.$$

Let us start with the first-order condition with respect to $\overline{\pi}$, which is straightforward:

$$\frac{\partial L}{\partial \overline{\pi}} = 2(1 - q)[\overline{\pi} - (1 - \alpha)\tilde{i}_t^V + 2(1 - \delta)(1 - q)[\overline{\pi} + (1 - \alpha)\tilde{i}_t^V]$$

$$+ 2q[\overline{\pi} - (1 - \alpha)\tilde{i}_t^H] + 2(1 - \delta)q[\overline{\pi} + (1 - \alpha)\tilde{i}_t^H]$$

$$= 2\overline{\pi} - 2(1 - \alpha)E[\tilde{i}_t^\omega] + 2(1 - \delta)\{\overline{\pi} - (1 - \alpha)E[\tilde{i}_t^\omega]\}$$

$$= 2(2 - \delta)\overline{\pi} = 0 \Rightarrow \overline{\pi}^c = 0,$$

3. This means assuming that

$$\frac{1}{\alpha}\frac{a_y}{a_d} > -\tilde{i}_t^V.$$

Although $\tilde{i}_t^V$ is an endogenous variable, it is possible to show that the assumption can always be met by choosing a_y large enough.

where the superscript c stands for the commitment solution. Thus, in the full commitment case, the central bank chooses policy so as to achieve a zero average rate of inflation. Since all price setters take into account average inflation, there is no benefit, only costs, for the central bank to choose a positive average inflation.

This does not mean that monetary policy is impotent. If we compute the marginal benefit of increasing $\tilde{\imath}_t^V$ at neutral interest rates and $\overline{\pi}$, we find

$$\frac{\partial L}{\partial \tilde{\imath}_t^V}\Big|_{\tilde{\imath}_t^H = \tilde{\imath}_t^V = \overline{\pi} = 0} = 2(1 - q)\lambda \alpha a_d a_y (b\Psi)^2 > 0,$$

which implies that the central bank will choose $\tilde{\imath}_t^V < 0$ (since we are minimizing the objective).

The exact solution is

(16) $$\tilde{\imath}_t^V = -a_y \frac{q\lambda \alpha a_d (b\Psi)^2}{\lambda(ba)^2[q(\Psi a_d)^2 + 1 - q] + (2 - \delta)(1 - \alpha)^2}.$$

The central bank sets i_t^V below $i_t^{d,V}$ in order to increase the private sector's incentives to insure against the sudden stop. The cost of this policy is that the exchange rate depreciates in the V regime. To offset the effect of this policy on average inflation, the central bank chooses $\tilde{\imath}_t^H > 0$ (see equation [11]), so that policy is tighter in the H regime and output is lower.

Note that as a result of its attempt to increase precautioning against the V regime and hence increase $\tilde{y}^V$, the central bank tolerates some instability in inflation and exchange rates.

10.5   The Central Bank Without Commitment

Let us now study a central bank that cannot commit to the interest rate choices of date t, prior to this date. Two biases arise from the lack of commitment. First, if the central bank's preferences are as stated in equation (14) it will choose interest rates to completely stabilize the exchange rate ("fear of floating"). Second, if the central bank's preferences are distorted so as to always prefer to increase output, as in Barro and Gordon (1983), then the fear-of-floating problem is made worse. The central bank loosens in the H state and tightens in the V state, while inducing a positive average rate of inflation. This is exactly the opposite of the policy dictated in the commitment solution.

10.5.1   Fear of Floating

Suppose that the central bank chooses interest rates in each state (H or V) to minimize the loss function in equation (14). Then in H it solves

$$\min_{\tilde{\imath}_t^H} L^H = \lambda(ba\tilde{\imath}_t^H)^2 + [\overline{\pi} - (1 - \alpha)\tilde{\imath}_t^H]^2 + (1 - \delta)[\overline{\pi} + (1 - \alpha)\tilde{\imath}_t^H]^2$$

while in V it solves

$$\min_{\tilde{i}_t^V} L^V = [\bar{\pi} - (1 - \alpha)\tilde{i}_t^V]^2 + (1 - \delta)[\bar{\pi} + (1 - \alpha)\tilde{i}_t^V]^2.$$

Compared to the loss function in V of the previous section, the main change is that there is no output term. This follows from our assumption in equation (10) that there is no aggregate demand channel whereby lowering interest rates increases output. The loss function in H is the same as in the previous section.

It is easy to verify that the solution to these two problems (that is consistent with the rational-expectations requirement that $E[\tilde{i}_t^\omega] = 0$ is to set $\tilde{i}_t^H = \tilde{i}_t^V = 0$, with $\bar{\pi} = 0$. Note that at $\bar{\pi} = 0$, inflation and the exchange rate are fully stabilized by choosing $\tilde{i}_t^H = \tilde{i}_t^V = 0$, with $\bar{\pi} = 0$. In addition, the output gap in H is equal to zero.

While the policy stabilizes both inflation and the exchange rate, the cost is that output drops too much in the sudden-stop state, V. The central bank essentially ignores the insurance channel of monetary policy and focuses purely on maintaining a stable exchange rate.

10.5.2   Exacerbating the Problem: Barro-Gordon

We now modify the central bank's objective function to introduce an expansionary bias a la Barro and Gordon (1983):

$$(17) \qquad\qquad L = -\lambda \tilde{y}_t + \pi_t^2 + (1 - \delta)\pi_{t+1}^2.$$

The $\tilde{y}_t$ term now reflects the central bank's preference to always raise output. We drop the squared-output term since it does not change our message.

The choice problem in H is

$$\min_{\tilde{i}_t^H} L^H = \lambda b \alpha \tilde{i}_t^H + [\bar{\pi} - (1 - \alpha)\tilde{i}_t^H]^2 + (1 - \delta)[\bar{\pi} + (1 - \alpha)\tilde{i}_t^H]^2.$$

This gives the first-order condition

$$(18) \qquad\qquad \tilde{i}_t^H = \frac{\delta}{2 - \delta}\frac{1}{1 - \alpha}\left[\bar{\pi} - \frac{\lambda b \alpha}{2(1 - \alpha)\delta}\right].$$

Note that a larger value of λ (greater preference for increasing output) leads to a lower interest rate choice. A higher value of $\bar{\pi}$ offsets this tendency.

The choice problem in V remains the same as in the fear-of-floating case since output, as of date t, is fixed:

$$\min_{\tilde{i}_t^V} L^V = [\bar{\pi} - (1 - \alpha)\tilde{i}_t^V]^2 + (1 - \delta)[\bar{\pi} + (1 - \alpha)\tilde{i}_t^V]^2.$$

The first-order condition is

$$(19) \qquad\qquad \tilde{i}_t^V = \frac{\delta}{2 - \delta}\frac{\bar{\pi}}{1 - \alpha}.$$

Since in equilibrium, we must have that $E[\tilde{\imath}_t^\omega] = 0$, it follows from equations (18) and (19) that

$$\overline{\pi} = \lambda \frac{qb\alpha}{2(1-\alpha)\delta} > 0.$$

Replacing this expression back into equations (18) and (19), we find that $\tilde{\imath}_t^H < 0$ and $\tilde{\imath}_t^V > 0$:

$$\tilde{\imath}_t^H = -(1-q)\lambda \frac{qb\alpha}{2(1-\alpha)^2\delta} < 0,$$

$$\tilde{\imath}_t^V = \lambda \frac{qb\alpha}{2(1-\alpha)^2\delta} > 0.$$

The central-bank preference for increasing output has a perverse effect in our model. Since lowering interest rates in H increases output, the central bank sets $\tilde{\imath}^H < 0$. As in Barro-Gordon, the anticipation of the low interest rate in H raises the private sector's inflation expectations and leads to $\overline{\pi} > 0$. In V, the central bank sees no output benefit to changing interest rates since output is predetermined by the sudden-stop supply. However, since the average rate of inflation is now positive, the central bank is faced with an exchange rate that depreciates at date t. To counter this, the central bank raises the interest rate in V. In equilibrium, this leads to a lower $\tilde{\imath}_t^{d,V}$ and an even tighter sudden-stop supply. The crisis is thereby exacerbated.

10.6   Implementing Optimal Policy through Inflation Targets

Given the time inconsistency of the central bank, what should its mandate be? That is, how should the central bank's objectives be modified so that it internalizes the insurance dimension of the sudden-stop problem? In this section we highlight two possibilities. First, inflation targets can be made state dependent: stringent (low) in H and loose (high) in V. Second, the central bank's mandate can overweight the inflation of nontradables in the measure of inflation that it targets. Since output contracts in the V regime, there is deflation in nontradables. The inflation-targeting central bank offsets this by lowering interest rates and causing the exchange rate to depreciate (leading to inflation in tradables). This incentive increases by placing a larger weight on nontradables.

10.6.1   State-Contingent Inflation Targets

We continue with the linear-output specification but modify the central bank's objective function to introduce a state-contingent inflation penalty term of κ^ω, for $\omega \in \{H, V\}$:

(20) $L = -\lambda\tilde{y}_t + (\pi_t - \kappa^\omega)^2 + (1-\delta)(\pi_{t+1} - \kappa^\omega)^2.$

A positive κ means that inflation is less costly for the central bank, while a negative κ penalizes inflation further.

The choice problem in H is

$$\min_{\tilde{\imath}_t^H} L^H = \lambda b \alpha \tilde{\imath}_t^H + [\overline{\pi} - \kappa^H - (1 - \alpha)\tilde{\imath}_t^H]^2 + (1 - \delta)[\overline{\pi} - \kappa^H + (1 - \alpha)\tilde{\imath}_t^H]^2.$$

This gives the first-order condition

$$\tilde{\imath}_t^H = \frac{\delta}{2 - \delta} \frac{1}{1 - \alpha} \left[\overline{\pi} - \kappa^H - \frac{\lambda b \alpha}{(1 - \alpha)\delta} \right].$$

Note that, everything else being constant, a larger value of κ^H leads to a lower interest rate in H.

The choice problem in V is

$$\min_{\tilde{\imath}_t^V} L^V = [\overline{\pi} - \kappa^V - (1 - \alpha)\tilde{\imath}_t^V]^2 + (1 - \delta)[\overline{\pi} - \kappa^V + (1 - \alpha)\tilde{\imath}_t^V]^2.$$

The first order condition is now

$$\tilde{\imath}_t^V = \frac{\delta}{2 - \delta} \frac{\overline{\pi} - \kappa^V}{1 - \alpha}.$$

As before, since in equilibrium we must have that $E[\tilde{\imath}_t^\omega] = 0$, we obtain

$$\overline{\pi} = \lambda \frac{q b \alpha}{2(1 - \alpha)\delta} + (1 - q)\kappa^V + q\kappa^H.$$

We note that in the commitment solution $\overline{\pi}$ is equal to zero. Imposing $\overline{\pi} = 0$ yields a constraint across κ^ω:

$$\kappa^H = -\frac{\lambda b \alpha}{2(1 - \alpha)\delta} - \frac{1 - q}{q}\kappa^V.$$

If there is a strong Barro-Gordon inflation bias (high λ), then κ^H can be made low in order to offset this bias. Similarly, to the extent that the central bank has a loose inflation target in V (if κ^V is high), κ^H can be set low so the net result is a $\overline{\pi}$ of zero.

Substituting this κ expression back into the first-order conditions for interest rate choices allows us to solve for the optimal interest rate choices

$$\tilde{\imath}_t^H = \frac{\delta}{2 - \delta} \frac{1}{1 - \alpha} \frac{1 - q}{q} \kappa^V$$

and

$$\tilde{\imath}_t^V = -\frac{\delta}{2 - \delta} \frac{1}{1 - \alpha} \kappa^V.$$

By choosing $\kappa^V > 0$ (and hence $\kappa^H < 0$), the central bank will follow a state-contingent policy as dictated in the social optimum, with $\tilde{\imath}_t^H > 0$ and $\tilde{\imath}_t^V < 0$.

In equilibrium, this leads to a higher $\tilde{\iota}_t^{d,V}$ and a looser sudden-stop supply. The crisis is thereby lessened.

Before we conclude this section, note that both the state-contingent inflation target and the nontradable-inflation overweight solutions act through the inflation terms of the central-bank objective. If we were to introduce a contemporaneous output effect of a change in $\tilde{\iota}^V$, these recommendations would remain, but there would be an additional channel open: we could now also achieve the desirable effect by raising the weight of output in the central bank's objective during V regimes.

10.6.2   Nontradable Inflation Target

Let us now introduce an infinitesimal (in the sense that it does not feed back into aggregate demand) nontradable good, whose inflation is determined by a simple Phillips curve:

$$\pi_t^N = \overline{\pi} + \tilde{y}_t.$$

We modify the measure of inflation that the central bank targets to be a weighted average of π_t^N and the tradable inflation of π_t that we have been using so far. The central bank's objective function is

(21) $L = -\lambda \tilde{y}_t + [\beta \pi_t^N + (1 - \beta)\pi_t - \kappa^\omega]^2$
$$+ (1 - \delta)[\beta \pi_{t+1}^N + (1 - \beta)\pi_{t+1} - \kappa^\omega]^2.$$

β is the weight on nontradable inflation. We normalize the $t + 1$ (noncrisis) inflation rate on nontradables to be zero. Finally we set $\kappa^V = 0$ (leaving $\kappa^H \neq 0$).

The choice problem in V is

$$\min_{\tilde{\iota}_t^V} L^V = [\overline{\pi} + \beta \tilde{y}_t^V - (1 - \beta)(1 - \alpha)\tilde{\iota}_t^V]^2$$
$$+ (1 - \delta)(1 - \beta)^2[\overline{\pi} + (1 - \alpha)\tilde{\iota}_t^V]^2$$

The first-order condition is

$$\tilde{\iota}_t^V = \frac{\overline{\pi}[1 - (1 - \beta)(1 - \delta)] + \beta \tilde{y}_t^V}{(1 - \alpha)(1 - \beta)(2 - \delta)}.$$

The choice problem in H is

$$\min_{\tilde{\iota}_t^H} L^H = \lambda b \alpha \tilde{\iota}_t^H + [\overline{\pi} - \kappa^H - \beta b \alpha \tilde{\iota}_t^H - (1 - \alpha)\tilde{\iota}_t^H]^2$$
$$+ (1 - \delta)(1 - \beta)^2\left[\overline{\pi} - \frac{\kappa^H}{1 - \beta} + (1 - \alpha)\tilde{\iota}_t^H\right]^2.$$

This gives a solution for $\tilde{\iota}_t^H$ that is linearly increasing in $\overline{\pi}$, decreasing in λ, and decreasing in κ^H.

As in the previous section, we can always choose κ^H so that $\overline{\pi} = 0$. That is, when we impose the equilibrium condition that $E[\tilde{\imath}_t^\omega] = 0$, we arrive at a relation for $\overline{\pi}$ in terms of κ^H. We simply choose κ^H so that $\overline{\pi}$ equals zero.

Given this κ^H, $\tilde{\imath}_t^V$ is proportional to $\beta \tilde{y}_t^V$. Since $\tilde{y}_t^V < 0$, we can implement $\tilde{\imath}_t^V < 0$ by choosing $\beta > 0$. Since $E[\tilde{\imath}_t^\omega] = 0$, this means that $\tilde{\imath}_t^H > 0$, which is achieved by setting $\kappa^H < 0$.

By increasing the weight on nontradables in the measure of inflation that the central bank targets, the central bank follows a state-contingent policy as dictated in the social optimum. Again, in equilibrium, this leads to a higher $\tilde{\imath}_t^{d,V}$ and a looser sudden-stop supply.

10.7   Reserves Management

Since crises are characterized by dollar shortages (see equation [2]), there is scope in the model for managing international reserves in order to ease these shortages. Our model provides a natural motivation both for centralized holding of reserves and for holding them in the form of dollars.

We assume that the central bank has a small amount of international reserves at date t. These reserves can be injected at date t or saved for use beyond date $t + 1$, when they yield $\gamma > 0$ utils per unit of reserves. The latter represents the opportunity cost of using the reserves early, and should be interpreted more broadly as the value of precautioning.

We contrast how the results of section 10.4 and section 10.5.1 change upon the introduction of international reserves. The loss function in both cases is modified to

$$(22) \qquad L = \lambda \tilde{y}_t^2 + \pi_t^2 + (1 - \delta)\pi_{t+1}^2 + \gamma R_t,$$

with R_t the amount of reserves injected.

Recall that in section 10.4 we solve for the interest rate choices that the central bank commits to in minimizing the loss function, while in section 10.5.1 we solve for the sequentially optimal interest rate choices given this loss function.

There is no value in injecting reserves in H. Since there is no dollar shortage, the action has no effect on either prices or output. Reserves will be hoarded because failing to do so has an opportunity cost γ. In the V regime, the action increases dollar supply and relaxes the vertical constraint (10) to

$$(23) \qquad \tilde{y}_t^V = R_t^V - a_y + a_d \tilde{\imath}_{t|t-1}^{d,V}.$$

One can see from this expression that R_t^V enters exactly as $-a_y$ in all the expressions. In particular,

$$(24) \qquad \tilde{y}_t^V = \Psi b(R_t^V - a_y - \alpha a_d \tilde{\imath}_t^V).$$

As we discussed earlier, the optimal policy considers the dependence of $\tilde{y}_t^V$ on $\tilde{\iota}_t^{d,V}$ (which enters through expectations), while the no-commitment case does not.

The introduction of international reserves-management considerations does not change any of the main qualitative conclusions with respect to monetary policy in either the commitment or no-commitment case of sections 10.4 and 10.5.1, respectively. In particular, it is still the case that $\bar{\pi} = 0$ in both cases, that $\tilde{\iota}^H = \tilde{\iota}^V = 0$ in the no-commitment case, and that $\tilde{\iota}^H > 0$ and $\tilde{\iota}^V < 0$ in the commitment case.[4]

However, reserve injections are a substitute for (countercyclical) monetary policy. To see this, note that in the commitment solution for $\tilde{\iota}_t^V$ in equation (16), $\tilde{\iota}_t^V$ is decreasing in a_y. Since R_t^V enters as $-a_y$ in all expressions, the reserve injection increases the optimal $\tilde{\iota}_t^V$.

The most interesting new result comes from the first-order condition with respect to R_t^V. From equations (22) and (24), the solution for R_t^V in the commitment case is

$$(25) \qquad R_t^{V,c} = -\frac{\gamma}{2\lambda(b\Psi)^2} + a_y + \alpha a_d \tilde{\iota}_t^V.$$

From equations (22) and (23), the solution for R_t^V in the no-commitment case is

$$(26) \qquad R_t^{V,nc} = -\frac{\gamma}{2\lambda b\Psi} + a_y + \alpha a_d \tilde{\iota}_t^V$$

Note that $b\Psi = b/(b + a_d) < 1$, so the first term is more negative in the commitment case. Also, since for any equilibrium level of R_t^V, $\tilde{\iota}_t^{V,c} < \tilde{\iota}_t^{V,nc}$, we have that $R_t^{V,nc} > R_t^{V,c}$. That is, the central bank with no commitment not only will use too little monetary policy but also will inject reserves too aggressively.

There are two factors behind this result. First, injecting reserves both increases output and decreases $\tilde{\iota}_t^{d,V}$. Ex post, the central bank considers the output benefit, but ignores the effect on $\tilde{\iota}_t^{d,V}$. Ex ante, the central bank accounts for the second effect: the lower $\tilde{\iota}_t^{d,V}$ decreases the private sector's incentives to insure against the sudden-stop shock. The latter effect makes the commitment central bank inject less reserves than the no-commitment one.

The second factor has to do with the time inconsistency of monetary policy. In the no-commitment solution, the central bank has to offset a larger crisis caused by the inadequate monetary policy. As a result, it over-injects its reserves.

The latter factor is remedied indirectly by solving the monetary policy time-inconsistency problem as we have discussed. The former factor, on the

---

4. These statements assume that $R_t < a_y$, so that there is insufficient international reserves to eliminate the sudden-stop shock.

other hand, requires further modification to the central bank's mandate so that it increases the value it assigns to hoarding reserves during the V regime.

10.8 Final Remarks

We have analyzed monetary policy in an environment of sudden stops. Sudden stops are times when a country is financially constrained in the international financial market. In this context, lowering or raising domestic interest rates has only small effects on the tightness of this financial constraint, but such action does have significant effects on the domestic borrowing capacity of agents. Moreover, the anticipation of such actions is important in determining precautionary actions that agents take against sudden stops.

From this viewpoint, we have derived positive and normative results for monetary policy and reserves management. We have highlighted a new time-inconsistency problem and its interaction with the conventional stabilization bias. Finally, we have suggested how an inflation-targeting framework can restore incentives, so that central banks behave optimally.

Our model is clearly very stylized. In particular, our assumption that the country faces a vertical supply of funds during sudden stops is extreme. But it is important to realize that our main conclusions do not depend on this extreme. We could consider a more general model in which the supply of funds was not completely inelastic in the V regime. In this case, the V regime would have both an aggregate-demand channel and the insurance channel we have highlighted (i.e., lowering $\tilde{i}_t^V$ leads to a contemporaneous increase in $\tilde{y}_t^V$). Importantly, relative to the H regime, the output-inflation trade-off will still turn steeper (although not vertical) during the V regime, and hence the central bank will be prone to favor inflation over output targets more than in the H regime. Moreover, as long as the insurance channel is present, this reaction will remain suboptimal.

Insurance against sudden stops affects many policy decisions in emerging markets, from reserve management to liquidity ratio requirements. It seems only natural that optimal monetary policy be analyzed in the same light, as in this paper. Moreover, it is important to understand the interaction of monetary policy with other insurance policies (as we have with reserve policies). We hope that our framework provides a starting point for such an integrated approach.

References

Barro, Robert, and David Gordon. 1983. A positive theory of monetary policy in a natural rate model. *Journal of Political Economy* 91 (4): 589–610.

Bernanke, Ben, and Alan Blinder. 1988. Credit, money and aggregate demand. *American Economic Review* 78 (2): 435–39.

Bernanke, Ben, Mark Gertler, and Simon Gilchrist. 1999. The financial accelerator in a quantitative business cycle framework. In *Handbook of macroeconomics,* ed. John Taylor and Michael Woodford, 1341–96. Amsterdam: Elsevier.

Bulow, Jeremy, and Kenneth Rogoff. 1989. A constant recontracting model of sovereign debt *Journal of Political Economy* 97 (1): 155–78.

Caballero, Ricardo, and Arvind Krishnamurthy. 2001. International and domestic collateral constraints in a model of emerging market crises. *Journal of Monetary Economics* 48 (3): 513–48.

———. 2002. A vertical analysis of monetary policy in emerging markets. MIT, Department of Economics. Mimeograph.

———. 2003. Excessive dollar debt: Financial development and underinsurance. *Journal of Finance* 58 (2): 867–93.

Calvo, Guillermo. 1998. Capital flows and capital-market crises: The simple economics of sudden stops. University of Maryland, Department of Economics. Mimeograph.

Calvo, Guillermo, and Carmen Reinhart. 2002. Fear of floating. *Quarterly Journal of Economics* 117 (2): 379–408.

Christiano, Lawrence J., Christopher Gust, and Jorge Roldos. Forthcoming. Monetary policy in a financial crisis. *Journal of Economic Theory.*

Diamond, Douglas, and Raghuram Rajan. 2001. Liquidity shortages and banking crises. University of Chicago, Graduate School of Business. Mimeograph.

Dooley, Michael. 2000. A model of crises in emerging markets. *The Economic Journal* 110 (460): 256–72.

Gertler, Mark, Simon Gilchrist, and Fabio M. Natalucci. 2001. External constraints on monetary policy and the financial accelerator. New York University, Department of Economics. Working Paper.

Holmstrom, Bengt, and Jean Tirole. 1998. Private and public supply of liquidity. *Journal of Political Economy* 106 (1): 1–40.

King, Mervyn A. 1994. Monetary policy in the UK. *Fiscal Studies* 15 (3): 109–28.

Kiyotaki, Nobuhiro, and John Moore. 2001. Liquidity, business cycles, and monetary policy. London School of Economics. Mimeograph.

Lorenzoni, Guido. 2001. Interest rate stabilization and monetary control: A reconciliation. Princeton University, Department of Economics. Mimeograph.

Svensson, Lars E. O. 1999. Inflation targeting as a monetary policy rule. *Journal of Monetary Economics* 43:607–54.

———. 2000. Open-economy inflation targeting. *Journal of International Economics* 50:155–83.

Woodford, Michael. 2002. Inflation stabilization and welfare. Princeton University, Department of Economics. Mimeograph.

Comment   Ben S. Bernanke

This very interesting paper highlights the potential interaction in emerging-market economies between the monetary policy regime and the effects

Ben S. Bernanke is the Howard Harrison and Gabrielle Snyder Beck Professor of Economics and Public affairs at Princeton University and a member of the Board of Governors of the U.S. Federal Reserve System.

of adverse shifts in the portfolio preferences of international investors ("sudden stops"). It raises the possibility that inflation targeting may serve as a form of commitment device for monetary authorities in those economies—not as a mechanism for committing to price stability per se, as is usually the case in the inflation-targeting literature, but rather as a means to commit to responding in a particular way to the sudden stop in capital inflows. Specifically, the authors argue, adopting inflation targeting can be viewed as a commitment *not* to defend the exchange rate in a crisis. If that commitment is credible, then the ex ante incentive of domestic agents to be long in dollars (by forgoing dollar-denominated liabilities as well as holding dollar assets) is increased, mitigating the severity of the dollar shortage caused by the crisis. In short, the authors argue that adopting inflation targeting before the crisis may be an antidote to the "fear of floating" problem stressed by Calvo and Reinhart (2002).

The model used to illustrate this point is highly stylized, which is both a strength and a weakness—a strength, because it makes the basic economic idea extremely clear; a weakness, because it thereby ignores some complicating aspects of the problem that are likely to be crucial in real economies. One particularly important omission is any consideration of what caused the sudden stop in the first place. (The paper assumes that sudden stops are exogenous, but as ever-more-discriminating international capital markets make episodes of pure contagion less likely, that assumption does not seem particularly attractive.) If the source of the crisis is, say, ongoing fiscal instability, then an inflation-targeting regime may well be infeasible, for reasons of fiscal dominance. Another source of crisis discussed in the literature is the combination of a poorly supervised banking system and a government that is unable to commit to not bailing out the banking system if it fails (a moral hazard problem). In such a situation a general bank run can provoke a fiscal crisis and hence a sudden stop. Monetary policy would have little power to ameliorate this type of crisis, however, because banks in particular would have no incentive to be long in dollars, knowing that they will be bailed out in any case. The correct response to this type of problem is some combination of bank supervision (e.g., limiting exposure to dollar liabilities) and fiscal commitment devices to moderate the government's moral hazard. The general point is that whatever factors create the potential for sudden stops will also likely affect the feasibility and desirability of the solution proposed here.

Another drawback of the stylized nature of the model is that its empirical plausibility is difficult to assess. For example, an implication of the model is that when the central bank defends the exchange rate (the time-consistent solution), we should see deflation in nontradables. (This result provides the basis for equating inflation targeting in nontradables prices to a commitment to devaluation.) Because in practice nontradables prices cannot be insulated from the exchange rate (a depreciation affects wage demands, the costs of inputs, and inflation expectations), I would guess that a sudden stop would typically lead to inflation in nontradables as well as tradables. Some analysis of the data is called for. If a crisis does typically lead to inflation in nontradables, and if, moreover, the nontradables inflation rate in a crisis is difficult to forecast, then setting a quantitative inflation target in advance for nontradables, as recommended by the authors, may not be particularly useful. Another empirical issue relates to the ability of the central bank to hit an inflation target in the time frame relevant to an international financial crisis; generally we believe that central banks can control inflation only with a lag of months, not days or weeks. In short, determining the practical relevance of the policy recommendation of this paper will require a good deal more empirical analysis and quantification.

My remaining comments concern some issues relating to the micro-foundations of the model. First, the authors appeal to models of credit-market imperfections in which collateral is used to mitigate agency costs. It seems to me that the collateral that would be relevant for borrowing from abroad would be denominated in dollars, not in pesos; but the authors assume that the assets relevant to the domestic demand for investment goods, A_t, are peso assets rather than dollar assets. This assumption would seem to be of some consequence for the analysis, since only if these assets are in pesos is the value of domestic collateral affected by devaluation. A related point concerns the ex ante holdings of dollar assets by domestic investors, which confers a social benefit (being a form of insurance) in this model. But dollar holdings by domestics may also be viewed as a form of capital flight; and in a world of capital-market imperfections, in which domestics are presumed to have superior local information, the fact that domestics are not investing in the home market should involve deadweight losses, which are ignored here.

Second, I also had some concerns about the pricing assumptions in the model. The authors distinguish two types of producers of domestic goods: "fast" pricers, who tie their prices to the exchange rate, and "slow" pricers, who set their prices in advance according to their expectation of the exchange rate. I understand the reasons for these assumptions, but I wonder if they are entirely sensible economically. First, domestic goods and imported investment goods are not perfect substitutes, so it is not evident that pricing should be such as to keep the expected real exchange rate constant. Second, because the actual exchange rate may differ radically from the expected exchange rate in a crisis, it seems unreasonable to assume that even very "slow" pricers do not reset their prices when a crisis occurs. Allowing repricing in a crisis would certainly affect some of the results of the model.

To reiterate my main impressions, I found the paper stimulating and useful. More quantitative analysis is needed to translate this stylized model into concrete recommendations for policy. But at a more qualitative level, the paper offers another compelling argument for why emerging-market countries should abandon exchange rate pegs, which have not served them well in recent years, in favor of inflation targeting or other monetary policies that focus on domestic macroeconomic stability.

Discussion Summary

Jose De Gregorio suggested that the conclusions depended importantly upon the assumption of a model in which there is no effect of exchange rates on output. He proposed that the result might be quite different if, for example, an expenditure-switching effect were allowed for.

Mark Gertler pointed out that the main reason for the limited interest rate effects in the model was the segmentation between the markets for domestic and foreign currency funds—that is, the absence of arbitrage between these two markets.

Michael Bordo argued that financial development and a measure of fiscal stability were necessary preconditions for the successful adoption of a nominal anchor in emerging economies.

In response to Bernanke's comments, *Ricardo Caballero* pointed out that a major reason for fear of floating was the need to maintain control of inflation expectations. He stressed that the paper did not aim to explain particular historical episodes, but to provide a framework to think about inflation targeting in the presence of capital flow volatility. Credible inflation-targeting regimes are new to emerging-market economics. He emphasized that the distribution of inflation between tradable and nontradable goods depended on the response of inflation expectations to a devaluation; during currency crises the pass-through from nominal exchange rates to domestic prices could be very different from that of other periods. Regarding the importance of the domestic interest rate even when most of the borrowing occurred in foreign currency, he pointed out that during market segmentation episodes monetary policy affected the domestic dollar rate. When used correctly, monetary policy alleviated the inefficiency due to market segmentation by reallocating external resources from times of high foreign capital inflows to times of low capital inflows. The more general underlying theme was the sudden segmentation of markets during financial crises, which was most extreme during collapses of the banking sector. Because a sudden stop could be interpreted as a crash in the value of an asset—namely, the value of the country's collateral—the paper was more broadly applicable to the question of how monetary policy should respond to asset market crises. The particular challenge posed by this model was the risk that monetary policy might be losing its effectiveness during the crisis, and this risk carried implications for the conduct of policy prior to a crisis.

Contributors

Laurence Ball
Department of Economics
Johns Hopkins University
3400 North Charles Street
Baltimore, MD 21218-2685

Ben S. Bernanke
Board of Governors of the Federal
    Reserve System
20th Street and Constitution Avenue,
    NW
Washington, DC 20551

John Berry
Bloomberg News
1399 New York Avenue NW, 11th floor
Washington, DC 20005

Olivier Blanchard
Department of Economics, E52-357
Massachusetts Institute of Technology
50 Memorial Drive
Cambridge, MA 02142-1347

Michael Bordo
Department of Economics
New Jersey Hall
Rutgers University
New Brunswick, NJ 08901-1284

Ricardo J. Caballero
Department of Economics, E52-252a
Massachusetts Institute of Technology
50 Memorial Drive
Cambridge, MA 02142-1347

Stephen G. Cecchetti
International Business School
Brandeis University
P.O. Box 9110
Waltham, MA 02454

José De Gregorio
Banco Central de Chile
Augustinas 1180
Santiago, Chile

George W. Evans
Department of Economics
1285 University of Oregon
Eugene, OR 97403-1285

Martin Feldstein
National Bureau of Economic
    Research
1050 Massachusetts Avenue
Cambridge, MA 02138

Mark Gertler
Department of Economics
New York University
269 Mercer Street, 7th Floor
New York, NY 10003

Marc P. Giannoni
Columbia Business School
3022 Broadway, Uris Hall 824
New York, NY 10027

Marvin Goodfriend
Federal Reserve Bank of Richmond
701 East Byrd Street
Richmond, VA 23219

Jiri Jonas
International Monetary Fund
700 19th Street, NW
Washington, DC 20431

Junhan Kim
Research Department
The Bank of Korea
110 3-Ka Namdaemun-Ro Chung-Ku
Seoul 100-794, Korea

Mervyn King
Bank of England
Threadneedle Street
London EC2R 8AH England

Donald L. Kohn
Board of Governors of the Federal
   Reserve System
20th Street and Constitution Avenue,
   NW
Washington, DC 20551

Arvind Krishnamurthy
Kellogg Graduate School of
   Management
Northwestern University
2001 Sheridan Road
Evanston, IL 60208

Thomas Laubach
OECD, Economics Department
Country Studies 1 Division
2 rue André Pascal
75016 Paris, France

N. Gregory Mankiw
Council of Economic Advisers
The White House
1600 Pennsylvania Avenue, NW
Washington, DC 20500

Bennett T. McCallum
Graduate School of Industrial
   Administration
Carnegie-Mellon University
Pittsburgh, PA 15213

Laurence H. Meyer
The Center for Strategic and
   International Studies
1800 K Street, NW
Washington, DC 20006

Frederic S. Mishkin
Graduate School of Business
Uris Hall 619
Columbia University
New York, NY 10027

Edward Nelson
Research Division
Federal Reserve Bank of St. Louis
411 Locust Street
St. Louis, MO 63102

Athanasios Orphanides
Division of Monetary Affairs
Board of Governors of the Federal
   Reserve System
20th Street and Constitution Avenue,
   NW
Washington, DC 20551

Glenn D. Rudebusch
Economic Research
Federal Reserve Bank of
   San Francisco
101 Market Street
San Francisco, CA 94105

Stephanie Schmitt-Grohé
Department of Economics
Duke University
P.O. Box 90097
Durham, NC 27708

Niamh Sheridan
International Monetary Fund
700 19th Street, NW
Washington, DC 20431

Masaaki Shirakawa
Bank of Japan
2-1-1 Hongoku-cho, Nihonbashi,
    chuo-ku
Tokyo 103 8660 Japan

Christopher A. Sims
Department of Economics
Princeton University
104 Fisher Hall
Princeton, NJ 08544

Frank Smets
European Central Bank
Kaiderstrasse 29
D-60311 Frankfurt am Main,
    Germany

Lars E. O. Svensson
Department of Economics
Fisher Hall
Princeton University
Princeton, NJ 08544-1021

Martin Uribe
Department of Economics
Duke University
Durham, NC 27708-0097

John C. Williams
Macroeconomic Research
Federal Reserve Bank of
    San Francisco
101 Market Street
San Francisco, CA 94105

Michael Woodford
Department of Economics
Columbia University
New York, NY 10027

Author Index

Ábel, István, 357n4, 374n22
Akerlof, George, 369n17
Altig, David, 115, 118, 134
Amato, Jeffrey D., 114, 117, 118, 120, 124,
    128, 130, 133
Anderson, T. W., 213n13

Backus, David, 21n3
Ball, Laurence, 6–7, 196, 203n2, 251, 273,
    371n21
Balvers, Ronald J., 203n2
Barro, Robert, 331, 424, 434, 435
Basu, Susanto, 118
Batini, Nicoletta, 175
Begg, David, 359n7
Benhabib, Jess, 283, 300, 301, 302
Bernanke, Ben, 10, 21n4, 27, 74n46, 93,
    123, 124n34, 204, 249, 251, 252, 270,
    273, 312n1, 312n3, 321n7, 342n6,
    355n2, 360n8, 366n16, 369, 387, 399,
    406, 425
Blejer, M. L., 312n3
Blinder, Alan S., 123, 135n44, 313, 425
Blume, Lawrence E., 202
Boivin, Jean, 118, 122, 124, 124n34, 130,
    133n39, 163n1
Bomfim, Antulio, 202n2
Bootle, R., 320
Brash, Donald T., 400
Bray, Margaret M., 202
Brayton, Flint, 211, 215
Broaddus, J. Alfred, Jr., 332

Brock, William, 300, 301, 307
Bufman, Gill, 366n16, 404n41
Buiter, Willem H., 211
Bullard, James B., 202, 239, 240, 241
Bulow, Jeremy, 426

Caballero, Ricardo J., 9–10, 424, 426,
    427n2, 429, 431
Calvo, Guillermo A., 96, 115, 383n28, 424,
    426, 443
Čapek, Ales, 379
Carlstrom, C. T., 239
Carroll, Christopher D., 203n2
Cecchetti, Steven G., 4–5, 173, 179, 265, 328
Cho, I.-K., 240, 241
Christiano, Lawrence J., 21n4, 22n6, 29,
    102, 114, 118, 123, 130, 134, 139,
    203n3, 425
Clarida, Richard, 20n2, 21n4, 23n7, 27, 52,
    70, 85, 96, 107, 124, 125, 301
Clark, Peter B., 174n5, 205
Clifton, Eric V., 272, 395
Clinton, Kevin, 371
Cogley, Timothy, 124, 328
Corbo, Vittorio, 270, 272
Cosimano, Thomas F., 203n2
Craine, Roger, 225n16
Currie, David, 21n3

Debell, Guy, 357n3
Dennis, Richard, 85n4
Deppler, Michael, 371

Diamond, Douglas, 425, 425n1
Dickens, William, 369n17
Dittmar, Robert, 175n6, 187
Dixit, Avinash K., 126
Dooley, Michael, 426
Drew, Aaron, 388, 400
Driffill, John, 21n3

Easley, David, 202
Edge, Rochelle, 118
Ehrmann, Michael, 179, 265
Eichenbaum, Martin S., 102, 114, 118, 123, 130, 134, 139
Eichengreen, Barry, 357n5
Eliasz, Piotr, 124n34
Erceg, Christopher J., 115, 117n27, 128, 164, 202n2, 416
Estrella, Arturo, 355n1
Evans, Charles L., 102, 115, 118, 123, 130, 134, 139, 210, 214
Evans, George, 202, 209, 237n2, 239, 240, 241, 242, 243

Feldstein, Martin, 12, 15–16, 323
Ferguson, R., 332
Fischer, Stanley, 389
Flodén, Martin, 20n2
Flores-Lagunes, Alfonso, 173
Friedman, Benjamin M., 201–2n1, 209
Friedman, Milton, 106
Fuerst, T. S., 239
Fuhrer, Jeffrey C., 118, 134, 211, 212n12, 328

Galí, Jordi, 20n2, 21n4, 23n7, 27, 52, 70, 85, 96, 107, 124, 125, 134, 205n5, 212, 225, 301, 328
Gaspar, Vitor, 225
Gavin, William T., 175n6, 187
Gertler, Mark, 7, 20n2, 21n4, 23n7, 27, 52, 70, 85, 96, 107, 124, 125, 134, 205n5, 212, 225, 301, 321n7, 425
Giannoni, Marc P., 3, 22, 36, 37, 37n22, 38n24, 94, 94n2, 96, 96n3, 105n14, 109, 109n16, 109n17, 112nn20, 21, 22, 118, 123, 124, 130, 133n39, 150n60, 156, 160, 163n1, 168
Gilchrist, Simon, 425
Gilovich, Thomas, 256n3
Goodfriend, Marvin, 7, 8, 10, 106, 164, 170, 314n4, 318n5, 320n6, 321n7, 328, 330n12, 332
Goodhart, Charles A. E., 174n5, 205

Gordon, David, 424, 434, 435
Gray, Jo Anna, 301
Greenspan, Alan, 312, 321
Gurkaynak, R. S., 318n5, 324n9
Gust, Christopher J., 21n4, 22n6, 203n3, 425

Haldane, Andrew, 312n3, 394
Hall, R. E., 331
Henderson, Dale W., 115, 117n25, 128, 164, 416
Holmstrom, Bengt, 425
Honkapohja, Seppo, 202, 210, 237n2, 239, 240, 241, 243
Hrnĉîř, M., 359n6
Huang, Haizhou, 174n5, 205
Hyginus, Leon, 272

Ireland, P., 318n5, 330n12

Jackman, Richard, 251
Jensen, Christian, 86
Jewitt, Ian, 211
Johnson, David R., 272n9
Jonas, Jiri, 8
Jonsson, Gunnar, 20n2, 52
Judd, John F., 125

Kerr, William, 21n4
Kilian, Lutz, 125
Kim, Junhan, 4–5
Kimball, Miles S., 118
King, Mervyn A., 2, 10, 20, 23, 31, 59n39, 78, 93, 169, 174n4, 175, 185, 249, 265, 312n3, 426
King, Robert G., 165, 170, 328, 330n12
King, Robert J., 21n4
Kiyotaki, Nobuhiro, 425
Kohn, Donald L., 8, 312n3
Kozicki, Sharon, 202–3n2
Krause, Stefan, 173
Krishnamurthy, Arvind, 9–10, 424, 426, 427n2, 429, 431
Kuttner, Kenneth N., 268n6
Kydland, Finn E., 36, 187
Kysilka, Pavel, 386

Landerretche, Oscar, 270, 272
Laubach, Thomas, 114, 117, 118, 120, 124, 128, 130, 133, 205n6
Layard, Richard, 251
Leeper, Eric M., 49n34, 301
Leiderman, Leonardo, 366n16, 404n41

Leitemo, Kai, 65n42
Lengwiler, Yvan, 205
Levin, Andrew T., 22n6, 90, 115, 117n25, 128, 164, 202n2, 209n9, 416
Levine, Paul, 21n3
Liederman, L., 312n3
Loayza, N., 312n3
Lorenzoni, Guido, 425
Loyo, Eduardo, 284, 296, 300
Lucas, Robert E., 202

Mahadeva, Lavan, 359n6
Mankiw, N. Gregory, 165, 177n7, 196, 203n2, 273
Marcet, Albert, 202, 210, 236n1, 241
Marimon, R., 239
McCallum, Bennett, 22, 39n25, 73n45, 85, 86, 88, 89, 107, 118n28, 312nn2, 3
McFarlane, Ian J., 401
McGough, B., 239
Meyer, L. H., 312n1, 349
Mihov, Ilian, 123
Mishkin, Frederic S., 10, 13, 98, 204, 249, 253, 263, 268n6, 312n1, 355n1, 357n5, 370, 383n28, 387, 396, 398, 404
Mitra, Kaushik, 202, 239
Moore, Geoffrey R., 134, 328
Moore, George, 211
Moore, John, 425
Muth, John F., 201n1

Natalucci, Fabio M., 425
Nelson, Edward, 85, 88, 107, 118n28
Neumann, Manfred J. M., 250, 268n6, 272, 272n9, 312n3
Nickell, Stephen, 251
Nicolini, J. P., 241

Obstfeld, Marice, 300, 301, 307
Orlowski, Lucjan T., 358, 398
Orphanides, Athanasios, 5–6, 13, 203n3, 205, 205n6, 216n14, 222n15, 329
Orr, Adrian, 388, 400

Parkin, Michael, 179
Perry, George, 369n17
Persson, Torsten, 55
Posen, Adam S., 268n6
Prescott, Edward C., 36

Rajan, Raghuram, 425, 425n1
Ramey, G., 214, 242, 243
Reinhart, Carmen, 424, 426, 443

Reis, Ricardo, 177n7, 196, 203n2
Roberts, John M., 97, 212n12, 215
Rogoff, Kenneth, 175, 300, 301, 307, 426
Roldos, Jorge, 425
Romer, C. D., 314
Romer, D. H., 314
Rotemberg, Julio J., 21n4, 22n6, 27, 30n17, 46n31, 73n45, 86, 99n8, 102, 122, 124, 126, 130, 131, 133, 134, 135, 135n44, 149, 163n1, 169
Rudd, Jeremy, 212n12
Rudebusch, Glenn D., 125, 166n3, 187

Sack, B., 318n5, 324n9
Sargent, Thomas J., 21, 22, 45, 124, 201, 202, 203nn2, 3, 209, 210, 236n1, 240, 241, 296, 328
Savastano, M. A., 357n5, 396, 404
Savin, Nathan E., 202
Saxton, J., 312n2
Schaechter, Andrea, 357n3
Scheater, Andrea, 252, 253
Schmidt-Hebbel, K., 312n3
Schmidt-Hebbel, Klaus, 270, 272, 370
Schmitt-Grohé, Stephanie, 283, 300, 301, 302, 329
Sheridan, Niamh, 6–7, 262n5
Sherwin, Murray, 388
Siklos, Pierre L., 357n4, 374n22
Simon, Herbert A., 202n1
Sims, Christopher A., 7–8, 202, 202n1, 284, 288n3, 289
Škreb, Marko, 370
Smets, Frank, 70, 115, 118, 225
Šmidková, K., 359n6
Söderlind, Paul, 48, 51, 178n9
Soto, R., 312n3
Staiger, Douglas, 215
Steinson, Jon, 96
Sterne, G., 312n3
Stevens, Glenn R., 401
Stiglitz, Joseph E., 126
Stock, James H., 215, 371
Stone, Mark R., 252, 253, 357n3
Summers, Larry, 369n18
Svensson, Lars E. O., 3–4, 13, 20n2, 23, 24, 25, 25n10, 27, 31, 41n26, 49, 52, 55n38, 68, 70, 72n43, 79n47, 86, 87, 93, 94n1, 105, 139n48, 142n54, 169, 174, 175, 177, 178, 184, 187, 228n17, 250, 273, 301, 302, 312, 312n3, 328, 387, 388, 397, 426
Swanson, E., 318n5, 324n9

Tabellini, Guido, 55
Tapia, M., 312n3
Taylor, John B., 22, 32n19, 46n31, 47n32,
    72, 73, 73n45, 86, 125, 202n2, 204,
    213n13, 329
Taylor, Johy B., 24
Tetlow, Robert J., 203n2
Tinsley, Peter A., 203n2
Tirole, Jean, 425
Tomita, Toshiki, 288
Townsend, Robert M., 202
Turnovsky, Stephen, 225n16

Uribe, Martin, 283, 300–301, 302, 329

Vestin, David, 70, 175n6
Vickers, John, 93
Vigfusson, Robert J., 29
Volcker, Paul, 204, 219–20
von Hagen, Jurgen, 250, 268n6, 272, 272n9,
    312n3
von zu Muehlen, Peer, 203n2

Wallace, Neil, 21, 22, 45, 296, 301, 307
Walsh, Carl, 55
Watson, Mark W., 215, 371
Whelan, Karl, 212n12

Wieland, Volker, 22n6, 203n2, 209n9
Williams, John C., 5–6, 13, 22n6, 90,
    205n6, 209n9, 215, 216n14, 222n15,
    329
Williams, N., 240, 241
Wong, Chorng-Huey, 272
Woodford, Michael, 3–4, 13, 20n2, 21,
    21n4, 22, 22nn5, 6, 23n7, 27, 27n11, 28,
    29, 30, 30n17, 31, 34, 36, 37, 37n22,
    38n24, 41n26, 46n31, 47n32, 50, 52,
    66, 70, 72n43, 73n45, 74n46, 85, 86, 94,
    94n2, 96, 96n3, 97nn4, 5, 98n7, 99n8,
    101, 102, 103n12, 105n14, 106, 107,
    107n15, 109, 109nn16, 17, 112nn20, 21,
    22, 115, 117n24, 118nn28, 29, 122, 123,
    124, 126, 130, 131, 133, 134, 135,
    135n44, 138n47, 139n48, 141n52,
    142n54, 149, 150n60, 156, 163, 163n1,
    169, 202, 300, 301, 307, 330n12, 414,
    417, 426
Wouters, Raf, 115, 118

Yates, Anthony, 175
Yun, Tack, 27n12

Zelmer, Mark, 252, 253, 357n3
Zha, Tao, 49n34

Subject Index

Australia, 251, 252t; inflation targets and exchange rates in, 400–404
Average inflation, 247–49

Banks. *See* Central banks
Bivariate results, for inflation targeting, 268–72

Canada, 251, 252t
Capital flows. *See* Sudden stops
Central banks: ability to control inflation paths of, 300–301; adoption of inflation-targeting frameworks by, 19; best practices for designing, 173–74; inflation-targeting, 1; inflation targeting vs. price-path targeting and, 174–75; social loss function and, 49–51; transparency and, 66–67; without commitment to interest rate choices, 434–36. *See also* Federal Reserve; Monetary policy
Chile, inflation targets and exchange rates in, 400
Closed economies, results of hybrid targeting for, 182–84
Commitment, 191–92
Constrained discretion, 13, 20–21
Cost-push shocks, 96–102
Currencies. *See* Exchange rates
Czech Republic: changeover from fixed to floating exchange rates in, 354–58; comparing inflation in, with non-

inflation-target floaters and, 380–84; hitting and missing inflation targets in, 377–80; inflation targets and exchange rates in, 397–98, 403–4; introduction of inflation targeting in, 359–63; preliminary experiences with inflation targeting in, 372–74. *See also* Transition economies

Deflationary models, 284–89
Determinacy of equilibrium, 3, 44–45, 77; hybrid rule for ensuring, 61–64; necessary and sufficient conditions for, 83; under specific targeting rule, 65–67
Discretion, 191–92; constrained, 13, 20–21

Efficient simple rule, 222–25
Equilibrium, indeterminacy of, 44–48. *See also* Determinacy of equilibrium; Optimal equilibrium
Equivalent price-level targeting rule, 68–71, 79
ERM2 system, monetary policy within, 405–9
European Monetary Union (EMU), 9, 253–54; inflation targets and exchange rates in, 401–3
Exchange rates, inflation targets and, 396–405
Explicit inflation targeting, implementing, by Federal Reserve, 331–32

Explicit instrument rules, 24, 79; commitment to, 71–76, 77–78; defined, 23n7

"Fear of floating," 10, 424
Federal Reserve: Greenspan era of, 319–21; implementing explicit inflation targeting in, 331–34; implicit inflation targeting practiced by, 8, 321–23; inflation targeting and, 311–13; prioritizing long-run inflation and, 323–27; short-run inflation targeting and, 327–31; Volcker disinflation period of, 315–19. *See also* Central banks; Monetary policy; United States
Finland, 251, 252t
Fiscal policies, deflationary traps via "Ricardian," 284–89
Forecast paths, 64
Forecast targeting, 23, 48–49; constructing, 49n34; dynamic-programming procedure for, 51–52
Forward-looking policy making, disadvantages of, 20–23

General targeting rule, 23, 94n1
Greenspan, Alan, 319–23
Growth, output, inflation targeting and, 262–65

Habit persistence, 117–22
Hungary, 354; comparing inflation in, with non-inflation-targeting floaters and, 380–84; hitting and missing inflation targets in, 377–80; inflation targets and exchange rates in, 397–98, 404–5; introduction of inflation targeting in, 365–68; preliminary experiences with inflation targeting in, 374–77. *See also* Transition economies
Hybrid rule, for ensuring determinacy, 61–64
Hybrid targeting: loss comparison for, 187–90; results for closed economies of, 182–84; results for open economies of, 184–88; rules, 5; theory of, 176–82
Hybrid-targeting regimes, 175

Imperfect knowledge, 202; inflation expectations and, 207–11; monetary policy and, 220–26
Implicit inflation targeting, by Federal Reserve, 8, 321–23
Implicit instrument rule, defined, 23n7

Implied reaction functions, 24
Indeterminacy, of equilibrium, 44–48
Inflation: average, 257–59; efficient policy response to, 222–25; persistence, 262; stabilizing, with reserves or tax backing, 289–96; variability, 259–62
Inflation expectations: formation of, 203–4; imperfect-knowledge solution for, 207–11; least squares inflation forecasts and, 212–15; model for examining, 204–5; perfect-knowledge benchmark for, 206–7; perpetual learning and, 211–20
Inflation-forecast targeting: benefits of, 93–94; as optimal monetary policy, 3
Inflation inertia, 102–6
Inflation persistence, least squares learning and, 215–16
Inflation targeting, 250–51; benefits of, 250; bivariate results of study of, 268–72; comparison of studies of, 272; as constrained discretion, 13; defined, 1; exchange rates and, 396–405; as framework, 10; improving, 297–98; interest rates and, 265–68; methodology for studying, 255–57; output growth and, 262–65; process of, in United Kingdom, 12; pros and cons of, 296–97; sample of countries for studying, 251–55; unanswered questions about, 1–2. *See also* Federal Reserve; Sudden stops; Transition economies
Inflation-targeting central banks, 1
Inflation-targeting regimes, 1; flexible, 1
Inflation targets: in Australia, 400–404; in Chile, 400; in Czech Republic, 377–80, 397–98, 403–4; in European Monetary Union, 401–3; exchange rates and, 396–405; in Hungary, 377–80, 397–98, 404–5; implementing optimal policy through, for sudden stops, 436–39; learning with known, 226–30; in New Zealand, 399–400; in Poland, 377–80, 397–98; setting, and transition economies, 388–94; in transition economies, 396–405
Instrument rule: explicit, 23n7; implicit, 23n7
Interest rates: inflation targeting and, 265–68; in optimal equilibrium, 40–44; stabilization objectives for, 106–14
Israel, 399

Japan, deflation in, 288

Knowledge, imperfect, 202; inflation expectations and, 207–11; monetary policy and, 220–26

Learning: least squares, 215–16, 235–38; in monetary policy, 238–40; perpetual, 202, 211–20
Least squares inflation forecasts, 212–15
Least squares learning, 235–38; inflation persistence and, 215–16

Modified loss function, minimization of, 55–61, 78
Monetary policy, 173–74; disadvantages of purely forward-looking policy making for, 20–23; in ERM2 system, 405–9; imperfect knowledge and, 220–26; inflation-forecast targeting as optimal, 3; learning in, 238–40; optimal, 3; optimal, under perfect knowledge, 207. *See also* Central banks; Sudden stops
Monetary policy rule, defined, 23

New Keynesian model, 3
New Keynesian Phillips curve, 97, 177n7, 196
New Zealand, 252, 252t; inflation targets and exchange rates in, 399–400
Norway, 253

Open economies, results of hybrid targeting for, 184–88
Optimal equilibrium: determinant, 44–45; forward-looking model for, 27–32; highest-level policy specifications for, 25–26; indeterminate, 44–48; interest rates in, 40–44; intermediate-level policy specifications for, 26; lowest-level policy specifications for, 26; responses to shocks, 32–35; sequentially constrained, 53–55; from "timeless perspective," 35–40
Optimal monetary policy, 3
Optimal policy rule, 156
Optimal target criteria, 96–122
Output growth, inflation targeting and, 262–65

Perfect knowledge: benchmark model of, 206–7; optimal monetary policy under, 207

Perpetual learning, 202, 211–20; least squares inflation forecasts and, 212–15
Poland, 354; comparing inflation in, with non-inflation-targeting floaters and, 380–84; hitting and missing inflation targets in, 377–80; inflation targets and exchange rates in, 397–98; introduction of inflation targeting in, 363–65; preliminary experiences with inflation targeting in, 374–75. *See also* Transition economies
Policy making, disadvantages of forward-looking, 20–23
Policy rules, 76–77; criteria for, 24–25
Price-level targeting, 174–75, 192–93
Price-path targeting, 174–75, 192–93
Prices, sticky, 114–17
Price stability, origins of, in United States, 313–23

Rational expectation models, 201–3
Reaction functions, 24; implied, 24
Reserves, stabilizing inflation with, 289–96
Retail Prices Index minus mortgage interest payments (RPIX) inflation rate, 12, 93
Ricardian fiscal policies, deflationary traps via, 284–89

Shocks: cost-push, 96–102; inflation, and economy following, 216–20; optimal equilibrium responses to, 32–40. *See also* Sudden stops
Slovak Republic, 354–55
Social loss function, discretionary minimization of, 49–51
Spain, 251, 252t
Specific targeting rule, 77, 78–79, 94n1; commitment to, 64–71; defined, 23–24; determinacy under, 65–67; hybrid rule related to, 67–68; price-level, commitment to equivalent, 68–71
Sticky prices, 114–17
Sticky wages, 114–17
Sudden stops, 9–10; implementing optimal policy through inflation targets for, 436–39; literature on, 425–26; model of, 426–29; monetary policy and, 424–25, 429–32; optimal policy for, 432–34; reserves management for, 439–41
Sweden, 251, 252t, 253
Switzerland, 253

Targeting: defined, 23; forecast, 23. *See also* Hybrid targeting; Inflation targeting; Price-path targeting

Targeting rules: general, 23; specific, 23–24

Target levels, 23

Target variables, defined, 23

Taylor rules, 3, 32n19, 267, 284

Transition economies, 9; changeover from fixed to floating exchange rates in, 354–58; deciding speed of disinflation in, 388–94; determining responses by central banks to deviations of inflation from targets in, 394–96; inflation targets and exchange rates in, 396–405; lessons and problems of inflation targeting in, 384–405; operational aspects of inflation targeting in, 384–88; preliminary experiences with inflation targeting in, 368–84; setting inflation targets and, 388–94. *See also* Czech Republic; Hungary; Poland

Transparency, central-bank decision making and, 66–67

United Kingdom, 251, 252t; central bank in, 13; committee process of inflation targeting in, 13–14; inflation in, 11; process of inflation targeting in, 12

United States: comparison of model with actual policy of, 145–56; deflation in, 288; Greenspan era of, 319–21; implementing explicit inflation targeting in, 331–34; inflation go/stop monetary policy period of, 314–15; optimal policy for model of, 136–45; origins of price stability in, 313–23; small quantitative model of, 122–36; Volcker disinflation period of, 315–19. *See also* Federal Reserve

Variables, target, defined, 23

Vector autoregression (VAR) model, 122–26

Vigilance, dissecting benefits of, 225–26

Volcker, Paul, 203, 312, 315–19

Wages, sticky, 114–17